"Update of a classic..." "More than a sparkling update of a classic, E[d] Nash brings his direct marketing reader a veritable hitchhiker's guide to th[e] information superhighway. If it's new, dynamic and it's working right now it's in this book!"—**Bob Teufel**, *President, Rodale Press, Inc.*

"Totally comprehensive..." "If you want to totally understand Direct Ma[r]keting, read this totally comprehensive book. Once again Ed has broug[ht] our discipline out of the shadows of traditional advertising."—**Stan Braun stein**, *Executive Vice President, MBS/Multimode, Inc.*

"Covers the gamut..." "Covers the gamut of radical changes in the scop[e] and function of direct marketing in a practical how-to way. An indispen[s]able guide."—**Nat Ross**, *Adjunct Professor, Marketing, New York Unive[r]sity*

"Best single overview..." "The best single overview—both conceptua[l] and practical—of direct marketing as a key component in integrated ma[r]keting programs. I have selected it as the text for my next direct marketin[g] class."—**Karl Lendenmann, Ph.D.**, *Director of Planning and Research Bozell/SKS, Instructor, University of California, Irvine*

"For neophytes and pros..." "This book is a 'must read,' not only for th[e] neophyte who needs to know where direct marketing is now but also fo[r] the pro who needs to know what's ahead as our industry embarks on th[e] superhighway."—**Lee Epstein**, *President, Mailmen Inc.*

"A must-read..." "A must-read for anyone interested in improving the pe[r]formance of direct marketing programs. Covering essentials of both strateg[y] and implementation, it is a primary and advanced text on how to do dire[ct] marketing right!"—**Keven J. Clancy, Ph.D.**, *Chairman, Copernicus Ma[r]keting Strategy Group, Professor of Marketing, Boston University*

"Of great value in training..." "I found Ed Nash's book to be of grea[t] value both for myself and in training members of my staff. I cannot imagin[e] a better reference book for the seasoned veteran or neophyte."—**Charle[s] Wickham**, *Senior Vice President, Disney Publications*

DIRECT
MARKETING

DIRECT MARKETING

STRATEGY, PLANNING, EXECUTION

EDWARD NASH

FOURTH EDITION

McGRAW-HILL

NEW YORK SAN FRANCISCO WASHINGTON, D.C. AUCKLAND BOGOTÁ
CARACAS LISBON LONDON MADRID MEXICO CITY MILAN
MONTREAL NEW DELHI SAN JUAN SINGAPORE
SYDNEY TOKYO TORONTO

Library of Congress Cataloging-in-Publication Data

Nash, Edward
   Direct marketing : strategy, planning, execution / Edward L. Nash.—4th ed.
     p.   cm.
   Includes index.
   ISBN 0-07-135287-2
   1. Direct marketing. I. Title.
   HF5415.126.N37 2000
   658.8'4—dc21   99-054038

McGraw-Hill

A Division of The McGraw-Hill Companies

2 3 4 5 6 7 8 9 0 AGM/AGM   0 9 8 7 6 5 4 3 2 1 0

ISBN 0-07-135287-2

This book was set in Garamond by Pro-Image Corporation. Printed and bound by Quebecor/Martinsburg.

McGraw-Hill books are available at special quality discounts to use as premiums and sales promotions, or for use in corporate training programs. For more information, please write to the Director of Special Sales, McGraw-Hill, Professional Publishing, Two Penn Plaza, New York, NY 10121-2298. Or contact your local bookstore.

This book is printed on recycled, acid-free paper containing a minimum of 50% recycled, de-inked fiber.

*To my wife Diana, and my daughter Amy,
who have been my motivation to "fill the
unforgiving minute with sixty seconds
worth of distance run." (—from Kipling's IF)*

CONTENTS

Preface to the First Edition

Direct marketing is not only a technology, it is a process. It not only seeks to make a sale, it builds profitable customer relationships.

In doing this, any medium may be used—not only direct mail, but newspapers, magazines, radio, television, matchbook covers, and other media not yet dreamed of. The defining characteristic is not the method of reaching the prospect, or even the method by which the prospect responds to us. It makes no difference whether the inquiry or order comes to us by mail, phone, Mailgram, interactive cable, or a visit to a retail location.

What is essential is that the customer's name and address be "captured," to be recorded on a list which becomes the heart of the marketing process. The mailing list is the means by which we fulfill our obligations to the customer or prospect; provide satisfactory service; collect payments due us; and make subsequent offers of products, services, or information.

Those of us who make our living in direct marketing entered the field from widely divergent directions. Among us are mail-order entrepreneurs seeking profits from the amazing leverage of direct marketing; advertising executives fascinated by its measurability; academicians captivated by its logical and scientific foundations; writers and artists pursuing its virginal creative opportunities; and suppliers of paper, printing, and other services who have discovered its present immensity and its future potential.

Lately our ranks have been joined by skilled practitioners in financial, packaged goods, retail, and other marketing methods who have suddenly been called upon to apply the direct marketing process in one way or another to their own fields.

In the advertising agency business, I have worked with people who have approached this business from all these varied perspectives. There has always been the need to train new people who voluntarily chose or accidentally stumbled into this unique and immensely satisfying field.

I originally conceived this book as a means of sparing myself the trouble of explaining the basic principles of direct marketing over and over again.

The book gradually expanded into a guide for anyone who must conceive, plan, or execute all or part of a direct marketing program.

My intention is to take the reader step by step along the road to eventual success in any direct marketing endeavor. For novices, it is the basic training needed to succeed in this fast-moving field. For specialists, I do not presume to teach about their own field, but to provide a sense of context— how their specialty interrelates with every other area of this business. For everyone, I offer some new insight and wide abstractions about my particular forte, direct marketing strategy. Though not every reader may agree with all my hypotheses on strategy, it is my expectation that this book will at least initiate starting points for the identification of each reader's own strategic conclusions.

In addition, I have tried to apply some of the writing principles of the field to the book itself. If the book is interesting and fast-moving, that is because the subject is interesting and fast-moving. If the book is long, that is only because there is a lot to say. If the book is lively and conversational, that is because I believe that the style of the written word should not differ significantly from that of the spoken word.

I welcome you, the reader, to *Direct Marketing,* the book. If you are new to the field, I welcome you to that, as well. May you find both as stimulating and satisfying as I do.

New York, 1982

Preface to the Second Edition

"The more things change, the more they remain the same," reads an old French proverb. In the last five years, since the publication of the first edition of *Direct Marketing,* our field has undergone vast changes—but, in many ways, it is still the same.

Many years ago, when copywriters were the sages of what was then called "mail order," successful advertising was built on instinct—a writer's instinct for a phrase, an entrepreneur's instinct for a product, a designer's instinct for an attractive mailing package or advertisement.

Later the field "progressed" from an art into a science; the computer became king. Lists could be processed. Results could be modeled and forecast. Profitability could be tracked for each individual key number. Catalogs could be designed by calculating profit potential per square inch.

Today, we've come full circle. Those who dare to break the rules achieve the greatest breakthroughs, while copycat catalogs and formula advertising fades into oblivion. Once again, creativity rules.

The new strength of creativity is that we know more about our own instincts and more about the consumers' instincts. And we know more ways to bring the two together.

In this second edition, you'll find frequent references to the use of psychology—in research, in understanding consumer needs, and in communicating with the consumer. Today we can plan products to meet unspoken and highly personal emotional needs; we can deal with fears and anxieties, with aspirations and fantasies, with sensual satisfactions and subtleties of self-imagery. We can touch on issues that cannot be expressed in words, only with pictures. And thus, we can cater to the needs not only of the body but also of the soul.

This recognition of psychology is present in many of the revisions and updates throughout the book. It has resulted in virtually a new chapter on research, whole new sections on creativity, and a complete revision of past theories about using television—the most emotional medium of them all.

Psychology has made it possible for us to replicate the magical instincts of the creative greats of yesteryear, to logically analyze illogical needs, and to precisely calculate the best way to fulfill a vague emotional desire.

To the tens of thousands of readers who bought the first edition and are coming back for more, I promise not to disappoint you. The changes will make reading the new book worth your while.

To new readers, who may be discovering this field or my writings for the first time, this book will give you a basic foundation in the principles—old and new—that make the difference between success and failure, between amateurism and professionalism.

New York, 1986

Preface to the Third Edition

As I write these words, the rest of this revision has long been completed and at the publisher. This preface was delayed because my father was hospitalized and, after five weeks, passed away. We buried him two days ago. I ask the reader's understanding if he is very much on my mind.

My dad and I were very different. He printed words. I write them. Our interests were different, as was our style. Yet I cannot ignore the fact that his ideas and spirit are part of me, and that I cannot seek different goals without at least understanding the ways we were the same.

I see this lesson applying to direct marketing, which I have seen grow and expand and become more sophisticated in the same way. Yet we who love this field do not do it justice if we fail to understand its roots. Those roots are in the mail-order business, and always will be.

There is no question that the field has grown up. The earlier prefaces record that progress: first, acceptance into the world of general advertising, then at least token integration. There are no longer challenges to our size. Every statistic shows that direct mail as a medium, and direct marketing in its many forms, are among the fastest-growing segments of the entire economy. And there is no question that our methods work. Where once we listed with pride the handful of Fortune 500 companies who had some involvement in our field, now it is difficult to find one that does not.

But what is still missing is respect. Respect for the ways in which we are different. Respect for the knowledge that may be based on tests of old-fashioned products but that are still valid. Respect for the judgment and instincts of those who have made it their life's profession.

Though experience has proven the value of direct marketing, too many of the entrenched practitioners of general advertising lack the respect for this less familiar (to them) discipline. Two of my present clients are the largest and best-known advertisers in their respective categories. One of them thinks nothing of spending a million dollars on a television spot, but sets direct mail budgets so tightly that they can rarely afford more than a letter and reply card. The other is a leader in using visual imagery to build brand equity, but allows only stock photos to be used for the mail medium. In both cases direct marketing has been relegated to the more junior executives who have more to lose if they go 5 percent over their budgets than they can gain if they should double expected sales goals.

Many companies wouldn't place an ad in a trade magazine without careful planning and professional help. But they don't hesitate to trim their budgets by using freelance writers to do conceptual planning, and art studios to write direct-response copy. This is somewhat like building a customized house without an architect. It's done all the time, but the house looks it, and the roof leaks.

No wonder I still meet people who dispute the experience of direct marketing by saying they tried something and it didn't work. Their mail-pieces are often nothing more than an ad in an envelope and lack the unique relationship-building aspect of direct mail. And when they do write a letter, it sounds like an ad rather than a one-on-one communication. The lists are wrong. The offer adds no real motivation or immediacy. The copy platform is nothing more than "50¢ off." *Of course* their tests didn't work, any more than it would work to run a letter as a magazine ad or an ad as a television spot.

One problem is the proliferation of specialties. Today you'll find shingles hung out for financial specialists, customer loyalty specialists, database specialists, infomercial producers, and interactive technicians. There are analysts, telemarketers, order entry firms, computer processors—all of them offering their services on a piecemeal basis to experienced and inexperienced direct marketing users alike.

While in the hospital my dad was a victim of this kind of specialization. Pulmonologists, cardiologists, urologists, neurologists, surgeons, and others each poked and prodded and performed their own procedures. To find out his status I had to speak to each of them separately, none of whom could give me the whole picture. They each did their own job as well as they could. They each pronounced their own treatment successful and the patient cured of that ailment. The hospital looked at all the charts and called me to say he had therefore improved and was ready to come home. Later that same day they called to say he was dead. How many direct marketing projects die the same way, for lack of an experienced, competent leader with a clear, strategic approach to the objective?

In every field, the analogy to a chain's weakest link holds true. A sound system, for instance, is no better than its weakest component, regardless of what the others cost. Yet companies continue to waste the power and precision of direct marketing in all its forms by not recognizing that it is more complex than it looks. Direct marketing requires the same standard of professionalism, the same top management interest and involvement, as any other marketing or communications activity.

There are many who say that direct marketing has arrived. Maybe so. But where have we arrived? And what is the next destination? Is size the standard? Or acceptance by famous advertisers? No, the standard is, always was, and always will be: will it work, will it be worthwhile, will it make a contribution? For direct marketing, and direct marketers, to make it work, we must know and respect our roots. That's what it's all about. That's what this book is all about.

New York, 1994

Preface to the Fourth Edition

In 1970, ten years before the first edition of *Direct Marketing* was published, Alvin Toffler wrote his insightful book *Future Shock*. Among other things, he predicted that the rate of change in both science and lifestyle would be geometric, not linear.

Those who doubt it need only compare this fourth edition with the three editions that precede it. There have been more changes to deal with between editions three and four than between the first edition and the third combined.

I have been fortunate enough to be involved in many of the innovations the industry takes for granted now. As a junior copywriter, I saw the first efforts to add visual imagery to what was once totally a copywriter's world. As marketing head of a correspondence school, I experimented with alternatives to gummed labels for addressing. As President of a record club, I made the investment decisions and hired the talent to convert from punched cards to tape and floppy-disk-driven main-frames. This in turn enabled us to develop one of the first computerized analysis tools to give us weekly forecasts of profitability on each and every ad and mailing.

Later I was part of the first acquisition of a direct marketing agency (Rapp & Collins) by a general agency, DDB, and later headed a major start-up for BBDO, where John Caples participated as "Creative Director Emeritus." These positions immersed me in the job of applying direct marketing methods to mass advertising clients. In return, I had the opportunity to learn about and use their research methods and psychological imagery and apply these sciences to direct marketing clients. As a result, BBDO Direct created the first direct marketing commercials that used dramatizations and music as well as sales pitches—for ITT Longer Distance, Weekly Reader's Book Club, and AARP.

Later, running an independent agency, I spent six years helping Procter & Gamble develop their mailing lists and creating applications for a score of their brands. It wasn't until much later that what we were doing became known as "Database Marketing."

But all of this pales in comparison to the changes in the last few years. The size and scope of direct marketing programs today is awesome. The analytical processes and fulfillment capabilities of suppliers has expanded to match.

My first job, at 17, was as an assistant for an account executive, who went on to become one of the best-known and respected direct marketing leaders, Stan Rapp. Later I was hired as a junior copywriter for the largest ad agency in the mail order field, Schwab & Beatty, which had all of 25 people. Their senior copywriter was the now-famous Tom Collins. Eventually Foote Cone & Belding created the Rapp & Collins agency. Capitol Record Club, which I headed, was their first account.

Today some direct marketing agencies have more offices around the world than these early agencies had employees. Some count their staff by the thousands and their billings in the billions. Yet the fundamentals of what works and what doesn't haven't changed at all. Whales and minnows share the same basic needs. Their size doesn't change the environmental principles they need to survive.

While direct marketing clients, agencies and programs have grown larger and more complex, the human beings they communicate with have changed relatively little. Consumers' needs are basically the same; we just understand them a bit better. Practical benefits and value are still outweighed by self-image. Considered purchases must still be supported with long copy argument. Impulse purchases must still be facilitated with easy-to-use response mechanisms, whether they be via mail, phone call, or a click on a web page. And one of the inviolate commandments of direct marketing still demands that the responder be motivated to do it now because "later means never."

The development of direct response television eventually attracted experts in that media who could add dramatic values that proved to make a difference. The development of the Internet as a marketing media has similarly put a premium on those who can manipulate its underlying technology. But creative appeals have not changed, nor has the need for sound, strategy-driven copy and layout, nor have the ultimate influences on profitability—allowable margin, response rates, and advertising cost per response.

For instance, the reader of this edition will find the chapter on design totally revised in response to the software systems that have replaced thumb-nail sketches and rubber cement. Yet there is no change in what makes an ad or mailing piece easy to read and effective.

The Internet is mentioned in almost every chapter, and the chapter on how marketers can profitably use e-commerce is the largest in the book and took the longest time to write. While the technology is different, the creative and economic principles are the same as most other media. This writer's task was not made easier by the weekly announcements of new methods and new applications.

Though the Internet has enormous potential as both a media and a distribution channel, I saved the last chapter for the one that I believe represents an even greater potential for direct marketers and direct marketing service providers. That is globalization—the adaptation of communications, products, and distribution systems to sell our products and services virtually anywhere in the world. While this globalization was growing rapidly on its own, the Internet has accelerated its growth. The smallest and newest kitchen-table direct marketing business, with virtually no added effort or expense, can get Internet orders from consumers and businesses all over the world—some from countries most foreigners can neither spell nor find on a map.

The Internet is a great new marketing opportunity. Anyone can play, but the survivors will probably be the first, the fastest, the most creative, and the best-financed.

International marketing is more than an opportunity; it is a necessity. The interest in export is greatest in those countries that have the greatest need to do so. Often, they are also the countries whose pay scales are vastly lower than those in their marketing targets. Most companies are already facing competition from international competitors, and direct marketing has proven to be the fastest and most effective means to enter other markets.

Global marketing is not an option, but an imperative. I summarized this more briefly in a recent speech: "You are in global competition whether you want to be or not. You don't have to go there, but they're coming here!"

Ed Nash
New York 1999

Statements of Appreciation

FIRST EDITION, 1982

Where does one begin to thank those who have taught the lessons or provided the opportunities to enable one to write a book like this?

There are the people who trained me at various points in my own career: Tom Collins, Mel Fauer, Lee Friend, Ray Hagel, Alan Livingston, Stan Rapp, Dave Reider, Vic Schwab, Warren Smith, Sam Sugar, Aaron Sussman, and George Violante. They can be said to have been my teachers, and every client with whom I have ever worked, every specialist and staff member who has ever worked with me or for me, has also been my teacher. So have been the authors of the books which came before mine, the lecturers whose talks I attended, and the brilliant men and women who invented some of the theories I only report. These include Richard Benson, Mike Fabian, Jerry Hardy, Rose Harper, Si Levy, Ben Ordover, Maxwell Sackheim, Robin Smith, Robert Stone, Frank Vos, and Lester Wunderman.

I must extend my warmest appreciation to the staff of the Direct Marketing Association, whose manuals, materials, and advice proved invaluable. These include, among many others, Richard Brennan, Karen Burns, Bob DeLay, Bonnie DeLay, Richard Montesi, Ed Pfeiffer, Bonnie Rodriquez, Marilyn Ross, Laurie Spar, Donna Sweeney, Merrill Tomlinson, Ruth Troiani, Sue White, and Dante Zacovish. Pete Hoke, the publisher of *Direct Marketing* magazine, offered not only advice and information, but also encouragement when I needed it most.

More immediately, there are those who provided specific information or who helped me by reviewing specific sections of the manuscript: Renee Birnbaum, Sol Blumenfeld, Susan Bynum, Tom Collins, Joel Feldman, Tom Garbett, Hal Glantz, Lloyd Kieran, Ellen Kraus, Carol Ladanyi, Marge Landrau, Jeramy Lanigan, Craig Mansfield, Walter Marshall, Fran McCown, Murray Miller, Charles Orlowski, Fred Rola, Murray Roman, Joe Shain, David Shepard, Iris Shokoff, and Mike Vigil.

My executive assistant, Caroline Cohen, supervised the endless hours of typing, proofing, and working with the editorial and production specialists at McGraw-Hill. I would never have met the final deadlines without her help. I would like to thank my editor, William Newton, who has been superb.

Having saved the most important for last, I now thank my patient and loving wife, Diana, who provided the inspiration and encouragement to start this project in the first place, and to keep it going night after night, week after week, as what started as a labor of love seemed to become a monstrous burden and an impossible chore. She made it all worthwhile, and still does.

A word of apology to my five-year-old daughter, Amy. When she's old enough to read this passage, perhaps then she'll understand why Daddy was spending so much time at "the typewriter" (sic) instead of with her.

To all of you, for all your contributions, thank you.

SECOND EDITION, 1986

For all the people who guided me and helped me write the first edition of this work, my appreciation has not diminished. However, the list has grown longer.

Today I must thank Brian Anderson, who pioneered the new method of broadcast buying reported here for the first time, and Lucille Guardala, who wrote the television commercials which demonstrated that direct-response broadcast standards should be no lower than those of general advertising.

I must thank Sheron Davis, Fran Kahn, and Jeff Kintgen of BBDO's research division, who helped to adapt some of the most sophisticated, psychological research techniques to the unique needs of direct marketing.

Many of the executives at BBDO Direct helped me review the facts and update examples from the first edition to this. Lois Seiden contributed much to the chapter on print media. Lloyd Kieran wrote the computer program to solve the need for a statistical validity table that could be used and understood easily. Cindy Benes-Trapp conceived the jacket. Sharon Ross provided the patience and care needed to work with McGraw-Hill's demanding editors and production specialists, and the planning to keep the whole project on schedule amid a hundred other priorities.

Many industry leaders reviewed chapters for me and submitted suggestions. I am particularly indebted to Dave Shepard, Jules Silbert, Stan Fenvessey, and Ed Burnett.

My daughter, Amy, will be ten when this is printed, and can already type out a good ad on her own. But my wife, Diana, has not grown older at all. She is as young and beautiful as when I first met her, and she remains the source of my strength and inspiration when I take on projects like this.

This new edition would never have been commissioned by the publisher if it had not been for the many readers of the first printing whose word-of-mouth advertising made possible the next printing, and the next, and eventually this new edition. I must, above all, thank those men and women—many of whom are just entering this wonderful field—for contributing their own new ideas, new energy, and new opportunities for us all.

THIRD EDITION, 1994

To thank everyone who has contributed in one way or the other to the writing of this book would require a book in itself. Every client has taught me something as I have worked with them. Every employee has given me something back, even in the questions they ask. Every other book and magazine article and lecture has added to the knowledge that I have assembled here.

Some names do come to mind though, in no particular order. Bill Harvey of Next Century Media and Tim Hawthorne of Hawthorne commercials, who provided much of the material for the chapters on Interactive and Infomercials respectively. Judy Black, Bozell's media futurologist, who helped with both. My friend Bob Wientzen, now president of Advanced Promotion Technologies, who hired me to do a project for P&G seven years ago and challenged me to cope with and contribute to the world of database marketing as applied to packaged-good companies. Tricia McGivney, formerly my assistant and now list manager at Bozell Direct, who fielded the foul balls so I could concentrate on serving clients and completing this edition.

And, last and best, my wife Diana, who has helped me and encouraged me and kept my spirits up through good times and bad.

In short, I extend my thanks to all those to whom the previous editions were dedicated: "To my teachers—everyone for whom I have ever worked, or who has ever worked with me or for me. Each has taught me something new about direct marketing or, more importantly, about life."

FOURTH EDITION, 1999

As with previous editions, there are many who contributed one way or the other to this new edition.

The Direct Marketing Association's Information Central division, an irreplaceable resource, processed dozens of requests at their modest fees. The U.S. Postal Service's direct mail educational publications were invaluable. *DM News*' archival website gave me the facts to bring every item up to date, just as its newspapers do when I'm preparing for a client presentation.

I am particularly indebted to Joseph Furgeile, who heads a respected consulting company specializing in financial planning and analysis. Mindy Gardner, a partner in OmniTalent.com, took on the voluminous job of checking the Internet chapter for accuracy and omissions. David Strauss of Western Media and Pam O'Dell of PJO Media were valuable resources on media planning.

Chuck Polle of InterOmni and Dave Rosenthal of Shepard provided valuable material on new printing techniques, as did the Agfa Corporation. Adobe was very helpful in sending information about new graphic software. Team Nash's Art Director, Anna Martino, spent hours helping me simplify the complexities of the many computer graphics tools she uses as comfortably as I would type a letter.

In a less direct way Pam Kieker, head of Virginia Commonwealth University's direct marketing certificate program, and Pierre Passavant who heads New York University's program, also made major contributions—by inviting me to teach at their institutions. So did Vito Fortuna of the USPS who arranged for my lectures at Postal Forums and other USPS-sponsored venues. These experiences as a teacher of advanced direct marketing subjects made me aware of several areas where the previous edition could be improved, not only in content but in clarity. Every line of this edition has been reviewed and, where necessary, rewritten to make it easier for a newcomer to the field to understand.

Mary Beth Barber, a journalist and dramatist, worked with me as a researcher and editor. Over six months, she first contacted various sources to assemble data for each chapter, then reviewed my manuscripts as I completed one each weekend. She tracked down hundreds of facts and company names—a much more difficult task than it might appear, because so many mergers and name changes have taken place. Every reader will benefit from her annoying (to me) but essential questions, particularly "Will your reader know this phrase?"

I also have to thank Team Nash's Marcia Mata who organized the research materials and who took on added responsibilities servicing our Latin American clients so I could find the time to deal with this book. Luciana Ambrozano pitched in wherever she was needed, handling word processing and contact chores, always with a smile.

I could not have done it all without the continued love and support of my wife and daughter. As winter turned to Spring and my weekends were still spent chained to my laptop instead of walking with them on the beach at Amagansett, their understanding, sympathy, and encouragement became essential.

My ultimate appreciation goes to you, the reader, and the 100,000 readers of the three previous editions and dozens of translations who came before you. If it wasn't for your support, this newest edition would never have been commissioned. I thank you, and I hope this book helps you find the same success and satisfaction I have found in this measurable, logical, wonderful field of direct marketing.

DIRECT MARKETING

INTRODUCTION

"All the armies of the world are not as powerful as an idea whose time has come." This liberal translation of the famous Victor Hugo quote applies to direct marketing as it stands today—years after the first edition of this book was written.

In the last five years since the third edition was published, the rate of change in direct marketing makes Alvin Toffler's predictions in "Future Shock" look downright conservative. The rate of change has been geometric, not only in size and scope but in technology.

Mechanical paste-ups have given way to Quark and Adobe software. I must confess that I miss the smell of rubber cement and the wide racks of mechanicals with their acetate and vellum overlays. A zip disk lacks the sensory involvement with production components, and the sense of completion when it's all turned into color proofs.

List selection is still (or should be) driven by instinct and experience, but new regression analysis formulations and a vast array of list enhancement opportunities make it infinitely more complex and more precise.

The Internet Opportunity

The Internet has multiplied the speed and reach of interactive communications, opening opportunities that were only fantasies two decades ago. To companies and investors who spurned direct mail but have invested billions in the Internet, it is a tool with such a vast potential that they can't take the risk of not being involved. At this point the Internet produces more "big ideas" than "good ideas," more sales than profits. It has made millionaires—not from CPOs (Cost per Order), but from IPOs (Initial Public Offerings). For now it is the dynamic demonstration of chaos theory at work. But, as I sit here and write this, the traditional giants of communication such as AT&T and IBM and Cablevision are quietly preparing to bring order to the Internet. They are laying fiber-optic cables, searching for new transmission processes on phone lines and TV cables, and acquiring companies that will round out their capabilities. Within a few years the Internet will be available anywhere, and instantly. Through phone lines, on your TV cable, in your car, and in your pocket.

To veteran direct marketers the Internet is just another medium, subject to the whims or human nature, the needs of body and soul, the impulse and considered buying patterns of the marketplace. While we have had to learn what's different, just as we did with television, so should the Internet specialists learn all that is not different. To help, an entire chapter has been added—the longest in the book. The reader who seeks to master the opportunities of the Internet should read the entire book, not just the chapter!

Internet Zealotry

In the past few months, I have heard two different Internet enthusiasts predict the end of all magazines, all retail stores, all newspapers and even the postal system. This is possible, but not in a free world where people have different preferences on how and where to shop. Wise businesses still choose to serve all their potential customers by using all possible distribution and communication channels.

To paraphrase a statement I once heard about a philosophical movement: "Direct marketing has finally come into its own; we have our own lunatic fringe." In our case, it is the sensation-seeking lecturers who predict that "one day all advertising will be direct marketing," that "all retailing will be mail order," that "infomercials can sell anything," or that "everyone will shop through interactive video connections."

This over-zealousness deserves what Gilbert and Sullivan in *The Mikado* called making "the punishment fit the crime." In their case, it would be to make them pool their IPO proceeds and buy an island where they could run their own technocracy. There they would be made to stay in individual cells—with slow computers—bothering each other with e-mails and impressing each other with cute website names and clever graphics.

Globalization

Almost lost in the excitement about the Internet is another opportunity that represents an even greater potential: globalization! Businesses all over the world have finally gotten the message that there are more customers and more buying power outside their borders than within them. Also, many have discovered that the best way to open new markets is not by challenging change-resistant retail systems, but by going straight to the consumer through direct marketing.

All over the world, more and more consumers are developing both the buying power and the aspirations to become direct marketing customers.

They want what they see on television. They know the world's top brands. And they are willing to pay more for the quality, design and imagery of almost any product from a land far away.

The Internet has helped, of course. Even the tiniest home-made website can be reached by anyone in the world with a modem. But that doesn't mean that a buyer can find them without other advertising. Each and every direct response medium has a role to play to generate traffic for an Internet store.

Even without the Internet, catalogs are now being printed in a score of languages. Merchandise is being shipped from one country to another all over the world. The size of the country, or the company, has little bearing on its overseas potential.

One great boost for international marketing is the new attitude of most of the world's postal systems. While they may have monopolies on local delivery, they compete fiercely for international shipments. As happens with all competition, even mailing a package has become simpler, faster and less expensive.

Direct Marketing: "Good News"

The overall progress of direct marketing which I described in the previous edition still stands. Today, direct marketing is an idea so timely that it almost has a life of its own, so popular that it has spread through every kind of business and every country of the world, so effective that despite a proliferation of well-meaning amateurs it chalks up so many victories and successes that a half-dozen trade publications can't cover them all.

One measure of its success is that it is now the basis for a score of sub-disciplines. "Database marketing" is now a basic tool of some of the largest packaged-goods companies. "Relationship marketing," "one-on-one marketing," "maxi-marketing," "integrated marketing," and others all offer interesting extensions and variations of its basic techniques.

Companies that once scoffed at "mail order" and "junk mail" have since opened their own direct-to-the-consumer sales operations. Who would ever have guessed that both Procter & Gamble and General Foods would have fully-staffed direct marketing divisions, that Bloomingdale's and Neiman-Marcus would be known to many consumers as the names of mail-order catalogs, that IBM, Apple, and Compaq—unable to ignore the growth of the mail-order computer company created by Michael Dell—would decide to join the fray and create their own catalogs? Who would have guessed that a field in which one "rule" was that you couldn't sell anything over $10 by mail would be used effectively by banks, stockbrokers, and automobile companies, by jewelers, tourism promoters, and real estate ventures?

Direct Marketing: "The Bad News"

The truth is that even with enormous advances in analytical and computer capabilities, most direct marketing attempts still fail to achieve their potential or, worse, fail to work at all. Companies with minor successes stop there and fail to exploit their breakthroughs with further testing. Financiers still fail to properly value two of direct marketers' most powerful assets: a responsive database and an established "brand equity."

To master direct marketing and take full advantage of its potential, marketers must understand that all of its current applications are rooted in the art and science of a once-scoffed-at field called mail order. One cannot pretend to be a direct mail or database practitioner without having a solid understanding of how magazine subscriptions, book clubs, office supplies, and credit cards are sold, without appreciating the thinking and testing behind a mailing for Publishers' Clearing House, a magazine ad for Columbia Video Club, a television spot for Ginsu knives or Marshall Islands coins. Only then should anyone attempt to plan or execute even the simplest e-commerce or database application.

The direct marketing discipline can be preserved and profited from only if its roots are respected and understood. Only by building upon the foundations of the past, can today's innovators succeed in using direct marketing as it should be used.

A BRIEF BACKGROUND

Only 20 years ago, direct marketing was considered a specialty to be employed by book publishers, record clubs, magazines seeking subscriptions, correspondence schools, and sellers of kitchen gadgets and low-priced fashions. No one then would have guessed that it was destined to become a marketing tool utilized by more than half of the *Fortune* 500 companies.

Anyone looking through old magazines will find early examples of what was then called mail-order advertising. Many of the classic advertisements of all times were mail-order ads: "They laughed when I sat down to play" . . . or Charles Atlas's bully kicking sand in our hero's face, or "Do you make these mistakes in English?"

Advertisements were crowded with small-type copy, appealing to every human desire. The most mundane products were offered as keys to fame, success, popularity, riches, admiration, sex appeal, security, and eternal happiness. Mailing pieces began to utilize the simplest kinds of personalization, such as a prospect's handwritten name on an invitation to subscribe to *Business Week*. And mailing lists progressed, slowly and painfully, from typed labels to Scriptomatic cards to rooms filled with trays of ink-covered Elliott addressing stencils. Clerks pushed long metal rods through trays of hole-punched stencils to select prospects by elementary categories, then refiled them manually.

It all seems primitive today, and yet in those early efforts a solid foundation already was being laid for direct marketing as it is today. The earliest advertisements, as far back as I have been able to search, all include the one tiny element that has made it possible for a copywriter's art to become a marketer's science, that has enabled modern writers to declare what works and what doesn't with a sense of certainty unknown to most other kinds of advertising.

The Incredible Key Number

That tiny element is, simply, the key number. This is the common denominator of every type of direct marketing activity, in every medium, for every product, in the years that have passed as well as those that are yet to come.

The incredible key number, carried in coupons, reply cards, and, today, in internet "cookies" is what makes direct marketing unique. It is the foundation of our knowledge, the key to our science, the signpost to our future.

The early giants of our field—Maxwell Sackheim, Victor Schwab, John Caples—did not have to rely on a client's subjective opinion to gain acceptance and fame for their advertising. They *knew* it worked. The clients knew it when the responses, bearing the key numbers of advertisements that they or their agencies prepared, poured out of mail sacks. The advertising community knew those ads were "great" the same way we know today: by seeing them repeated, over and over again, in ever-expanding media schedules.

As the reservoir of knowledge grew, copy-oriented executives looked to other areas for response improvement: price testing, media testing, and premiums. Products began to be created just for mail-order advertising. Sherman & Sackheim created the Little Leather Library and then another innovative proposition, the Book-of-the-Month Club. An innovative retailer named Sears started to develop a catalog offering merchandise to railroad station agents, and another industry was born. In later years, Lester Wunderman helped Columbia Broadcasting System (CBS) create the now-famous concept called the Columbia Record Club. Jerry Hardy, creator of the original Time-Life Books concept, later became president of the Dreyfus Fund and revolutionized the financial industry by selling mutual funds by mail without using stockbrokers.

As the industry emerged, computers and optical scanning devices counted the same incredible key numbers and produced a wealth of data showing marketers not only how many coupons were returned from a particular advertisement, but how many people bought how much and what they paid for it. Simple concepts such as cost per order gave way to precise forecasts of return on advertising investment. The key number led not only to new ads and new mailing lists, but also to the creation of entire new businesses.

The Miracle of Statistical Projectability

One reason for the rapid evolution of the industry is its unique ability to test new ideas with minimal downside risk. The key to this strength is statistical projectability. Direct marketing is a statistician's paradise, for all the practices of this mathematical application are used daily as an intrinsic part of its marketing and its operations.

If a test mailing to a valid sample produces a 5 percent response, there is a reasonable probability that the rest of the list or similar lists will, within a predictable margin of error, produce the same result. It is therefore possible, by spending relatively small amounts, to accurately determine the best copy, offer, or list for a given proposition, or even to test one product against another. The same principle is present in magazine advertising, where regional editions and split runs can provide a very accurate reading of which ad "pulls" the best or whether the publication itself is potentially profitable.

Precise forecasting is another tool, made possible because thousands of prospective customers turn the pages of a magazine or look in their mailboxes in a frighteningly predictable manner. They elect to rush to the phone or put our coupon aside—each acting independently—until a precisely graphable "later." The total pattern makes it possible for direct marketing to be more of a science than any other field of advertising or marketing.

OTHER ADVANTAGES OF DIRECT MARKETING

The predictability of direct marketing, arising out of its measurability and the science of statistics, is only one of the unique elements of this field. Others are (1) concentration, (2) personalization, and (3) immediacy. Businesses built on direct marketing live with these advantages every day, for they are what makes the existence of such businesses possible. And any company planning to apply direct marketing techniques to its established business or to enter the direct marketing field must first understand how these advantages work and how to apply them to their objectives.

Concentration

Concentration is a media concept. It is the ability to take promotional dollars and direct them to the most likely prospects with great accuracy.

When general advertisers, seeking a larger share of a market, blanket entire communities with newspaper, magazine, and television messages, selectivity is necessarily very limited. Readership surveys and Simmons data make it possible to achieve relative efficiencies, but not anywhere near the precision targeting available to direct marketers.

The "rent-up" campaign for Starrett City, a major housing development in Brooklyn, New York, is an excellent example of this capability. Previously the conventional approach had been used—ads in the real estate section of the prestigious *New York Times.* The fixed budget produced low awareness, no perceptible attitude changes, and—most important—a lack of new leases from the target audience: middle-income families with children.

The new effort switched the same dollars into a different media pattern. Instead of the *Times*, with distribution throughout the metropolitan New York area and its affluent suburbs, the designers of the campaign switched to the mass-audience *New York Sunday News*, using preprints distributed only in those areas of Queens and Brooklyn where the client's development presented a distinct advantage. Instead of being just one ad among many, the preprint format offered a full-color, high-impact story and a response coupon asking for an appointment.

This concentration enabled the client—with the same media budget—to rent out the balance of the 25,000 apartments in Starrett City. Later, because of a change in objectives, direct-response television was used to target prospective tenants in a specific income range.

When General Electric wanted to promote its wide line of television sets and other video products, it turned to direct mail. Where general media would have spread a diluted message to a general audience, the direct mail campaign offered high-tech products with explanations of engineering excellence to lists of people who would understand and appreciate technological advantages, while featuring beautiful cabinetry and design in mailings to new home owners and people who subscribed to magazines such as *Architectural Digest*.

Direct mail offers even greater concentration, by offering even greater selectivity. From tens of thousands of mailing lists an advertiser can select those people who have identified themselves as being interested in buying products of a certain type in a particular price range, and buying them through the mail. In addition, one can select—instead of or in addition to so-called buyers lists—an incredible range of community and individual characteristics compiled from census, Simmons, and telephone directory data.

The search for selectivity and segmentation reached new heights with the development of database marketing. Beginning with questions such as "Do you smoke?" this field quickly evolved into category usage and brand preference for virtually every product. Interests and personality indicators made it possible to apply the principles of direct marketing to other fields: automobiles, packaged goods, investments, travel, with hardly any limitation.

Personalization

Another cornerstone of direct marketing, particularly within the direct mail media, is the ability to personalize communications. Not only can we select very specific audiences for concentrated promotions, we can address them in a manner that dramatizes our conviction that the product or service we are offering is particularly right for each person who gets our message.

Addressing a person by name is one obvious example, which can range from a label showing through an envelope window to a much more dramatic display: giant ink-jet letters, computer-addressed salutations, or simulated handwritten fill-ins on envelopes or invitations.

Of much greater effectiveness is personalization incorporated in the concept of the mailing itself. A *Newsweek* mailing talks openly about the kinds of subscribers they are looking for, and the characteristics indicated by the address of the recipient. *Reader's Digest,* in a sweepstakes promotion, lists the names of winners in the same or nearby towns. Business mailings refer to the industry type or sales volume or number of employees, as indicated by Dun & Bradstreet (D&B) mailing lists.

One mailing to promote weekend car rentals for Avis included one paragraph that showed through the envelope and dramatized the kinds of weekends the prospect might take. The examples changed depending on the location of the prospect. Different weekend suggestions were written for each zip-code group to make the appeal as real as possible.

A Lanier promotion for word-processing equipment used not only computer personalization, but also a half-dozen variations in the printed brochure to illustrate the specific applications of a new product to each of several industries. Only the cover and a couple of pages changed, but the mailing became more relevant when the recipient's industry was boldly displayed. "How this new product can save time and money for advertising agencies (or engineering firms, or law offices)" is much more likely to be read than any general appeal.

Today, the novelty of seeing one's own name in an ad or mailing piece is often perceived as mere gimmickry. But there have been two important advances in personalization.

The first is personalized imagery: a letter that is not from a company trying to sell something, but from an actual person who is sharing his or her sincere enthusiasm for a product or service. This approach has proven particularly effective in database applications.

The second is the recognition that relevance is the handmaiden of personalization. It is far more effective to select and segment lists in such a way as to enable reference to their community, their occupation, or their interests. One application is to refer to known interests in relation to the product being offered. For instance, "Next time you go bowling, you'll feel better and look better with . . ."

Immediacy

The third and most vital element of direct marketing is *immediacy.* Conventional advertising invests millions of dollars to establish product awareness and positive attitudes. It can establish a desire; but it can't fulfill it.

On the way to buy an advertised product, our prospects may be exposed to competing messages, conflicting desires, alternative uses of discretionary spending power. The store may not have our client's product, or the salesclerk may not know where it is, how to use it, or why the customer should buy it.

The decline of selling skills in retailing is one of the great forces propelling the growth of direct marketing. Advertisers who count on the wisdom of store buyers or the ability of store salespeople to move their products may find that even the finest products can become marketing casualties.

Direct marketing messages, in all media, ask for the order now, or at least for a response that enables us to ask for an order on the next communication. General advertising's objective is *awareness* and *attitude*. Direct marketing's is the third A—*action*.

There is a wide spectrum of actions we can ask for. The ultimate is to ask for a sale: a mail order, a subscription, a membership, or a contribution. We can ask for it on a loose "send-no-money-now" trial basis or on a hard "check-with-order" basis.

We can establish a contact, by making an appointment or providing a less specific motivation to bring our prospect to a retail outlet or a showroom, or we can arrange to have our salesperson visit the prospect's home or office.

On the less committed end of the spectrum, we can offer a booklet or sample as a means of identifying prospects that are worth the expense of additional mailings, phone contacts, or personal visits.

Immediacy is a strength of direct marketing, but it is also a requirement. Our promotions are successful only to the extent that we facilitate immediate action. It is for this reason that our copy disciplines find ways to urge action now, rather than later; that our offer disciplines require simple, easy-to-use, sometimes pre-filled-out reply forms; that our media planners place a premium on bound-in insert cards or other easy-to-use reply devices. A sacred rule of direct marketing is that response devices must be easy to use because, if they are not used immediately, they may never be used." In direct marketing, as we'll explain in Chapter 2, "later" means "never."

THE REVOLUTION IN DIRECT MARKETING

Earlier I pointed out that direct marketing is being accepted as a fundamental marketing tool in a growing variety of businesses—from giant multinational financial corporations to local retailers offering an interesting new product to their customer lists or a specialized item in the shopping sections of national magazines.

The greatest attention has been given to the companies starting or acquiring direct marketing businesses, or deciding to offer their existing product line by mail order. But the most important development, and one that has proven to have the greatest role in the widening importance of this field, is the fact that the techniques of direct marketers can be valuable even for businesses that do not utilize any type of mail-order distribution. The principles of direct marketing are already widely in use in financial institutions of every kind. The largest manufacturers of office equipment are rapidly discovering how lead selling can increase the efficiency of powerful sales organizations who never needed it before. Oil companies, telephone companies, and hotel chains are using it. Applications of direct marketing have been developed for automobile companies, appliance manufacturers, toy makers, and camera manufacturers. And packaged-goods companies of all sizes have embraced direct marketing's most advanced application—database marketing as an ongoing strategic marketing tool. The list is unlimited.

The Two-Way Discovery

Just as the world of general marketing is discovering the tools of direct marketers, we in direct marketing have made a discovery of our own. We, as an industry, once looked down our noses at the undefinable, unmeasurable, seemingly unscientific methods of general advertising. Suddenly we have all, in our own ways, woken up, rubbed our eyes, and looked around to make an incredible discovery: We didn't know all the answers!

As we educated the barbarian practitioners of communications techniques that lacked the almighty key number, our pontifications were interrupted by the startling realization that maybe, just maybe, all these giant marketing organizations with years of experience investing larger budgets than most direct marketers even dream of might just have something to teach us after all.

Little by little, direct marketing specialists became exposed to the workings of general advertising. Executives with packaged-goods experience came to work for direct marketing agencies and clients. Realizing the growing importance of direct marketing as a tool for every kind of advertiser, major advertising agencies such as Young & Rubicam and Doyle Dane Bernbach purchased the most famous specialized agencies in this field and worked with them to bring both general and direct marketing clients the combined expertise of both disciplines.

Today the field has changed completely. Yes, the basic principles are still intact—and still correct. The old books are still correct; they're just not complete. Today there are new tools and new sciences that enabled us to reach levels of professionalism never before attainable. There are five such areas that I consider extremely important:

1. Computer technology
2. Strategic planning
3. Structured creativity
4. Predictive research
5. Nonverbal communication

The Coming of the Computer

The availability of computer systems has been to the direct marketing industry what airplanes have been to transportation. No development has had such a far-reaching, truly revolutionary impact on our way of doing business.

The computer's first applications in our field were similar to those in every other field of business. They saved us time. Mailing lists were transferred to punched cards, which could be sorted and filed easily. Customer records could be maintained on magnetic tape and, later, instantly recalled for billing, shipping, and promotional mailings. The cards gave way to tape, and the tape to floppy disks. Punched cards became high-speed printouts and ink-jet labelers that operated faster than the eye could see. Labels became heat-transfer fill-ins and, eventually computer-typed and laser-printed letters.

The ability to file and retrieve data changed the procedures, the personnel, and the profitability of direct marketing. But this was only the beginning. These first applications of the computer were, in effect, only simpler, faster ways to do everything we always used to do before. The real excitement was yet to come.

Responses, once laboriously broken down by ledger cards, are now not only tallied but compared to expectations, sorted by test cells, forecast to infinity, factored for relative customer quality, analyzed for trends, and tracked for profitability through the life of the customer relationship. Regression analysis and other sophisticated mathematical methods predict with uncanny certainty which postal areas and which combinations of personal characteristics are most likely to produce an optimum profit.

Sophisticated firms now use computers for "modeling"; that is, for printing out scenarios based on subtle changes in pricing or renewals. This is done most often in the magazine field, but in other direct marketing fields as well.

Both customer lists and prospect lists can now be subjected to infinite selectivity, merging, purging, matching, eliminating of present customers, and screening of individual names or census tracts for likely credit risks.

A merchandiser now, for instance, can go through the company's customer list and make an offer only to those who have purchased an item in a specific category, in a specific time frame, and within a chosen price range. The customer can be selected by neighborhood, credit experience, sex, or any other deducible factor. Once the customer has been selected, a computer letter can refer to past purchases or known interests.

Computerized list segmentation has made it possible for mailings to be directed to those most likely to respond, sparing others from unwanted offers and advertisers from unnecessary expense.

Credit can now be extended more easily, on the basis of more reliable data. Screening of bad credit risks can be based on past experiences in a half-dozen areas. And we can be more creative than ever in displaying our customer's name and other data with dramatic, computer-driven printing methods.

Thanks to the computer, our industry can be not only more accurate than ever but also more personal. The technology invented to process enormous volumes of data and keep track of millions of customers has made it possible for us to treat each one individually and to be more personal than ever in our offers, our appeals, and even in the products we develop.

The Emergence of Strategic Planning

Another great evolution has been the growth of strategy as a recognized factor in direct marketing.

When the bulk of mail-order ads promoted a single product or self-help book, each advertisement stood on its own to a much greater extent than today. We concerned ourselves with building sales, not reputations, with very few exceptions. The occasional farsighted advertiser—such as Book-of-the-Month Club—established an identity in copy style and layout. The legendary Oscar Ogg painstakingly drafted calligraphic-style layouts for the Book-of-the-Month Club that accurately portrayed the respectability and sincerity of this mail-order institution.

Most firms, however, searched for the elusive "hot product," wrote headlines and copy that promised the moon, and relied on research methods that can be fully described as "Let's run it somewhere and see if it works."

Things are very different today. The market is bigger. The options are more numerous, and the stakes are gigantic. There are over a hundred direct marketers with sales volumes over $100 million, and many more aiming to join their ranks. Total consumer sales attributed to direct marketing (not counting database marketing's effect on retail sales) exceed $150 billion dollars—$92 billion in products, $27 billion in financial services, $31 billion in other services such as long distance, internet, and air shipping. Add to this $78 billion in business products and services and $60 billion in fund-raising. Yes, the rewards are greater, but so are the risks. Fortunately, the tools to work with have improved also.

The success of a product today begins in its very design. You can't take a product off a retail shelf and expect it to succeed in a mail-order ad without some special advantage. That's why many products are designed especially for mail-order markets and are "Not available through stores."

The offer is more than just a good price. It involves calculations of market potential and advertising cost. It requires consideration of returns, credit, premiums, trade-ups, and additional items that can be sold.

Media are much more complex also. What's the size of the universe? Can multimedia support methods expand it? Is there a core market that can be segmented out for special attention? Should our strategy "skim off" the most likely prospects from a large audience, or concentrate on squeezing every sale out of a smaller target market with what we call a high-penetration strategy?

Creative copy is no longer the starting point. Brilliant headlines are no longer enough. Professionals in this field resolve questions of positioning, emotional appeal, benefit extension, and credibility before the first word of copy comes out of a word processor.

Today marketing strategy involves long-range objectives seldom considered in the past. Every advertisement not only brings in orders but also creates impressions that will influence the result of future offers by your firm. Every customer relationship is a value in itself, to be treated as carefully as if you were running an exclusive retail shop. Furthermore, it is likely that you will face direct, effective competition within months after your success has become well known.

Structured Creativity

Another great change that is rapidly sweeping this industry, and many other industries as well, is the emergence of *structured creativity*.

When I was running the Capitol Record Club, I remember Capitol's president, Alan Livingston, telling our board, "You can't have a hundred-million-dollar corporation dependent on whether or not four or five dope addicts get their act together and give us a hit single."

The same advice applies to direct marketers. We can't build and maintain multimillion-dollar businesses on the occasional brainstorm of the rare and unpredictable genius who comes along from time to time. If you're running a Doubleday or a Time-Life or a CBS, you need new ideas and new products when you need them, not when an idea happens to be available.

The solution to this dilemma was found in the development of techniques to stimulate and evaluate new ideas on a dependable basis. Some of the early attempts at this included positive thinking and what we now call "brainstorming" in various forms. "Synectics," a method of problem solving based on creative thinking, offered an original approach to problem definition and formal creativity that in turn inspired many spin-offs and variations.

During the initial planning stages for a new client or introduction of a new product, I often recommend that some type of open-ended structured creativity session be part of the plan. These sessions always include both client and agency personnel, as well as some objective but talented people not steeped in the client's business. Sometimes they are run by a skilled staff member as an "idea-generation lab." Often we bring in outside facilitators.

Such sessions produce hundred of ideas. Many of them are unusable, a necessary by-product of any free-thinking creative process. But, without exception, one or two brilliant approaches emerge which would not have been created in any other way. Some of these have, in turn, become spectacular direct marketing successes.

Seeing the Future: Predictive Research

The fourth major revolution has been the recognition of the potential of *predictive research*.

In a field where, for years, only "split-run testing" was respected, research has finally come into its own. For years classic packaged-goods research methods produced the wrong answers for direct marketers. Recently, focus panels and interviews have been able to get meaningful reactions to a proposition and determine which advertising approach will work best in the media marketplace. But this has worked only with research methods that have been specifically adapted to the needs of direct marketing.

Chapter 4 will reveal some of the techniques used today, if not to pick winners at least to eliminate losers and give our split-run tests a better chance to come up with a winner.

Nonverbal Communication

Of all the "secrets" direct marketers have learned from their interaction with general advertisers, none has had as much impact as the recognition of the role of nonverbal communication in advertising.

In a field where the rule used to be that "copy is king," art directors, photographers, and researchers with training in psychology now make significant contributions to direct marketing communications in all media.

Progressive direct marketers now recognize that consumers get impressions from every aspect of a communication, not just from the headlines and the copy. A cluttered, messy, cheap-looking layout makes the company and the product seem cheap, and all the verbal assurances and guarantees in the world won't overcome the impression.

If every mailing piece yells "Bargain!" and "Clearance!" eventually the recipient gets the impression that bargain is the nature of the company, and expectations of a quality product steadily diminish and finally disappear. On the other hand, if a company has built a reputation over the years, by the overall impression it conveys and by its actions in providing good products with good service, then future communications are more likely to succeed. The appearance of an ad, the character and personality communicated by the photographs or graphics used, can do more to enhance or destroy credibility than any words.

Indeed, many messages can be communicated with images and photographs more dramatically than with words. If you said, "Use this product and find happiness," people would not take you seriously. If you said, "Romance can be yours if you follow the advice in this magazine," you would lose all credibility. Yet advertisers can "say" such things, and prospects "read" exactly these messages when the message is conveyed pictorially. A happy couple using your product associates happiness, the couple, and the product in the eye and mind of the reader.

Like any new tool, nonverbal communication must be understood and practiced to gain the best results. As a result, the creative process today is more difficult than it used to be, but also infinitely more capable of solving any marketing problem.

Other Important Developments

The five developments discussed above are not the only major changes going on. They are, however, the ones responsible for the present scientific and professional level of direct marketing. Even as I write this, other changes have emerged that are having dramatic and far-reaching consequences in the direct marketing world.

The telephone is one change, as both an ordering opportunity and a selling tool. Credit cards are another, bringing advertisers the ability to offer "credit" terms while getting cash payments. The Internet—though still in a state of change itself—is challenging direct marketers to make full use of its unique capabilities. Globalization is still another—the tendency for direct marketing businesses, like all business, to extend across the world's borders. Only rarely can a successful direct marketing proposition in one country not be transferable in some way to others around the globe.

INTEGRATED MARKETING

For years there was a wall between the disciplines of general advertising and direct marketing. Today those walls have come tumbling down, and advertisers can demand and expect direct marketing based on the combined experience of general advertising and direct marketing. In many agencies, direct marketing is a strategic element routinely considered when new campaigns are planned. Conversely, the resources of the general agency—sophisticated research methods, precisely measured media planning, and brilliant creative departments—are available to back up the direct marketing group. It is not, as has existed before, a coexistence or mutual toleration, but a total assimilation that retains the strengths of both. It is not a matter of hanging the name "direct marketing" on a general agency department, or vice versa. In the old days direct marketing used reason to generate action; general advertising harnessed emotion to influence awareness and attitudes. Today each discipline has learned to respect the other.

Reason and Emotion

Direct marketers have always been the masters of reason. We excelled at lengthy advertisements that involved the reader, proclaimed benefits, made promises, overcame objections, and asked for the order. Our advertisements in all media argued with the prospect. Sometimes we yelled our story with bold-type newspaper headlines, and sometimes we used loud, strident broadcast announcers. The highest state of the art was "17 reasons why. . . ."

At the same time, general advertisers had mastered the art of emotion. Photographs associated a smile with a product and good times with a company name. They brought tears to our eyes and smiles to our faces, creating emotional involvement far beyond those that are possible using written communication alone.

Modern direct marketers learned to use *both* reason and emotion. We tested our ideas explicitly, adding photographs that communicated emotional ideas that might lack credibility in verbal form. Significant lift factors were noted. The use of nonverbal, photographic communication in an emotional message is now tracked and tested just as precisely as any other kind of copy.

Action and Awareness

Direct marketers have always concentrated on the immediate goal of action-coupons (or phone calls) now! The old rule was "Every ad stands alone. There's no such thing as cumulative effect."

General advertisers, on the other hand, concerned themselves with changes in aided and unaided awareness, and measured the positive and negative associations consumers had with a brand name. They cared about frequency of impression and multimedia impact. They tracked the extra value people would pay for a trusted name, and knew the effect of building long-range reputation even while they urged people to buy a product at their supermarket or department store. General advertisers emphasized the long-range attitude of the consumer, while we direct marketers concentrated on making a fast buck.

Today, both kinds of advertising have to do both. Some stimulus to immediate action helps general advertising to pay off. Some concern with long-range awareness helps direct marketing propositions to remain viable for a longer period.

Every communication has an "awareness" by-product. It's free. But it can be positive or negative. You can build product image and company name, as well as the overall image of direct marketing, with every communication—or you can hurt all three. The difference is a little extra planning and a long-range view.

We know from third-party propositions and from support advertising that impressions are transferable. In third-party propositions, the endorsement of a company trusted by the consumer makes it possible to sell everything from luggage and diamond rings to insurance policies that might not be successful otherwise. In support advertising, we know that we can place TV spots or radio commercials calling attention to a newspaper ad or mailing, and have a response rate greater than advertisements in either media would produce independently. Why has it taken us so long to accept that every time we send out a mailing we create attitudes that will affect the response to every future mailing?

We have always concerned ourselves with the 5 out of 100 people who responded to a mailing. We have ignored the rest. But 30 or 40 others probably opened the envelope and read at least part of the contents. They may not have ordered *this time*, but they have formed some impression of the product and the company. If it's good, they're more likely to say yes next time. If it's bad, they may not even open the envelope on the next effort. Taking the long-run view will pay off in future campaigns.

A WISH FOR THE FUTURE

Despite the increased use of direct marketing by major companies and agencies, few, other than mail-order advertisers, have integrated its basic strength into their overall business planning. To realize its full potential, its principles must be incorporated not as a "below the line" secondary activity, but as a fundamental corporate marketing strategy. Direct-marketing planning should be the guideline for setting the marketing budget in the first place. Logic and common sense support budgeting this way:

1. *Identified customers.* The repeat customers, who produce most of any company's sales and profits, should get priority. Avoiding the loss of one customer is more profitable than gaining three new ones. And it is easier to get present customers to buy 10% more, than to get 10% more customers. In the first place, you need only to mail to ten households; in the second,

you must mail to 50 or 100. The "catch" is the phrase "identified." You can only apply this to customers who have given you their names and addresses, so on-pack and other offers to obtain this data must be part of this activity.

2. *Identified prospects.* Known users of competitive products, heavy users of the category, and imminent purchasers—if they are known—should be the second priority. These households or businesses don't need to be sold on the category, only on your brand. Many prospects are available through Metromail and other database programs. Others can be searched out with your own promotions.

3. *Probable suspects.* People with demographic or other characteristics who statistically "look like" your present customers. These people have a better chance of responding to your advertising than the general public.

4. *Mass advertising.* The budget that is left over should then be spent on mass advertising, which, in terms of accountable advertising, can best be justified if it includes offers designed to identify more customers, prospects, and suspects. Like the first three categories, mass advertising can build brand equity, positive attitudes, and name recognition as a bonus.

A NOTE ABOUT HISTORY

In this edition and in all the previous ones, I have tried to maintain a continuity between the lessons of the past, the methods used today, and an idea of what the future holds. For more than 25 years in this business, I have worked with many different kinds of companies and helped develop many new applications. The ones that fail are usually those that are so intent on where they want their business to go that they have forgotten where they came from or where they are at the moment. A sailor can't select a course just on knowing a goal; you have to first find your bearings.

Direct marketing's roots are in mail order. It is where direct mail became an advertising medium. It is where great copywriters found that their instincts about people counted as much as their knowledge of the product. It is where the basic math of Cost Per Response first became the standard measurement of every direct marketing effort, as it still is today and will be tomorrow.

To anyone who thinks this book may spend too much time on direct marketing's background and history, I offer you one reminder:

"Those who have forgotten the mistakes of the past are condemned to repeat them."

2

STRATEGIC PLANNING

If you hand a mailing piece to a group of direct marketers, you will have a scene reminiscent of the Indian tale of several blind men describing an elephant. Just as the blind men will comment on different aspects of the elephant, direct marketers will focus on different parts as well. Somebody will describe a brilliant letter, another will comment on a clever headline, still another will rave about an original format or an exciting layout. Someone else may overlook the communications vehicle altogether and note an attractive offer or appealing product.

Direct marketing is no *one* of these things. It is all of them together: a sum more powerful than its ingredients, a harnessing of the forces of art, science, psychology, and common sense to achieve a marketing objective.

When a marketer is planning a new venture, or trying to improve an existing one, the elephant fable inevitably comes into the picture. Creative advisors suggest new headlines. Merchandisers look for new products. List brokers critique the list choices.

The newest form of direct marketing—the Internet—is no exception. One advertiser, disappointed by the results of his paid banners and buttons, asked for help. My observation was that it violated every direct marketing precept. There was no audience selection. No apparent benefit. No immediacy. The Internet expert, like most specialists, focusing only on her own field—added flashing lights and graphic motion—without fixing any of the underlying problems.

Each new field utilized by direct marketing has gone through the same phase. Direct response television, database marketing, infomercial marketing—each went through a stage where "specialists" ignored the lessons of human nature and relied solely on the new media. Each eventually discovered that the strategic direct marketing principles that have created some of the world's most successful corporations apply to every product, every medium, and every market segment—in every country in the world.

STRATEGY DEFINED

The one critical element that must be understood to master this field is *strategy*. But first we must agree about what strategy really is. Am I using strategy in the sense that military planners use it when planning or discussing wars won or lost? Yes. In the sense that Machiavelli wrote about, in his advice on how to manipulate masses and topple princes? Yes. Will we deal with it in the dictionary sense of *harnessing combined resources to achieve a selected goal?* Yes.

Further, we will see how and why strategic planning is the great essential difference between amateurism and professionalism in direct marketing and, probably, in most other fields as well.

What's Different?

Many people in the field deal with their first direct-marketing application after years of experience in general advertising and marketing. Though they may be respected professionals in the art of "indirect" advertising, they often experience difficulties adjusting to the very different and often difficult requirements of direct marketing.

Targeting. While general advertisements must find a common denominator among most readers or viewers of their message, direct marketers are concerned only with logical prospects—perhaps only 5 or 10 percent of the overall audience. Also, some customers are worth more than others. The widely-accepted 20-80 rule says that 20 percent of your customers create 80 percent of your business. Therefore we must be sure that we attract those who are prospective customers. Our measurement is not what percentage of the overall audience or circulation we reach, but what percentage of those who are likely to purchase the product or service.

Concentration. We concentrate our advertising budget and our creative attention on the targeted readers or viewers, not on averages. For instance, while an average audience may best be reached with one simple, easy-to-retain idea, a genuine prospect often needs (and demands) as much information as possible. This leads to longer copy, larger mailings or advertisements, and longer TV formats. How long? Long enough to make the sale. In direct marketing, our efforts usually are not measured by impressions and changes in attitude, but by actual sales—whether by phone, mail, Internet or in retail stores.

Involvement. Those who work in direct mail or in longer-format mass media enjoy a luxury unknown to general advertisers: sufficient space or time to tell the whole story. But it is also an obligation. We must use it to involve readers and to hold their interest, through an interesting story, intriguing illustrations, fascinating information, or involved formats like stamps, cards, coupons, or other items.

Personalization. The ability to personalize in direct mail is infinite—not just by being able to simulate a letter or refer to the reader by name, but by making the message as relevant as possible to the reader's own interests. This of course does not apply to direct mail alone. Local newspaper ads often produce higher response rates if they include references to the city. Magazine ads do better if geared to the publication and the special interests of its readers. Websites often have greetings with the customer's name, and references to past transactions.

Response-Ability. Because we are going after a response and not just an impression, we want to make it as easy as possible for the prospect to respond. That's why coupons or website order pages must be easy to fill out. Forms must allow prospects to write phone numbers that are legible. There should be enough room to legibly print names and addresses. Even when we are seeking a retail transaction, it pays to give the address of the local dealer, or to provide a clip-out reminder of the purchase intention for the customer's future reference. Huge phone companies and the local plumber use one proven response technique in common—a reminder sticker to put on your phone or your refrigerator.

Accountability. No matter what we are selling or how it is to be purchased, it always requires a response, and that response must be measurable. That is the only way we can test one list or medium against another; the only way we can continue to say "I know" that this worked and that didn't. Direct marketing is the ultimate in accountable advertising—one attribute that has enabled this field to evolve and grow as it has.

Test-Ability. Direct marketing uses research to help develop ideas or to understand why one ad worked and another did not. However, it is not usually accepted as a substitute for testing—the actual tabulation of responses to determine what works and what doesn't. Split runs, test markets, and relatively small samples are used to determine what the consumer will really respond to. Executives trained in direct marketing will usually try several products or marketing approaches in relatively inexpensive test campaigns, holding back the bulk of the marketing budget until actual results can be measured and projected.

FIVE ESSENTIAL ELEMENTS OF STRATEGIC PLANNING

The first step in any marketing endeavor is to determine a basic strategy. There are five elements of strategic planning in direct marketing:

1. Product
2. Offer
3. Media
4. Distribution
5. Creativity

No single one of these elements is all-important or unimportant. Each demands careful study, perceptive problem definition, innovative solutions, and logical decision making. They apply whether planning a major launch of a giant new program or starting a kitchen-table mail-order business. They are universal and, when used with some imagination and lots of hard work, can increase the profitability of any size or type of direct marketing endeavor.

While many of these examples refer to direct marketing's roots in classic mail order, they are the foundation for direct marketing. It is necessary to understand the keys to mail-order success in order to be successful in its newer applications. The experience outlined in this book is based on the development of this field in the United States, but despite some variations necessitated by logistics, the principles apply anywhere in the world and have been reconfirmed on every continent.

PRODUCT STRATEGY

Originally, most businesses were based on the idea that a product is a fixed, inflexible entity that is developed by one area of a business, then handed to a sales or marketing department with the order: "Now you guys figure out how to sell it!"

Today the emphasis has been reversed, with product-development teams directed to find products or services to meet marketing opportunities. In place of the old dictum to consumers "We made it, you should buy it," we now have "You want it, we'll make it."

Direct marketing has been a pioneer in this approach. The ultimate application today is a product that is designed and priced "from scratch" exclusively for direct marketing. Dell, Gateway and Apple Computers all demonstrate this goal. All of these companies encourage you to configure the ideal computer for your needs—how much hard-disk space, RAM, what processor speed, modem speed, number and types of ports, drives, etc. Tell them what you want and they will make it for you!

Mail order products are often designed to provide appealing offers that can be sent on a trial basis, with both product and packaging that looks good on a printed page. They are priced to permit credit sales, introductory offers, and repeat sales in subscription or club programs. They are often exclusive to direct marketing; at least in the version offered they are "Not available in stores."

The giants of our industry have their best marketing teams developing and testing new products for sale to their house lists—product sales that benefit from the reputation of the company and the expertise of its management. For most direct marketers the options are more limited, however. A retail product can be adapted for mail-order sales. A group of printed publications can be repackaged as a direct marketing program. A successful overseas proposition can be tailored for introduction in another country. Popular retail product—such as books or flowers—can be offered with greater convenience or greater selection by phone or website.

Product Selection

The first consideration in product strategy is, of course: Do you have the right product in the first place? The most skillful direct marketer can't sell a product that has no appeal at all—not to any market segment, at any price, by any distribution method.

Every one of my New York University classes has included at least one person who has a product he or she wants to sell by mail order, usually only because retailers have expressed no interest at all. As each class progressed, it became obvious that the product could not be sold by itself. The market simply wasn't large enough to justify creating the business or the product.

But all is not lost. Often the most oddball product can be successful in some specialty catalog, perhaps as one of a hundred items offered. If a catalog gets a 3 percent response from its past customers, this item needs only 1/100th of 3 percent—3/100 of 1 percent of the catalog mailing—to pay its way for the catalog company.

It's not difficult to get your product into a catalog, because people are always on the lookout for new items to freshen their merchandise mix. And if the product is successful in one catalog, it will be repeated in the next. As surely as the sun rises, competitors will note that the product was repeated and come after you to include it in their catalogs.

Theoretically, a start-up company can introduce its first product this way and reinvest the income in additional products, or in its own catalog business. With its own catalog or new products, it may then have a "back-end" to make solo mailings profitable where it would not have been on a one-shot basis.

From the cataloger's point of view, product selection is the key strategic element, the one ingredient that must be right before the company begins to fine-tool pricing, list selection or creative style. However, a weak product can often be "saved" by using some of the approaches described below.

Changing a Product without Changing It

The most economical way to revise a product is to change it without actually adding anything to it. There are several ways to make "changes" in direct marketing.

Positioning is a whole sub-science, so important that half of Chapter 9 is devoted to the subject. Briefly, it involves a general advertising technique for a product or service: presenting it with a different image, aiming it at a different market segment, or by selling it at a different point in the buyer's decision-making process. This last technique is my own invention, which I call *horizontal positioning*. It will be discussed in more detail in Chapter 9.

One example of conventional or *vertical* positioning is a campaign from a few years back to sell Avis used cars as "The New Car Alternative." Avis was appealing to new-car buyers instead of the conventional used-car market. An example of horizontal positioning was Doubleday Book Club's "Fantasy" advertisements that sell prospects on the idea of reading for the sake of reading itself, rather than on book clubs in general or on their particular book club offer.

The "breakout" technique is another valuable tool of the trade. This involves taking a component of the basic package and isolating it to be featured as part of the offer. You can spot the breakout technique in mailings or advertisements that promote product elements as premiums—for instance the plastic case for a card series. Sometimes the companies might offer a reference service's binder or an index section. Credit card companies use the breakout techniques all the time. You'll notice offers that feature an illustrated card, or are associated with a charity. They highlight other features rather than the tired but fundamental benefit—instant credit. Many products have attachments, accessories, manuals, or even service contracts that can be broken out and featured as ways of giving new life to old offers.

Multiple-part products can be taken apart, or put back together, to make what appear to be entirely different offers. A catalog of socket wrenches and tools with individual prices would probably not be successful in general markets, yet "100-Piece Tool Sets"—1,000 assorted nuts and bolts as a bonus for fast action!—are offered in full-page ads in dozens of publications.

I remember a variation I once did for Walter Black's Classics Club, a book club that basically offered three books for $1 with a subscription to others. I chose to add an element that dramatized the combined end product: "Build a fine collection of great classics like this," referring to a photo of a shelf of the beautifully bound books. It worked so well that the panel eventually became the theme for an ad that ran for years.

On the other hand, a set of encyclopedias can be sold volume by volume, or a Barbie doll can be sold with an offer that presents new doll outfits each month for the enthusiastic user. A manufacturer of pots and pans can sell a deluxe set of pots, or a subscription to a pot-a-month club, or a basic set with other kitchen equipment added, or the set of pots along with "The coffee pot free just for trying this amazing offer."

None of the products in these examples have changed. They have just been repositioned, redescribed, or recombined to make them seem fresh and different.

Turning Lemons into Lemonade

One of the most interesting approaches to revitalizing a stale proposition is the dramatization of a product feature that has been either buried in body copy or left out of advertisements completely. My first direct marketing boss, Victor Schwab, called this "turning lemons into lemonade." You can build an ad around any aspect of a product or service. This includes the major features, and the minor ones. Ads can promote not only the new improvements, but also old features that have been taken for granted.

Don't presume that the customer knows everything there is to know about your product. Reintroduce it, and look for every benefit that can legitimately be dramatized. Is the product small? Stress space saving and portability. Does it lack the bells and whistles that competing products offer? Talk about simplicity and ease of operation. Is it an older model? Write that they don't make products like this anymore, and that this model is in limited supply.

Is your company not the largest in its field? You may be able to stress personal service or family ownership—the idea that the company principals are intimately involved, read every letter, and stand behind every one of their products. Are your prices a bit high? Then make a plus out of it and feature the idea that not everyone appreciates extra quality; this offer is only for those who do, and are willing to pay for it. Is your magazine thinner than others? Then perhaps it has more selective editorial matter and can be read quickly. Is your charity the smallest in its field? Then stress how the work is probably more personal.

I have never seen a marketing proposition where there wasn't some feature that lent itself to dramatization.

All this presumes that the claims given in the examples above are legitimate. If your product doesn't offer the customer some real value or advantage of some sort, then maybe you should start all over again with a new product. You can add all the sugar you like, but if the lemons were rotten in the first place no one will want to drink your lemonade.

Enhancing Perceived Value

Your product strategy isn't limited to the extremes of developing whole new projects on one hand and repositioning or reassessing your product on the other. It always pays to invest by adding some genuine value to enhance the product's perception. Such additions are "paid for" by reduced order cost resulting from greater advertising response, and they can be tested easily and inexpensively.

Premiums are a simple addition. So is utilitarian packaging such as a carrying case or storage container. If you're planning to send follow-up mailings anyway, why not include a newsletter that you can mention as an added benefit in your initial offer? A cosmetic firm's customized beauty makeover can include an "Insider's Fashion Forecast" newsletter, for example. Or a plants-by-mail service can include a magazine that doubles as a catalog. Both of these examples add value to the basic proposition.

Some other value add-ons include a very strong, long-term guarantee—a feature that can become a powerful advertising appeal in itself. A manufacturer can feature some type of support service. A cookbook publisher can offer a telephone service for recipe help!

Product planning requires basic decision-making at the onset. Company officials have to have a commitment about what the product or service is, and how they want it perceived. It can't be all things to all people. It can be the best *or* the cheapest, traditional *or* innovative, entertaining *or* educational. To try to be everything at once is to be nothing.

Whether you reposition it, change it, dramatize a new feature, or invent something entirely new, the product itself must respond to research and test results in the same manner as every other ingredient of this five-part marketing equation. Unfortunately the product is often the last consideration of many advertisers, who prefer to place blame on the ad or the medium rather than looking at their own product.

OFFER STRAGEGY

Of the five critical marketing elements, offer strategy is the one most easily revised for a fast-result improvement. Even the slightest change in price—whether it's in bold or buried in body copy or a coupon—can have dramatic effects on front-end performance.

Price-cutting is often a cop-out for real strategic planning. Anyone can cut prices. The real marketing accomplishment is to increase sales without cutting profit margins.

Expressing the Price

Not only the price itself but also the way the price is expressed can drastically influence the cost per order. For example, let's say a monthly magazine has a newsstand value of $3 per copy, or $36 per year. The subscription offer is set at $18 per year. Here are some of the ways this offer can be expressed:

- One year for only $18   Basic price statement
- $1.50 per copy   Basic price expressed by unit
- Half price   Price expressed in fractions
- Six issues free   Savings dramatized by units
- Save $18   Savings expressed numerically
- Save 50 percent   Savings expressed in percentages

Note that all these offers represent exactly the same $18 price. Only the means of expression varies. Of course, most of these statements must comply with Better Business Bureau (www.bbb.org) standards and Federal Trade Commission (FTC) (www.ftc.gov) regulations and, if used to sell magazines, will be subject to the additional standards of the Audit Bureau of Circulation (ABC) codes (www.accessabc.com). For more information, check out their web sites. Details about their regulations and guidelines are available on these pages.

Another example of price variation is a gift or service free with a subscription. The customer pays the full $36 and receives a premium that costs the publisher $18 but may have a much higher perceived value. For example, *The New York Times* offered a free $25 membership in a discount dining plan rather than cut its subscription price. Cellular phone services offer free or low-priced phones rather than cut the monthly minimum payments.

Price Sensitivity

One test I conducted for a film-processing client shows how sensitive pricing and price expression can be. The numbers are altered for confidentiality, but the relationships are correct. The offer is an introductory 35-mm film-processing order, with a sliding scale of prices ranging from $1.99 for a 12-exposure roll up to twice that for 36-picture rolls. The objective was to attract film-processing customers who could then be sold additional processing at progressively higher prices. Table 2-1 shows what happened.

This test demonstrates several important lessons. In the first place, you can see how important offer expression can be. The cost per order ranged from $2 to $19. If the 1-cent sale was your control offer and produced 10,000 orders at a cost of $12 each, the half-price offer would have produced 24,000 orders at $5 each. If your allowable margin at $3.50 was $10 per order (based on anticipated re-orders), the 1-cent sale offer would have produced a $30,000 loss; the half-price offer would have produced a $78,000 profit, even after reducing the margin by 75 cents per order.

The 99-cent offer, which had a higher average price but a $3 higher cost per order, would have resulted in a profit of $15,000. It is often the case

TABLE 2-1
TEST RESULTS OF A FILM-PROCESSING OFFER

Price statement	Twenty-print price	Average price (all sizes)	Cost per order	Margin	Units	Net	Contribution
Basic, $1.99 up	$1.99	$3.50	$19	$10.00	6,315	($9.00)	($56,835)
Film, only 39 cents	1.39	2.50	14	9.00	8,571	(5.00)	(42,855)
1-cent sale	1.00	2.50	12	9.00	10,000	(3.00)	(30,000)
$1 off	.99	2.50	9	9.00	13,333	—	—
99-cent offer	.99	2.50	8	9.00	15,000	1.00	15,000
Half price	.99	1.75	5	8.25	24,000	3.25	78,000
39-cent limited offer	.39	2.20	2	8.70	60,000	6.70	402,000

that a client finds a satisfactory offer like this one and stops experimenting, therefore never finding a more profitable offer, such as the half-price one in this example.

The more daring 39-cent offer would produce far more orders—60,000 in this example—and a very dramatic $402,000 profit. This is true if the "back end" doesn't deteriorate and the margin holds up despite the poorer-quality orders. In most cases there would be some deterioration of quality, but not enough to offset the dramatically higher number of responses at a much lower order cost.

It is a mistake, however, to look solely at cost per order as the ultimate indicator of profit. As is further discussed in Chapter 8 on Math, there are times when a higher cost per order may result in a lower net profit per order—if you include the enhanced marketing costs—but many more orders and a better overall *return on investment* (ROI). Plans should aim at total profit measured against investments, not just profit per item sold.

Elasticity of Price

In setting a pricing strategy, price elasticity must be taken into account. There are customers who must have certain products and will pay almost any price to get it. If there are enough of these customers, companies can set their price very high.

Inelasticity is more often the rule, however. If you are selling a strictly discretionary purchase—a product or service that people can live without—then it is likely that you are asking your customer to make an impulse decision.

Just look at some of those executive toys in the airline gift catalogs. No one really *needs* a battery-operated travel alarm that plays your favorite tune and tells you what the time is in 12 time zones. However, for $5 or $10, few of us would have trouble justifying such a purchase in our own minds. We could probably talk ourselves into it for $29.95. But for $129.95? Suddenly it becomes a considered purchase instead of an impulse one, at least for most of us. This is an example of an *inelastic* price. It can stretch only so far, and no further.

Price Break Points

When setting a selling price, consider currency break points. In the United States, 99 cents will do better than $1.20, $4.99 much better than $5.50, $10 better than $11, and $19.95 much better than $21.

On the other hand, often you can approach such a break point with no noticeable decline in results. If you're at $8.95, you can often move up to $9.95 with a negligible decline in response rate. But in my experience, price the product at $10.95 and watch for a 20 to 30 percent drop-off in the response rate.

If you must raise prices 10 percent, I suggest you try 20 percent instead—keeping the currency break-point concept in mind. In some recent tests,

I've found that prices like $6 and $12 may cost some orders, but not enough to offset the profits from this slightly higher price.

You'll notice in these examples I use both rounded (e.g., $5) and broken (e.g., $4.95) prices. Frankly, I suspect that the consumer is smarter than most people think and that no one is fooled by the nickel difference and perceives $4.95 as a significantly lower price. My feeling is that prestige-related offers should use the rounded figures, price-appeal offers the broken prices.

However, I have no definitive recommendation. I posed this question in the first edition of this book 17 years ago and no one has come forward with new information on this subject. There have always been more important things for my clients to test. Whether the client with the $10 subscription price should charge $9.95—or whether the $9.95 marketer has unnecessarily sacrificed a treasure in nickels—is a question I'll leave for others to decide. My advice is to decide what's appropriate for your own business and stick to it.

Add-on Pricing

I'm often asked about shipping and handling costs, which are a frequent complaint raised in customer correspondence. Should you set your price at $10 plus $2.50 postage and handling, or should it be $12.50, or a flat $10? This is a question I *have* tested. It's a perfect example of how the consumer has a way of surprising us.

The tests indicate that a price of $10 plus shipping and handling will do about the same as $10, without statistical significance one way or the other except losing $2.50 in income per shipment. The only "bad" price would be $12.50 "including shipping" which would do about 10 percent worse than either alternative. It appears safe to conclude that consumers don't mind paying for shipping costs as an add-on.

The Almighty "Free!"

No discussion of pricing would be complete without homage to the almighty "Free!" I call it almighty because, when I was a young copywriter at Schwab & Beatty, no use of the word ever escaped being capitalized by my copy chief, as if the word represented a deity deserving of respect.

In a way the treatment is deserved, because even in this day of FTC-specified qualifications and rampant consumer skepticism, "Free!" is still the single most powerful word in the vocabulary of direct marketing offers.

The film-processing price test I described earlier was an exercise necessitated because the most famous film offer of all time—the one developed for Film Corporation of America—was specifically barred by the FTC. That offer was "Free film—send $1.00 for postage and handling." The customer was sent film only to discover that it apparently had to be processed by the same company—for an additional cost.

That doesn't mean a company can't genuinely give something to a customer for free, given that there are no strings attached. More recently, my client Video Professor regularly used a genuine free sample offer in their advertising. Their computer-training CDs and videotapes were so well-written that sampling did generate sufficient orders to be profitable.

The power of the word *free* is such that it often makes possible two-step offers in which a customer is offered a free booklet, free information, a free trial, or a free short-term subscription, while the company builds a mailing list for later solicitation. The enormously successful Time-Life Books operation initially built its business on one offer: free examination of the first book in a series.

One variation is what magazines call the "comp-copy offer," which is shorthand for "complimentary initial copy sent on trial." Most comp-copy offers are free only to respondents who do *not* eventually subscribe. If they do, the first issue is made part of the subscription. There's a good reason for doing this. ABC rules will not count a free copy in the magazine's circulation figures, a dilemma that's bound to make any magazine advertising department unhappy.

Having subscribers include the first issue isn't really giving it "free." The customer ends up paying for it. As a result, the "true comp-copy offer" has evolved, which makes the first issue free whether or not the respondent elects to cancel, regardless of circulation figures.

A healthy approach to this dilemma was developed by one magazine. They developed an initial "collector's issue" which was offered as the free incentive. These could be printed in quantity and sent out to new subscribers promptly, without waiting for the next issue date. The regular issues then all counted as circulation for advertising purposes.

The alternative impressed me for another reason. Magazine ads that try to refer to specific editorial content will disappoint many subscribers if the free trial issue doesn't include a story on the same subject. But the special issue can include all the articles referred to in advertising, thus paying off the implied promise of editorial examples.

Time magazine's development of exciting premiums such as almanacs or videotapes are offered in much the same way, and enable the magazine to make an honest free offer.

Other Considerations

There are many other considerations besides price to consider when planning offer strategy. Many of them are discussed in Chapter 6 on propositions.

One question is credit. Depending on the nature of the product and the audience, you may or may not want to establish a credit relationship with your customer. "Send no money now" is a powerful result-builder, especially when used with a full guarantee. But it involves sending out bills, setting up credit-evaluation procedures, and writing off some percentage of bad debt. Installment sales and credit cards have their own unique problems, as do cash-on-delivery (COD) shipments. Yet in at least one country "bill me" and COD are the standards.

Contests and sweepstakes are another aspect of offer strategy, ones that can have dynamic but dangerous consequences. The "lift" of a sweepstakes can be like a narcotic; it makes you feel good for the moment, but you can get hooked on it. While sweepstakes have been very important for many advertisers, they create a whole new set of problems in terms of poor-quality responses, high costs, and the need to come up with bigger and better contests in order to maintain the hyped sales level.

The effects show up in everything from bad debt to poor renewals to lower list-rental income. "Sweepstakes-sold" is, to a sophisticated advertiser, a warning that the magazine or list whose circulation is offered consists largely of people who like to enter contests, not necessarily of people truly involved in the subject of the magazine, product, or service sold. Some of the largest magazines in the world have seen their advertising revenue decline after using sweepstakes to maintain an artificially high circulation.

The Time Factor

The most overlooked factor in planning offer strategy is *time*. Usually an advertiser must make some type of advertising or premium investment, such as a discounted product, to attract a customer. We often refer to "buying" a customer, as it is not uncommon to deliberately lose money on a customer-acquisition offer by selling an item for $10 that costs the company $15 and sells normally for $20. In this case, if the advertising cost was $10 we have "bought" a customer for $15.

How fast we get back that $15 depends on what type of proposition we set up, the popularity of our products, and the effectiveness of our creative material. In other words, the same factors that go into planning customer acquisition strategy go into back-end strategy.

Most advertisers aim for a first-year break-even on each customer. They want to recover their initial investment within twelve months of the initial solicitation. They start developing a satisfactory return on investment in the second, third, and subsequent years. Renewals, repeat purchases, list-rental income, trade-ups, and cross-sell projects bring in profits over a period of years. Sometimes the break-even point does not occur during the first year at all, but only after two, three, or even four years.

This time factor accounts for the great profitability of magazines, mail-order catalogs, and club operations that have been in business for many years. They control the "mix" of old and new customers so as to produce a stable profit. Too many new customers may lower the profit margin for that year. To be a "hero" for the bean counters watching the bottom line, all one has to do is cut back on new-customer acquisition and let the profits from old customers overwhelm the cost of acquiring new ones. Obviously, the company pays for this decision in the long run, and could be out of business eventually. In general, longevity equals stability.

Price increases must be introduced with caution. New customers may be willing to pay the higher price, but the balloon can burst when customers who came in at an old, lower price are asked to renew at the new, higher one. Buyer resistance from old customers can set back any financial gains from the price increase for a period of two or three years, until the mix of new customers brought in at the higher price improves the bottom line.

Mathematical Models

All of these approaches can be evaluated with the aid of mathematical models. While I recommend using consultants who specialize in mathematical modeling, it is possible to set up a workable model on an in-house computer using Lotus or Excel spreadsheets. I prefer to leave it to specialists.

But it's not as easy as it sounds.

No matter who manages it, your basic data must be programmed and entered. Order cost, promotion expenses, conversion rates, renewal rates, cancellations, and bad debts all must be taken into account. Current data can be projected into a model of the next few years showing profitability, cash flow, sales volume, and production requirements.

With a good program, you can try out any scenario until you find the one that best suits your company's objectives and capabilities. For example, let's say you want to consider lowering a price but you expect that product costs per order will increase. You open your spreadsheet file and enter that conversion and payment expectations go up 5 percent but that you expect response rates to go down 10 percent. The entire business plan, utilizing these revised profit and loss estimates, can be printed out in minutes.

How well you plan will determine how good your estimates are. Subtle changes can have the most profound—and sometimes the most surprising—impact on your entire business. Any company that fails to think through offers and try new ones is missing a bet. In the mysterious alchemy of direct marketing, the right offer is the indispensable catalyst that activates every other ingredient. It is the key ingredient in turning the paper we write our plans on into gold.

MEDIA STRATEGY

In direct marketing, the medium is the market. We generally do not use lists or publications to reach predetermined market segments. Each list, publication or broadcast audience is a market in itself.

Conventional advertisers pick out cities or market segments and plan schedules to build awareness within these target groups in the most efficient manner possible. Readership studies, audience profiles, and Simmons data are correlated with circulation figures in order to obtain a cost per page per target audience. This might be 200 or 300 percent higher than a publication's cost per page for general circulation, depending on the selectivity.

In direct marketing, we usually don't care whether a new customer comes to us from one city or another or even in one month or another (except for circulation guarantees or fiscal year profitability goals). A customer is a customer is a customer. Since the U.S. Postal Service, UPS or Federal Express make up our distribution system, we do not have to worry about proximity to retail outlets or distributor routes. Therefore our strategies are concerned not with geographic markets but with media markets. Since every medium is subject to precise testing and result measurement, we can determine the most effective medium objectively instead of subjectively.

The Media Universe

Direct marketers often refer to a media "universe," meaning the maximum of known lists, publications, and other media that can be expected to be productive for a given product or service. Planning our strategy requires a full understanding and precise identification of the media universe for a given product.

At one time, the identification of a media universe was largely a product of instinct. Advertisers would go through magazines and look for those with a suitable editorial environment or with advertisements for a large number of repeat mail-order advertisers. Instinct still has its place, but today the investigative tools are more sophisticated. Every advertising agency has reference lists for its clients that note competing advertisers—including the magazines or television shows where it has ads or commercials. Simmons and other services identify the demographics, interests, and media preferences of users of virtually every product or service.

No product has an unlimited universe, because no product appeals to everyone. A universe is limited in width by the range of lists and publications available. Its depth is limited by the intrinsic appeal of the product, the offer, and the creative strategy.

Consumer Reports presents a classic example of how to expand a media universe. In 1977 and 1978, their universe consisted of about 10 million names on mailing lists and one national publication: *TV Guide*. A new creative approach that appealed to women as well as to men enabled them to dramatically increase the number of publications that were profitable. At one point, over 30 magazines and dozens of newspapers were on their media list. Both radio and television became major media sources as well.

A media universe, like the planetary universe, contracts and expands. In fact, "expanding the media universe" is the strategic objective of many of my firm's consulting assignments.

For a large advertiser intent on maximizing its facilities and reputation, planning may begin with the availability of a media category that has not responded to otherwise successful propositions. Direct marketers, for example, will develop short-term offers for some media, special products for others, and different credit terms for still others. A magazine might try a short-term offer in an impulse medium such as package inserts. A book club might offer a pre-selected group of books instead of a choice in a television offer that requires phone response. A mail-order firm might require credit card payments or ask for additional information when advertising in a publication that has previously produced poor credit experience.

Support is another way of expanding a universe—running advertisements in one media calling attention to a mailing, a website or a Sunday supplement. Support will be fully discussed in Chapter 16 on broadcast media. Broadcast is the most common support medium, but not the only one.

No Lists?

There is an abundance of mailing lists for most propositions. Sending material to a different list is usually the basis of a new test program. As the reader will see in Chapter 14 on mailing lists, there are thousands of lists and infinite ways to combine, select and segment them for most products. However, with some products and in some countries this is not the case.

In several countries, there are still no list brokers to bridge the gap between list owners and potential renters. And there is a lack of confidence that lists will be used once and not copied. But the lists are there— subscribers, members, credit card holders, and more. There are also opportunities to distribute mail door-to-door, and to build your own mailing lists by advertising in other media.

"No lists" usually also means "no competition," "high response rates," and "an opportunity to dominate the category." Like many problems, it is an opportunity in disguise. This is discussed in more detail in Chapter 22, Global Marketing.

Core Lists and Publications

In direct marketing, media and list-buying strategies are not as concerned with numbers as they are with *relevance*. If you are selling fishing reels, a small list of known buyers of fishing equipment is worth more than a list of demographically selected prospects—i.e., males, 35 and over, non-urban. And if your company is a mail-order business, then a list of people who have bought such products through the mail is worth more than a list of patrons of local sporting-goods shops.

Magazine audiences are selected in the same way. A publication directed at fishing enthusiasts is likely to do well for the fishing-reel proposition. If the bulk of the magazine's readers are "direct-mail-sold," they are more likely to respond than readers of a publication bought primarily from newsstands.

Interestingly, this is the opposite criterion from that used by packaged-goods advertisers, who generally prefer newsstand readers. These readers buy their magazines from stores or stands, and typically buy other products in retail stores. It is also presumed that readership per newsstand-sold copy may be higher than subscription copies.

Core lists are lists of relevant buyers of related products, or are lists that are composed of the most logical or most productive lists from the past. Similar publications are called *core publications*. These core media usually are the most productive for any product or service.

Pilot Testing

In a typical media schedule, lists and publications are assembled into categories related to the potential markets for a product or service. For example, categories that might be included for a female-oriented product are "Women's Homemaking," "Women's Career," "Women's Lifestyle" (such as *Cosmopolitan*), and "Women's Special Interests." Mailing list categories might include "Subscribers to Women's Magazines," "Cosmetics Plan Expires," and "Book Club Members."

These categories are assembled according to the logical relationships affecting the particular product being sold. If the product is particularly costly, the price range or products might be more relevant than the product itself in assembling a list universe.

If you were selling a power saw, a media universe might include "Mail-Order Tool Buyers," "Mechanics-Type Magazine Subscribers," and "Home Repair Catalog Inquirers." Usually advertisers of things like power tools would devote the bulk of their media plan to repeat insertions in lists or proven publications. Test advertisements or mailings would be scheduled in new lists or publications within the same category. Other tests would be dedicated to probing related categories not previously tested.

The objective here is to limit risk. We want to test the new categories without committing so much of our budget that the new categories, if unsuccessful, would offset the profitability of the roll-outs and test extensions.

Risk Limitation

It is important to limit the number of untested variables. What is being tested—the x factor—is the category of publication. This is, therefore, not the place to also test untried space units, new formats, or new creative strategies.

If your control ads have worked with a full page, small space is not the way to test a new category. In space, the way to minimize risk is usually to use a publication in the proper category that has small circulation but has been proven successful for other direct marketers. If you must use a larger-circulation, more costly magazine, then look into regional editions. Provided you are not penalized with a "back-of-the-book" position, calculations from a regional insertion can usually be interpolated to project what the cost per order would be on a national basis. It is important to adjust your cost figures to reflect the difference between the higher per-thousand regional rate and the national rate.

Mailing lists are much more flexible, since it is typically less costly to test a new list versus an ad in a new publication. The principles are the same, however. The lists tested should be proven within each category. The types of lists should be comparable. For instance, don't compare "hot-line" names—the most recent buyers of the list-owner's product—against a group of lists composed of year-old names. And like print advertising, make sure the test printing-costs are adjusted to compare what the mailings would have cost for a large-quantity rollout.

Testing will be more fully explored in Chapter 5. For now, it is only necessary to understand how a media program is put together—a very different process than that used by general advertisers.

CPM, CPP, OPM, and CPR

When planning a media program for your proposition, don't fall into the trap of presuming that cheap is good. A low CPM (cost per thousand) circulation is no bargain if the list or publication doesn't pull in the quantity and quality of buyers you need.

Some publications have a low CPM, but low readership. If readers only skim the publication, there is less chance that your advertisement will be noticed. Others have a very small, "digest" page size. If you need space to show your merchandise or tell your story, such a small page is not worth as much as a page in a publication of conventional size.

If you have access to computerized readership data compiled by Simmons or another research firm, you will be able to study the circulation analysis of a publication or a broadcast buy in terms of CPP (cost per thousand prospects). Such data offers more than a breakdown of readers by age or education. It can tell you whether the readers have bought an item in the product or service category recently, whether they have noted that they intend to, and whether they have ever bought by mail. Information about other members of the family may also be available. It might note whether another member of the family has joined a book club, for instance. With this kind of data, the CPP for a magazine campaign can be compared with what it would cost to reach prospects through other media. Surprisingly, CPP analysis often indicates that magazines or broadcast can be as cost-efficient as direct mail, and *vice versa.*

Micro-Marketing

Increasingly, with certain luxury consumer products or business-to-business services, a marketing program must be directed to very few prospects.

When such prospects can be identified using specialized direct mail lists, the marketing choices are obvious and limited. A different approach is required when the audience can be reached only by using broader lists or media.

When broader lists are used, media efficiency is not the ultimate standard. There will always be a waste factor of irrelevant names. For instance, an insurance mailer seeking veterans built an enormous business using lists with a good proportion of veterans. But these lists also contain the names of many non-veterans. The mail is addressed to "Dear Veteran," and simply ignores the non-veterans who may receive the piece. The non-veterans are not a concern in this strategy.

This attitude must often be adopted for print media and broadcast campaigns as well. The campaign concentrates on those who are prospects and ignores those who may not be. In some cases, only a handful of readers or

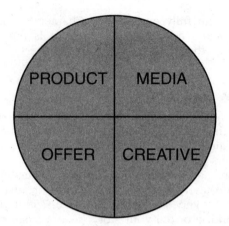

PRODUCT
   What is it really?
   What are its benefits?
   Does it enhance self-image?
   Can it be improved?
   What are its positioning options?

OFFER
   What distribution channel?
   Retail? Mail order? Agent-sold?
   Pricing? Premium? Credit?
   One-shot. Two step? Trade-ups?
   Continuity? Subscription?

MEDIA
   Who might buy it?
   How do I reach them?
   Mail? Internet? Telemarketing?
   Newspapers? Magazines?

CREATIVE
   Targeting. This is for you!
   What it will do for you.
   How it will make you feel.
   Why it works. Proof. Guaranteed.
   Action. A deal! Now not later.

Figure 2-1. Parts of the whole—four basic components of direct marketing strategy.

television watchers will be legitimate prospects, but they are the ones that count.

Ultimately, OPM (orders per thousand) becomes a planning factor. OPM is an index of how many orders (or inquiries or donations or subscriptions) are produced from promotion efforts in the various media. OPM is an index of responsiveness. It provides a standard of reasonableness. That is, if we double the cost of the mailing package, is it reasonable to presume that we can double the OPM? In some cases the answer will be *yes*; in others *no*.

CPM and OPM figures are both superseded by one universal index: CPR (cost per response). CPR—sometimes called CPO, for cost per order, or CPL, for cost per lead—is the indicator of "front-end" effectiveness, the relationship between responsiveness and cost. It is obtained simply by dividing the advertising cost by the number of responses.

The "quality" of respondents takes into account various kinds of conversion efforts: how many inquirers will buy, how many book club applicants will honor their commitment, how many interested people will see a salesperson and become customers. It also eventually takes into account the size of orders and the length of the relationship with renewal rates, frequency or renewals, etc. This eventually leads to projected ROI—return on advertising investment. A good strategic plan should consider these factors and forecast them for each and every media recommendation.

Other Media Considerations

A media strategy must consider all of the above factors and build a logical testing plan that reflects the acceptable degree of risk as compared with the need to exploit a productive campaign as quickly as possible. Time is a major aspect of strategy.

One must consider turn-around time: the time it will take to get the results from one effort, and whether you can then act fast enough to exploit the next peak season.

Response formats are an important factor in publication advertising. Does your proposition need a bind-in card to facilitate a quick, impulsive response? That limits your media options somewhat.

Secrecy is important. If you are testing a new product, use direct mail outside your competitor's home base. It is less likely to be noted. Even if they do see it, they have no way to determine how big your test is. In today's marketplace, a big success can be "ripped-off" in weeks and copied by a competitor. Keep your success stories under your hat.

Competition is another factor. You don't want to be in the same issue with a direct competitor unless you have a much more powerful offer. Mailing lists usually are rented on a protected basis, meaning that no competitor can use the same list in the same 30-day period.

You must also consider what type of space unit is needed to present the creative story. If you are offering a choice of 50 books or magazines or records, you'll obviously need a larger unit than if you have a simple message.

Editorial content also is a factor. Does it create a climate beneficial to your offering? Does its own reputation enhance or diminish the credibility of its advertisers?

A media strategy usually must combine caution in testing with aggressive risk-taking to exploit a success before it is copied. Your media strategy must be uniquely tailored to your own product, your market, and current availabilities.

DISTRIBUTION STRATEGY

One overlooked element of marketing strategy is the distribution method itself, whether it's retail or direct mail. Too often it is presumed that the method of getting the product to the customer will be the same as for all of the other company's products, or the same as that used by the company's competition.

In fact, some of the most exciting marketing breakthroughs have taken place because corporations have been willing to re-think this basic question for one or more of their product lines or services.

Distribution is an element of marketing, but too many organizations keep distribution outside of the marketing director's responsibility or authority. In such cases, though, it should still be one of the considerations in determining marketing strategy, even if the marketing department has to negotiate with a different part of the company to launch a new test plan.

On the broadest scale, there is the question of whether or not to use direct-marketing methods at all. Often this is the fundamental decision.

Take the example of a company selling an industrial product or service directly to businesses, using sales representatives. Over the years the better salespeople have left, and the company has had difficulty replacing them. Do they drop the product line? Or do they consider alternatives? They can sell the product in rural and marginal areas directly by mail. They can use telephone operators to solicit reorders from previously sold customers rather than use the valuable time of the remaining sales force. They can solicit leads, using their sales force for calls on pre-qualified interested prospects rather than waste their time on cold canvassing. With sales calls exceeding $300 each, this can be a profitable approach even if the sales force is strong and effective.

Database Marketing

Database marketing provided the missing link between mass advertising and direct marketing, enabling us to apply our learning to new goals selling cars, appliances, clothing, hardware, or groceries. There are no longer any limits to the products, services and types of distribution that can benefit from the principles of direct marketing. The goals are different: influencing retail distribution, fighting for "share of market," building retailer loyalty by providing specialized customer support.

Let's consider products that traditionally have been sold in the conventional retail manner. Shelf space is hard to get for new products from new companies. Store personnel unfamiliar with the products are unable to explain features or answer customers' questions. And discount chains are squeezing the price margins mercilessly.

Many companies have chosen to introduce such products through mail order, selling directly to the consumer. They can target their efforts to those customers most likely to be interested, concentrate their efforts on explaining how the product works, and offer proof of performance. And they can give people incentives to try the product immediately.

Products concerned with personal embarrassment lend themselves extremely well to direct mail. Sensitive issues such as incontinence, impotence, thinning hair and teenage skin problems can be dealt with in great detail through the privacy of direct mail, whereas most customers would hesitate to discuss such problems with a retail sales clerk. If the product is a good one, word of mouth will start to work for the company and eventually retailers will *ask* for the product.

Products that traditionally have been sold through direct marketing can also benefit from a re-thinking of the basic distribution method. For example, the American Management Association traditionally sold their courses as "one-shots." Circulars made the offer of individual courses and asked for cash with the order. They eventually found they could do better with some courses if they issued a catalog offering all the courses and convert inquiries with a mail series and phone calls.

Some large organizations are geared for selling by continuity (periodic automatic shipment), and resist changing to a club system (negative option) even when research shows that their customers would prefer it. Others built their business with clubs but quickly recognized the potential of continuity publishing and single-package promotions. By using these approaches, they expanded their business dramatically. When I ran Capitol Record Club, our most profitable venture was not the club itself but boxed sets of music by Nat King Cole, Frank Sinatra, and other popular artists.

Magazine publishers can consider putting their product in books. Publishers can consider part-works (newsstand-sold segmented periodicals) or seminars. These concepts are explained further in Chapter 6 on propositions.

Financial institutions have found that once they have a customer relationship, it pays to offer as complete a package of services as possible. They can often recruit new customers more easily with these services than for their basic banking relationship. Rethinking the basic proposition of what a bank or an insurance company or a stockbroker *does* has led to greater marketing flexibility and greater consumer choice.

Of course, it is not necessary to use mail order or lead-selling systems to use direct marketing. In recent years, many advertisers have been using direct mail effectively to support retail sales or to supplement direct-selling organizations.

Automobile manufacturers and packaged goods companies use the principles of direct marketing to encourage test drives or product trial, as well as the loyalty of their existing customers. Avon, Mary Kay, Clinique and Yves Rocher have all created major direct mail and Internet programs to generate additional sales of products that were originally designed to be sold only through person-to-person selling.

It is these applications that have benefited most from database marketing, a direct offshoot of direct marketing. This method is the subject of an entire book I have written on the subject—*Database Marketing* (*McGraw-Hill*)—and differs from general direct marketing primarily by its ability to select and address prospects individually and by household, rather than by media segment. Chapter 20 of this book is a presentation of the basic elements of this powerful by-product of direct marketing.

CREATIVE STRATEGY

No aspect of direct marketing is more discussed than the creative side. This is the glamour part of the industry. It's what makes direct marketing an art as well as a science. However, for purposes of planning, creative strategy (the copy and layout) is the last consideration—not because it is the least important, but because it is the most flexible.

The Need for Flexibility

The crafts of the writer and the artist demand versatility. It is no trick to produce every advertisement in one distinctive style, no matter how effective it might be. This kind of advertising strategy is like an actor with no range beyond his or her own personality, or an artist who paints the same subject in the same style over and over again. A true genius requires the ability—and more important, the *willingness*—to adapt one's skills to fulfill any objective.

A creative department must be able to solve the creative requirements of any product, any offer, any media. The copywriters must be able to adjust style and vocabulary to any market segment, to change length to any size advertisement or letter, and to write headlines and conceive illustrations that attract any desired audience.

In the old days, a copywriter's task was clear-cut. Benefits were offered, dramatized and guaranteed. Attributes were proclaimed, proved and glorified. Selling propositions were stated, restated, and stated yet again—in visual presentations crowded with copy and liberally sprinkled with exclamation points.

Today the creative process is infinitely more subtle. The old-fashioned "hard-sell" approaches can still work in the short run, but they are shortsighted. Hard-sell copy picks up core markets—the easy prospects—but fails to build credibility or develop positive attitudes for the future.

"Future Respondents"

Today, we not only look at the 2 to 5 percent of people who respond to a mailing piece or the much smaller percentage of a magazine's audience who respond to an advertisement. We must consider that our advertisement is being seen and noted by a much larger percentage of readers or viewers who, though not responding now, are prospects for future promotions. Today, just as general or "awareness" advertisers find situations where it is desirable for them to ask for a response with direct marketing techniques, we in direct marketing must consider the awareness- and attitude-building factors in our response-seeking advertising.

International Silver's American Archives division happened to run a half-page list-building advertisement offering a condiment set for $4.99 in the same issue as a full-page advertisement picturing an elegant silverware service available at retail outlets. Starch reports for the issue indicated that the half-page mail-order advertisement had higher "Noted" and "Read Most" scores than the full-page advertisement intended solely for those purposes. I had a similar experience with an ad for ITT's telephone services. People do read direct-mail advertisements. My theory is our ads get better readership because we are "open for business." General ads are like "window shopping."

Ninety percent of communication is non-verbal, and "first impressions" are based not only on what you say, but how you say it. An analogy I have used frequently is that copy style is like tone of voice, whereas layout is like body language. Both communicate credibility or the lack of it, and say as much about your company and its product as anything in your basic copy platform.

When planning a creative strategy, you must consider not only those who respond today, but also those who may respond in the future.

Emotional Factors

The concepts expressed in the previous section of this chapter gradually evolved into a whole new approach to strategic planning. Some years ago, when I was President of BBDO Direct, I had the opportunity to take packaged-goods methods and apply them to the direct marketing field. Many such methods required understanding the psychology of human perceptions and communication.

With BBDO's help, I was able to incorporate many of these general advertising methods into the basic procedures of the direct agency, adapting them to the creative work plan used for every new assignment. The results were incredible. We found that by using photography more psychologically and developing emotional themes relating to the prospect's self-image, we were able to produce significant lift factors. These will be discussed in more detail in Chapter 4 on research and Chapter 9 on creative tactics.

For now I will just say that the choice of strategy must consider not only the practical reasons for buying a product, but also emotional needs, not only immediate action-inducing elements, but also the imagery of the product.

While our primary objective is always an immediate response, our results are influenced by the imagery, awareness and brand equity created by general advertising. Our efforts in the mail, magazine pages, television tube or computer screen can add to or detract from those factors.

I have been privileged to work with many clients whose budgets permitted substantial research programs. One consistent result of a hundred focus panels and a thousand interviews is that the reputation of the advertiser is a critical factor in the consumer's decision to respond or not respond. At the same time, the price a customer is willing to pay is a direct result of "brand equity"—the confidence in a brand name that is the result of repeated product and user images.

Just as some image advertisers are slowly learning to respect the advantages of asking for a response, so must sophisticated direct marketing users learn that imagery and brand equity contribute to the long-term acceptance of our offers.

CHOOSING A STRATEGY

This chapter has dealt with strategic alternatives in five areas: product, media, offer, creativity, and distribution method. In preparing a strategy, it is important to consider all five of the basic elements and to make definite, clear-cut decisions. Many of the choices will be difficult, but they must be made.

I have found that the worst strategy in any of these five areas is any so-called "safe" strategy. If you are competing against General Motors, it is folly to produce cars just like theirs at the same prices. Somewhere you have to take a chance and be different in as many respects as possible. Lee Iacocca did not achieve Chrysler's great marketing turnaround by doing the same as everyone else.

It is essential to keep in mind that when one of these five elements is changed, all of them must be reviewed. Raise the price and a two-step distribution method may do better than a one-step. Use television and an emotional appeal may out-pull a logical one. Use a different list, or different media, and an entirely different combination may be necessary.

I've seen mailings which were literally an ad in an envelope, which makes no more sense than reading a direct mail letter aloud on television. Direct marketing's principles may be universal, but their application demands flexibility and, above all, creativity.

Later in this book we will note how each communication medium has its own strengths and weaknesses. Each has a relative degree of credibility, personalization, newsworthiness, interactivity, immediacy, and message capability.

There are many ways to help make strategic decisions. A written plan is essential. Research can help. And when the alternatives are boiled down to a few significant fundamentals, you can always use split-run testing to let the consumer tell you the best way to go or which market is the best to aim for.

If you are introducing a new product, saving an old one, or looking for a major breakthrough or market expansion, then you must be willing to rethink all five main strategic areas.

Your strategy will, of course, be influenced by your corporate personality. In World War II, General Patton and Field Marshall Montgomery became archetypal examples of two different military strategies.

Patton was aggressive: a man who seized every opportunity, took risks, bent the rules of warfare, and plunged ahead as fast as his tanks could go. His forces seized bridges, bypassed pockets of resistance and exploited opportunities as they occurred. British Field Marshall Bernard Montgomery was known for his cautious, logical, carefully planned campaigns, based on the best intelligence available. He planned carefully, regrouped slowly, and moved his forces ahead step by step, with due care to logistics and supply lines.

One of my banking clients was a Patton-type company. They would test one or two fundamental approaches and, if successful, roll out a major national campaign so fast that the competition was unable to copy the concept. Another corporation I know is a Montgomery-type company, with each direct mail program studied and planned and poked at for such a long time that, by the time the test gets in the mail, the competition has copied their concept, and reaped the profits from a similar program.

While I regard myself as a Patton fan, I will not say that the Montgomery approach isn't right for some companies. I won't venture an opinion as to which approach was the best then, or which would be best for your company now. But I will urge you to consider not only the direction in which you want to go, but also how fast or how cautiously you want to proceed once you set your direction.

Strategy requires the selection of goals and the defining of objectives. Tactics are the methods of achieving those goals. Planning is the conscious decision-making process that must precede any act of creation. Execution is the effective use of all three, implemented with excellence. No matter what role you play in your business, you must understand how these elements interact.

THE MARKETING PLAN

Only a written plan brings everyone involved into the total strategy. Even the greatest media buyers or copywriters cannot do their best work in a vacuum.

Only a written marketing plan documents strategies and test objectives as originally conceived, so that results obtained months later can be properly evaluated.

Only a written plan makes it possible to obtain useful professional advice from coworkers and consultants. Without it, any expert is only reacting to the scanty information and predigested prejudice of his or her client.

Most important, only a written plan enables everyone to fully think through every essential element that affects decision making—not only the big decisions, but countless day-to-day implementation choices vital to the final results.

HOW SHOULD A PLAN BE PREPARED?

In the following sections I'll describe the "what" of a marketing plan. But "who" should write it, and "how" should it be assembled are questions that need to be addressed as well.

Ideally the head planner should be a marketing strategist, no matter what his or her title is within the business. The planner may be the boss, a product manager, or an outside consultant, but one person has to be responsible for assembling and coordinating the preparation of the plan.

But seldom can one person write the entire plan. A team is needed. Each component of the overall plan should be prepared by a specialist in the particular area being covered. An initial briefing is needed to begin the project, and frequent consultation with other members of the marketing-planning team will better focus the final result.

Much of the detailed assembly of information can be delegated by the team leader. The decision-making of the essential elements of a plan cannot be delegated, however. Nor should one person make the decisions unilaterally. Just as it is impossible for most writers to be objective about their own writing, so it is with marketers. Planning must be an open, honest dialogue among professionals whose integrity precludes both personal ego or a need to please client or boss.

The leader who is too directive will not get honest opinions from those who could provide important ideas and information. As William Wrigley said, "When two people in a business always agree, one of them is unnecessary."

On the other hand, if the planner is not directive enough, the plan will be aimless or contradictory. A balance must be achieved between these two extremes for a well thought-out and successful plan.

The format of the plan is not critical. It can be written in simple outline form, or in an exhaustive narrative format with charts, tables, and exhibits. I have seen and endorsed excellent plans written in only a few pages, as well as one for a major national corporation that required 300 pages to summarize a year of research and planning.

Once written, a plan should be updated from year-to-year, adding new competitive information, new marketing data, and the real-world lessons of research, results, and testing.

BASIC PLANNING ELEMENTS

The basic elements of a marketing plan are, in the broadest sense: product description, marketing environment, objective, strategies, and economic considerations.

Product Description

The first section of a marketing plan is generally a statement describing the product or service. It sounds a great deal simpler than it is.

The perception of a product or a service may be thought of as being organized into ascending levels.

Attributes.   The obvious first level of product description is its basic attributes. What exactly are we offering? What is its size, material, and function? How does it work? In what ways is it better made, better designed or more reliable than previous products designed for the same purpose. Although you might attach samples or photographs of the product, it helps to verbalize each and every attribute, including the color, the feel, the weight, even the sound it makes when it operates.

Technical Data.   Be sure to include the technical advantages as well—the nitty-gritty scientific details that most people wouldn't understand. For one thing, you may find it necessary to communicate with professionals or enthusiasts who would appreciate the differences. For another, a discerning copywriter might make something big out of the smallest detail.

How was the product made? How does it work electronically, chemically, or mechanically? Exactly what happens inside, where the customer can't see but the writer can describe? Is the product made of a scarce material? Tell about it. Is there hand-craftsmanship, or exacting precision tooling, or rigorous quality control? How long will it last? How long will it operate? How is it better than the competition?

David Ogilvy's famous Rolls-Royce ad about its loudest sound being its electric clock might never have been written if some planner hadn't first verbalized this attribute.

Practical Benefits.   When writing copy, or even when presenting product information to your own sales staff, every attribute should be translated into a benefit. So the car has a more powerful engine. Ho hum! But translate that into faster starts, quieter performance, extra power for safe passing, or for climbing the steepest hills.

Sometimes I demonstrate this with a coffee mug. The unimaginative participants see only a handle. But after some encouragement the class is calling out benefits. "The opening is large so it's comfortable," one student cries out. "You won't burn your hand," says another. "It's strong, so it won't break off," cries another.

Emotional Benefits.   In some ways the most important considerations are the emotional points. What real or imagined need does the product fill? What will it do for the buyer? How might it change the customer's self-image or image to others? What benefit might it add to the customer's life: comfort, convenience, spare time, confidence, prestige, wealth, romance, beauty?

Take any of the preceding points and, as a psychologist would, ask the magic question: "How do you feel about that?"

You'll find the car-buyer likes the feeling of more power, whether or not it's ever used. You'll find the macho coffee mug buyer doesn't want to be embarrassed by spilling coffee because of an unsteady grip on one of those tiny tea cup handles.

Fantasy. Even the simplest products can be taken to the fantasy level. The car-buyer expects new sexual conquests. The buyer of the sturdy coffee mug responds to the idea of peace of mind—no worry about spilling on clothes, furniture, etc.

Some might say this approach doesn't apply to intangible consumer products like telephone services, retail stores, websites, banking services, or insurance. These things are not as easy to explain as for a new car, for instance. But the less tangible the product or service and its advantages, the more important it is to work at describing just what it is we are trying to sell.

Business-to-business marketing is not immune from the fantasy approach, except that we generally are concerned with its flip side—fear. Losing one's job, because of a bad decision, is a powerful negative fantasy.

Self-Esteem. In recent years, learning from general agency psychological research, we have learned that there is a still higher level that marketers must deal with—the question of self-esteem or self-image.

Early copywriters used to talk about "the coffee table effect." The idea was that people would buy art books or encyclopedias to leave on a table and impress their friends, family or neighbors. The next generation and its researchers discovered that there was only one person these buyers really wanted to impress—the man or woman they saw in the mirror.

The art books were bought because buyers wanted to *feel* cultured. The encyclopedias were bought because they wanted to think of themselves as good parents. The ultimate, literally, application of this self-esteem motivation is advertising for life insurance and pre-paid funeral arrangements, the benefit being the pride of feeling like a good, responsible family head.

The Classic Product Description Example

Perhaps the best way to dramatize the levels of product description is to share with you an exercise that I sometimes use to train copywriters. The assignment: Describe a pencil.

"It's yellow. There's black lead inside a wooden tube. There's a point on one end and an eraser on another." How many writers would stop right there?

Another might go on to describe how the pencil lead is made, what kind of wood it's encased in, or the country of origin of the rubber eraser. Still another writer might describe the manufacturing process, relate how long the manufacturer has been in business, or dramatize the many types of pencils offered by the company.

Better. But then along comes the scientific writer, who has painstakingly used up a pencil to find out how many times it can be sharpened, how long it will hold a fine point, and—after hours of work—exactly how many words can be written with a single pencil.

Much better. But we can still do more, by trying out competing pencils and determining whether ours "lasts 20 percent longer." That's a lot of work, surely, but nobody has ever said advertising is easy.

Even with all this we've only just begun, for advertising is an art as well as a science, and our prospective customer is emotional as well as logical. Imagine for a moment the psychological satisfactions— the security of being able to erase errors easily, the peace of mind in knowing that the pencil will not leak or stain or smear.

Further, imagine what using a pencil says about those who prefer it. These drawing tools would reinforce their own self-images that they are practical, conservative, frugal, and have the courage to admit that they can make mistakes.

Let's carry the copywriting art one step further and, adding a sense of poetry, suggest that such a pencil as ours might enable its possessor to write a moving play, develop a brilliant business idea, or compose a touching love letter. Thus our buyer might achieve—by buying a pencil—fame, riches, and romance.

How Is the Product Perceived?

Exactly what do people think about what you're selling? The product-description section is the place to include all relevant research on how your product or service is presently perceived by various components of your customer base. Both quantitative (such as surveys) and evaluative research (such as focus panel sessions) should be summarized here. The purpose is not to summarize the research itself, but to present conclusions of the research.

What consumers *believe* about your product can be just as important as what it really is. Perception is an aspect of reality. If the product is perceived as better or different than it really is, an abundance of returns and complaints can result. A retailer is forced to improve the product or reveal the shortcomings in the promotions. The brilliant entrepreneur Joe Sugarman often includes a sentence in his long-copy advertisements pointing out features that a product is lacking, then adding a line making light of it, such as "Of course, at this price you can't expect everything."

If your product is perceived as worse than it really is, a good writer can make sure that every concern is overcome in the copy presentation. The knowledge that these perceptions exist and the decision to deal with them must be elements of the marketing plan.

"People Like Me."   Research has shown that people have an idea of what sorts of people use different kinds of products. If the sort of people they are or would like to be use a certain product, they identify with the product.

In many research projects we find that, even after screening the participants for interest in the product category, and after discussing the advantages of the product for nearly an hour, most people are still not ready to buy it. When we probe for hidden objections, one phrase comes up repeatedly: "It's not for me." They explain this only as "not seeing them-selves" driving, owning, wearing or using the product or service.

One objective of image advertising is exactly that—to associate the prod-uct with the self-image of prospective buyers. BBDO pioneered this ap-proach with television advertising for General Electric which over the years "widened the band of acceptance." Today GE is a brand almost everyone is proud to own. BBDO's advertising for Pepsi-Cola was not addressed to younger audiences, as you expect, but to people of every age who think of themselves as younger, as youthful in spirit and interests.

If people see themselves as "sophisticated" or "macho" or "chic," or as part of an "in" group, they will desire a product they perceive as sophis-ticated, or macho, or chic, or "in." If people perceive a product as silly, or only for old folks, or kids, or poor people (again, depending on self-image) they may shy away from the product regardless of how much they really would like to have it. This can apply to individual brand names or to entire categories of products or services.

Self-image buying can best be influenced through advertising with non-verbal elements. Illustrations and situations depict a typical user in such a way that the prospect wants to identify with the subjects in the ad. This has now been applied to direct marketing efforts. It has produced some aston-ishing results.

This product-image concept is not necessarily achieved by taking ap-pearances upscale. In one program we found that parents thought that home delivery of disposable diapers was not for them, but for wealthy or lazy people. We lifted response by 50% just by adding photos of families of modest means using the service.

Our plan must not only note what is known about a product and how it will be perceived, but also identify the consumer's impression of what kind of people buy it. Tactics must be developed so the product seems right for all those "people like me" out there in the marketplace.

MARKETING ENVIRONMENT

The marketing environment is the cumulative total of every external factor (elements not controlled by the marketer) that might influence the devel-opment of marketing strategy. As you'll see, it includes competition, media, distribution, government regulations, and economic trends.

Competition

The competitive situation is a constant and continuing factor in your own strategy development. Every legitimate information-gathering process should be used, and all information recorded.

The first step is obvious. Start collecting every tear sheet and direct-mail sample that falls into your possession from any source. Ask media repre-sentatives for back issues known to contain competitive advertising. Ask your staff, your suppliers, and even your friends and relatives to send you anything they happen to get in the mail that might relate to your product. Then use the reference sources described later in this chapter.

The marketing plan should summarize the current knowledge about each competitor's activity and draw conclusions about what appears to be their strategies, their offers, and their copy platforms. I consider this type of "reverse engineering" of an ad or direct mail package so important that it is a central part of my advanced course at NYU.

When you get samples of the competition's ads or mailings, analyze what they are doing. Spell out, in writing, what audience they seem to be aimed at, and how they are positioned against your product. Reconstruct their copy platform, by listing each and every point used in the copy of each competitor. If there are many competitors, set up a chart and compare who is saying what.

Look for the evolution of the appeals, offers, and copy claims. This is often very revealing, especially if you don't make the common mistake of underestimating your competition. The safest course is to presume that if point A has been added or point B left out since last year, it may have been done because of research, testing, or results that would apply just as well to your product.

For example, as I write this, a staff member is going through every jewelry catalog on behalf of a Brazilian gemstone client entering the U.S. market. Rather than guess what will sell here, we are counting types of jewelry, price ranges, and types of stones to learn from the experience of those who are already active here. Will it be exactly the same for our client? No. Will it increase the probability of a successful new catalog? Definitely, yes!

Today the sources of information are greater than they have ever been. However, there is still a need to build your own files of competitive activity, as it is still difficult to get full data about direct mail used in most business categories.

Magazine Advertising.   Using reference services such as PIB (Publishers' Information Bureau) based in New York, magazine advertising can be tracked over a long term. This resource will tell you what magazines other advertisers are using, in what months, and in what size units.

However, it will not tell you what the ads look like or how their copy has evolved. If you are concerned with a competitor who advertises in magazines, you will want to examine their most-used magazines on a regular basis.

Don't just look at one ad. It is particularly important to examine copies of these publications at newsstands and compare several copies to see if there is a split-run test—different creative treatments or offers being promoted to see which is the most successful. These differences should be carefully logged to see which split is repeated. It is safe to presume that the ad repeated is the one that proved to be most successful.

Broadcast Advertising.   Like magazine advertising, broadcast advertising has similar information posted by New York-based Competitive Media Reporting (CMR). CMR has a number of different services to track broadcast advertising, including lists by month of the day-parts, and major markets used by direct-marketers, as well as all other advertisers. The organization tracks what ran, on what stations, the length of the variety of commercials, how many times the commercial aired, and approximately how much the advertisers paid.

Some of their information analysis is compiled into monthly reports, while others are tracked daily. CMR has computer-based resources that provide daily updates of television commercial occurrences, as well as a web-based service where members can view competitor's commercials in stop-motion video.

Direct Mail. Direct mail has become much more trackable in recent years, at least with direct mail packages. While it is valuable to see what the competition is doing and what kinds of offers and promotions they are using, it is still virtually impossible to learn what lists are being used and what quantities are being mailed.

However, you can get information on what lists are available, through list brokers, SRDS and MIN (Marketing Information Network). MIN has more than 29,000 list data cards which can be accessed by computer. The information is updated every three months. Agencies and list brokers are the most common users of this service. They use the computerized search engines to find appropriate lists using very specific terms, and then use the information to make recommendations to their clients.

Target Marketing magazine, published by Denny Hatch, produces both a series of monthly newsletters called *Who's Mailing What* and a yearly *Directory of Major Mailers and What They Mail*. The newsletter editors read thousands of pieces of direct mail each month. The directory provides detailed information about the companies sending the mailers, including a list of what they mailed out during the year. Subscribers can read through the various listings and order photocopies of the mailers from the publication, but there is no indication of what lists were used.

Another recent improvement in data gathering is a service provided by John Cummings and Company (Armonk, NY) called DBM/SCAN. Originally a tracking service for database marketing activities by packaged-goods products, it has been expanding into automotive and other categories. They call DBM/SCAN a "competitor intelligence service" that provides a survey of activity in a particular product category along with copies of samples, on a fee basis or through an annual subscription.

General Business Information

By all means order the product, subscribe to the service, or join the club or plan offered by your competitor. In fact, join it several times yourself or through different people in your office. See how the competition responds to different actions on your part such as prompt payment, slow payment, and no payment. Note every date you receive or send something.

While you're at it, send in similar dummy memberships for your own product or service. You may be surprised at the results, particularly if your fulfillment is being done at another location or by an outside service.

There are other ways to investigate what others are doing. Vary your answers on database questionnaires to see what kind of mail arrives. Have people in your office log on to different competitive websites, enter the same website in different ways (such as a direct link versus clicking through another website), and fill out on-line forms in different ways to see how contacts are handled.

On top of this, use all the conventional research techniques for business information. Get annual reports. Look up articles that may have appeared in the business press or newspapers. Read books, articles, and interviews written by your competitors or their agencies. If your competitor has a website, study it. And seek out news stories and articles about the company.

There are many easily accessible resources, especially on the Internet. Utilize Internet resource portals like Ad Talk (www.adtalk.com) and the New York Public Library's information page on how to find market research information (www.nypl.org/research/sibl/market/market.htm.) This links to numerous others, including on-line articles and governmental resources. Other resources include:

American Demographics   www.demographics.com

A commercial site with search engines to find summaries of data or services that can be purchased.

U.S. Census Information   www.census.gov

Site published by the federal government that lists up-to-date census information.

Business and Industrial Data   www.ntis.gov/naics

Reports and market data classifications compiled by the National Technical Information Service of the US Census Bureau.

EDGAR databases   www.edgar-online.com

Industry information from SEC filings.

Gov. Info Sharing Project   govinfo.kerr.orst.edu

An academic/governmental project from Oregon State University with lots of information and statistics.

D. Flanagan Research Page   home.sprintmail.com/~debflanagan

A research resource for free information available on the web, compiled by an ambitious small businessperson.

Boise State Research Page   www.idbsu.edu/carol/busness1.htm

Great compilation of resource links, compiled by an employee of the Boise State University library.

Today there are several fine magazines and newsletters covering news and developments in the direct marketing field. I particularly recommend

DM News, Direct, Direct Marketing and *Target Marketing* – each of which has a unique perspective. The field is now so widespread and fast-moving that one must read all of these just to keep up with what's happening.

Friday Report and *The DeLay Letter* are some excellent newsletters of particular value to senior executives, advertising agencies, consultants, and others in the service industry. The former provides excellent coverage of talks at meetings and conventions. The latter features exclusive interviews with industry executives and "inside" information not generally available elsewhere. There is surprisingly little duplication between them.

It's amazing what people sometimes disclose in the course of seminars or business meetings. A unique and valuable source of direct-marketing information is the enormous library of cassettes available from *Direct Marketing* magazine. Order and listen to every cassette with speeches by your competitors and by representatives from their advertising agencies.

The Direct Marketing Association (DMA) is a gold mine of valuable information about the industry in general, and well worth the membership fee. One of their lesser-known services is a library of contest entries that can be visited in New York or purchased on CD-ROM. These entries are in bound books that include statements of objectives, mailing plans, samples, and results. If your competitor has submitted campaigns for awards, this can be a surprisingly beneficial reference source.

Members can also obtain computerized summaries of news items, contest entries, and other data about types of direct marketing programs at a very reasonable processing fee. Those interested can search by industry, specific company, or marketing method through their database—search capabilities that are now available for DMA members through the Internet.

In fact, all of these publications and resources now offer much of their information on the Internet. These are some URLs you will find useful:

Direct Marketing Association	*www.the-dma.org*
DM News	*www.dmnews.com*
Direct Marketing	*www.hokecomm.com*
DRTV News	*www.dmnews.com*
Teleservices News	*www.dmnews.com*
International DMNews	*www.dmnews.com*
Direct Magazine	*www.directnewsline.com*
Advertising Age	*www.adage.com*
Who's Mailing What	*www.whosmailingwhat.com*
Target Marketing	*www.targetonline.com*
Friday Report	*www.hokecomm.com*
Response	*www.responsemag.com*
IMarketing	*www.dmnews.com*

Another valuable source is the list-rental information issued by your competitors and available in Standard Rate and Data Service (SRDS) or through list brokers. Often they indicate the number of customers brought in within a given period of time, the size of their total list, the average sale, the source of the names, and a demographic breakdown. The cards issued by some brokers will list companies that use each list regularly, which is very valuable. Some allowances are necessary because they are presenting the data in the most favorable light to rent their lists, but some valuable data still can be deduced.

The Media Universe

This section is the place to record compilation of the mailing lists and publications that might be relevant to your particular proposition.

SRDS publishes various catalogs of publications and mailing lists, as well as a web-based service that allows users to search with modern computer search engines. Go through these SRDS publications and begin to assemble, in categories, the various media that you might someday hope to use. Indicate the basic costs for print media, presuming a standard space unit. Also indicate what you might spend on mailing lists. Figure not only the list cost but also an estimated package cost. You may find that certain media categories are so large that it's worthwhile to tailor strategies specifically to find ways of making those categories work.

Certainly the information on what media your competition has used and repeated should be taken into account here, as well as the media they tried and evidently discontinued. There's no dishonor in learning from someone else's experience.

Don't make the mistake, however, of presuming that a medium has been "used up" by a competitor. International Masters Publishing has followed Betty Crocker into markets all over the world The staff found that a quality product, the right offer, and a good creative strategy can make even the most saturated media pay off for their "My Great Recipes" cards. Atlas Editions, in turn, followed them. Don't let the competition scare you off. Go where the action is. Just find ways to be better than they are.

Time is a factor in media selection, as well as cost. When you are formulating your marketing plan is the time to estimate how long it will take to get into the various media categories with your ad or mailing—and how long it will take to read the results. Turn-around time will be important because you always will want to read the results of one mailing or ad in time to make a decision on the next.

To summarize, you should, for each medium listed, estimate costs for a standard unit, record apparent competitive experience, indicate the lead time in preparing an ad or mailing, and finally indicate how fast you should be able to read the results.

Fulfillment

This term applies to the steps needed to convert responses into shipments and sales. All responses need to be entered into a database and receive some type of reply, whether those responses arrive on the Internet, by phone, mail or cable-TV click-through. Obviously, the content and context of those replies depends on the nature of the business.

Magazine subscription companies require not only the mailing of the publication, but procedures for billing and eventually renewals. Fund-raisers must enter the donation and send appropriate thank-you letters. Companies that sell through agents or salespersons need a lead distribution system that tracks conversion rates, and the number of people who purchase the service or item after being contacted. Packaged-goods companies count redemption of store coupons or use other research methods. And catalogers and other mail-order marketers must deal with packaging, shipping, returns, customer service, and other mail-order issues.

Companies must provide for adequate handling of the responses, whether by mail, phone, or at retail establishments. Many otherwise successful promotions have failed because the phone lines were busy or the operators improperly trained. And there are cases of major direct marketers who have gone out of business because of poor computer planning. The attitude of some Internet developers is particularly shocking when they brag of enormous click-throughs that could not be connected to their sites because their servers were over-loaded. The Victoria Secret Superbowl advertisement that led viewers to the Internet site was a perfect case-in-point. The simplest direct-marketing pre-test would have enabled the technicians to know the number of Internet viewers expected and plan for greater capacity.

Fortunately there are consultants who specialize in these issues, and suppliers who have gained substantial experience in handling such functions. With very few exceptions, I usually recommend letting outside suppliers handle fulfillment, at least during the first couple of years of a new direct marketing venture.

The decisions about who shall be in charge of fulfillment should be part of the plan shared with all participants in the planning process. Sharing of information often will help to identify steps that might otherwise be overlooked in the fulfillment process. For more on this see Chapter 19 on fulfillment.

Economic Trends

Are there economic trends that affect your business? Here's the place to spell them out in narrative, figures and charts. If your product is sensitive to the economy as a whole, include pertinent economic indicators such as the Consumer Confidence Index, the Dow-Jones Index, and Housing Starts. These are the tables I most often find relevant to mail-order predictions.

Is your product related to a specific hobby, interest, or fashion? Then spell out available information and speculate about the life-cycle of the interest. Usually the best time to ride in on a new fad is near the beginning. Usually once it becomes so popular that general magazines and Sunday supplements deal with it the fad is almost over.

Timing is critical. CBS brought out *Popular Gardening Indoors* just in time for indoor gardening to be yesterday's enthusiasm. International Silver introduced a CB (citizens-band) necklace and a gorilla pendant just in time for CB radio to fade and for the remake of *King Kong* to have come and gone.

Unless your product can be issued on a timely basis with fast turn-around media, save your money. You can make a fortune if you're one of the first to offer collectibles, but you can lose your shirt if you're one of the last.

THE MARKET

In direct marketing we deal with "media universes," "target markets," or "audiences." We try to quantify these markets by age, education, and income; by zip code and census tract; by demographics and psychographics. But this is just the beginning of defining a market.

Your Customer Is Not a Statistic

The first lesson to remember is this: your customer is not a statistic. The buyer is not packaged in neat demographic profiles waiting for your message to arrive. There is only one common denominator that you can count on—interest in your product.

Interest can be developed, with the help of the right creative strategy, among people who compose virtually any statistical unit; but their interest is individual. What they do have in common is that *they are accessible at an economical cost through a common list or other medium.*

An average age or income is useless unless it is related to the accessibility of those characteristics through various media. Too narrow a definition, such as "people who like hummingbirds," also is useless, unless there are substantial numbers of publications or lists directed to such interests. Inaccessible statistical profiles are academic exercises.

Watch out for what I call "circular research." After years of positioning a product toward older people, a research study will show that older people have been buying the product. The research doesn't show what could have been—or still could be—if the total market potential were considered and different creative efforts were aimed at alternate lists or media. *The Marketing Revolution* by Kevin Clancy and Robert Shulman (Harper Business, 1992) provides an enlightening discussion as to how and why new customers may not look like present customers.

Although statistical data is a keystone of packaged-goods marketing, it is often just an idle curiosity for direct marketers. This is a fundamental difference between a typical packaged-goods marketing plan and a direct marketing plan.

The Lifestyle Approach

Logical reasoning will take you further than statistics in a direct marketing plan, and should be the starting place for the market section of a plan.

Begin with the product: its function, its purpose, and its benefits. Who needs it? Who might be persuaded to need it? What absolute limitations are there? What essential prerequisites exist with regard to where the prospective customer is in his or her life, career, or avocation?

One exercise used by some major agencies is the "ideal-prospect" scenario. Imagine an ideal buyer. Make up a story about where he or she lives, what he does, how his job is going, how he's getting along with his wife, what his ambitions are, what he does in his spare time. Does he have a beer after work at the local pub? Does he build craft projects in his workshop on Sunday afternoons? What are his political preferences? What's his favorite movie, TV show, or magazine?

Just letting your imagination go wild in this way will help you—and the copywriter—to zero in on what's really important and relevant about the market characteristics for your particular product. What's the chance that the relevant characteristics of the ideal direct marketing respondent are only age, income, and education? Not very likely. In fact, none of these are relevant for some services and products.

Where there are common demographic denominators, they should be taken into account. Usually these common denominators are pure speculation until a full range of list and media and positioning tests has been run.

Media Choices

Before you select particular lists, publications or websites, you must first decide which category will best present your product.

Each media category has its strengths and weaknesses. Decide if you need color, sound, ease of response or fast-turnaround time. Table 3-1 shows some of these capabilities.

Common Media Characteristics

Reading media and list results is an art form in itself. While a media universe may be conceptualized arbitrarily at the beginning of a marketing program, it must be reshaped when the result figures are available.

TABLE 3-1
CAPABILITIES OF MAJOR DIRECT-RESPONSE MEDIA

Medium	Advantages	Disadvantages
Direct mail	Reaches all households Selectivity and personalization Most suitable for testing Most flexible Second highest response rates Contains all action elements	Second most expensive Long startup time Profile analysis Potential limited

TABLE 3-1
CAPABILITIES OF MAJOR DIRECT-RESPONSE MEDIA (*Continued*)

Medium	Advantages	Disadvantages
Telephone	Powerful "one-on-one" capability	Dangerous with prospects
	Fastest response time	No visual appeal
	Selectivity	Most expensive CPM
	Flexibility	55% household reachability
	Excellent for research and profile analysis	
	Can increase average order size substantially	
	Highest response rates	
	Powerful upgrade-sell	
Magazines	Reach mass or class	Less space to tell story
	Adds reputation of publication	Less personal
	Good color reproduction	Slower response
	Long ad life	Less selectivity than mail or phone
	Low CPM	
	Test inexpensively	
	Moderate lead time	
	Shortest startup time	Poor color
Newspapers	"Newsy" image	Poor ROP production
	Fast response	Poor selectivity
	Wide variety of formats	No personalization
	Broad local coverage	Rates vary
	Inexpensive to test	Sometimes affected by local conditions
Television	Emotional capacity	Limited copy time
	Powerful demonstration capability	No permanent response device
	Fast response	Difficult to split-test
	Wide choice of time buys	Network time scarce
	Can reach all U.S. households	Limited time available in second and fourth quarters
	Strong support medium	
Radio	High-frequency, inexpensive	No response device
	Many profiles can be isolated by choice of show and time	Limited copy time
	Short startup times	No visual appeal
	Powerful support medium	
Internet	Instant access	Low penetration
	24/7 availability	Frequent crashes
	Interactivity	Awkward scrolling
	Personalization	Demands patience

After adjustments have been made for media format, competition, regionalization, date, and position (in print media), a clear picture starts to come into focus. Usually some list or publication categories—or some Internet websites, search engines or portals—are clear winners, others are clear losers, and some are marginal.

The pay-off comes from looking beyond the obvious and searching out what winners and losers have in common. Astute analysts and strategic planners insist on reviewing editorial content of magazines, sources of mailing lists, and the entire competitive environment before drawing conclusions about what works and what doesn't.

Common sense goes a long way toward identifying abstractions about successful media. Direct marketing results are always subject to logical analysis and interpretation. Beware of the blaring exception to logic. Every time I have been stumped by a seeming contradiction to an otherwise clear pattern, the villain has been not mistaken logic, but the unreliability of available testing procedures. I've found that a magazine that was supposedly a split run sent most of ad A to newsstand dealers and ad B to subscribers. Though the print run was 50-50, a large percentage of the newsstand copies were returned unsold, thus depressing that side of the split.

I've seen mailing-list suppliers—accidentally or intentionally—provide the most recent names rather than a typical cross-section, thus making a marginal list look better than it really is. If something looks odd, don't act on the test results until the contradiction can be explained or until a retest can be arranged under tight supervision.

All test results and conclusions should be summarized in the marketing plan. The market portion of the plan should include all relevant data and all speculation about possible buyer profiles. It should include the history, the interpretation, and a statement of objectives for the future.

THE STRATEGIES

Strategic planning is possible only when the product, the market, and the environment have been clearly identified. There is always more than one possible strategy. Alternatives should be developed and then reviewed according to pre-established criteria, and then the best strategy selected. Often it is possible to test more than one fundamental strategy. Consumer response will determine which is the most effective. The selection of strategies depends on several considerations: budget, timing, market conditions, and the inherent personality of the corporation making the decision.

One important determinant is a sub-statement of the objective: the goal. Both should have been listed in the preliminary material. Usually the objective is general, such as "Expand media universe," "Open youth market for product," or "Lower cost per order." The goal, however, is specific: "Expand media universe by $500,000" or "Reduce cost per order by 25 percent." The more ambitious the goal, the more daring the strategy that can be justified and the greater the downside risk merited. If the goal is modest, strategies should avoid daring new concepts or bold offers and stick to logical progressions from existing control ads and packages.

Testing Approaches

Let's say, for example, that we are dealing with an existing and reasonably successful proposition that is ready to break into the big time. Our survey of the product, the environment, and the possible markets has identified several areas for possible improvement. Maybe the proposition has worked well in women's magazines in full-page black-and-white ads. The goal is to double sales for the next year.

We would probably list a variety of possible strategies, including a price change, a premium addition, the use of credit cards, a new creative strategy to widen the appeal of the product, and some new media and formats. The trick is to test all these approaches in a short period of time in preparation for a massive rollout in a later prime season.

The first step would be to list and evaluate all of the possible strategies for testing. The key factor would be the likelihood that the change would result in the desired improvement. Some possibilities would be ruled out in favor of others. Perhaps some form of predictive research would be used to help select those variations most likely to appeal to the potential customer.

It is likely that no matter how tight the decision-making process, there will be a variety of possibilities. The testing strategy should isolate test ads or mailings into three categories: media or list tests, simple offer or format tests, and basic creative concept tests.

One creative concept should be selected to be the control ad or mailing piece. Generally this is the most logical and proven approach. This control is the vehicle for testing one medium or list against another. Where possible, all offer and format variations also are tested within one or two media: a core list and an expansion list, for example. The basic control might run in 10 or 20 purely media test cells. The variations might take two of the media and test four or five variations against each, and then the basic creative format testing might be tried. The result would form a Grid Test like the one shown in Table 3-2.

While the individual "cells" (combinations of list and version) are only sent to 5,000 names each, the totals for each list and version are large enough to be statistically reliable. This way you are able to test many more options, can take some creative risks, and therefore increase the possibility of developing a breakthrough.

One consideration in split-run publication testing is the normal inability of publications to match advertisements to bind-in cards. This can be done by combining variation testing to the card itself. In this way simply pre-printing and pre-mixing the cards before supplying them to the publication can permit an infinite number of test variations.

Another way is to set up a transfer code, where the ad describes some option (perhaps choice of premium). The letters designating the choice vary

TABLE 3-2
GRID TEST MATRIX

	List 1	List 2	List 3	List 4	List 5	Total
Creative A Offer A	5M	5M	5M	5M	5M	25M
Creative B Offer A	5M	5M	5M	5M	5M	25M
Creative C Offer A	5M	5M	5M	5M	5M	25M
Creative A Offer B	5M	5M	5M	5M	5M	25M
	20M	20M	20M	20M	20M	

If 20,000 was the minimum sample size for a valid test, ordinarily only 5 variables could be tested in a 100,000-piece mailing. Grid testing permits nine variables, increasing the change of finding a significant winner.

not only by the premium but also by which version of the ad they appear on.

Split run tests can easily be set up for banner copy. The banners can be rotated on an alternate basis to give you a perfect test of copy or offer. It pays to vary several messages to test which is most successful, then take the best and try them on other sites.

With simple adjustments and interpolation, it is possible to calculate what any of the ads or mailings would have done in any of the lists or publications. Testing is further discussed in Chapter 5.

The Product Viability Test

One frequent situation is the need to prepare a test strategy for a brand-new product or concept. Under such circumstances, budgets generally are more limited and the need for more information is less demanding. What is needed here is not an estimate of the best copy or the ultimate media universe, but a quick answer to the query, "Does this product have any life at all?"

In such cases the test program is confined to larger samples of four or five very logical media, usually in direct mail. Only lists that represent categories large enough to sustain the business by themselves are tested. It will do the client no good to learn that a small list is highly successful if the list category cannot supply the needed volume.

It is vital to determine at what price the product or service can sell. Usually the creative concepts are limited to very basic approaches, perhaps a general discount certificate package and a sweepstakes approach. Within each basic list, both approaches are tested, as well as some basic product or price concept.

One purpose of the test is to produce a large enough customer base to get a reading on back-end performance. If a 5 percent response is expected and a 10,000-customer base is considered minimal to get a valid reading, then this initial mailing would require 200,000 pieces, depending on the reliability needed. Don't panic. Chapter 5 explains this in detail. As Table 3-2 shows, this can be spread over five lists of 20,000 names, each to be mailed one of four different mailing packages, thus giving us 20 test cells of 10,000 names each.

If the test is intended to enable a now-or-never decision on a new product, then it is also necessary to test any basic alternative medium. For instance, if competitors previously have used package inserts and broadcast to a larger extent than direct mail, then the control approach should be adapted for these media also. While direct mail may be the best medium for testing variations, it is still necessary to include all basic media categories. Both broadcast and package inserts are, by themselves, large enough media to support enormous businesses.

ECONOMIC CONSIDERATIONS

A marketing plan should stand by itself as a source document and as a working plan. Therefore the plan should include all pertinent economic considerations, perhaps in an appendix.

All information on costs, allowable margins, and past results should be recorded. I also find it helpful to do a simple chart showing the response needed to produce a break-even cost per order. The table should have different columns for minimum responses if the mailings have a different per-item cost. See Table 3-3.

Such a chart is helpful for creative people, who occasionally have to be reminded that the more expensive the package, the larger the response must be to break even. Sometimes for a product with a limited market and a large unit-sale, the same chart will justify spending the money on a high-penetration, multiple-part mailing program.

Another piece of information that should be included is a statistical validity indicator. A simple table is called for, listing the minimum size sample

TABLE 3-3
RESPONSE RATE NEEDED AT VARIOUS TARGET CPOs, %

Direct mail, cost per thousand	$10	$50	$100
$200	2	0.4	0.2
300	3	0.6	0.3
400	4	0.8	0.4
500	5	1.0	0.5
600	6	1.2	0.6

that is needed to produce a 90 or 95 percent confidence level at various response rates and allowable error margins. This requirement will be covered in Chapter 5, Testing, in more detail.

All of the economic assumptions should be detailed here as well. What are the basic costs for product and premium? What return, trade-up, and collection assumptions are being made? What overall budgets are established, and what profit and loss (P&L) is it expected to produce?

The availability of such economic considerations in the marketing plan makes it possible for everyone concerned in promotion to look at the overall picture. It might, for example, show that a modest back-end improvement in units sold per customer or in renewal rate might lead to more significant profit improvement than lowering the cost per order. This data would lead to appropriate strategies for back-end improvement.

LEGAL CONSIDERATIONS

Today, more than ever, an attorney should be consulted at the earliest stages of preparing a marketing plan. It is almost impossible for any lay person to be thoroughly familiar with every nuance of national and state government regulations and restrictions, and with various courts' interpretations of the law.

Different applications of postal regulations can make a significant difference in your total financial picture. For instance, companies operating with nonprofit status are entitled to dramatically reduced postal rates. Other companies might benefit from sending merchandise out under classifications that require much less postage than parcel post.

The Federal Trade Commission (FTC) is concerned about consumer protection. They require that commitments be spelled out clearly and completely, that product representations be honest and in no way misleading, and that words such as *free* or *guarantee* be handled in very precise ways. Even the size of type is often specified.

If you are dealing with banking, insurance or investment services, you will have to be apprised not only of federal rules and regulations, but of state ones as well. Some states are more restrictive than others, and some have procedures that cause considerable delay in granting approvals.

Some specific areas of great importance include procedures for notifying customers in the event of shipping delays, rules regarding merchandise substitution, and the parameters of "dry testing"—announcing a product before it is actually produced.

A knowledge of the FTC "thirty-day rules" that apply to delayed shipments and that require specific notices and actions is extremely important. One prominent marketer spent years in lawsuits because at a critical point he elected to notify customers of a delay by phone instead of mail. While most marketers would consider a phone-notice better service, it has only recently become acceptable, provided certain records are kept. Logic or common sense cannot be relied upon when interpreting government rulings.

"Unordered merchandise" is an area of particular sensitivity, as are the various practices involving unauthorized billing. If you sell on credit, Regulation Z of the Treasury Department regarding differentials between single payment and multiple payment plans may apply. If you are in the financial area, the Securities and Exchange Commission (SEC) will have much power over what you can and cannot say.

Be sure you consult the latest bulletins issued by the DMA Committee on Ethical Standards. Robert Posch's chapter in the *Direct Marketing Handbook* (McGraw-Hill, 1992) is very helpful, as is his full-length treatise, *The Direct Marketing Legal Advisor* (McGraw-Hill, 1983).

The DMA has encouraged direct marketers to be sensitive to the issue of consumer privacy. One of its more recent actions is to allow consumers to write to the DMA and place their name on a "do not mail" list. The DMA encourages mail-list compilers to utilize this resource when updating their mailing lists.

The association has also published a list of guidelines intended to protect consumers from having personal information passed on to other direct marketers or used in an unethical way. Sharing financial data like credit-card and checking account numbers is an obvious no-no, as is the release of medical data shared between a medical provider and patient.

Following these guidelines is not only courteous, it's common sense and will protect direct-marketing businesses from entanglements with the government. The Better Business Bureau provides some guidance at www.bbb.org, as well as the DMA's helpful information pages at www.the-dma.org.

The laws governing direct marketing have changed rapidly, and so I deliberately did not attempt to give specific advice in this book, as it is intended to span a number of years. Keep in mind that whatever strategies you devise will have to be within the bounds of government regulations, industry ethical standards, and simple fairness to the customer. Define those standards now before you've finalized your marketing plan so you won't risk going over the line in the letter or spirit of your marketing proposition.

IMPLEMENTATION

Now, at last, it's time to get down to action. The background has been clarified and the strategies chosen. All that remains is the implementation of the plan. This section of the marketing plan includes all the basics that in less professional approaches are likely to compose the entire plan. This section is a blueprint for action.

Basic Scheduling

This section should start off with a simple statement of the purpose of the plan. If the purpose is a viability test, a universe probe, a search for breakthrough creative concepts, or a rollout of a proven approach, this is the place to say it. Then set up the plan to do it.

Media schedules, timetables, and budgets are basics that should be included here in appropriate detail. If testing grids or keying systems are called for, include them. If product changes or revisions in the fulfillment system are necessary, this is the place to lay them out.

Further, with each step, this is the place for detailing responsibilities: who will do it, who will approve it, and by what date it must be approved.

Creative and Offer Concepts

Creative and offer concepts should be separately outlined. They should approximate the same form as an advertising agency work assignment, containing everything copywriters need to start their work. For each offer and creative concept there should be a simple statement of the objective and goal for that one version, and an explanation of the strategy chosen for specified ads or mailing pieces.

Any revisions in the basic copy platform should also be mentioned next to each creative concept, as well as any special economic considerations, cost limitations, timing problems, or other factors. Sensitivities—legal matters, styling considerations, and subjective client preferences—should also be noted for the benefit of the creative team.

A positioning statement also should be included, with special emphasis on any ways advertisements are expected to differ from previously established positioning. This positioning statement should refer specifically to copy style, level and tone, as well as to graphic style and image. Often this type of detail is not part of the basic marketing plan, but is added later in the form of individual strategy statements for specific advertisements, mailings, and broadcast commercials.

The final step is a statement of result targets: how the program as a whole is expected to affect the profit-and-loss sheet. This is the place to temper the goals and make allowances for the probability that not every new format is going to beat the control.

Budgeting

The budget should be prepared on the "task method." This means that recommended cost estimates should be provided for achieving the objectives stated in the plan. The task-based budget should be stated even if it is unlikely that the necessary monies will be appropriated. Possible budget shortcuts and abridgments should be included if it is possible that the task-based budget is in excess of management's expected overall costs.

Where there are alternatives, their effect should be clearly expressed. If a smaller test budget will require a second stage of extension testing and a season's delay in the rollout, it should be graphically depicted, as should the risks and economic effects of such a delay.

If it is not yet possible to forecast results from recommended mailings or media insertions, a range of possible CPRs (Cost Per Response) should be shown, with the economic effect of each worked out and shown.

It's a mistake to end a marketing plan with the cost of implementing the plan, for many executives scan the last pages first. The final wrap-up should restate the sales and profit expectations. This keeps the final focus on what is to be gained, not on what investment is required.

Timetable

The wrap-up is the schedule. How long will everything take? What are the key decision points? What answers are needed by what dates in order to move everything along? Who is expected to do what?

More marketing plans are killed by inaction than by deliberate rejection. If you want your marketing plan to have the approval of your management, then make it very clear who is expected to approve what, by what date, so that at least the blame will be clear if someone sits on your proposal.

Perhaps a note about overtime factors is in order. Often as little as a one-week delay in the early stages of a program will result in escalated production costs incurred for overtime and rush services. If you have the figures available, they make a dramatic footnote for the timetable section of a marketing plan.

Whether your plan is a complete statement of every element and alternative (as outlined here) or a simple design for the next mailing, put as many details in writing and add data as you go along. The simplest plan is better than none, providing it is a written document that everyone can agree upon in advance and look at later.

THE MARKETING PLAN FORMAT

In the previous pages of this chapter I have outlined what kind of information should go into a marketing plan and explained why the background data is as important as the strategy itself—both in creating the strategy and in reviewing it.

Here's the format of the plan in more conventional marketing language:

Title
   Marketing Plan for period for Xyz Company Product Line.
   Prepared by Name, date

Introduction
   Why the plan was prepared
   Qualifications of the preparers

Product Description
   Attributes—basic and technical
   Benefits—Practical and emotional
   Emotional and psychological imagery
   Positioning

Marketing Environment
   Competition –media used, copy points
   Government regulations—dos and don'ts
   Known problems and opportunities

Market Potential
   The media universe
   Profile of prospective customers
   Product, offer, or positioning changes
   Results of previous list and media tests
   Available demographic or psychographic data

Strategic Planning
   Objectives of marketing program
   Goals: quantified objectives, within time frame
   Strategic alternatives
   Criteria for selection
   Recommended prioritized strategies

Implementation
   Basic campaign outline
   Test grid, if applicable
   Media or list recommendation
   Offer or creative concept
   Budgets
   Timetables
   Result targets

The writing style of a marketing plan should be as simple as possible. The object is to impress the boss or client with the soundness of the thinking, not with the number of words. An outline form, with bulleted points and telegraphic copy style, is very appropriate as long as it is clear.

Loose-leaf binders are recommended, as are copies of the plan in digital formats. They permit updating, revision, and addition during the course of a campaign. New data, new ideas, and result reports should all be added to the basic marketing plan during the course of the year, so that the plan is not just a historical record of an original intention but a living, working document of a campaign in progress.

Smaller Companies

When lecturing about the importance of testing, I invariably am challenged by executives from a smaller company who believe that they can't afford to do split-run testing. It is true that the opportunities are more limited, but they are there. Most of my clients, regardless of size, start up with limited budgets and testing is always an option.

The key is the realization that testing does not necessitate complete new creative executions for every test. The key is to test concepts first, particularly offers and overall creative positioning. This can often be done with window envelopes, with flexible brochures, with laser printing of a head-line or letter, or with a buck slip which is different in different versions. Magazines and newspapers have regional editions and split runs. The Internet is infinitely flexible. You can often test two or three ideas without increasing costs at all, as long as you plan for it.

Major Corporations

The planning process is, of course, influenced by the budget available. While the elements and processes may be the same, the resources permit steps that smaller companies cannot afford.

Data Analysis. Some companies spend tens or hundreds of thousand of dollars on what is now called "data mining"—intensive computer searches for trends, patterns or marketing segments. While the process is substantially the same as the simpler computer matching and regression analysis available from major list-compilers and service bureaus, it is supposed to have much greater promise. It has not yet been demonstrated that the greater size of the computer or the consulting firm offering such services necessarily justify the substantially greater costs.

Research. Larger companies, particularly those that have honed their skills on retail-distributed products and mass merchandising, will often include a round of focus panels or interviews as part of the process. I believe in research, but frankly I have seen more bad research projects than good ones. Researchers using packaged good results will always come up with the wrong results unless they understand what is different about direct marketing. Why? Because as direct marketers we can't ask people to read our copy and comment unless we first determine if they would read it voluntarily. Because we are only concerned with the small percentage of people who will eventually respond to our offer, the opinions of others simply don't count at all. Because we don't care what is "liked" or even "recalled" our objectives are more immediate.

Budgeting. While such companies have "deep pockets," they are usually less flexible in budgeting. I have seen many examples of direct marketing programs that, when finally authorized, are severely under-budgeted, and where there is no allowance for testing before a roll-out. The result is an untested self-mailer sent to millions of homes which, even if it does work, might have worked much better if tested. But many companies still operate this way. One cause is that executives in such companies learn that doubling response might get them a pat on the back, while going over budget by even 10% will get them fired.

Until such corporations recognize the "new budgeting" described in the first chapter, the most successful direct marketing ventures will continue to come from smaller and mid-sized companies.

EVALUATING A MARKETING PLAN

For many executives, particularly in larger businesses, the preparation of a marketing plan is left to an advertising agency, a consultant, or staff members. The real task for such executives—one that is just as important as writing the plan—is the plan's evaluation.

If the plan has been prepared as outlined here or in a similar format, it is a self-contained document that includes all relevant background material. The evaluator should be able to take one binder on an airplane or to a poolside lounge chair and read through the plan without reference to outside data.

The first thing evaluators should note is whether all pertinent considerations have been taken into account. If they have, the other pieces should logically fall into place. The evaluators should then ask whether the plan looks ahead. Does it provide marketing and creative direction for the future?

If the plan is for a presently successful campaign, are there provisions for testing ads and mail pieces for future seasons when the present control will eventually wear out?

The budget will be important, of course, especially as it fits into overall corporate budgets. However, it should be considered only in terms of downside risk. Even the unsuccessful portions of a campaign produce some orders.

Is the plan legal? Does it follow the spirit as well as the letter of the law? It may be helpful to send the copy platform to lawyers for review early on rather than waiting for finished copy.

Most important, is it unique? Does it present fresh, original, creative thinking? Is it identical to your competitor's plan except for the product name? A good executive should expect some new approaches and some challenging ideas, as well as obvious marketing logic.

After the plan has been completely reviewed, one final test remains. In some ways this may be the most important. Call in the people who wrote the plan and approved it. Look them in the eye and ask them this one question: "Do you really think this plan will be successful?"

The people who wrote the plan should really believe in it. You have a right to expect them to believe in it and to have enthusiasm about it. If they don't, start looking for new people and a new plan.

RESEARCH

One of the most significant results of the influence of general advertising disciplines on the traditional processes of direct marketing has been the increasing role of research. In previous editions of this book I strongly urged the greater use of traditional research methods, and lamented the fact that most direct marketers didn't use this valuable tool. In the 21st Century, as direct marketing continues to grow and refine the tools of its trade, there is more acceptance of this basic ad-making step perfected by our cousins in the world of image advertising. But, with this increase in use, there is a new urgency to "do it right."

Direct Marketing's Different Needs

I continue to advocate the use of focus panels, interviews and other methods to determine the "why" of successful and unsuccessful campaigns. But my enthusiasm has been tempered by the tragic results of bad research, generally performed by those who have not learned or who refuse to appreciate the differences between mass advertising and direct marketing.

I have seen a customer cross-sell program cancelled by a packaged goods advertiser because the recall factor was not up to the standards of their other advertising. Shocked, I tried to point out that our program was designed to generate trial through special offers, while the millions they spent on other media was designed for brand recognition. I argued that the goals were not the same, that they couldn't be compared by the same criteria. To no avail. A program that generated tens of thousands of letters and hundreds of thousands of product trials was stopped cold by bad research.

Another company in the telecommunications field used one-on-one interviews in connection with a cellular phone project. They came to the conclusion that "short letters would be better than long ones," despite the need to include vital details about the phone, the rates, the territory, and why the customer should have a cellular phone in the first place. As this was contrary to every direct-marketing experience, we asked to attend the next group of interviews. We noted that they displayed several mailpieces and asked which one the interviewee liked best. Adding up the answers, the short letters were the winners.

At the next session we asked the interviewer to ask, towards the end of each interview, "Now that you are familiar with this program, is it something that you personally would be interested in buying?" Separating the comments of the "yes" people from the others we came to a very different conclusion. Potential buyers—people really interested—preferred the longer letters. They wanted more information, not less. This has been repeated with other products and the result has been the same. Always. Without exception.

In the real world only one or two out of a hundred people would be expected to sign up for the program. Yet the researchers, using packaged-goods standards for products bought in a retail outlet, valued everyone's reaction equally. These researchers, like many others I have encountered, failed to recognize that in direct marketing the only opinions that count are those of potential buyers.

That does not mean that research should not be used. Those who use research wisely will find that it often can make the difference between the success or failure of a new campaign. It can provide the edge needed to revive a failing proposition or to ensure the success of a new product. Knowing the difference between good and bad research methods (and researchers) can be as valuable an asset to a direct marketer as it is to a mass marketer.

RESEARCH VERSUS TESTING

It is important to differentiate between research and testing. The two terms are often used interchangeably, and therefore misused. This book deals with each in separate chapters.

For the most part, direct marketers rely on testing—an art and a science that has always been a unique strength of the industry. Testing—as we use the term—refers to producing an advertisement, mailing piece, or commercial and putting it in the media. The results are compared against other similar campaigns. These tests produce some responses and partially pay for themselves.

Yet there is an inherent problem. Testing may tell us *what* works, but never *why*. Like a good accountant, results can tell us what we did wrong, but not what we should do instead. It can tell us *who* is buying a product, but not *why* they are buying it. It can tell us that our proposition appealed to some people on one mailing list, from one type of community or among subscribers to one publication, but not the *reasons* for the difference.

Research, on the other hand, involves a learning process. It does not produce orders or leads, so it is usually treated as an expense. Companies who would not hesitate to try out a new direct-mail package or invest in the production expense of a new advertisement often freeze up when it comes to approving several thousand dollars for a research project.

Research should be as fundamental a part of an advertiser's annual budget as production costs or creative fees. It should be looked on as an investment, not an expense.

Research as an Investment

The question should not be "Do we need research?" but "How much and what type of research do we need?" Direct marketers should think about this example: If a company was considering adding a sweepstakes, the management wouldn't look at $15,000 in prizes and expenses as a cost, but as an investment because of the potential increase in return. If the company mails out a million pieces, the cost of this contest would be $15 per thousand pieces. The question then is not whether $15,000 is affordable, but whether $15 per thousand is a reasonable cost. If the million-piece mailing costs $300 per thousand, the $15,000 would represent a 5 percent increase in mailing cost. The question then is whether you can reasonably expect a 5 percent lift in response, say from 1 percent to 1.05 percent. In that case the expectation is reasonable, and you might try the sweepstakes.

On the other hand, a million-dollar prize would cost $1000 per thousand at the quantity in this example, and would require a 333 percent lift—a 4.3 percent response instead of 1 percent. That is unlikely, although not impossible. As the mailing quantity increases, the ratios improve dramatically, making even ten million a wise investment for companies who will use this prize for ten or twenty-million mail pieces.

Why all this talk about sweepstakes economics in a chapter on research? Because the arithmetic is exactly the same. And so are the examples. Substitute a research investment of $15,000 and ask yourself the same question: "Is there a reasonable probability that this investment will pay for itself in added response?" Depending on the size of your total budget, decide whether a particular research proposal will help you to develop a product improvement or a new creative theme. Then determine whether it can give you a response increase sufficient to pay for the cost of the research. If the cost is out of line with the response needed to justify the expense, or vice versa, pass it up. Otherwise, you have just as good a chance of finding a new breakthrough from a research investment as you do in trying a new format or offer variation.

PURPOSES OF RESEARCH

There are many different research techniques, going far beyond the simple "focus panel" most advertisers are familiar with. Most full-service direct marketing agencies and advertisers have consultants on staff to advise them about which research method is most appropriate for a specific objective. First, however, we have to identify the objectives that are most appropriate for research. Some broad areas are:

- *Market research,* which seeks to understand the marketing environment, including its various geographic, demographic, and psychographic segments.

- *Creative research,* which seeks to identify new creative themes and prioritize copy points.

- *Predictive research,* which seeks to narrow the number of approaches that are brought to the testing stage.

- *Post-test analysis,* which analyzes test results or compares respondents and non-respondents to identify marketing and creative steps for the future.

Market Research

Market research attempts to both identify and understand the prospects for the product or service being offered. While testing will eventually tell us which lists, publications or broadcast programming will produce the most responsive audience with the least cost, market research tells us who the likely prospects are, independently of how we can reach them.

Researchers can tell us not only the *who*—in terms of age, income, education, and geographic location—but also the *why.* Why do some people crave our product while others couldn't care less? Why do some people see it one way while others see it very differently? We can learn about lifestyles—the psychographic indicators of how our prospects live; what kind of work they do; their hobbies, sports, and interests; their tastes and preferences. Information like this makes mailing list selection less subjective and more scientific than direct marketers of the old school ever thought possible.

Research also can answer such questions as: What do our prospects know, or think they know, about our product or service? How do they react to it? Do they understand it? Does it need more explanation? Are there undesirable features that should be eliminated, or other features that can be added? Do customers really need what we have to offer? And—an entirely different question—do they *know* they need it?

And what about the offer? Pricing is a suitable subject for research, but as I've observed so far the results have not been satisfactory. People may tell you whether they would or would not buy a product at a certain price, but the information has not proved reliable compared to offer testing. I wouldn't recommend eliminating all offer research however. Research will help to identify premiums, uncover a need for a better guarantee, or determine reactions to elements of the proposition other than pure pricing.

Finally, researchers can answer two vitally important questions about our prospects: What is their self-image, and what is the image they have of people who use products like ours? This "user-imagery" question is discussed in more detail later in this book, and can be very significant in determining product positioning and the use of visual communication in all forms of advertising.

Segmentation Tools

Great strides have been made in developing research tools that help us to segment the market for products according to geographic, demographic, or psychographic information. These tools are not always linked to specific brands or products, but nevertheless they are able to provide clues to the interests and lifestyles of prospects.

Simmons. One valuable tool is Simmons, probably the leading consumer analysis company. Long used as a tool by general advertising media departments, it provides a continuous survey of people around the country and relates their interests, hobbies, purchasing histories, and intentions to purchase specific products. This data is compared to the audience's exposure to particular publications and other media.

Agencies and companies who have this service on computer can customize the data by comparing various statistics to find correlation. For instance, if women who frequently buy hosiery are likely to travel or read, we know something about what kind of lists are likely to work for a hosiery club, and what kind of situations should be shown in illustrations. It also gives us the information it was originally designed for as an index to measure the likely effectiveness of print media schedules.

Simmons studies have always included characteristics such as whether a prospect purchased anything by mail or joined a book club. A few years ago they also developed a purchase log that tracks actual purchases rather than just rely on memory. Interestingly, many more participants logged in mail-order purchases than stated they had bought by mail.

Geo-demographics. Geo-demographics, a research tool developed specifically for the direct marketing industry, is now very much in use by all types of advertisers. This method involves studying available census data about different geographic units—zip codes, census tracts, or even smaller units such as postal-carrier routes—and relating them to demographic or lifestyle indicators.

Such data has long been available on a demographic basis, enabling direct mailers to select high-income areas, home-owning areas, or areas with large families. The newer applications relate to lifestyle data, and were obtained by reducing over 1000 available variables into fewer than 100 significant indicators. Some of the companies in this field add their own proprietary data as well.

Some segmentation methods include Claritas' Prizm and CACI's Acorn. These, and others, enable an advertiser to analyze lists and locate significant variables to increase the probability of success. Some of these are lifestyle indicators that define geographic areas. Claritas' Prizm categories present these geographic clusters in easily-understood lifestyle terms. They are found in Table 4-1.

Such information not only helps us to use otherwise marginal mailing lists, but provides us with a feeling for the type of people who are buying our product. This naturally can lead to changes in the substance and style of the advertising communications prepared for these markets. Often such data reminds us to be less clever, less subtle, and more in touch with basic needs and desires.

Creative Research

Focus panels, field interviews, and questionnaires can give advertisers a chance to get a current reading on the thinking of the marketplace. Advertisers can check on whether their messages are understood, determine the jargon used by readers and viewers, and uncover objections that otherwise would go unanswered. Most important, research can identify opportunities that might otherwise be missed.

Today's creative directors must be objective enough to realize that they are not omniscient and should make full use of modern research. But research directors must recognize that their methods are a source of creative inspiration, not a substitute for it.

Creative research, as the name suggests, is concerned with the creation of advertising messages rather than with overall marketing questions. Of course, the areas of major interest do overlap, and the same research project often may have objectives relating to both areas.

The definition of creative objectives is best done in relation to a creative philosophy that seeks answers to test the applicability of a specific strategy.

Awareness.   If there is little awareness of the product, we need to "Create a need" with educational copy addressed to those consumers entering the market. Virtually every product needed such an approach at some time, and even established products can be sold to some market segments in this way. Research can tell us where and when this approach is needed.

Is the consumer aware of the category, but not of our brand? This requires a different approach. Are consumers aware of the product, but not of its advantages? Has the public been exposed to misinformation that should be corrected? Or is the product one that is already needed and wanted? In this last case, our problem is to stress offers that can motivate immediate action. Research can answer these questions.

Attitudes.   What are people's preexisting attitudes toward the product or service? What do they associate it with? Often we find a basic problem of credibility. People know our claims, but don't believe them. An entire advertising program was built around dramatization of the guarantee for one such case. Scientific explanation was used in another. Credibility was achieved in yet another with the help of a respected spokesperson.

TABLE 4-1
PRIZM LIFESTYLE SEGMENTATION

Cluster name	Demographic description	% of Households
URBAN		
U1 URBAN UPTOWN		
Urban Gold Coast	Professional Urban Singles & Couples	0.59
Money & Brains	Sophisticated Townhouse Couples	1.12
Young Literati	Upscale Urban Couples & Singles	0.94
American Dreams	Established Urban Immigrant Families	1.40
Bohemian Mix	Bohemian Singles & Couples	1.48
U2 URBAN MIDSCALE		
Urban Achievers	Mid-Level, White-Collar, Urban Families	1.60
Big City Blend	Middle-Income Immigrant Families	1.12
Old Yankee Row	Empty-Nest, Middle-Class Families	1.31
Mid-City Mix	African-American Singles & Families	1.08
Latino America	Hispanic Middle-Class Families	1.23
U3 URBAN CORES		
Single City Blues	Ethnically Mixed Urban Singles	1.74
Hispanic Mix	Urban Hispanic Singles & Families	1.56
Inner Cities	Inner-City, Solo-Parent Families	1.94
SUBURBAN		
S1 ELITE SUBURBS		
Blue Blood Estates	Privileged Super-Rich Families	1.18
Winner's Circle	Executive Suburban Families	2.15
Executive Suites	Upscale White-Collar Couples	1.32
Pools & Patios	Established Empty Nesters	1.85
Kids & Cul-de Sacs	Upscale Suburban Families	2.93
S2 THE AFFLUENTIALS		
Young Influentials	Upwardly Mobile Singles & Couples	1.35
New Empty Nests	Upscale Suburban Fringe Couples	2.06
Boomers & Babies	Young, White-Collar Suburban Familes	1.11
Suburban Sprawl	Young, Suburban Townhouse Couples	1.50
Blue-Chip Blues	Upscale Blue-Collar Families	1.93
S3 INNER SUBURBS		
Upstarts & Seniors	Middle Income Empty Nesters	1.28
New Beginnings	Young, Mobile City Singles	1.19
Mobility Blues	Young, Blue-Collar/Service Families	1.48
Gray Collars	Aging Couples in Inner Suburbs	1.97
CITY (MEDIUM-SIZED/2ND CITY)		
C1 2ND CITY SOCIETY		
Second City Elite	Upscale Executive Families	1.89
Upward Bound	Young, Upscale White-Collar Families	1.83
Gray Power	Affluent Retirees in Sunbelt Cities	2.03

TABLE 4.1
PRIZM LIFESTYLE SEGMENTATION (*Continued*)

Cluster name	Demographic description	% of Households
C2 2ND CITY CENTERS		
Middleburg Managers	Mid-Level White-Collar Couples	1.72
Boomtown Singles	Middle Income Young Singles	1.03
Starter Families	Young Middle-Class Families	1.58
Sunset City Blues	Empy Nests in Aging Industrial Cities	1.68
Towns & Gowns	College Town Singles	1.39
C3 2ND CITY BLUES		
Smalltown Downtown	Older Renters & Young Families	1.83
Hometown Retired	Low-Income, Older Singles & Couples	1.20
Family Scramble	Low-Income Hispanic Families	2.19
Southside City	African-American Service Workers	1.97
TOWN		
T1 LANDED GENTRY		
Country Squires	Elite Exurban Families	1.33
God's Country	Executive Exurban Families	2.63
Big Fish, Small Pond	Small Exurban Families	1.37
Greenbelt Families	Young, Middle-Class Town Families	1.48
T2 EXURBAN BLUES		
New Homesteaders	Young, Middle-Class Families	1.66
Middle America	Midscale Families in Midsize Towns	2.23
Red, White & Blues	Small Town, Blue-Collar Families	1.80
Military Quarters	G.I.s & Surrounding Off-Base Families	0.42
T3 WORKING TOWNS		
Golden Ponds	Retirement Town Seniors	1.62
Rural Industria	Low-Income, Blue-Collar Families	1.70
Norma Rae-Ville	Young Families, Bi-Racial Mill Towns	1.37
Mines & Mills	Older Families, Mine & Mill Towns	2.24
RURAL		
R1 COUNTRY FAMILIES		
Big Sky Families	Midscale Couples, Kids & Farmland	1.48
New Eco-topia	Rural White/Blue-Collar/Farm Families	0.90
River City, USA	Middle-Class, Rural Families	1.78
Shotguns & Pickups	Rural Blue-Collar Workers & Families	1.91
R2 HEARTLANDERS		
Agri-Business	Rural Farm-Town & Ranch Families	1.45
Grain Belt	Farm Owners & Tenants	2.25
R3 RUSTIC LIVING		
Blue Highways	Moerate Blue-Collar/Farm Families	2.04
Rustic Elders	Low-Income, Older, Rural Couples	1.88
Back Country Folks	Remote Rural/Town Families	2.18
Scrub Pine Flats	African-American Farm Families	1.52
Hard Scrabble	Families in Poor Isolated Areas	1.99

Once you know what the problem is, creative directions emerge from logical thought processes. Otherwise, there is a tendency for some creative people to pursue cleverness for the sake of cleverness. Sound solutions to identified problems always produce better results.

Needs.   We can also learn from research what the consumer's real needs are, and how our product or service can fulfill these needs. Such needs usually deal with emotional and imagery issues, as well as real, tangible concerns.

A mobile telephone, for example, enables one to keep in touch when traveling. But is that the real need? Research shows that it may also be an executive toy, a symbol of success, or a gadget to fulfill curiosity and enhance self-esteem. In such cases the needs of the office are a way of justifying the purchase, but are not the primary motivator. This leads advertisers to create ads using illustrations to enhance self-image.

In fund-raising, most creative appeals are based on the good work of the philanthropy. But some research seems to indicate that reward and recognition for the donor are equally important. Philanthropists want to achieve something more than a sense of doing a good deed. They often want others to know they have done that good deed. Some research even indicates that a philanthropist may be buying "immortality" and "dis-alienation." This may explain why appeals for children often do better than those for adults, and why people seem to respond to being part of a "crusade"—figuratively joining hands with others to accomplish a noble goal.

These are just a few examples of research that reveal customers' emotional needs which might otherwise be overlooked in the creative process.

Intentions.   The potential buyer's intentions are another area of interest. Do we have to create a need? Or fulfill it? Do we have to persuade our prospect to buy our particular brand rather than a competitor's? Or is our problem simply to overcome inertia with a sale or special offer, to get them to act now rather than later?

Very often I find that the subjective judgments of clients and agency staff are correct, but for only a limited segment of the market. Research sometimes reveals market segments with unanticipated problems or unforeseen opportunities that require different approaches.

Behavior.   When we've identified the families—or companies, in the case of business products—as our prospects, it is valuable to know how they previously handled the problem solved by our product or service.

For example, if we are selling long-distance telephone services, we discover different behavior among different market segments. Some families may send cards or write letters as alternatives to long-distance calls. Others simply make such calls very briefly or infrequently. Of course you want to concentrate on the heavy users.

Imagine you're selling a lawn product. It's helpful to know whether the present prospect spends countless hours pulling up crabgrass, suffers with a poor-looking lawn, or uses an expensive service that is more costly than yours. Your choice of creative strategy becomes very clear with such information. You know whether to base it on "Save time and trouble" or "Get a better lawn" or "Save money." A good direct-response ad or mailing will include all these copy points, but a choice must be made as to which to emphasize to attract the prime prospect in the first place.

Execution.   Some research methods also can be helpful in perfecting the execution of the creative theme or concept finally selected.

Simple interviews or focus panels may not be helpful in telling you whether an ad is "liked" or whether the panel members would "respond." But these techniques can tell you whether your message comes across as it's meant to or whether people will stop to read your ad at all.

Such creative research can be a good investment if there is a great deal at stake in a successful ad or mailing. This is especially true when there are differences of opinion within a client's or an agency's organization. Some quick research can quickly break a deadlock or resolve a disagreement.

User Imagery.   Probably the most significant development in creative research is the application of "user imagery" in the field of direct response. This method seeks to influence the image prospective customers have of who buys a product or service. "Do people like me use this? Do I associate myself with others who use this product?"

Such imagery is readily apparent in ads for products, such as perfume or clothing, that suggest a lifestyle that many consumers would like to adopt as their own. Virtually every kind of product or service has a "brand personality." Buyers perceive some to be "right-for-me," whereas others are "not-for-me."

My firm has supervised imagery studies for direct-marketing clients in fields such as banking, air express, investments, credit cards, book clubs and magazines, and we have never failed to find a creative opportunity. Sometimes an imagery study influences the entire basic thrust of the campaign.

There was a time when old-fashioned copywriters perceived research as a hindrance. Today's writers and artists welcome both the stimulation of research and the sound creative strategies that come from it. Research has made the creative task more professional. It enables the creative team to put more energy into expression than speculation. Most important, a solid creative plan based on research takes the guesswork out of the creative process.

Predictive Research

One of the most common reasons that research has not been used adequately in direct marketing is the relative weakness of predictive research, or pre-testing methods. While pre-testing has been used extensively in the general advertising world—where test market campaigns have been the only interim step before a national rollout—no research method has approached the effectiveness of the split-run and sampling methods that are an integral part of direct-marketing methodology.

However, even the largest advertisers cannot afford unlimited split-run testing. Sample sizes and the number of cells in a direct mail campaign should have some relationship to a total budget. Print advertising is limited by the flexibility of the print media being tested. When color ads or brochures are involved, production costs can quickly become prohibitive if several four-color executions are being tested against each other.

Predictive research techniques range from simple screening methods to complex physiological investigations involving voice pitch, eye movement, and even brain waves. More than 50 different approaches to copy testing are used by general agencies.

In my experience, pretest techniques do not pick winners. They are no substitute for split-run testing to find the one perfect ad or mailer. What they do is identify the losers. If there are a dozen possible concepts for a campaign and only four can be tested, pre-testing can eliminate the half-dozen least likely to succeed. With only six left to choose from, the odds greatly improve that the client and agency will pick the three or four most likely to make a difference.

I have seen pre-testing methods used for naming a new product, selecting a spokesperson and establishing priorities among the elements of a copy platform. It can be too costly to test every possible element if four-color printing, high-quality television production or complex mail formats are involved.

It's important to note the limitations of pre-testing research. The results typically provide only an index of relative appeal, never an absolute figure. In other words, you may learn which ad will attract the most people compared to the other ads, but not whether any of them will bring in the number of customers you need.

Post-Testing

An axiom of direct marketers is that we always know what went right or wrong after the results of a split-run. Theories abound to account for breakthrough results or to explain why certain campaigns ended up at the bottom of the response rankings. Hindsight is a gift possessed by all practitioners in this field.

While research can't determine who will actually respond to a *future* campaign, it can find out why people responded to a *previous* offer. We can uncover the differences in the attitudes, feelings, motivations and perceptions of those who responded and those who didn't. Telephone surveys, in-depth interviews and mail questionnaires can be used to answer this question.

In some cases we can learn what appeal most influenced the buying decision of the responders. Sometimes it is not the one we featured, and future efforts can thus be strengthened by emphasizing the reasons people respond to the ad. Or we may find that a key point that could have brought in customers was overlooked by the non-responders, possibly because of the layout or because it was expressed too subtly by the copywriter.

We can ask hypothetical questions to the non-responders to guide us in future efforts. What if we lowered the price? What if we offered a guarantee? What if you didn't have to send money now and could just try it? What if we included a free training course? What if you knew that many other people like you had already bought it? What if you knew that this offer was being made by a well-known corporation? What if the offer appeared in a respected magazine or a favorite webpage or channel? A key element that could affect future efforts can be identified if we know the non-responder might have acted differently when given different information. The only other way to uncover this element would be by repeated trial and error.

Such questions should, of course, be asked of people who remember getting the offer, who have some conceivable use for the product or service, and who are qualified as prime prospects. The opinions of others are irrelevant. Especially unimportant are those who say—even *swear*—that they didn't get the mailing. They are as reliable as the large percentage of consumers who swear they never ordered by mail, phone or the Internet, even though their names are on our customer lists.

RESEARCH METHODS

Up to now we have been discussing what can be done with research, and why direct marketers should use it with much greater regularity and effectiveness than in the past. The next part of this chapter touches on available research tools divided into two broad categories, *qualitative* and *quantitative.* They are listed here to give you some understanding of the large variety of available research tools that can be adapted for direct marketing, followed by an introduction to some of the newer nonverbal research methods.

Too many advertisers ask their advertising agency or research firm for "just a couple of focus panels" or "a questionnaire." This is like asking for a self-mailer without first determining the offer or even the right medium.

Research is a great industry today, with countless companies in the field. Many have unique or proprietary methods, and several have successfully applied these methods to the problems of direct marketers. The first place to start a research project is with the specialist at your ad agency, a consultant, or your own experienced staff member. The choice of research methods should be determined after the objectives are established. As I said earlier, good research can be helpful, but bad research can be disastrous.

QUALITATIVE METHODS

There are two broad categories of qualitative research: group discussions, sometimes called *focus panels,* and individual interviews, which may take place at potential customers' homes, offices, on the street or even on the telephone.

Focus Panels

Focus panels are the antithesis of direct marketing's scientific testing methods. They are not subject to measurement at all. Individual panel members may be atypical of the market as a whole, and there is almost never a definitive resolution to any question. Yet their value is immense.

Basically, focus panels are like group therapy sessions. They typically involve between 6 and 12 people who engage in an open discussion. A moderator, who must be more of a psychologist than a researcher, guides the group into areas of interest to the advertiser. Clients who are in a position to influence the direction of the discussion watch the whole proceeding, through a two-way mirror or on closed-circuit television.

Planning.   The first step for a focus panel is a consultation with a research specialist and the preparation of a plan. This plan must include several vital subjects: overall objectives, geography, composition, screening criteria, and a discussion guide.

The objectives may be open-ended, and their creators must recognize the limitations of the focus panel. A focus panel objective cannot be quantifiable, as in "Determine percentage of market familiar with client's trademark." A realistic objective would be, "Obtain consumer reactions to client trademark." It cannot be selective, as in "Select which advertisement to run." It can be subjective, as in "Determine comprehension of new advertising execution."

Some of the most productive panels have the most open-ended objectives. One panel simply asked people if they would open a particular direct mail package—and how they felt about the contents if they did. Others sought attitudes toward new book clubs or other direct-marketing ventures.

Geography is another consideration that advertisers and researchers should decide beforehand. Most focus-panel researchers are affiliated with testing services around the country, and are in a position to obtain screeners, panels, and focus group rooms across the country.

Usually it is possible to assemble panels representing different lifestyles and demographics within almost any city. Sometimes a researcher will recommend a suburban location if that is where the market is for the particular product or service. More often a researcher will sample groups in a variety of areas to get a good cross-section of opinion. Conducting panels in different cities can result in some surprises.

The general characteristics of the individuals in the group is referred to as the group's composition. Groups can be selected within any age, income, education, or lifestyle parameters. Often there are very significant and differing reactions depending upon age, sex, or lifestyle. For example, women who work outside the home and full-time homemakers may have different reactions to a product.

Sometimes different groups are selected based on their attitudes towards products. A magazine may want to explore the attitudes of groups who logically should read the magazine but never have, of newsstand buyers who have never subscribed, and of former subscribers who failed to renew. Obviously each of these groups should reveal very different attitudes toward the magazine.

How many groups should one have, then? Some arbitrary choices have to be made, especially because a professionally done focus group can cost between $3000 and $6000, not including the travel expenses of the moderator and marketing personnel. Holding two different panels in each of three cities can cost between $15,000 and $30,000. I recommend limiting the number of panels and reserving some money. You may want to schedule additional panels after the first reports have been studied. The additional panels can then concentrate on target groups or focus topics that require further exploration.

Screening Criteria.   Once location and composition have been established, it is necessary to establish screening criteria, the key determinant of a panel's usefulness. Usually direct-marketing focus groups should be composed of people who have bought by mail. People who are hostile to mail-order will be useless, and their opinions and attitudes will color the comments of the rest of the panel.

Other criteria include employment, media readership, and history of purchasing similar products. The criteria questionnaire should also include a question designed to eliminate competitors, people in related fields, or members of the news media who might compromise the trade information exposed to the focus panel participants.

"Screeners" employed by the research firm telephone lists of people supplied by the client or assembled from local directories. They telephone hundreds of people until they can get the handful needed for each product—people who are qualified according to the criteria established, and who are willing to participate in a panel in return for a nominal payment. The more restrictive the screening criteria, the more people must be called in order to assemble the panel.

Discussion Guide.   The discussion guide is the step that requires the most work. Researchers usually will not prepare the guide until they have been awarded the contract.

The discussion guide is basically an agenda—a step-by-step guide to the various topics as they are to be exposed to the focus-group participants, including a list of product samples or promotional materials to be shown to the groups.

There is no one right way to prepare a guide. Moderators develop styles that fit their own personalities, and no two are alike. Some are analytical. Some are flamboyant. Yet most of them have some elements in common. The following composite of common denominators is based on the many panels I have observed.

Opening Remarks. The first objective is to relax the participants and to set the ground rules for the next couple of hours. Most moderators encourage the members of the group to be honest in their opinions and feelings. A casual environment is established, with refreshments and light conversation. A joke or two doesn't hurt.

Introductions are made for two reasons. One is to help the participants to feel comfortable with one another. The other is to make it easier to relate individuals' backgrounds to their comments when audio or video tapes are reviewed during the analysis.

Most moderators disclose the presence of observers on the other side of the mirror. Almost all advise participants that the discussions are not being judged nor rated, and that there will be no resolution to the topics. Panel members are told that one person's opinion is as good as any other's, and that there is no pressure to obtain agreement.

Attitudinal Exploration. The next step is to inquire about general attitudes toward the product category, buying by mail order, or other relevant topics. Questions are open-ended and designed to elicit background for the more specific comments that will come later.

Psychoanalytic methods are used to encourage amplification during this stage: "Mmm-hmm, I see"; "Why do you feel this way?"; "Can you tell us more about that?"; "Who else feels this way?" All these comments are used to draw out the group's feelings and attitudes.

Development Stages. The main topic is introduced in a variety of ways. If the product being investigated is a magazine, the panel may be asked where they get information about a certain topic or how they learned certain things. They will be led into mentioning magazines in general and the specific magazine being studied in such a way that the magazine being explored is concealed from the focus panel. These indirect methods are used in order to forestall any bias and to elicit comments that might be withheld out of courtesy if the sponsor were known right away.

Often competing advertisements or products are presented. Sometimes the advertiser's name is blacked out. This is done to obtain comments about the product or advertisement that is uncolored by positive or negative attitudes the panel members have developed toward the brand name.

One focus panel explored attitudes toward conventional mail-order propositions and identified positive and negative reactions. The moderator purposely explored the negative attitudes. The sponsor's proposition—which overcame many of the objections of conventional mail-order—was then introduced. The features of the new proposition would have been less evident if they had not been contrasted with the previous ones.

Subject Exploration. About halfway through the session the subject of the panel is unveiled in the same casual manner in which the previous queries were presented. By now the group should be warmed up, and comments should come freely.

One technique is to show a commercial or read the headlines of an ad or mailing piece and then ask the participants to quickly jot down the points they recall that were important to them. Comments are solicited later as to what these points were and why they were important. It is important for participants to write down their observations. Otherwise panel members tend to echo the first comments they hear rather than expose their own honest reactions.

Sometimes several ads are shown and the panelists may be asked to rate the likelihood that they would buy the product on a zero-to-ten scale in the same manner. They are then asked for their scores and the reasons for their judgements.

Interest Indication.   This step has been added since the previous edition of this book, and is based on a technique used by the Direct Marketing Research Center in New York. It's purpose is to draw out the extent of genuine interest of the participants. In one case a focus group was asked, "OK. If the client makes it in the color you want, takes out the feature you don't like, prices it as the level you indicated, who here would buy this?" To press the point even further, sometimes a mock offer is added: "What if I could sell it to you right now for half that price?" Even more dramatic bargains are offered if necessary. Nothing is actually sold. They just want to separate the talkers from the buyers.

The screening step determined which participants were really prospects for such an item. They want to know which of them, having been exposed to the message, would now consider becoming a customer. Those opinions and reactions are reviewed separately and compared with the balance of the group to isolate the differences. They argue that without this step results are skewed by those who do not and never will have the intention of purchasing your product or service. (For example, the "buyers" group generally preferred creative executions with benefits, read more copy, and liked longer letters and brochures. With advertisements, they also preferred long copy treatments.)

The Re-direct.   Up to this point, the moderator has been in complete charge, pursuing a line of questioning previously worked out with the client. Then thirty minutes or so from the end, the moderator makes an excuse to leave the room, invites the group to have some refreshments, and proceeds to the room where the clients have been watching. In hurried conference, the moderator and the clients exchange ideas on how the next segment should be handled.

Clients may ask that a particular person's viewpoints be explored further, that a point be stressed, or that a major change be introduced: "Stress the guarantee and see if that changes anyone's mind"; "Tell them who is behind this new product and see if it adds credibility"; "Would they join this club if they didn't have to pay anything up front?"

The moderator rejoins the group and finishes the session using the requested approaches. The client, agency, and research people discuss their observations immediately after each session. Often they revise the discussion guide before the next session. Sometimes new layouts or package designs are created between one session and the next in response to comments.

The Write-Up.   When everyone is back home, the researcher's work begins anew with a comprehensive written summary of the results of the various focus panels or interviews. Correlations are made with the backgrounds of the focus panel members, and patterns and differences are observed from one group to the next. These written reports are extremely valuable and usually are circulated to all interested parties.

Individual Interviews

Sometimes group interviewing may be impractical. Perhaps it is impossible to identify enough prospects in a given geographical area to form a group. At other times the subject investigated may be too technical, too diverse in its applications to different individuals, or too personal to discuss in group sessions.

In these situations, the most common approach is the in-depth individual interview, based on the same kind of comprehensive discussion guide as that just outlined for focus groups. And as with focus panels, a critical element is the determination of whom to interview. Another is the training and skill of the interviewer.

Individual interviews can take several forms, ranging from a simple run-through of a questionnaire to open-ended discussions. These discussions can be highly complex. Some companies interview doctors on medical subjects or engineers in their areas of interest and pay them for their time. In some cases, interviewers go door-to-door or stop people on street corners or in shopping centers.

Individual interviewing can cover all the areas and all the steps used in focus panels. Its weakness is that it does not provide the cross-stimulation that occurs when respondents spark each others' reactions. As a result, it may be harder to get to respondents' real feelings.

One advantage of the personal interview is that the interviewer can probe into personal issues—emotional reactions, selfish desires, sexual associations—which some respondents might hesitate to discuss in front of a group. Individual interviews also lend themselves to physiological and psychological methods that would not be practical in groups. Some of these are discussed later in this chapter.

QUANTITATIVE METHODS

Quantitative research, as the name implies, endeavors to measure the various components of the marketing equation.

For general advertisers, such measurements often are the only index other than sales figures of the effectiveness of an advertising investment. For direct marketers, the needs for quantitative research are more limited, as new directions or concepts often can be tested more economically through exploratory split-run advertising and mailing than through research. However, there are some notable exceptions.

One company uses telephone interviewing of people on new mailing lists to gauge the probability that the list will succeed. Another uses Simmons data on magazine readers to determine the best combination of print media for specialized products and services. Some agencies also use audience composition data to buy broadcast time, as discussed more fully in Chapter 15.

For a quantitative study to be meaningful, it must be statistically reliable. The sample size must be large enough to be meaningful within the guidelines of statistical validity. Such studies can be conducted by telephone, which provides speed and the ability to conduct a truly national sample. Or they can be made in person at home, at the office, or in any public place. The common denominator of such studies is that they always end up with numerical rankings rather than simply lists of observations and conclusions.

In some research efforts, quantitative studies are used to set priorities among observations produced in earlier qualitative studies. For instance, one method invites consumers to complain about a product or category rather than simply state their preferences. A list of perceived problems arises from the qualitative step—which are then included in quantitative research.

The resulting study lets business people know how often a problem occurs with products or services (either their own or other similar ones) and how important the problem is to the consumer. But the best results also show a problem's pre-emptibility—the likelihood that an advertiser can position the product as the only answer to the problem.

In-Person Interviews

As with all research, the first question to consider is with whom do you want to talk. The second is where. At home? At the office? At a factory gate? A supermarket? At an elegant shopping area? To some extent the choice of place will determine your success at finding the mix of respondents needed for the particular survey.

Door-to-door interviews can give you a mix in a specific geographic area, but the diversity may not be wide enough. Such interviews are also time-consuming, and many people do not like to open their doors to strangers, particularly in urban areas.

Fixed-site interviews, sometimes called "intercepts," provide a good mix of people with some common denominator. If they are conducted at a shopping center, you know you are talking with someone who shops at a center with a particular image—fashion, bargain, etc. If you are in front of an office building or a factory, a different set of demographic probabilities comes into play.

You are also able to talk with people at the time when a certain type of purchase or activity is on their minds. For example, an amusement park is a good place to talk about attitudes toward recreational activities, and a bank is a good place to discuss financial questions.

Telephone Interviews

Some packaged-goods organizations have established the correlation between telephone responses, response rates, and actual marketplace experience so finely that they can make decisions about major direct mail programs from a few hundred phone calls. While I am still uncomfortable with this approach, I am impressed by its potential.

It is now relatively simple to make several hundred phone calls from one central location to selected prospects throughout the country. Lists of customers, names from mailing lists, or respondent information from a mailing or advertisement can be used. The calls can be made quickly and important information can be compiled in less than 24 hours by using a telephone survey.

One purpose of telephone interviews is to measure the probability of converting respondents to paying customers. You can ask people who have replied to different offers or different media sources, "Now that you've seen the free sample, do you intend to continue?" A relative index like this would take months to determine by any other method.

Another purpose of telephone interviews is to obtain information about a sample advertisement mailed to a specific list. The mailing can be sent "cold" and followed up with a telephone call asking whether the recipient recalls receiving it and what his or her impressions are. Or it can be sent in a sealed envelope with a written request that it not be opened until the call is received.

Though telephone surveys have limitations in the areas of cost and depth capabilities, no other method can give you answers so quickly.

Mailed Questionnaires

To many, the word *research* brings to mind *questionnaire*. Yet mailed surveys are one of the least reliable research methods. There are three dangers in such surveys.

One, they *seem* simple to prepare, and therefore too many advertisers fail to retain professional researchers to handle them, resulting in unreliable research.

Two, they are often too difficult or time-consuming to answer, resulting in skewed responses. Typically there will be disproportionate ratio of responses from people with nothing better to do—people who may not be typical prospects.

Three, the most likely respondents are not typical of the whole group or the group you'd like to direct the questions to. For example, if you are promoting web pages and ask the question, "Is your company using web marketing, and how?" those who are *not* have less interest in answering and won't send the questionnaire back, skewing the results. On the other hand, if you ask "Are you satisfied with your new car?" those with a gripe will be sure to reply.

The solution to the first problem is obvious—work with a professional. The second problem is more difficult to solve. I recommend validating that the people who sent back the questionnaire are typical of the whole prospect list, not just people with lots of time on their hands or venting their need to brag or complain. This can be done by following up a mail questionnaire with a telephone survey to non-respondents that attempts to determine on a spot basis whether non-respondents are substantially similar to respondents. Once this has been established, mail questionnaires can be used freely.

The third question is almost unsolvable, except that survey users should always identify their results as percentages of those responding. And those reading such results should be wary of the conclusions.

Mailed questionnaires are unlike in-person interviews. You cannot control how an individual receives the questions. For example, if you ask about unaided recall in one question, there is nothing to stop the reader from scanning a list later in the questionnaire. Also, you don't know whether the questionnaire has been filled out by the prospect or by the prospect's spouse, secretary, or janitor.

If you do use questionnaires, here are five suggestions to help make them more effective:

1. *Make it easy.* The ease of filling out the form is a critical factor. Except for unaided recall questions where you should ask for a one-word reply, everything else should be answerable by making a simple check mark or circling a number. Don't ask for complicated rankings. Put touchy queries such as those about age into groups rather than asking for specific data.

2. *Make it interesting.* Begin with the "meat" of the survey, and use any illustrations, trademarks, headlines, or product packages in the earlier questions. Ask the dry (and sometimes too personal) questions about age, education, and so on at the very end. Also, include some questions that the respondent will enjoy reading or answering even if they are not very important to you.

3. *Make it personal.* Wherever possible, include a letter addressed to the individual, make it clear that only a small number of people are being sent this form, and that every answer represents tens of thousands of consumers.

4. *Make it important.* Explain, if it is true, that a major corporation is postponing a multimillion-dollar new-product launch until the person's opinions have been received, or that it is the practice of the company to investigate and act on this type of information in the name of good consumerism. The questionnaire also should look important. This is not the place to skimp on paper quality or typesetting.

5. *Make it profitable.* Most researchers use some type of premium: a small gift either promised in return for the questionnaire or enclosed with the quiz. The future gift is difficult because it requires disclosure of the name and address of the respondent. I prefer a small cash gift—perhaps a $2 bill, which is an interesting oddity in itself, or a check for $5 or $10. When sending questionnaires to business prospects, you can suggest that they may want to donate the gift to their favorite charity if there is a policy prohibiting the acceptance of such incentives.

One company uses questionnaires to pretest new products even before they have been fully developed. Descriptions—not promotional copy—of half-a-dozen product concepts are given in three or four paragraphs each. Customers are asked to register their reactions this way:

☐ Would order

☐ Might order

☐ Some interest

☐ No interest

The questionnaires are sent to people on the company's own mailing list. Once the responses have been ranked, the company knows which product concept is the most interesting to their customers and which is the least.

Mathematical Analysis

Various segmentation methods are available to compare geographic areas. Based on the idea that "birds of a feather flock together," they surmise group dynamics from the common denominators of postal zones, census tracts, and various sub-segments of each. Today, with the evolution of database marketing, similar information and applications can be based on individual households to a degree never before possible.

Over 100 million individual households in the U.S. have provided some kind of lifestyle and product-usage information. Direct marketers can look at specific ages and marital status for millions more, as well as all the census and other information compiled by residence location.

While no one supplier owns all of the data, an extensive system of cross-licensing and data sharing has evolved so that virtually any existing data—from a half-dozen sources—can be overlaid onto your own list or onto an especially relevant outside list. Some of the suppliers who specialize in this are First Data, InfoSource/Donnelley Marketing, Database America, DirecTech, MBS/Multimode, Axciom/Direct Media, Polk and Experian. These companies seem to be merging and renaming themselves daily, so don't be surprised if the names change. Your direct-mail list-broker can help you to determine which of these companies can best help you to meet your needs.

Your buyers can be pinpointed by first enhancing your list with this data and then preparing a "penetration index"—a ranking of which data most frequently corresponds with your best customers. Sometimes called a *regression analysis*, this method matches characteristics and then uses one of several mathematical formulae to develop a profile of the list segments. This can be further analyzed in terms of market share, profitability, potential, and other goals. Once this data is available, you can select media and lists with the highest indexes.

RESEARCH ON NONVERBAL COMMUNICATION

Perhaps the most exciting frontier of research and its applications to direct marketing is nonverbal communication. It is only fitting that new developments in the art of communicating visually—without words—should be accompanied by new research methods.

The applications of psychology to all forms of advertising have led to some powerful breakthroughs that are only beginning to be applied to direct marketing. Foremost is the recognition that people cannot—or will not—always express themselves in words. Many people are not capable of expressing their feelings verbally. In addition, some feelings cause guilt or embarrassment, such as "I'm sick and tired of reading to my child every night," or "I'm not sure I'm smart enough to invest in stocks," or "I like this car because it makes me feel sexy."

Such feelings can be the key to new advertising strategies, but they are difficult to ferret out in conventional interviewing. For this reason a great many methods have been developed that enable advertisers to identify reactions which may be too difficult or personal for prospects to express verbally.

Physiological Methods

Measurement of involuntary reactions to stimuli can be done by several methods in common use today. The sight of an advertisement, a commercial, an illustration, or even a simple benefit statement are a few examples of researched stimuli.

Brain Wave Measurement. An electroencephalograph records spontaneous electrical activity in the brain when the subject is shown different items. The results show attention and arousal in different ways and to different degrees—responses that indicate whether the person tested found the stimuli favorable or unfavorable.

Eye-Movement Tracking. An optical device records exactly what the eye is looking at, how long the focus is maintained, and the sequence in which the message is perceived. This method presumes that greater attention to an element of an ad or mailing piece denotes greater interest.

Galvanic Skin Response. This method utilizes a psychogalvanometer which, when in contact with the subject's fingertips, records the rate of sweating every 2½ seconds. More sweating indicates the degree of arousal, which indicate the frequency and intensity of the subject's feelings about the subject matter. I have seen demonstrations of this method that later correlated very closely to split-run test results, closely enough to eliminate sure losers. The theory here is that arousal may indicate good or bad feelings, but no arousal is always a sign that the ad won't work.

Pictorial Methods

In general or direct marketing it is essential to measure the perceptions that people have of a company, a category, a product, and of themselves. Self-imagery has been shown to be a factor in buying decisions, and any information about the prospect's self-image will help in planning the campaign.

Customers have clear impressions of who shops at a particular store, who wears a certain kind of fashion, and who travels in a certain kind of transportation vehicle. If they think your product is not for "people-like-me," all the logical convincing in the world will not get them to send in the coupon or make a purchase. In this case you must change their impression of the product.

One approach is to inquire what kind of automobile (or bird or animal) a product connotes and then compare it with one that the prospect identifies with personally. If you're in the investment business, symbols of strength and wisdom are desirable. If you're selling an upscale product you don't want downscale images, and vice versa. I have seen a bank associated with foreign cars (a negative association in this case, as the bank was considered an outsider in the community). I have seen another bank associated with winos and bums. While shocking at first, these images indicate the presence of a problem that is solvable, and that would not have been solved if the problem had not been identified.

Photo-images are an incredibly precise measurement. One agency uses a proprietary method called Photosort. In this method, photographs of people are shown to individual prospects who are asked to sort them into groups. Each group represents a different brand, or a different way of cleaning a house, or a different website. The photographs represent previously identified personality and character attributes, and are rated according to the prospect's personal preferences. The result is a detailed score of the personality traits most associated with the product or service.

No matter which technique one uses, the more sophisticated and psychological the research method, the more important it is to have professionals administer the program and interpret the results.

New Approaches

Some research approaches are particularly applicable to direct marketing's selectivity and versioning capabilities, such as the ones advocated in *The*

Marketing Revolution by Kevin Clancy and Robert Shulman. The authors point out that all customers are not alike, and averages of likes and dislikes are not as valuable as understanding the mindset of the people who would respond to product advantages or creative positioning. What counts is not what most people think, but what the thoughts are of those people who are likely to buy the product or service.

Research can also point out that your present customer base is not necessarily the one most profitable to market to. Often it is more productive to open up a whole new segment than to squeeze the last few buyers from an overworked demographic group. Most direct marketers, accustomed to knowing *what* works best and *what* their best markets are, through testing, have no idea of the value of research. It can open new insights on what profitable markets and segments they are *not* reaching. Research can be an exciting source of ideas, inspiration, and understanding—and the only way to answer the question "WHY?"

5

TESTING

The measurability of direct marketing is such an integral part of this business that the word *testing* is commonly used. Direct marketers talk of testing media, testing copy, and testing an offer. We run test campaigns, dry tests, split-run tests, element tests, and concept tests.

In its simplest form the word can be used as a synonym for *try*, as in running an advertisement in a publication or using a mailing list for the first time and seeing if the results fulfill our expectations. In its most complex form, two- and three-dimensional grid tests can be constructed to simultaneously read media, offer, and copy variables on a new business proposition.

If you mail to an entire mailing list the first time you try it, you aren't testing, you're gambling. If you put your entire budget in the newest medium—such as infomercials in the recent past and the Internet currently—and ignore all the established media which are equally interactive, you are putting all your chips into only one of the casino's games.

The defining characteristic of "testing" in direct mail is the minimization of downside risk. Because direct mail is believed to be subject to the rules of statistical predictability, you should be able to mail as few as 3000 or 5000 pieces and determine a range of response rates—the number of customers who inquire or actually purchase your service or product—that might be expected from the entire list.

Most books on direct marketing, including every edition of this book, have statistical validity tables to help determine the answer to this question. These tables are all based on formulas derived from game theory, the laws of chance, algebraic interpretations of sampling practice, and established formulas of statistical probability. Unfortunately most of them have been difficult to put to practical use and have required many pages of explanation.

While the principles of testing are unchanged, I have tried to make the application as easy as possible. Lloyd Kieran, a respected direct marketing consultant in Laguna Niguel, California, prepared an easy-to-use set of probability tables exclusively for this book. Most tables in other books list response rates and tell you how many samples you should mail. I instead chose these to show what variations you can expect at typical sampling and test-extension quantities, and the projected response rates.

These tables first appeared in the second edition of this book. While here the tables calculate up to a 12 percent response rate, the tables in another of my books, *Database Marketing* (McGraw-Hill), range as high as 30 percent, reflecting experience in this expanding application of database marketing.

PROBABILITY TABLES

One of the great advantages of the direct mail-medium is its predictability. If a direct marketer has information about past direct-mail efforts, then it is possible for him or her to accurately forecast the results of a rollout. However, some simple rules must be followed.

When projecting the results of a planned mailing, one must keep in mind the basic rule of comparing "apples to apples." For example, it is essential to roll out a new mailing with the same package as used in the test. If you make any substantial change, the predicted results will no longer be as accurate.

The laws of statistical probability will apply only if variables are minimized and measured like to like. There are some variables that cannot be controlled, however. Time is one example. Even though you mail exactly the same package a second time to exactly the same lists, you cannot overcome the time differential. You can minimize the variable—by mailing at the same time of year, for example—but it is impossible to change the fact that the package was mailed in two different years. There is always some difference, however small. If the economy or competitive conditions have changed dramatically from one year to the next, the time factor will mostly likely make a significant difference.

Probability Table Description

The probability tables in Tables 5-1, 5-2 and 5-3 are based on a standard statistical formula for predicting a future outcome based on sample results. In all, there are three tables: one for a 95 percent confidence level, a 99 percent confidence level and a 90 percent confidence level. I generally use the 95 percent table. Each table shows the following:

- Sample sizes, ranging from 1000 to 100,000 pieces, expressed in thousands

- Response rates, expressed as percentages, ranging from 0.5 percent to 12 percent, in 0.5 percent increments
- Percent variation—margin of error expressed as a percentage of the response rate
- Low projection—the test response rate less the margin of error
- High projection—the response rate plus the margin of error

How Probability Tables Work

The easiest way to understand the tables is by example. Let's assume you mailed 5000 pieces and achieved a 2 percent response rate. You can now predict a future response rate if you replicate the test *exactly*. Now refer to Table 5-1, which has a 95 percent confidence level. In the column for the 2 percent response rate on the line for a 5000 sample, you will see a percentage variation of 19.4 percent in the "% Var." column. That means if you replicate the test exactly, you can expect to achieve a 2 percent response rate, plus or minus 19.4 percent, 95 times out of 100 replications. (There is the statistical probability that 5 times out of 100 replications you will *not* achieve that response rate, plus or minus 19.4 percent. However, 95 times out of 100 are pretty good odds.)

Then, looking in the "Low" column, you will see 1.61 percent. That projection is the low end of the range, or 2 percent less 19.4 percent. Looking in the "High" column, you will see 2.39 percent, which represents 2 percent plus 19.4 percent, the high end of the range. In other words, if your test mailing was 5000 pieces and it achieved a 2 percent response, you can expect to achieve a rollout response as low as 1.61 percent and as high as 2.39 percent, or somewhere in between. Your confidence (or odds) of attaining that result is 95 times out of 100.

Let's assume that a 95 percent confidence level isn't good enough. Refer to Table 5-2, which has a 99 percent confidence level, and you will see that the margin of error has changed to 22.1 percent. The response rate now can be projected in a range from 1.56 percent to 2.44 percent, 99 times out of 100, if the test is replicated exactly. While the differences in the two response rate ranges may seem small at first glance, it is important to note the difference between the margins of error for a 95 percent confidence level and a 99 percent confidence level. Note that the former is 19.4 percent, the latter 22.1 percent. This differential can sometimes be significant.

Let's complete our example now with a look at the 90 percent confidence level, using the same example of a 5000 piece mailing and a 2 percent response rate with Table 5-3. In this case the margin of error is 16.3 percent, and the range of the response rate will fall between 1.67 and 2.33 percent. While the projected response rate range is tighter, the confidence is not as great, for that response rate range can be expected only 90 times out of 100—not quite as good as a 95 percent confidence level, and certainly not as good as a 99 percent confidence level.

When you examine the tables in detail you will see a pattern emerge that helps to clarify the concepts of margin of error and confidence in the pro-

TABLE 5-1
DIRECT MAIL PROJECTION TABLE

95% Confidence Level—Standard Deviation: 1.960 (Page 1)

ANTICIPATED PERCENT RESPONSE

Sample Size (000)	.5% ±%	Variance Low	High	1.0% ±%	Variance Low	High	1.5% ±%	Variance Low	High	2.0% ±%	Variance Low	High	2.5% ±%	Variance Low	High	3.0% ±%	Variance Low	High
1.0	87.4%	.06%	.94%	61.7%	.38%	1.62%	50.2%	.75%	2.25%	43.4%	1.13%	2.87%	38.7%	1.53%	3.47%	35.2%	1.94%	4.06%
2.5	55.3%	.22%	.78%	39.0%	.61%	1.39%	31.8%	1.02%	1.98%	27.4%	1.45%	2.55%	24.5%	1.89%	3.11%	22.3%	2.33%	3.67%
5.0	39.1%	.30%	.70%	27.6%	.72%	1.28%	22.5%	1.16%	1.84%	19.4%	1.61%	2.39%	17.3%	2.07%	2.93%	15.8%	2.53%	3.47%
7.5	31.9%	.34%	.66%	22.5%	.77%	1.23%	18.3%	1.22%	1.78%	15.8%	1.68%	2.32%	14.1%	2.15%	2.85%	12.9%	2.61%	3.39%
10.0	27.6%	.36%	.64%	19.5%	.80%	1.20%	15.9%	1.26%	1.74%	13.7%	1.73%	2.27%	12.2%	2.19%	2.81%	11.1%	2.67%	3.33%
12.5	24.7%	.38%	.62%	17.4%	.83%	1.17%	14.2%	1.29%	1.71%	12.3%	1.75%	2.25%	10.9%	2.23%	2.77%	10.0%	2.70%	3.30%
15.0	22.6%	.39%	.61%	15.9%	.84%	1.16%	13.0%	1.31%	1.69%	11.2%	1.78%	2.22%	10.0%	2.25%	2.75%	9.1%	2.73%	3.27%
17.5	20.9%	.40%	.60%	14.7%	.85%	1.15%	12.0%	1.32%	1.68%	10.4%	1.79%	2.21%	9.3%	2.27%	2.73%	8.4%	2.75%	3.25%
20.0	19.6%	.40%	.60%	13.8%	.86%	1.14%	11.2%	1.33%	1.67%	9.7%	1.81%	2.19%	8.7%	2.28%	2.72%	7.9%	2.76%	3.24%
25.0	17.5%	.41%	.59%	12.3%	.88%	1.12%	10.0%	1.35%	1.65%	8.7%	1.83%	2.17%	7.7%	2.31%	2.69%	7.0%	2.79%	3.21%
30.0	16.0%	.42%	.58%	11.3%	.89%	1.11%	9.2%	1.36%	1.64%	7.9%	1.84%	2.16%	7.1%	2.32%	2.68%	6.4%	2.81%	3.19%
35.0	14.8%	.43%	.57%	10.4%	.90%	1.10%	8.5%	1.37%	1.63%	7.3%	1.85%	2.15%	6.5%	2.34%	2.66%	6.0%	2.82%	3.18%
40.0	13.8%	.43%	.57%	9.8%	.90%	1.10%	7.9%	1.38%	1.62%	6.9%	1.86%	2.14%	6.1%	2.35%	2.65%	5.6%	2.83%	3.17%
45.0	13.0%	.43%	.57%	9.2%	.91%	1.09%	7.5%	1.39%	1.61%	6.5%	1.87%	2.13%	5.8%	2.36%	2.64%	5.3%	2.84%	3.16%
50.0	12.4%	.44%	.56%	8.7%	.91%	1.09%	7.1%	1.39%	1.61%	6.1%	1.88%	2.12%	5.5%	2.36%	2.64%	5.0%	2.85%	3.15%
60.0	11.3%	.44%	.56%	8.0%	.92%	1.08%	6.5%	1.40%	1.60%	5.6%	1.89%	2.11%	5.0%	2.38%	2.62%	4.5%	2.86%	3.14%
70.0	10.5%	.45%	.55%	7.4%	.93%	1.07%	6.0%	1.41%	1.59%	5.2%	1.90%	2.10%	4.6%	2.38%	2.62%	4.2%	2.87%	3.13%
80.0	9.8%	.45%	.55%	6.9%	.93%	1.07%	5.6%	1.42%	1.58%	4.9%	1.90%	2.10%	4.3%	2.39%	2.61%	3.9%	2.88%	3.12%
90.0	9.2%	.45%	.55%	6.5%	.93%	1.07%	5.3%	1.42%	1.58%	4.6%	1.91%	2.09%	4.1%	2.40%	2.60%	3.7%	2.89%	3.11%
100.0	8.7%	.46%	.54%	6.2%	.94%	1.06%	5.0%	1.42%	1.58%	4.3%	1.91%	2.09%	3.9%	2.40%	2.60%	3.5%	2.89%	3.11%

TABLE 5-1
DIRECT MAIL PROJECTION TABLE (Continued)

95% Confidence Level—Standard Deviation: 1.960 (Page 2)

Sample Size (000)	3.5% ±%	Variance Low	Variance High	4.0% ±%	Variance Low	Variance High	4.5% ±%	Variance Low	Variance High	5.0% ±%	Variance Low	Variance High	5.5% ±%	Variance Low	Variance High	6.0% ±%	Variance Low	Variance High
1.0	32.5%	2.36%	4.64%	30.4%	2.79%	5.21%	28.6%	3.22%	5.78%	27.0%	3.65%	6.35%	25.7%	4.09%	6.91%	24.5%	4.53%	7.47%
2.5	20.6%	2.78%	4.22%	19.2%	3.23%	4.77%	18.1%	3.69%	5.31%	17.1%	4.15%	5.85%	16.2%	4.61%	6.39%	15.5%	5.07%	6.93%
5.0	14.6%	2.99%	4.01%	13.6%	3.46%	4.54%	12.8%	3.93%	5.07%	12.1%	4.40%	5.60%	11.5%	4.87%	6.13%	11.0%	5.34%	6.66%
7.5	11.9%	3.08%	3.92%	11.1%	3.56%	4.44%	10.4%	4.03%	4.97%	9.9%	4.51%	5.49%	9.4%	4.98%	6.02%	9.0%	5.46%	6.54%
10.0	10.3%	3.14%	3.86%	9.6%	3.62%	4.38%	9.0%	4.09%	4.91%	8.5%	4.57%	5.43%	8.1%	5.05%	5.95%	7.8%	5.53%	6.47%
12.5	9.2%	3.18%	3.82%	8.6%	3.66%	4.34%	8.1%	4.14%	4.86%	7.6%	4.62%	5.38%	7.3%	5.10%	5.90%	6.9%	5.58%	6.42%
15.0	8.4%	3.21%	3.79%	7.8%	3.69%	4.31%	7.4%	4.17%	4.83%	7.0%	4.65%	5.35%	6.6%	5.14%	5.86%	6.3%	5.62%	6.38%
17.5	7.8%	3.23%	3.77%	7.3%	3.71%	4.29%	6.8%	4.19%	4.81%	6.5%	4.68%	5.32%	6.1%	5.16%	5.84%	5.9%	5.65%	6.35%
20.0	7.3%	3.25%	3.75%	6.8%	3.73%	4.27%	6.4%	4.21%	4.79%	6.0%	4.70%	5.30%	5.7%	5.18%	5.82%	5.5%	5.67%	6.33%
25.0	6.5%	3.27%	3.73%	6.1%	3.76%	4.24%	5.7%	4.24%	4.76%	5.4%	4.73%	5.27%	5.1%	5.22%	5.78%	4.9%	5.71%	6.29%
30.0	5.9%	3.29%	3.71%	5.5%	3.78%	4.22%	5.2%	4.27%	4.73%	4.9%	4.75%	5.25%	4.7%	5.24%	5.76%	4.5%	5.73%	6.27%
35.0	5.5%	3.31%	3.69%	5.1%	3.79%	4.21%	4.8%	4.28%	4.72%	4.6%	4.77%	5.23%	4.3%	5.26%	5.74%	4.1%	5.75%	6.25%
40.0	5.1%	3.32%	3.68%	4.8%	3.81%	4.19%	4.5%	4.30%	4.70%	4.3%	4.79%	5.21%	4.1%	5.28%	5.72%	3.9%	5.77%	6.23%
45.0	4.9%	3.33%	3.67%	4.5%	3.82%	4.18%	4.3%	4.31%	4.69%	4.0%	4.80%	5.20%	3.8%	5.29%	5.71%	3.7%	5.78%	6.22%
50.0	4.6%	3.34%	3.66%	4.3%	3.83%	4.17%	4.0%	4.32%	4.68%	3.8%	4.81%	5.19%	3.6%	5.30%	5.70%	3.5%	5.79%	6.21%
60.0	4.2%	3.35%	3.65%	3.9%	3.84%	4.16%	3.7%	4.33%	4.67%	3.5%	4.83%	5.17%	3.3%	5.32%	5.68%	3.2%	5.81%	6.19%
70.0	3.9%	3.36%	3.64%	3.6%	3.85%	4.15%	3.4%	4.35%	4.65%	3.2%	4.84%	5.16%	3.1%	5.33%	5.67%	2.9%	5.82%	6.18%
80.0	3.6%	3.37%	3.63%	3.4%	3.86%	4.14%	3.2%	4.36%	4.64%	3.0%	4.85%	5.15%	2.9%	5.34%	5.66%	2.7%	5.84%	6.16%
90.0	3.4%	3.38%	3.62%	3.2%	3.87%	4.13%	3.0%	4.36%	4.64%	2.8%	4.86%	5.14%	2.7%	5.35%	5.65%	2.6%	5.84%	6.16%
100.0	3.3%	3.39%	3.61%	3.0%	3.88%	4.12%	2.9%	4.37%	4.63%	2.7%	4.86%	5.14%	2.6%	5.36%	5.64%	2.5%	5.85%	6.15%

TABLE 5-1
DIRECT MAIL PROJECTION TABLE (Continued)

95% Confidence Level—Standard Deviation: 1.960 (Page 3)

	ANTICIPATED PERCENT RESPONSE																	
	6.5%			7.0%			7.5%			8.0%			8.5%			9.0%		
		Variance			Variance			Variance			Variance			Variance			Variance	
Sample Size (000)	±%	Low	High	±%	Low	High	±%	Low	High	±%	Low	High	±%	Low	High	±%	Low	High
1.0	23.5%	4.97%	8.03%	22.6%	5.42%	8.58%	21.8%	5.87%	9.13%	21.0%	6.32%	9.68%	20.3%	6.77%	10.23%	19.7%	7.23%	10.77%
2.5	14.9%	5.53%	7.47%	14.3%	6.00%	8.00%	13.8%	6.47%	8.53%	13.3%	6.94%	9.06%	12.9%	7.41%	9.59%	12.5%	7.88%	10.12%
5.0	10.5%	5.82%	7.18%	10.1%	6.29%	7.71%	9.7%	6.77%	8.23%	9.4%	7.25%	8.75%	9.1%	7.73%	9.27%	8.8%	8.21%	9.79%
7.5	8.6%	5.94%	7.06%	8.2%	6.42%	7.58%	7.9%	6.90%	8.10%	7.7%	7.39%	8.61%	7.4%	7.87%	9.13%	7.2%	8.35%	9.65%
10.0	7.4%	6.02%	6.98%	7.1%	6.50%	7.50%	6.9%	6.98%	8.02%	6.6%	7.47%	8.53%	6.4%	7.95%	9.05%	6.2%	8.44%	9.56%
12.5	6.6%	6.07%	6.93%	6.4%	6.55%	7.45%	6.2%	7.04%	7.96%	5.9%	7.52%	8.48%	5.8%	8.01%	8.99%	5.6%	8.50%	9.50%
15.0	6.1%	6.11%	6.89%	5.8%	6.59%	7.41%	5.6%	7.08%	7.92%	5.4%	7.57%	8.43%	5.3%	8.05%	8.95%	5.1%	8.54%	9.46%
17.5	5.6%	6.13%	6.87%	5.4%	6.62%	7.38%	5.2%	7.11%	7.89%	5.0%	7.60%	8.40%	4.9%	8.09%	8.91%	4.7%	8.58%	9.42%
20.0	5.3%	6.16%	6.84%	5.1%	6.65%	7.35%	4.9%	7.13%	7.87%	4.7%	7.62%	8.38%	4.5%	8.11%	8.89%	4.4%	8.60%	9.40%
25.0	4.7%	6.19%	6.81%	4.5%	6.68%	7.32%	4.4%	7.17%	7.83%	4.2%	7.66%	8.34%	4.1%	8.15%	8.85%	3.9%	8.65%	9.35%
30.0	4.3%	6.22%	6.78%	4.1%	6.71%	7.29%	4.0%	7.20%	7.80%	3.8%	7.69%	8.31%	3.7%	8.18%	8.82%	3.6%	8.68%	9.32%
35.0	4.0%	6.24%	6.76%	3.8%	6.73%	7.27%	3.7%	7.22%	7.78%	3.6%	7.72%	8.28%	3.4%	8.21%	8.79%	3.3%	8.70%	9.30%
40.0	3.7%	6.26%	6.74%	3.6%	6.75%	7.25%	3.4%	7.24%	7.76%	3.3%	7.73%	8.27%	3.2%	8.23%	8.77%	3.1%	8.72%	9.28%
45.0	3.5%	6.27%	6.73%	3.4%	6.76%	7.24%	3.2%	7.26%	7.74%	3.1%	7.75%	8.25%	3.0%	8.24%	8.76%	2.9%	8.74%	9.26%
50.0	3.3%	6.28%	6.72%	3.2%	6.78%	7.22%	3.1%	7.27%	7.73%	3.0%	7.76%	8.24%	2.9%	8.26%	8.74%	2.8%	8.75%	9.25%
60.0	3.0%	6.30%	6.70%	2.9%	6.80%	7.20%	2.8%	7.29%	7.71%	2.7%	7.78%	8.22%	2.6%	8.28%	8.72%	2.5%	8.77%	9.23%
70.0	2.8%	6.32%	6.68%	2.7%	6.81%	7.19%	2.6%	7.30%	7.70%	2.5%	7.80%	8.20%	2.4%	8.29%	8.71%	2.4%	8.79%	9.21%
80.0	2.6%	6.33%	6.67%	2.5%	6.82%	7.18%	2.4%	7.32%	7.68%	2.3%	7.81%	8.19%	2.3%	8.31%	8.69%	2.2%	8.80%	9.20%
90.0	2.5%	6.34%	6.66%	2.4%	6.83%	7.17%	2.3%	7.33%	7.67%	2.2%	7.82%	8.18%	2.1%	8.32%	8.68%	2.1%	8.81%	9.19%
100.0	2.4%	6.35%	6.65%	2.3%	6.84%	7.16%	2.2%	7.34%	7.66%	2.1%	7.83%	8.17%	2.0%	8.33%	8.67%	2.0%	8.82%	9.18%

TABLE 5-1
DIRECT MAIL PROJECTION TABLE (*Continued*)

95% Confidence Level—Standard Deviation: 1.960 (Page 4)

Sample Size (000)	9.5%			10.0%			10.5%			11.0%			11.5%			12.0%		
	±%	Variance Low	High	±%	Variance Low	High	±%	Variance Low	High	±%	Variance Low	High	±%	Variance Low	High	±%	Variance Low	High
1.0	19.1%	7.68%	11.32%	18.6%	8.14%	11.86%	18.1%	8.60%	12.40%	17.6%	9.06%	12.94%	17.2%	9.52%	13.48%	16.8%	9.99%	14.01%
2.5	12.1%	8.35%	10.65%	11.8%	8.82%	11.18%	11.4%	9.30%	11.70%	11.2%	9.77%	12.23%	10.9%	10.25%	12.75%	10.6%	10.73%	13.27%
5.0	8.6%	8.69%	10.31%	8.3%	9.17%	10.83%	8.1%	9.65%	11.35%	7.9%	10.13%	11.87%	7.7%	10.62%	12.38%	7.5%	11.10%	12.90%
7.5	7.0%	8.84%	10.16%	6.8%	9.32%	10.68%	6.6%	9.81%	11.19%	6.4%	10.29%	11.71%	6.3%	10.78%	12.22%	6.1%	11.26%	12.74%
10.0	6.0%	8.93%	10.07%	5.9%	9.41%	10.59%	5.7%	9.90%	11.10%	5.6%	10.39%	11.61%	5.4%	10.87%	12.13%	5.3%	11.36%	12.64%
12.5	5.4%	8.99%	10.01%	5.3%	9.47%	10.53%	5.1%	9.96%	11.04%	5.0%	10.45%	11.55%	4.9%	10.94%	12.06%	4.7%	11.43%	12.57%
15.0	4.9%	9.03%	9.97%	4.8%	9.52%	10.48%	4.7%	10.01%	10.99%	4.6%	10.50%	11.50%	4.4%	10.99%	12.01%	4.3%	11.48%	12.52%
17.5	4.6%	9.07%	9.93%	4.4%	9.56%	10.44%	4.3%	10.05%	10.95%	4.2%	10.54%	11.46%	4.1%	11.03%	11.97%	4.0%	11.52%	12.48%
20.0	4.3%	9.09%	9.91%	4.2%	9.58%	10.42%	4.0%	10.08%	10.92%	3.9%	10.57%	11.43%	3.8%	11.06%	11.94%	3.8%	11.55%	12.45%
25.0	3.8%	9.14%	9.86%	3.7%	9.63%	10.37%	3.6%	10.12%	10.88%	3.5%	10.61%	11.39%	3.4%	11.10%	11.90%	3.4%	11.60%	12.40%
30.0	3.5%	9.17%	9.83%	3.4%	9.66%	10.34%	3.3%	10.15%	10.85%	3.2%	10.65%	11.35%	3.1%	11.14%	11.86%	3.1%	11.63%	12.37%
35.0	3.2%	9.19%	9.81%	3.1%	9.69%	10.31%	3.1%	10.18%	10.82%	3.0%	10.67%	11.33%	2.9%	11.17%	11.83%	2.8%	11.66%	12.34%
40.0	3.0%	9.21%	9.79%	2.9%	9.71%	10.29%	2.9%	10.20%	10.80%	2.8%	10.69%	11.31%	2.7%	11.19%	11.81%	2.7%	11.68%	12.32%
45.0	2.9%	9.23%	9.77%	2.8%	9.72%	10.28%	2.7%	10.22%	10.78%	2.6%	10.71%	11.29%	2.6%	11.21%	11.79%	2.5%	11.70%	12.30%
50.0	2.7%	9.24%	9.76%	2.6%	9.74%	10.26%	2.6%	10.23%	10.77%	2.5%	10.73%	11.27%	2.4%	11.22%	11.78%	2.4%	11.72%	12.28%
60.0	2.5%	9.27%	9.73%	2.4%	9.76%	10.24%	2.3%	10.25%	10.75%	2.3%	10.75%	11.25%	2.2%	11.24%	11.76%	2.2%	11.74%	12.26%
70.0	2.3%	9.28%	9.72%	2.2%	9.78%	10.22%	2.2%	10.27%	10.73%	2.1%	10.77%	11.23%	2.1%	11.26%	11.74%	2.0%	11.76%	12.24%
80.0	2.1%	9.30%	9.70%	2.1%	9.79%	10.21%	2.0%	10.29%	10.71%	2.0%	10.78%	11.22%	1.9%	11.28%	11.72%	1.9%	11.77%	12.23%
90.0	2.0%	9.31%	9.69%	2.0%	9.80%	10.20%	1.9%	10.30%	10.70%	1.9%	10.80%	11.20%	1.8%	11.29%	11.71%	1.8%	11.79%	12.21%
100.0	1.9%	9.32%	9.68%	1.9%	9.81%	10.19%	1.8%	10.31%	10.69%	1.8%	10.81%	11.19%	1.7%	11.30%	11.70%	1.7%	11.80%	12.20%

TABLE 5-2
DIRECT MAIL PROJECTION TABLE

99% Confidence Level—Standard Deviation: 2.236 (Page 1)

ANTICIPATED PERCENT RESPONSE

Sample Size (000)	.5% ±%	Variance Low	High	1.0% ±%	Variance Low	High	1.5% ±%	Variance Low	High	2.0% ±%	Variance Low	High	2.5% ±%	Variance Low	High	3.0% ±%	Variance Low	High
1.0	99.7%	.00%	1.00%	70.4%	.30%	1.70%	57.3%	.64%	2.36%	49.5%	1.01%	2.99%	44.2%	1.40%	3.60%	40.2%	1.79%	4.21%
2.5	63.1%	.18%	.82%	44.5%	.56%	1.44%	36.2%	.96%	2.04%	31.3%	1.37%	2.63%	27.9%	1.80%	3.20%	25.4%	2.24%	3.76%
5.0	44.6%	.28%	.72%	31.5%	.69%	1.31%	25.6%	1.12%	1.88%	22.1%	1.56%	2.44%	19.7%	2.01%	2.99%	18.0%	2.46%	3.54%
7.5	36.4%	.32%	.68%	25.7%	.74%	1.26%	20.9%	1.19%	1.81%	18.1%	1.64%	2.36%	16.1%	2.10%	2.90%	14.7%	2.56%	3.44%
10.0	31.5%	.34%	.66%	22.2%	.78%	1.22%	18.1%	1.23%	1.77%	15.7%	1.69%	2.31%	14.0%	2.15%	2.85%	12.7%	2.62%	3.38%
12.5	28.2%	.36%	.64%	19.9%	.80%	1.20%	16.2%	1.26%	1.74%	14.0%	1.72%	2.28%	12.5%	2.19%	2.81%	11.4%	2.66%	3.34%
15.0	25.8%	.37%	.63%	18.2%	.82%	1.18%	14.8%	1.28%	1.72%	12.8%	1.74%	2.26%	11.4%	2.21%	2.79%	10.4%	2.69%	3.31%
17.5	23.8%	.38%	.62%	16.8%	.83%	1.17%	13.7%	1.29%	1.71%	11.8%	1.76%	2.24%	10.6%	2.24%	2.76%	9.6%	2.71%	3.29%
20.0	22.3%	.39%	.61%	15.7%	.84%	1.16%	12.8%	1.31%	1.69%	11.1%	1.78%	2.22%	9.9%	2.25%	2.75%	9.0%	2.73%	3.27%
25.0	19.9%	.40%	.60%	14.1%	.86%	1.14%	11.5%	1.33%	1.67%	9.9%	1.80%	2.20%	8.8%	2.28%	2.72%	8.0%	2.76%	3.24%
30.0	18.2%	.41%	.59%	12.8%	.87%	1.13%	10.5%	1.34%	1.66%	9.0%	1.82%	2.18%	8.1%	2.30%	2.70%	7.3%	2.78%	3.22%
35.0	16.9%	.42%	.58%	11.9%	.88%	1.12%	9.7%	1.35%	1.65%	8.4%	1.83%	2.17%	7.5%	2.31%	2.69%	6.8%	2.80%	3.20%
40.0	15.8%	.42%	.58%	11.1%	.89%	1.11%	9.1%	1.36%	1.64%	7.8%	1.84%	2.16%	7.0%	2.33%	2.67%	6.4%	2.81%	3.19%
45.0	14.9%	.43%	.57%	10.5%	.90%	1.10%	8.5%	1.37%	1.63%	7.4%	1.85%	2.15%	6.6%	2.34%	2.66%	6.0%	2.82%	3.18%
50.0	14.1%	.43%	.57%	9.9%	.90%	1.10%	8.1%	1.38%	1.62%	7.0%	1.86%	2.14%	6.2%	2.34%	2.66%	5.7%	2.83%	3.17%
60.0	12.9%	.44%	.56%	9.1%	.91%	1.09%	7.4%	1.39%	1.61%	6.4%	1.87%	2.13%	5.7%	2.36%	2.64%	5.2%	2.84%	3.16%
70.0	11.9%	.44%	.56%	8.4%	.92%	1.08%	6.8%	1.40%	1.60%	5.9%	1.88%	2.12%	5.3%	2.37%	2.63%	4.8%	2.86%	3.14%
80.0	11.2%	.44%	.56%	7.9%	.92%	1.08%	6.4%	1.40%	1.60%	5.5%	1.89%	2.11%	4.9%	2.38%	2.62%	4.5%	2.87%	3.13%
90.0	10.5%	.45%	.55%	7.4%	.93%	1.07%	6.0%	1.41%	1.59%	5.2%	1.90%	2.10%	4.7%	2.38%	2.62%	4.2%	2.87%	3.13%
100.0	10.0%	.45%	.55%	7.0%	.93%	1.07%	5.7%	1.41%	1.59%	4.9%	1.90%	2.10%	4.4%	2.39%	2.61%	4.0%	2.88%	3.12%

TABLE 5-2
DIRECT MAIL PROJECTION TABLE (Continued)

99% Confidence Level—Standard Deviation: 2.236 (Page 2)

ANTICIPATED PERCENT RESPONSE

Sample Size (000)	3.5% ±%	Variance Low	High	4.0% ±%	Variance Low	High	4.5% ±%	Variance Low	High	5.0% ±%	Variance Low	High	5.5% ±%	Variance Low	High	6.0% ±%	Variance Low	High
1.0	37.1%	2.20%	4.80%	34.6%	2.61%	5.39%	32.6%	3.03%	5.97%	30.8%	3.46%	6.54%	29.3%	3.89%	7.11%	28.0%	4.32%	7.68%
2.5	23.5%	2.68%	4.32%	21.9%	3.12%	4.88%	20.6%	3.57%	5.43%	19.5%	4.03%	5.97%	18.5%	4.48%	6.52%	17.7%	4.94%	7.06%
5.0	16.6%	2.92%	4.08%	15.5%	3.38%	4.62%	14.6%	3.84%	5.16%	13.8%	4.31%	5.69%	13.1%	4.78%	6.22%	12.5%	5.25%	6.75%
7.5	13.6%	3.03%	3.97%	12.6%	3.49%	4.51%	11.9%	3.96%	5.04%	11.3%	4.44%	5.56%	10.7%	4.91%	6.09%	10.2%	5.39%	6.61%
10.0	11.7%	3.09%	3.91%	11.0%	3.56%	4.44%	10.3%	4.04%	4.96%	9.7%	4.51%	5.49%	9.3%	4.99%	6.01%	8.9%	5.47%	6.53%
12.5	10.5%	3.13%	3.87%	9.8%	3.61%	4.39%	9.2%	4.09%	4.91%	8.7%	4.56%	5.44%	8.3%	5.04%	5.96%	7.9%	5.53%	6.47%
15.0	9.6%	3.16%	3.84%	8.9%	3.64%	4.36%	8.4%	4.12%	4.88%	8.0%	4.60%	5.40%	7.6%	5.08%	5.92%	7.2%	5.57%	6.43%
17.5	8.9%	3.19%	3.81%	8.3%	3.67%	4.33%	7.8%	4.15%	4.85%	7.4%	4.63%	5.37%	7.0%	5.11%	5.89%	6.7%	5.60%	6.40%
20.0	8.3%	3.21%	3.79%	7.7%	3.69%	4.31%	7.3%	4.17%	4.83%	6.9%	4.66%	5.34%	6.6%	5.14%	5.86%	6.3%	5.62%	6.38%
25.0	7.4%	3.24%	3.76%	6.9%	3.72%	4.28%	6.5%	4.21%	4.79%	6.2%	4.69%	5.31%	5.9%	5.18%	5.82%	5.6%	5.66%	6.34%
30.0	6.8%	3.26%	3.74%	6.3%	3.75%	4.25%	5.9%	4.23%	4.77%	5.6%	4.72%	5.28%	5.4%	5.21%	5.79%	5.1%	5.69%	6.31%
35.0	6.3%	3.28%	3.72%	5.9%	3.77%	4.23%	5.5%	4.25%	4.75%	5.2%	4.74%	5.26%	5.0%	5.23%	5.77%	4.7%	5.72%	6.28%
40.0	5.9%	3.29%	3.71%	5.5%	3.78%	4.22%	5.2%	4.27%	4.73%	4.9%	4.76%	5.24%	4.6%	5.25%	5.75%	4.4%	5.73%	6.27%
45.0	5.5%	3.31%	3.69%	5.2%	3.79%	4.21%	4.9%	4.28%	4.72%	4.6%	4.77%	5.23%	4.4%	5.26%	5.74%	4.2%	5.75%	6.25%
50.0	5.3%	3.32%	3.68%	4.9%	3.80%	4.20%	4.6%	4.29%	4.71%	4.4%	4.78%	5.22%	4.1%	5.27%	5.73%	4.0%	5.76%	6.24%
60.0	4.8%	3.33%	3.67%	4.5%	3.82%	4.18%	4.2%	4.31%	4.69%	4.0%	4.80%	5.20%	3.8%	5.29%	5.71%	3.6%	5.78%	6.22%
70.0	4.4%	3.34%	3.66%	4.1%	3.83%	4.17%	3.9%	4.32%	4.68%	3.7%	4.82%	5.18%	3.5%	5.31%	5.69%	3.3%	5.80%	6.20%
80.0	4.2%	3.35%	3.65%	3.9%	3.85%	4.15%	3.6%	4.34%	4.66%	3.4%	4.83%	5.17%	3.3%	5.32%	5.68%	3.1%	5.81%	6.19%
90.0	3.9%	3.36%	3.64%	3.7%	3.85%	4.15%	3.4%	4.35%	4.65%	3.2%	4.84%	5.16%	3.1%	5.33%	5.67%	3.0%	5.82%	6.18%
100.0	3.7%	3.37%	3.63%	3.5%	3.86%	4.14%	3.3%	4.35%	4.65%	3.1%	4.85%	5.15%	2.9%	5.34%	5.66%	2.8%	5.83%	6.17%

TABLE 5-2
DIRECT MAIL PROJECTION TABLE (Continued)

99% Confidence Level—Standard Deviation: 2.236 (Page 3)

ANTICIPATED PERCENT RESPONSE

Sample Size (000)	6.5%			7.0%			7.5%			8.0%			8.5%			9.0%		
	±%	Variance Low	High	±%	Variance Low	High	±%	Variance Low	High	±%	Variance Low	High	±%	Variance Low	High	±%	Variance Low	High
1.0	26.8%	4.76%	8.24%	25.8%	5.20%	8.80%	24.8%	5.64%	9.36%	24.0%	6.08%	9.92%	23.2%	6.53%	10.47%	22.5%	6.98%	11.02%
2.5	17.0%	5.40%	7.60%	16.3%	5.86%	8.14%	15.7%	6.32%	8.68%	15.2%	6.79%	9.21%	14.7%	7.25%	9.75%	14.2%	7.72%	10.28%
5.0	12.0%	5.72%	7.28%	11.5%	6.19%	7.81%	11.1%	6.67%	8.33%	10.7%	7.14%	8.86%	10.4%	7.62%	9.38%	10.1%	8.10%	9.90%
7.5	9.8%	5.86%	7.14%	9.4%	6.34%	7.66%	9.1%	6.82%	8.18%	8.8%	7.30%	8.70%	8.5%	7.78%	9.22%	8.2%	8.26%	9.74%
10.0	8.5%	5.95%	7.05%	8.2%	6.43%	7.57%	7.9%	6.91%	8.09%	7.6%	7.39%	8.61%	7.3%	7.88%	9.12%	7.1%	8.36%	9.64%
12.5	7.6%	6.01%	6.99%	7.3%	6.49%	7.51%	7.0%	6.97%	8.03%	6.8%	7.46%	8.54%	6.6%	7.94%	9.06%	6.4%	8.43%	9.57%
15.0	6.9%	6.05%	6.95%	6.7%	6.53%	7.47%	6.4%	7.02%	7.98%	6.2%	7.50%	8.50%	6.0%	7.99%	9.01%	5.8%	8.48%	9.52%
17.5	6.4%	6.08%	6.92%	6.2%	6.57%	7.43%	5.9%	7.05%	7.95%	5.7%	7.54%	8.46%	5.5%	8.03%	8.97%	5.4%	8.52%	9.48%
20.0	6.0%	6.11%	6.89%	5.8%	6.60%	7.40%	5.6%	7.08%	7.92%	5.4%	7.57%	8.43%	5.2%	8.06%	8.94%	5.0%	8.55%	9.45%
25.0	5.4%	6.15%	6.85%	5.2%	6.64%	7.36%	5.0%	7.13%	7.87%	4.8%	7.62%	8.38%	4.6%	8.11%	8.89%	4.5%	8.60%	9.40%
30.0	4.9%	6.18%	6.82%	4.7%	6.67%	7.33%	4.5%	7.16%	7.84%	4.4%	7.65%	8.35%	4.2%	8.14%	8.86%	4.1%	8.63%	9.37%
35.0	4.5%	6.21%	6.79%	4.4%	6.70%	7.30%	4.2%	7.19%	7.81%	4.1%	7.68%	8.32%	3.9%	8.17%	8.83%	3.8%	8.66%	9.34%
40.0	4.2%	6.22%	6.78%	4.1%	6.71%	7.29%	3.9%	7.21%	7.79%	3.8%	7.70%	8.30%	3.7%	8.19%	8.81%	3.6%	8.68%	9.32%
45.0	4.0%	6.24%	6.76%	3.8%	6.73%	7.27%	3.7%	7.22%	7.78%	3.6%	7.71%	8.29%	3.5%	8.21%	8.79%	3.4%	8.70%	9.30%
50.0	3.8%	6.25%	6.75%	3.6%	6.74%	7.26%	3.5%	7.24%	7.76%	3.4%	7.73%	8.27%	3.3%	8.22%	8.78%	3.2%	8.71%	9.29%
60.0	3.5%	6.27%	6.73%	3.3%	6.77%	7.23%	3.2%	7.26%	7.74%	3.1%	7.75%	8.25%	3.0%	8.25%	8.75%	2.9%	8.74%	9.26%
70.0	3.2%	6.29%	6.71%	3.1%	6.78%	7.22%	3.0%	7.28%	7.72%	2.9%	7.77%	8.23%	2.8%	8.26%	8.74%	2.7%	8.76%	9.24%
80.0	3.0%	6.31%	6.69%	2.9%	6.80%	7.20%	2.8%	7.29%	7.71%	2.7%	7.79%	8.21%	2.6%	8.28%	8.72%	2.5%	8.77%	9.23%
90.0	2.8%	6.32%	6.68%	2.7%	6.81%	7.19%	2.6%	7.30%	7.70%	2.5%	7.80%	8.20%	2.4%	8.29%	8.71%	2.4%	8.79%	9.21%
100.0	2.7%	6.33%	6.67%	2.6%	6.82%	7.18%	2.5%	7.31%	7.69%	2.4%	7.81%	8.19%	2.3%	8.30%	8.70%	2.2%	8.80%	9.20%

TABLE 5-2
DIRECT MAIL PROJECTION TABLE (Continued)

99% Confidence Level—Standard Deviation: 2.236 (Page 4)

ANTICIPATED PERCENT RESPONSE

Sample Size (000)	9.5%			10.0%			10.5%			11.0%			11.5%			12.0%		
	±%	Variance Low	High	±%	Variance Low	High	±%	Variance Low	High	±%	Variance Low	High	±%	Variance Low	High	±%	Variance Low	High
1.0	21.8%	7.43%	11.57%	21.2%	7.88%	12.12%	20.6%	8.33%	12.67%	20.1%	8.79%	13.21%	19.6%	9.24%	13.76%	19.1%	9.70%	14.30%
2.5	13.8%	8.19%	10.81%	13.4%	8.66%	11.34%	13.1%	9.13%	11.87%	12.7%	9.60%	12.40%	12.4%	10.07%	12.93%	12.1%	10.55%	13.45%
5.0	9.8%	8.57%	10.43%	9.5%	9.05%	10.95%	9.2%	9.53%	11.47%	9.0%	10.01%	11.99%	8.8%	10.49%	12.51%	8.6%	10.97%	13.03%
7.5	8.0%	8.74%	10.26%	7.7%	9.23%	10.77%	7.5%	9.71%	11.29%	7.3%	10.19%	11.81%	7.2%	10.68%	12.32%	7.0%	11.16%	12.84%
10.0	6.9%	8.84%	10.16%	6.7%	9.33%	10.67%	6.5%	9.81%	11.19%	6.4%	10.30%	11.70%	6.2%	10.79%	12.21%	6.1%	11.27%	12.73%
12.5	6.2%	8.91%	10.09%	6.0%	9.40%	10.60%	5.8%	9.89%	11.11%	5.7%	10.37%	11.63%	5.5%	10.86%	12.14%	5.4%	11.35%	12.65%
15.0	5.6%	8.96%	10.04%	5.5%	9.45%	10.55%	5.3%	9.94%	11.06%	5.2%	10.43%	11.57%	5.1%	10.92%	12.08%	4.9%	11.41%	12.59%
17.5	5.2%	9.00%	10.00%	5.1%	9.49%	10.51%	4.9%	9.98%	11.02%	4.8%	10.47%	11.53%	4.7%	10.96%	12.04%	4.6%	11.45%	12.55%
20.0	4.9%	9.04%	9.96%	4.7%	9.53%	10.47%	4.6%	10.02%	10.98%	4.5%	10.51%	11.49%	4.4%	11.00%	12.00%	4.3%	11.49%	12.51%
25.0	4.4%	9.09%	9.91%	4.2%	9.58%	10.42%	4.1%	10.07%	10.93%	4.0%	10.56%	11.44%	3.9%	11.05%	11.95%	3.8%	11.54%	12.46%
30.0	4.0%	9.12%	9.88%	3.9%	9.61%	10.39%	3.8%	10.10%	10.90%	3.7%	10.60%	11.40%	3.6%	11.09%	11.91%	3.5%	11.58%	12.42%
35.0	3.7%	9.15%	9.85%	3.6%	9.64%	10.36%	3.5%	10.13%	10.87%	3.4%	10.63%	11.37%	3.3%	11.12%	11.88%	3.2%	11.61%	12.39%
40.0	3.5%	9.17%	9.83%	3.4%	9.66%	10.34%	3.3%	10.16%	10.84%	3.2%	10.65%	11.35%	3.1%	11.14%	11.86%	3.0%	11.64%	12.36%
45.0	3.3%	9.19%	9.81%	3.2%	9.68%	10.32%	3.1%	10.18%	10.82%	3.0%	10.67%	11.33%	2.9%	11.16%	11.84%	2.9%	11.66%	12.34%
50.0	3.1%	9.21%	9.79%	3.0%	9.70%	10.30%	2.9%	10.19%	10.81%	2.8%	10.69%	11.31%	2.8%	11.18%	11.82%	2.7%	11.68%	12.32%
60.0	2.8%	9.23%	9.77%	2.7%	9.73%	10.27%	2.7%	10.22%	10.78%	2.6%	10.71%	11.29%	2.5%	11.21%	11.79%	2.5%	11.70%	12.30%
70.0	2.6%	9.25%	9.75%	2.5%	9.75%	10.25%	2.5%	10.24%	10.76%	2.4%	10.74%	11.26%	2.3%	11.23%	11.77%	2.3%	11.73%	12.27%
80.0	2.4%	9.27%	9.73%	2.4%	9.76%	10.24%	2.3%	10.26%	10.74%	2.2%	10.75%	11.25%	2.2%	11.25%	11.75%	2.1%	11.74%	12.26%
90.0	2.3%	9.28%	9.72%	2.2%	9.78%	10.22%	2.2%	10.27%	10.73%	2.1%	10.77%	11.23%	2.1%	11.26%	11.74%	2.0%	11.76%	12.24%
100.0	2.2%	9.29%	9.71%	2.1%	9.79%	10.21%	2.1%	10.28%	10.72%	2.0%	10.78%	11.22%	2.0%	11.27%	11.73%	1.9%	11.77%	12.23%

TABLE 5-3
DIRECT MAIL PROJECTION TABLE

90% Confidence Level—Standard Deviation: 1.645 (Page 1)

ANTICIPATED PERCENT RESPONSE

Sample Size (000)	.5% ±%	Variance Low	High	1.0% ±%	Variance Low	High	1.5% ±%	Variance Low	High	2.0% ±%	Variance Low	High	2.5% ±%	Variance Low	High	3.0% ±%	Variance Low	High
1.0	73.4%	.13%	.87%	51.8%	.48%	1.52%	42.2%	.87%	2.13%	36.4%	1.27%	2.73%	32.5%	1.69%	3.31%	29.6%	2.11%	3.89%
2.5	46.4%	.27%	.73%	32.7%	.67%	1.33%	26.7%	1.10%	1.90%	23.0%	1.54%	2.46%	20.5%	1.99%	3.01%	18.7%	2.44%	3.56%
5.0	32.8%	.34%	.66%	23.1%	.77%	1.23%	18.9%	1.22%	1.78%	16.3%	1.67%	2.33%	14.5%	2.14%	2.86%	13.2%	2.60%	3.40%
7.5	26.8%	.37%	.63%	18.9%	.81%	1.19%	15.4%	1.27%	1.73%	13.3%	1.73%	2.27%	11.9%	2.20%	2.80%	10.8%	2.68%	3.32%
10.0	23.2%	.38%	.62%	16.4%	.84%	1.16%	13.3%	1.30%	1.70%	11.5%	1.77%	2.23%	10.3%	2.24%	2.76%	9.4%	2.72%	3.28%
12.5	20.8%	.40%	.60%	14.6%	.85%	1.15%	11.9%	1.32%	1.68%	10.3%	1.79%	2.21%	9.2%	2.27%	2.73%	8.4%	2.75%	3.25%
15.0	18.9%	.41%	.59%	13.4%	.87%	1.13%	10.9%	1.34%	1.66%	9.4%	1.81%	2.19%	8.4%	2.29%	2.71%	7.6%	2.77%	3.23%
17.5	17.5%	.41%	.59%	12.4%	.88%	1.12%	10.1%	1.35%	1.65%	8.7%	1.83%	2.17%	7.8%	2.31%	2.69%	7.1%	2.79%	3.21%
20.0	16.4%	.42%	.58%	11.6%	.88%	1.12%	9.4%	1.36%	1.64%	8.1%	1.84%	2.16%	7.3%	2.32%	2.68%	6.6%	2.80%	3.20%
25.0	14.7%	.43%	.57%	10.4%	.90%	1.10%	8.4%	1.37%	1.63%	7.3%	1.85%	2.15%	6.5%	2.34%	2.66%	5.9%	2.82%	3.18%
30.0	13.4%	.43%	.57%	9.4%	.91%	1.09%	7.7%	1.38%	1.62%	6.6%	1.87%	2.13%	5.9%	2.35%	2.65%	5.4%	2.84%	3.16%
35.0	12.4%	.44%	.56%	8.7%	.91%	1.09%	7.1%	1.39%	1.61%	6.2%	1.88%	2.12%	5.5%	2.36%	2.64%	5.0%	2.85%	3.15%
40.0	11.6%	.44%	.56%	8.2%	.92%	1.08%	6.7%	1.40%	1.60%	5.8%	1.88%	2.12%	5.1%	2.37%	2.63%	4.7%	2.86%	3.14%
45.0	10.9%	.45%	.55%	7.7%	.92%	1.08%	6.3%	1.41%	1.59%	5.4%	1.89%	2.11%	4.8%	2.38%	2.62%	4.4%	2.87%	3.13%
50.0	10.4%	.45%	.55%	7.3%	.93%	1.07%	6.0%	1.41%	1.59%	5.1%	1.90%	2.10%	4.6%	2.39%	2.61%	4.2%	2.87%	3.13%
60.0	9.5%	.45%	.55%	6.7%	.93%	1.07%	5.4%	1.42%	1.58%	4.7%	1.91%	2.09%	4.2%	2.40%	2.60%	3.8%	2.89%	3.11%
70.0	8.8%	.46%	.54%	6.2%	.94%	1.06%	5.0%	1.42%	1.58%	4.4%	1.91%	2.09%	3.9%	2.40%	2.60%	3.5%	2.89%	3.11%
80.0	8.2%	.46%	.54%	5.8%	.94%	1.06%	4.7%	1.43%	1.57%	4.1%	1.92%	2.08%	3.6%	2.41%	2.59%	3.3%	2.90%	3.10%
90.0	7.7%	.46%	.54%	5.5%	.95%	1.05%	4.4%	1.43%	1.57%	3.8%	1.92%	2.08%	3.4%	2.41%	2.59%	3.1%	2.91%	3.09%
100.0	7.3%	.46%	.54%	5.2%	.95%	1.05%	4.2%	1.44%	1.56%	3.6%	1.93%	2.07%	3.2%	2.42%	2.58%	3.0%	2.91%	3.09%

TABLE 5-3
DIRECT MAIL PROJECTION TABLE (*Continued*)

90% Confidence Level—Standard Deviation: 1.645 (Page 2)

ANTICIPATED PERCENT RESPONSE

Sample Size (000)	3.5% ±%	Variance Low	Variance High	4.0% ±%	Variance Low	Variance High	4.5% ±%	Variance Low	Variance High	5.0% ±%	Variance Low	Variance High	5.5% ±%	Variance Low	Variance High	6.0% ±%	Variance Low	Variance High
1.0	27.3%	2.54%	4.46%	25.5%	2.98%	5.02%	24.0%	3.42%	5.58%	22.7%	3.87%	6.13%	21.6%	4.31%	6.69%	20.6%	4.76%	7.24%
2.5	17.3%	2.90%	4.10%	16.1%	3.36%	4.64%	15.2%	3.82%	5.18%	14.3%	4.28%	5.72%	13.6%	4.75%	6.25%	13.0%	5.22%	6.78%
5.0	12.2%	3.07%	3.93%	11.4%	3.54%	4.46%	10.7%	4.02%	4.98%	10.1%	4.49%	5.51%	9.6%	4.97%	6.03%	9.2%	5.45%	6.55%
7.5	10.0%	3.15%	3.85%	9.3%	3.63%	4.37%	8.8%	4.11%	4.89%	8.3%	4.59%	5.41%	7.9%	5.07%	5.93%	7.5%	5.55%	6.45%
10.0	8.6%	3.20%	3.80%	8.1%	3.68%	4.32%	7.6%	4.16%	4.84%	7.2%	4.64%	5.36%	6.8%	5.12%	5.88%	6.5%	5.61%	6.39%
12.5	7.7%	3.23%	3.77%	7.2%	3.71%	4.29%	6.8%	4.19%	4.81%	6.4%	4.68%	5.32%	6.1%	5.16%	5.84%	5.8%	5.65%	6.35%
15.0	7.1%	3.25%	3.75%	6.6%	3.74%	4.26%	6.2%	4.22%	4.78%	5.9%	4.71%	5.29%	5.6%	5.19%	5.81%	5.3%	5.68%	6.32%
17.5	6.5%	3.27%	3.73%	6.1%	3.76%	4.24%	5.7%	4.24%	4.76%	5.4%	4.73%	5.27%	5.2%	5.22%	5.78%	4.9%	5.70%	6.30%
20.0	6.1%	3.29%	3.71%	5.7%	3.77%	4.23%	5.4%	4.26%	4.74%	5.1%	4.75%	5.25%	4.8%	5.23%	5.77%	4.6%	5.72%	6.28%
25.0	5.5%	3.31%	3.69%	5.1%	3.80%	4.20%	4.8%	4.28%	4.72%	4.5%	4.77%	5.23%	4.3%	5.26%	5.74%	4.1%	5.75%	6.25%
30.0	5.0%	3.33%	3.67%	4.7%	3.81%	4.19%	4.4%	4.30%	4.70%	4.1%	4.79%	5.21%	3.9%	5.28%	5.72%	3.8%	5.77%	6.23%
35.0	4.6%	3.34%	3.66%	4.3%	3.83%	4.17%	4.1%	4.32%	4.68%	3.8%	4.81%	5.19%	3.6%	5.30%	5.70%	3.5%	5.79%	6.21%
40.0	4.3%	3.35%	3.65%	4.0%	3.84%	4.16%	3.8%	4.33%	4.67%	3.6%	4.82%	5.18%	3.4%	5.31%	5.69%	3.3%	5.80%	6.20%
45.0	4.1%	3.36%	3.64%	3.8%	3.85%	4.15%	3.6%	4.34%	4.66%	3.4%	4.83%	5.17%	3.2%	5.32%	5.68%	3.1%	5.82%	6.18%
50.0	3.9%	3.36%	3.64%	3.6%	3.86%	4.14%	3.4%	4.35%	4.65%	3.2%	4.84%	5.16%	3.0%	5.33%	5.67%	2.9%	5.83%	6.17%
60.0	3.5%	3.38%	3.62%	3.3%	3.87%	4.13%	3.1%	4.36%	4.64%	2.9%	4.85%	5.15%	2.8%	5.35%	5.65%	2.7%	5.84%	6.16%
70.0	3.3%	3.39%	3.61%	3.0%	3.88%	4.12%	2.9%	4.37%	4.63%	2.7%	4.86%	5.14%	2.6%	5.36%	5.64%	2.5%	5.85%	6.15%
80.0	3.1%	3.39%	3.61%	2.8%	3.89%	4.11%	2.7%	4.38%	4.62%	2.5%	4.87%	5.13%	2.4%	5.37%	5.63%	2.3%	5.86%	6.14%
90.0	2.9%	3.40%	3.60%	2.7%	3.89%	4.11%	2.5%	4.39%	4.61%	2.4%	4.88%	5.12%	2.3%	5.37%	5.63%	2.2%	5.87%	6.13%
100.0	2.7%	3.40%	3.60%	2.5%	3.90%	4.10%	2.4%	4.39%	4.61%	2.3%	4.89%	5.11%	2.2%	5.38%	5.62%	2.1%	5.88%	6.12%

TABLE 5-3
DIRECT MAIL PROJECTION TABLE (Continued)

90% Confidence Level—Standard Deviation: 1.645 (Page 3)

Sample Size (000)	6.5% ±%	Variance Low	High	7.0% ±%	Variance Low	High	7.5% ±%	Variance Low	High	8.0% ±%	Variance Low	High	8.5% ±%	Variance Low	High	9.0% ±%	Variance Low	High
1.0	19.7%	5.22%	7.78%	19.0%	5.67%	8.33%	18.3%	6.13%	8.87%	17.6%	6.59%	9.41%	17.1%	7.05%	9.95%	16.5%	7.51%	10.49%
2.5	12.5%	5.69%	7.31%	12.0%	6.16%	7.84%	11.6%	6.63%	8.37%	11.2%	7.11%	8.89%	10.8%	7.58%	9.42%	10.5%	8.06%	9.94%
5.0	8.8%	5.93%	7.07%	8.5%	6.41%	7.59%	8.2%	6.89%	8.11%	7.9%	7.37%	8.63%	7.6%	7.85%	9.15%	7.4%	8.33%	9.67%
7.5	7.2%	6.03%	6.97%	6.9%	6.52%	7.48%	6.7%	7.00%	8.00%	6.4%	7.48%	8.52%	6.2%	7.97%	9.03%	6.0%	8.46%	9.54%
10.0	6.2%	6.09%	6.91%	6.0%	6.58%	7.42%	5.8%	7.07%	7.93%	5.6%	7.55%	8.45%	5.4%	8.04%	8.96%	5.2%	8.53%	9.47%
12.5	5.6%	6.14%	6.86%	5.4%	6.62%	7.38%	5.2%	7.11%	7.89%	5.0%	7.60%	8.40%	4.8%	8.09%	8.91%	4.7%	8.58%	9.42%
15.0	5.1%	6.17%	6.83%	4.9%	6.66%	7.34%	4.7%	7.15%	7.85%	4.6%	7.64%	8.36%	4.4%	8.13%	8.87%	4.3%	8.62%	9.38%
17.5	4.7%	6.19%	6.81%	4.5%	6.68%	7.32%	4.4%	7.17%	7.83%	4.2%	7.66%	8.34%	4.1%	8.15%	8.85%	4.0%	8.64%	9.36%
20.0	4.4%	6.21%	6.79%	4.2%	6.70%	7.30%	4.1%	7.19%	7.81%	3.9%	7.68%	8.32%	3.8%	8.18%	8.82%	3.7%	8.67%	9.33%
25.0	3.9%	6.24%	6.76%	3.8%	6.73%	7.27%	3.7%	7.23%	7.77%	3.5%	7.72%	8.28%	3.4%	8.21%	8.79%	3.3%	8.70%	9.30%
30.0	3.6%	6.27%	6.73%	3.5%	6.76%	7.24%	3.3%	7.25%	7.75%	3.2%	7.74%	8.26%	3.1%	8.24%	8.76%	3.0%	8.73%	9.27%
35.0	3.3%	6.28%	6.72%	3.2%	6.78%	7.22%	3.1%	7.27%	7.73%	3.0%	7.76%	8.24%	2.9%	8.25%	8.75%	2.8%	8.75%	9.25%
40.0	3.1%	6.30%	6.70%	3.0%	6.79%	7.21%	2.9%	7.28%	7.72%	2.8%	7.78%	8.22%	2.7%	8.27%	8.73%	2.6%	8.76%	9.24%
45.0	2.9%	6.31%	6.69%	2.8%	6.80%	7.20%	2.7%	7.30%	7.70%	2.6%	7.79%	8.21%	2.5%	8.28%	8.72%	2.5%	8.78%	9.22%
50.0	2.8%	6.32%	6.68%	2.7%	6.81%	7.19%	2.6%	7.31%	7.69%	2.5%	7.80%	8.20%	2.4%	8.29%	8.71%	2.3%	8.79%	9.21%
60.0	2.5%	6.33%	6.67%	2.4%	6.83%	7.17%	2.4%	7.32%	7.68%	2.3%	7.82%	8.18%	2.2%	8.31%	8.69%	2.1%	8.81%	9.19%
70.0	2.4%	6.35%	6.65%	2.3%	6.84%	7.16%	2.2%	7.34%	7.66%	2.1%	7.83%	8.17%	2.0%	8.33%	8.67%	2.0%	8.82%	9.18%
80.0	2.2%	6.36%	6.64%	2.1%	6.85%	7.15%	2.0%	7.35%	7.65%	2.0%	7.84%	8.16%	1.9%	8.34%	8.66%	1.8%	8.83%	9.17%
90.0	2.1%	6.36%	6.64%	2.0%	6.86%	7.14%	1.9%	7.36%	7.64%	1.9%	7.85%	8.15%	1.8%	8.35%	8.65%	1.7%	8.84%	9.16%
100.0	2.0%	6.37%	6.63%	1.9%	6.87%	7.13%	1.8%	7.36%	7.64%	1.8%	7.86%	8.14%	1.7%	8.35%	8.65%	1.7%	8.85%	9.15%

TABLE 5-3
DIRECT MAIL PROJECTION TABLE (Continued)

90% Confidence Level—Standard Deviation: 1.645 (Page 4)

ANTICIPATED PERCENT RESPONSE

Sample Size (000)	9.5%			10.0%			10.5%			11.0%			11.5%			12.0%		
	±%	Variance Low	High	±%	Variance Low	High	±%	Variance Low	High	±%	Variance Low	High	±%	Variance Low	High	±%	Variance Low	High
1.0	16.1%	7.97%	11.03%	15.6%	8.44%	11.56%	15.2%	8.91%	12.09%	14.8%	9.37%	12.63%	14.4%	9.84%	13.16%	14.1%	10.31%	13.69%
2.5	10.2%	8.54%	10.46%	9.9%	9.01%	10.99%	9.6%	9.49%	11.51%	9.4%	9.97%	12.03%	9.1%	10.45%	12.55%	8.9%	10.93%	13.07%
5.0	7.2%	8.82%	10.18%	7.0%	9.30%	10.70%	6.8%	9.79%	11.21%	6.6%	10.27%	11.73%	6.5%	10.76%	12.24%	6.3%	11.24%	12.76%
7.5	5.9%	8.94%	10.06%	5.7%	9.43%	10.57%	5.5%	9.92%	11.08%	5.4%	10.41%	11.59%	5.3%	10.89%	12.11%	5.1%	11.38%	12.62%
10.0	5.1%	9.02%	9.98%	4.9%	9.51%	10.49%	4.8%	10.00%	11.00%	4.7%	10.49%	11.51%	4.6%	10.98%	12.02%	4.5%	11.47%	12.53%
12.5	4.5%	9.07%	9.93%	4.4%	9.56%	10.44%	4.3%	10.05%	10.95%	4.2%	10.54%	11.46%	4.1%	11.03%	11.97%	4.0%	11.52%	12.48%
15.0	4.1%	9.11%	9.89%	4.0%	9.60%	10.40%	3.9%	10.09%	10.91%	3.8%	10.58%	11.42%	3.7%	11.07%	11.93%	3.6%	11.56%	12.44%
17.5	3.8%	9.14%	9.86%	3.7%	9.63%	10.37%	3.6%	10.12%	10.88%	3.5%	10.61%	11.39%	3.4%	11.10%	11.90%	3.4%	11.60%	12.40%
20.0	3.6%	9.16%	9.84%	3.5%	9.65%	10.35%	3.4%	10.14%	10.86%	3.3%	10.64%	11.36%	3.2%	11.13%	11.87%	3.1%	11.62%	12.38%
25.0	3.2%	9.19%	9.81%	3.1%	9.69%	10.31%	3.0%	10.18%	10.82%	3.0%	10.67%	11.33%	2.9%	11.17%	11.83%	2.8%	11.66%	12.34%
30.0	2.9%	9.22%	9.78%	2.8%	9.72%	10.28%	2.8%	10.21%	10.79%	2.7%	10.70%	11.30%	2.6%	11.20%	11.80%	2.6%	11.69%	12.31%
35.0	2.7%	9.24%	9.76%	2.6%	9.74%	10.26%	2.6%	10.23%	10.77%	2.5%	10.72%	11.28%	2.4%	11.22%	11.78%	2.4%	11.71%	12.29%
40.0	2.5%	9.26%	9.74%	2.5%	9.75%	10.25%	2.4%	10.25%	10.75%	2.3%	10.74%	11.26%	2.3%	11.24%	11.76%	2.2%	11.73%	12.27%
45.0	2.4%	9.27%	9.73%	2.3%	9.77%	10.23%	2.3%	10.26%	10.74%	2.2%	10.76%	11.24%	2.2%	11.25%	11.75%	2.1%	11.75%	12.25%
50.0	2.3%	9.28%	9.72%	2.2%	9.78%	10.22%	2.1%	10.27%	10.73%	2.1%	10.77%	11.23%	2.0%	11.27%	11.73%	2.0%	11.76%	12.24%
60.0	2.1%	9.30%	9.70%	2.0%	9.80%	10.20%	2.0%	10.29%	10.71%	1.9%	10.79%	11.21%	1.9%	11.29%	11.71%	1.8%	11.78%	12.22%
70.0	1.9%	9.32%	9.68%	1.9%	9.81%	10.19%	1.8%	10.31%	10.69%	1.8%	10.81%	11.19%	1.7%	11.30%	11.70%	1.7%	11.80%	12.20%
80.0	1.8%	9.33%	9.67%	1.7%	9.83%	10.17%	1.7%	10.32%	10.68%	1.7%	10.82%	11.18%	1.6%	11.31%	11.69%	1.6%	11.81%	12.19%
90.0	1.7%	9.34%	9.66%	1.6%	9.84%	10.16%	1.6%	10.33%	10.67%	1.6%	10.83%	11.17%	1.5%	11.33%	11.67%	1.5%	11.82%	12.18%
100.0	1.6%	9.35%	9.65%	1.6%	9.84%	10.16%	1.5%	10.34%	10.66%	1.5%	10.84%	11.16%	1.4%	11.33%	11.67%	1.4%	11.83%	12.17%

jections. Simply stated, confidence decreases as sample sizes and response rates decrease. Conversely, confidence increases as response rates increase and as sample sizes increase. Putting it another way, if you expect a relatively low response rate, be sure to use a sample large enough to enable you to have confidence in the results. Otherwise you may have a test that cannot be projected to a satisfactory degree of acceptance.

Using Probability Tables in Planning a Mailing

Let's assume you are planning a test mailing that will ultimately lead to a large-scale rollout. You anticipate a response of 3 percent. Now refer to the 3 percent column in Table 5-1. By scanning down the column, you see that a 10 percent error margin is possible with a mailing of 12,500 pieces, and a replication of that test projects a yield of between 2.67 and 3.33 percent.

But let's say that the break-even point for this proposition is a response rate of 2.8 percent. So the next mailing, based on the 12,500-piece test, could possibly come in as low as 2.67 percent. Your company's profits—and perhaps your job—depend on results no less than 2.8 percent. If you scan down the column, you will see that to be statistically sure of no less than 2.81 percent you will need a test of 30,000 pieces. Anything less is, to use the gambling example, "betting against the odds."

After reviewing the 95 percent tables further, you see that you can use a smaller test sample if your anticipated response rate is higher. For example, a 4 percent response rate would require a mailing of only 10,000 pieces to fall within the ±10 percent margin of error (Table 5-1). However, a lower anticipated response rate—for example, 1 percent—would require a much higher test mailing quantity (40,000 pieces for a 1 percent response rate) to have validity within your parameters (Table 5-1).

The decisions you make before your test mailing are quite important because your rollout decision will be based on the test results.

Using Probability Tables to Evaluate a Mailing

Having accomplished a test mailing, you can then evaluate the results in terms of a projection. Let's assume you mailed 10,000 pieces and achieved a response rate of 2.5 percent. Table 5-4 shows what you can expect at different confidence levels.

The margin of error appears to be less at a lower confidence level and greater for a higher confidence level. The example in Table 5-4 is based on a 2.5 percent response rate and a test quantity of ten thousand. If you get 2.5 percent response on the test and are satisfied with a confidence level of 90 percent (that is, 9 times out of 10), then you can plan on a rollout response of between 2.24 and 2.76 percent. However, if you want to be more certain, look at the 99 percent confidence level (99 times out of 100), and note that you need to work with a wider range in your rollout response.

TABLE 5-4
TESTING

	Confidence level, %	Margin of error, %	Projected low response, %	Projected high response, %
Table 5-3, p. 1	90	10.3	2.24	2.76
Table 5-1, p. 1	95	12.2	2.19	2.81
Table 5-2, p. 1	99	14.0	2.15	2.85

Construction of Probability Tables

For those who are interested, the probability tables use a standard statistical formula for large samples. Using certain factors, we can determine the margin of error as follows:

Let E = margin of error (expressed as a decimal variable—plus or minus—to be added or subtracted from the response rate)
r = response rate (expressed as a decimal)
n = sample size
S = standard deviation

The formula for margin of error is as follows:

$$E = \sqrt{\frac{(r)(1-r)}{n}}(S)$$

To determine the sample size for a given margin of error, the formula just given is converted to the following:

$$n = \frac{(r)(1-r)(S)^2}{E^2}$$

The tables were constructed on a personal computer, using Lotus 1-2-3. The Lotus formula for determining the margin of error, expressed as a percentage, is as follows:

{@SQRT[E$66*(1 − E$66)/($B7*1000)]}*196/E$66

(E$66 and $B7 are cell addresses with constants.)

Testing

Theoretically, statistical probability tables are absolutely reliable. After testing the proper sample and getting acceptable results, a company should be able to roll out any number of pieces it wishes. In practice, a favorable test result usually is followed by a test extension—a cautious re-mailing to a larger quantity—before a company's entire program is committed to a new mailing package, offer, or audience. There are several theories as to why this is a favored plan of action.

I received a letter from a California marketer who suggested a reason for this lack of confidence. He wrote that many in the direct-marketing industry "lack faith in the competence or honesty of the list broker or list source . . . everyone has at least one horror story of salted lists or computer foul-ups." The same writer suggests mailing lists should always be physically inspected in their original formats. "That way, when they think they are mailing 10,000 needlepoint catalogs to sewing hobbyists, they will learn before, not after, the mail is dropped that what they really had was 10,000 car dealers."

This writer may or may not be correct. More likely, the root of the dilemma may lie in the fact that we are dealing with a fluid environment. A mailing sent out even a few months after a test might encounter changed attitudes, economic circumstances or competitive activity, not to mention weather, news events, and other influences that affect direct marketing results.

Another theory suggests that list owners use their freshest names for tests, while an extension or rollout necessarily includes earlier ones as well.

TESTING METHODS

It is important to remind clients or your company's management that a test is a test, and that the costs of smaller press runs and the proportionately higher creative and production costs are not the basis for determining the eventual cost per response. In larger quantities, printing will cost less per item. Even postage will be reduced due to automation discounts.

Test vs. Rollout Costs

My company just submitted a bid to a client which included all fees and costs, which came out to $1.06 each at the 30,000 test quantity, 63¢ at 100,000 and 54¢ at 300,000. In most cases, a test will lose money because of the higher test cost, but the mailing will be very profitable at the rollout cost. That's why we always request rollout information and submit prices at the rollout quantities as well as at the test level. All projections of cost per response must be based on the projected rollout cost.

Some clients and managers have to be reminded what testing is about. A test is successful if it identifies any combination of media, offer and creative factors which are profitable enough to justify a rollout. Within the last year we did such a direct-mail test for a company which only used newspapers, radio and television. The tests pointed to a clear winner with the direct-mail package, but it was never rolled out because the CEO, looking only at the overall test costs and response—not the reduced rollout costs and the most successful lists and offers—told the ad manager "See, I told you direct mail wouldn't work!" The manager, not having learned the fable about the Emperor's new clothes, chose not to challenge his superior who would rather be right than rich.

That was the end of their direct-mail experiment. We estimated that it could have made them an additional twelve million dollars in annual profit.

But they'll never know that. The best way to avoid this happening to you is to be sure that everyone understand the expectations and standards of success *before* the test takes place.

Grid Testing

The quantity used for each test being conducted, whether of copy or lists, is called a "test cell." Each test cell is assigned its own key number. If five new lists were being tested, you would have five test cells. If other mailers were being sent to previously tested groups of names, each separately keyed group would be called a "rollout cell" or an "extension cell."

Often a variety of tests will be conducted simultaneously—perhaps new concepts, offer variations, and new lists. The test quantities can be enormous if the combination of anticipated response rates and required error-limit require large samples. Testing many variables also requires large test quantities. In the interest of minimizing downside risk, an alternative method is needed. That alternative is grid testing, a method I developed when I was a partner in the original Rapp & Collins agency.

Under the grid method, each test cell is still the minimum quantity indicated in the discussion of sample size earlier in this chapter. The difference is that each cell may represent more than one variable, as long as the total number of cells for each variable meets the minimum sample-size test.

Let's say we have three copy tests and three list tests, and that a sample size of 60,000 is indicated. Ordinarily that would require a mailing quantity of 540,000 pieces—nine cells of 60,000 names each. However, if you structure the test as shown in Table 5-5, you can cut the total mailing quantity, and therefore the total test investment, by two-thirds.

Note that the total mailing required is only 180,000, yet there is a 60,000 quantity against each variable being tested. The totals to the right and below the grid are meaningful. But don't be tempted to draw conclusions from the totals in each cell, unless you do so within the much wider error margin of the smaller quantity.

For more substantial testing programs, economies can be achieved by not testing every variable in every list. If every variable is tested on one list and every variable is tested against a control somewhere in the grid, results

TABLE 5-5
TESTING

		Lists		
Copy	A	B	C	Total
X	20,000	20,000	20,000	60,000
Y	20,000	20,000	20,000	60,000
Z	20,000	20,000	20,000	60,000
Total	60,000	60,000	60,000	180,000

can be interpolated. For instance, look at a 95 percent confidence level and a 1 percent response. At 60,000 you can be sure the rollout will be between .92 percent and 1.08 percent, and it is more likely to find significant differences between the factors being tested. At 20,000, it falls to between .86 percent and 1.08 percent. This means that a cell showing a 1.08 percent response is not necessarily any better than one that shows .86 percent.

Production Economies in Testing

The grid test is one way to lower the investment in testing. There are other ways as well—methods that depend on what is being tested.

List tests require only changes in the key number. Offer tests should require changes only in those areas where the offer appears. Substantial production economies can be effected by not showing the offer on the four-color brochure or other color-printed elements. A premium versus no-premium test can be accomplished by keeping the entire package the same and only adding a buck slip (a slip of paper stating the offer), by changing the reply device, and by adding a paragraph to the letter. It isn't necessary to do an entirely new package for every variation.

When CBS Publishing introduced a new gardening magazine, we wanted to try several fundamental approaches: a conventional announcement package, a how-to positioning for beginners, and an "exotic plants" positioning for advanced gardeners. This was accomplished very inexpensively by designing an envelope with an open-back cellophane window and a brochure in which each page stressed a different appeal. The brochure was designed so that it could be folded so the page with the appeal being tested was visible through the back-page window. Only one press run of the brochure and envelope was required, and the letter changes were simply laser variations.

I developed a Weight Watchers package that varied only in one insert and in the response card, part of which showed through a window of the outer envelope face. Everything else remained the same, except for the opening paragraph of the letter. A minimal production budget permitted two very different appeals to be tested: one dramatizing the social aspect of weight-reduction groups, the other the eating pleasure of the varied menus.

In general, a new program should be testing broad concepts and not creative executions. Laser printing, variable inserts and other versioning methods can permit you to determine the most effective positioning and list factors. A dozen variables can thus be tested for less than the cost of two or three separate executions.

List Sampling. When testing a mailing list, it is essential that the names tested be representative of the entire list. In Chapter 14, Mailing Lists, there is a discussion of why Nth-name samples are the most accurate way of doing this. Just divide by the number of samples (n) needed. If you have 750,000 names on the list and you need 50,000 for your test, n is 15. This system will provide a true cross-section of the entire list, if it is supplied correctly by the list owner. Any shortcuts, such as taking a single geographic area or a fifth zip-code digit, add a considerable measure of risk.

Also read the discussion in Chapter 14 of the relative merits of hot-line names, active customers versus expires, and other factors. All these list characteristics must be taken into account when testing lists.

PRINT MEDIA TESTING

Whereas direct-mail testing opportunities are limited only by imagination and economics, newspaper and magazine testing is limited by the production capabilities of the publications.

There are two principal objectives of testing in magazine space. One is to test a magazine as a medium. The other is to test the ad and vary copy, offers, or products.

Testing in Magazines

In Chapter 15, Print Media Planning, there is a lengthy discussion of the pilot-testing theory applied to magazines. It deals with grouping magazines in constellations, and testing the most representative magazine in each group.

Using only one portion of a magazine rather than the entire publication often can minimize downside risk further. Some magazines permit you to buy one-half of the circulation across the board on a national basis. Many magazines will permit you to buy one or more sections of the country. Either plan will enable you to run an advertisement and discover a magazine's response rate without having to buy the entire circulation. Often regional insertions are placed in the back of a magazine, where response would be materially less than the same ad placed nationally. Adjustments must be made in such tests for seasonal or position variations and for the higher cost of the smaller circulation, just as you would in a direct mail test.

As little as ten-thousand dollars can test full-page ads in the largest magazines such as *Time* and *TV Guide* in small regional or city editions. A mere one thousand dollars can test small-space advertisements in hundreds of smaller specialty magazines.

The small-budget advertiser can start with a fractional unit and work up, little by little, to larger sizes and even spectacular-sized units. Some of the largest firms in the direct-marketing business started in just this way. The only difference between them and advertisers with more substantial budgets and wider-reaching test programs is the element of time. The larger firms compress step-by-step testing of smaller advertisers into one season by testing 10 or 20 variables at once. This enables them to quickly establish a multimillion-dollar business rather than build it gradually by reinvesting profits.

A-B Split-Run Testing

There is no more accurate way to determine which magazine advertisement is the best than split-run testing. Whether you are testing an offer, a copy approach, or one product or business against another, this testing approach will always give you a clear and meaningful basis for decision making.

SRDS, Standard Rate and Data Service, defines *split run* this way: "A technique to measure the relative strength of different copy approaches . . . for example, by means of coupon returns from equally divided portions of a specific edition or issue of a publication's circulation, each identical except for the varying copy approaches." Some require that a full page be purchased for the test. Others offer A-B split runs on fractional units. The SRDS listing of split-run opportunities appears in Table 5-6.

To run a test, simply prepare two different versions of your advertisement, each with a different key number, and place both of them in the publication as a split insertion on the same date. Usually an extra fee is charged by the publication.

The publication probably is printed "two-up" on one or more enormous web or rotogravure presses. The magazines either are bound separately and the streams of finished magazines merged, or a double magazine comes off the press and is sheared in half after binding.

In either case, every second magazine has a different advertisement. When looking through a pile of magazines on a newsstand, you can typically see ad A in one magazine, B in the next, A in the one following, and so forth. These magazines are sent throughout the country to magazine distributors or mailed out to subscribers in the same fashion, leading to an absolutely perfect sampling of the whole: 50 percent for one, 50 percent for the other. The validity of this type of test is virtually unchallenged, provided that the difference between test results is large enough.

What result size is "large enough" to be meaningful is a controversial question. One commonly used guide for determining statistical significance in split-run print advertising involves "significance factors"—the percentage difference between two alternatives at a varying total number of responses. At least one well-known direct-marketing company relies on this type of table, despite the fact that some statisticians appear to be at a loss to identify the underlying mathematical formula.

The chart in Table 5-7 is widely used and simple to understand. Just combine the total response to the two versions of your ad—usually the control and the variation—and you'll have the total response figure. Then divide the numbers for each split to produce the percentage of the total response. Look up the total response figure in the left-hand column and refer to the significance figure in the right column.

If your test result—expressed as a percentage of total response—is greater than the figure listed, then you have a significant improvement. The test ad should become your control ad in the future. If the test result and the control figure is not greater than the significance figure, then you have a "tie" with the control. You can use the new advertisement or not, basing your decision on non-statistical considerations such as its long-term effect

TABLE 5-6
CONSUMER MAGAZINES WITH SPLIT-RUN ADVERTISING RATES

Ability Magazine	Money
American How-To	Mother Earth News
The American Legion Magazine	Motor Trend
American Park Network	Mountain Bike
Albion Sports Communications Inc.	Muscle & Fitness
Atlantic Monthly	National Enquirer
Baby Talk	National Lampoon
Bicycling	National Speed Sport News
Bon Appetit	New Age
Bride's Magazine	New Woman
Capper's & Grit	The New York Review of Books
Car Craft	Newsweek
Child	Northwest Airlines World Traveler
Chocolatier	Organic Gardening
City Pages	Our Sunday Visitor
Conde Nast Traveler	Parents
Cover Magazine	Parents Baby
Elegant Bride	Parents Expecting
The Elks Magazine	Penthouse
Emerge	People Weekly
Esquire	Performing Arts Network
Essence	Petersen Magazine Network
Family	PGA Tour Partners
Family Circle	Petersen's Photographic
Family Digest Baby	Playbill Magazine
Family Digest Magazine	Playboy
Fast and Healthy	Power & Motoryacht
Flex	Prevention
Fortune	Reader's Digest
4-Wheel & Off-Road	Redbook Magazine
Four Wheeler	Rodale's Scuba Diving
Gardening How-To	The Rotarian
Generation	Scene
Gentlemen's Quarterly	Scouting
Glamour	Secure Retirement
Golf For Women	Self
Golf Magazine	Shape
Good Housekeeping	Ski Magazine
The Guide Package	Skiing Magazine
Guns & Ammo	SmartMoney
Healthy Kids	Sport
Hemispheres	Sports Illustrated
Hot Rod	Stanford
Hunting	Teen
Journal of Accountancy	TV Blueprint
Ladies' Home Journal	TV Guide
Lindy's Sports Annuals	TV Plus
Maclean's	US Airways Attache Magazine
McCall's	Vegetarian Times
Men's Fitness	Woman's Day
Men's Health	Working Woman
Mode	Writer's Digest
Modern Bride	Yankee
Modern Maturity	YM

TABLE 5-7
SIGNIFICANT FACTOR IN SPLIT-RUN
ADVERTISING (95 PERCENT
CONFIDENCE LEVEL)

Total responses (both sides)	Factor
50	64.24
100	60.00
200	57.07
300	55.77
400	55.00
500	54.47
1,000	53.16
1,500	52.56
2,000	52.23
3,000	51.83
4,000	51.58
5,000	51.41
10,000	51.00
20,000	50.71
30,000	50.58
40,000	50.50
50,000	50.45
100,000	50.31

on the image of your product and company. Some companies with extensive schedules will elect to use such "tie" ads to alternate with other ads and thus avoid the "fatigue" factor.

A respected university professor gives his students a simpler rule of thumb. He says that each side of a split must have at least 100 responses to be meaningful. This is a quick standard, but not one I am comfortable with. I believe the circulation and the number of responses must be taken into account just as they are in direct mail. While this is no more scientific, I use the same statistical tables as for direct mail with one exception. Because magazine-circulation advertising costs only a tenth of most direct mail, I simply add a zero to the sample size charts. If a magazine's circulation is one million, and I am using an A-B split-run so each "side" is 500,000, I use the direct mail table for 50,000.

Multiple Split-Run Testing

The A-B split provides a reliable comparison of one advertisement against another in a given publication. But what happens when there are a half dozen valid concepts to be tested in magazines?

Multiple split-run testing, sometimes called telescopic testing, is designed to solve this problem. It combines the A-B split just described with the availability of regional editions of magazines. If a magazine has four re-

TABLE 5-8
MAGAZINE GEOGRAPHIC EDITIONS

West	Ad A versus ad B
South	Ad A versus ad C
Northeast	Ad A versus ad D
Midwest	Ad A versus ad E

gional editions, you can test four different ads against your control ad. For an example see Table 5-8.

The results of such a test might be as shown in Table 5-9. The hodge-podge of result figures can quickly be made meaningful. One way is to calculate the "lift factor" for each insertion, independent of the results of the control ad A, as shown in Table 5-10. Another way is to adjust the ad A results to a national average, calculating the adjustment against all of the other numbers and restating the figures accordingly.

Either of these techniques compensates for geographic or distribution variations and enables you to read the results correctly. Similarly, the various advertisements can be indexed, with the control ad designated 100. Table 5-10 shows an example of an adjusted-result report, including all the preceding factors and the figures adjusted against the control. Note that the greatest lift resulted from ad C, although ads B and E had lower cost-per-response (CPR) figures because of regional variation.

Referring to the significance chart in Table 5-7 we see that at this level of total response we need only a 54 percent factor for the new ad to be declared a valid winner. Ads B, C, and E all are valid winners. Statistically, ad D also is equivalent to ad A, though it did not beat it.

Some magazines have many editions throughout the country. For example, *TV Guide* has 109 local editions. *Time* has a number of ways to break up their national distribution. You may choose among the 11 regional additions, or the 51 state editions (including the District of Columbia). They also have 50 spot-market editions by metropolitan area—ten major metro areas that include the ten largest cities in the U.S., and 40 non-major metro areas for other less-dense urban areas. As a result, it is possible for sample sizes to get too small to be meaningful. In such cases the practice has been to group the editions by regional demographics, with each group containing

TABLE 5-9
MAGAZINE TEST COMBINING REGIONAL EDITIONS AND A-B SPLIT

Edition	Control	Response	Variation	Response
West	Ad A	351	Ad B	416
South	Ad A	297	Ad C	376
Northeast	Ad A	328	Ad D	302
Midwest	Ad A	345	Ad E	420

TABLE 5-10
REGIONAL SPLIT-RUN TEST ANALYZING "LIFT FACTOR"

Edition	Cost	Control	Number	CPR	Test	Number	CPR	Lift %
West	1,836	A	351	$2.62	B	416	$2.21	18
South	2,856	A	297	4.81	C	376	3.80	26
Northeast	3,060	A	328	4.66	D	302	5.07	(7)
Midwest	2,448	A	345	3.55	E	420	2.91	21
Total	$10,228		1,321	$3.86		1,514	$3.37	

a mix of urban, rural, and geographic areas (eastern, and western) of the country.

Flip-Flop Testing

Unfortunately, many magazines don't have split-run testing facilities, particularly those with circulations that are not large enough to enable them to be printed in the two-up process. Very few newspapers offer this service, although most magazine sections of Sunday papers do.

The best available technique is *flip-flop* testing, and even this requires geographic editions. *The Wall Street Journal* is sold in three editions, but is printed for seventeen different regions, and each region can carry separate copy. *USA Today*, which I have found to be a very effective direct-response medium, offers copy changes in their 25 print sites throughout the country. A local newspaper might have a city and a suburban edition that can be used this way for a test.

In this kind of testing you run ad A in one edition and ad B in the other on the same day. Then a week or two later you reverse the ads, running B where A ran and vice versa. By running two ads and reading the combined total response rates rather than individual ones, the distortion factors offset each other. One edition or region might be stronger than another. The ad that runs the first time will probably do better than the second ad in each section, because it has "creamed" the market somewhat. However, this qualification applies to both ads and both editions. The total response rate of ad A compared with ad B should be valid.

Full-Page Bind-Ins

There are times when the best testing medium may be full-page bind-in cards, although they are too costly for most advertisers. This type of unit is called "hard space," as compared to an ordinary advertisement, called "soft space."

The bind-in cards are preprinted by the advertiser and supplied to the publication for insertion in the magazine. The unit can include a perforated reply card, gummed areas for tokens or stamps, numbers for sweepstakes, pop-ups, or a variety of other techniques not possible with a conventional soft-space unit.

As the cards are preprinted and pre-mixed by your own printer, virtually any number of variations can be tested simultaneously. This is an excellent technique for major advertisers whose potential investments are so large that 6, 8, or 12 concepts must be tested before a major campaign is launched.

While the cost of the space and printing may seem high compared with the publication's circulation and the cost of a conventional page advertisement, it generally produces a high enough response rate to equal or exceed the orders per dollar expended on a conventional unit. The unit is atypical in that the ad must be designed to utilize both sides of the bound-in card. Some advertisers have gotten around this requirement by placing a separate advertisement for a different product from their company on the reverse side of the page.

If you are selecting a publication for this type of testing, you'll want to pick one that is sold mostly by subscription rather than newsstand. Newsstand-sold magazines have a much greater waste factor than those sold mostly by subscription. Though your space rates are based on actual circulation, you still have to print enough card units for the magazine's total press run, including the unsold newsstand copies. This inflates your overall cost.

Bound-In Reply Cards

A more common format for major advertisers is the combination of a single- or double-page advertisement with a bound-in reply card, usually called an *insert card*. This is a very successful unit, producing four times the result of a page alone with an average cost increase only two or three times higher. But it does have limitations as a test vehicle.

With few exceptions, there is no way to match cards to an alternative A-B split. If the card is to match the page, it is impossible to be sure that the cards are inserted in synchronization with the page.

One solution is to confine the test to the card alone without changing the advertisement for the page. This is really only suitable for testing offers or minor proposition variations. If it does not appear on the page, several different offers can be featured on the card itself. For instance, it is easy to test one card with a premium featured and another with no premium at all to determine the lift factor of the premium. Or you can test factors like simplified commitment copy, the availability of a trade-up option, or a requirement for respondents to provide their own stamp as opposed to business-reply mail.

Another way to do split testing when insert cards are involved is to use a transfer code. This is a useful device when several basic concepts are being tested for a proposition that usually is successful only when an insert card is used. In this case, the insert card is constant and the ads change, with as many variations as A-B splitting and regional editions permit.

One version of the transfer code is to offer a choice of options, asking respondents to use a designated letter for one option and a different letter for the other. For example, in one ad for books the customer is asked to select A for a black binding and B for a brown one. In the other, C represents black while D represents brown. The customer is asked to place the letter in a designated space on the insert card so as to indicate the choice.

Better still, if you have product order numbers, put an A after each number on ad A, a B after those in ad B, and so on. These letters are later translated into key numbers, and the results are analyzed as with any other split run.

Where a choice is not available, a premium can be used instead. The respondent can be asked to place a designated letter on the card for a free poster, for example.

The most direct and straightforward approach of all seems to work as well as the others, but it may depend on the type of product being offered. This is a simple statement on the printed page that says "To help us evaluate our advertising, please put this key number in the space indicated on the reply card."

Deliberate Underspacing

If a proposition usually works in a page but doesn't do well as a half-page, we say it is *underspaced*. The same consideration applies to format as well as space size. If a proposition works best with an insert card or a bound-in multipage unit, and we run a simple black-and-white page, we have underspaced the ad.

Deliberate underspacing is one way that an advertiser with a modest budget can enjoy the benefits of multiple testing. He or she just needs to use regional editions and A-B splits for a smaller unit than would otherwise be profitable, while the overall results will be disappointing and the risk and investment have been limited.

Another technique is the use of half-page black-and-white ads in Sunday supplements of newspapers in a few regions before investing in a full-page, full-run, full-color advertisement. The trick with all of these underspacing approaches is to keep your focus on the original objective and the original expectation.

NEWSPAPER PREPRINTS

The possibilities for copy testing in preprints are infinite. You can have your own printer produce as many different versions of your advertisement as cost and statistical validity permit and then deliver them, premixed, to newspapers for insertion in their Sunday editions. The only limitation would involve trying to mix formats, as the insertion equipment can only be set to handle one size and thickness of your preprint and they can't be interspersed.

The problems with preprint copy testing don't appear at the publication. They come at your printer. It is essential that someone visually check the shipment of inserts after they have been mixed and before they are sent out to the newspapers.

Some printers don't have the presses to automatically "stream" the different versions together on press, and they rely on something they call *hand spanning*. This means that they pack the inserts from different stacks or skids, one handful from this stack, another from that stack, and so on. This is adequate for a test, if it's really done. Unfortunately, there are too many temptations for the individual supervisor to take shortcuts and invalidate your test.

For instance, in a four-way split, if the press is doing only two versions at a time, the printer should store the entire run of the first two versions and wait for the production of the second two versions before packing anything. But unless the printer has adequate floor space, this may not happen—and no one is going to tell you. There are many scrupulous and careful printers who would never permit this to happen, but caution still requires that your own inspector check the skids before they are shipped.

Another caution might be to include a pure-key test if possible, with no changes other than the code number itself. The results should be identical, within statistical error limits. If they're not, you'll know that something is wrong. However, it will be too late to do anything about it other than change printers in the future. The on-site inspection is still the preferred choice.

Picking the Right Newspapers

With the exception of a few large cities with more than one newspaper, this medium provides a very broad range of demographics in their readership—rich and poor, educated and not, mail-order buyer and retail buyer.

The key variable, then, is geographic characteristics—median income, education, buying power, etc. Size of market is often the most influential characteristic. For a test, pick a variety of papers in different-sized markets: one or two large cities, several medium ones, and a handful of smaller towns. In all cases the newspapers should be those which can demonstrate a large number of repeat insertions by other mail-order advertisers, with rate structures that are competitive with newspapers with similar circulations in similar markets.

Within these broad parameters, availability will be the prime consideration. On key dates you may find that your competition has already reserved space, or there may be too many other advertisers scheduling preprints on the dates you want. You will have to check availabilities and weigh the tradeoffs of preferred dates versus preferred markets in making your selections.

Format Tests

One of the old maxims of testing was that it was possible to split only within a given format—one preprint versus another, one full page versus another. Few magazines would permit tests of small-space units. However, just as rate cards are not always indicative of the rates available to direct-response advertisers, so they are not always the best guide to what kind of splits are available. If your own budget or your agency has enough buying power and influence, and if your media specialist is respected by the media and a good negotiator, virtually anything is possible.

Some examples of possible negotiated tests:

- Black-and-white versus color
- Large space versus small
- Card versus no card
- "Square" third page versus vertical column
- Multiple splits in publications that supposedly offered none
- One position versus another in the same publication
- Custom-tailored geographic segmentation

Such tests are not generally available, and if available, it's usually only on a limited and confidential basis. But they can provide definitive answers very quickly to media strategy questions that might otherwise take years of trial-and-error approaches to resolve. Find out if these options are available at all. As they say in the Bronx: "It don't hoit to ask."

BROADCAST

This is the place to use the "best-foot-forward" approach. Testing should begin on those stations most likely to succeed, where experience shows that your own propositions or those of other direct marketers have been successful.

Direct-Response Testing

There can be substantial differences in response by type of market, so a variety of stations should be included in a test schedule: urban, rural, East, West, South, Midwest, independent stations, network affiliates, and cable stations. Often there are patterns showing that one type of station works better than others. More often the key variable is the willingness of stations to establish a rate structure and make available time slots that will be cost-efficient, regardless of type of market or programming for that station.

Dayparts. The time of day is usually the most constant and controllable variable other than the station itself. The time of day is the most effective selector of audience segments. Weekend mornings reach parents whose children are watching children's shows. Afternoons reach homemakers at home, enjoying the never-ending stream of soap operas and talk shows. News programs and adventure shows reach a higher number of men. Late-night programming seems to find older people, or at least restless ones.

Programming adjacencies offer even more precise selections, for certain shows seem to attract audiences with predictable affinities.

Other Testing.   Other than the station, type of show and time of programming, there are often times when it is necessary to test other factors, such as frequency, length of commercial, or the content of the commercial itself.

The technique most used is a variation of flip-flop testing discussed earlier in this chapter in the section on print media. A different phone number is assigned to the new campaign. The new one is run in alternate weeks on several stations, beginning with the new campaign on half the stations and the old one on the other half. Half the stations are running A-B-A-B-A, while the others are playing B-A-B-A-B. This tends to offset differences by station and by whether a commercial is played earlier or later in the schedule.

This test method generally is used to test entirely new commercials. Occasionally it's used to test frequency—the optimum numbers of airing per week. It would not be possible to test prices or other offer variations this way. Such testing requires a "paired-market" test—using similar metropolitan areas with similar demographics and audience characteristics.

Audience Valuation

More sophisticated techniques, discussed in Chapter 16, attempt to evaluate specific audience segments in order to predict the success of potential television schedules. The result is a specific allowable media cost for audiences targeted by different stations.

To initiate such testing, spots are placed at various times during a particular week, and then the actual audiences reached by the spots must be subjected to computerized analysis. This type of analysis requires access to all the audience evaluation tools used by general advertising. The analysis is difficult and complex, but produces a media planning tool that reaches far beyond the old standard of pure cost per response. This method has made it possible to effectively target narrow-audiences, such as for upscale, lifestyle, and cultural propositions.

Support Broadcast

As will be discussed in Chapter 16, *support* broadcast—spots referring the audience to an ad, a mailing or an Internet URL—is very different from *direct-response*. They are very different in their purposes and methodologies Testing their usefulness or refining scheduling for the two broadcast mediums are just as different.

The choice of markets in support broadcast is dictated by the media to be supported. Within each market, however, there are usually several stations to choose from, and within each station, there is a choice of dayparts and frequency.

Often it is necessary to use every station in a market in order to reach the 300 or so gross rating points most direct marketers feel is a minimum for effective media support. Gross Rating Points are the percentage of TV sets tuned to a program, multiplied by the number of spots. It is usually the total of the GRP ratings of each airing at a station carrying the spot. As support spots must be aired in a precise pattern during three or four days adjoining the appearance of the ad or mailing being supported, it may be difficult to secure availabilities and most stations will not sell such time at direct response rates.

Usually the first objective is to test the effectiveness of support broadcast itself. The standard technique is to select between six and ten similar markets, supporting some of them at one frequency level, others at a higher level, and some without any support at all.

To calculate for testing purposes, the costs of the broadcast are added to the costs of the preprints or direct mail being supported. The total advertising cost is divided by the number of responses received. The combined cost-per-response figures can then be compared for each market, and conclusions can be drawn as to whether support costs are justified and at which GRP level. Similarly, an ongoing campaign can test various daypart concentrations, commercial lengths, or even different creative appeals.

I advise readers considering any type of broadcast testing to reread Chapter 16, and to keep in mind the objective of a broadcast support test. Support advertising cannot be expected to lower cost-per-response (CPR), although sometimes it does. A more reasonable expectation is to extend the media being supported—a higher level of orders at the same CPR, or a CPR that is higher than unsupported preprints or direct mail, but still less costly than other media alternatives.

Infomercial Testing

This, too, is covered in more detail in the Broadcast chapter. This "long form" of DRTV broadcast is the wild card of direct-marketing media. As this form has become more popular, it has become increasingly difficult to buy half-hour units at reasonable time periods at reasonable prices.

Media buying for infomercials is an exercise in frustration. The established multi-product marketers have sewn up the better time spots. The new advertiser is offered time at 2:30AM on little known cable stations or rural local stations. And every purchase of airtime must be paid in full, in cash, in advance. There is little room for trial and error.

In this sector, any discussion of what's ideal would be purely academic. You have to see what you can get and take your chances. My approach is to work with media companies who buy a great deal of such time. Although their best time slots will go to their current clients, they at least have access to the better stations and experience on what will work and what rates to pay.

The only suggestion I can make here is to avoid putting all your eggs in one basket. Try several time periods and several types of stations. If you can't afford more than a few placements, then save your money and use short-form one and two minute spots to get started.

Internet Testing

As with infomercials, everyone knows of the great successes, at least in stock prices. What doesn't make headlines is that the field is littered with the corpses of under-capitalized, under-marketed entrepreneurial ideas.

This edition has a whole chapter devoted to the Internet. When the fantasies of instant riches calm down, the Internet—especially the World Wide Web—will prove to be a significant factor in direct marketing. The caution for all who choose to utilize this media is to remember that the rules of human nature and the experiences of direct marketing still apply. Technology alone won't do it.

To limit these remarks to testing, I will only point out that there are enormous parallels between the development of this field and that of cable television. Both media forms initially quoted circulation in terms of access or impressions. Both had enormous amounts of unsold time available to aggressive bargainers. And both eventually discovered that having access is not the same as having audiences—that having the right content to attract the right audience is critical.

There are infinite opportunities to experiment with links, shopping malls, buttons, banners, and preferred positions. Most reach their audiences by including their message in a portal or browser homepage. And many successful pages rely on deceit, trickery or curiosity to get Internet users to their used car, air travel, music or other service instead of the one they might have sought.

My suggestion is to work with one of the more established web-media marketers and try a variety of sizes, sites and creative appeals. Test not only the media opportunities but also the product, offer, and creative elements as discussed in direct mail. Test those same factors in other direct-marketing media, and integrate it all so they work together to reach your audiences.

Judge them all by the same standards—not "hits" or even "click-throughs" but sales. After all, you don't measure direct mail by how many people see it or read it, but by responses that turn into *profitable* sales. The clock is already ticking on the Internet's leave of absence from this aspect of reality.

TESTING STRATEGY

Now that we've covered how to test in each medium, let's look at the basic philosophy that applies to any and all kinds of testing. The first step is to plan the test. How many versions to run? What factors are likely to be the most important? This has to be in proportion to your goals and your ability to use the information you gain. The approach to this depends on the personality of your company.

What to Test

What you should test depends on your budget, mailing size, objectives, and willingness to assume risk. It is easy to test a wide variety of mailing lists, or a simple direct-mail variation. Each split costs very little to execute. It is more costly to test different TV commercials, color magazine ads, and total mailing concepts. The cost of testing should be in relation to the size of the expected benefits.

Changes that affect the product being offered or the way the product is positioned create the greatest difference in results. Offer changes run a close second, with very dramatic differences resulting from changes in price, premium, commitment, terms, and other factors.

Creative changes are next, with very broad differences sometimes resulting from a change in headline or illustration, or in print and direct mail formats. Layout revisions or different copy treatments of the same theme usually show very little difference, presuming they were professionally executed in the first place.

The big differences—200 and 300 percent lift factors—almost always come from product positioning, offer changes, or the selection of different lists or publications.

As it's too expensive to test everything, the selection of what to test has to be done methodically. First, consider test opportunities within your basic mailing or media schedule—publications you are using anyway that make testing feasible. Then list the things you would like to test, in the order of expected result improvement.

In a recent mail-order product introduction, I still had 12 possible ad variations even after focus panel reviews and predictive research. There were 8 testing opportunities, between direct mail and a Sunday supplement regional—A-B split. When the opportunities were reviewed, all the copy alternatives were set aside in favor of testing product and offer variations. We chose to test creative executions in the second round after the other elements were firmed up.

Evolutionists versus Fundamentalists

Another issue is how boldly to test. One school, which I'll call the evolutionists, advocates strictly "readable" testing, with all elements in an ad or mailing piece identical except the single factor being tested. If you are testing a headline, they will tell you, don't change the layout anywhere, and leave every element of type size and color exactly the same. The justification of this approach is "When the results come in, what conclusions will I be able to reach?" If more than one element changes, the ability to make a final pronouncement on what works or doesn't work is muddied.

The fundamentalists, on the other hand, are looking for the big breakthrough, the dramatic result, regardless of whether or not they ever know why one approach works and another one doesn't. Noted publishing consultant Dick Benson advocates testing one creative resource against another.

His advice was not to try to work out an overall testing plan that leads to definitive knowledge, but to pit one supplier against another and see which approach does the best.

In my opinion the best approach depends on what you have to lose. If you are running a successful business, then changes should be evolutionary. You can then build upon experience that can be used in other mailings and for other products. On the other hand, if you're in trouble, go for broke with completely fresh, way-out approaches.

For most clients, I prefer the evolution approach. I find that even the best creative directors are pressured by the fundamentalist system into looking for creative gimmicks and major departures, sometimes overlooking the less exciting but more profitable breakthroughs that can occur from a simple coupon revision or offer change.

If your packages are coming from different agencies or creative sources, what have you learned? That one source is always better than the other? Not really. I believe it is more important to build a base of what one of my clients calls "company knowledge" that can be implemented by any in-house or outside resource.

Which Medium to Test In

Each medium has its unique advantages. Direct mail offers great flexibility if you are testing a wide variety of offers, and great economy if the basic color circular can remain the same with only the letter and reply card changing. It also offers a very low profile, if you don't want your testing activity to be spotted by your competition.

Print media, on the other hand, let you test broad creative concepts very dramatically and inexpensively in black-and-white magazine or supplement splits. Such basic design differences cost less to execute in art, type, and production in print media than in direct mail.

Broadcast is expensive to test, with each commercial variation costing thousands of dollars. And it is very difficult to get a reading of one element against another. I prefer to use television only after the best offer and creative approaches have been determined by testing in mass magazines or newspapers.

It's possible to do broad testing in media units other than those that will eventually be the most profitable. Larger units such as bind-in cards, or smaller ones such as black-and-white fractional units, may give a reading that will project accurately to color pages with bind-ins or other units that will be the mainstay of the basic campaign. The added CPR, because of the less-efficient unit, should be considered an R & D (Research and Development) expense. I recommend that clients set aside a budget for such testing.

An interesting advantage of print advertising is its virtually certain transferability into other media, including direct mail. A print-tested concept almost always proves successful in direct mail and broadcast. A direct mail concept, on the other hand, hardly ever translates into any other medium.

When to Break Out the Champagne

When introducing a new product or trying to improve an established one there is a natural impatience to measure the results. Part of this is the desire to use the knowledge as soon as possible. Part is just plain curiosity.

"Doubling" is a convenient way to read results, as earlier returns usually are not reliable indicators of eventual results. The doubling date is sometimes called the "half-life" point, a term borrowed from the world of nuclear physics. This is the point where half the total responses are in. The final result will be double the responses at that time.

Direct mail results start dribbling in immediately. Nothing is significant, however, until the first Monday after a first-class mailing or the third Monday after a bulk-rate mailing. With first class, half the results usually are in two weeks after the first large Monday mail. With third class, this point comes three or four weeks later.

Now that I've presented a formula, let me warn you against counting on it. Mail delivery is nothing less than erratic. It varies at different times of the year and in different post offices. A local campaign will get results faster than a national one. Carrier presorted mail travels faster. Mail with business reply envelopes may linger a few days at your local post office on the way back to you.

Print Results

Magazines and newspapers also have predictable patterns. Daily papers are read immediately or never, and so the half-life point is less than a week away. In a local Sunday paper, you can usually double the results that are in as of the following Thursday. (But for a national schedule you have to allow more time for the mail to arrive from across the country.)

Most monthly magazines have a doubling point three weeks after the first heavy Monday, or about four weeks after the magazine's on-sale date. An earlier, less reliable, 20 to 25 percent point may be reached after two weeks for those who insist on making early forecasts.

Weekly magazines have a similar pattern. Once the returns start arriving, the halfway point is reached about 12 days later, or about two weeks after the publication first went on sale.

"Hard space," such as business reply insert cards, will come in faster than soft space, which requires the respondent to hunt for an envelope and stamp. Inquiries or responses to free offers will come in faster than those that require the writing of a check or the filling in of a credit card number. Telephone orders will come in faster, but with a similar pattern.

Magazines with mostly subscription readers are usually received throughout the country at the same time. The responses will come in as much as a week faster than responses from a newsstand-sold magazine that is picked up by readers over a month's time.

Magazine response curves also vary by the editorial content. A magazine with a long, particularly interesting article may be saved for weeks, keeping the responses coming in for a longer time. A shelter book—meaning a magazine dealing with home decorating—may be kept and referred to, while a news magazine usually is read the day it arrives. All these factors affect response curves.

To develop your own forecasting patterns, I recommend tracking the results of your ads in each magazine on a daily basis, logging in the results separately by whether they come in by mail, phone and Internet. Then chart these results on graph paper until you discover the pattern that fits your product, market and the media you use.

Broadcast, Internet and Telephone

There is no curve in broadcast media or in telephone selling. Most responses come in within hours or they don't come in at all. On telephone or Internet orders received in response to a radio or television offer, at least 90 percent will arrive in the first three or four hours. I've been told that the "half-life" point for mass e-mail is about six minutes after the transmission! When a mail-in offer is used on broadcast, the response curve is the same as with a daily newspaper.

In telephone selling the responses are, of course, instantaneous. Each day's tallies can be obtained by phone to give you an immediate indication of the success of the scripts used that day.

Internet response-curves will vary dramatically. Banner ads on a browser or ISP "pop-up" can give you results in a day. But a difficult to find URL that depends on search engines can take months to generate a significant number of orders. But an Internet retail site, like ValueAmerica, will have half their orders within a few days of their large-space newspaper ads or television commercials, with the balance drifting in over a month as if it were a catalog.

Rollout Strategies

Once the results are in, there is usually little time to analyze them and make decisions. Closing dates will compel decisions as to whether to repeat print or broadcast insertions and run more ads or to send out more mailings. Competitors already will be considering "ripping-off" your best ideas. Seasonal factors will add even more pressure to do something in a timely manner. A successful test has to be exploited quickly or your competitors will do it for you.

Some cautions should be observed. A new approach may work because it is fresh and new, not because it is better. It may work the first time it is run or mailed, but not again. Some ads tire more quickly than others. An approach may not work because of some unusual coincidence. Whenever results seem illogical, always check the medium in which the ad ran. Perhaps a competitive ad ran in the same issue, diluting your responses. Maybe a major news event distracted readers, or a weather aberration kept them from reading the paper or watching television at all.

TABLE 5-11
ORDER PROJECTIONS
(Typical order flow pattern based on one company's experience. Pattern
will vary depending on media used, type of product or service and
whether payment is required.)

Week	Gross week %	Cumulative gross %	Gross orders	Cumulative gross orders
1		0.00	0	0
2	12.450	12.45	2,546	2,546
3	20.110	32.56	4,112	6,658
4	15.709	48.27	3,212	9,870
5	8.578	56.85	1,754	11,624
6	6.666	63.51	1,363	12,986
7	5.089	68.60	1,041	14,027
8	5.217	73.82	1,067	15,093
9	5.718	79.54	1,169	16,262
10	3.592	83.13	734	16,997
11	2.344	86.47	684	17,680
12	3.249	89.72	664	18,345
13	3.168	92.89	648	18,992
14	2.363	95.25	483	19,476
15	1.530	96.78	313	19,788
16	1.000	97.78	204	19,993
17	1.156	98.94	236	20,229
18	0.063	99.00	13	20,242
19	0.280	99.28	57	20,299
20	0.250	99.53	51	20,351
21	0.094	99.63	19	20,370
22	0.062	99.69	13	20,382
23	0.000	99.69		20,382
24	0.062	99.75	13	20,395
25	0.032	99.78	7	20,402
26	0.000	99.78		20,402
27	0.031	99.81	6	20,408
28	0.031	99.84	6	20,414
29	0.000	99.84		20,414
30	0.031	99.88	6	20,421
31	0.031	99.91	6	20,427
32	0.000	99.91		20,427
33	0.032	99.94	7	20,434
34	0.000	99.94		20,434
35	0.000	99.94		20,434
36	0.031	99.97	6	20,440
37	0.000	99.97		20,440
38	0.000	99.97		20,440
39	0.000	99.97		20,440
40	0.031	100.00	6	20,446
	100.000		20,446	

Weekly result reports should report both actual orders received and projection based on estimates or on past experience. Such a report would show: A. Orders received. B. Cumulative orders. C. Projection based on estimated completion. At the half-way point (in this example 4 weeks) you can rely on the data for your next mailing. Of course a complete sales report will also show payments, returns, and what items were sold. Source: Joseph Furgiuele, FURGIUELE & COMPANY, INC.

Another decision that will depend on corporate personality is whether to act on half-life figures or wait until final results are in and back-end experience is gained.

Usually the best approach is somewhere in between. Unrepeatable opportunities—a key season, a difficult-to-get insert card or back-cover position—should be reserved at an early date, because the opportunity is perishable. But other factors are constant. Successful lists can be re-used with increased quantities. A productive Internet buy can be extended and expanded. With broadcast, you can drop the weak stations and add a larger number of new stations, gradually building up the schedule.

My own observations are that the risk-takers do better in the long run, and that a winning proposition should complete its rollout within a year. Taking longer to complete the rollout means that marketing circumstances may change, mitigating the success of the early results. Remember that timing is a factor in the original test results as well, and next year may not be as good as this year. The old maxim about making hay while the sun shines is very applicable to the field of direct marketing.

THE
PROPOSITION

Except for changing the product itself, nothing can make as big a difference as a change in the basic offer, known as the proposition. While there are exceptions, this is still the rule. Changes in the price, the terms, the guarantee, the way the product is combined or segmented—all of these create more changes in result tabulations than most changes in copy and layout. The rule stated another way: "The substance of the offer outweighs the form of its presentation."

PRICE OFFERS

Does price make a difference? You bet it does. We'll start with the simplest category: a business selling a single product or service directly to the consumer in a "one-step" approach that asks for the order on the initial contact. This category includes how the order comes in, whether by mail, by phone, by Internet click at the customer's office, through the Internet from a home computer, at the customer's front door, over the counter at a retail store, at a trade show, or at a county fair.

Hidden Price. If the product is new, has a new feature, or answers a real need, you may want to de-emphasize price until after the benefits have been fully presented. In such a case the price may be buried in the last paragraphs of the main copy. One correspondence school concealed its tuition under a flap on the enrollment form. A magazine used a sealed envelope to be sure the price was the last and not the first information communicated. Credit card, insurance and bank offers use this device consistently. They feature the attractive initial fees and terms up front, and hide the continuing terms in small type at the back of the letter or brochure.

Featured Price.   "Giant wall map, only $1" can be a powerhouse offer. If the price is the news, then scream it out at the beginning, right in the headline of an ad, the superscript of a letter, or the display on a television commercial or Internet banner. Most general advertising, other than by retailers, usually can't feature price because of legal restrictions, but direct marketers—like retailers—can and should.

Comparative Price.   Did the product previously sell for more? Is it the equivalent of a retail product that sells for a higher price? For example, would your book club titles cost more in "publishers' original editions? " Then by all means let the consumer in on this fact. The more striking the comparison, the more prominent it should be. But make sure it's legitimate and make sure you can prove the claim. Government and industry self-regulators are frowning on stretched comparisons justified by a few token sales at a higher price.

Introductory Price.   If you're offering a new product or service, an introductory offer is a great way to get attention and encourage immediate action. Publishers have had great success with "pre-publication offers."

Discount Offers.   If the offer can be expressed in terms of a comparison with a previous price, a retail price, a newsstand price or other prices elsewhere, then consider expressing that price in percentages or fractions. "Half-price" will usually do better than "Originally $10, now $5."

Savings Feature.   Consider featuring the savings in a price comparison, rather than the low price. "Save $11" can be a stronger lead than "Now only $19."

CREDIT PROPOSITIONS

Credit is costly, not only in "no-pay" sales, but in interest costs if you carry your own receivables, or in financing discounts or credit card charges if you don't. Don't forget paperwork processing, billing, postage, and the cost of added returns. But the availability of credit in its many forms can be as valuable a sales stimulus as a product enhancement or price reduction.

Whether or not you offer credit is a fundamental decision that will be affected by the value of your product and the nature of your market. In some product-market combinations, not offering credit is not an option— the proposition will not work without it. With others it may be a marginal consideration requiring extensive testing of whether the front-end lift is worth the back-end cost and complications.

Free Trial Offer

Credit combined with a guarantee is the strongest credit proposition available. Its powerful benefit is the implication that you have such confidence in your product that you are willing to let the consumer use, read, examine, or try it before deciding whether to return or pay for it.

As returned merchandise can be a significant expense for you, it is necessary to consider the cost of the product and the expected retention rate before trying this offer. If you do try it, then make the most of it by emphasizing "Free trial," "Send no money now," and "Use it for 10 days at our risk." If you plan to refurbish and reship returned merchandise, use the term "Free examination." There are legal problems in reshipping "tried" merchandise.

Conditional Free Trial

Essentially the same as the previous offer, the conditional free trial has one vital difference: The offer is subject to acceptance. A clause in the coupon can state this reservation. The marketer can then apply a variety of credit-screening techniques. Here are some examples.

- *Internal match.* Previous bad-pay customers, or those who have already taken advantage of a "one-time only" or "one-to-a-family" offer, can be eliminated by computer matching, usually by address.

- *External match.* Prospective customers can be checked against lists maintained by credit compilers such as TRW, Experian, and local credit bureaus. The Credit Index (formerly Hooper-Holmes) compiles a master "deadbeat" list of people who have failed to meet their commitments to other direct marketers.

- *Zip-code characteristics.* The credit history of previous respondents from the specific postal area or like postal areas, defined in clusters, can be considered a high-risk area or low-risk. This data is sometimes tempered by the media source, meaning that the credit experience of certain publications is permitted to over-ride the negative credit experience of the zip code.

- *Individual indicators.* Substantial credit differences can result from the types of information provided in the coupon. Although a full credit application—inquiring about employment and banking histories—might be theoretically desirable, it would depress the response rate severely. Bad-pay prospects often can be screened out simply by asking for additional information, such as a phone number or a signature.

A separate question is what to do with customers whose orders are rejected. The orders should be acknowledged in the interest of courtesy if not profitability. I prefer honest replies, advising the customers that their previous history prevents shipping their orders on credit and asking for prepayment, credit card payment, or additional information. In Germany, the order is simply shipped C.O.D. (cash on delivery) instead of on credit.

Installment Sales

Installment sales can often be profitable with a large enough unit sale or where a credit relationship already exists. The most common application of installment sales is a simple three- or four-part billing, usually used with a trial offer. Businesses using installment sales also can require that a deposit be paid or that the order be charged to a credit card, a debit card or a new or existing charge account.

Care should be taken to comply with Regulation Z requirements—a government ruling regarding full disclosure of interest terms. Even if there is no credit interest, but you give a premium or discount for cash, there is a presumption that the installment payments include interest and a disclosure statement is still legally required. I personally negotiated with the Treasury Department for a waiver for magazine offers, but other products may still be subject to this requirement.

Charge and Credit Cards

One of the greatest boosts to the direct marketing industry is the ability to utilize charge and credit cards in direct marketing. In many countries credit-card holders do not represent a majority of the population, but they do represent a significant percentage of consumer spending power. Simply acknowledging the acceptance of bank debit cards—stating the acceptance of credit or debit cards instead of listing the credit card option alone—can widen the coverage even further. See Figure 6-1a—a "straight" mail-order coupon payable by check, money order or credit card.

Obviously cards will be most effective when used with offers that are appropriate in both market and price range. But another important consideration is the response element itself. A credit card offer requires space for number, expiration dates, and the name of the card used. The customer may get frustrated trying to squeeze the 15 digits into a small space. A solution for print-media advertisers is to offer a conventional coupon asking for a check with the order, and then to offer the credit card option only with phone orders, as in *"For credit or debit card orders call 800. . . ."*

Telephone orders have other advantages for all media. They offer an excellent opportunity to "trade up" a send-no-money proposition to a credit-card order. The phone operator is simply scripted to offer a premium for doing so.

COD Sales

Cash-on-delivery (C.O.D.) sales are a form of credit sales only in that the consumer is able to order without enclosing payment in advance. Either

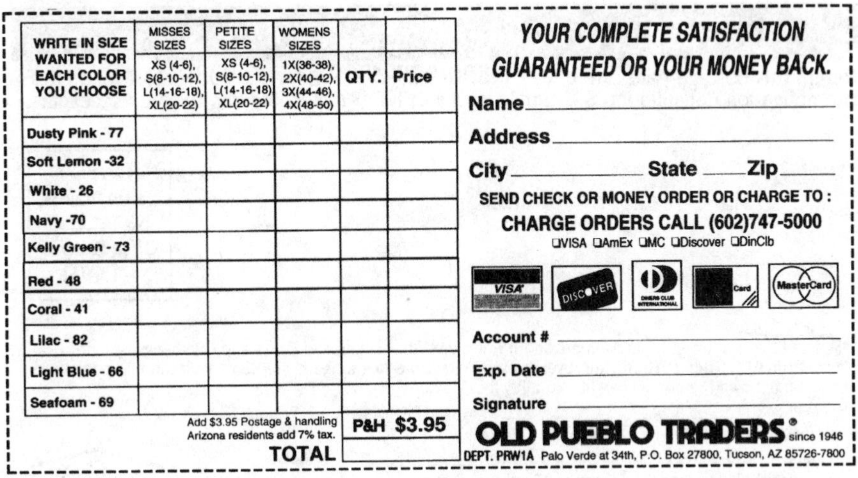

WRITE IN SIZE WANTED FOR EACH COLOR YOU CHOOSE	MISSES SIZES XS (4-6), S(8-10-12), L(14-16-18), XL(20-22)	PETITE SIZES XS (4-6), S(8-10-12), L(14-16-18), XL(20-22)	WOMENS SIZES 1X(36-38), 2X(40-42), 3X(44-46), 4X(48-50)	QTY.	Price
Dusty Pink - 77					
Soft Lemon -32					
White - 26					
Navy -70					
Kelly Green - 73					
Red - 48					
Coral - 41					
Lilac - 82					
Light Blue - 66					
Seafoam - 69					
			Add $3.95 Postage & handling Arizona residents add 7% tax.	P&H	$3.95
			TOTAL		

YOUR COMPLETE SATISFACTION GUARANTEED OR YOUR MONEY BACK.

Name

Address

City State Zip

SEND CHECK OR MONEY ORDER OR CHARGE TO :

CHARGE ORDERS CALL (602)747-5000

☐VISA ☐AmEx ☐MC ☐Discover ☐DinClb

Account #

Exp. Date

Signature

OLD PUEBLO TRADERS® since 1946

DEPT. PRW1A Palo Verde at 34th, P.O. Box 27800, Tucson, AZ 85726-7800

Figure 6-1a. MAIL ORDER. "Payment or credit card."

the U.S. Postal Service or United Parcel Service delivers the package and collects payment with this method. It is one alternative that some marketers use when selling impulse products to people who do not have an appropriate credit card, especially when orders are taken by telephone.

C.O.D. requires extensive and costly paperwork, and refusals tend to be excessive for several reasons. Sometimes the customer doesn't have the cash available when the order is delivered. At other times no one is at home,

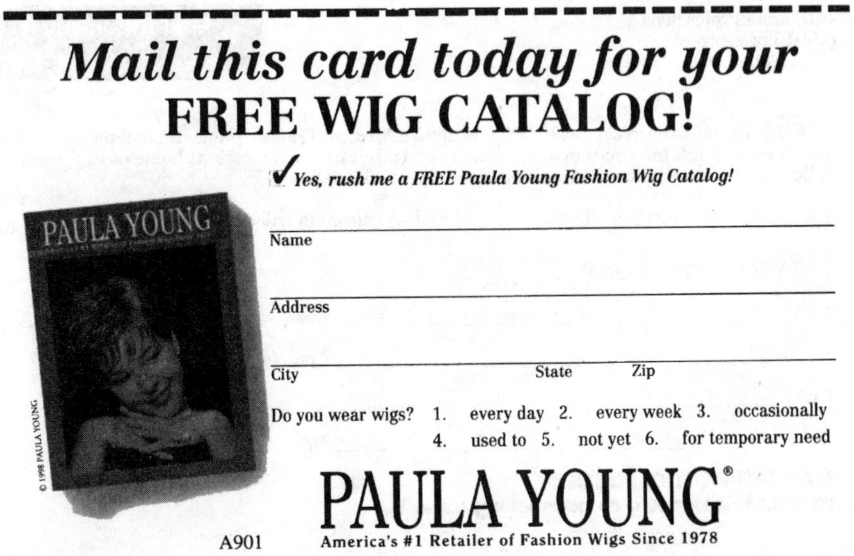

Figure 6-1b. FREE CATALOG "No obligation."

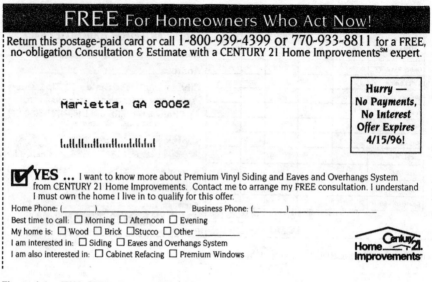

FREE For Homeowners Who Act <u>Now</u>!

Return this postage-paid card or call 1-800-939-4399 or 770-933-8811 for a FREE, no-obligation Consultation & Estimate with a CENTURY 21 Home Improvements℠ expert.

Marietta, GA 30062

lulllllullllllllllllllll

Hurry —
No Payments,
No Interest
Offer Expires
4/15/96!

☑ **YES** ... I want to know more about Premium Vinyl Siding and Eaves and Overhangs System from CENTURY 21 Home Improvements. Contact me to arrange my FREE consultation. I understand I must own the home I live in to qualify for this offer.
Home Phone: (_____)_____ Business Phone: (_____)_____
Best time to call: ☐ Morning ☐ Afternoon ☐ Evening
My home is: ☐ Wood ☐ Brick ☐ Stucco ☐ Other _____
I am interested in: ☐ Siding ☐ Eaves and Overhangs System
I am also interested in: ☐ Cabinet Refacing ☐ Premium Windows

Home Improvements Century 21

Figure 6-1c. TWO-STEP "Expert consultation."

At-Home Professions
2001 Lowe Street
Fort Collins, CO 80525

Mail this reply card for free facts

YES! I want to earn up to $30,000 a year as a Medical Transcriptionist. Send me your color brochure and full information about how I can train at home to work at home or in a medical office as a Medical Transcriptionist and earn up to $30,000 a year.

I am under no obligation. There is no cost and no salesman will call.

Dept. SPM49

PLEASE PRINT CLEARLY

Name _____ Age _____

Address _____ Apt. No _____

City _____

State _____ Zip _____

MAIL THIS REPLY CARD TODAY.
It's your first step to a money-making career!

M172

Figure 6-1d. LEAD GENERATION "Send full information."

FREE ISSUE/SAVINGS CERTIFICATE

YES!

☐ **Send my FREE issue of CHILD.** If I like it, I'll receive 12 issues in all for $8.97 – *I save 74%*. If CHILD doesn't meet my expectations, I'll return your bill marked "cancel" and keep my FREE issue without further cost or obligation.

← *Best Buy!*

☐ 24 issues for just $15.94. *Save 77%!*   HEMD9

Name

Address   Apt. No.

City   State   Zip

PLEASE TELL US YOUR CHILD'S AGE: **YOUR CHILD'S DATE OF BIRTH**
1st Child: Month_____ Year_____
2nd Child: Month_____ Year_____

Cover price $2.95. Rates good in U.S. only. Please allow 6 to 8 weeks for delivery of the first issue.

Figure 6-1e. SUBSCRIPTION "Receive 12 issues for. . ."

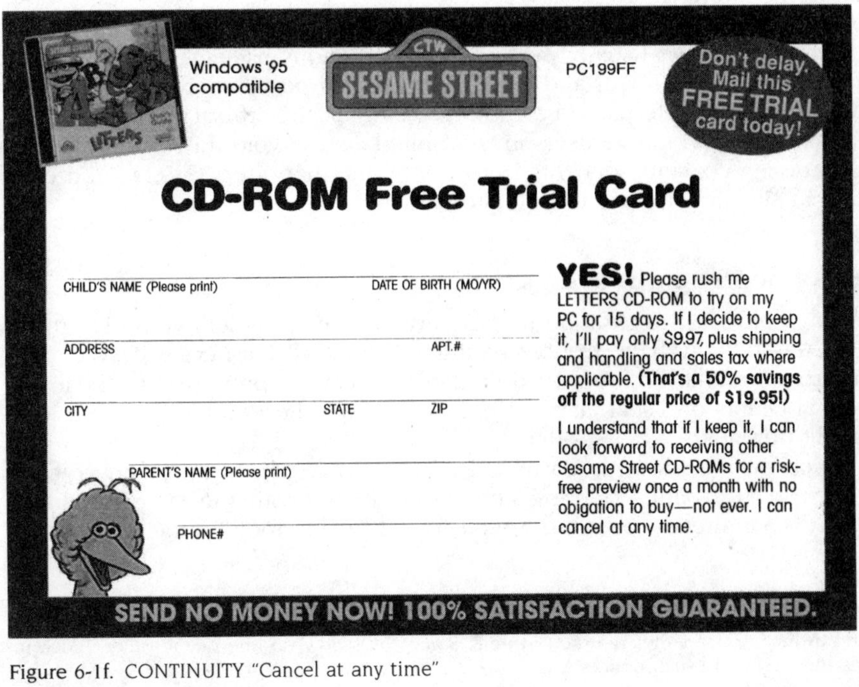

Windows '95 compatible   SESAME STREET   PC199FF   Don't delay. Mail this FREE TRIAL card today!

CD-ROM Free Trial Card

CHILD'S NAME (Please print)   DATE OF BIRTH (MO/YR)

ADDRESS   APT.#

CITY   STATE   ZIP

PARENT'S NAME (Please print)

PHONE#

YES! Please rush me LETTERS CD-ROM to try on my PC for 15 days. If I decide to keep it, I'll pay only $9.97, plus shipping and handling and sales tax where applicable. **(That's a 50% savings off the regular price of $19.95!)**

I understand that if I keep it, I can look forward to receiving other Sesame Street CD-ROMs for a risk-free preview once a month with no obigation to buy—not ever. I can cancel at any time.

SEND NO MONEY NOW! 100% SATISFACTION GUARANTEED.

Figure 6-1f. CONTINUITY "Cancel at any time"

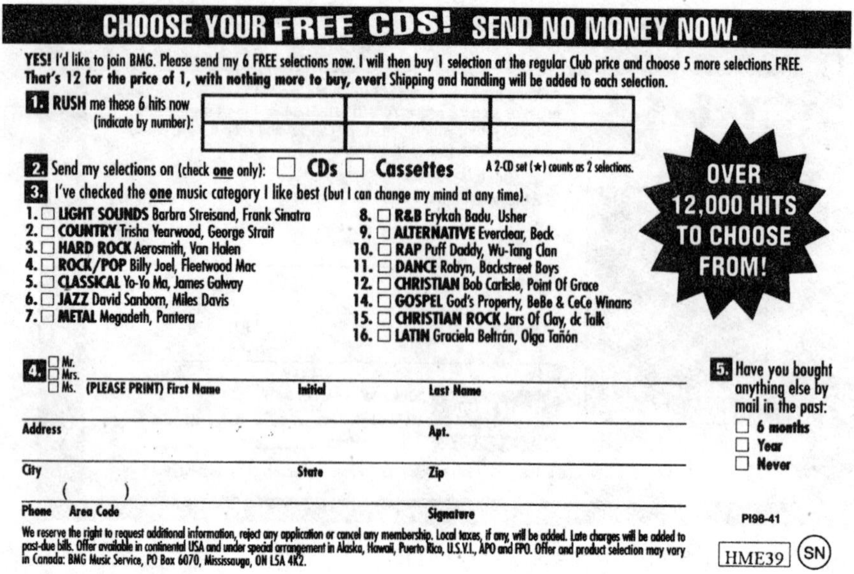

Figure 6-1g. CLUB Negative option/Commitment*

and it is too much trouble to arrange redelivery or to pick the package up at the post office.

Often the impulse to buy has simply cooled off, particularly as the C.O.D. collection process usually presents an anonymous package with a request for immediate payment and unexpectedly high postal charges. Even when all C.O.D. costs are passed on to the customer, the refusal rate generally is so high that most advertisers in the United States avoid this technique. Out of a dozen consulting clients I have only one that offers C.O.D., and even in that situation we are testing alternatives.

Easy or Pre-approved Credit

An age-old retail technique that is very effective for demographic groups that traditionally have trouble getting credit at all is offering easy or pre-approved credit. Pre-approved credit offers can be presented to those potential clients on lists that have been computer-checked by TRW and local credit bureaus.

Such mailings have been used by banks for years. In fact, they've been over-used by banks offering checkbook loans, with the cliché opening, "You have already been approved for $2000 in credit." One opportunity

---

*Many "clubs" still require a commitment to buy more AND permission to ship a selection if an advance notice is not returned in time. Some clubs now do one or the other. BMG, for instance, sends 19 such notices a year.

area not yet exploited is the offer of pre-approved credit to prospective mail-order buyers of jewelry, collectibles, or similar high-ticket items.

Low Down-Payment

If you're offering credit or installment sales, a low down-payment can be as important as a low price, particularly if it reflects an advantage to the consumer. One correspondence school lowered the down-payments at three different points in the conversion series to add news value to its series of enrollment mailings.

Low Interest

As an alternative to a price reduction, a dramatically low interest rate can get attention and stimulate sales. If you are competing with department stores that carry their accounts at 12 or 18 percent interest, an offer of an installment item at 6 percent might have greater appeal than an equivalent price reduction.

GUARANTEES

A guarantee of some sort is not an option in direct marketing. It is a necessity. We are asking consumers to trust us by placing orders and sometimes sending payment for items they have never actually seen. It is necessary to return that trust by standing behind the product and services we offer with the most liberal return or refund policies possible.

I believe it is not at all coincidental that the companies with the most generous policies seem to be consistently among the most successful.

Norm Thompson, a very professional catalog house featuring classic casual wear, makes this guarantee:

"YOU BE THE JUDGE™"

When we say "You Be the Judge™," we mean just that! Every product you purchase from Norm Thompson must live up to your expectations, not ours. If at any time a product fails to satisfy you, return it to us, postage prepaid, and we'll either replace the item, or refund your money in full, whichever you wish.

This is definitely not a 2-week guarantee. It's good for the normal life of the product. (You being the judge of what that normal life should be.) We'll stand behind everything we sell to the fullest extent . . . no ifs, ands, or buts.

Sears Roebuck & Company puts the same idea in more succinct language with this guarantee statement that they credit as a major contributor to Sears success:

SATISFACTION GUARANTEED OR YOUR MONEY BACK.

Unconditional Guarantee. The two statements quoted above are examples of unconditional guarantees. While a small minority of customers may abuse such a guarantee by returning obviously used and abused merchandise or by falsely claiming dissatisfaction, the guarantor is usually more than compensated by the goodwill and added sales from the majority of its customers.

Conditional Guarantee. If you must limit your guarantee, the law requires that you label limitations precisely. Some types of guarantees are:

- *Time limit.* This is the most common type of guarantee. The time limit is stated in a sentence such as "If not satisfied, return within 10 days for full refund."

- *Repair or replacement only.* This form of guarantee includes an assurance that the item will work, rather than that the customer will be satisfied with it.

- *Liability limit.* In situations where a customer might claim secondary damages, the guarantee takes the form of a limit on liability. For example, "Liability limited to replacement of film," as used by a film processing company.

- *Usage condition.* For some products the guarantee may be written in a form such as "When used according to instructions" or "Providing it has not been dropped or abused." This is used often for fragile items.

Double Guarantee. While most financial officers will welcome this idea like an attack of eczema, its "lift" power is so substantial it merits its consideration with most products offered to civilized audiences. "Double your money back" will be abused, but by so few people that you still come out ahead. Like any other offer, it must be tested first.

Competitive Guarantee. If you believe your product is as good as any competitor's try this: Offer to send them your competitor's product as a replacement, or free, if they don't like yours. One variation of this was tried by *Newsweek*: "Try *Newsweek* for 3 weeks without cost. If you don't like it, we'll ask *Time* to send you their best offer."

Dramatized Guarantee. You don't have to offer to eat your hat or roll a peanut down the street with your nose if your customer isn't satisfied, but it is a good idea to find a way to dramatize your guarantee. For example, "Bring this coupon to our store; if our prices are not the best in town, we'll pay for the gas you used to drive here."

"Keeper" Offer. When you're offering a premium, you can dramatize confidence in your product by telling buyers they can keep the premium, even if they elect to return the purchase.

Trial Subscription.   If your product is sold serially, as magazine subscriptions and continuity programs are, you can give buyers the right to cancel either "at any time" or after examining the first shipment.

Value Protection Guarantee.   Some organizations selling collectibles or investments have advertised a willingness to buy back the item in the future if it has lost value or has not achieved a specific gain in value. Such offers should be made only by large, well-financed companies that can deliver on the claim. Anyone recklessly making this kind of guarantee may run into a personal charge of mail fraud. The "limited-liability" protection of a corporation won't help anyone charged with fraud.

CONTINUITY PROGRAMS

The most successful mail-order propositions generally involve the establishment of a customer relationship that extends beyond the initial transaction. Continuity is one of the most critical, and unfortunately most neglected, aspects of the direct-marketing profitability equation.

A retailer can establish good customer relationships by providing the service, quality, and environment to support the simple invitation *"Come again."* A catalog marketer accomplishes repeat sales in the same manner, except that the company image is created by the catalog and service.

Many direct-marketing propositions offer either a series of products such as books, videos, or skin-care items, or a product that is segmented or serialized to facilitate continuity programs. Anyone promoting via direct marketing should look for ways to combine, break apart, or add to existing products in order to make some type of continuity offer possible. Examples include a vacuum cleaner company that sells replacement bags, a publisher of a computer manual that offers an update newsletter, and a reference service that sells quarterly or annual updates. See Figure 6-1f.

Subscription

The word *subscription* is most frequently associated with magazines. This form of publishing is not only the most common user of this proposition, but also one of the most sophisticated. The technique can be applied to other products as well.

A magazine is basically an information or entertainment product sold in installments over a period of time. The most common time period is a year, but most publications are willing to discount rates for longer subscriptions—two, three, or more years.

Shorter subscriptions often are used as introductory offers, to make a trial inexpensive for a new customer. One innovation is the variable-term introductory subscription, which permits a new subscriber to choose any number of copies at a low price per copy.

Subscription selling is probably the longest customer relationship in direct marketing. As a general rule, 50 to 60 percent of first-year subscribers will renew for a second term; 70 to 90 percent of renewed subscribers will then renew again for subsequent terms—on to infinity. This renewal rate is partly influenced by the professionalism of the renewal series, but obviously depends to a much greater extent on the reader's satisfaction with the magazine's editorial content.

The defining characteristics of subscription sales are that the term is fixed and the service is billable at its inception. Subscription propositions are sometimes offered to the consumer as "item-a-month" or "pay-as-you-go" plans, where the total price is committed but payable in monthly installments. The same technique can be applied to a library of books, a set of collectibles, or collections of linens or tableware. See Figure 6-1e.

Automatic Shipment Plans

Unlike subscription selling, the automatic shipment plan seeks not one large sales transaction but a series of individual ones. The customer is asked to participate in a sales plan that provides for the sale of individual units at a predetermined interval—a month, or six weeks, or sometimes annually. The most famous examples are the various libraries or sets of books offered by Time-Life Books, Grolier, Meredith, Harlequin, and other major publishers.

In this type of continuity plan the customer agrees to buy a unit per interval. It differs from other continuity plans in that the customer only has the option to accept the purchase or quit the program. The units could be books in an encyclopedia set, cosmetic samples, components of a teaching plan for children, parts of a desk set or matched luggage, annual diaries or yearbooks, or items in a collectible series. It could even be a service such as furnace inspection or window cleaning. The possibilities are infinite.

Here is a typical example from a Gevalia® Kaffe ad:

> Yes, I would like to try one pound of Gevalia Kaffe for $10.00, including shipping and handling, and receive with it a hunter green, soft white, or jet black 10-cup Automatic Drip Coffeemaker (retail value $44.95) as a free gift.
>
> Please send Gevalia Kaffe—two 1/2-lb. packages of the type(s) I have indicated. I understand I will continue to receive additional shipments of Gevalia approximately every six weeks, plus a special holiday shipment. I may cancel at any time after receiving my introductory shipment without obligation. The coffeemaker is mine to keep regardless of my decision.

Note that in this case the customer is offered the first shipment of coffee at a substantially reduced price, with return privileges, and may cancel at any time. The free coffee maker is a keeper, a premium that may be retained whether or not the customer decides to continue with the program. Sometimes such coupons provide for accelerated shipments at a later date or the right to "load up" subsequent books once credit is established.

The essential principle is that the customer authorizes automatic shipments and agrees to pay for them or return them. Usually the customer does not have the right to return a single shipment without canceling the program—a pressure to induce acceptance of the entire series.

The psychology of this principle is that inertia—one of the most powerful elements of human psychology—is converted from a negative buying force to a positive one. Customers no longer have to say "yes" to buy the product; instead, they must say "no" to not buy it. This is the underlying psychological principle of all continuity plans.

Club Plans

Though some firms use the word club rather liberally to describe any type of continuity plan and even non-continuity membership plans, the technical usage of the term should be reserved for the negative option concept as originated by the Book-of-the-Month Club.

The defining characteristic of the club concept is its addition of choice to the basic automatic shipment plan. In a conventional club, automatic shipment is not limited to one pre-selected product each interval, but a choice is provided—usually by means of a club bulletin or advance announcement. The club "member" is free to accept a recommended item (often called a "selection of the month"), select an alternative, or choose no item that month.

Your investment is significant—both the advertising expenses and the inducement offered to persuade people to join. To make this investment pay out, two problems must be anticipated.

1. How do you get the members to respond to each announcement bulletin?
2. What is to keep members from always declining purchases?

These are very valid concerns, and they have led to some ingenious solutions that now apply to many types of direct marketing propositions.

1. The negative option
2. The positive option
3. The commitment
4. The membership plan

Negative Option

Basically, the negative option refers to the customer's need to say no in order to keep a pre-selected shipment from arriving in the mailbox. It applies to continuity programs in which the definition of *no* can be "Pass this shipment only," "Cancel entirely," or a choice between the two types of refusal. In clubs, the negative applies only to the selection. It provides the leverage to overcome inertia and force a reply. The consequence of not replying within a reasonable time period is that the selection will arrive and have to be paid for or returned. Some writers have successfully presented this feature as a positive benefit, stressing its convenience and its contribution to self-discipline.

The purpose of negative option is emphatically *not* to ship unwanted merchandise, for that is to no one's benefit. It would result only in returns, no-pays, and cancellations. The objective is simply to overcome inertia and force a conscious, considered decision. Usually about 25 percent of club members will take the selection (if it is a desirable one) and another 25 to 50 percent will take an alternate. The figures vary widely from business to business and interval to interval, depending on the attractiveness of the product offered and the soundness of the presentation. Negative option can force a decision, but it can't force a sale.

Note that I used the word *interval* rather than *month* or *year*. The original Book-of-the-Month Club concept has evolved into many book or record clubs that offer 15, 16, or even 18 different announcements per year.

Positive Option

To make this presentation complete, we must touch on the antithesis of negative option. Theoretically, a continuity plan might be constructed wherein the customer is sent pre-shipment announcements, but need not reply. A commitment, discussed below, might apply and so the customer would have to buy something eventually. In principle, such a plan should have a higher initial response because it would attract people who don't want to be bothered with making a decision or sending a notice every month. In principle, the commitment should offset the loss-of-inertia reversal.

Commitment

A commitment is simply an obligation for the customer to buy a minimum number of units or a minimum dollar volume within a limited time period, traditionally a year or two. There have been clubs that tried to eliminate the commitment, just as some have tried to operate without negative option. While it might be possible to dispense with one, there is no way to operate without both. Figure 6-1g, on page 140, combines incentives for joining with negative option, but no commitment.

Why would customers accept the obligation of a commitment? For the same reason that they accept the negative option—an attractive inducement. A back-end obligation such as "I agree to buy as few as four more CDs at regular club prices in the next three years" is the price the customer pays for a front-end reward such as "seven CDs for 1 cent."

Note that the customer is as sensitive to the commitment as to the inducement. Large advertisers continuously test "three books for 98 cents" versus "four books for 10 cents" and similar offers. They also test whether the commitment on a given offer should be one item more or less, and whether the obligation should be fulfilled within one year, two years, an unlimited time period, or once every three months.

Membership Plans

Most continuity plans offer the customer what Capitol Record Club called "Savings in Advance." Membership plans flip this concept around and, incredibly, offer the customer a pay-now, save-later option.

The way these usually work is that members are invited to join a plan, sometimes called a club, which will give them some immediate benefits or the right to future benefits in return for a fee paid at the onset. Because a fee is paid at the beginning, this type of plan is more like a subscription than any other type of continuity plan. There are several basic applications of this scheme, each of them with variations that may or may not be interchangeable.

Discount Buying Service.   The customer is asked to pay a fee in advance. Membership then entitles the customer to buy from a catalog at presumably bargain prices not available to the public. Usually the company counts on the membership fee to cover or at least defray advertising costs. The profit depends on the markup from subsequent sales.

Catalog Subscription.   If a catalog has intrinsic value in itself, it can be the heart of a membership plan. Typically, it is a "magalog," a term coined by Maxwell Sroge Associates that essentially means the blending of magazine editorial content and catalog product offers.

This catalog format often is quite effective, even when mailed conventionally. Not only are the editorial pages a reason to keep the catalog and read it more carefully, but they generate interest in the product or service category, educate the reader, and create desire for the products. It is particularly effective in specialty catalogs dealing with outdoor apparel, hobbies, and technical subjects such as computer software.

A typical variation is to put a price on such a catalog and make it available at that price to anyone, but to send it free to buyers. Some magalogs have even been sold on newsstands.

Customized Service.   Another membership approach is based on providing some type of personal service to the customer in return for the membership fee. The personal service would lead to offers of related products.

One dramatic example was the Sarah Coventry Personal Beauty Plan, which invited the customer to send $25, a photograph, and the answers to a questionnaire. The photograph was enlarged and sent back with a professional face makeover, using real cosmetics on an acetate sheet. The colors recommended were available only in their own line of cosmetics. The application of this method is only helped by modern computer technology, which makes it possible to produce personalized horoscopes, career plans, investment analyses, life expectancy predictions, and diet plans—all as part of related mail-order programs.

An interesting and recent variation of customization (though not part of a continuity program) was advertised by a weight-reduction product called Ultra Slim-Fast. Readers were invited to send in a photograph of themselves and answer some questions about weight-reduction goals. In return they received a computer-generated picture showing their own picture at their desired weight. New technology such as this provides a constant challenge and opportunity to direct marketers developing the propositions of the future.

Most current membership plans have everything built in except some type of automatic shipment element. The real challenge for such companies is to find a way to combine the up-front appeal of their present propositions with the back-end profitability of some of the other continuity plans outlined here.

DATABASE BUILDING

What was once called *two-step marketing* is now generally referred to as *database building*. Database marketing has opened up many new applications of direct marketing, particularly in packaged goods, automotive, appliance and other marketing areas that had not previously used direct marketing. But basically it is the first step of any form of a "two-step proposition." The only difference is that a traditional direct marketer usually has a specific second step in mind, while the database marketer often builds a list as a marketing tool without having tested specific applications.

In my book *Database Marketing: The Ultimate Selling Tool* (McGraw-Hill, 1993), I cover this subject in much more detail. But I also point out the truth that database marketing is rooted in classic mail order. To master the newest forms of this marketing art one should understand its history and have some experience with it.

The previous sections of this chapter have dealt with offers that "ask for the order" for a product or service at the initial contact. Certainly the most qualified name on a mailing list is that of someone who has already made a purchase. But even catalog marketers will run advertisements in media other than direct mail, simply offering the catalog. This type of ad is a two-step list-builder or—to use the modern expression—an example of database building. See Figure 6-1b for an example.

The general objective of database building is to locate new prospects—through leads, inquiries, or sample requests—to be followed up later with a more intensive sales effort than would be affordable on a large-scale basis, since many consumers contacted would be marginal or unqualified prospects. The later follow-up might be through a personal visit by a salesperson, an invitation to a showroom or sales event, a telephone call, or additional direct mail like elaborate conversion packages, a videotape, or a series of selling letters.

This two-step technique is used by many of the largest corporations in the direct-marketing business. Encyclopedia publishers offer a free booklet which is delivered by a salesperson. Insurance companies offer books of maps or gardening guides, also brought by a sales representative.

Financial institutions offer free information or a prospectus, which is then followed by an intensive series of mailings and telephone calls. Real estate developers invite prospects to make an appointment to see model homes; the sales effort begins at the site. Or pipe tobacco may be offered in a 25-

cent trial size to introduce the product, with the hope that the flavor will sell itself.

Free Information.　The simplest and most logical two-step plan is the offer of free information. The pitch can be strengthened by further definition of the information, such as, "Send for free information about the amazing new XYZ device, including pictures, diagrams, detailed operating instructions, and our pay-as-you-go installment purchase plan." See Figure 6-1d.

Free Booklet.　When your advertising is aimed at an earlier horizontal positioning stage, it is often effective to offer a booklet about the generic subject rather than the specific topic. North American Coin & Currency, for instance, offers the "Gold Guide" rather than asking for an investment right off the bat. The guide, of course, sells not only the generic advantages of precious metal investments, but also the particular services offered by its publisher.

Free Planning Kit.　Another way to make offers more attractive is to make up a "kit" of everything the client may need regarding a need. Planning a vacation or diagnosing a lawn problem, for example. I developed a series of meeting and convention planning kits for Marriott Hotels to produce very hard leads instead of the usual contest entries or booklet requests. Offers of these guides would appeal only to sales managers or other executives who were seriously planning a major meeting.

Free Videotape.　With the proliferation of VCRs, videotapes have become one of the most effective ways to respond to a lead or to get one in the first place. Now that videotapes cost little more than a good color brochure, it is an option that should be utilized.

Free Book on Related Subject.　Books that emphasize topics related to the advantages of your product are great marketing tools. Lanier, for instance, offered a copy of a book called *Time Management* along with information about their dictating equipment. The subject set the stage for saving time by dictating, and the book had a perceived value of $300 or so.

Free Gift.　Here's the classic insurance offer again. "Just send us your birthdate and we'll send you a free book of maps"—or a tool kit, gardening guide, or some other popular item. The thinking here is that supposedly everyone is a prospect for insurance, it is not capable of being presold, and all you want is to get the salesperson in any door.

Free Survey.　"Let us survey your telephone costs." "Let us check your roof for leaks." "Let us inspect your car's tires." All of these offer a genuine service that should appeal only to people who feel they have a need for such a survey or service. Hence the leads should be good ones, and the service profitable to offer. See Figure 6-1e.

Free Sample. If your product lends itself to sampling, and if it is really so good that it sells itself, then consider giving it away in small units. Tobacco companies have handed out samples of new cigarette brands. Soap companies have placed samples on doorknob hangers. Why not offer a free sample and send it along with an effective selling message by mail or salesperson?

Free Catalog. Some companies just send their catalogs to every logical mailing list. When the catalog is costly or the lists are marginal, a two-step offer is sometimes preferable. Space advertising is an excellent way to get fresh names for a catalog business, just by offering the catalog. These catalog inquiry names often are better than buyer names from other catalog companies. See Figure 6-1b.

Choice of Booklets. A choice of booklets (or catalogs or samples) is an accurate way of identifying which of several products or services someone is most interested in. I have frequently recommended this device for database building.

Nominal Cost. All the above propositions can not only be offered on a "free" basis, but they can also be sold for a quarter, a dollar, or other "bargain" price. Even the slightest charge qualifies the inquiry and makes it worth following up.

List-Building Offer. Some merchandisers, instead of offering a catalog or other information in their promotions, go right ahead and sell some product that is an example of their line and that represents an unusual value. You'll find clothing merchandisers advertising in *The Wall Street Journal*, for instance. Often these ads don't produce a profit over the cost of goods and advertising, but they do produce a list of qualified buyers for the company's full line of products—a solid list for a lower cost per name than a straight "free catalog" offer.

LEAD SELLING

In a lead selling system, two-step initial transactions are completed by a dealer, agent, or salesperson rather than by the company's own direct mail.

Lead Flow Considerations

In supporting a sales organization, it is often necessary to maintain a steady supply of leads throughout the year for all members of the sales force. This introduces a new consideration into media planning, as it is often necessary to mail or advertise during seasons that might be comparatively unresponsive. It is more important to keep the conversion rate high in most cases than to maximize the cost-per-lead figures.

Often more leads come in from one part of the country than the others. Sometimes they're from the West or rural areas. Other times it may be the Southeast or urban areas. The areas that had a smaller response need supplemental programs. Sometimes regional publications or local compiled lists are used in order to keep the sales force content. At LaSalle Extension University we called this a "local support program."

Too many leads sent to one salesperson will be "burnt off." The salesperson will prejudge the names and pick and choose on a hunch which ones are the easiest to sell. Most of the time these hunches are wrong. But too few leads sent to salespeople will cause them to quit their jobs because they are not making enough money.

There is a chicken-and-egg dilemma in terms of planning for lead selling. Do you plan your lead supply to satisfy your sales force? Or do you allocate your sales territories and dealerships to reflect the lead flow? This is a matter to be resolved between the sales force manager and the direct marketing manager, preferably without bloodshed.

Lead Freshness

One question that everyone agrees on is that leads must be followed up promptly. Every day that passes before a prospect is contacted by a salesperson will noticeably reduce the conversion rate. In some cases I have advised companies to set up systems for computer transmitting or faxing leads to dealers or sales offices to avoid the delay of postal transmission. The advent of the Web and e-mail makes this even easier today.

If a company's computer system takes too much time to get leads processed, it is often advisable to bypass the computer initially and send a manual lead to the sales force. A copy can be sent to the computer department for data entry on a more convenient schedule.

Lead Distribution

Usually a lead is supplied on some type of computer form. The forms should obtain as much information as possible to help the salesperson relate to the prospect. Besides the name, address, title (if a business lead), and phone number, the lead should include the date entered, the company's SIC (Standard Industrial Classifications) code or business classification, and the exact nature of the inquiry. The salesperson should know what ad or mailing piece the prospect responded to and in what publication the ad appeared.

The person who receives the lead should have one copy for filing and another to be transmitted back to the computer center for tabulation. The report form should indicate the date of contact and initial disposition of the potential customer, and all notes should be tabulated into sales reports.

In my opinion, a lead should be supplied with some type of expiration date. Perhaps the lead can be exclusive for a given period and then become nonexclusive, with other dealers or the company's own mail conversion effort cutting in after a deadline. My experience has proved that salespeople will convert more if they have only a limited time to contact the prospect.

The computer should be programmed so that lead distribution is not automatic. Whether you are dealing with salespeople or dealers, the transmission of additional leads should be contingent on the prompt reporting and effective handling of leads previously sent. The computer should automatically cut off lead flow if the open lead ratio is too high or if subsequent confirmation questionnaires indicate that reporting wasn't accurate.

Cutting off lead flow should not be left to the discretion of the sales manager, who should concentrate on getting the sales staff who are lagging behind to shape up or ship out. Unassignable leads should be sent to a dealer or salesperson in an adjoining area or converted by mail order rather than sent to an uncooperative or ineffective salesperson.

Appointment Assignments

Some organizations that sell one product or service directly to the public—vinyl siding contractors, carpet companies, or security system installers—use a more controlled method. Rather than providing their salespersons with leads, they have their own telemarketing department call each prospect, re-qualify them, and schedule appointments.

Large national phone services can do this on a national basis. They keep track of sales performance, days off, routes and schedules. Typically sales representatives are given three or four such appointments. When there are more leads than sales representatives in a given area, the company recruits more sales staff as quickly as possible. Where the reverse occurs, leads are given only to those with the best conversion records.

Lead Reports

Both the local and headquarters sales managers should have reports that indicate exactly how many leads have been distributed, how many are "open" or uncontacted, and how many have been sold. The dollar volume of the sales should be related to the dollar cost of the leads, if possible. Such reports should be cross-tabulated by type of product, type of prospect, salesperson, or dealer. The initial promotion should also be noted with codes indicating which mailing list, what media, and other necessary coding.

The frequency of these reports—whether it's weekly, monthly, or quarterly—depends on the ability of management to find time to read and study the results. I prefer to reduce the frequency of reports and really study them rather than release frequent reports only to have them stacked on a windowsill.

These reports are not historical curiosities. They are blueprints for action. It is essential that the management respond by changing advertisements, schedules, products, or salespeople as necessary.

QUALITY OF LEADS AND INQUIRIES

The quality of leads can be fine-tuned like a stereo set. For instance, as the volume of leads goes up the quality goes down and vice versa. The slightest change in the advertisement or mailing piece can produce significant changes in lead quality. So can changes in the publication, station, web-page link or mailing list used.

We refer to the relative "hardness" and "softness" of leads. A hard lead is super-qualified and ready to buy. A soft lead may be someone requesting a free gift. Usually we operate between the two extremes and adjust the lead flow and quality to meet immediate needs in the marketplace and to satisfy the concerns of the sales organization. Figure 6-1b is an example of a "soft" lead. Figure 6-1e, which asks to arrange a "consultation" is much "harder."

Exactly what kind of leads are needed will vary at times. Sometimes there will be too many that don't pan out into sales. Other times there won't be enough leads to keep the sales staff busy.

Lead Hardeners

If dealers or salespeople complain about the quality of leads, here's how to bring in leads that have been "hardened" through changes in advertisements or mail packages:

- *Mention price.* Indicate what the product will cost.

- *Mention sales call.* Say someone will call.

- *Tell more.* Reveal more information about the product, including any potential negatives.

- *Ask for more information.* Get the telephone number and the best hours to call. If conducting business direct marketing, ask how many employees the company has, as well as other information that might be useful.

- *Charge something.* Even a token amount for a booklet or sample will smoke out the real deadbeats.

- *Require a stamp.* Don't use a business reply card or envelope. Let the prospects buy the stamps—maybe even supply their own envelopes.

- *Narrow the offer.* Make it very relevant to the product or service you are selling.

Lead Softeners

If more leads are needed, here's how you can loosen up the lead quality and obtain more leads from the same promotion expenditures:

- *Tell less.* Leave something to curiosity.

- *Computerize the response coupon.* Fill in the names and addresses of the prospects on the material to be sent back. Give them less to do.

- *Add convenience.* Supply the stamp, the envelope, and maybe even a pencil.

- *Give more.* Add a gift or premium, maybe one that has value independent of the product offered.

- *Charge less.* Make it free, free, free.

- *Ask less.* The fewer questions, the better.

- *Add a prize.* A sweepstakes is the ultimate quality-softener.

Don't forget that the choice of media will also have a material effect on lead quality. The low-cost-per-lead publication or list may be composed of teenagers or others who send for everything. Study the source data and change mailing and media schedules to improve quality. Fine-tuning the media is just as important as fine-tuning the coupon copy.

CONTESTS AND SWEEPSTAKES

One sure way to boost the number of responses is a contest or sweepstakes. A prize of as little as $10,000 has been known to lift response rates between 30 and 50 percent. Larger prizes, selected creatively, have done even better.

If you use a contest, consult a contest management company such as Ventura Associates or D. L. Blair to help you select prizes, set up rules, and administer the contest. The legal restrictions are very exacting, and an independent management and judging organization will be well worth the small cost.

The best way to calculate the value of a sweepstakes is to include the cost of the prizes in the overall budget of the mailer. The larger the mailing, the less significant the sweepstakes cost on a per-mailer basis. For example, a mailing of 10 million pieces with a $100,000 contest costs only an additional $10 per thousand pieces. It needs only a slight lift over a non-sweepstakes package to be profitable.

The problem with sweepstakes is not in initial cost but in the quality of the leads. The added lift of a sweepstakes package represents a large number of people who are forced into a yes-or-no decision on the product offered with the sweepstakes.

Sweepstakes produce a noticeable deterioration in the quality of business produced, not just in the initial acceptance, conversion or payment. The weakness is all the way down the line. Using sweepstakes with magazine offers reduces the customer payment rate, the initial conversion rate, and subsequent renewal rates. The only remedy is to continue to offer more sweepstakes, with current customers as well as future new offers. For managers faced with maintaining sales levels originally set with sweepstakes offers, sweepstakes seem like an addiction.

Lately sweepstakes have been losing their novelty and have needed larger and more interesting prizes in order to remain effective. Some variations have artificially hyped response by concealing the "no" alternative in deliberately confusing formats. This is a form of deception that will cost its user a great deal in back-end performance. Customers won't come back, and suddenly sales and leads will drop in double-digit percentages.

The purpose of a sweepstakes is to gain readership and generate a yes-or-no decision from the prospect on the product offer, usually a trial subscription to a periodical. It is a strategic anomaly of sweepstakes that adding more product information usually depresses response rather than increasing it as might be expected. This oddity is why there are so many sweepstakes offers that feature the contest to the virtual exclusion of the product.

REFERRAL OFFERS

Get-a-friend (GAF) or member-get-member (MGM) propositions are useful for almost any type of product or service. Their effectiveness depends heavily on the genuine satisfaction the original customer derives from the product or service. There is no way to "bribe" a customer into recommending a proposition that has not been pleasing. But if an offer is genuinely good, GAFs are a way of accelerating the word-of-mouth publicity that would ordinarily take place anyway. There are several types of GAFs or MGMs, as discussed below.

Name Requests.   These are simple requests for names and addresses of people who would be interested in the proposition. They can be very fruitful in building a mailing list, particularly if you also request permission to mention the referrer's name in your initial letter. Such requests can be simple printed notices on the back of statements or inexpensive inserts. Most advertisers do not offer an incentive for such names so the leads are not lessened.

Pass-Alongs.   Pass-alongs are simple brochures included in a product shipment that describe the basic proposition along with a request to either mail it or give it to a friend. The order form might include space for the present customer's information so that a thank-you gift can be sent if the pass-along generates an order. Computerized identification codes can also be used to track pass-alongs.

Sales Brochures.   In this case, customers are asked to function practically as sales agents by showing the product to a friend or neighbor and soliciting orders in return for a commission, prize, or merchandise credit. Some companies have used this technique very effectively, creating an unofficial army of part-time salespeople. One of our Brazilian clients, DeMillus Lingerie, pays 25% commission offered in their catalog to anyone.

This approach is most effective when the original customers have reason to feel smart about the purchase and feel they are doing their friends a favor. The sense of passing along a good thing is an essential ingredient—even more critical than the value of the incentive.

I don't know of anyone who has successfully sent out mailings devoted only to MGM offers. In most cases they are financially successful only when they are included as a catalog page or package insert, essentially getting a "free ride" from another form of advertising.

Front-End Referrals. Recent tests for clients at my company have shown surprisingly strong responses to requests for names as part of the front-end prospect mailing. In continuity promotion for a packaged-goods company, we generated two referral names on one-half of the new customers—on average one referral per order. These names, when sent in a mailing mentioning the referrer's name, produced a 20 percent response, a major contributor to the success of the proposition

I would not suggest this for video clubs and other propositions that have generous up-front offers and high credit risk, at least not across the board. In my experience, only customers who have proved that they honor their agreements and pay their bills should be sent this type of referral marketing materials. The theory is that good credit customers produce good credit referrals, and vice versa.

***

The proposition is the heart of any direct-marketing effort. It requires concentrated creativity that is independent of the more glamorous tasks of designing interesting headlines or colorful mail pieces. Many companies unfortunately seem to restrict their outside creative sources to implementing existing offers. Why bring in agencies or consultants to write fresh headlines, when their talent can have a much greater impact creating fresh offers as well?

Offers can be any combination of those outlined here, or others that are created on a company-by-company basis. There is no limit to the new, imaginative offers that can be presented to the public. It is precisely the new offer that will have been created while this book is on press or after it is published that will be the most exciting in the industry. Its very freshness will help it to be effective.

The search for offers requires constant monitoring not only of your competitor's propositions, but also of what's going on in the whole field of direct marketing—in the United States and around the world. It requires your best talent, your most courageous thinking, and your most daring testing.

"BACK-END" MARKETING

The many direct-marketing efforts used to gain first-time customers—as discussed in the previous chapters—are sometimes referred to as *front-end promotions*. The equally vital techniques for making these acquired customers continual buyers of our products services are called *back-end promotions*.

In direct marketing, back-end promotions are particularly vital. Each new customer usually represents a sizable investment in advertising cost. If the customer takes no action after an initial contact and possible purchase, the direct marketer loses some of the advertising investment. Customers don't have to walk out of the store to abrogate this investment. They don't even have to make a negative decision. If they simply do *nothing*, the effect is the same. Our hard-won customers start to fall by the wayside from the very first contact.

Perhaps these prospects simply inquire but don't buy. That's understandable. But what about the customer who orders and decides not to keep our product? Or the one who—worse yet—keeps it and doesn't pay for it? What about the retail customer who tries our product or service once, but never again?

HARNESSING INERTIA

One principle that helps us understand the dynamics of customer behavior at the back end is *inertia*. Merriam-Webster's Collegiate® Dictionary, Tenth

Edition, defines *inertia* as "a property of matter by which it remains at rest or in uniform motion in the same straight line unless acted upon by some external force." Inertia is a characteristic that describes human behavior as well. It can work for you or work against you in the field of direct marketing.

Inertia is your ally if your proposition is a "club" with negative option, or a series of publications or products sold on a "ship-till-forbid" basis. It is your ally in the travel field if your customers have your company's reservation-line number in their pockets or by their phone. It is an ally if you are in banking and the customers have authorized any type of automatic investment or savings—particularly with payments charged to an existing checking or charge account. Inertia works for you in the packaged-goods field if your brand is accepted, respected, and is the first the customer reaches for under normal circumstances. It works in the retail or catalog field if your business is the first place customers go to for certain items. It works on the Internet if your site is book-marked or if you have reason to return to it repeatedly.

There are negative aspects to human inertia as well. In fact, it is one of the most formidable obstacles to be overcome for most marketers. If forces in customers' lives have pushed them away from your product or service, it's hard to get them back.

Imagine this scenario. A customer returns from a hard day's work, greets the family, kicks off his or her shoes, and collapses into a favorite chair to look at the day's mail. There are magazines to read, a letter from an old friend, a bill that demands attention, and an assortment of mail from both local and national advertisers. One of them is yours.

Your letter asks buyers to buy something that they have somehow managed to live without. It asks them to decide which of several models or subscription terms is right, to calculate not only the price but shipping costs and sales tax, to remember sizes, to find a charge card or write out a check—all right at that moment. Or perhaps it asks them to go to their computer, boot up their Internet access, look for your URL, wait for irrelevant pictures to down-load, and then learn more about your offer. Lotsa luck!

Some might say, "If people want my product, they'll go to the trouble to write a letter or deal with a complicated order form." That may be correct in theory or in an ideal universe, but inertia gets in the way. No matter how good your deal, you will lose business because some people will put it off until later, and then just never get around to it. In direct marketing, "later" means "never."

Overcoming Procrastination

All this brings us to another important principle that should be kept in mind when planning back-end promotions: *procrastination*. As more fully discussed in Chapter 9—Creative Tactics, the need for immediacy or urgency applies just as much to the back end—but with greater opportunities for effective application. Expiration dates, limited supply, impending price increases and special introductory offers all have greater credibility with a previous customer than with a front-end prospect.

EFFECT ON ALLOWABLE MARGIN

Chapter 8—Marketing Math explains the concept of *allowable margin*: the portion of the selling price available for a combination of advertising (new-customer acquisition cost) and for contribution to advertising and overhead. The importance of back-end improvement becomes obvious after one has determined the lifetime value of a prospect name added to a marketing database .

Chapter 8 direct-marketing math explains the concept of *allowable margin*: the portion of the selling price available for a combination of advertising (new-customer acquisition cost) and for contribution to advertising and overhead. The importance of back-end improvement becomes obvious after one has determined the lifetime value of a prospect name added to a marketing database.

Let's postulate a product with a $100 sales price and a $40 allowable margin (after product cost and other expenses). The advertising cost per order is $30, so we make $10 or 10 percent on the initial sale.

Now let's add the simplest type of back-end promotion—a "bounce back" accessory offer shipped with the product. There's no postage, no list costs, and a $250/M brochure. Response rates on present customers are very high, so we can plan for 25%. At this rate, the CPR is only $10. If the accessory is a $50 item with a $30 allowable, our profit per order is $20 each. As one out of four of the original customers ordered the accessory, we have an added $5 profit per average customer—a 50% increase! Now offer another accessory in the mail, and then another one through telemarketing, and the original $10 continues to multiply.

It is the profitability of "back end" promotions that make it possible for a retailer to send catalogs to outside lists though they lose money on every new customer, or for magazines to sell new subscriptions at half their regular rate.

It is imperative that all direct marketers—at least the marginal ones—understand these back-end concepts. One reason is that there are business propositions that appear to be patently unprofitable, unless you understand the dynamics of the back end. There are magazines that lose money or, at best, break even on the first-year subscription customers. But the magazines make up for it with advertising or renewals. One company I am familiar with sold incredibly low-priced maps or books—prices so low there was no way to make a profit from these sales. But the company's real aim was to amass sizable lists for promoting their other products and for renting to other direct mail users.

The most recent example of back-end promotions is the Internet. Many successful Internet companies give away services and software to customers—things like free computer games, free software, free e-mail, free mapping and addressing services, free language-translation services. The list goes on. The expenditures on these promotions are expected to eventually be offset by the revenue from other sources like advertising, Internet-service provider fees and e-commerce transactions.

The balance of this chapter will be devoted to describing a score of possible back-end promotions. Almost all of them are adaptable—at least in theory—to virtually every type of product or service.

Re-Selling Efforts

Every field has some type of what I call the "re-sell." The retail clerk tells the customer, "That looks wonderful on you!" The packaged goods company prints a re-sell message on the box or label. The restaurant reprints a good review in their menu—a way of saying, "You've made a good choice in coming here." Direct marketing is no different.

In its simplest form, the re-sell effort can simply be a restatement of the basic appeals that motivated the customer to purchase from the original advertisement, commercial, or mailing piece. The less the purchase is considered, the greater the need to re-sell at the point of delivery.

For example, one company advertised a revolutionary way to rid one's backyard of mosquitoes and other insects without electrical grids and the noisy sound of bugs being zapped all night long. This sounded appealing. I ordered one with great anticipation for a bug-free summer. It arrived with no re-sell material to remind me of my expectation, only with operating instructions. It turned our the item was basically an electric fan that was supposed to suck in insects which happened to fly by and dropped them in a tray of water—to drown.

The original appeal had presented the idea of relaxing in a hammock without annoying insects—a concept that greatly appealed and succeeded in getting me to order the product. But at this equally critical point in the selling process—the initial opening of the package—the focus was now on the operational instructions, with no reminder of the initial pitch. Instead the material focused on how to empty the water tray that would be filled with assorted bug carcasses, and how to scrape off the bugs that stuck to the bottom. Ugh! Of course, it went back.

A re-sell insert is an essential continuation of the selling process. It should remind the customer of the ultimate benefit, of why he or she ordered it in the first place. It should restate guarantees, and urge the customer to try the product for a reasonable amount of time before deciding. It might use a kind of peer pressure—testimonials from others that have ordered the same item and were delighted. A few positive words from other satisfied customers certainly help to delay a possible decision to return a purchase.

If an item requires complicated assembly or operating instructions, care should be taken to make the use of the item as easy as possible, even at the expense of rewriting the instructions completely or using extra paper and graphics.

If an item was sold as a prestige-giving asset, perhaps with some type of club membership or air of exclusivity, this should be carefully restated and consistently presented. Symbols such as "membership cards" may be silly to some people, but others treasure them.

Re-sell involves considering the entire first impression—not just when the customer is first presented the product in an advertisement, but also when the product is received. Book club members in a research panel I attended compared opening a mail order shipment to opening a Christmas present. When the package is presented exactly how they expected it from the advertisement—or even enhanced in some way—the customer will be pleased. If it's not, our once-happy customer may not see the benefit of the product but only the box it came in. Opening a package is an event. Make it a happy one.

The imagery that was involved in motivating the original purchase should be carried through consistently in every part of the selling process, and in every stage. The shipping package, the wrapping, the bills or shipping documents should all be presented as if they were an advertising representation of the product. They should conform to the original theme that captured the customers' attention in the first place. It is amazing how often a well-presented product advertised in a sophisticated magazine is sent in a battered manila shipping envelope with tacky, uncoordinated inserts.

If you must generate additional income by accepting package-insert enclosures from other companies, then at least be fussy and accept only the ones that have offers and appearances that enhance your own product. Bargain offers of pantyhose—no matter how meritorious in their own right—simply have no place in the initial shipment of a Zubin Mehta recording to a new member of the classical division of a mail-order music service.

TRADE-UP PROMOTION

"Here's the shirt you asked for, sir," says the clerk in the haberdashery store. "Let me show you a beautiful tie that will go perfectly with it."

"As long as you're buying such a fine car," the automobile saleswoman says, "I'm sure you'll want the premium radio with surround stereo and CD player."

Trade-ups have long been accepted in retailing and in early mail order. It is an opportunity often ignored by today's newer applications—particularly in database and Internet marketing. Yet they represent one of the easiest profit potentials for most propositions.

The front-end application is simple. "Check this box and we'll send you the deluxe edition for only $5 more." The deluxe edition might mean a better binding, an extra section, or stamped initials—features that are inexpensive to produce, but add value to the product.

The back-end application of a trade-up isn't as simple to present. It often means devising accessories, companion pieces, or refills of some kind. Encyclopedias offer yearbook subscriptions. Some products come in large economy sizes. Service companies offer an extra premium for a longer term. Direct-marketing offers on products sold at retail stores do double-duty. In addition to the immediate income, they also produce the customer's name and address, thus enabling promotions through the mail or e-mail.

Perhaps one of the most innovative examples of a trade-up offer is the way sophisticated magazine advertisers are using direct-response television combined with inbound telephone. The two-minute television ad offers an introductory subscription at half the newsstand price: "One year for only $12." The customer calls an 800 number and the telephone operator takes the necessary information including name and address. Then comes the trade-up offer. "Instead of the one-year offer, ma'am, I can enter your subscription for two years for $20—a savings of 58 percent off the newsstand price."

For $5 collectible-coin advertisers, I suggested offering a silver version for $50 for interested customers who called in. More than 10 percent accepted the trade-up, the equivalent of ten unit sales of the original coin. The 10 percent customer conversion doubled the total dollar volume. This one trade-up idea made several propositions successful which otherwise might have been discontinued.

In magazine circulation promotion, this technique sometimes is called *renewal at birth*. The trade-up effort can be an elaborate mailer or bill insert, or something as simple as a line on the invoice that says "Check here for greater savings."

There are trade-up applications for virtually every product or service, and because they cost very little in terms of advertising since they usually enjoy a "free ride" with an invoice or shipment, they are as close as one ever gets in this business to "a sure thing."

COLLECTION LETTERS

When you are selling on credit, sometimes the sale is the easiest part of the marketing problem. Collection efforts, like in any kind of direct mail, can vary greatly in effectiveness. Three key factors are *convention, progression,* and *immediacy.*

Convention

The mainstay of any collection effort is, of course, the invoice. It should look like an invoice and be worded like an invoice—not like a colorful promotion piece. The most effective bill is a computer-printed invoice, complete with account numbers, computer codes, the exact amount to be paid, and a due date.

An initial invoice can include some gentle references to memberships in national credit bureaus, or a reminder that promptness counts when building a credit reputation. In my opinion it should always include an addressed reply envelope, though not necessarily one with postage paid by the addressee.

Convention is the governing force here, as in any kind of direct-mail layout. People expect a bill to look a certain way. If it looks like a bill, reads like a bill, it will be treated like a bill. Do not try to do more with this part. This is not the place to confuse your customer with sweepstakes and added promotions.

However, even a simple bill should maintain the imagery selected for the initial promotion. It should be well-designed graphically and typographically, in a manner consistent with the company image.

Progression

Subsequent bills traditionally take on added urgency. Some methods of inducing payment include a gentle "Please pay" in handwriting, or a "Past due" in a rubber-stamped impression. These will always have a place in any series of collection letters. A friendly note with a message like "Have you overlooked our invoice?" or "Is there anything wrong?" is always appropriate as well.

Flattery can get you somewhere in collection letters during the initial progression stage. "We appreciate your good payment record with us and we're sure this late payment must be an oversight," is a nice way to induce customers to pay.

The threatening approach has become over-used in the second stage of the progression of collection letters. Typically such letters range from "Before I turn this account over to our collection manager. . . " to letters from collection agencies or lawyers that start with "Please be advised that. . . ."

I prefer a more sincere approach, things like handwritten letters, perfumed notes, or a touch of humor. Most severe collection approaches are no longer legal or particularly effective. A really heavy threat usually won't bring in enough money at that late stage to be worth the bad will that the letter creates. Let the outside collection agencies or lawyers do the threatening. When all else has failed, you may as well turn the account over to collection specialists and let them do their thing in their way—which is much more powerful than the roughest letter any direct-mail company would want to send out.

Immediacy

The urgency principle applies in collection letters as in any other kind of promotion. Letters can have the deadline theme, as in "Last chance to renew without interrupting your subscription," "Last chance to reinstate your subscription," or "Last chance to pay and maintain your present excellent credit rating with us."

Billing letters are designed to collect money as their primary purpose, of course. But the main objective is to collect the money without endangering the basic customer relationship.

Notations such as "If you have already paid this invoice, please disregard this request" may reduce the level of frustration from the bill recipient somewhat, but customers still get very annoyed if they receive bills for accounts that already have been paid. Many companies wait a full month after the first bill to give customers a chance to make payments before getting the next bill. In this way the prompt payers—the largest and most valuable group of customers—are spared the annoyance of getting the second bill at all.

CONVERSION EFFORTS

How do you turn an inquiry into a sale? A trial subscription into a full-term one? An unused credit card or charge account into an active customer? A catalog request into a catalog sale? A simple kit buyer into a steady customer? An occasional customer into an active member of your marketing database? The answer: every way you can.

Conversion is the payoff effort to every type of two-step promotion. The first response, sometimes called the *acknowledgment package,* is traditionally an all-out effort to make every point you have to—in every way possible—to make the sale now or never. This is where the blue-chip brochures, broadsides, samples, letters, and testimonial flyers come in and usually pay off. This is the opening curtain, the background, the plot, the grand climax, and the finale all rolled into one.

Your prospects asked for this package, in one way or another. They sent the card, made the phone call, sent an e-mail or clicked "Yes" on your website. They have identified themselves as prospects. They are almost sure to open the package and at least look through it. You have their names, addresses, and other information that makes it possible to highly personalize the communication you send them. With a high-order ratio expected, you can afford to do it right. This is no time to hold back.

Assuming that you have pulled out all the stops, your marketing problem here is not just to overcome buyer concerns but to deal with your real obstacle: *procrastination.*

The recipients who don't want your product or service because of the cost or other reasons aren't going to be persuaded to buy something they don't really want, no matter what you do. The pre-sold prospect will buy it whether you send a bundle of mimeographed pages or an elaborate sales package. The real target is the person in the middle. The key to successfully marketing products is to capture the prospect who needs your product but can live without it, who would like to have it someday but has more pressing needs, who definitely wants to buy it but who has put the order form in a huge "to do" pile and who might fill it out and mail it "someday."

For this prospect, you need "the works"—facts, proof, guarantees. More importantly, you have to overcome inertia. The key to making the conversion effort work is to provide effective motivations for acting now rather than later. Some examples:

■ A packaged-goods advertiser offers a unique gift for purchasing several packages of their product by a certain date—enough for the customer to get used to the flavor and buy it out of habit.

- A shoe company offers a free wallet "this month only" for first-time orders from its catalog or for those who bring in coupons from the Sunday newspaper.

- A photo processor includes a coupon good for a 50-cent credit or a free enlargement on the next order, if the coupon is received by a certain date.

- A car rental company offers a free roadmap book the first time its newly issued credit card actually is used by the customer, as long as it is before an expiration date.

- Political and philanthropic fund-raisers provide a moral incentive to act now. Their best appeals are for things like funds to finance a special effort in a key state; or to get a tractor to a needy village in time for harvest; or to feed a particular hungry child whose name, background, and photograph are enclosed.

- In one of the highest-unit sales efforts around, a precut home fabricator offers pre-season specials. The offer is different each season—price discounts during one, free insulation during another, and bonus garages during a third. All of this is for acting now, *this season*, rather than the next.

If the acknowledgment package is too heavy to go by first-class mail, a fast and simple letter is usually in order, thanking the customer and promising the requested information. This is sometimes called a *keep-warm letter*.

However, even with every possible device in the initial acknowledgment package, only 40 to 60 percent of the potential business will be derived from the order form it contains. The rest come later, if a direct marketing company is doing its job. The initial package should be just the beginning of a series of follow-up communications designed to remind and re-sell the customer.

The main purpose of these mailings is to re-stress urgency and to make an order form available at the time when the prospect finally is ready to follow through on the original inquiry. Wouldn't it be easier if you knew when the customer would be ready? Sure, but there is no way to anticipate that moment. That moment can depend on the customer's personal finances, biorhythm, astrology, or simply on a change of mood.

Follow-ups can take many forms, but all should be aimed at combating inertia. They can include carbons of the original letter, reminders of special-offer expiration dates, and announcements of new special offers with new deadlines. To make each mailing look different, they should stress different points. One may have a testimonial emphasis, another may dramatize the guarantee, and still another may be a sincere letter from a company officer.

How many efforts should a conversion series include? As many as you need to do the job. As long as the allowable margin continues to exceed the order cost, try another mailing. You can always cut back if the last one doesn't pay. Usually my clients end up with between six and eight mailings in this type of series. Some companies that have large lists and sophisticated analysis methods have refined follow-up communication to the point of varying the eventual number of follow-ups according to the potential customer or list source. High-quality leads from business magazines or particularly relevant websites or mailing lists will justify more efforts than those from less desirable sources.

When I was marketing director of LaSalle Extension University, the number of mailings in my conversion series varied according to the course being sold, but were never less than a half-dozen efforts. Our best approach was to gradually make it easier to enroll, with lower initial payments or shorter commitments with each effort, but never lowering the overall tuition.

Table 7-1 shows a typical conversion mailing series—a composite of several successful ones. It's a good starting point for your own experimentation with conversion techniques.

If the value of the order is high enough, this series may be supplemented by telephone calls that follow up the key points in the letters and make the same offers. "Did you get our letter?" "Do you have any questions? These service-oriented calls can be very effective if they are done well. However, care should be taken so that resentment about the telephone intrusion doesn't hurt overall response. Phone selling will show a quick lift in directly attributed sales, but it could depress the overall return depending on the script, the skill of the caller, and the sensitivity level of the customers.

These follow-ups can be sent by e-mail or fax, but only if the customer indicates they prefer such communications. Filling in a fax number on an order form doesn't mean they want your faxes.

What happens after letter Number 10? Do you write the name off and dispatch it to direct-marketing limbo? No, just move it into a general file of previous inquiries to be solicited all over again, once or twice a year. House

TABLE 7-1
TYPICAL CONVERSION MAILING SERIES

	Effort	Theme	Offer
1.	On receipt: first-class mail	Thanks: information on way	None (This is a keep-warm letter.)
2.	On receipt: bulk mail	Basic acknowledgment	Premium for fast action by date
3.	Two weeks	Carbon copy	Premium reminder
4.	Four weeks	Testimonial	Premium expiration
5.	Eight weeks	Letter from president	Premium extension
6.	Twelve weeks	Guarantee	Easy payment or low down payment
7.	Sixteen weeks	New premium announced	New premium
8.	Twenty weeks	Benefit theme	New premium reminder
9.	Twenty-four weeks	Questionnaire (Include referral request.)	Premium expiration
10.	Thirty weeks	Last chance	Prices not guaranteed later

lists that include former customers, inactive members, and subscription expires always become the most effective and profitable mailing list for subsequent promotions. This is without exception. Each name goes full-circle and becomes ready for the whole gamut of front-end approaches.

RENEWAL SERIES

Whether you have a home repair service, a term insurance policy, a membership of some sort, or a periodical subscription, renewals are the key to profitability.

For magazine subscriptions—one of the most demanding of all direct-marketing fields—the first attempt to convert a trial offer to a full-rate subscription is called a *conversion* because the introductory offer is customarily at a lower price than the ongoing renewal rate. Perhaps 50 percent of initial subscribers "convert," and 80 percent of those who have already converted "renew."

The same type of ratio applies to any renewal effort. Because the expected response rate is so high, it is once again economically feasible to devote a great deal of effort to this process. As in conversion or collection efforts, it is not uncommon to use a six- or eight-letter series over a period of months.

The most effective opening renewal notice is the simplest. Many publishers today use a "turnaround document," a simple notice and card designed to be mailed back to the publisher. To be consistent with the convention theory discussed in Chapter 11 on layout, I prefer that such cards be as official looking as possible.

One technique is to avoid asking customers for yes-or-no decisions. Instead, ask them how many years of renewal or how many refills they want, or whether they want the plain or deluxe edition this year, or if they would prefer the product in blue or red. This technique is based on one of the earliest examples of sales psychology used by Coca-Cola. The company advised restaurants to ask whether a customer wants "a large or small Coke" rather than "Do you want something to drink?" It is now accepted practice to invite a current member or subscriber to choose the "large or small" renewal without featuring "none." After all, the customer can express the negative choice by not responding at all.

Many companies combine renewal and billing efforts by asking for renewal only when they ask for payment, at least in the first few mailings. Then they offer the "Bill-me-later" alternative later in the series of mailings. Whether to try this option and when to separate the billing and renewal options are details that differ from one company to the next and should be tested, analyzed, and modeled financially.

A typical series begins about four months before the expiration of the series, unless the subscription was so short that only a few months have gone by since the first issue was received. After the first renewal effort, skip a cycle—that is, wait two months instead of one—before sending out the next effort. Many renewals are received on the first effort, some sooner than others, and you want time to get the responses before sending out the next mailing. Perhaps 25 percent of the total response will come in from that first mailing. Sending the second bill later will save the cost of answering letters from people telling you that they have already paid or renewed, as well as saving the company the cost of postage from those unnecessary second bills.

The subsequent renewal efforts can then get a bit more urgent, with specific references to forthcoming expiration dates, missed issues, or possible reinstatement. It is sometimes advisable toward the end of the series to re-sell the benefits of the product all over again. Use sincere appeals, questionnaires, or other dramatization of the basic selling themes to gain the customers' attention.

As with conversion efforts, the length of the series may vary according to the source. Analysis can determine how many letters are justified for different groups of members or subscribers.

Some interesting experiments have been conducted with early-response incentives. The classic renewal series might offer a full-price renewal at the beginning of the mailing series and switch to a special introductory offer when the name gets placed in the expired file. Some companies have tried the reverse. A special incentive is offered for early renewal, justified by "saving us the trouble and expense of sending more notices." The approach is a very creative one, though few publishers have used it. I suspect that the cost of sending the incentive to all subscribers (even those most eager to renew) might not be justified by the added renewals. Also, the added renewals at the beginning of the series may simply be accelerated responses that are offset by a lower response rate later on.

For example, a premium or discount may cost $1 and result in a 10 percent increase in response. The effective premium cost of the increased response isn't just $1, it's $11. That's because the same premium has to be given to the original ten customers who would have responded anyway, as well as to the one additional customer that represents the 10 percent response increase.

It is a shame that renewal efforts, like billing and conversion efforts, are not given more attention. Some companies use professional creative sources for their front-end material but feel that the back-end letters are so simple they can handle it themselves. Yet the truth is that such back-end efforts demand the same care and expertise as any other part of the promotion. In fact, the net effect on profitability is usually greater than can be achieved by increasing front-end response.

One additional approach to renewals is to build the renewal process into the proposition. There are three ways that might apply, in principle, to other businesses as well.

One is the book club bonus-books system, in which the membership continues after satisfaction of the initial commitment. An offer such as "One book free for every two you buy" is sometimes dramatized with bonus coupons.

The second is the automatic shipment authorization, in which the publisher of an annual—say an encyclopedia yearbook—has built into the original agreement an authorization to ship and bill the product each year. Usually the customer is granted the option of returning the book without further obligation or shipments.

The third is the automatic renewal technique, where the original offer guarantees "the lowest rate available" for future renewals, and builds in the order for renewal. The only problem then is billing. One major advertiser has used such an offer without a material decrease in initial response. This advertiser later found that the automatic renewals held up, but that excess returns and complaint correspondence made the revised offer unprofitable.

The same general principles apply to non-mail-order applications, such as packaged-goods database programs. For example, new customers of a product for infants were given a catalog of deeply discounted merchandise premiums that could only be obtained with proofs-of-purchase. A liquor offer sent to users of competing brands included not only an incentive for trial, but also a mini-catalog of clever gifts that could be earned for subsequent purchases. Various cigarette companies and even a manufacturer of motor oil have published catalogs containing merchandise that could be earned the same way. And what else are all the frequent-flyer, guest, and buyer programs but incentives to renew the commitment to a brand?

REACTIVATION TECHNIQUES

An attempt to keep a former relationship active or to reinstate it is a form of renewal, but it is actually closer to the front-end promotion in theory and practice. Every front-end approach—including both the creative and offer approaches—can be used to woo former customers. The only change would be a reminder to the customer of the previous contact.

One client, Avis Rent-a-Car, had millions of "Wizard Reservation Numbers," but found that a large percentage of these accounts was completely inactive. The gamut of programs developed to reactivate these members ranged from free gifts with the next rental to simply reissuing the stickers bearing the numbers. (The numbers originally were sent on labels, with instructions to affix them to a credit card, overlooking the fact that the labels would be discarded when the cards expired.)

Another interesting example was an RCA (now BMG) Music Service mailing that referred to the inactive club date and type of music the listener preferred—all in giant ink-jet type showing through an envelope window. "To Mrs. Jones—our 1997 classical music member." This type of "We've missed you" technique is used by many large mailers. My experience has shown that reactivation efforts are so profitable that this technique belongs in any direct-marketing program.

Beneficial Finance's credit card had millions of cards issued but relatively few in use. We designed a program to reactivate members with a large-scale contest promotion: the more you use it, the more chances you have to win. Later, Discover Card made the same offer to its cardholders. American Express, which constantly analyzes usage patterns for credit reasons, uses the same information to identify inactive cardholders and contacts with appropriate letters and even phone calls. Land's End sends a particularly involving letter: "Have we failed you in any way?"

REFERRAL PROMOTIONS

Prospect lists are valuable assets to any company, and database building is an important activity to be considered. List-building activities come in many forms, but the most common are member-get-member (MGM) and get-a-friend (GAF) offers.

In the simplest form, you ask customers for a list of friends who might like to receive a catalog, learn about your service, or receive news about your activities. Such a request can be minimal—a postscript on a letter or brochure in direct mail, a message on a grocery package, or a simple display in a retail store.

One common theory is the "birds-of-a-feather" idea. Good customers tend to send in names of other potentially good customers. Bad customers tend to send in names of other potentially slow payers. Therefore, requests for names often are included only in package inserts, mailings to converted buyers, or early-stage invoices—never with past due bills or bills in initial conversion packages. More ambitious programs actually recruit present customers as salespeople to some extent. Record clubs often enclose a brochure that a club member can give to a friend. Such brochures contain the basic offer and an order form or membership application. The only difference is that there is a space for the recommending member's name and address. The sponsoring member is usually offered a free gift or credit for recommending the new member.

Typically these promotions are multiple-page pamphlets because the brochure has to contain the entire sales story and an application or order form. The same brochure may have two order forms—one for the new customer and another detachable flap containing the offer to the sponsoring member.

Some political candidates mail their core supporters and ask them to each get five or ten new contributors by distributing the enclosed envelopes and pamphlets. This is a notably successful technique if there is genuine enthusiasm for the particular candidate. The same idea often is effective for religious fund-raisers.

One of my most successful referral promotions was for Pampers Express. A simple offer of a free teddy-bear to both the present customer and to any referred name who joined the program resulted in half the customers referring names—an average of two new names per original customer. As half of the referred names eventually joined, the offer produced one-third of our client's membership!

Incentives to sponsoring members may include just about anything. I've seen bonus books and records, gifts matching those given to the new member, simple premiums, contest entries, and silver dollars. The gift can be as much as you are willing to pay for a new customer or member, minus the allocated costs of the promotion.

CROSS-SELLING

- You are an insurance agent with a list of people who have bought life insurance. How do you sell them accident insurance, property insurance, and retirement plans?

- You are a bank with a large number of checking account customers. How do you sell them savings accounts, Christmas clubs, traveler's checks, and mortgages?

- You run a neighborhood gas station and have taken the trouble to get the addresses of customers who come to you for gas. How can you sell them auto repairs, tires, and oil changes?

- You are a toiletries manufacturer who has built a list of buyers of your perfume brand. How can you get them to try your line of cosmetics?

These are just a few of the many types of cross-selling opportunities. They exist in virtually every field. If you have satisfied customers but you don't have a second product to promote, find one. It is often worthwhile to develop a new product or act as a retailer for someone else's product to take advantage of the tremendous opportunity that cross-selling offers.

The basic principle to utilize with cross-selling promotions is, once again, inertia. The present relationship is a bond to build upon, which is a far easier process than establishing a new relationship.

The application of this principle demands that you first remind the present customer of the existing relationship. Then make the new offer appear to be a continuation by keeping the same or similar name, copy style, graphics, and offer structure.

One of the best cross-selling case histories I know was created for a large New York banking institution. As automobile and other loans were paid off, the bank sent out highly personalized mailings inviting customers to continue to make the same monthly payments as before, but as deposits to their own savings accounts rather than loan payments. The mailing piece included a computer-printed letter, a computer-filled account form, and a series of coupons bearing the customer's name and account number and the amount of the previous monthly payments. This mailing tailored the promotional savings-account product to the active loan accounts by utilizing the familiar payment-coupon format. It is an excellent application of both the inertia concept and the principle of convention.

Another example in the financial field that I reported as a trend in the previous edition of this book is now standard practice. Investment brokers like Merrill Lynch and Smith Barney dramatize the liquidity of their investment vehicles by issuing checkbooks and credit or debit cards capable of accessing the holder's entire net worth.

A simpler example of cross selling is one used by Time-Life Books. This enormous, highly sophisticated organization produces "libraries" of books on various subjects—animals, boating, history, cooking, and others—all sold by ship-till-forbid subscription. Once a relationship has been established with any one of these libraries, the subscriber is cross-sold other libraries, single books, videos, magazine subscriptions, or other products of the Time Warner family.

Simpler efforts use statement stuffers describing one library that are inserted with shipments and invoices for others. A unique technique of Time-Life is to make a cross-sell offer on a perforated extension of the billing invoice. The necessity for handling the extension when paying the bill assures its being noticed and relates it directly to the customer's present point of contact with Time-Life Books.

Cross selling presumes, of course, that your product and service have been well received. I know of one converse example: a photo-finishing concern that changed its name periodically to attract customers who had negative experiences with the company under its original name.

Cross selling not only introduces customers to other products, but can help to attract new customers as well. Mailings and on-pack messages offering free samples of other products or savings coupons are perceived as adding value to the first offer.

REORDER SOLICITATIONS

Giant mail-order corporations devote the bulk of their marketing activity to sending catalogs and mailing pieces to their vast, scientifically segmented mailing lists. Merchandising departments are constantly looking for new items and analyzing previously sold ones. Mailing lists are segmented by type of purchase, unit sale, type of product, and original source—all to enable direct marketers to vary the frequency and scale of the promotions sent to each group of customers. Catalog sales companies sometimes only send their sale catalogs to price-oriented buyers. Buyers of certain types of merchandise are offered specific specialty catalogs.

One of the advantages of a website "catalog" is that it can appeal to all these special groups at the same time, simply by enabling the customer to select the category they are most interested in. For instance, a travel agent invites viewers to either scan current special values or to access availabilities for a specific destination and date.

The number and scale of catalogs has evolved over years of testing and now ranges from simple flyers to full-color volumes, as well as localized versions for various regions and seasonal ones for spring, summer, winter, and pre-Christmas.

Many smaller companies have a fall pre-Christmas catalog as their most important and profitable effort. Unless they have segmented active buyers who merit year-round promotions or have seasonal merchandise, these companies can barely sustain an entire catalog for the spring season. If designing and producing a second catalog isn't profitable, the first one can often be revitalized by adding a sale theme, or restricting the size of the mailing compared to the pre-Christmas effort.

Of course every "free-ride" opportunity should be taken advantage of. Statement stuffers—four- to eight-page flyers enclosed with bills—are often extremely profitable, as are bounce-back solicitations enclosed with merchandise shipments. Some types of companies (photo developers, for example) have built their entire back-end business on bounce-backs enclosed with processed film. Often their promotions include some type of extra incentive, such as coupons good with the next film-processing order sent in by a certain date, and credit certificates for unprocessed prints.

Other types of companies offer opportunities to conveniently enter a contest or sweepstakes and, most often, bonus certificates given for frequent use. These certificates can be used in virtually any kind of business. They involve enclosing some type of value voucher with each shipment, or some type of card that has to be punched or validated in some way. When a certain number of certificates are saved or the card has been completely punched, they may be redeemed by the customer for another item free.

Back-end promotions require a strong commitment to positive thinking. If you are sending out your first catalog, don't get discouraged if the results seem disappointing. That's only a starting point. Take the result figures apart piece by piece. Some lists or list segments probably were profitable even if the overall mailing wasn't. Some items in the catalog or some pages probably did well even if the total result was in the red. Find your strong points and build on them, even if they steer you into an entirely different product line or market than you had originally intended. A little objectivity can go a long way in direct marketing.

LEAD SELLING

All the principles discussed to get leads also apply to using leads. Converting inquiries by direct mail is a two-step proposition. In such a case, the lead-selling effort is basically the conversion system outlined previously.

More often, leads are used because the second step is not only by mail but also through some type of personal selling. Once a lead has been obtained, it is turned over to a telephone or field selling organization for further contact. This contact person, in turn, can go directly for the sale at that time, or try to establish an appointment in the prospect's home or office.

The simplest type of lead-selling system is one used by virtually every marketer of office equipment. Once it is obtained, the lead information is simply transcribed onto a multiple-part document and turned over to a company sales agent or a local independent dealer. The dealers or sales agents are expected to report on the disposition of the prospect (sold; no interest; bought other), but no added pre-selling support is given to the dealer at all.

An effective lead system, in my experience, should not rely on the sales agent or dealer. I recommend sending a conversion-type series of letters to the prospect in addition to contacts by the sales force or dealer.

These mail efforts can be designed to persuade the prospect to visit the dealership or to call the salesperson for an appointment. Sometimes the efforts simply keep the prospect interested in the product or service until the salesperson makes contact.

International Gold Corporation had been giving dealer names to phone inquirers without any follow-up at all when I was invited to design a new Krugerrand marketing system. The one I made provided for capturing the names and addresses of callers and forwarding the name to not one but three dealers, who then had to compete to make the sale. A five-step follow-up series was sent to the prospect, not only selling the inquirer on the basic proposition, but also asking for the order on behalf of any of the three recommended dealers. All the dealers had to do was give price quotes and arrange for delivery. Our confidence level in the dealer organization was relatively low in this particular case, necessitating a particularly high degree of pre-selling.

Even sophisticated sales organizations have conflicting priorities and varying attitudes. Salespeople sometimes have to be convinced to follow up leads. I saw a very dramatic example of this when different offices of a major business-equipment company were given the same type of leads. Some offices were enthusiastic about leads and followed up every one; others were skeptical and put in a minimal effort. The conversion rate in the enthusiastic offices was 300 percent greater than in the others. We determined the difference to be the attitude of the office managers, whose enthusiasm or lack of it was picked up by the sales force.

Salespeople and dealers are human beings, and like other human beings they don't want to be rejected any more than anyone else. This simple psychological fact results in "pre-screening," when a salesperson eliminates certain prospects from his list of leads before contacting them. This is what happens when a salesperson sorts through business-to-business sales leads and decides, "This company isn't large enough," "This title isn't that of a decision maker," or even "This handwriting indicates someone I don't want to do business with."

When I was vice president, marketing, of LaSalle Extension University, in the years before government regulations crippled the correspondence-school business, I had inherited a classic system. Inquirers simply received a catalog by mail; everything else was left to the salespeople. They eventually converted about 15 percent of the leads sent to them. At the same time, a mail-order conversion sequence was signing up 10 percent of the leads from rural areas where we had no sales representative, completely by mail, without having to pay a substantial sales commission.

Our new system gave the leads to salespeople for only 60 days. They had this initial period to make their sales on a protected basis. After that, we cut in the mail-order sequence that included monthly letters, brochures, and a variety of premiums and trial offers, just as we had done in the rural areas. The results were amazing. We picked up an additional 5 percent conversion in mail-order sales even after the sales force had supposedly "worked" the leads. What was more amazing was that the average salesperson's conversion ratio increased from 15 to 20 percent. Counting the mail-order conversions, we were now getting 25 percent conversion instead of 15 percent. You can imagine the phenomenal effect this had on the bottom line.

It seems salespeople increased their efforts for two reasons. One, they could no longer procrastinate because they would eventually lose their protected exclusivity. Two, they didn't want to be embarrassed by the number of new enrollees generated by the mail-order activity—enrollees that were from leads they supposedly had worked.

Did salespeople resist this new system? Sure. But only until they found that, despite their worst expectations, they were making more money. Also, we were able to sell them on the idea by demonstrating that the higher conversion total would make it possible for us to significantly expand the lead-procurement budget and provide each salesperson with a greater flow of leads than before—which we did. This simple change in the back-end follow-up system helped LaSalle to grow threefold in only two years.

A very recent example is the lead management system used by MCI. Their "sales force" for residential customers was a well-trained telephone marketing organization operating out of regional centers. The need to keep a steady flow of leads was an integral part of their system. Large-scale mailings were broken down into weekly flights in each call-center territory. If a mailing was particularly successful, the rate of mailing was slowed down so the sales team could catch up on all the leads. The reverse was also true—if the lead response was slow, more mailings would be sent out.

An ideal lead system should be flexible. Too few leads discourage a dealer or salesperson. Too many results in the leads being "burnt off"—not given the full attention they would deserve if the salesperson had more time for each potential customer. New computer systems make it possible to issue leads to sales territories automatically, to adjust lead flow according to past conversion experience for individual dealers or salespeople, and to adjust territory size by spilling over surplus leads to salespeople in adjoining territories. Ideally, there should also be an early-warning system for the sales and marketing managers if any territory receives too few leads. With timely information, territories can be revised, salespeople can be transferred, and supplementary lead-generation systems can be activated so as to provide leads in a dry area.

SPECIAL SITUATIONS

There is no way to anticipate every situation that may arise in the course of running a direct marketing business, but here are four unusual ones that may be of help to some readers of this book: cancellations, handling credit turndowns, out-of-stock situations, and dry-run testing.

Cancellations

Many subscription, continuity, and club relationships most typically end in a cancellation of some sort. Rather than the company dropping them because the customers are characterized as unproductive or slow payers, the customer writes "Cancel" on an invoice or returns an automatic shipment.

In the past, the cancellations were entered, the records dropped from the active file, and that was that. I have suggested to several clients that they make one last effort to reactivate the customer, usually by telephone. A well-trained phone operator calls and asks if there is a problem, expresses concern, and asks for another chance. Often the cancellation was a correctable annoyance, such as too frequent mailings of a product "of the month," or an objection to too many scent strips in a magazine. This simple step not only pays in restored business, but also identifies potential dislikes by many customers and can lead to the correction of the annoyances and irritations that generated the cancellation requests in the first place.

Credit Turndowns

Inevitably a certain number of new orders—other than prepaid ones—have to be turned down because of credit risk. This may be because the customer appears on a bad credit index or because of probability, as indicated by zip-code experience or other factors. I've seen some companies just ignore such credit orders. Others send brutally frank letters. My own recommendation is to try to save the situation by tactfully switching the credit request to a cash order.

When turning down a credit order, first attribute the turndown to lack of credit information rather than to bad credit information or zip-code probabilities, two responses that are bound to create ill will and futile correspondence. Then, instead of a cold turndown, offer a special cash deal. One music club declined to send the advertised "6 CDs for $1" but instead offered a no-strings-attached plan that let the customer select one free CD for every one purchased, on a cash-with-order basis. While this generated less than half the orders from the standard proposition, the alternative was no orders at all from these credit-risk customers.

Out of Stock

A common situation with catalog houses and other mail-order vendors of products is the out-of-stock situation. FTC requirements specifically spell out standards and procedures for notifying customers if an item can't be shipped within 30 days, and require companies to give the buyer an opportunity to cancel the order. These procedures should be followed to the letter not only because it's the law, but also because it's good business. As I noted earlier in the book, the FTC describes a number of their rules and regulations on their webpage at www.ftc.gov.

Even 30 days is too long to keep customers waiting when they have ordered something they want for themselves or to give as a gift. Don't substitute an item or send a different size or color without explicit authorization from the customer, and don't keep customers waiting for suppliers to replenish inventory. A prompt, no-nonsense letter explaining the situation is in order, along with a reply card giving the customer the option of waiting, canceling, or selecting an alternative. A substitute should be specifically recommended if possible. If the unit sale is large, a phone call may be in order, preferably followed by a written notice and response card.

Dry-Run Testing

Dry-run testing—offering a product that isn't ready to ship—is another problem for advertisers. There are times when we want to test various factors before the product is complete—factors like sizes, packaging, premiums, and prices.

A dry-run direct-mail test for *Bon Appetit's* "*Wine Journal*" was able to determine whether or not to offer a leather-bound trade-up edition, whether to offer a premium, and which of several price levels would be most effective.

Such offers appear to be acceptable if they are clearly labeled as preview or prepublication offers, and if no prepayments are accepted. If credit card charges are solicited, it should be made very clear, and scrupulously arranged for, that no credit charges will be processed until the item is ready to ship. And while not necessarily a legal requirement but certainly an ethical one, these test orders should be fulfilled when the product is finally ready to ship at the lower of the new price or the price originally offered. As government regulations vary from time to time and state by state, check with your attorney or with one of the law firms that specialize in direct marketing. The DMA can send you a list of them if you decide to use dry-run testing.

As you can see by the wide variety of techniques presented here, there is as much room for creativity and strategic planning in back-end promotions as in the more glamorous and highly visible front-end promotions. "Back-end" techniques are not just an adjunct to a good marketing program. They are a vital and integral part of direct marketing which can affect your profitability as much or more than "front-end" acquisition programs.

MAIL ORDER
MATH

In earlier chapters I have described direct marketing as both art and science, but it is first and foremost a business. And as in any business, the fundamental objective is profit.

In direct marketing, each individual promotion can be evaluated in terms of profit or loss. Each proposal that requires a mailing list, advertisement, TV schedule or fee paid to an Internet service can be examined as if it were a subsidiary business, and decisions can be made to expand that one particular business, or to close it down. The underlying principles of mail order mathematics should be understood by anyone planning or executing any kind of direct marketing program.

To a certain extent, mathematics is a connection to reality. It cannot be faked. Too much money spent on a mailing piece may turn a profitable program into a losing one. If you modify a headline or offer and improve response rates by 10 percent your profits will increase geometrically—by much more than 10 percent.

Success often depends on the ability to respond quickly to result information. But some forms of direct marketing give us answers faster than others. The mail order business may seem to be simple, but profitability usually depends on whether or not customers reorder. Lead or inquiry-generation programs depend on conversion rate. Clubs and continuity plans must be able to forecast subsequent purchases and attrition rates. In database marketing, customer value or the value of a share point must be evaluated. And with all the glamour of and excitement about new interactive methods, the relationship between costs and income will ultimately mean more than projections of hits or clicks. In the long run, profits will outweigh investor optimism.

Each marketing process requires its own evaluation steps, yet all share the same foundations—the arithmetic of basic mail order. And they all begin with the same first step—Cost per Response, or the investment in obtaining the inquiry, order, coupon redemption or Internet click that begins the customer relationship.

THE BASICS

Cost per Response (CPR)

CPR can refer to cost per lead, cost per member, cost per subscriber, cost per click-through or any variation that is relevant for a particular business. You will see it called CPO for Cost per Order, CPL for Cost per Lead, but the formula is always the same. Simply divide the cost of the advertising by the number of responses:

PROMOTION COST ÷ RESPONSES = COST PER RESPONSE

Basic Profit Calculations

There is more to "advertising costs" than the money paid for mailings or other types of advertising. Though some costs are non-recurring development expenses, they should not be overlooked in budgeting. Others may seem like insignificant minor items, but they add up by the end of the year. It is best to anticipate every expense to avoid surprises at year-end.

Table 8-1 is a brief summary of some Operating Costs, Advertising Costs and—the other side of the coin—Income.

Promotional P&Ls (Profit and Loss)

While businesses using direct-marketing techniques consult all the same accounting reports that any business has, it is also customary to look at each promotional effort as a business in itself.

TABLE 8-1
ECONOMIC ELEMENTS THAT AFFECT THE BOTTOM LINE

Cost	Advertising	Income
Fixed Costs	Media Buys	Sale Price
"Goods Sold"	Mailing Lists	Shipping Fee
Incremental Costs	Computer Services	Units per Sale
Fulfillment Costs	Creative/Production	Trade-ups
Shipping Costs	Printing/Mailing	Conversion
Credit + Returns	Postage/"Nixies"	List Rentals

When I was President of Capitol Record Club, a CFO watched overall trends and filed reports with the parent company on what happened last quarter. The financial executive who I spent much more time with was the Director of Marketing Analysis, whose job it was to look forward and participate in decision-making. This position was held by Glenn Cavender, a baseball player turned accountant, who saw each media insertion and member mailing as an opportunity for a base hit or a home run.

Each promotion had its own pro-forma plan against which results were tracked. To fit this company's unique needs, we designed a weekly report that not only projected total responses after a few weeks of results, but predicted conversion rates and buying patterns based on the geographic and music characteristics of the respondents, to predict the three-year P&L—on each ad and each mailing!

Every company will have its own marketing analysis needs. Some smaller ones concentrate on cash flow. Some larger ones on Return on Investment. The example in Table 8-2 is from a hypothetical spread sheet used by Joseph Furgiuele in his class at New York University. While it may seem complex, it is elementary compared to the factors considered for client projects.

Allowable Margin

Allowable margin (AM) is a common short-cut used in the direct marketing business. It is short-hand for one figure which includes profit and advertising expense. It is simple enough that any staff or agency member can focus on advertising effectiveness without concern for factors which they have little influence over. Basically, it is what is left after you have paid for the product, shipped it, and written off any credit losses. In its simplest form, it is the amount of money available for advertising and profit for a given product after you have deducted every other expense.

For example, let's say a widget costs 50 cents to make, 25 cents to package, and 25 cents to ship. The $1 total is subtracted from the selling price. If the selling price is $2, the AM is $1.

Many advertisers also add a charge per unit for administration or overhead before figuring the margin. If you have to allow 10 percent for overhead, then that 20 cents is deducted from the $2 selling price, making the allowable margin only 80 cents.

Allowable margin should always be figured on an incremental basis. A hotel or phone company or Internet provider has most of their expenses in fixed costs. To handle new business, they have to add very little in additional (incremental) expense. Burdening the AM figure with overhead that has already been covered may be better on a profit per customer basis, but it leads to less aggressive growth.

Profit Leverage

Deducting the cost per response from the allowable margin gives the profit per response (PPR). In its simplest form, if the figure is positive, you have

TABLE 8-2
PROMOTION P&L CALCULATIONS
Elements of a financial plan or analysis.
(Ordinarily these would be listed across the top of a spread
sheet. Specific media or lists would be listed down the left
side.)

Item	Example
List Name	Acoustic Guitar Magazine
Selection	Active Subscriber, Male
Quantity Mailed by Key	12,663
Gross Orders	303
Gross % Response	2.40%
Cash Orders	24
Credit Orders	276
Credit Paid	35
% Credit Paid	12.67%
Net Orders	62
Gross Revenue	$7,277
Net Revenue	$1,488
Package CPM	$185.00
Actual List CPM	$146.15
Postage CPM	$165.00
TTL Promo CPM	$496.15
TLL Promo Cost	$6,267.98
P&L	(4,779.98)
Projected Gross Orders	459
Projected Gross % Response	3.64%
Projected Net Orders	312
Projected Net Revenue	$7,497
Projected P&L	$1,229.21
Projected Net Revenue per Order	$3.93
Projected Net Revenue per M Mailed	$97.30

Courtesy of Joe Furgiuele, FURGIUELE & COMPANY, INC.

a successful mailing; if it's negative, you have an unsuccessful one. In practice, "successful" is usually not a matter of being "in the black," but of reaching some goal—return on investment, circulation level, market share, or other calculable goal. The allowable margin concept is not typically used in ordinary accounting practices, but is a traditional approach in direct marketing and provides a simple rule of thumb for planning and evaluating promotions.

It is important to be aware that the impact of increasing or decreasing response rates—and the inverse relationship on cost per response—produces a geometric impact, not a linear one, on the bottom line. Table 8-3 illustrates this in detail. In this case, allowable margin is fixed and the cost per order is the only variable.

TABLE 8-3
GEOMETRIC LEVERAGE: EFFECT OF CPO ON PROFIT
(Example $5 margin and $50,000 advertising budget)

CPO ($)	Orders	Margin	Profit
6	8,333	41,665	(8,335)
5	10,000	50,000	0
4	12,500	62,500	12,500
3	16,666	83,330	33,330
2	25,000	125,000	75,000
1	50,000	250,000	200,000

Notice how a modest change in the CPO makes a dramatic difference in profitability. This is why it pays to seek better response rates. The use of "margin" (allowable for advertising and profit, or sale price after deducting all expenses except advertising) simplifies marketing calculations.

The geometric leverage of direct marketing has a simple explanation. As results improve, you not only get more profit per order but you get more orders.

Though this sound obvious, in practice it is often over-looked, especially in companies dominated by accountants instead of by marketers. "What," they say, "spend 20 percent more on a mailing package? So what if it's full-size, full-color and professionally created by experts instead of by amateurs!"

Yet a 20 percent increase in response actually increases profits by 114 percent, as illustrated in the example in Table 8-4. Spend an extra 20 percent in advertising cost, which is $4,000, and the profit is "only" $11 million,

TABLE 8-4
LEVERAGE: 20% DIFFERENCE IN RESPONSE RATE PRODUCES 114% DIFFERENCE IN PROFITS

	Plan	+20% sales	+20% sales +20% ad cost	−20% sales
Sales	$80MM	$96MM	$96MM	$64MM
Less Promotion Cost	20	20	24	20
Less Direct Expense	41	49	49	33
Less Fixed Costs	12	12	12	12
Total Costs	$73MM	$81MM	$85MM	$65MM
Profit	$7MM	$15MM	$11MM	($1MM)
Profit Plan vs. Plan		+$8MM	+$4MM	−$8MM
		+$114%	57%	−$114%

The direct expense is 50% cost of goods plus 1,000, increasing or decreasing as a function of sales. In actual practice, the decrease in sales may also result in unsold inventory, not reflected here.

which is "only" 57 percent. Spend $4MM more for $8MM more income resulting in $4MM more profit—57 percent more than the original plan. That should be worth investing in some new creative resources!

CUSTOMER ACQUISITION COSTS

What does it cost to get a new customer? Often it's more than the money you make on the first sale. This is the same as retail stores advertising "loss-leaders," or e-commerce companies losing money to build a dominant share of the market.

Tables 8-5, 8-6 and 8-7 compare three approaches to acquiring a customer. Table 8-5 is a one-step direct sale to a rented list. Table 8-6 is a one-step space ad; and Table 8-7 is a two-step approach, running an ad offering a catalog and then sending the first catalog. In all three examples, the cost per name investment results in someone who actually buys something, so it is really Cost per New Customer.

Other companies have reported better or worse figures than these examples. I find that some co-op mail is often more productive than these figures, and, obviously, the figures will reflect the media or list choices, the product offered, and the creative execution.

ANALYSIS MODES

Table 8-8 shows a typical comparison of test costs versus rollout costs. You cannot appraise a test based on the test cost. Always make your decisions

TABLE 8-5
THE COST OF ACQUIRING A CUSTOMER: ONE-STEP DIRECT SALE-LIST RENTAL

	Variable costs	Example 1	Example 2	Example 3
Total mailings		1,000,000	1,000,000	1,000,000
Response rate		2%	1%	2%
Total responses [new buyers]		20,000	10,000	20,000
Average order size		$50	$50	$100
Gross sales		$1,000,000	$500,000	$2,000,000
Margin before advertising	35%	$350,000	$175,000	$700,000
List rental cost, per name	$0.60	$600,000	$600,000	$600,000
Profit contribution [loss]		($250,000)	($425,000)	$100.000
Profit (cost) per name		($12.50)	($42.50)	$5.00

Source: Catalog Age, 1997/DMA Statistical Fact Book

TABLE 8-6
THE COST OF ACQUIRING A CUSTOMER: ONE-STEP DIRECT
SALE-SPACE AD

	Variable costs	Example 1	Example 2	Example 3
Total circulation		1,000,000	1,000,000	1,000,000
Response rate		0.1%	0.05%	0.05%
Total responses [new buyers]		1,000	500	500
Average order size		$19.95	$19.95	$39.95
Gross sales		$19,950	$9,975	$19,975
Margin before advertising	35%	$6,983	$3,491	$6,991
Space ad cost, per 1,000 names	$10	$10,000	$10,000	$10,000
Profit contribution (loss)		($3,017)	($6,509)	($3,009)
Profit (cost) per name		($3.02)	($13.02)	($6.02)

Source: Catalog Age, 1997/DMA Statistical Fact Book

TABLE 8-7
THE COST OF ACQUIRING A CUSTOMER: TWO-STEP CONVERSION

	Variable costs	Example 1	Example 2	Example 3
Step 1: Catalog inquiry				
Total circulation		1,000,000	1,000,000	1,000,000
Response rate		0.05%	0.5%	1%
Total responses (catalog inquiries)		500	5,000	10,000
Advertising cost per 1,000 names (query generator)	$10	$10,000	$10,000	$10,000
Loss		($10,000)	($10,000)	($10,000)
Cost per name		($20)	($2)	($1)
Step 2: Catalog mailing to inquiries				
Mailings to requestors		500	5,000	10,000
Response rate		1.6%	5%	7.5%
Total responses (catalog orders)		8	250	750
Average order size		$75	$75	$75
Gross sales		$600	$18,750	$56,250
Margin before advertising	35%	$210	$6,563	$19,688
Advertising cost (per catalog in mail)	$0.50	$250	$2,500	$5,000
Advertising cost (query generator)		$10,000	$10,000	$10,000
Profit contribution (loss)		($10,040)	($5,937)	$4,688
Profit (cost) per name		($1,255)	($23.75)	$6.25

Source: Catalog Age, 1997/DMA Statistical Fact Book

TABLE 8-8
TEST VERSUS ROLLOUT COSTS

Test package	Quantity	CPM	Response	CPO
Cost	10,000	$600	4.2%	$14.29
Rollout cost	100,000	$270	4.2	6.43

based on what it will cost to roll out. In direct mail, printing rates are always higher in small quantities. In print media, national rates are lower than for regional tests. In television, you can use larger markets or cable stations with better costs than smaller local stations.

If you are testing with a limited investment, be sure to base your evaluation on what the campaign will cost in a rollout, rather than on the higher costs of the small test campaign.

If you are testing during a relatively less-efficient season, estimate what response you would expect in the better season when you would run the full campaign.

If you are testing a variety of offers or creative appeals, or if you are testing a variety of lists, publications, stations or websites, focus on what works, not on the overall results.

Table 8-9 would apply equally well to any medium. In this analysis, line 3 represents a cost per inquiry, calculated from a magazine's cost per thousand circulation and a response rate. For magazines, it would be simpler to divide the space cost by the number of responses and get the same figure, without having to refer to circulation or response percentage. This example would be more applicable to direct mail; a cost-per-thousand figure would appear on line 1 and a response rate on line 2.

Line 4 takes into account the cost of the mailings designed to convert the inquiry into a sale, multiplying it by the number of mailings in line 5. This case indicates only four packages at an average cost of $400 per thousand. Telephone conversion costs might also be added at this point, along with the costs of a computer firm to handle the incoming mail.

TABLE 8-9
CONVERSION RATE IMPACT (TWO-STEP EXAMPLE)

1. Magazine CPM	$18.00
2. Response to ad	0.3%
3. Cost per inquiry	$ 6.00
4. Cost per conversion effort	0.40
5. Four conversion efforts	1.60
6. Total cost of inquiry and conversion	7.60
7. Cost per order:	
10% conversion	76.00
15% conversion	50.67
18% conversion	42.00

Line 6 combines the cost of acquiring the lead (line 3) and converting it (line 5) to produce combined cost of inquiry and conversion series.

Line 7, then, is merely a projection of what the eventual cost per order would be at various conversion rates. You can see how dramatically changes in the conversion rate affect the CPO. Increased conversion effort costs are usually insignificant compared with the profitability of increasing the percentage rate, which is why six- and eight-part conversion series, with added telephone efforts, have become commonplace in this type of promotion.

Table 8-10 includes every factor applying to the profitability of a direct mail promotion, presuming a simple cash offer with 40 percent of the customers electing to pay by credit card and the others by check. It also indicates a 5 percent customer correspondence factor, 10 percent returns, and 3 percent bad debt.

Note that this analysis shows the profit and loss (P&L) in terms of total dollars rather than unit costs. While CPR and AM figures are handy for planning, P&Ls should always be in terms of real dollars.

Back-End and Front-End Analysis

The terms *front end* and *back end* apply to analysis as well as to planning. Front end measures the initial cost of attracting the inquiry or first order,

TABLE 8-10
SIMPLIFIED PROFIT AND LOSS WORKSHEET FOR
DIRECT MAIL PROMOTION
100,000 Packages Costing $280 per Thousand, 3.2% Response or 3200 Orders

	Unit value, dollars	No. of units	Total dollars
1. Selling price	$32.95	3200	$105,440
2. Plus shipping and handling	1.95	3200	6,240
3. Gross order value	34.90	3200	111,680
4. Minus returns (10%)	34.90	320	11,168
5. Net sales	34.90	2880	100,512
6. Cost of goods (delivered)	7.31	2944	21,521
7. Order processing, shipping, returns costs, customer service, and credit fees	4.53	3200	14,494
8. Premium (keeper)	1.20	3200	3,840
9. Promotion (CPO)	8.74	3200	27,968
10. Bad debt (3%)	34.90	86	3,001
11. Overhead (15%)	5.24	2880	15,091
12. Total expenses			85,915
13. Profit	5.07	2880	14,597
14. Profit % to net sales			14.5%

whereas back end evaluates how well those inquiries convert to a buyer status. The sum of the front end (inquiry cost) and back end (conversion cost) is the total cost of acquiring a new customer.

While great emphasis usually is put on obtaining the lowest possible cost per front-end response, ultimate success in attracting new customers depends just as much on back-end factors. The marketing manager must know the "quality" of customers attracted; how effectively they were converted to initial and subsequent purchases; whether they paid; and how long they stayed active as customers, members, contributors, or subscribers.

Sometimes a direct marketer increases response rates with a sweepstakes or an exceptional premium, only to find that the performance of the newer responders lowers profit rather than raising it. More often I've found that an added response rate up-front more than compensates for back-end deterioration. But there is no one "right answer" for all cases. Either way, it is essential to monitor back-end performance to adequately evaluate how your promotions are working.

SEGMENTATION ANALYSIS

In the most elementary form of segmentation analysis, direct marketers evaluate individual lists, publications, or stations, but not entire campaigns. In any campaign, some media perform better than others. It is axiomatic that in future seasons we will expand our usage of those that did well, seek other similar media, and drop those that did poorly. The criterion is profitability. By using CPR and AM, we can quickly tell which are likely to perform satisfactorily in the future. This seemingly simple and logical process is the key to the success of any application of direct marketing. It is unfortunate that many of the new users of this methodology omit this crucial process and therefore never realize its full potential.

Simply list all the media sources in inverse order of cost-per-response—those with the lowest CPR first. For those at the top of the list, look for additional media with similar audience characteristics. For the ones on the bottom, drop them or find a new proposition to appeal to them. For those in the middle, proceed cautiously with test extensions. For many years of direct marketing's history, this was the "secret" that built giant catalog and publishing companies. But then came along segmentation, in progressively more complex forms.

Internal Segmentation

This is the analysis of a medium by its inherent characteristics that can be placed into categories. For example, the results of an ad in a magazine or in *The Wall Street Journal* can be related to the publication's geographic editions. Perhaps an ad in the full circulation produced marginal results, but had varying results in different regions and would be profitable if only the West Coast editions were used.

A run-of-station buy on a television station may also be marginal, but a breakdown of the results by different dayparts might show that it would be very profitable if the time slots bought were weekend only, nighttime only, or whatever the proposition and resulting analysis called for.

Direct mail is especially responsive to internal segmentation. With both house lists and rented lists, it is possible to break down results into a wide variety of segments: recency of purchase, size of purchase, type of purchase, original source, and demographic data. Credit card and insurance companies usually also have age, income, marital status, and similar data available.

Any available characteristic can be analyzed in terms of relative responsiveness. Either assign key numbers in advance to predetermined segments, or arrange to analyze respondents in comparison with the characteristics of the total list used. Often the results are surprising, with totally unexpected factors producing significantly different results.

There is room for imagination in defining segments. One client suggested converting birth dates into astrological signs and looking for patterns according to the supposed characteristics of different signs. Another suggested an age or age-of-children breakdown, on the theory that people at different points in their life cycle will have different purchasing proclivities. The latter idea sounds more reasonable than the first, but part of the fun of this business is, to use a recent New York Lottery slogan, "Hey, you never know."

External Segmentation

This refers to the analysis of characteristics that are not intrinsic attributes of the media. Generally applicable to direct mail, this form of analysis has proven to be a valuable tool for telemarketers and Internet advertisers as well.

There are many degrees of external segmentation. The simplest one is the identification of areas of the country that produce significant variations in response rates or in customer quality. In its purest sense, this would involve tracking the number of mailings, calls or other contacts from a particular zip code and determining whether the response from the individual zip code was ultimately profitable. Unfortunately, such samples tend to be much too small to analyze in this pure sense.

The most scientific application of this approach is cluster analysis, as popularized by Claritas and now available from several other companies. Their refinements group zip codes together according to the latest available census data, as updated by commercial projections of population trends. This is discussed in more detail in Chapter 5 on Testing.

Responses, mailing quantities, and eventual pay-up rates today can be assembled into zip-code patterns according to any and every type of data available in the latest U.S. Census.

All the obvious parameters—age, income, education, home ownership, etc.—can be included, as can less obvious characteristics. For instance, Claritas found that *Field & Stream* was most effective when they sent their mailings to zip codes with a high incidence of freezer ownership!

Knowing some critical characteristics enables a refinement of list purchasing beyond gross list selection. Desirable areas can be selected and undesirable ones purged. In print media, tougher credit standards can be applied to zip code clusters that are likely to produce poor-quality business. The added cost of a select or suppress factor when buying lists is very small compared to the savings involved.

Zip code analysis is not the only method of external segmentation. It is possible to match lists according to individual names, such as length of residence, single- or multiple-family occupancy, and ethnic last-name indications.

Financial institutions have been able to use what may be the ultimate form of external segmentation to predetermine the potential customers to whom they will mail offers of preapproved lines of credit. Names of prospective customers are sent to major credit bureaus such as Experian to check acceptability of credit, based on information in the organization's files. While many good prospects are screened out because of lack of available credit data, those who do match are already qualified. Credit cards, preapproved "instant-loan" plans, and other financing instruments are often sold this way. While the front-end cost per response is sometimes disappointing, the back end quality is not.

Decile Analysis

A refinement of segmentation analysis, *decile analysis* is the practice of statistically analyzing the responsiveness of each segment of a mailing program. Divide the segments into 10 groups, each representing 10 percent of the total. Then list them in descending order of profitability. The top-performing segment, 10 percent of the total, might bring in 20 percent of the sales or profits. The two top deciles combined, or 20 percent of the total, might yield 35 percent of the total profits. These are imaginary numbers, but exemplify a typical list and how to analyze it.

This type of analysis generally shows each segment individually and on a cumulative basis. You can readily determine which sources should be dropped and the optimal size of your advertising budget. If you mail too small a percentage of the total, the fixed costs will not be covered. If you mail too large a percentage, you will be reaching down into the less profitable segments.

The risk/return ratio also is obvious. There is a point at which the next 10 percent of advertising investment would yield a much smaller percentage in profit increase, a factor to be considered in terms of overall objectives. For example, some magazines will use lower-ranking sources that produce an apparent loss because their objective is to maintain circulation levels, not to optimize subscription income. Decile analysis technically refers to sorting the result figures into 10 parts, but the practice and the name have been applied to breakdowns of 20, 50, or more segments as well.

Dimensional Analysis

In a hypothetical analysis of mailing lists, list categories, or other media sources arranged by profitability, it is presumed that some will do much better than others. Though the overall result may be good or bad, within those results are some lists that are exceptionally good and others that are very poor. Another possibility is that all may be good or bad, but with relative degrees of performance.

The usual practice has been to draw a line somewhere and decide which lists or groups are worth mailing to in the future and which are not. However, if each source is further broken down by zip code clusters or some other external factor, it is highly probable that the line will be diagonal rather than horizontal.

The best way to explain that diagonal line is by example. Imagine that a cluster analysis or a state grouping indicates that some parts of the country or demographic groups do 25 percent better than the average and others 25 percent worse, and that these groups are shown across the top of a report. Down the side you have the lists themselves, the SIC codes for a business list, or the decile groupings or list categories. If these percentages are applied to the lists—either individually or collectively—this additional factor will be overlaid on top of the list results. This type of grid analysis most often combines list results with a geographic analysis.

The chances are that even the best lists will have some areas that would be better omitted, and that even the worst lists will have some segments or parts of the country that should produce a satisfactory profit.

It is theoretically possible to refine mailing-list results on a three-dimensional base. For example you can compare and weight results for the lists themselves, for demographics, and for other factors such as size of market or weather (for a gardening or recreational product like skiing equipment). House lists can be similarly refined based on recency, frequency, and unit sale—the three most important characteristics of customer lists.

Regression Analysis

Suppose you had interest data from Polk, category and brand usage from Donnelley Marketing, a subsidiary of First Data, and individual purchase history from your own transactions. These can all be combined in a list and then subjected to detailed analysis. This is the key to what is now called *modeling* and uses a mathematical probability process called *regression analysis*.

The details of regression analysis, and its variations, are more appropriate for a book on mathematics. Mathematicians, computer services experts and database consultants specialize in providing these services, either directly to agencies and advertisers or as subcontracted services to list compilers.

Generally, regression analysis consultants will provide such an analysis on a fixed or hourly fee basis, or as part of a continuing relationship with an agency or list supplier. The fees they quote will depend on the complexity of the analysis, and on the number of factors to be considered. If the client does not already have the data to be analyzed, they will arrange the necessary overlays through list compilers and charge the client the additional costs.

The process compares the known characteristics of your customers with the characteristics of other mailing lists. Mathematically, the matches are noted, counted and compiled. The result is a "penetration analysis"—a ranking of those characteristics that were matched most frequently and the other lists which shared them.

MORE ECONOMIC CONSIDERATIONS

Here are some other terms that everyone in this business should be familiar with.

Conversion Rates

If you are offering a free booklet and then converting leads into sales, you will be concerned with conversion rates. The same term applies to a credit order, a trial subscription, or a membership. These transactions are not considered sales until they actually have been paid for.

If you have 1000 inquiries and 200 of them become buyers, you have a conversion rate of 20 percent. As an algebraic equation, this would be expressed

$$\frac{\text{Buyers}}{\text{Inquiries}} = \frac{\text{Conversion Rate } (x)}{100}$$

This kind of simple equation is resolved by cross-multiplying 100 times buyers which equals X, and the unknown conversion rate times inquiries. You then divide both sides by the number of inquiries in order to isolate the unknown X factor. But it is not necessary to use this equation.

On a calculator, simply enter the number of buyers and divide by the number of inquiries, then move the percentage point two places to the right. This will give you the conversion rate. If your calculator has a percent key, press that rather than the equals key, and the two places will automatically be moved over for you.

Renewal Rates

Renewal rates are determined in the same manner as conversion rates. The term is generally used in analyzing the profitability of a subscription or service sold on an annual basis. Typically between 40 and 60 percent of first-year subscribers renew for the second year. Of these second-year subscribers, perhaps 80 to 90 percent will renew in subsequent years. In the circulation field, these subscribers then are called *renewed renewals*, or RRs.

Attrition (or Retention) Rates

If you are selling a proposition on a continuity basis, or in a club that requires a purchase every month or cycle, you will have to deal with attrition. This is the number or percentage of "starters" (initial customers or subscribers) who drop out at the end of each cycle by canceling, failing to meet a purchase commitment, or not paying. Typically 50 percent or so will not "convert" during the first cycle by not making the first purchase. This number drops off by 5 or 10 percent in subsequent cycles—that is, as a percentage of those who survived the first-cycle attrition.

While the phrase Attrition Rate is in common use, I prefer to focus on the positive side of this coin. The opposite of Attrition Rate is *Retention Rate,* meaning the number of customers who do renew and keep buying. The profit from continued buying by a shrinking number of the original customers adds up as each successive year's new customers are added to the mix.

In mature direct-marketing businesses, all the profits come from retained customers. The key management decision is to decide how much of these profits to reinvest in "buying customers" (front-end acquisition costs) each year. A manager can always make one year's profits look good by cutting back on customer acquisition—the direct-marketing equivalent of a farmer selling off his seed corn for a quick profit, but leaving nothing to sow for the next year.

Units per Response

In calculating profitability, take into account the number of units per sale. This can vary substantially, and can make the difference between success and failure. Usually a single-unit offer that has a gift appeal will produce anywhere from 20 to 50 percent more units than orders—the result of customers who buy an extra item for a friend or family member.

This factor can be manipulated in several ways—you can offer discounts for multiple orders; you can feature matching or accessory items; and you can offer your product only in larger sizes or sets. Increasing the number of units per sale—if it can be done without depressing the number of sales—is often easier than achieving a comparable increase in front-end responses.

Average Take

In a catalog or club, you know that not everyone will buy from every mailing. A *take* is the decimal fraction of your customer total that buys an item from each cycle. If you expect 20 percent of your customers to make a single purchase, the average take is 0.2. If half the customers make one purchase, then the take is 0.5. The club I ran, Capitol Record Club, combined a tight definition of "active member" and strong incentives for multiple purchases. The result was an exceptional 1.2 "take" per cycle.

Name Value

All financial projections should provide an allowance for the value of a name—either for future sales as part of a company's house list, or as a contributor to list rental income. This factor is an estimate of the net value as a rental name only. The name value is the net result of rentals to other companies. That value is an estimate of the number of times you or your list manager believes such a name would "turn" times the net income, after brokerage and computer costs.

Time Value

Some advertisers plan to break even the first year, then make their profits on subsequent years' reorders or renewals. Continuity plans and clubs make large up-front investments with the intention of pulling ahead months later as additional purchases are made.

The value of the money tied up in advertising and premium investments should always be taken into account in long-range planning. Whether you borrow money from a bank or you are investing your own funds, the current earning value of money is a factor to be considered. If your money can earn interest or dividends at 10 percent, then $1 invested now has to return $1.10 a year later just to break even. All long-term planning should be weighted for this time-value factor. Similar tables show when it might be more profitable to take 90 cents now rather than $1 later—the reverse consideration. Your banker or accountant can supply such data easily.

CATALOG ANALYSIS

If you are mailing a catalog or any type of multiple-item proposition, you will want to analyze not only the total proposition, but also the profitability of each individual item in the catalog.

Space Allocation

This involves treating each page or fractional page-unit as if it were an advertising promotion of its own.

Divide the cost of the entire catalog by the number of pages. For instance, if the catalog costs $90,000 and has 48 pages with 3 pages used for covers and ordering information, then each page is worth $90,000 divided by 45, or $2000. Similarly, half a page is worth $1000, a quarter-page $500, and a tenth of a page $200. In calculating the profitability of each item, the cost of the space has to be added to the cost of goods and to shipping and overhead costs.

If an item is very profitable, you will want to not only repeat it in future catalogs, but also to enlarge the space used to feature it. If an item is unprofitable, you can either drop it or reduce the size of the space allocated to it.

Product success will vary widely, depending on the positioning of the catalog merchandiser and the lists used. The results-per-item are examined individually and by category to guide future selections and spacing. It is important to look for patterns—product type, price range, style, uniqueness, or markup percentage—so as to find the unique key to each catalog's profit potential.

Often it pays to do a separate calculation of this type for major list categories. It may even be desirable to produce separate catalogs with different merchandise for different list segments.

Catalog Profit and Loss

Whether catalogs are sent by mail or displayed on a website, they are subject to the same economic factors as we have been discussing for direct mail. Table 8-11 shows some average highlights of average consumer and business to business catalogs.

Table 8-12 shows average circulation figures and other information, while Table 8-13 includes some average statistics on lifetime value—the annual value per customer and life span averaging reports from a number of catalog companies. Typical results of catalog mailing are shown in Table 8-14.

These tables are just a few highlights from a 235-page detailed study prepared by the Direct Marketing Association in cooperation with W. A. Dean and Associates. The study is a comprehensive analysis of practices

TABLE 8-11
CATALOG PROFIT AND LOSS HIGHLIGHTS

P&L highlights (as a % of net sales) 1997 median figures	Consumer	B to B
Gross Sales	109.0%	102.5%
Returns	−9.0%	2.9%
Net Sales	100.0%	100.0%
COGS	44.1%	49.8%
Marketing Expenses	27.9%	14.0%
Operating Expenses	17.4%	12.9%
G & A Expenses	11.9%	14.0%
Operating Income	10.3%	10.8%
List Rental Income	1.1%	0.4%

W. A. Dean and Associates/DMA State of the Catalog Industry Report

TABLE 8-12
CATALOG CIRCULATION STATISTICS
(Median figures reported)

Circulation	Consumer	B to B
Annual Circulation (000)	4,856	700
Number of Mailings	12.0	7.0
Order Size	$82	$290
Sales per Book Mailed	$2.00	$4.00
Orders per Year (000)	120.0	43.9
Response Rate	2.7%	3.9%

W. A. Dean and Associates/DMA State of the Catalog Industry Report

and trends in all aspects of the catalog business including a forecast of econometric factors through the year 2003, when catalog sales are expected to reach 19 billion dollars a year in the U.S. alone. The report sells for $395 to members and $495 for non-members and is available from the DMA (www.the-dma.org) or at their book center at 301-604-0187.

RETURN ON INVESTMENT

Increasingly, the standard of measurement is *return on investment,* or ROI. Sophisticated companies with diverse product lines and distribution methods rely on this standard to determine where to allocate their resources. Investors and bankers, deciding which companies to buy stock in or lend money to, also look at ROI. Brylane's catalog expert Jules Silbert defines it as the net profit earned in a year divided by the average amount invested in the business during that year. In direct marketing, this investment consists of the average inventory, the accounts receivable, the plant and equipment, and the average amount of cash needed to cover payroll and other current expenses.

The Return on Investment Model

To simplify an understanding of return on investment analysis in the direct-marketing business, Brian Hopkins uses two models: one for simple mail-

TABLE 8-13
AVERAGE LIFETIME VALUE STATISTICS FOR CATALOG

LTV statistics	Consumer	B to B
Median $ Value per Customer	$89	$498
Average Life Span	4.3 yrs	4.3 yrs

W. A. Dean and Associates/DMA State of the Catalog Industry Report

TABLE 8-14
CATALOG MAILING RESULTS

List description	Mail qty	Average sale ($)	Response rate	Gross orders	Gross sales	Margin @ 25%	Selling* cost per M	Selling cost	Profit $
House List	500,000	$89	6.8	34,000	$3,026,000	$756,500	$710	$355,000	$401,500
Tested A	100,000	$88	5.4	5,400	$475,200	$118,800	$790	$79,000	$39,800
Tested B	100,000	$79	5.1	5,100	$402,900	$100,725	$790	$79,000	$21,725
Tested C	100,000	$82	4.7	4,700	$385,400	$96,350	$790	$79,000	$17,350
Tested D	60,000	$63	4.3	12,580	$162,540	$40,635	$790	$47,400	–$6,765
Tested E	60,000	$75	3.9	2,340	$175,500	$43,875	$790	$47,400	–$3,525
Tested F	50,000	$76	3.0	1,500	$114,000	$28,500	$790	$39,500	–$11,000
New List G	5,000	$50	3.0	150	$7,500	$1,875	$790	$3,950	–$2,075
New List H	5,000	$50	3.0	150	$7,500	$1,875	$790	$3,950	–$2,075
New List I	5,000	$50	3.0	150	$7,500	$1,875	$790	$3,950	–$2,075
New List J	5,000	$50	3.0	150	$7,500	$1,875	$790	$3,950	–$2,075
New List K	5,000	$50	3.0	150	$7,500	$1,875	$790	$3,950	–$2,075
New List L	5,000	$50	3.0	150	$7,500	$1,875	$790	$3,950	–$2,075

*Includes printing, mailing, postage, list rental (where applicable). Lists D, E and F are included to maintain volume until better lists are found.
Source: Team Nash, Inc.

ONE-STEP DIRECT MAIL
RETURN ON INVESTIMENT WORKSHEET

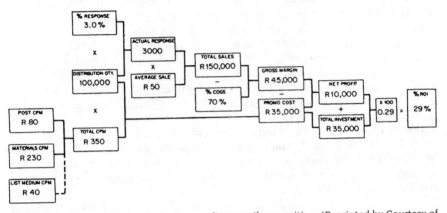

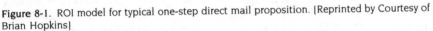

Figure 8-1. ROI model for typical one-step direct mail proposition. [Reprinted by Courtesy of Brian Hopkins]

order sales, and another for two-step or lead-generating businesses. Hopkins, a prominent direct-marketing practitioner in South Africa, works with a wide variety of business and consumer organizations that now use these models. Although they are expressed in rands, they could just as well be in dollars, pesos, reais, yen or eurodollars.

Figures 8-1 and 8-2 are shown with examples filled in for specific applications. Basically, measuring the ROI calls for an analysis of the interplay

TWO-STEP DIRECT MAIL
RETURN ON INVESTIMENT WORKSHEET

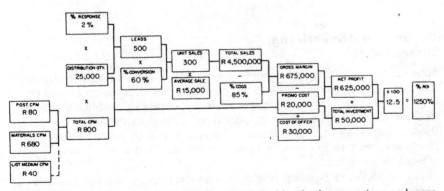

Figure 8-2. ROI model for typical two-step proposition, adding leads, conversions, and space for cost of offer. [Reprinted by Courtesy of Brian Hopkins]

of expenditure, market size, potential response, and potential contribution or profit. A variance in any of these four factors will have an impact on the return on investment.

In these models, advertising expenditure is referred to as PROMO COST, which in turn is made up of a cost-per-thousand rate. The classic M in CPM stands for 1000 as it has since the Roman Empire, though CPK might be in use in some remote part of the world. In print or broadcast, this figure may be the media cost. In direct mail, it is the product of the mailing components: postage (POST CPM), printing and lettershop (MATERIALS CPM), and list rental costs (LIST MEDIUM CPM). The circulation, audience, or mailing quantity is shown as DISTRIBUTION QTY in this model, and is multiplied by the response rate (% RESPONSE).

GROSS MARGIN is the potential contribution, calculated from the value of each AVERAGE SALE. The percentage cost of sale or cost of goods sold (% COGS) is subtracted from total sales to arrive at the gross margin. The % COGS figure represents either the total of manufacturing or distribution costs and overhead, or a marginal cost factor.

To determine return on investment (ROI), subtract the total promotional cost from the gross margin to arrive at the NET PROFIT. Then divide this figure by promotional cost or total investment to arrive at a ROI factor. Simply multiplying by 100 then provides the % ROI figure.

Figure 8-1 shows the chart figured for a typical direct mail campaign. Figure 8-2 is a modification providing for two-step marketing. Two blocks have been added: LEADS and % CONVERSION to determine the number of sales (UNIT SALES).

Another block appears in this example—COST OF OFFER—which is applicable to either one- or two-step marketing. This factor provides the cost of the incentive to respond: a booklet, premium, loss leader, initial introductory shipment, or whatever else was an expense to sell the customer.

This model is a handy way to quickly test the interrelationships between different costs, response rates, media costs, and other factors. For instance, it often shows that the higher response rates of direct mail do not always justify its expense compared to media such as magazine and broadcast advertising when calculating the overall expenses versus responses.

Return on Advertising Investment

Sometimes we refer to ROAI, meaning *return on advertising investment*. In this model, advertising is looked at as an incremental investment—a correct consideration for a product or service that has other distribution channels. The profit on direct-marketing sales is compared to the cost of enabling those sales to get the ROAI figure. The goal is usually not to simply be "in the black," but to generate a better investment ratio than other possible uses of those funds.

This calculation is often useful in encouraging a company to offer its services in the mail-order channel for the first time or to use direct marketing to expand its market area. For local retailers, this is often a way to "go national." For national marketers, it is often a way to enter foreign markets. In both cases, the geographic areas with the greatest ROAI will be the safest areas to enter conventional distribution as well.

ROAI figures are generally encouraging, due largely to the fact that the advertising is "paid for" by the portion of the retail price that otherwise goes to distributor and retailer mark-ups, or to rent and personnel for a retailer.

ACCOUNTING PRACTICES

Direct marketing is like any other business, in that the rules of conventional accounting hold true despite its uniqueness. The following are some considerations that the direct marketer will want to learn more about from an accountant or tax adviser.

Inventory Valuation

What you invest in stock in a warehouse ties up capital and is often subject to taxation. Drop-ship or installment shipping arrangements may be more desirable.

Year End Tax Treatment

If advertising is expensed rather than capitalized, it may be possible to reduce current-year taxes by sending out mailings at the end of one year—an expense—and taking the resulting sales in the next year. This would defer taxes and make available more capital for mailing.

Capitalized Advertising

If earnings growth is your objective (as with publicly-held companies), it appears reasonable to capitalize advertising costs, making them a current-year asset in the year they are paid for, and then write off the expense during the years when the income is produced. This would be most applicable to programs with long-term customer relationships.

Member Value

Direct marketing expenditures—both advertising costs and premiums to attract customers—should be treated as an investment in future sales. If money is put into building a new retail outlet, the expense is capitalized and spread over many years. Yet the money spent on bringing customers into a mail-order "store" is often treated as an expense for accounting purposes, leading otherwise sophisticated companies to bunch up their advertising at the beginning of a fiscal year so as to get back their yield in the same yearly accounting period. This attempt to satisfy artificial accounting criteria leads to poor investment decisions. Recognition of "member value" or "customer value" as an accounting practice—particularly in club and continuity programs—would offset advertising expense and give the reader of an annual report a more accurate picture of a company's fiscal situation.

Reserves

Holding reserves is another accepted practice, to allow for inventory write-offs, returns, or bad credit, thus reducing current-year tax obligations.

Hidden Assets

One of the great frustrations of direct marketing executives is the extent to which major corporations fail to recognize the real strengths of a direct marketing business.

For instance, a direct marketing firm's greatest asset is its mailing list, which should be computed at a value based on the capitalized value of its list-rental income and internal solicitation potential. If a direct marketing company is sold, its list is the asset most in demand. Yet most accountants fail to give it any value in computing assets or profits.

Similarly, control of key media positions such as options on back covers or insert card positions is a substantial hidden asset. So is fulfillment software that works smoothly, result data that guides a company in its marketing decisions, and trained, loyal personnel. Direct marketers accommodate figures to accounting methods. Perhaps someday accountants will find a way to return our cooperation and appropriately value the industry's greatest assets.

Putting It All Together

Eventually all the separate considerations and calculations add up to a plan and later to a result analysis. Refer to Table 8-14, is a sample of a typical plan, showing a variety of lists or other media, projections based on past results where known and on reasonable expectations where there is no prior experience. Note that the bulk of the promotion is sent to house lists which produce not only the highest response rate but also the highest unit sale. The promotion or selling cost is lower because no list rental costs are needed. Continuations of previously tests lists come next, with forecasts based on previous testing. Then some new lists are added. The ration between proven lists and test lists is a fundamental management decision—more testing if growth is the objective, less if maximum profit is the objective.

For a major catalog company, such a report would probably include several categories of house lists, based on recent sales history, some rollouts of proven lists, some modest test extensions where a previous test was marginal (perhaps trying a new selection factor), and a much wider range of test lists grouped into categories.

* * *

This chapter was not meant to be a course on algebra, statistics, accounting, economics, or business math. There are excellent books are available on all those subjects. To acquire more advanced knowledge of the math and finance of the direct marketing field, I suggest that readers enroll in the DMA's courses on math and finance that are offered in major cities throughout the country. There are also excellent courses now available at many universities. I have been particularly impressed with the math and finance course at NYU, taught by noted consultant Joseph Furgiuele, who contributed several of the illustrative tables.

Keeping Up to Date

You will notice that some of the examples in this chapter and elsewhere are reprinted by permission of the DMA from their Statistical Fact Book. The limitations of scheduling guarantees that any example or industry statistic will not be the latest information by the time the book is actually printed and purchased. I therefore strongly recommend that serious direct marketers purchase the latest copy of the DMA Statistical Fact Book, as well as join and participate in DMA events.

CREATIVE TACTICS

In a *New York Times* interview, the artist Willem de Kooning said "I see the canvas and I begin!" His results were bold, spontaneous brushstrokes with no comprehensible theme or subject—results that would be absurd in advertising.

The late Victor Schwab, co-founder of Schwab & Beatty, used to quote Corey Ford's story about the rider who jumped on his horse and rode off in all directions—an allusion to copywriters who sat down at their typewriters and wrote subjective copy without adequate planning.

One of the great copywriters, Tom Collins, a co-founder of Rapp & Collins, took the pro-planning position a step further, with fewer words. His credo: "Advertising is hard!"

CREATIVE PLANS

Brilliant ideas and sudden inspirations come to people who have done their homework, who have done the basic conceptual thinking that is essential before trying to write copy or design layouts.

The largest ad agencies require their account staffs and writers to prepare "creative strategy statements" or "creative work-ups." This is the first step in the ad-making process—*after* the marketing plans have been written, *after* the product and its positioning have been selected, *after* the offers have been finalized, and *after* the media or list schedule has been determined.

Preparing the creative work-up is the step that comes before the fun starts: the exciting, challenging, stimulating, fulfilling process of creating the advertisement or mailing piece to meet prescribed positioning and tactics.

A large advertiser may want a formal copy platform to be reviewed in meetings with several supervisors. A smaller advertiser may write a list of copy points on a pad, talk it over with a co-worker, and sleep on it before selecting creative priorities. The process in the two cases is identical: (1) develop alternative concepts, and (2) select and prioritize.

I find that a creative plan has a very practical business function as well, for both ad agencies and in-house creative departments. At Team Nash, we always submit the plan to the client for approval, just as we do schedules and estimates. It serves to define the project and limit the degree of revisions. If the client later changes his or her basic strategy, we expect to get paid for what we've done executing the first strategy and then re-estimate the schedule and fees.

Positioning

The single most important creative decision in the making of a successful ad or mailing piece is positioning. This concept can apply to basic marketing strategy or to the writing of a single mailing piece. It can be constant—the same for all products created by a company and for all media and offers—or it can vary from campaign to campaign and from mailing to mailing.

First developed as an aspect of packaged-goods marketing and popularized by Rosser Reeves, positioning has become a basic part of advertising jargon. It is like the weather: Everyone talks about it, but no one knows how to change it.

In direct marketing, we do have the ability to change our positioning. We can measure the results and make dramatic changes from one advertisement to another. We can, in effect, be all things to all people, just not at the same time.

The difference is that we are usually not starting with a product that has built its awareness and associations over years. Each direct-marketing effort can modify its own position, and seek out and sell the portion of the market segment attracted to that position.

Perception as the Standard

Before going into the various kinds of positioning, I first want to point out that positioning is not necessarily related to reality. Instead, it is a function of perception.

From a pure marketing standpoint, it is not important whether your product is the best of its kind. What is important is whether people *think* it is the best. Positioning in the marketplace means positioning in the mind. Though it is easier and more ethical to place a product where it should be placed on the basis of merits, its position in the marketplace is not necessarily dictated by reality. The ratings in *Consumer Reports* magazine often shoot down our previous conceptions of which brands are the best, while pointing out little-known brands that really are.

VERTICAL POSITIONING

The classic approach to positioning is based on this definition of the term: *the portrayal of a product in its proper status vis-à-vis other products.* A hierarchy is presumed; the most obvious categories are price and quality. The products are classified as good, better, best or cheap, cheaper, cheapest.

Value is, of course, only one possible spectrum of positioning. A camera can be easy-to-use as opposed to one with more controls, or a portable computer can be lightweight as opposed to being more powerful. Soap can be gentler or stronger. An Internet business service can be a ready-to-use no-brainer where all the thinking has been done for you, or a service that can be highly customized for the technologically advanced customer. Automobile brands can be positioned as safer or faster, sportier or more comfortable. Indeed, such companies go beyond tailoring their advertising to different appeals and actually design models that can be positioned to different consumer preferences.

It has been said that the essence of the creative process is choice. Certainly, it is the fundamental decision that must be considered in positioning. All the conventional uses of this discipline involve some type of relative placement over or under others. I call this "vertical positioning" to differentiate it from horizontal positioning, described later in this chapter.

Product Placement

Within the sphere of vertical positioning, product placement is a more common consideration than its companions: offer placement, audience placement, and media placement.

Product placement is a function of how the product is presented in relation to competing products. It involves choice: choice about what real attributes are selected for prominent attention, or choice about the images, associations, and conventions that are to be attached to the product's public perception.

A product can be "New!" or it can be "A Tradition Since 1829." It can be "Solid"—"Built to Last," or it can be "Lightweight and Portable." It can be "Bigger" or "Compact."

A camera can be super-simple—Just point it and shoot"—or it can offer the ultimate in dials, knobs, gadgets, and other controls for maximum flexibility.

None of these positions is necessarily right or wrong, but all of them are different, and all of them give you something to say about your product that differentiates it from the competition. The position that is almost always wrong is "right in the middle," with a committee-designed concept that tries to be all things to all people at the same time.

Offer Placement

Book clubs constantly maneuver against each other with offers such as six for $1 or three for 49 cents, and magazines present their introductory subscription prices in countless variations. (See Chapter 6.)

The offer is a positioning consideration as well. The examples above are attempts to offer the lowest price—or at least to appear to. This is the most common direction, but it is not the only one and certainly not always the best one.

A full-price offer sets your product apart. So does, "A little more expensive, but worth it." There is a subtle difference, with not so subtle results, between "Regular price 50 cents" and "$1, but for you, half-price." The first is just cheap; the second is a bargain. It may not be logical, but neither is human psychology.

The offer is another way of placing your product. A high price is presumed to represent high quality. Too low a price is presumed to be cheap. A price slightly higher or lower than the competition can be fine provided the placement is justified. A price dramatically higher is a way of appealing to snobbery. A price dramatically lower may allow a product to be bought on impulse, or it may not be believable at all. This applies not only to pricing but also to introductory or trial offers that result in *de facto* new prices.

Personally, I prefer to go after the "slightly higher" position in most cases, with a good-quality story to justify the added cost and some premium or discount for immediate action. It is usually easier to point out the better features in a high-priced product than to explain why the cheaper product is low-priced.

Audience Placement

The classic audience positioning is related to age, income, education, occupation, and other demographic or geographic characteristics.

A product may be salable to many audiences, but a given advertisement in a given medium usually has to choose one audience segment as its primary objective. Within any given medium—magazine or newspaper, direct mail or television—there is a wide variety of audiences. How else can you explain the success, within one publication, of many widely varied promotions? Which audience you reach is a function of both copy and art, and both of these aspects can be adapted to attract whichever audience segment is desired.

Some headline styles and typefaces connote elegance. Others imply news or bargain images. Some appeal to most women, others to most men.

Older people are more willing than younger ones to read long copy messages, provided the type is legible. Color makes a difference, and so does the choice of illustrations. The age and apparent personality of a model, for instance, will attract similar readers and repel dissimilar ones.

Psychographic considerations are, in my opinion, a more important aspect of audience placement than demographic ones. The lifestyle and life stage of the prospect is usually a more sensitive positioning selector for direct marketers than age, education or income.

For example, more dramatic result differences occur from aiming a message at newlyweds, new parents, homeowners, and retirees than from any demographic selectors. On a finer level, positioning a product as one for people who value independence, macho sex appeal, culture, or other psychological delineators is the most dramatic difference of all.

Such emotional placement is the ultimate audience selector. Conventional market segmentation would never lead you to write an ad with this headline: "Lonely?" Yet lonely people who are precisely targeted by such a headline may be just the right audience for self-confidence courses, dating services, dance lessons, or even bowling alleys.

Size

The size of your medium is one way to position your communication. This is particularly true in newspapers or magazines, where you say a lot about what you are selling by the space unit you select. This also applies to the location of this ad within the publication.

A back cover, front-of-book position, or one adjacent to respected national advertisers, usually does better than being placed with small-space discount advertising. There are several cases where position more than made up for the savings in paying lower-priced remnant or discount rates.

A double-page spread or a full-page newspaper ad tells the reader, before a word is read, that this message is BIG! It's important! It also says that the advertiser is substantial, or else they couldn't afford such a large-space unit.

This doesn't mean that everyone should use large advertisements. A philanthropy might prefer a smaller, half-page unit to convey a humbler and more appropriately frugal image.

Size is not usually a factor in direct mail or on the Internet, nor is length a positioning (or negative) factor on television or radio. While greater size or duration may permit a more effective sales message if used for that purpose, sheer size will not add credibility except in print.

In direct mail, the size effect is infinitely more flexible, as described in Chapter 12 on Direct Mail Formats. A personal message can be conveyed one way, an ethical or financial message another. A bargain catalog is presented one way; an expensive collectible another. A sweepstakes offer aimed at young mothers calls for a very different format selection than a business-products proposition addressed to presidents of corporations.

HORIZONTAL POSITIONING

Horizontal positioning is the newest dimension in positioning—one that I personally identified and validated through testing. It adds a new perspective: time.

Horizontal positioning refers to the point in the consumer's decision-making process chosen as a starting point for an advertising message. It can deal with any of the four basic parameters: product, media, offer, and audience. It is a supplement to conventional positioning, not a substitute for it. This leads to a positioning grid, such as that illustrated in Fig. 9-1, offering a matrix of placement opportunities rather than one dimension or another.

The spectrum of horizontal positioning begins at the left side of the chart with "create a need." At the right is "overcome inertia." In between are "fulfill a need," "sell competitively," and "motivate by value." All of these are primary appeals that should be chosen as creative starting points as carefully as other positioning factors. Let's review them one at a time, in the order of their evolution in the mind of the consumer.

Create a Need

Does anyone remember carbon paper? Not too many years ago, that was how we made duplicate copies of letters. Today xerography is the standard, and most manufacturers sell competitively against other copiers. But when copiers first appeared on the market, specific product features, pricing, and other approaches would not have been as relevant as the merits of the product generically.

But now that photocopying has become commonplace, what if you can offer a new, lightweight copying machine with an unusually low price? The expected strategy would be to dramatize the price or the features and compete with the established copier companies. But there is another strategy that may do much, much better and is certainly worth testing: create the need—meaning sell the category—before you sell the individual product.

For example, take our lightweight low-priced copier. Instead of featuring product benefits or pricing, aim the message at the "new-user" market. Imagine ads with a headline such as, "Why every home should have a copier." Describe general uses for the home: keeping tax records, preparing

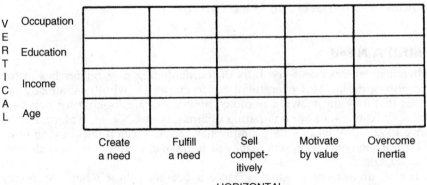

Figure 9-1. The positioning grid.

shopping lists, making copies of valuable papers. Or imagine a similar version of this message in a school newspaper: "How a copier can help your grades."

Such an ad doesn't begin with the product at all, except as a general product category. It stops the reader who hasn't considered such a purchase and says, in effect, "Hey, you! You need one of these!"

Once that point has been established, the role of this particular copier and its suitability for home use becomes very relevant. Then it is a simple matter of the particular product being in the right place at the right time, and in our case for the right price. A lead-procurement version might, in fact, simply offer a booklet about the uses of copiers in the home. The sales call or follow-up literature would promote the particular product.

At any given time and in any given marketplace, there are always some individuals in the market in each stage of the decision-making process. Which one should be selected will depend on just how many potential buyers are at each stage.

New Triers

We are all very aware of the "new trier" market—those who are usually the first to buy a new technology or fashion. Once it was microwave oven buyers. Today it might be users of digital cameras or broadband phone lines for faster Internet access. These people purchase new items for a number of reasons, mostly because they feel they need the latest thing. But "you need this new item or service" can also generate sales for products that appear to already have widespread acceptance.

For instance, home computers and cellular phones are widely accepted—but not by everybody. For many homes, the way to sell such products is still to create desire, perhaps by designing product variations specifically for those who are still non-users.

The incredible success of the iMac is a perfect example. It was introduced as one self-contained unit, with no hardware to install, the minimum number of components to plug in, as easy to use as a typewriter used to be, and for less than $1200. It was a brilliant stroke for this late-trier market—available in a choice of five fruit-colored flavors!

Fulfill A Need

Obviously, at this point, the bulk of the marketing possibilities lies in the creation of desire. However, there are some people who have already decided that they must own a home computer and are looking for one with the right features, or are comparing different brands, or are waiting for the price to come down. Or they simply have to be pushed into buying now. All these segments represent stages of horizontal positioning, and all exist side by side.

For an investment product, I wrote a headline, "Just what *are* money market accounts, anyway? And why should I keep my savings in one?" This is the create-a-need position and, according to research with beginning investors, was the headline that was most appealing and would generate the most interest and readership. Obviously it was aimed at those investors who were new to this category.

Fulfilling a need is probably the most common position in advertising, and it appears to be the starting place for those advertisers who do not employ strategic planning in general, or positioning in particular. They have the presumption—sometimes misguided—that the world already knows it needs what you are trying to sell.

In the money-market example, a need had to be created. In other positions, "fulfill a need", the need already exists. The consumer is aware of it, and advertising only has to announce that there is now a way to satisfy that need.

Using the copier example, this position leads to advertising that says, "Looking for a compact, attractive, low-priced home photocopier? Here it is."

"Motor's Auto Manual Helps You Fix Any Car Fast" presumes that there are people who: fix their cars; and want to save time, even though it also states a benefit. These classic ads run in publications whose readers want to fix their own or others' cars and believe they can do it. For that segment, the ad offers help.

For a more general, less handy portion of the population, the need might have to be created in the first place, with something like, "Make Money, Have Fun—Now Anyone Can Fix Cars." Here the theme is a generic one, and the desire is being created rather than fulfilled.

The difference is whether the customer knows they have a need prior to reading the ad. Time-Life began an ad for its American Wilderness library with a glorious mountain scene and the word "Escape!"—fulfilling a psychological need. *Bon Appetit* tempted readers with a close-up photo of a scrumptious chocolate cake, appealing to a sensual need to enjoy the food one eats. The Dreyfus Tax Exempt Bond Fund appealed to a universal need with its headline "Zero Tax." All these examples were winners, proven by split-run testing.

Sell Competitively

This middle position is probably the single most common general-advertising position.

Most advertisers generally presume that a product is needed and wanted, and that the only consideration is which brand to buy. Using the copier example, such ads might have the theme, "Why the XYZ copier is the one you need for home use because of this unique feature."

Most advertising presumes that a portion of the media audience already knows it has a need (say transportation), wants to fulfill that need (by buying a car), and has only to choose (which car to buy). For automobiles, that is probably correct.

In any category where your product or service has a genuine improvement over others or even over previous versions of yours, it can be very effective to sell the new features which, presumably, the competitive product or the one the customer now owns doesn't have.

Competitive selling can be very aggressive and may, in fact, be most powerful when it challenges competitors by name. You've seen car ads do this, but very few direct marketers seem willing to meet the competition head-on. Those who do are often very successful.

Financial management is one of the sectors where direct marketers challenge the competition in their advertising. Equitable's Money Market Account was introduced as "the new alternative" to certificates of deposit, while savings banks were countering with ads attacking mutual funds. Today, on-line stockbrokers compare their rates openly, not only with the full-service brokers such as Merrill Lynch, but with other Internet brokers.

Motivate by Value

Price emphasis is another distinctly separate aspect of horizontal positioning—the aspect most common to retail-establishment advertising. It is the easiest, least imaginative, and usually least profitable form of advertising, saying in effect, "Buy now, because we're cheap."

In direct marketing, pricing motivation is usually manifested by announcements such as that you can now get 13 records for 1 cent from the Columbia Record Club, six books for 99 cents from The Literary Guild, or a Sharper Image closeout on a travel alarm for only $24.99.

The limitations of price emphasis are obvious. For one thing, it is only effective if the pricing is genuinely attractive. And attractive pricing may cut into allowable margin so severely as to make the offer unprofitable.

It is more preferable, and a much greater challenge, to find motivations, positions, and appeals that will sell a product without resorting to price emphasis. Good marketing and advertising are capable of doing this. Price emphasis should be a last resort after all conventional price options have been fully explored.

Notwithstanding this admittedly utopian goal, pricing and offers will produce a dramatic variation in response rate and CPR, virtually without exception. This is why major advertisers always give price testing a high priority in the selection of ads or mailing pieces to be tested.

A music club, using split runs in *TV Guide*, tested 30 offers, including "Take 8 Free," "Take 9 Free," "Take 10 Free," "Take 12 Free," and "7 for $1.00."

A mail-order film processor entering the mail-order field began with a seven-way offer split in newspaper-inserted envelopes. These offer tests included "This certificate good for one dollar off our already low prices." "1¢ Sale. Pay for processing your first roll at our regular low price. Pay only 1¢ for processing your second roll." "Half price. Yes—take 50% off our already low regular prices for film processing." (See Table 9-1.)

The position based on price, discount, premium, or introductory offer may be the least imaginative from the creative viewpoint and the most obvious from the strategic planning standpoint, but it is still the easiest and fastest way to produce a dramatic change in advertising response.

TABLE 9-1
TEST RESULTS OF A FILM-PROCESSING OFFER

Price statement	Twenty-print price	Average price (all sizes)	Cost per order	Margin	Units	Net	Contribution
Basic $1.99 up	$1.99	$3.50	$19	$10.00	6,315	($9.00)	($56,835)
Film, only 39¢	1.39	2.50	14	9.00	8,571	(5.00)	(42,855)
1¢ sale	0.99	2.50	12	9.00	10,000	(3.00)	(30,000)
$1 off	0.99	2.50	9	9.00	13,333		
99¢ offer	0.99	2.50	8	9.00	15,000	1.00	15,000
Half price	0.99	1.75	5	8.25	24,000	3.25	78,000
39¢ limited offer	0.39	2.20	2	8.70	60,000	6.70	402,000

Overcome Inertia

The middle three positions are already used often and effectively. The forgotten positions are at the two extremes. The create-a-need position is discussed above. The other extreme is overcoming inertia, or to put it another way, basing the fundamental theme of the advertisement on immediacy.

In retail advertising, the immediacy concept is based most frequently on a sale, a closeout, a discount, or a cents-off coupon good for a limited time only.

In direct marketing, when immediacy is the position, the offer, the copy, and the layout must all be developed with the dramatization of immediacy as a primary objective.

This position is driven by the inertia theory. In brief, it presumes that at any given time in the life cycle of an established product, there are people who have never heard of the product, others who have tried and rejected it, and still others who have bought or are about to buy it. In addition, another large, very significant market segment has heard of it, likes it, intends to buy it someday, and just hasn't gotten around to it yet. This last segment is the prime target of this position. Its intent, in very simple language, is to flag these people down, grab them by the shoulders, and yell, "Do it now! Don't put it off a minute longer!"

The Save the Children advertising campaigns were a clear example of this. After years of exposure to their advertisements and that of other child-sponsorship philanthropies, a large audience was ready and waiting, according to a Yankelovich survey. All that had to be done was to overcome inertia.

The ads presumed prior knowledge and went right for the order—*now*—with headlines like "Fill out this coupon now and save a child." This simple position change, first tested in split runs, was very successful.

Telegram approaches, with their abbreviated sentence structure and implied urgency, communicate immediacy in style, but so do handwritten messages and other devices described later in this chapter. The difference is that they are dominant rather than supportive themes.

Deadlines are, of course, one of the most effective methods of all, whether real, as with a limited quantity or special offer, or implied, as in, "Please reply by date indicated."

Many magazines, for example, promote their subscriptions once or twice a year, when their replacement or growth needs require it. Often these offers promise savings of between one-third and one-half off the newsstand price.

Such offers might be more effective if, instead of relying solely on price, they moved the position to that of immediacy. This would mean making the reduced rate a true special offer, good only for the 60 days or so of the promotion.

POSITION SEGMENTATION

Research can be very helpful in determining the most effective positioning for a given product or proposition. One method is to mail questionnaires or conduct telephone interviews with buyers or customers to determine which feature or appeal motivated them to buy.

In some cases the conclusions are obvious, as when one approach is clearly and consistently the most appealing. However, direct-marketers must be careful to avoid what I call "the average trap," where results are pooled together to indicate a one-size-fits-all solution which, like some apparel with the same description, fits no one.

For example, a very inexpensive car might be the choice of young people who can't afford anything else, and also of more affluent, older people who use it as a second car. If you were to look only at the average, you would mistakenly conclude that your market was somewhere in the middle.

General advertisers relying on mass media make this mistake frequently. The business-school classic is Packard, once the leaders in luxury cars, which during the depression mistakenly moved to mid-price cars, the one category that didn't survive. In direct marketing—direct mail particularly— we are freed of the need to play the averages and can direct different messages to different geographic segments.

Research Matrix

A useful tool is a *research matrix*, such as the hypothetical example in Fig. 9-2. This is for a product such as a camera, and compares two ranges of responses: modernist self-image, and desired complexity.

Each dot represents one of 25 interviews with people who bought the product. It is clear here that buyers who consider themselves modern, or triers of new products, bought the new item because of its ease-of-use. However, buyers who consider themselves traditional also bought the product, but in their case they were attracted to some of the new controls and options that it concluded.

Here again, an averaging of the interviews might lead to an incorrect middle position. The same kind of grid can be prepared to visualize other

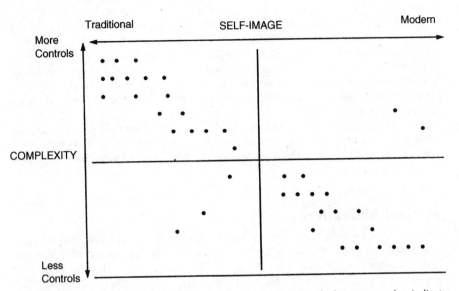

Figure 9-2. Hypothetical Research Matrix. Forty respondents ranked on two scales indicate pattern of preferences.

research responses—say, the correlation between ages and feature desired, or price preference and intended product use.

This case clearly demonstrates that, to the extent media and list planners can identify cost-efficient ways of reaching people with the specified self-images, different positioning is needed.

ESTABLISHING A POSITION

How do you determine which position is right for your advertising campaign? How do you revise a position that has been firmly established in the consumer's mind? The following section will help you answer these questions.

Locating the Correct Positioning

First, when do you do it? Some advertisers go through the positioning exercise only at the inception of a new product launch. Others consider positioning only when a basic ad program starts to fail. Of course, positioning is one of the considerations that should be raised at such times, even though most advertisers will instead concentrate on revising lists and media. It is incorrect to presume that an entire publication or list no longer works when, in fact, what could really be happening is that the relatively small portion of each medium that has been responding is no longer doing so to the same extent as before.

A different position may "talk to" a different segment of the same media universe. It may hit an emotional "hot button" with a larger percentage of the original audience segment than before. More likely, the number of prospects who were reached by the original horizontal position has declined. Advertising must then address itself to those who have moved to a later point or to those just entering the market who must be addressed at an earlier position placement.

Relocating either the horizontal or the vertical positioning can radically alter your entire marketing picture, significantly increasing response rates and substantially increasing the size of the total media universe, which is in some ways more important.

Vertical Alteration

Advertising can be adjusted vertically in very subtle ways not immediately discernible to previous users or to competitors. An important requirement is that present audiences are not lost in the search for a slightly higher or lower demographic profile. Revising copy style and graphic appearance are simple ways to alter vertical positioning.

You can move a product upscale or downscale by changing typefaces, copy vocabulary, graphic image, and the selection of models or actors used in the advertising. For multi-product companies, of course, the selection of featured products will make a material difference in the type of customers produced for later promotions.

Beer and cigarette advertising have adopted the concept of vertical positioning in dramatic ways. There is the "Marlboro man," that attached a masculine image to a cigarette brand that once had a "sissy-image." Virginia Slims appealed to an emerging feminist market with "You've come a long way, baby."

Some brands of beer—such as Heineken and Beck's currently—position themselves for the white-collar suburbanite entertaining in the home. Others aim for the larger blue-collar beer market, with scenes set at ball games, bowling alleys, and bars, that show macho spokesmen and imply that viewers could be as tough as truck drivers or construction workers if they would just drink more of this particular brand of fermented hops.

Using research methods, direct marketers can determine whether prospects—business or consumer—believe a product or service is "for people like me." Because we know that people want to associate with brands and products that reflect their self-image, we can position our products visually by carefully selecting the kind of people we show in our ads, mailings, or other communications. Split-run tests have proven that the addition of the right photograph can produce dramatic improvements in the results of direct-response advertising.

Horizontal Alteration

Almost always, changing horizontal positions requires a fundamental change in advertising concept. At times it is possible to broaden an existing advertisement by adding appeals to other horizontal placements, but usually entirely new ads, mailing pieces, or commercials are required.

An early ad for Black's Classics Club offered works by Aristotle and Bacon as a premium for joining the Classics Club, presuming there was already a desire to know the classics—namely, fulfilling a need.

Later ads changed the picture considerably. At one time they ran an illustration suggested by me which positioned such books as "furniture," showing a shelf of classics with the line, "Start now to build this fine home library." Later ads by the brilliant Len Reiss created a different image, and sold readers on the educational and cultural satisfaction of reading such great classics. These approaches are both examples of moving the proposition back to an earlier position—creating the desire to read the classics rather than presuming the need existed already—so as to appeal to new audience segments.

Franklin Mint's Franklin Library division at one time relied on television commercials in which several reviewers guessed at the value of these finely bound books followed by an announcer who intoned "Wrong! It only cost . . ." This was a dramatic and well-done exposition of the value position. Challenged to find a commercial to replace this tiring spot, I moved to the first position, creating the need. The bindings and value story were relegated to a secondary position behind a dramatization of a young man reading and getting pleasure out of one of the classics offered: *Moby Dick*. This spot proved successful at opening a whole new market segment for Franklin Library by dramatizing what should be obvious: that great books are also great to *read*!

Let's look at another example—the simple calculator. When calculators first came out they could be sold by creating a desire for them among non-calculator users or by fulfilling the need of office calculator users for a small portable model. One ad would sell their usefulness, the other would presume knowledge of what a calculator does and stress size, weight, and portability.

Eventually, many calculators came into the market, and smart advertisers abandoned their earlier ad themes and moved into competitive selling (if they had a superior product) or into the pricing position (if price was a viable appeal). Even while new, sophisticated calculators at unbelievably low prices were flooding the retail market, direct marketers still reaped huge sales. Older, higher-priced models took the route of overcoming inertia, placing materials with attractive reasons to "act now" in prospects' hands via space ads and direct mail.

At any given time, even today, each and every horizontal position can be used by some manufacturer. The desire to utilize such marketing appeals impelled research and development departments to find ways to make their products better or cheaper in some way, to some market. Examples are children's educational calculators, game calculators, race handicapping calculators, programmable calculators, and miniature calculators the size of a business card.

Let me make clear that, in direct marketing, you are not limited to a single position for all of your marketing efforts. A position can be adopted for a specific medium or list as the best position for the particular target audience.

For instance, Consumers Union has used a food-oriented product position for women's lists and magazines, an automobile-related position for male lists and publications, and a home-repair emphasis for lists of homeowners. A direct mail campaign I created for General Electric positioned television sets as technologically superior for one kind of list, but as attractive furniture for another. The choice of which of their wide product line to feature varied to fit the particular market segment.

As new products are developed, marketers are called on to find different ways to appeal to new audiences. In return, manufacturers are called on to innovate, improve, and economize in order to please the consumer. This free, competitive interplay of marketer and manufacturer is the strength of America's capitalist economy, and the search for better advertising is its catalyst.

THE IMAGERY TRIANGLE

One theory, which has been particularly useful in creative planning, has been the Imagery Triangle. It has been included in research projects and been the basis for split-run testing. It has worked for most of my clients and may be useful to any direct marketer planning a creative project.

In brief, it is based on the idea that the prospect must have three clear images in mind before he or she can feel confident about responding to a direct marketing offer. These are product image, self-image, and company image. When planning, we assign different percentages of emphasis to each corner and plan the creative accordingly.

Product Image

The lower-left corner of Fig. 9-3 represents the product story, or "What does this do for me?" This is the basic product presentation that most companies and copywriters handle superbly, and is the foundation of the simplest trade announcement or catalog blurb as well as major packaged-goods database campaigns.

When the product is new, or has an attractive new feature, by all means it should have the major emphasis, with 60 or 70 percent in that direction. When it is established, you need not spend as much time explaining the basics such as how it works or what it's used for, and should stress product only if there was some new feature or benefit. Certainly this changes as the product goes through different stages of its lifecycle.

However, no matter how prominent the feature, some space must be devoted to company image or self-image, if only as insurance for the future. With today's fast-changing product evolution, virtually any product feature is bound to be imitated or surpassed by a competitor in a season or two. Your protection is to establish a self-image position or clear trust in the company that can serve as an advantage even after other edges have been lost.

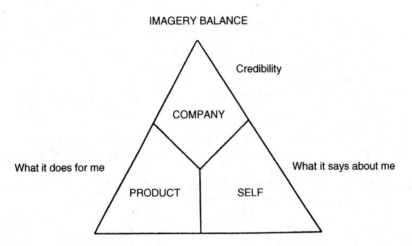

Figure 9.3. The Imagery Triangle.

For example, imagine a bank issuing a credit card with a new feature—perhaps private club privileges at airports, or credits towards stays at resort hotels. Either of these would be very attractive to frequent flyers who can't possibly use all the "miles" they've accumulated for plane trips by billing on their credit card. But eventually another card-issuer might offer the same feature. To win customers that stay, you need a fundamental positioning image; features alone aren't enough.

Self-Image

The lower-right corner of the triangle designates the percentage of attention for self-image, or "What does it say about me?" Putting it another way, "How does this buying decision enhance my self-esteem, my own image of who I am?"

For years, direct marketers thought that impressing others was a consumer motivation. The idea of the "coffee-table book" came into vogue. The pictorial element of an advertisement was designed to show "others" admiring your good taste.

We sold Bibles and encyclopedias in the same way, assuming that most customers would never open them, convinced that our customers simply wanted to impress others with their devoutness or scholarship. We knew it wasn't to help the children in the family pursue these goals because in most cases the buyer's children were too young to read.

Later research revealed that neither neighbors nor family were the real underlying motivation, although the latter might be offered as an excuse. The real reason was the buyer's need to reinforce his or her *own* self-image as a devout person or as a good parent, as the case might be.

Successful brands all have clear positioning images, which usually correspond to the buyer's own self-image. They are more youthful, more traditional, more elite, more popular, more technical, or more carefree—and they appeal to consumers who see themselves in the same way.

Today, many products and services are basically parity offerings. Their advantages over past or competitive versions may be too tiny to make much of a fuss about. In these cases, only the ability to appeal to self-image distinguishes one from the other.

When self-image must be stressed, photos of appropriate people using the product or service become important in the creative presentation. Prospects should look at an advertisement and sub-consciously think, "This person is just like me," or "I want to be more like this person." It's much easier to appeal to an individual's self-image with pictures than words.

Company Image

If product image is "What does it do for me?" and self-image is "What does it say about me?" then company image is credibility: "Can I believe the advertiser's answers to the first two questions?" Company image establishes the credibility needed, to some extent, for any marketing proposition.

To the extent that the offer is a costly one, or involves personal safety, this is a major issue. To the extent that the product is intangible, or in an area where the customer has learned to be skeptical, it may well need to occupy 40 to 50 percent of the message.

One client offered precious-metals investments in an environment where some less reputable firms had poisoned trust in this proven inflation hedge. Their solution was to arrange a partnership with a well-known bank to store the gold bullion, which could not be delivered because usually it was sold on margin. The ad: "Monex offers something new in gold investments— the gold!"

Similarly, magazine agents encountered skepticism among some consumers about their huge sweepstakes mailings. Publishers' Clearing House ran heavy schedules on television showing real winners. American Family used well-known celebrities Dick Clark and Ed McMahon to add credibility, showing them both in television advertising and in direct mail.

Even the largest companies must sometimes devote space to establishing their credibility, especially when appealing to a new market segment or entering a new field. For example, when Sears bought Coldwell Banker and Dean Witter, they insisted on adding the Sears name, but did nothing at all to justify the new brand. Instead, their catalog image diminished the credibility of these high-end brands. They should have dedicated a percentage of every direct marketing communication to changing their own image.

When a company is new and has no image, they must create one by spending more of their advertising emphasis in this area. Techniques might include photos of their building or their founder, mentions of their resources, details of their awards, descriptions of their quality control, and testimonials from their satisfied customers.

Imagery Balance

When used as one element of a creative plan, so-called *imagery balance* dictates the relative emphasis to be given to each of the three elements in creative planning. If an element such as the reputation of the company or the features of the product is already strong, little emphasis is needed. If one of the images is unclear, more emphasis is needed.

In practice each of our clients and our account team agree on a percentage to be placed in each of the three image corners, adding up to 100 percent in all. While some propositions may seem to require a great deal of attention in all three segments, choices must be made. The most attention should be given to those areas that are the least clear.

For instance, an established company such as IBM or Time-Life would be given only 5 percent in the company image corner of the imagery triangle, not because it is unimportant but because it can be presumed. Even this percentage is a reminder to prominently display the logo and company name. For an unknown company, particularly one asking for investments or promoting a personal health product, this figure might be 25 or 35 percent.

Where a product is brand new and has distinct and obvious advantages, the product should be the hero. The same applies where a product has new and exciting features. Where there is no product story, then self-image often is the key. At any rate, self-image is one factor that always must be present to some degree.

In using this method, I have occasionally had the opportunity to test different percentage allotments in split runs, and have found significant differences in results. Sometimes different market segments require different image combinations. A magazine's expired subscribers may want to know what's new. New prospects may need to have the features of the magazine related to their self-image, or they may require some knowledge of the credentials of the publisher.

EIGHT TACTICAL ELEMENTS OF CREATIVE SUCCESS

In addition to the Imagery Triangle, there are eight additional areas that should be thought through, talked over, and carefully chosen. These are:

1. Audience targeting
2. Product presentation
3. Involvement devices
4. Convenience factors
5. Immediacy incentives
6. Speed of delivery
7. Credibility
8. Style

Once the basic marketing plan has been completed—including the positioning decisions—it is necessary that these eight factors be considered
for each individual mailing or advertisement that is to be tested or rolled
out at each stage of a program. The back-end follow-through to obtain
payment, renewals and reorders are also involved, not only the front-end
solicitation of orders or inquiries.

These steps do not have to change with each separate test or each letter
in a sequence. Within a fixed combination of the eight factors there is room
for dozens of different copy and layout executions. In my experience, however, fundamental conceptual differences will produce a greater difference
in results than different creative executions of the same concept.

In some organizations the selection of these concepts is left to the copywriter or copy-art creative team. In others it is selected by the account
person or product manager, and included as part of the specifications for
a creative execution. In either case it should be a separate and distinct
process, participated in or at least reviewed by both marketing and creative
personnel. Agreement should be reached before anyone "jumps on a word
processor and rides off in all directions."

AUDIENCE TARGETING

Once you have selected your audience, you have to figure out how to get
to them. If you have picked your lists and media correctly you know you
are reaching your potential customers, but you don't know whether they
are seeing your message.

The classic AIDA formula—attention, interest, desire, action—begins
with the concepts of *attention* and *interest.* Another way of saying this is
"How do you get the right people to stop and read your advertisement or
open your letter, in the midst of dozens of competing advertisements or
mailing pieces?"

Attention Appeals

The obvious way to target an audience is simply to announce whom your
message is for. A money market fund begins its ad, "A new alternative for
people who have $2500 in a savings account or certificate of deposit." You
can't get much more specific than that.

A book club directed at new market entrants begins, "If you've never
joined a book club before, maybe its because you never knew about. . ."

Here are some other, less wordy applications of this type of headline:
"Hard of hearing?"; "Good news for denture wearers!"; "For women with
narrow feet."

Appeals to Needs

If your product or service appeals to too broad an audience, you won't
have much luck applying this principle. "Readers!" or "For people who like

to dress well" may be too general. In most cases you'll do better getting the attention of your audience by addressing their needs, both physical and emotional. Such needs include the entire range of human desires and emotions:

- Independence
- Importance
- Self-image
- The respect of others
- Energy and health
- Wealth and security
- Pride and satisfaction
- Adventure and excitement
- Tranquility and escape
- Eating well; dressing well
- A good job, a nice home, a healthy family
- Love and affection, sex and romance
- Being amused, excited, and entertained
- Being smarter, or at least appearing smarter
- Being happy, or at least happier
- Doing good, feeling good, looking good, and maybe even being good

Take, for example, a product or plan that helps readers stop smoking. The broad "attention" approach would be simply "For people who want to stop smoking." But let's say you want to talk to smokers who have not yet made that decision. You could write a headline about health or long life, or you could state that food tastes better to nonsmokers. You could say that the reader would look better without nicotine stains or smell better without smoky hair and clothing, and point out how this improvement could lead to new friends, a better job, or a new romance. A multi-product company can feature different products to meet different appeals. For instance, a book club can appeal to any of these needs by featuring one book or another.

Try this exercise with any product, and you'll be amazed at how many needs your product can fulfill. Then make a deliberate choice before you start to write a headline.

The Floating Audience Appeal

Sometimes with an unusual product it's important to let a product find its own audience by appealing to curiosity, snobbery, or independence. Some examples: "Why is *Rolling Stone* the most misunderstood magazine in

America?"; "What is *Ms.* magazine, and why is it saying all those terrible things?" Any ad that says "X—it's not for everyone" fits into this category.

PRODUCT PRESENTATION

Chapter 3, The Marketing Plan, suggested that you describe your product or service from every possible viewpoint, and gave the example of how as simple a product as a pencil can be described from physical, historical, scientific, emotional, and psychological perspectives. The time to make that exercise pay off for you is when you are ready to present your product.

Once the product has been described, you can then select certain attributes or appeals around which to build your advertising. The choices may depend on the positioning decision made for a specific ad or mailing piece. They may depend on your understanding of the nature and needs of the target audience. They may vary depending on the available media and the format you have to work with. For example, decorator colors would not be as demonstrable in a black-and-white ad as in a color one, and a product that has an impressive action or motion would come across better on television than in print.

Feature Dramatization

Finding a way to dramatize one or more attributes of the product or service is another creative tactic. This can be done as a logical presentation, as in, "Seventeen reasons why you should read *U.S. News & World Report*," or a dramatic one, such as, "See how this wonder knife cuts through solid steel."

Dramatization often involves exaggeration—giving an example or case history that is accurate but atypical. Demonstrating that your glue can lift a suspended elephant or pull a freight train has nothing to do with your prospect's intended use, but serves to dramatize the attribute of strength. The case history of a homeowner who built a whole new wing with the help of a do-it-yourself book may not echo the typical prospect's intention, but it will serve to dramatize the attribute of the book's usefulness.

While working on the introduction of a money market fund, I discovered the importance of dramatizing liquidity in the form of the check-writing feature of such funds. This appeal proved to be indispensable, even though operating data indicated that very few such investors ever took advantage of the feature. They just wanted to know it was there in case of a sudden emergency or opportunity.

Unique Selling Proposition

The concept of the *unique selling proposition* (USP) is most important in general advertising where a single association is needed to aid recall, but it is also useful to direct marketers. It is most relevant at two levels of horizontal positioning: (1) creating a need, and (2) competitive selling.

In creating a need, the USP is often a generic concept for an entire category of products. In such instances the ad must point out the desirability of your product as compared with the product in prevailing use.

Television's USP when first introduced—a visual image—was sufficient to sell a great many sets by companies that are no longer major players in the television-manufacturing business. In order to sell competitively today, electronic manufacturers constantly search for new USPs such as color-correction signals, room light-adjustment devices, remote control units, and built-in accommodation for cables, recorders, game controls, computer attachments, and phone hookups. The computer industry is now undergoing a similar change; examples include the multi-colored iMacs and the built-to-order Gateway personal computers.

Selling Benefits

Most important, every product attribute must be interpreted in terms of benefits, whether the product is generically unique, competitively unique, or not unique at all.

Never assume that a customer knows why a certain feature is important. No matter what you're selling, look for interpretations of product attributes as potential planks for your copy platform. For example, a Krugerrand coin contains exactly 1 ounce of pure gold—an attribute. Because the price of an ounce of gold can be found in the daily paper, it is easy to determine its value—a benefit. An appliance may have a plastic body for lightness, a metal body for sturdiness, or a glass body so that you can see how it works or keep it clean easily. No matter what the attribute, thinking in terms of benefits can lead to important and effective selling points.

Building an Edge

In direct marketing, we presume that the market and its needs are the given, and any product can be adapted to fit. Therefore, where there isn't a unique selling proposition or a product with a feature or benefits that can be dramatized, we can always invent one.

Even with an ongoing business, there is always some way to give it an edge. Add a guarantee, a service, or a way to update the product. Invent an accessory, an attractive display case, or some element that will make the product a bit easier or more effective to use. Or give it an intangible edge: peace of mind, confidence, pride, or certainty.

The power of marketing can and should be used as a two-way street—not only to sell consumers on using new products, but also to motivate manufacturers to improve products to meet consumer needs and desires.

Getting to the Point

The specifics of a copy platform are governed by the attitudes of the consumer. These attitudes have changed over the years and will continue to change.

If you look at the typical buyer scenario suggested in your marketing plan, it probably will be evident that this prospect is very different from the prospect who was enticed into reading such long copy messages of yesteryear as The John Caples classic, "They laughed when I sat down to play the piano." In the eyes of direct marketing copywriters, today's consumer is distinguished by laziness, impatience, and procrastination.

Many consumers are reluctant to seek out information on different brands and to analyze which is best. You must bring the facts to them. They don't want to wade through long copy messages to find reasons why your product is the one they should buy. You must make your message interesting and rewarding to read. Furthermore, when presented with the facts, consumers don't want to interpret them. You must do it for them.

Most consumers not only don't want to read long copy messages in advertising and direct mail, they don't want to read your ad or direct mail at all—no matter how short the message. Ads such as "Forty-nine reasons why you should buy . . ." usually are not as successful today as they once were, precisely because your prospect won't keep reading until he/she finds the one reason that would really be convincing. If you've got something to say, you'd better say it up front, simply and clearly.

A classic philanthropic ad read, "For $16 a month, you can help Rosario Torres. Or you can turn the page." The motivations were buried in the body copy. Most readers just turned the page. It was later discovered, in split-run testing, that this ad did only one-third as well as a new advertisement built on the concept of involvement. To quote from Victor Schwab's poetic rendering of a consumer's advice to writers, "Tell me quick, and tell me true, or else my love, to hell with you."

INVOLVEMENT DEVICES

Assuming that your prospect has been stopped and has enough interest in your product to hesitate before turning the page, linking to another website, or tossing the letter in the wastepaper basket, how do you hold that interest long enough to get your whole message across? The key need here is some way to "involve" your prospect. Here are some ideas.

Quizzes

"Do you make these mistakes in English?" is an old classic that ran for years. Another is, "Should you invest in a tax-exempt bond fund?" Both ads ask a question and offer information that stimulates the reader's desire to learn the answer.

Checklists are a variation: "Which of these important stories have you missed because you haven't been subscribing to . . . ?" Another variation is a headline with a simple yes-or-no request.

Fascination

Every once in a while a copywriter has an opportunity to hold the reader's interest through the sheer eloquence of the story being presented. Often such a message is an entertaining narrative, an intriguing case history, or step-by-step instructions on building a craft project or cooking a sumptuous recipe. A message that is rewarding in itself because it entertains or informs can be one of the best ways to hold a prospect.

Boardroom Reports, the publisher of *Bottom Line Personal* and many other newsletters, uses a format that relies heavily on what publisher Martin Edelston calls "fascinations." As articles are published, provocative lines are abstracted, such as "What food should you never eat on an airplane?" These are tested to see which are the most effective. They then become the headlines and copy of their advertising in every medium. These newsletters, with over a million subscribers, are the proof of the success and power of this method.

Value

A coupon that graphically appears to have value in itself will involve the reader of an ad or mailing piece. While "checks" must be used carefully in a way that will not deceive the reader, any item that in fact can save the reader money does have value and should look valuable. No one wants to throw away an envelope that contains a valuable certificate. Fewer still will toss out one that has a coin showing through a window, contains a bona fide check (even for a token amount like 10 cents), or has a real postage stamp on the reply envelope.

I have received mailings containing a $2 bill commemorative stamps, packets of seeds, and good-luck charms—all attempts to get me to pay attention to a message by offering me obvious and immediate value.

Personalization

Nothing is as fascinating to a person as his or her own name. All evidence shows that the more frequently and prominently it appears in direct mail, the better the mailings will do.

Even more effective is evidence that the advertiser is addressing not just a name, but a person. Messages can be made "special" by including an address, past purchase information, political affiliation, or other data—the more relevant the better. The Internet has the capability of infinitely personalizing messages by combining unique data from "cookies" with data from classic direct-mail sources. Good personalization involves not only using the prospect's name often but using it well, with as much relevance as computer technology, available data, privacy-law and good taste permit.

Play

Tom Collins quotes the saying, "Within every person there is a child, and that child likes to play." This is the underlying reason why stamps, stickers, and tokens of all kinds lift response more often than not. *U.S. News & World Report* achieved a major breakthrough by using a Westvaco-patented reply card that told the addressee, "Press here to subscribe." A trick fold popped out a picture of a handshake, indicating that the prospect was accepting the offer.

Other mailings ask readers to scrape off a coating, lift a flap, scratch a surface to release a scent, pull a strip to reveal a message in a window, look for a lucky number, examine a photograph through a colored filter, or moisten a surface to reveal an invisible-ink message. Corny? Sure. But these kinds of play devices are used because they work.

Completion

The brilliant direct-mail innovator Sol Blumenfeld identified the concept of "completion" as a factor in direct mail response devices.

This is the true magic of stamps, peel-off labels, and tokens used in marketing—particularly in direct mail. The "yes" or "no" stamp is not just a toy; it is a tool that fulfills the prospect's compulsive need to finish an apparently incomplete design.

Imagine a response card that shows a picture of a man looking into empty space with his arm outstretched and—yipes!—a hand missing! How can you resist pasting in the stamp that (1) adds the hand, (2) places the magazine being held by the hand in a position where the man appears to be reading it, and (3) coincidentally, indicates your acceptance of the publisher's proposition?

Try this experiment to see for yourself the power of completion. Draw a circle or a square on a blackboard, with one segment omitted. Leave a piece of chalk nearby and watch how visitors to your office feel a need to finish the shape.

Here's a simple method for mail pieces. Start to tell a story on an envelope, and leave it unfinished, or even in mid-thought. The completion urge will get your reader inside faster than any plea to "see inside." For the same reason, I always insist that direct mail letters be typed with the last paragraph on each page interrupted in the middle of a sentence—a powerful way to get people to turn the page and keep reading.

Choice

Perhaps one of the most successful involvement devices is the simplest: choice. "Which records do you want for only . . . ?"; "How many weeks of this magazine shall we send you for . . . ?"; "Do you want the red or green display case for your recipe card file?"; "Do you want your contribution to help a needy boy or a needy girl?" Or simply, "Yes or no?"

CONVENIENCE FACTORS

"Make it easy to respond" has always been a fundamental requirement for DM advertising. In fact, convenience is one of the cardinal reasons for the growth of direct marketing as an industry.

After all, shopping by mail or on the web means you don't have to use your precious time and even more precious gasoline to drive downtown. You don't have to look for a parking space, push through crowds, fumble through shelves and racks, and reason with a salesperson that knows nothing about sales and sometimes less about courtesy.

You see what you want in an ad or a catalog. You fill out a coupon, make a phone call or click on an Internet link. In a matter of days, someone from the Postal Service, UPS, FedEx, or other shipping service brings it to your door. If you don't like it, you just pop it back in the mail.

The concept of convenience must be extended into every type of response advertising, and there are several ways that responding to such advertising can be made even easier.

Coupon Readability

Coupons, commitments or guarantees should be crystal-clear in style, meaning, and typography.

Some art directors seem to think that a coupon is a necessary evil, to be kept to a minimum size regardless of how much copy is to be included. Not so. The coupon is the place to summarize your selling theme. It deserves as much space as needed to be clear and easily readable. Some very successful ads I've been involved with have used an entire page as one giant coupon.

The coupon should be easy to fill out. Lines and spaces should be large enough so a consumer can write his or her name, address, city, state, and zip code comfortably without abbreviating or printing in tiny letters. If someone writes illegibly, you're out an order. If another prospect gets frustrated trying to write in a cramped space, you're out another order. And if a third consumer has to look for a pair of eyeglasses in order to read the small type in the coupon, you're out a third order.

What a shame! Why put the right offer in the right medium, hold the attention of the right people through the copy and into the coupon, and then lose them because of simple readability problems?

Ease of Response

Most sales are impulse responses to some extent, and every second of delay minimizes your chance of getting a reply.

Format has a lot to do with ease of response. Soft-space ad coupons should be easy to tear out—not buried in the gutter of a magazine or the middle of a page.

Bind-in cards, flaps, and tip-ons all are worth more than their added expense in increased response, not because they attract attention, but because they make it easy to respond.

In direct mail you can make it even easier to respond by providing an envelope or a reply card. Advances in computerization allows direct marketers to fill in the general information on a reply form. Business-reply mail will save your prospect a trip to the post office or the stamp machine.

Some successful mailings have included a small pen or pencil so the prospect can fill out the mailer immediately, without fumbling around for a writing utensil. If a choice is involved in your offer, stamps, tokens, labels, and other devices can be used to make selection and ordering simple as well as interesting.

Internet order forms are also subject to the need for ease of response. In fact two-thirds of customers going to "shopping cart" ordering pages never order—presumably due to confusion or frustration.

I personally spent over an hour today trying to order two books from Amazon.com. Between the error messages "failed to load" and "must have your password," I was thoroughly frustrated. I would have given up except that my wife needed those books for a class she was teaching. Ordinarily I would have just placed the order by phone.

I spent 40 minutes with their customer service department, but the company would not take a phone order. They preferred to waste my time and theirs to get the order over the web rather than accept the order on the telephone. It was not an experience that I enjoyed.

Avoiding Calculations

It is safe to assume that most of your prospects don't like to do math. Yes, some veteran mail-order buyers can tackle a major catalog and calculate a maze of shipping costs and sales-tax rates that depend on the items ordered, shipping weights, and varying routes. But I can't help wondering how much more business some of these catalog companies might do if the costs were all calculated in advance and included in parentheses next to each item.

If you're expecting multiple orders, don't confront your reader with a need for multiplication and postage calculations. Instead, make it simple and present predetermined totals as much as possible.

Consider this example: "Send me _____-widgets at $1.49 each, plus 50¢ postage and handling (additional widgets, add 35¢ postage and handling); Ohio residents add 5% sales tax." Instead, try this:

[ ] Send one widget for $1.49, plus 50¢ shipping. Total $1.99

[ ] Send three widgets for $3.99 (a 10% saving!) plus $1.20 shipping. Total $5.19

[ ] Send five widgets for $5.99 (a 20% saving!) plus $1.90 shipping. Total $7.89

[ ] Ohio residents please add 5% sales tax—7¢ for one, 20¢ for three, 30¢ for five.

Note that this example limits choice of quantity, but encourages larger unit sales through both simplification and the discount. We have calculated shipping costs, multiple-order prices, and totals except for Ohio residents— and for them we've calculated the percentage-based sales tax.

Ease of Payment

The easier it is to order, the greater the likelihood of impulse purchases. In many cases, selling on credit and including in the coupon the option "Bill me later" is worth the risk. The risk can be excessive for high cost goods, of course. But for lower cost ones the number of impulse purchases outweighs the risk.

Credit cards are a godsend to the direct marketing business. They make it easy for prospects to pay, and easy to order. For most people, credit cards are more convenient to use than checkbooks. They pull out the cards, copy the numbers, and send their orders on the way. Even more significant, credit cards have enabled the majority of mail-order buyers to pay by telephone or on an interactive website.

Ultimate Interactvity

Permitting a customer to inquire or order by telephone is the ultimate convenience. A phone is always handy, and dialing ten or eleven digits of a toll-free number takes far less effort than mailing most reply cards.

Phone services and web servers are open twenty-four hours, seven days a week, just as mailboxes are. Your phone operator also can answer simple questions, do calculations, advise whether an item is in stock, and take credit card payments over the phone. Mail-order companies with advanced interactive web pages are increasing their ability to do the same.

Ironically, the anonymous telephone operator who is trained to be courteous, knowledgeable, and quick, is rapidly replacing the personal service that most retail salespeople used to provide on a face-to-face basis.

Our audiences have become less literate, less legible and less patient We have come a long way from the days when neat, handwritten letters were exchanged between sellers and buyers who treated each other with respect for literacy as they transacted their business. Today, in the age of the computer, we are well advised to make our messages easy to read, easy to understand, and easy to respond to.

IMMEDIACY INCENTIVES

One evangelical fundraiser sent its past supporters an imitation telegram with this short message: "Urgent. Please send $20 by return mail. Will explain later."

This may be the purest and shortest known implementation of the immediacy criterion in direct mail. It contains all the basic elements: urgency, copy, command terminology, graphic expression, and deadline. All these conceptual elements should be included in direct marketing copy when there is justification for them.

Urgency Copy

Ideally, the immediacy concept should be an intrinsic part of the basic proposition. Even if immediacy is not intrinsic, there are many ways to convey a sense of urgency. The telegraphic message in the example above is a one approach. News headlines, or words such as *now, new,* and *introducing* have a similar effect.

The need for prompt action can be related to the proposition, if justified with reminders about limited quantity or possible price increases. In such cases it pays to dramatize the result of inaction, as in, "Why pay more later?"

Try dramatizing the imminent savings, comfort, or other advantages of the product or service offered, as well as the costs, discomfort, and disadvantages of putting off a decision. Some examples: "Winter is coming sooner than you think. Order this coat now so you'll be ready for the first frosty day"; "Send your contribution today. A child's hunger has no patience."

Command Terminology

One copy approach that seems to be consistently effective is what I call "command terminology." This is the simple second-person declarative sentence: "Do it today," "Send it now," or simply "Mail this coupon." Somewhere, before a copy message has been completed, it is important to answer the reader's unspoken question: "So what do you want from me?" The answer should be a command: a statement of exactly what you want the person to do. In the AIDA copywriting formula, "action" is the payoff. The request for action should be as much like a command as good taste permits.

When I was marketing director of LaSalle Extension University, we had the opportunity to run a great variety of headlines dramatizing the tangible and intangible advantages of the school's educational courses. The most consistently effective approach for this market was the use of command headlines such as "Be an Accountant" or "Learn Auto Repair."

Adding Immediacy

How do you make a layout look like it has news value? The key is recency. An old message doesn't demand immediate attention or action. A message that is hot off the presses conveys the impression that it is worth reading and acting on immediately.

Imagine that you are driving your car, looking for a parking space, and suddenly you see one near what appears to be a little-used driveway. Stenciled in faded letters is the warning do not park here. It looks as if it has been there for a long time. Many people would ignore it. However, as you pull into the space, someone knocks on your window and hands you a note with the same message. Suddenly it's immediate. You are likely to pay attention to it and heed the warning.

Some media have immediacy built in. Radio and television are prime examples, particularly because of the possibility of positioning commercials near news programs. Newspapers are more immediate than magazines, weekly magazines more immediate than monthly ones.

In direct mail, a telegram format is the ultimate immediacy. "Air mail" seems more urgent than other classes of mail. Even though all first-class mail now goes for the same rate, a simple red-and-blue diagonal border around an envelope or reply card similar to the air-mail style still conveys the idea of speed, promptness, and importance.

Handwritten notes appear more recent—and thus more immediate—than printed letters. Rubber stamps or facsimile stickers also convey urgency. An interesting direct mail technique is to put part of the text, the postscript, and some marginal annotations in facsimile handwriting to suggest that they are afterthoughts.

Immediacy can be conveyed in print advertising by setting the ad in a typewriter face, or the headlines in crayoned hand lettering. One retailer ran sales ads in such type with hand-printed or typed copy and photos with visible cut marks—a concept called *calculated crudity*.

The more finished the ad, the more permanent it looks—and therefore the less immediate. The trick is to strike a balance between the graphic respectability you want to convey and the need for immediacy. It isn't easy, but it is possible.

Deadline

The most important of all immediacy elements is the deadline. If the proposition permits, you can say "Offer expires on November 8." Setting a specific date is the strongest deadline of all.

"Offer expires in 10 days" is good, but not quite as strong as a specific date. Yet it may be preferred in some cases. I often recommend an undated deadline when there is risk that the mailing may not get out on time, or the ad is expected to change hands as prospective customers present it to other prospective customers.

Where there is no genuine offer deadline, there are ways to suggest it. For instance, in a market where prices are rapidly increasing, you might say, "This price not guaranteed unless reply received before _____ -." or more simply, "Please reply by _____ -."

Other deadlines can be related to supply rather than date: "Only 5000 plants available at this price." Sweepstakes often include a bonus for early entry—a proven stimulus to the total response. Some propositions offer a premium or discount to the first few thousand people who reply.

The common denominator is the same in all these examples. Set a deadline or give a reason for action *now*. In direct marketing, it is now or never.

Speed of Delivery

Since a cardinal rule of direct marketing is to add immediacy to encourage the prospect to act now rather than later, direct marketers should do the same for customers. It is only fair, and good business, to pay off this sense of immediacy by turning on the service, shipping the merchandise, sending the information, or providing whatever you're selling as soon as possible.

Don't wait to send letters back and forth to fulfill the customer's expectations. When the phone is involved, use on-line transfers to turn a phone inquiry into an in-home appointment or installation. Use UPS, Federal Express, Priority Mail and other quick-service shipping companies to get your merchandise shipped in a day or two rather than take weeks with parcel post.

CREDIBILITY

The consumer today has probably never been more distrustful. Automobiles are recalled. Popular packaged foods turn out to have dangerous ingredients. Why should consumers trust a product they have never seen but have only read about in an ad or mailing piece, a form that is transient by its very nature?

Some credibility is provided in newspaper or magazine advertising by the implied endorsement of the publication the ad appears in. But this is less relevant in newspapers and, because of the lack of acceptance standards in many stations, almost nonexistent in broadcast. It is hard to convey believability when your TV spot is adjacent to advertising for a psychic hotline.

The element of credibility is a must item on any copy checklist. Fortunately, there are many ways to provide it.

Advertiser Reputation

Nothing is quite as effective as sponsorship by a company that has built a good reputation over the years. If your company is well known, then make it clear that you stand behind the product being offered, and put the company name in a prominent place. If your company is owned by or affiliated with a well-known substantial company, be sure to feature that company name. Split-run testing indicated a 25 percent lift for a new magazine introduction that featured the name of the broadcast network that owned the magazine over an identical ad that did not. When Condé Nast introduced *Self,* the publisher's marketing staff felt their other magazines were better known than the publishing name. The opening campaign showed covers of *Vogue, Glamour,* and *Mademoiselle* rather than the Condé Nast name.

If your company is large or reputable, has won awards, or is licensed by the government, then by all means say so. If it's a new company and you are just starting out, then make something of that. Say that your president reads every letter, or that the item is your only product.

The Bandwagon

People flock to see why a store or restaurant is crowded. If your product is selling well, then say so. Tell them that your direct marketing business is prospering, that thousands of people have used your product, that certain big companies or some famous personalities such as so-and-so have bought it. Everyone loves a winner.

Endorsers

If your company isn't well known, or even if it is, consider finding an endorser—a well-known spokesperson who offers instant identity and therefore believability for your message. Where would National Liberty have been without TV celebrity Art Linkletter's endorsements during their peak growth period? Or American Family Publishing without Ed McMahon?

Corporate Personalization

Your spokesperson doesn't have to be a movie star or a national celebrity. It can be your own chief executive officer. A CEO who looks and sounds sincere might provide an ideal image in your advertising. Look at Ben & Jerry's Ice Cream, or Gloria Steinem's *Ms.* magazine ads. A personal message from the founder or the publisher can have a very nice ring—both in copy style and at the cash register.

Testimonials

Testimonials once were the mainstay of mail-order advertising. It is surprising how few advertisers make good use of them today, since they are still very effective. There is nothing quite like an honest face and the signature of someone in a nearby part of the country to add believability.

The problem is that testimonials are difficult to come by. In our lazy, non-literate age, unsolicited testimonials are few and far between. When you do get one, you may not be able to get a release to use it in advertising. MCI recently hired my company just to solicit testimonials for their wide range of products. It was costly, but the statements that were turned up were worth gold.

One packaged-goods client has proven this element to be critical to achieving the necessary response rate. Eventually we used laser printing to feature testimonials from each prospect's own state, changing our local testimonial from state to state. And we even included testimonials and photographs of real people using the product, people who had similar lifestyles to our prospective customers.

Outside Guarantors

A guarantee is always helpful, and is more helpful if the guarantor is well known. If your company isn't well known, consider getting an outside source to back up the guarantee and ensure that money will be refunded if the customer is not satisfied. Perhaps an insurance company such as Lloyds of London or a local bank can endorse the guarantee. Perhaps an independent testing laboratory can vouch for the product claims. A newspaper clipping that cites the effectiveness of your product's principal ingredient could be quoted. An industry association may grant you its "seal of approval."

"Why Are You Being So Good to Me?"

To the extent that your offer sounds "too good," it may be perceived as unbelievable. Don't blame today's consumer for asking "What's the catch?" when the word *free* shows up.

Offer qualifications should be clearly stated up front, not just as required by law, but as a matter of good business. Split-run ads have confirmed that the various rules and laws requiring club commitment and return policies be spelled out in detail actually help response rather than hurt it.

CREATIVE WORK PLANS

In most agency and advertiser organizations, the pressure of daily work and the need to meet deadlines inevitably lead to shortcuts in the creative process. The worst shortcut is to start turning out mailing pieces and advertisements even when creative tactics have not been thought through.

The only way to keep creative work on target is to use a creative work plan for each and every project. Here are some elements that might be included:

General Information

- Client or product
- Project number
- Media or list type
- Size and format
- Schedule and deadlines
- Assignments and required approvals
- Personalization or versioning options
- Image triangle—suggested emphasis

Product Information

- Attributes and benefits
- Positioning

- Objective or offer
- Dramatization or demonstration possibilities
- Support of claims; guarantees; endorsers
- "What will this do for me?"

Market Information

- Demographics—age, education, etc.
- Psychographics—personality, interests, and others, if known
- Prospect dramatization (describe typical prospect)
- Self-image considerations
- "What does it say about me?"

Company Information

- Required logos and tag lines
- Credibility supports, if needed

Response Stimulators

- Immediacy factors; reason for acting now
- Order or inquiry details
- Response device; card; envelope needed; etc. . . .

Your approach should reflect the values and unique style of the organization or the organization's creative director. But the approach must be in writing, and it must be prepared in advance and agreed to by the account supervisor or product manager.

10

COPYWRITING

Up to now we have dealt mostly with the science of advertising—the planning, the research, and the strategic and tactical considerations that precede writing the first word of copy.

It is as if the navigators have now set the course, and the pilot is ready to take over the responsibility of getting the plane into the air. Or the architect and engineers have completed the plans for a new office building, and the artisans are now ready to break ground.

Copywriting is the original "art" of advertising, especially mail-order writing. All the historic greats of the field started as copywriters, and all the classic direct-marketing advertisements are essentially expressions of the copywriter's art.

An old-timer in the field once told me, "Copy is king." This is an exaggeration today, but copy is still the fountainhead of great innovations in direct marketing. The experience of copywriting is extremely valuable—perhaps indispensable—to those whose creativity would extend to the whole process of direct-marketing management.

"ADVERTISING IS HARD"

Vic Schwab emphasized the importance of relating product benefits to human needs. In his classic *How to Write a Good Advertisement* (Harper & Row, 1962), he listed several basic needs: better health, more money, greater popularity, improved appearance, more comfort, more leisure, pride of accomplishment, business advancement, social advancement and increased employment, among others.

David Ogilvy added story value, with text and illustration, subheads, and captions, all telling a story that bridges the common interests between the producer of a product and its potential consumer. The Ogilvy style, with book-like typefaces, sentence or title headlines, easily readable layouts and dramatic illustrations, has become instantly recognizable. Above all, Ogilvy ads have been literate, showing proper respect for English language structure and punctuation. I believe these ads were unusually effective because they treated the consumer with respect and invited the reader to respond in kind to the message and product.

Bill Bernbach was the first to adapt advertising style to its media context. Recognizing that advertising almost always appears in an entertainment medium—whether in the pages of a magazine or adjoining a television show— he added the dimension of entertainment to advertising itself. As a result, followers of his approach often include touches of humor, suspense, pathos, conflict, or contradiction to make them at least as appealing as the editorial or programming content they adjoin. It's a lot easier to get your point across if people *want* to read or watch your message.

Tom Collins, co-founder of Rapp & Collins, summed it up with an aphorism reminiscent of Will Rogers: "Advertising is hard!" This classic understatement says it all. There's no easy route to successful advertising. The stroke of creative inspiration is a rare phenomenon that comes only to those who have been immersed in research, planning, strategy, and tactics.

The hard work of marketing scientist and creative artist pays off in successful advertising. The quickie advertisement tossed off by a freelance or inexperienced in-house ad department may be an ad technically, but it will never realize the true potential of direct marketing done the hard way, the slow way, the sure way.

A SIMPLE FORMULA

Every writer has heard of the AIDA formula. As a reminder, the words stand for *A*ttention, *I*nterest, *D*esire, and *A*ction. This is the basic set of rules that guided me when I first wrote copy.

I was once asked by Murray Raphel, the well-known specialist in retail marketing, for my own formula. With all homage to AIDA, I offered the "five S's" formula. The letters stand for "Stop 'em! Show 'em! Seduce 'em! Satisfy 'em! Sell 'em!"

Stop 'em. Write a headline that flags down the likely prospects from all of the readers or viewers out there.

Show 'em. Communicate nonverbally as well as verbally. Use pictures, photos of people, and visual images to reinforce the headline.

Seduce 'em. Appeal to the highest psychological level, not just material benefit. Try emotional needs, fantasy, self-image.

Satisfy 'em. Deal with real needs and problems, and show how the product or service fulfills those on every level.

They Laughed When I Sat Down
At the Piano
But When I Started to Play!~

ARTHUR had just played "The Rosary." The room rang with applause. I decided that this would be a dramatic moment for me to make my debut. To the amazement of all my friends, I strode confidently over to the piano and sat down.

"Jack is up to his old tricks," somebody chuckled. The crowd laughed. They were all certain that I couldn't play a single note.

"Can he really play!" I heard a girl whisper to Arthur.

"Heavens, no!" Arthur exclaimed. "He never played a note in all his life. . . But just you watch him. This is going to be good."

I decided to make the most of the situation. With mock dignity I drew out a silk handkerchief and lightly dusted off the piano keys. Then I rose and gave the revolving piano stool a quarter of a turn, just as I had seen an imitator of Paderewski do in a vaudeville sketch.

"What do you think of his execution?" called a voice from the rear.

"We're in favor of it!" came back the answer, and the crowd rocked with laughter.

Then I Started to Play

Instantly a tense silence fell on the guests. The laughter died on their lips as if by magic. I played through the first few bars of Beethoven's immortal Moonlight Sonata. I heard gasps of amazement. My friends sat breathless—spellbound!

I played on and as I played I forgot the people around me. I forgot the hour, the place, the breathless listeners. The little world I lived in seemed to fade—seemed to grow dim—unreal. Only the music was real. Only the music and visions it brought me. Visions as beautiful and as changing as the wind blows clouds and drifting moonlight that long ago inspired the master composer. It seemed as if the master

musician himself were speaking to me—speaking through the medium of music—not in words but in chords. Not in sentences but in exquisite melodies!

A Complete Triumph!

As the last notes of the Moonlight Sonata died away, the room resounded with a sudden roar of applause. I found myself surrounded by excited faces. How my friends carried on! Men shook my hand—wildly congratulated me—pounded me on the back in their enthusiasm! Everybody was exclaiming with delight—plying me with rapid questions. . . "Jack! Why didn't you tell us you could play like that!" . . . "Where did you learn?"—"How long have you studied?"—"Who was your teacher?"

"I have never even *seen* my teacher," I replied. "And just a short while ago I couldn't play a note."

"Quit your kidding," laughed Arthur, himself an accomplished pianist. "You've been studying for years. I can tell."

"I have been studying only a short while," I insisted. "I decided to keep it a secret so that I could surprise all you folks."

Then I told them the whole story.

"Have you ever heard of the U. S. School of Music?" I asked.

A few of my friends nodded. "That's a correspondence school, isn't it?" they exclaimed.

"Exactly," I replied. "They have a new simplified method that can teach you to play any instrument by mail in just a few months."

How I Learned to Play Without a Teacher

And then I explained how for years I had longed to play the piano.

"A few months ago," I continued, "I saw an interesting ad of the U. S. School of Music—a new method of learning to play which only cost a few cents a day! The ad told how a woman had mastered the piano in her spare time at home—and *without* a teacher! Best of all, the wonderful new method she used, required no laborious scales—no heartless exercises—no tiresome practicing. It sounded so convincing that I filled out the coupon requesting the Free Demonstration Lesson.

"The free booklet arrived promptly and I started in that very night to study the Demonstration Lesson. I was amazed to see how easy it was to play this new way. Then I sent for the course.

"When the course arrived I found it was just as the ad said—as easy as A.B.C! And, as

the lessons continued they got easier and easier. Before I knew it I was playing all the pieces I liked best. Nothing stopped me. I could play ballads or classical numbers or jazz, all with equal ease! And I never did have any special talent for music!"

Play Any Instrument

You too, can now teach yourself to be an accomplished musician—right at home—in half the usual time. You can't go wrong with this simple new method which has already shown 350,000 people how to play their favorite instruments. Forget that old-fashioned idea that you need special "talent." Just read the list of instruments in the panel, decide which one you want to play and the U. S. School will do the rest. And bear in mind no matter which instrument you choose, the cost in each case will be the same—just a few cents a day. No matter whether you are a mere beginner or already a good performer, you will be interested in learning about this new and wonderful method.

Send for Our Free Booklet and Demonstration Lesson

Thousands of successful students never dreamed they possessed musical ability until it was revealed to them by a remarkable "Musical Ability Test" which we send entirely without cost with our interesting free booklet.

If you are in earnest about wanting to play your favorite instrument—if you really want to gain happiness and increase your popularity—and not once for the free booklet and Demonstration Lesson. No cost—no obligation. Right now we are making a Special offer for a limited number of new students. Sign and send the convenient coupon now—before it's too late to gain the benefits of this offer. Instruments supplied when needed, cash or credit. U. S. School of Music, 1644 Brunswick Bldg., New York City.

U. S. School of Music,
1631 Brunswick Bldg., New York City.

Please send me your free book, "Music Lessons in Your Own Home", with introduction by Dr. Frank Crane, Demonstration Lesson and particulars of your Special Offer. I am interested in the following course:

Have you above instrument?. . . . .

Name. . . . .
                (Please write plainly)

Address. . . . .

City. . . . . State. . . . .

Pick Your Instrument

Piano	'Cello
Organ	Hawaiian and
Violin	Composition
Drums and	Sight Singing
Traps	Ukulele
Banjo	Guitar
Tenor	Hawaiian
Banjo	Steel Guitar
Mandolin	Harp
Clarinet	Cornet
Flute	Piccolo
Saxophone	Trombone
Voice and Speech Culture	
Automatic Finger Control	
Piano Accordion	

Figure 10-1. This classic advertisement by John Caples is an excellent example of the power of long-copy advertising and the effectiveness of the story-telling format. Containing over 1000 words in a 7 × 10 inch ad, it nevertheless was so effective that it ran for almost twenty years.

Sell 'em. Ask for the order, in a way that is simple to follow, reinforces the basic message, and assures satisfaction.

In this book, we deal with creative plans, tactics and directions—all of which have to be done first. But the fine art of copywriting is probably best known for its tricks of the trade—how to get ideas, how to write a headline, how to make sure copy is read. Once upon a time, before we all got involved in strategies and psychology and research—when people used to read more and had better vocabularies—these skills were the foundation of direct marketing creativity. They may not dominate the substance of our communications today, but they still provide the style. And without readable, colorful and interesting writing, none of our strategies will ever be communicated at all.

THE DIRECT DIFFERENCE

Writers trained in general advertising often have a difficult time working in direct marketing. Even when the objective has nothing to do with recall and imagery, their general-advertising training often gets in the way. That's why real direct-marketing writers and creative executives are in such demand and often command higher salaries than general agency equivalents. And it's why a young beginner, directed by a skilled direct marketer, will often turn out advertising that will out-pull other ads done by a supposed heavyweight convert from a general-advertising background.

It is rare that I do not have—or at least know of—an opening for a good direct-marketing creative. I probably see a hundred portfolios a year from writers and artists. These portfolios often contain outstanding and well-known advertising for major general advertisers. But when I look at the handful of direct mail pieces tucked into the back cover, they are almost always disappointments.

The creative person unfamiliar with direct marketing often produces parodies of what the writer thinks a direct mailing or direct-response ad or TV spot should be. The personalization is minimal, or used in a trite fashion. The letter is almost an afterthought, written more like an advertisement than a letter. Adding "Dear Mr. Jones" doesn't make it a letter.

The bright Internet specialist usually invites me to view his website. Often I am impressed with the innovative graphics. But rarely do I find any trace of salesmanship in the messages—that is, if I can get the page opened in the first place without my computer crashing. All their skills at using sound, motion and visual graphics are useless if the prospective employer (and the consumer) doesn't have the bandwidth or the patience to view it.

The biggest difference is in the use of the space itself. General copywriters are trained to get across one idea, clearly and cleverly, in a manner that will be recalled by viewers and will influence their attitudes. In a ten- or thirty-second commercial—or a magazine page that will be turned quickly—they have one shot to make an impression and get an idea across in a form that will stick. And so they should in mass advertising.

But direct response, regardless of the medium, and direct marketing, regardless of the objective are different animals. Our purpose is not to leave an impression but to generate a positive decision to buy and a motivation to act—not later, but right now. Our job is not to make an impression, but to make a sale. Direct marketing is not only advertising, and it is not only sales. It is the bridge between the two, and must incorporate elements of both.

For one thing we either have more space, as in direct mail, or we are willing to use the space we have, as in long-copy magazine advertisements. We are not limited to one idea, but have the space to work in appeals to all segments of our audiences. We do not stop at making an impression, but go on to amplify, demonstrate, justify, motivate, and ask for an action. The writer must work harder to cover the entire sales message rather than just one point. And the art director must work with the writer, with neither one dominating, because art and layout must be the vehicles for the selling message, not ends in themselves.

Although there are many award programs in the direct marketing industry, and despite having served as chairman of the DMA's Echo Awards, the only award that counts is the end result. Leave out a selling point, and it shows on the bottom line. Put the body copy in reverse type, or against a distracting background, and the phones don't ring as often. Write a headline that's so subtle you're counting on the prospect to figure it out, and you may as well start looking for another job since your client will be looking for another agency. In direct marketing, the only reality is results. And like it or not, your career, like mine, is governed only by the answer to the boss' or client's question: *What have you done for me lately?*

GET READY, GET SET . . .

Regardless of what other role you might play for your client or in your agency organization, for the purposes of this chapter you are now a copywriter. Even those company presidents who occasionally exercise their right to toss off an ad of their own are, at the time and place of writing, copywriters and only copywriters.

Whether your starting point is your own inspiration, an informal discussion, or a carefully prepared "project assignment" with marketing plans, briefings, and spelled-out creative specifications, the copywriter's first two steps are the same: *define the assignment* and *abstract the information.*

Define the Assignment

Are you creating concepts for discussion, or finished copy for a concept that has already been agreed upon? What are the medium and the space unit? Is there a formal marketing plan for the entire product line? Have creative tactics and positioning been worked out for this particular project, or are you expected to propose them? (If the latter, get agreement on them before you submit headlines or copy. You'll save yourself a lot of false starts and wasted time by doing so.) Also, what is the history of this project? Why is a new ad needed? How do the audience, medium, positioning, and strategy differ from previous ads? What is the result history of those ads?

The more you can learn, the more you can contribute. No data should be held back from the copywriter. If there is a need for secrecy about actual result figures and margins, then ask for some type of target or index figures that can be shared with everyone on the creative team.

Abstract All Information

Restate everything yourself, in your own words, in your own notes, and for your eyes only. Ignore the repetitious instructions and information you already know about, but spell out the key points you must add to your knowledge, and the key criteria expected of you for this assignment.

It is important that the elements of strategy and tactics, as well as all relevant product and market information, be digested and restated in your own words. This is necessary to integrate the data into your own mental processes, and to be sure you understand and can explain it.

Beat the Winner

Often a writer has a broad assignment: to find a way to improve results—either in quantity or quality—as compared to either a previous winning effort or a competitor's ad.

You know that your ad or mailing will be put up against a control package that may have beaten dozens of tests before. The medium is fixed. The offer is fixed. You must overcome the winner with pure creative superiority.

The first step is to take the other package apart creatively. This too must be done in writing, as a way of helping you to fully identify what is important about it. The best approach is what I call *reverse engineering*—a breakdown of copy points and elements used in the piece being studied. Read the competing copy paragraph by paragraph and draw conclusions such as these: What is the writer trying to say? What need is being appealed to? What position is being taken? What makes it work?

Figure 10-2 is an exercise I give my students at NYU to effectively translate theory into practice. All copywriters—whether they're new to the field or old pros—should do an exercise like this one every once in a while to improve their skills.

List all the elements. Then take the list and regroup it. What are the constants that must be in your package? Isolate the main themes. What does this package have that other tested packages did not have? Identify the variables—the optional appeals that you can retain or drop as you see fit.

Once you've done this you will be in a position to take the plunge: to gamble on what you think the strong points are and where you think the copy can be improved. Rather than trying an alternate approach or trying to please the client by being clever, begin with the basics and write out your own copy platform for the new effort.

The copy platform is the choice of appeals that you, as a writer, want to place your chips on. Take the ones you think are strong and see how you can make them stronger. Take the weak ones and drop them or turn them into positives. Then, as your edge, find the new copy points that you think will strengthen the previous effort and make yours the winner.

Check your benefits list and see what you can add. Look at your positioning options if they haven't been spelled out in advance. Even if they have spelled out, feel free to contest the client's or marketing planner's selection. Just don't ignore it. It's possible to disagree with another's ideas as long as you've made an effort to understand them.

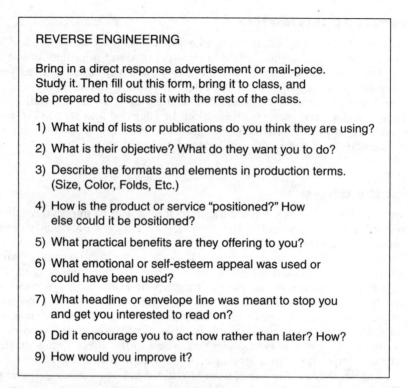

REVERSE ENGINEERING

Bring in a direct response advertisement or mail-piece.
Study it. Then fill out this form, bring it to class, and
be prepared to discuss it with the rest of the class.

1) What kind of lists or publications do you think they are using?

2) What is their objective? What do they want you to do?

3) Describe the formats and elements in production terms.
   (Size, Color, Folds, Etc.)

4) How is the product or service "positioned?" How
   else could it be positioned?

5) What practical benefits are they offering to you?

6) What emotional or self-esteem appeal was used or
   could have been used?

7) What headline or envelope line was meant to stop you
   and get you interested to read on?

8) Did it encourage you to act now rather than later? How?

9) How would you improve it?

"Reverse Engineering." This exercise is a homework assignment I use in my classes at NYU. It is an effective way to translate theory into practice and vice versa.

Figure 10-2

Three Secrets of Great Ad Writing

In real estate, the three most important considerations in selecting a property are location, location, and location. Similarly, the three great secrets of copywriting are research, research, and research.

Sure, any writer can fill up a page. The Blarney stone blesses all Irish and all ad writers with equal fervor. Consequently, it's no trick for any of us to spontaneously sound off for as many pages as we'd like on any subject we want. Politicians and debaters have been doing it for years, on whatever side of a subject is required. Making something out of nothing is a clever trick, not an art.

One common denominator of really fine copy is that it is "meaty"—filled with details, choice examples and clever anecdotes, all of which make points with examples rather than with broad and empty claims.

I have had to write copy on electronic capacitors, automotive additives, books on bridge (a game I had never played), and religious rituals that were unfamiliar to me. I knew nothing about these subjects before I wrote about them, and nothing soon afterward. While I was writing, however, I was steeped in each subject and knew enough to talk intelligently with experts.

Let's face it. If you can't talk about a subject in your own words, how can you write about it? If you haven't found out enough about the subject to interest you, how can you make it sound interesting to others? If you can't explain it to your spouse or best friend, how can you explain it on a web page or in a mailing piece you want other people to read?

Actors sometimes look at the camera and freeze at the thought of the millions of people who may soon be watching them. They have to be reminded to think, "I'm talking to just one person at a time." Copywriters too should heed this advice. If you can't talk to one person, you'll never talk to tens of thousands successfully. This means you must master each new subject with research, research, and more research.

First, get answers to every question that occurred to you when you read the briefing material or sat in on an orientation session. Don't be proud and stupid; be humble and smart. Let someone know what you didn't understand so you can get explanations of every point that isn't clear. No one is judging you, except by counting the coupons that will come in as a result of your efforts.

Study the product. If the product is a magazine, go back two years or more to find articles with a wide range of appeals, and write catchy summaries of each one. If it is a book, even an encyclopedia, go ahead and read it—or at least try to. As you read, make notes in copywriting form, as if you were writing a list of contents to be included in a mailing piece. Maybe you'll use it this way, and maybe not. But it's a great way to get examples for points you intend to make in your main copy message.

One hint: Note page numbers and sources as you write. Sooner or later a client or a lawyer is going to ask you for your sources, and it's a lot easier to make marginal notes as you go along. Some mailing pieces even add the page number to the copy, as a way of making the promise more specific.

After you have studied the product, head for the reference books. Go to the library, and look in the card files and in the *Reader's Guide to Periodical Literature* or other resource guides to get all the information you need on the subject. Do a web search, keeping in mind the sources of the material you find. Call associations or technical groups and see what they can offer you. One such inquiry led me to spend three days at the library of the Society of Automotive Engineering just to support one key point for an advertisement for LiquiMoly, an automotive product.

Don't just talk to the product manager or ad director. Ask to speak with— *insist* on speaking with—the engineers, editors, technicians, or other specialists who really know what's happening. When Procter & Gamble asked me to write a fund-raising mailing for The Free Store, Cincinnati's uniquely successful food distribution system for the needy, I visited the center personally. No briefing could have prepared me for the profoundly emotional experience of talking with the volunteers who work there and the people whom The Free Store helped. The resulting letter was one of my proudest and most successful efforts.

The more you know, the more you can write. Ideally, all the facts should be in the marketing plan, but it's more likely that the writer will be helping to write this section of the plan. In a small company without formal planning, you may go through the processes on your own without benefit of a formal strategic plan.

The Creative Work-up

You've defined the assignment. You've done your homework. Now you're ready to write—almost. Just one more thing—make a list.

This list is a simple one. Put down all the copy points you want to make, based on your selection of positioning. Include the creative tactics you've selected and how you'll dramatize the offer and product attributes, interpreting everything in benefits. Perhaps you'll have 20 or 30 basic points. Even if you know them all, write them down so that you can use the list later to help you sell the ad to the person who has to approve it.

Next put numbers or letters next to each point, indicating the relative importance of each. Which are major points? Which are minor? Which is the single most vital point to be worked into the headline? Which points should be clear to the reader, even if he or she reads only captions and subheads? Which ones are optional—to be left out if space limitations demand it? Answering these questions before writing the copy will allow the work to flow and ensure that you land on target, rather than continually starting over and over again. The Synergetic Work Plan in Fig. 10-3 can help keep these elements straight.

Harnessing Your Subconscious

Now put away your research. Put away your notes. Tape your list to a wall, and get away from it all. Take a nap. Take a walk. Play solitaire on your computer. Take whatever you need to let your mind digest all the research, strategy, and creative specifications. Sleeping on it works for some people. The point is to let your subconscious digest all the information you have acquired.

Your brain will, in effect, switch to "automatic" and integrate all this knowledge with everything else you've ever heard, seen, read, or been taught. You will make connections with the whole of your life experience much as a "method" actor creates a believable character for a role.

If your thinking has been logical and scientific, if you've been a sensitive observer of the human process, if you've allowed yourself to think, feel, and communicate on both an emotional and an intellectual level, if you have managed not to block out experiences as an adult or as a child, then

TeamNash INC *Synergetic Work Plan*

CLIENT AT&T Reach Out (states) PROJECT Fall 4-State Test   JOB # Preliminary

MEDIA Pre-analyzed Lists   FORMAT Direct Mail   DATE

---

1. OBJECTIVES

Primary: Induce Immediate Enrollments

Secondary: Maintain AT&T Standards

2. PROSPECT

Demographic: Frequent Intra-state Residential Caller

Psychographic: Probably socially active, extroverted, feels close to family and friends

3. PROSPECT POSITIONING

			XXXXXX	XXXXXX
Create Need	Fulfil Need	Complete	Value	Action

4. PRODUCT

Description: Route package, as briefed

Benefits: Savings on phone bills; greater usage for the same price

Offer:

5. PRODUCT PERCEPTION

Attributes: Package fee, varies by state

Practical Benefit: Immediate savings for Hi-po group, potential for others

Technical Benefit: Extent of savings greater or lesser depending on usage

Emotional Benefit: Feels able to make more and longer calls

Fantasy: Maintain closer relationship with friends and family, be liked and admired

Self Image: Smarter shopper, good manager

---

6. VALUE RELATIONSHIPS

xxx	Control		Care
xxx	Independence		Fashion
xxx	Pride		Admiration
	Aspiration		Security

7. DIRECT MARKETING ESSENTIALS

Prospect Involvement:
   Bill pre-analysis

Purchase Justification:
   Savings

Credibility Enhancer:
   AT&T's name and reputation

Immediacy Incentive:
   Possible waiting list
   First come, first served

Response Facilitator:
   Phone (800) and mail (postage paid)

8. IMAGERY BALANCE

COMPANY (Credibility)

10 %

60 %   30 %

PRODUCT (What it does for me)   SELF (What it says about me)

9. APPROVAL

Account Manager   DATE

Creative Director   DATE

Client   DATE

Figure 10-3. Most agencies have some type of formal planning document for creative assignments. This one incorporates horizontal positioning, product perception and imagery balance, as discussed in the previous chapter.

you will be able to draw upon the sum total of your entire life to help you understand, create, and express the ideas you need to do your job.

Your job is infinitely challenging: to make the complicated simple, the dull fascinating, and the mundane marvelous. You must bridge the communication gap between a lifeless product and a living consumer. The power to meet this challenge is already within you.

. . . AND GO!

Now you face the legendary blank sheet—the yellow pad or computer screen which has, at one time or another, intimidated not only ad writers but journalists, novelists, poets, and playwrights as well.

Presumably you have done your homework. You know the subject. You understand the assignment. You have a picture in your mind of whom you are talking to. You know what you want to say. Now, where do you start?

The Mental "Dump" Process

Computer technicians use the word *dump* to mean emptying the data stored in memory. Reporters and editorial writers call it "free-writing." It's a process I recommend for copywriters as well. The first attempt at writing should be not to write at all but to pour out everything that is on your mind about the subject at hand. It's a freeing process, if it is done right and honestly. You type, write, or doodle whatever comes to mind, including "What am I trying to say here?" or "I hate this job" or "I'd better wax my skis before I leave this weekend."

By getting random, irrelevant, and sometimes irreverent thoughts out on paper, you are freeing your mind to get to the task at hand. The results of this dump process is for your eyes only, and is simply a way of getting warmed up.

After a page or two of nonsense, resentment, or corn, the juices start to flow and random ideas show up on the page. The first few are often terrible. They are the clichés, the slogans that someone else has done before, or obscene plays on words that make fun of your task.

Some "pump-priming" phrases that have worked for other writers might be helpful: "The point I am trying to make is . . ."; "Imagine yourself . . ."; "Please buy my product because . . ."; "Here's how I'm going to change your life. . . .".

I find that this "dumping" process not only gets rid of the blocks; it gets rid of the obvious. After a few pages of stream-of-consciousness writing, the ideas start to be relevant to the selling job you have to do. The checklists start coming to life, played back by your subconscious mind. Sooner or later some really choice ideas start showing up. The first good ideas generate other good ideas, and soon the writer is on a creative "high," with usable phrases filling the pages. A genuine enthusiasm wells up. There is an anticipation, a sense of excitement. "Hey," you tell yourself, "this is going to be one of the best things I've ever written!"

Now you're ready. The hours or days of research, study, and planning pay off in a few hours of frenzied, productive writing.

If you build logically from the facts and begin to write, you will lack enthusiasm and that will show in your writing. If you jump in excitedly without having done your homework, the style will be there, but not the substance. The process I have recommended is certainly not the only approach, but it does offer one way for the direct-marketing writer (and artists as well) to set the mood for an advertisement that will be more than just satisfactory. It may just be great.

Begin at the End

This advice may seem strange, but it is sincere. The first thing to write is the coupon. Most writers save it for last and treat it as a necessary nuisance along with copyright notices. They are missing a bet.

Most people, when reading an ad, don't act on it immediately. Some tear out the ad and act on it at once. Most, however, tear out just the coupon and put it in a pile of bills to be paid or in a notebook, or just pin it to a calendar or bulletin board.

Later, when the time comes to write out the envelope and perhaps a check, the coupon itself is the only reminder of the reasons behind why they tore it out in the first place. The headline is gone. The pictures are gone. All that remains is the reply card or coupon.

Or you're on an e-commerce "shopping cart" page, filling in addresses and entering your credit card numbers. The more time you spend the more likely "Do I really need this?" will occur to you. No wonder 2/3rds of Internet shoppers drop out at this point without ordering.

At that point, which do you think will get a greater response? "Send me __ widgets at $4.95 each," or "Yes, I want to double my car's gasoline mileage without sacrificing speed or power, with your new Widget Wonderplugs (only $4.95 each), developed by the U.S. government for the space shuttle program. I understand that if I'm not completely satisfied I will get my money back by just . . ."

Writing the coupon first not only assures that it will get the important attention it deserves, but also will help you to crystallize the main point of your advertising copy. You win both ways.

The First Draft

Some writers prefer to visualize the entire ad, jotting down a headline and subheads in a sort of skeleton concept. This is a fast shortcut to presenting a finished idea, and comes in handy when several different conceptual treatments must be visualized for presentation. Unfortunately, many advertisements that begin in this manner don't hold up in the finished version. The copy execution simply lacks the spark of the original idea.

My recommendation is to write the first draft of the advertisement before working out a detailed visualization, and in some cases even before perfecting the headline or sub-heads. More often than not, good copy will suggest its own subheads, and any of them should be adaptable to main headlines.

There are as many approaches to the craft of copywriting as there are products to write about. My suggestion is to write the coupon first and the copy next, and then to extract the sub-captions and headlines from the body of the copy. If the copy is good, they'll be there. If they're not there, write new copy.

The first draft of a selling message should:

- Begin where the reader is
- Bridge the gap between attention and interest
- Create desire
- Fulfill need
- Provide positive benefits linked to product attributes
- Dramatize the offer
- Provide proof, assurance, guarantee, and a reason to act now

In short, it should include all the selling motivations that have been determined to be appropriate for the particular proposition, even though only one of them is emphasized as the basic positioning for the advertisement or mailing piece.

The first draft is for content, and should be worked on until every selling point has been included in the most logical sequence and in the most persuasive manner. Then some basic decisions have to be made.

Style

Ninety percent of all communication is said to be nonverbal. How you say something has far greater impact than what you are saying. The same is true in advertising.

Copy style is like tone of voice. Layout is like body language. The tone of voice of your message has to be chosen as carefully as the elements of the copy platform. Style can support your message or contradict it. The choice of style—and its appropriate use—is one of the finer points of the copywriting art.

Flow

Once you've gotten readers into your message with the right headline and illustration, how can you keep them reading? If it's a mail piece, the prospect has other letters to glance at. With magazine or newspaper ads, a hand is poised to turn the page at the slightest loss of interest. With TV or radio commercials, there are refrigerators to raid, washrooms to visit, and channels to change to the moment your message ceases to be appealing. The Internet is a maze of distractions, all urging you to click here or there before you have been exposed to the entire selling message. And your customer's hand never leaves the mouse or keypad, ready to "turn you off" by clicking in mid-sentence.

Tricks of the trade can help to create interest. Using numbers is one trick—"Three ways to be a better parent." Subheads breaking up blocks of copy into readable eyefuls is another. Still a third is a narrative style in which the message unfolds in sequence, as if you were describing the product to a friend.

Story Value

My favorite approach is to find a story to tell, preferably as if the writer of the letter was sharing an experience with a friend. Remember, corporations don't write letters, people do. I try to make the signer of the letter seem as real as possible, sharing emotional feelings.

When I first saw the results of the tests (or the low price, or the widespread acceptance, etc.) on this new product, I didn't believe it. I called to my assistant, Marcia: "Tell them to check it again!" She came back the next day, smiling. "They did check it," she said. "It does all that, and more. I tried it myself and it really works." Here are some excerpts from some of the many database conquest mailings I did for P&G products:

> "Greasy dishes! Greasy pots! Greasy plastic! I hate grease! I wish I could just make it disappear . . . After working or taking care of a family all day, no one wants to hassle with greasy dishes. That's why I really believe in . . ."

> "If you're like me, you love a clean, shining floor or countertop . . . or refrigerator. But you may not like the smell of the cleaner that you use to do the job . . . Too strong. Too harsh. Too much like a hospital . . . Well, if you're as tired of those harsh scents as I am, I've got terrific news . . .

You can also tell a story in the second person, asking the reader to imagine the experience of owning what you have to sell. A sentence beginning "Imagine . . ." has never failed me in the idea generation process.

> "Imagine how much fun it will be when you receive this wonderful item in the mail . . . taking it out of the carton . . . admiring its beautiful design . . . watching it perform its amazing functions . . . sharing the excitement with your friends. Why put off this moment a day longer than you have to?"

One of my "trademarks" is that my letters are often signed by a real person—a product manager genuinely proud of a new product, a quality engineer amazed at the great results. My daughter was the signer of a newsletter to teenagers about beauty products. And I even signed a letter myself about why I read *Yachting* magazine. Such letters practically ooze with sincerity, and the results prove that it's a worthwhile approach.

The great copywriters of yesteryear were all masters of story-telling. For example, "They laughed when I sat down at the piano . . ." written by John Caples of BBDO is often cited as a classic of direct response copywriting. (It is reproduced at the beginning of this chapter.) But you have to read the copy to see its real power –an example of the best in story-telling. After a half dozen paragraphs describing ridicule by his friends . . .

Then I Started to Play

"Instantly a tense silence fell on the guests. The laughter died on their lips as if by magic. I played through the first few bars of Beethoven's immortal Moonlight Sonata. I heard gasps of amazement. My friends sat breathless— spellbound! I played on and as I played I forgot the people around me. I forgot the hour, the place, the breathless listeners . . . Only the music was real. Only the music and visions it brought me. Visions as beautiful and as changing as the wind-blown clouds and drifting moonlight that long ago inspired the master composer.

"As the last notes of the Moonlight Sonata died away, the room resounded with a sudden roar of applause. I found myself surrounded by excited faces. How my friends carried on! Men shook my hand—wildly congratulated me— pounded me on the back in their enthusiasm. Everybody was exclaiming with delight—plying me with rapid questions. 'Jack! Why didn't you tell us you could play like that?"

Level

The level of copy should also be chosen deliberately. Copy level is related to vertical positioning. It should reflect the self-image of potential purchasers by not being too simplistic, but recognizing that their self-image is probably well above their actual reading comprehension. The writer has to walk a tightrope in order to appear literate on the one hand and to assume a minimal vocabulary on the other. The safe bet is to keep the vocabulary simple and the style colorful, to presume nothing and explain everything.

Nonverbal Messages

Today more than ever the copywriter must think visually as well as verbally. This involves much more than a choice of product illustrations or photographs to stop the right prospect. It recognizes that some copy points— particularly appeals to sensitive emotions, fantasies or self-image—are better expressed with visual images than with the written word. This is amplified in Chapter 11 on Layout, but visual communication should be a tool considered by all members of the creative team, not just the art director.

Getting Specific

In the musical *My Fair Lady,* Liza Doolittle sings, "Don't talk of love, show me!" Copywriters should heed this advice, especially in the final draft.

Don't say that a book is entertaining. Give a sample of the humor, or some other satisfying element. Don't say a product will save you time in the kitchen. Describe exactly what you can make, in how many minutes. Don't talk of something being informative. Start informing! Support your copy claims with specific examples, interesting examples, pertinent examples, and even more examples. Examples are what's interesting to your prospective buyer, and *that's* why you did all that research when you started.

Personalization

Once upon a time the word *personalization* meant mentioning the prospect's name as often as possible, or simply addressing the letter by name, as if that alone would equal the impact of a genuinely personal letter.

Today we know that it is more important to make the letter or other message as relevant as possible to the prospect's known interests, and to express that message in a sincere, conversational style, much as you might do if you were actually writing to a friend.

But that's only the beginning. Personal communication is a two-way street. In person, you would not tell someone about yourself without asking about their interests, nor should you do the opposite. In direct marketing copy you must do both as well. This applies particularly to letters, which by definition should have a personal style. To be "real," they should reveal something about the writer: "Greasy dishes. Greasy pots. Greasy silverware. I used to hate dealing with them all, until I tried . . ." "If you have dry hair like I do . . ." "'Who needs another pair of sunglasses' I thought, until I tried. . . ."

Stopping Power

Once the selling message has been worked out for both content and style, it's time to concern yourself with *stopping power:* the appeals you'll use to get the envelope opened, the ad noted, the TV viewer riveted to your commercial, the Internet viewer to stay on your site.

This final step in producing a really effective advertisement is the moment of truth in the craft of writing copy. The selling message may be superb, but if no one stops to read it, you've wasted your time and your client's money.

The headline must instantly flag down prospective buyers and intrigue them with an offer, a broad benefit, a need fulfillment, or a curiosity-provoking specific feature selected from the body of the advertisement. The range of headline opportunities will have widened considerably once the copy has been written.

My suggestion is to put off writing the headline. Instead, go paragraph by paragraph and write pithy sub-headlines with story value, curiosity, powerful benefits, and gripping emotional involvement. Then write captions for every illustration and try to come up with additional illustration ideas that will dramatize every major point. Each caption should translate the interest value of an illustration into a powerful selling point. All the subheads and captions, taken together, should add up to a convincing communication that will bring in the order even if the prospect doesn't read a word of the precious copy that spawned all these ideas.

If the research and planning processes are done right, the copy will be excellent. If the copy is excellent, the subheads and captions will be superb. The problem now should not be "coming up with a headline." It should be deciding which of several very fine, very persuasive subheads or captions to use as the main headline.

Of course, you can always write a headline as the first step, putting down on that blank sheet of paper the first thing that pops into your head after you're through studying the assignment. In my experience such headlines are often clichés or concept statements without benefit of the subjective integration, content assembly, style rewrite, and stopping-power processes recommended here. As always, the hard way is the sure way. That's why advertising is hard, and why it's right that it should be.

Making It Sing

The first draft is done. The content is complete, readable, right on target. Well done. But you're still not finished.

Of course, many writers polish up the first draft and call it an ad, and many such ads are successful. Yet what makes the difference between a good writer and a great one is what comes next.

Put the first draft aside until the next day, and forget about it. Go to a movie. Read a potboiler. Have fun. Then come back the next morning and look over the first draft as if you've never seen it before.

This time, look at it solely from the standpoint of style. Sit down and rewrite it completely, keeping the content but adding story value, entertainment, and fascination. Take the words you wrote yesterday, set them to music, and make them sing.

SOME GENERAL CONSIDERATIONS

No discussion of the craft of copywriting could be complete without providing the answers to some of the standard questions that have been raised over the last decade and will continue to be raised in the future. To those of us in the field, some of these questions have become downright boring. I address them here only in the hope of minimizing the number of times I will have to address them in the future.

How Long Should a Letter Be?

The answer: long enough to do the job. There is a story of a boy who asked the unusually tall Abe Lincoln how long he thought a man's legs should be. Lincoln's now-legendary answer was, "Long enough to reach the ground." How long should a letter be? Or an ad? Long enough to tell your story!

If you are giving away something free, with no strings attached, you don't need a long letter to make your offer. If you are selling something that a prospect has never seen before, you have to show it, explain it, tell how it works, and dramatize the benefits. If your readers know you, just give your name and a tag line. If they don't, you may have to put in your whole corporate history and financial statement.

Don't be afraid of long letters—or short ones.

The thing to remember is that it is not length in itself that gives effectiveness, it is the content. If you can cut a four-page letter down to two without losing a major selling point, chances are that the two-page letter will pull just as well with a slight reduction in CPR because of the printing costs saved.

On the other hand, if you can write a letter that is six, eight or twelve pages and holds the interest of your prospect, go ahead and try it. Some of the most successful direct-mail efforts are very long letters. The same applies to a speech, a book, or a website. Length is not significant. Content is.

Which Comes First, Format or Copy?

In the previous section, I advocated writing the copy before the headline, an admittedly "backward" approach that also involves writing the rough draft before sketching out a copywriter's "rough" of how the ad might look in the magazine, on your computer, or in the mailbox.

In print ads or television, the format is usually fixed. Writers are told that they have a page or 60 seconds to work with—and that's that. The format usually is dictated by media economics, and there is little ability to accommodate copy innovations.

Direct mail, however, is another matter. I am constantly amazed by clients or account reps who specify to the writer that a mailing piece should consist of "a four-page letter, 11 × 17-inch brochure, outer envelope, reply card, lift memo." There is nothing intrinsically wrong with such a format, but there is no reason to tie the writer's hands by dictating *any* format.

The format should grow out of the copy concept. The choice of brochure or booklet depends on copy flow and illustration requirements. Whether a mailing should be "all-in-one" or a group of small pieces—an invitation, a guarantee slip, a choice dramatization folder, a die-cut product representation—is a creative consideration that should await the writer's thinking process. Chapter 13 on direct mail production details the infinite variety of possibilities. For now, accept the idea that, in direct mail at least, the choice of formats should be a product of the creative process, not a specification.

To paraphrase Frank Lloyd Wright, "*Format* should follow function."

Handling Rush Jobs

A writer may ask, "All this is very nice, but where do I find the time to do this 'step-by-step process' when half the jobs I get are on 'rush' schedules?" The question is fair, and the problem is typical.

The first approach to rush jobs is to avoid them. Any account executive or product manager can appease a client or boss by saying yes to every request. The real professional will know when to say no, and will insist on giving creative sources adequate time to do their job properly.

The chance that something will go wrong in the execution increases dramatically with rush projects, and it is safer to risk offending a boss or client by saying no to an unreasonable request than to risk ending up with a product that suits no one. If the ad doesn't work, people will remember only the results. How fast you turned out the ad won't matter.

Accept a rush project only when you really want to, and when you are already so interested in the project and enthusiastic about the prospect of its working out well that you feel good about doing it. If that is the case, you'll find the time to go through each and every step listed above, taking less time for each.

Don't cut out research. Instead, have an apprentice do the research while you do other planning. Don't eliminate the sleep-on-it phase. Just condense it into a quick nap or a fast walk around the block. If you have a rush job, don't take shortcuts. Travel the tried-and-true route, but walk a lot faster.

The Curse of Cleverness

Just as all of us fall in love with our own corny jokes, copywriters are especially prone to falling in love with their own pet phrases. That's why we shouldn't begin with headline ideas and try to justify them with post-natal copy platforms. The planning must come first, the creativity later. That's also why copywriters cannot judge their own writing. Some element of objectivity is essential, whether it's from a supervisor, an account person, or a client's ad manager.

The greatest temptation to be clever rather than craftsman-like comes from peer-group pressure. Every art has its critics, and artisans tend to try to impress their critics instead of their customers. You've seen it in novels or poetry with eccentric but unreadable styles, in plays with obscure plots, in paintings and music whose themes were conceived under the influence of marijuana and only appreciated the same way.

In art and literature, people sometimes gain national attention and critical acclaim just by being different. This approach can also work in some fields of general advertising. In direct marketing, however, such acclaim—if it comes at all—will last only until the coupons come in. The only *real* critics in this field are the thousands of potential customers west of the Hudson River. They won't give 2 cents if your concept is cute or your execution different, but they will give $20 or more if you can convince them that your client's product is one that they need and want.

Sure, a clever ad or mailing may look good in your "book" when you apply for your next job. But wouldn't you be better off with fewer clever samples and a reputation for results that makes recruiters come to you?

Repetition: Right or Wrong?

Another area where battle lines are frequently drawn is repetition.

I don't mean the kind of repetition used by general advertisers, who find it desirable to repeat ad themes and brand names to reinforce awareness. I mean the key point that's flagged in the headline, mentioned in the subhead, illustrated and described in a photo caption, referred to in a brochure and lift letter, and then summarized in the body copy and on the response card.

Reiteration is a better word than *repetition* for what I am advocating, for there is no need to say the same thing again in the same way. There is a need to put your best copy claim forward in every part of your message, in any medium that might be seen by your prospect.

You have no way of knowing which part of your message is going to be read first. Some research shows that a postscript is the most-read and often the first-read part of a sales letter. In some cases, depending on format and graphics, the brochure may be read before the letter, or a supplementary flyer may be the first thing out of the envelope.

In an ad, people attracted to the illustration may read the caption before they read the headline. Others may read the coupon before the body copy. If you have a principal selling point, put it in every part of your ad that could conceivably be the part read first by potential customers.

Newspaper preprints and co-op mail inserts offer a clear example. Writers often put a great headline on page 1 of a four-page insert and use the back page for miscellaneous points. But when the insert slides out of the newspaper, the back is just as likely to be seen first as the front. Thus the principal selling theme must also be evident on page 4 as well, but perhaps worded differently.

Though repetition is desirable, there is no reason to present a selling point the same way over and over again. To avoid boring the reader, reword it. Give a different example or a different analogy. At the very least, use a fresh choice of words.

Presume that your first expression of the main theme is what stopped the prospects and got them to read your message in the first place. You know the message has appeal or they wouldn't be reading, so keep it in front of the readers' minds by reinserting it in each and every main segment of the ad, mailing, or TV commercial, and every page of your website. Be sure to make the message fresh at the moment of truth when you are asking your reader to fill out the coupon.

Isn't the Internet Different?

At times I've heard this same question for television, infomercials, and radio spots. Yes, the Internet is different, as a medium. Like every other medium it has its own set of advantages and limitations. But it is not immune to the laws of human nature that underlie the do's and don'ts of direct marketing. You still have to stop people, interest them, inform them, overcome objections, reassure them with guarantees and motivate them with an immediacy-laden offer. You still have to respect the laws of economics and invest money—not only on the web but in other advertising, mailings and TV spots—to get them to call up your URL in the first place. The Internet is unique, but so is each advertising medium. For more detail on how to utilize the Internet, read Chapter 21.

EVALUATING ADVERTISING COPY

In evaluating your own or someone else's advertising copy, here are some simple tests.

The Tightness Test. Try to cut the copy. Sit down with a blue pencil and see how much shorter you can make it without deleting a material selling point. If it's easy to cut, then the copy is soft, mushy, fatty, or whatever pejorative fits your style. If the copy is hard to cut without breaking up the flow or omitting an important point, then you've got tight, meaty, hard copy—the real thing.

Interchangeability. Take out the name of your product and see if you can use the same copy for a competitor or another product. Your ad should be uniquely appropriate to your proposition. If it fits others just as easily, the creative approach lacks a unique selling proposition.

The Glance Test. Give yourself 5 seconds to look quickly at the headlines, subheads, and captions. Is there enough meat to convince you that you want to read the rest of the ad? If not, then move your project back to GO, and do *not* collect $200.

Give yourself 10 to 15 seconds to read all the heads and subheads that call out to you in large, boldface type. Do they do a selling job in their own right? For instance, is a contents listing headlined "Table of Contents" or "The Secret of Eternal Life, and 88 other things you must know"? Every head, subhead, and caption should be a selling message in itself. These should make the sale even if the reader does not read one single word of body copy.

Intelligibility. Ask your secretary, the receptionist, and the elevator operator to read the ad. They don't have to be prospects and the ad doesn't have to interest them, but they should be able to understand what in the world you are talking about.

I have been amazed to discover that points I thought were obvious and clear were completely misunderstood by exactly the people who should have followed them without difficulty. Let people who have had nothing to do with the creation of the ad or mailing piece read it, and have them play back what they think you said.

I have heard writers defend their work by elaborating on copy points. My answer to this is "If you promise to accompany each and every copy of this ad or mailing and offer the same explanation, I'll approve it. Otherwise, make the ad stand on its own."

Actionability.   Now ask people to respond to the ad. Do they know exactly what to do, or do they start asking unnecessary questions? Is the coupon easy to fill out? Are the prices and any extra charges clearly understood? Is the phone number clear and legible, and is the fact that it's toll-free easily discernible?

You should be able to hand the ad to anyone in your office and say "Order this for me" with no further explanation. If someone has trouble ordering because he or she doesn't understand a point and an explanation is necessary, check through the response devices all over again.

A TRIBUTE TO COPYWRITERS

Maybe because I started as a copywriter, I expect writers to be the miracle workers of the advertising business. All the marketing planning and all the steps developing strategy and inventing tactics have one basic presumption: that copywriters can do anything.

Like the debating society member who can argue any side of the question, the copywriter must be prepared to sell any product to any audience with any positioning. For anyone who thinks writing copy is easy, let me offer a challenge—one that I use as a homework assignment in my NYU classes.

> First, take a product, any product—preferably one that you see being handled poorly—or take a fund-raising campaign for a worthy charity.
>
> Describe the product on every level—practical, scientific, and emotional—as discussed in the pencil example in Chapter 9. Imagine that you are the audience. Prepare a copy platform and write some ad concepts.
>
> Then adjust the style upscale or down. Vary the horizontal positioning, and rewrite the ad for an earlier position.
>
> Then change the size unit. What would you do differently in a small-space ad? In a double-page spread?
>
> Then change the medium. Rewrite the ad for television or radio. Or change the style so that it is appropriate for direct mail.
>
> Then dramatize a benefit, feature the offer, do an audience-selection ad, or lead with a premium.

The copywriter doesn't have to do all these things with every assignment, of course. Writers do have to have the inner conviction that their skills are ready and waiting and that they can produce winning direct marketing communications for any product in any medium at any positioning. Versatility is the mark of a truly professional writer. To paraphrase *Star Wars*: "May the skill be with you!"

CREATIVE DECISION CHECK LIST

How many ways can you change a direct mail package?
This idea-sparking list by Pat Friesen is a good place to start.

Offer Tests:
- ✔ Free sample vs. no sample
- ✔ Guarantee wording
- ✔ Response channels
- ✔ Free information vs. comparison-shopper's kit
- ✔ Methods of payment
- ✔ Send-no-money-now free trial
- ✔ Sample magazine vs. brochure
- ✔ Discounts
- ✔ Request for referrals
- ✔ Limited edition availability
- ✔ Incentives and free gifts

Format Tests:
- ✔ Solo vs. self-mailer
- ✔ Single shot mailing vs. series
- ✔ Pre- or post-mailing postcard
- ✔ Lift letter vs. no lift letter
- ✔ Free gift insert vs. no insert
- ✔ Window vs. closed faced envelope
- ✔ Classified vs. display ad
- ✔ Space ad with and without bind-in reply card
- ✔ Envelope size
- ✔ Tokens or stickers
- ✔ Live postage vs. pre-printed indicia or metered postage
- ✔ Solo mailing with and without sales brochure
- ✔ Tube vs. standard envelope
- ✔ Retention devices

Copy Tests:
- ✔ Brochure or ad headlines
- ✔ Personalization
- ✔ Envelope teaser vs. no teaser
- ✔ Opening paragraph in letter
- ✔ Letter length
- ✔ Use of testimonial copy
- ✔ Product benefit call-outs
- ✔ Photo caption vs. no captions
- ✔ The name of the response vehicle (Savings Certificate, Order Form, Reply Card)
- ✔ Handwriting in margins
- ✔ Pre-filled response vehicle

Layout & Design Tests:
- ✔ Charts and graphs vs. narrative numbers
- ✔ Photos vs. illustrations
- ✔ 4-colors vs. 1- or 2-color
- ✔ Type size & font
- ✔ Use of people/human elements in product photography
- ✔ Color, texture or weight of paper
- ✔ Age, sex, ethnicity of models

Source: Pat Friesen & Co., Creative and Strategy: (913) 341-1211

Figure 10-4

11

ART DIRECTION

At one time, the art director was considered to be a mere executor of creative strategies developed by marketers and copywriters. Today the industry generally recognizes that art directors can and should make a major contribution to the overall creative process. Exceptional art directors should be part of the creative team from the very inception of a project. They should be expected to contribute to strategic plans as well as make important contributions to the finished ad or mailing piece.

Visual Communications

While most artists have been trained in the techniques of graphics, they have more to offer. The bulk of this chapter addresses the problems of advertising layout, but it should be recognized that nonverbal communication as a major creative tool has increased the importance of the art function dramatically.

The art director can help to identify pictorial ways to communicate themes related to emotions, fantasy, or self-image. The mood of a photograph, the casting of models, and the direction during a photo shoot can be critical in suggesting intangible satisfactions to the potential customers who view the photos eventually in an ad. Subtleties such as props and settings can create highly effective messages in themselves—subtleties that can be validated with research. These characteristic apply to artistic illustrations, product shots and photographs with people.

In advertising, copy style is the equivalent of tone of voice and layout is the equivalent of body language. When a "user imagery" strategy is being employed, the people and expressions associated with the product are the key factors in the long-range awareness message. The selection of which people with what expressions is the major responsibility of an art director. If fantasy ideas are to be communicated, the imagination of the art director is the only limit. Subtle changes in typeface, size, location, and format can convey different images and stress different aspects of the final message.

The art director should be capable of taking the same copy and adapting it to any positioning, any image, any emphasis, any medium, any audience. The same message can be laid out to stress the headline, the illustration, the copy, the coupon, the offer, the lead item, the end product, the endorser or the guarantee. It is up to the art director to make the selections necessary to convey entirely different moods—elegance, bargain price, stability, excitement.

Communicating Imagery

The role of the art director has become all the more critical with the increasing use of direct response advertising to also influence brand images. Also, many elements of emotion and self-imagery are better communicated visually than verbally.

Emotional Messages.   It is obvious that that the closer the advertiser comes to an emotional "hot button," the more difficult it is to communicate in words. Perhaps a product really does make the user imagine his or her self as younger, bolder, sexier. Fine. But if you explicitly make those promises in a headline, you will be greeted with incredulity. In our society you can do or aspire to anything. But you can't talk about it, at least not in public, and certainly not with strangers.

So, you can show models being popular and having fun, but you can't say "Have more fun!" You can have the owner of your new car exchange seductive glances with a passenger and create an easily-read suggestion, but if you put the same idea in words many people will be offended.

Self-Image.   If you are appealing to people who see themselves as "thoroughly modern," then show the product in use with the latest styles and settings. If your prospect wants to "think of themselves as traditional or conservative," then pick your models and scenes accordingly.

Apparel and cosmetic catalogers understand the critical impact that the choice of models can have on the garments they display. One cosmetic ad manager told me "It's all casting. Everything else is detail." The personality conveyed by the model or spokesperson becomes the personality of the brand, store, or company.

One common direct marketing project involves popularizing a product or service that was originally marketed to a select core market. It is very difficult to find a message that says, "Now this is available to little guys like you." Whether the new prospect is a small business, a less affluent investor, or a less sophisticated prospect for technical equipment, the issue is the same. Most verbal expressions will be in poor taste, and will produce poor response rates. The solution is to show it, not say it, by placing "people (or companies) like you" in your illustrations.

Copy-Art Teams

In recent years, direct-marketing agencies have started to establish copy-art teams as a part of the standard organizational structure. Long used by general agencies, the team approach keeps a balance between verbal and visual elements of the creative product. I recommend adding a strategist— an account supervisor, account executive or a product manager (if the work is being done at an in-house facility)—as an equal partner to keep focus on the client's preferences and the agreed-upon strategy. If the writer, artist and strategist are able to work together over a long period of time and on many different projects, their thinking processes become thoroughly synchronized. Eventually the roles become less distinct, and either party may come up with a headline or a critical visual idea.

FIVE LAYOUT PRINCIPLES

Not withstanding the opportunities for art directors to contribute to overall creative direction, it is still as necessary for an art director to know how to create a layout as it is for a copywriter to know how to write. The balance of this chapter will deal with basic execution questions. My work with art directors has led to the identification of five basic principles that all well-executed layouts have in common. These five Cs of advertising layout are *concentration, cohesion, convention, contrast,* and *convection.*

Concentration

Attention-getting ability is proportional to the size of the largest single element, not to the total size of the ad. A small-space unit with a single large element—a word, a headline, an illustration—will get more attention than a unit the same size or even larger with smaller elements. Reducing the number of elements by simplifying, combining or eliminating some of them will always result in a layout that is more inviting to view and usually more readable and more successful.

To understand this better, look at newspapers. The article perceived to be the most important is not the longest one but the one with the biggest, boldest headline or the largest photograph.

In any advertising layout, or in any art form for that matter, balance is dull. Everything can't be equal. An artist or the creator of an ad must make a deliberate choice as to which visual element should be the most important.

Some ads and catalog pages are cluttered with so many conflicting subheads competing for attention that the reader is bewildered. At the other extreme, I once had to create an ad that was only 2 inches on one column. I chose to use half the space for a 1-inch-high, black, bold headline: *Opium!*

This small advertisement for Evergreen's reprint of the Jean Cocteau classic achieved very acceptable order costs.

The essence of creativity is choice. And the first choice for an art director is, "What will be the lead, attention-getting element?" The headline? An illustration? Simulation of a news story, a personal letter, an article? If everything is important, nothing is important.

Some ads are built around a dominant illustration, perhaps a square halftone photograph taking up 60 percent of the page. Others have a clean, dominant headline that marks the obvious place to start reading and does not compete for attention with other elements of the same ad.

Imagine for a moment two billboards along a highway. One is 50 feet high and has a 5-foot-high message. The other is 25 feet high and has a 10-foot-high message. It is obvious that the size of the message and not the size of the billboard will determine from how far away motorists will see it, and subsequently how many will read the message.

Whether your unit is large or small, and whether your medium is print, broadcast, Internet or direct mail, it must attract attention by the inherent strength of the lead element, not by the total size of the page or printed piece, or by the total length of the message.

Cohesion

The space in any direction between elements of a graphic presentation should not exceed the space between the message and the border of the layout. This rule sounds simple and obvious, but it used to frequently be ignored in direct-response advertising.

Cohesion is often absent when it is most needed—in newspaper advertising. An ad "breaks up" if the space between the headline and the body copy is greater than that between the headline and the adjoining advertisement, or if the headline or closing copy is isolated by white space from the main selling paragraphs. Some advertisements might have been more effective if the agency had simply purchased less space instead of a standard unit and closed up all the elements.

Does this mean that "white space" doesn't belong in direct-response advertising? No. But white space, like any other styling, selling, or attention-getting element, has to be used in conjunction with all the other elements and not as an end in itself.

What should an art director do when a novice graphic artist produces a layout with an excess of divisive space? Here are some idea-starters:

1. Enlarge the most important element, probably the headline or key illustration, and tighten up the remaining elements.

2. Reset the body copy so it reads comfortably.

3. Move towards the center all the elements that are "floating," to create borders or more white space at the margins.

The principle of cohesion is vital in fractional-unit advertising. Layouts for such ads should always be pasted in the newspaper or magazine to see how the ad will look on a busy page. Don't cheat! Pick the busiest page, not the one you would most like the ad to appear on. There should never be more space between elements of your layout than there is between your layout and the next ad.

Convention

Pre-existing associations with design elements will influence attitudes towards new creative efforts. The principle in fine art called *convention* refers to the perceiver's past experience and associations as an influence on how new perceptions are evaluated.

For instance, imagine for a moment that an artist has taken a canvas and painted the bottom half green and the top half blue. Most viewers, when asked to guess what is being portrayed, would call it a landscape, with the green bottom representing grass and the blue top the sky. Add some white blobs in the top area and, depending on their size, they will be perceived as clouds or stars. A yellow blob might be seen as a sun or moon, depending on the total coloring. What you think the abstractions represent is influenced by what the colors or shapes *conventionally* represent in this context. Perceptions of quality, cheapness, bargain price, and elegance are all influenced by past experiences.

There are many types of visual conventions. The most relevant to advertising layouts involve color, proportional space, typography and pictorial associations.

Space Conventions. If you study department store windows, you'll note that a cluttered window is used to convey the feeling of a sale, while a stark, relatively empty window – perhaps only one or two manikins displaying new fashions—is used when the garments are exclusive and expensive.

A large space advertisement, a long-form television commercial or an over-sized multi-page or multi-media (eg: videotape) catalog or mail-piece conveys importance. In these cases, sheer size implies that the advertiser is a solid, substantial company.

Color Conventions. Psychologists have long believed that color affects attitudes and moods. Walls would never be painted red in an office where doctors wish to calm patients' anxieties. Similarly, color choices can tell something about personality. What is the color of your car? Or your favorite sport-shirt or blouse? These may be valuable tools in segmenting markets or attracting personality types most likely to respond to a particular offer. Interestingly, one cigarette company offered a mail-redemption gift with purchase of a cigarette lighter. The consumers who responded had to pick their first and second choice of colors—red, blue, green, yellow? By now the company knows exactly which color choices correlated most often to new users of their brand.

The intensity of color is also a factor. People discuss colors with words like *strong, loud, pale, intense, weak.* Some use of color is described as *soothing* or *comfortable* while other choices are *busy* or *irritating*. What is important to remember is that colors have an influence on the perception of the offer. Yes, a "loud" layout might attract attention, but is it the attention of the people you want to attract? Does the ad create the mood you need to make a sale?

We no longer think we have to send pink envelopes to get the attention of women buyers, but that doesn't mean black and red stripes are appropriate either. Some advertisers believe that bright yellow envelopes will out-pull white ones. I've found that light blue and kraft-like colors sometimes produce a lift effect. But the colors are not chosen in isolation. They must support the overall feeling of the message.

With computer graphics, we have unlimited ability to create unusual colors as well as innovative designs. But just because we can do something doesn't mean we should. We know that color effects attitudes and results, but we don't always know which color is best. While computers can execute some colors on the screen, they are not necessarily capable of being reproduced for your direct-mail piece. The colors on the computer screen are represented by points of lights. Colors on advertisements are ink on paper or other materials. The final printed products are limited to the available dyes and inks.

Designers working on the computer must know the corresponding colors to what they see on the screen and to the final product that depends on the printing process. Those who don't will mislead and disappoint clients time after time. Figure 11.1 demonstrates how certain printing processes are limited in range. For example, the range for the CYMK printing—the basic printing process—is more limited than the RGB colors visible on the screen.

The sure way to avoid any problem is to produce a color proof from film before starting the actual printing process. Ask the printer for the color proof that represents the final product, and show this to your client. Have the client sign this color proof—to protect yourself, the graphic artist and the print shop. While graphic artists will present layouts, designs, and "almost-ready" ads throughout the artistic process—varying from preliminary ink-jet printouts to proofs from a high-tech digital center—these are not generated from film, and will not represent the final color. Only the color proof produced from film can do this.

The safe bet is to avoid colors that call attention to the design rather than to the product, and to stick with safe, neutral tones. Even neutrals should be coordinated so all the colors work together. Avoid the temptation to make an offer insert "stand out" by creating something inappropriate, like putting the insert copy in white type on a red background that clashes with every other piece in an envelope. The colors used in the elements of a mail piece or the pages of a catalog, a brochure or a website should work together and complement each other.

Type Conventions. Typography is also associated with past perceptions, and conveys its own form of nonverbal communication as the "body language" of an advertising message.

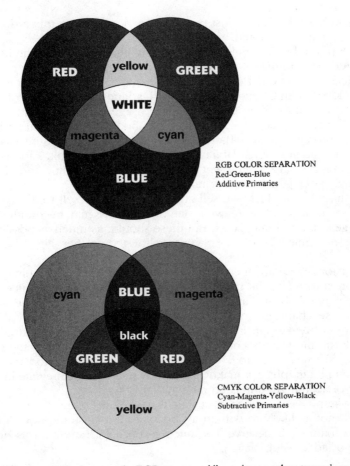

RGB COLOR SEPARATION
Red-Green-Blue
Additive Primaries

CMYK COLOR SEPARATION
Cyan-Magenta-Yellow-Black
Subtractive Primaries

Computer scanners and monitors use the RGB process, adding primary colors to produce tones and shades of color. However printing processes are subtractive, filtering out colors to try to get the same effect. The artist or printer must make adjustments so that the finished ad or mailing piece will match the colors seen on the monitor or on computer prints. Guides illustrating samples of 4-color process (CMYK)) and spot colors (PMS) provide a standard to communicate color objectives.

Figure 11-1

A sans serif typeface such as Univers or Helvetica is associated with modernity. A traditional book face such as Garamond, Caslon, or Times New Roman is the classic kind of face associated with books, magazines, and newspapers. These kinds of type suggest reliability and authority. The names of fonts that I have included here are of traditional typefaces, but almost every computer font has an equivalent, often with a different name, depending on the supplier. What is important is that type work together, with headlines and subheads and sidebars all suggesting a coordinated whole rather than chaos. Just because it is now easy to mix a dozen faces doesn't mean you should.

Type printed at an angle and non-cursive italic type give the impression of speed or imminence. Bold faces convey importance or loudness. Thin typefaces suggest quiet or restraint, or elegance or sophistication.

A bold Franklin Gothic face implies "Headline!" in most parts of the country. The presumption is that the ad's message is an important announcement. Century Schoolbook, a standard textbook face, seems appropriate for an educational message. Bauer Bodoni is a modernized serif face, with a good combination of readability and a contemporary look. Various pseudo-engraving faces are reminiscent of invitations and wedding announcements and suggest elegance and exclusivity.

Just like the products we sell and the people we sell to, every typeface has its own personality. As with tone of voice, we may need different faces to suggest different messages. But these should, as much as possible, be in the same "family" of faces or work well together. (See Fig. 11-2 on page 273.)

Occasionally an art director forgets that the primary criteria in type specification is to make the message easy to read. Put an abundance of space between lines of type and a sentence looks like separate one line statements. Use character spacing that is too wide and words aren't read as words, but break apart into individual letters. But the other extreme is just as bad; the message becomes difficult to read if the lines or the character spacing are too close together. Over-sized subheads or too much space between paragraphs can make a long copy message disintegrate into a busy clutter of seemingly unrelated paragraphs.

Typography is as much of an art form as any other aspect of design. Though not as likely to win an award as a cute illustration or a gimmicky website banner, it deserves as much respect and attention as any other aspect of advertising design.

Pictorial Convention. Both the choice of illustrations and their style constitute another form of body language. A picture of a spokesperson suggests sincerity and straightforwardness. A diagram or blueprint suggests that the product is well made. Luxury settings imply a luxury product, which is why expert photographers spend as much time finding the right props or locations as worrying about lighting.

As mentioned earlier, casting can be critical. This is often where we find the solutions for clients who ask us why something didn't work. A client who sold a product for infants had used a photo of a mother and a one-year old boy. But the child was dressed up so maturely that he looked two or three times that age. A catalog client used a fashion model that depressed the sale of any garment she was shown in. Later research found that readers didn't like the personality this otherwise attractive model suggested. A television spokesperson did an effective job describing an offer, but our research showed that his voice and posture suggested that he was an undertaker—not a good image for a seller of life insurance!

When designing advertising in any media form, remember that what people associate with illustrations can make a critical difference. Art directors are often amazed at the powers of observation of the people who view their messages. Pay careful attention to the details of props, settings, expressions, hair styles. If you are showing a product, set it up properly and show it being used correctly. Avoid anything that distracts from the imagery or product presentation you are trying to convey.

Illustrations tend to convey images and messages independently of the text and topics involved. It is important that these layout considerations be planned in accordance with the basic strategy and tactics so that the visual communication supports the copy.

Contrast

The chameleon, which survives by blending into its environment, should be the mascot of any art department—not as an inspiration, but as a reminder of the deadliest sin of advertising art.

The first law of layout: Be noticed. To be noticed in any medium your message must look different from its environment.

If your newspaper ad blends into the newspaper's editorial content or looks like just another advertisement, if your magazine ad looks like every other ad in the publication, if your website banner looks like decoration, or if your radio or television commercial blends into the program or into preceding commercials, you are throwing your money away.

Your advertisement must stand out. Your mailing must look fresh and different from the others in the day's mail. Your commercial must make people stop and take notice. Your Internet advertising must be more inviting that the information the viewer was looking for.

Boutique layouts that give a particular art studio or agency's work a distinctive look is good business for the agency, but not necessarily for the client whose money is being spent. The last thing in the world you want the prospect to say is, "Oh, isn't that clever. It's just like the ads for. . . ."

The artistic expression should not call attention to itself at the expense of the message. The object is not to make people say "What a clever (or pretty) ad!" or "What a clever designer (or agency)!" The object is to catch the reader's eye, to present the sales message clearly, and to use graphics to visually support that message. All this should lead to an immediate and positive action by the viewer in response to the proposition.

A corporate style is just as damaging. A corporate quality image or trade logotype may be desirable to establish identity, authority and credibility when a message is being read, but it should not stand in the way of getting attention in the first place.

If people think they know what your ad is going to say, they won't read it. If a bank, for example, sends out all its promotions in envelopes that look identical (perhaps to economize on printing costs), prospects will presume that the current mailing makes the same offer as the previous ones. The envelope will go unopened, the letter unread, and the proposition unconsidered.

Copy-catting is self-defeating in a dozen ways, not the least of which is that the advertiser being copied has probably moved on to another format just as you mimic the old one. *Newsweek* started looking for new ideas at a time when almost everyone in the field was planning to imitate their Mead-Digit subscription package, which featured the prospect's name, for the first time, in large bold type. Just about every week there was an announcement from another supplier who was installing the required equipment to create a similar subscription package. Just as often there were requests from clients who wanted to try the *Newsweek* approach. But what *Newsweek* knew—and the others didn't—was that the technique had already lost effectiveness.

Cycles seem to exist in advertising layout. Sam Sugar of Sussman & Sugar, Inc., a book-promotion agency, once observed that the first step for an art director is to review the publication an ad is going to run in and to determine what the current fad is—so you can go the opposite way!

The same thing happens in typography. Every typeface has had its fad. I have seen our industry overdose on Optima, Helvetica, Caledonia with descenders, Copperplate and Century Schoolbook. It's as if some secret newsletters, like the ones in the fashion world, are forecasting the "type style of the month," thus making the prediction come true. The smart move is to watch what everyone else is doing and find a way to make your own ads look distinctively different.

Convection

Once you've managed to attract the right readers to your message through your concept, copy and layout treatment, the job that remains is to keep them there long enough to get enough copy read to make the sale.

This is a matter of *flow* or *convection,* the art of designing the message in a manner that carries the reader along in a logical fashion from one element to the other, right to the coupon.

If you want to stop readers with a headline or illustration in an ad, then pay off the promise or curiosity in a subhead or in the first paragraph of copy. You then want the main copy to read in a manner that takes the reader to the point of action, to the coupon or to the phone number or a web URL (Universal Resource Locator).

In a mailing piece, you want the envelope or catalog cover to be opened and the reader to turn from one piece or page to the next in a logical manner. For instance, you seldom want the price to be among the first items noted.

Curiosity or a fantasy promise in a web banner might get the viewer to link to your website. But then the message should follow though in both content and graphic style. For instance, why frustrate the viewer with a come-on like "10 new ways to finance your business" and then link to a home page that shows a picture of a bank building and a menu of options that appear unrelated to the promise?

Support elements, like editorial sidebars, should be placed in a way that doesn't disrupt the primary copy flow. Items such as feature listings, testimonial panels, credentials, or detailed specifications should be there for those who want to know more but should be out of the mainstream.

If you are pulling for inquiries for an automobile, for example, the inclusion of technical specifications is necessary for some readers. For others it would be a distraction—a turnoff that would get them to stop reading altogether. Optional elements must be handled in such a way that they are optional *reading* as well.

Here's a simple test to see if your layout has convection. Draw a line down the main copy story to indicate how you think the reader will follow the message. Then ask someone else, perhaps an uninvolved writer or artist, to look at another copy of the same ad and draw a similar flow line. If the two lines are different, then perhaps the flow is not as obvious as you think it is.

The flow should be just as well-defined in a mail piece. The first thing prospects look at is their own names on the outer envelope, then they look again wherever their names appear. Nothing is as fascinating as our own image, signature, photograph, or other personalized feature.

The back of the envelope is less critical than the copy and image portrayed on the front. You cannot count on the reader to turn to the back, so the front should have enough incentive to get the envelope opened even if the back is never seen.

The rest of the elements should then be collated in a logical manner. If you don't want the price to be the first thing seen, cover it with a fold or flap. If the offer is sensational, then put the address at the top of the letter or near the address area, and let it be the first thing readers see when they open the envelope.

Otherwise the letter should be the first thing read. Just address the letter and let *that* be the envelope show-through. The addressed element will be the first thing seen when the mail package is opened. Everything else will be viewed after that.

If you want a color broadside to be the next thing read, then be sure it is the next thing viewed. Supplementary inserts should be smaller or less colorful so that they don't cover up or distract from the main pieces. If everything is equally important or equally interesting, you have no control over the flow of the message.

One trick of the trade that applies to both letters and long copy advertisements is the recognition that curiosity is a more powerful drive than pleas such as "see next column" or "see other side." Paragraphs should never be completed at the bottom of a column or a page, even though typists are often trained to do this. Instead, interrupt the last line in mid-sentence and, better yet, in mid-thought. Use the natural human desire to complete things as a force to encourage the continual reading of your sales message.

Don't build barriers within your ads. Subheads that are in a larger type size than the body copy will actually interrupt the reading of the copy rather than encourage it.

Bold borders that break up copy elements into panels will force the reader to "jump" from one to the other and leave half of them unread. It is better to use borders to separate optional reading elements or to separate your ad from others.

A photo can be a barrier also. Don't expect readers to continue reading a column of type if you distract them with a photo and caption in the middle of the column. Put them alongside the column rather than in its path. A popular technique is to place photos across a portion of two column widths so that the column of text is narrower, but continues down the page. Illustrations should support a copy point, not compete with it.

The five principles of concentration, cohesion, convention, contrast, and convection apply to all advertising, but their violation shows up faster and more directly in the measurable world of direct marketing than in general advertising.

OTHER SPECIFICS

Readability

Too many art directors focus on illustration and design, treating copy as a necessary evil. Such art directors will, if not supervised, treat the words as just another design element. They hide the type in as small a size as possible to fit their visual goals. They use an interesting but unreadable decorative type face, or put the words in reverse type (white on black, versus black on white) or superimposed on a busy photo or other background. Understanding the importance of readability is often the key difference between a potential creative director and a staff art director.

As mentioned earlier, too much line spacing or excess character spacing breaks up the thought and is hard to read. Crowding the lines or letters together by reducing normal spacing has the opposite but equally negative effect on readability.

A good art director shouldn't be too tricky with margins. Current software makes it easy to shape a copy block around an illustration or logo, but this sort of placement sometimes makes the copy difficult to read. Too wide a copy block is also a problem. The old rule which still makes sense to me is that the width of a copy in an advertisement should never be longer than the alphabet—26 characters. Newspaper columns have trained us to read narrow columns, so small-width copy blocks become another convention to deal with. Try it yourself—type some text, adjust the margin to different widths, and compare a wide copy block to a narrow one. See which one is more inviting to read.

One test that works: ask someone unfamiliar with the subject to read the ad aloud. If they don't hesitate or misread words, fine. Otherwise, either the typography is a problem or the copy is not well written. Readability is the obligation of everyone involved in the creative process.

Illustrations

One of the first questions is whether to use a photograph, a painting or drawing. There is no doubt about the answer; illustrations have been the subject of split-run testing. With all its realism, photography is clearly the winner, particularly with product illustrations.

That is not to say that there won't be occasions when drawings or diagrams will be the better way to make a point or to illustrate something that doesn't lend itself to photographs. Good artwork often can contribute to a unique style, set a mood, or dramatize a benefit better than a photo could.

When planning a photography shoot, you should strive for action, motion, and dimension. Even a straight product shot can be given a sense of action by surrounding it with props that make it appear to be in use or about to be used.

Depth—a product of lighting and camera angles—is essential if a photograph is going to "come alive" and do more than lie flat on the page. The standard is realism.

The concept of motion may be difficult to capture, but showing some sort of motion makes the difference between "posed-looking" shots and candid news photographs. A good model shouldn't look like a model if the designer and photographer apply this concept.

The art director should be involved with every basic decision when working with a photographer. When photographing people, the most important decision is the choice of models. This should never be left up to the photographer. Instead, go through the submissions of the model agencies yourself. The model should be able not only to look right, but to act right. Intangibles such as enthusiasm, contentment, tranquillity, and pride are all emotional states that are part of the message. Some models can be directed to convey an emotion. Others just sit and look pretty. I prefer to consider models who list membership in one of the acting unions, as this is an indication of some acting experience and ambition.

The standard for selecting models is not whether you find them attractive, but whether your prospects will relate to them. The ages and styles of models determine whether they are people the prospect can identify with, or if they can be perceived as authority figures. The choice depends on the theme of the advertisement. One mistake to be avoided, however, is selecting models who too faithfully reflect the target audience. Research tells us that people want to relate to models who represent their ambitions, not their realities. Prospects want to see themselves as a little younger, healthier, wealthier, wiser, happier, or thinner than they really are. Researchers call this "aspirational imagery."

Once the models have been hired, talk with them in person so that you can explain the nature of the shot and the kind of clothing and hairstyle that will be needed. It is amazing how little information agents and photographers give the models. It is well worth the time to tell them yourself.

Be at the photo session. In a still photograph, the setting must be staged and the actor must be directed with the same care as in a television commercial. See the shot through the camera as the photographer does (even though it may be upside down through the lens). You may see something that others may overlook—subtleties like scratches on your product or too suggestive a pose. And, of course, you and the art director should see the contact prints and select which shot should be blown up for final retouching.

Working with an illustrator is very similar, except that you see sketches of their work commissioned by you, rather than the details of a photography session. The illustrator will most likely work with a "swipe file" of photos and other ads. Get agreement on the subject, the style, and the apparel for illustrations that include people. I once had to reject an illustration because an artist dressed a character in a tuxedo in an ad for a mass-market book club. Another rejection showed retirees—pleased that they had invested in gold coins—drawn with insipid grins.

Cost control is always a problem. Negotiating art costs should never be left solely up to the art director, who is likely to be too sympathetic to the needs of peers in the art world. The art budget should always be previously approved by a product manager or account executive who has the total project budget in mind.

Costs have to be kept in perspective, and related to the value of the medium the illustrations are being used in and the total promotion budget. While I am usually the first to raise an eyebrow over the photography session that *must* be shot in the Caribbean or the commercial that can *only* be filmed in California, I will admit that there are times when such expenditures are justified.

Typography

Typography is the unheralded fine art of commercial layout. Of the tens of thousands of graduates of art schools, all are taught type as well as design and illustration, but only a handful—often relatives of printers or book designers—emerge with a genuine love for type.

Every creative organization should have at least one person who not only knows how to use typography but loves to work with it, for only that person will appreciate the infinite subtleties that go far beyond specifying type.

Sure, type must be selected and must fit the message to the available space, and anyone can be trained to count characters. The classic tool is a Haberule, which measures type lines by number of characters. But that has nothing to do with *designing* with type.

Type Has Style.   Each and every typeface has been designed to convey a feeling that is somewhat different from all other types that were designed before it (see Fig. 11-2). The simplicity of Futura has given way to the subtler shading of Univers, Helvetica, and Optima. The classic readability of Caslon has been joined by varieties of Baskerville, Bodoni, and Roman. There is an infinite variety of stylistic faces: the heaviness of Cooper Black, the playfulness of Kaleidoscope, the starkness of Stymie, and the stylistic games of playful Mediterranean faces like Memphis, Karnak, Cairo, and Delta. Note that these are original names for these styles; your computer or studio may have identical faces with different names. There are literally a thousand faces to chose from.

For an advertisement or mailing piece, a typeface must be selected that, overall, conveys the positioning selected for the project. It must have the

MODERN CONTEMPORARY	Futura Book *Univers Oblique* Helvetica Light **Optima Bold**
CLASSIC TRADITIONAL	Caslon Medium *Baskerville Inclined* **Bodoni Bold** Times New Roman
IMPORTANT STRONG URGENT	**Goudy Heavy** **Helvetica Black** **Impact** **Arial Bold**
INTERESTING PLAYFUL	Hobo Hip Hop Remedy Bauhaus

Figure 11-2. Type sets a tone that can support or distract from your advertising message.

flexibility to provide the shadings necessary for subheads, captions, emphasis, or parenthetical comments. And, of course, it must also be easy to read.

You can choose more than one face if you really know what you are doing, but mixing and matching typefaces is as dangerous as trying to match slacks and jacket rather than buy a suit. Sometimes separates come out fine and sometimes they look awful. But you can't go wrong wearing a suit.

Within each typeface there are usually light and bold styles, regular and italic, cursive and/or non-cursive versions, and an infinite range of sizes. There was a time when typography was limited by precise sizes. Now, with computer fonts, you can create any line width you want, and can condense or expand a typeface to your needs. Hand lettering can also create a variety of very worthwhile special effects.

Leading. Just as important as the selection of the type is the spacing between lines. This is called "leading" because of the rows of lead between lines in linotype printing from years ago. If you ordered an 8-point type and had no space between lines, it is set "solid" or "8-on-8." If it had 2 points of lead, it was called 8-on-10.

Solid leading is usually somewhat difficult to read, except in the case of some typefaces that are "small-bodied," with oversize ascenders and descenders. The eye supposedly reads reflected light, the white space around type, not the type itself. Therefore the spacing between lines may contribute more to readability than the size of the type. As a result, I usually prefer 11-on-12 to 11-solid or 12-solid, although it depends upon the typeface. The extra point of space between the lines separates them just a tiny bit to ease strain on the eyes. This book is set 10-on-11, for instance.

The size of type to choose for text copy is relative to the surroundings. In a publication like *TV Guide,* which uses fairly small type faces, you can safely use 6 on 7 for body copy. In newspapers or a large brochure, a larger face usually is more appropriate. The standard is the size readers expect as other forms of convention. There are some regulations regarding typeface size for particular text like disclaimers.

Kerning. Kerning is defined as the adjustment of space between adjacent letters. Computer fonts have automatic kerning, with the ability to adjust the space in between the letters in the different programs. An expanded kerning can make the text stand out and look important—think of the legal headings on court documents. A condensed kerning tightens the space between the letters, indicating a close and intimate mood, or just plain overcrowding. While kerning was not easily flexible in the past, computers have changed this. Very minor adjustments with kerning can make the difference between text fitting or not, with very little difference in appearance. Adjustments in font size and leading are used this way as well.

Age is an important determinant. Children like large type. Older people, whether they admit it to themselves or not, may have difficulty reading conventional type sizes and would prefer not to have to put on their reading glasses. Many advertisers whose propositions are aimed at older people go out of their way to keep typefaces large.

Another key factor is motivation. If the headline and initial subhead are so interesting that the prospect wants to read the rest of the copy, size will be irrelevant. In fact, it used to be customary in earlier direct-marketing ads to drop type sizes down every few paragraphs.

Condensing a typeface can often save space more effectively than going down to a smaller type size or decreasing leading.

Simplicity is the byword of good type design. A safe way to design an ad is to pick a readable book face and use the boldface for the headline and all subheads. Italic may work for captions, or a smaller size of the normal type. The body copy, subheads, and coupon copy could be the same size, with any insert panels a size smaller. You can't go wrong with this kind of design.

To be readable, lines of type can't be too long or too short. One rule says that lines should have a maximum of 50 characters. Another rule says 26 characters is ideal. The answer is not rules, but good judgment about what is readable, what is important, and what is inviting to read.

Designing Coupons

In Chapter 10, I suggested that writers work on the coupon first as a way of crystallizing the basic purpose of the advertisement. Although I do not give the same advice to art directors, the design of the coupon should nevertheless be assigned a great deal of importance.

I have seen too many art directors work out the placement of headlines, copy blocks and illustrations, and then just leave a blank area for the coupon. The coupon deserves more attention than that. The coupon is likely to be torn out for later use, and at that time becomes a self-contained selling piece and response form—every bit as important as the initial advertisement, if not more. It must contain the basic elements and positioning of the overall message.

Within the borders of the coupon or reply card, there should be a simple restatement of the basic offer, possibly combined with a spur to action. "Mail this card today to get your free copy" is the right kind of headline, as opposed to just "Mail this card."

The ordering copy and the address should be simple, legible, and to the point. There should not be crowding. Small type inspires distrust. This is not the place to use a "type-squeezer" or "shoehorn."

The "name, address, city" part of the coupon should be easy to fill out, leaving enough space for long surnames and addresses. If you are working internationally, rethink the lengths and sequence of the lines. Both names and addresses are usually longer.

Options or credit-card information also should be designed with great care. The placement and positioning of these elements in the layout will materially affect the response. For instance, if a credit option is built into the ordering paragraph and a cash-enclosed option is separate, you might have a 3:1 or 4:1 ratio for the credit responses. If the options are treated equally after the order paragraph, the response will switch to 2:1 for credit, or perhaps come in evenly. Presenting the options "( ) Check enclosed" and "( ) Bill me later" forces a decision and will increase your cash flow. Otherwise inertia pushes people to the option that does not have to be selected.

In a mailing piece, long commitments or credit terms can be contained in a stub or flap. This makes the ordering portion as simple as possible, yet still makes all sales and legal data visible at the time the coupon is filled out.

Don't be afraid of complicated coupons. The trick is to take the elements, conduct experiments, and find a way to simplify the elements. At one time, Columbia Music Club invited readers to: 1. Accept a long commitment; 2. Select a music division and write in the six-digit numbers of thirteen records; 3. Fill in their telephone numbers; 4. Choose cartridges, cassettes, tapes, or records; 5. Pick the first selection at a special discount; and 6. Use a "gold box" if they saw the offer on television. All within a standard-size coupon. The company did a good job of separating and simplifying these six necessary steps, and has been highly successful with similarly complicated coupons.

Telephone-ordering options can be highlighted with a small drawing of a telephone or with a large telephone number, if telephone ordering is desirable for the particular proposition.

Phone numbers or URLs must be clear and easy to read. They must not only be legible, but as easy to tear out as a coupon, not buried in the body copy.

Starch ad readership ratings show that ads with coupons or phone numbers usually have higher ratings than those that do not. Someone might use the comparison of the difference between window-shopping at a brightly lit open store, or a dimly lit one shut for the night. The ad with a clearly visible device is always "open for business." So why turn out the lights by hiding the coupon or phone number?

CATALOG DESIGN

The artist responsible for catalog design has a particularly challenging role. He or she must consider all the rules of good, clear communication and salesmanship not for one product, but for dozens or hundreds of different items. This requires a series of compromises.

For a mass-market, hard-sell merchandiser of relatively low price items, each page or item can have all the elements of a small ad—a headline, copy, feature insets or call-outs, product illustrations, and price features. Combine them together and you have a strong selling piece. But the image it conveys is that of a bargain-basement dollar close-out dealer. There are successful companies who do this well such as Damark and Lillian Vernon.

For better-quality or higher-priced merchandise, it is usually necessary to give more consideration to the overall image and positioning. After all, a catalog is like a retail store in that its appearance and reputation must attract the appropriate audience for the merchandise it offers. The right mailing list is like the right location. Potential customers will see the store or catalog. But that doesn't mean they will walk in or, with catalogs, that they will open the catalog and browse through it with a positive attitude. The catalog "brand," like a retail or packaged-goods brand, can add or detract from "brand equity"—the added perceived value which comes from image and reputation.

For catalogs, this image comes from the overall impression of the catalog. This impression is influenced by size, type of paper, and binding—saddle-stitch, perfect binding (flat edged), loose-pages or broadside. Most critical is the design of the pages, the presentation of the merchandise, and the choice of models, settings and photography style.

The design must support the chosen positioning. It is no accident that at first impression The Gap catalog appears to be a photo album of college students on Spring break. Nor is it a mistake that Neiman Marcus settings could be right out of Architectural Digest or Town & Country, or that L.L. Bean's outdoor-wear clothing and accessories adjoin canoes, snow shoes and hiking gear.

As with all direct mail, form should follow function. J. Crew uses large catalog pages to enable side-by-side presentations of their wide choices of color, texture and cut for most items. Tiffany and my jewelry client Amsterdam Sauer, both use 5 × 8 or smaller formats so that their most precious jewelry can be presented on separate pages, free of clutter and distraction and in appropriate settings and lighting schemes for each item.

To those starting a new catalog, let me suggest a shortcut: 1. Determine what magazine most of your audience subscribes to; 2. Study it and see what visual styles set it apart from other magazines; 3. Adapt the principles of that style to your catalog.

GRAPHIC TOOLS

Sometimes I miss the kind of art department that was prevalent ten years ago. The studio had rows of drafting tables with steel rules and T-squares. Dazzling racks of magic markers. Vertical shelves crammed with old mechanical paste-ups. Assortments of boards, acetates, vellum, and cover sheets that would become the next layouts and paste-ups. And—most nostalgic of all—the ever-present perfume of rubber cement.

With steady hand and grim concentration, the artists of yesterday wielded a ruling pen and an X-acto knife as skillfully as any surgeon using a scalpel. These skilled practitioners created the mail-order ads and mailing pieces that became the foundation of today's sophisticated direct-marketing industry. And then came computers.

The Computer Revolution

The earliest computers made it possible for anyone to change fonts and margins in a split-second, and to draw and store illustrations that could be moved, enlarged and re-shaped with the click of a mouse. In a matter of months programmers built elaborate software packages on that foundation, and issued the first editions of software that would change the world of design and graphic production forever.

Tracing the evolution of graphic programs is not easy because of the rapid growth in this field. Nor it is possible to offer a "current" list of the computer applications and software releases of the industry without becoming outdated within a couple of months. Therefore the reader must settle for a brief introduction of some of today's tools—a list that may be incomplete and out-dated by the time this book is printed and shipped from the publisher. It is meant only to provide a foundation for understanding what is available in this vast, ever-changing software world. The types of programs include page-layout, and photographic manipulation, and illustration software.

QuarkXPress™.   The cornerstone of the graphic-design industry. A page-layout program used for advertising, page-design products, direct mail, catalogs and books. The program is capable of very precise adjustment. This software lets the artist arrange alternate elements in a palette—easily shuffling different type treatments and illustration elements from any source—enabling the artist to use trial and error to reach the ideal combination. Many other computer software companies produce "plug-ins" that create different functions and tools for the program.

PageMaker® by Adobe®.   One of the first graphics programs, this software lets the artist use re-sizable and re-shapeable boxes to place written and visual elements within the margins of an advertising communication.

Adobe™ **Photoshop**™.   The ideal photo-editor. It allows an artist to manipulate photographs—photographs scanned from a conventional scanner, processed at a digital supplier, taken with a digital camera, imported from a photo CD, or downloaded from a source on the Internet. The artist can then enlarge it, crop it, silhouette it, or revise it—dot-by-dot (or "pixel-by-pixel" in computer terms) if necessary.

Adobe Type Deluxe™   This program assists the artist and the computer with the loading of typefaces stored on CDs, the hard drive or other discs. This program helps save memory by only having the needed fonts active at a particular time. Symantec Suitcase is a similar program.

Adobe Type Manager™   It's not a program that's used like the others exactly, but rather a tool that is "on" all the time. The ATM program "smooths-out" fonts that would appear rough or blurry without the program.

In addition, Adobe™ is one of the leading typeface distributors, offering thousands of fonts. Other producers of fonts include International Typeface Corporation™ (ITC), Agfa™, Emigree™, Bitstream™, Fontek™, Font Bureau™, Phil's™, Line Showings™ and Revelation™. Many of these come in condensed, bold, italic, condensed and super-condensed variations, and most of them are infinitely scalable in size and spacing. The artist has total flexibility. I asked one of my art directors what size font she used for an ad. It was 9.15, with 11.3 points of leading. That's precision!

Adobe Illustrator™   A variety of "tools" (see Fig 11.3) lets artists use pen, brush, spray-can, paint-bucket or whatever they can image to create free-form or aligned illustrations of any kind. Those using traditional art media can still do so and have their work scanned into a computer format.

Does all this make the art director's job easier? In one way, yes, for these tools provided unlimited flexibility to portray any content in any style. On the other hand, today's art director must develop not only taste but also the technical proficiency to harness and control these powerful tools.

Tomorrow's Technology

As advanced as today's art and photography tools may be, they are threatened by the same obsolescence that made the rubber cement jar a quaint antique. Software producers are constantly improving their product and releasing new versions. Digital cameras are becoming more and more sophisticated, and are currently commonly used in the advertising industry. In general, the new variations simplify processes, increase the number of graphic "tools," and give art directors greater creative freedom.

Today's art director must use several of the tools listed above to complete a single project. We just completed a new 5½ × 8 inch, two-sided co-op mail insert for one of our clients. This simple project, when completed, comprised more than a dozen elements in the form of text, graphics, photos and logos. The art director created the advertisement in QuarkXPress after using Photoshop and Illustrator to create and perfect the different elements. Often all three programs were open at the same time while she was producing the ad, and at least five different types of files were used to create the final product.

QuarkXPress is the most commonly used product these days by art directors. But they are all improving and advancing their capabilities. I don't wish to single out one program over another, but I have seen an advance release of Adobe™ InDesign™—Adobe™'s competitive product to QuarkXPress™—which is a good example of what to expect from graphic-designer software in the future (whether it's from Adobe™ or another company). The new Adobe™ product includes

- Integration with all other Adobe™ software, so files created from older software versions are always capable of being opened in this new software. It also opens QuarkXPress™ and other program files as well.

- New tools for the artist, including: the ability to have frames within frames (whether it's text or graphics inside the frames) to create different effects; new gradient tools that allow an artist to easily have text or graphics gradually lighten or darken (typically an Illustrator™ tool); bézier path tools like the ones found in Illustrator™ that allow the artist to edit

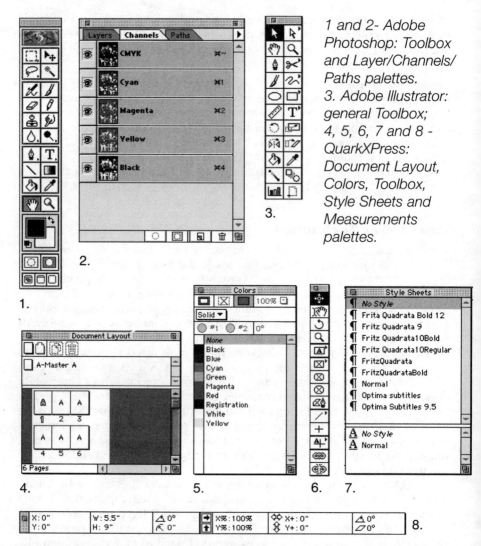

1 and 2- Adobe Photoshop: Toolbox and Layer/Channels/ Paths palettes.
3. Adobe Illustrator: general Toolbox;
4, 5, 6, 7 and 8 - QuarkXPress: Document Layout, Colors, Toolbox, Style Sheets and Measurements palettes.

Figure 11-3. Typical general control palettes, from the most used graphic softwares in printing design (Adobe Photoshop, Adobe Illustrator and QuarkXPress).

The palettes offer several tools that help the artist to achieve various and different objectives according to the necessities of each job.

Through them, it is possible to control all details such as selection of objects, text, patterns, colors, dimensions, measurements, style, scale and many other special effects, generated by the software commands or filters, depending upon the case.

Illustrator™-created graphics *after* they have been imported into In-Design™; and clipping paths that allow an artist to "mask" or hide parts of images while letting others show through. Want to hide a shadow on a photo? This used to be done only in Photoshop™, but now can be performed in the new software.

- Larger document capability—up to 18 feet by 18 feet. (Yes, *feet!*) The size capability accommodates catalog or magazine spreads up to ten pages at a time.

- Multiple-revision capability. Design changes made on one graphic or section of text are automatically updated throughout the file, if wanted. For example, a design change to a graphic on page one of a catalog is updated throughout the publication.

- Customizable short-cuts or "quick-keys" (keystrokes that correspond to complex processes) to increase an artist's speed, as well as the ability to use the same short-cuts from other programs that artists might be accustomed to.

- Instant zooming, from as little as 5% to as much as 4000%.

- Precision color controls that provide consistency from concept to final printing, and coordinate with the other programs that may be used.

- Multiple-language capabilities with 21 built-in dictionaries.

- Automatic re-sizing, when preparing ads for different publications.

- Automatic element assembly when sending art to a printer or other outside source. Each file created in these different layout programs require "links" to the graphics that have been inserted. Previously, art directors had to ensure all the graphics, fonts and color-management profiles were included with the file.

Undoubtedly Quark and other suppliers will be releasing their own improvements as well.

The Photography Headache

As emotional elements became more and more important in the world of direct marketing, so did the use of photography. Product shots were often supplied by the client or, in the case of catalogs, the various manufacturers. If they were not supplied, such photos could be easily and inexpensively taken by local photographers.

Advertisers with substantial budgets had no problems. They or their agencies could hire professional photographers, models, retouching experts or whomever they needed. But then greed stepped in.

Models—at least those represented by the large agencies—started demanding residuals and time limits on the use of the photos. Advertisers were expected to pay the modeling fee for a finite number of advertising uses, or for a limited number of mailings. These requirements were no problem for tests, but if the ad or mailing was successful there was suddenly a substantial added cost. For each added use we were expected to negotiate an added fee, often many times the original one. When we tried to offer a "buy-out" (unlimited use of the photos), the fees were even more ridiculous. Sometimes the fees requested were more than the total cost of the new mailing.

This was difficult enough, but then photographers joined in. They too wanted residuals—for photographs we specified, cast, directed and paid for! They demanded "creative royalties" for moving the lights around, loading the film, and aiming the camera.

Stock photos seemed like the answer. Dozens of expensive stock-photo catalogs piled up on the desks of art directors. The photos were available digitally in different resolutions—low for layout purposes or web pages (72 dpi, or dots per inch), and high for printing (300 dpi). The larger the file size, the more expensive the price. Most of the photo prices were as unreasonable as the modeling agencies and photographers, since they demanded absurd initial fees and limits on use. But in the early 1990s someone came up with a solution that worked for everyone—a brilliant combination of business innovation and technology.

The Stock-Photo Solution. Within one decade, PhotoDisc® (a division of Getty Photography) revolutionized the stock photo business. They not only solved the financial problems; they enabled greater efficiency and more flexible creativity than we could have dreamed of. Getty also has other photo services, but not all are necessarily royalty-free like PhotoDisc™. Some other stock-photo companies have followed their lead, like Digital Stock™ from Eyewire™. PhotoDisc's products include:

- Photos in high-resolution digital formats—no costly conversions from slides.

- Reasonable fixed rates that include all elements of the image, regardless of photographer or model.

- Over 70,000 photos to choose from, in books, discs or off the web.

- Subject search engines and the ability to download images from the Internet.

- CD-Roms, each with 100 to 150 photos or more in a specific category, available royalty-free with purchase.

- No charge for use of low-resolution images in preliminary layouts and reasonable fees for use that depended on image size and resolution, not on the media or use.

This may sound like an ad, but I've never met these people and have no business dealings with them other than as a customer. I am simply excited over the new freedom they have given to advertising and editorial art. By the time this book comes out, other stock photo houses will have also "seen the light." In the meantime, get on a computer and see this tool for yourself at www.photodisc.com.

FIRST-AID KIT FOR ART DIRECTORS

How to Spot a Bad Layout

If you are an art director who is on the firing line, or one of those who have to judge the art director's work, here are some telltale signs of a bad layout:

- The message doesn't stand out from other ads.
- The image is contradictory to the theme of the copy.
- The mood is completely inappropriate for the medium.
- The ad blends in perfectly with the publication.
- It reminds you of another mailing piece—whether you liked it or didn't.
- It's an expression of the latest fad.
- It's static. One phrase or illustration dominates without an easy transition.
- It's too busy. Readers jump from point to point, contrary to the flow of the message.
- The ad calls attention to itself. It's designed to win awards rather than sell the product.
- Everything is important, or nothing is important.
- The ad is hard to read. The type is too small or crowded.

Improving a Bad Layout

If a layout has been finished and still doesn't look right, here are some ways to improve the ad or mailing piece:

- *Exaggerate or emphasize something.* Emphasize the headline, the illustration, the coupon, even the body copy. Take it "out of proportion" and deliberately throw the design "off-balance." Balance is static. Direct-marketing ads need motion, action, and dynamism. Taking one element and filling 40 to 60 percent of the printed area with it will give you a whole new look.

- *Add people.* A spokesperson, a delighted customer opening a box and seeing your product, or a picture of a satisfied user can help a bad layout. People are interested in people.

- *Put the product in use.* Take it out of the package and show it being used. Add diagrams, sequence photos, or anything that will make the product come alive.

- *Change the typography.* Start all over and get an entirely different mood by working with different typefaces. Simplify the type and work within one family exclusively, or add one contrasting face for emphasis. Warm up the ad with a serif face and a cursive italic, or modernize it with a sans serif face and a non-cursive italic.

- *Pull the ad or mailing together.* Add white space at the edges, use borders or background tints with consistent line spacing, or try to get a clearer flow of ideas from one point to the next.

- *Break the ad up.* Isolate the important elements with internal space and internal rules, or make the copy more inviting to read with bolder subheads and minor illustrations, with indents and handwritten annotations.

- *Follow Thoreau's advice: "Simplify, simplify, simplify."* Take a complicated headline and isolate one pertinent phrase. Take a headline with lead-ins and subheads and combine them into one long simplified statement. Take optional elements and isolate them with different typefaces, panels, or tints. Talk to the writer, share your problem, and see if copy can be cut to give you the space you need to simplify, simplify, simplify.

12

DIRECT MAIL FORMATS

Format is a critical design element in direct mail, requiring the economical integration of creative and production processes to produce maximum communications impact.

In Chapter 11, we discussed art design and layout principles that apply to any form of communication: a simple newspaper ad, a full-color magazine spread, a computer letter, a full-color brochure, a simple buck-slip insert, the supers on a television commercial, or the screens or banners on a website.

In direct mail, the art director's job increases a hundred-fold, for the creative possibilities are multi-dimensional. The direct mail art director has to know all the disciplines and technology of the general advertising art director. In addition, he or she has to understand what can be done with paper, printing, computer forms, and imaging techniques, as well as the flexibilities and limitations of envelope fabricators, laser processes, and the machines that collate and insert mail.

In direct mail, you have the space you need to use every trick in the book of direct marketing psychology. You can dramatize and personalize, and you can provide incentives for immediate action. You can include samples or scent strips. You can take advantage of the play instinct with scores of involvement devices. You have all the space you need to ask for an order for the most complex or expensive purchase, to explain commitments or to ask for credit information. Direct mail is unlike space advertising or broadcast in that you do not have to fit your message into the format; you can fit the format to your message.

CONSIDERATIONS IN DIRECT MAIL FORMATS

The essential considerations in every direct mail design project include *response stimulation, personalization, involvement,* and *economy.*

Response Stimulation

No matter how you stop the reader—with curiosity, self-interest, a powerful offer, a dramatic benefit—the payoff is asking the reader to come to an immediate decision: to make a call, visit a store, or mail in a reply card. No matter what action is required, the writer must have it clearly thought out, so that the copy message leads up to it clearly and conclusively.

If a phone call is requested, then the phone number and what it entails should be stated in a separate insert or even a Rolodex® card, which can be affixed to the letter. If a store visit is the objective, then provide a coupon or reminder piece. It can be a simple inquiry, or a multi-question database builder. It can be a one-shot mail-order form ("Send me x; I enclose y dollars") or it can be a complex continuity membership. In any case, for the purposes of planning and of this chapter, they are all simply response devices.

Certainly, in traditional mail order, the response device is critical. I recommend planning the coupon text first, even before you write headlines or do layouts.

Ease of response is the first consideration. You want to make it as easy as possible for the prospect to fill out and mail your coupon. Pre-addressing the name and address with computer printing or with a label not only facilitates response, but ensures that you will retrieve key codes, account numbers, or other data.

If you are planning a catalog, it makes a difference if the order form is bound in the center, at the front, or at the rear. The worse alternative is to simply use a page in the catalog. While there are many styles and theories, I prefer to use a 4-page wrap with a strong message at the front, the address and featured items on the back. You can then use the inside of the front cover for a letter and the inside of the back cover for the order form. Some catalogers also use flaps on this cover page, perhaps with a special offer certificate on the front flap and an envelope comprising the rear one.

Incentives for fast response should be visible right on the response card, including any premiums for fast action, or offer expiration dates. You should work on the assumptions that your prospect may not mail this card for a few days and that the rest of the mailing will have been discarded by that time.

Like all other pieces in a direct mail package, the response device should be capable of standing alone and should provide sufficient incentive even if nothing else is read.

Even if a card can be a self-mailer, it usually is worth the extra cost to also provide an envelope. If confidential, financial, or personal questions are asked, an envelope is essential.

Often the response card is the lead insert; the first piece visible through the envelope window, and the piece personalized with the prospect's own name. This piece will be seen first. Therefore it is necessary to emphasize the positives about the offer, and to obscure any negatives (such as price) until the prospect has had a chance to read the other pieces in the envelope.

In other cases, the reply card may be nested inside letters and brochures and may not be the first thing seen at all. It is then necessary to help the prospect find the card. To accomplish this, you have to refer to the card. It should therefore have both a name and a color. For instance, "Send the reply card now" gives no help in finding the card in a complicated mailing. Instead consider, "Send the red super-value certificate . . ."

Many of the involvement devices that will be discussed below are intended to facilitate response, as are some personalization devices.

Personalization

Only direct mail, with the help of computer data and related high-speed printing technology, can facilitate the infinite range of personalization available today. It is one of this medium's most unique capabilities. Even web marketers, as of this writing, have been unable to send personal messages except to print the prospect's Internet screen name as in "Dear Nashnet."

Sorting.   As "relevance" is the key to personalization, not just repeating the prospect's name, segmentation is its simplest form. This can take place when lists are processed, permitting a message to be selected on the basis of demographic, geographic, or psychographic data. This personalization consists simply of inserting a different preprinted or laser-printed letter with each different list, or adding a special buck slip– a 3″ × 8″ insert so-called because it about the size of a dollar bill—to address a type of prospect. For example, a magazine might include a special insert for people who once subscribed, or a slip announcing that a forthcoming issue will have an important article on a subject that, according to the list the prospect is on, should be of particular interest.

Name Reference.   Another type of personalized direct mail design is the computer fill-in of the customer's name in the body of a letter, on the reply card that shows through the window envelope, or in other inserts.

It is also common to use a closed-face envelope, repeating the name and address on the outer envelope as well as on the contents of the envelope—usually the letter and reply form. This can be done on continuous forms, separately or at the same time as the letter, fabricating the envelope only after it has been addressed. The inserting is done either at the same time as fabrication, in a single manufacturing step, or later by optically matching the address or number codes. Some commercial lettershops now have equipment to laser-print prefabricated envelopes.

Combined with versioning, the possibilities are endless. Mary Kay's "Direct Support" program for its thousands of skin care salespeople featured the salesperson's address, phone and signature making millions of sales letters appear to be from the local representative.

Multiple Personalization.   It is common to design a form that permits a letter or an invitation to be produced on the same form as the response device. Most computer letter formats permit a maximum length of 22 inches and a width of up to 18-1/2 inches. With various side-by-side or front-to-back folding, bursting, and slitting processes available, it is possible to assemble, easily and inexpensively. a wide variety of personalized combinations. One of the most practical is an 8-1/2 × 14 letter including a certificate, response device, or invitation on the top or bottom. This can be attached, or slit off during processing. And either the letter or the stub can be used for addressing, to show through a window envelope. Another common format is to print full-size letters, side-by-side or top-and-bottom. This is useful when there is a complex form, such as a credit application that must be filled out.

For economy, even smaller sizes can be designed, printed one-up or two-up. Or several personalized pieces can be included in the same mailing. For instance, you can design a 6 × 8 inch personalized letter with a 6 × 3 inch response form. Such a simple format enables the printing of six sets on each 18 × 22 form. More complex formats are cut out of this same size.

One outstanding multiple format developed for International Masters by production expert Joel Gerbman used a 5-1/2 × 7-1/2 inch four-page letter, a 3-3/4 × 5-1/2 inch response slip, a 3-1/8 × 5-1/2 inch guarantee, and a 3-1/8 × 5-1/2 inch lift letter. Each was personalized with the prospect's name, and all printed out of a single 10-5/8 × 16-1/2 inch form and machine-collated with five other inserts.

Electronic Letter Writing.   In the mid-1970s, a variety of exciting new techniques was developed that took the art of personalization to new heights.

First Mead Digit, then Response Graphics, IBM, Xerox, and others developed various types of non-impact printing. Some worked by ink jet, spraying very tiny dots on a page at high speed so as to form letters, lines, or images. Newer methods used laser technology to achieve clearer, bolder type images.

The first applications were in the use of new and larger typefaces. Suddenly it was possible to put the prospect's name on the letter in inch-high capital letters, and facsimile handwriting or colored type. Suddenly you could print sideways or upside down, and thus open up new kinds of trick folds and seams to achieve special effects and new formats.

There was an explosion of creativity in personalization. Even more significant were the economic factors. Some of the new techniques could be attached to a printing press, permitting personalization, printing, folding, and assembly to take place in one high-speed motion. These ink jet, laser, and electrographic processes now permit great economy as well as unlimited creative flexibility. Today's options include personalized messages within the pages of a magazine, customized handwriting fonts that match the actual handwriting of the sender, high-definition photographs, simulated letterheads, and color laser messages. You can apply laser printing anywhere on a 17 × 22 inch sheet, making it possible to have versioned messages as well as addressing anywhere within a catalog, or to create totally versioned newsletters.

The best way to utilize these new techniques is to work very closely with graphic designers, printers, and computer houses that have the equipment available. They can show you the work others have done with their processes, and help you to work out your own format problems. Good suppliers are an important part of your direct marketing team.

Non-computer Personalization.   While the computer offers an infinite variety of sorting possibilities and letter-like or poster-like personalization, it is possible to get these effects in a simpler, more old-fashioned manner.

For years, *Business Week*'s control package was an invitation format, with the prospect's name handwritten. Avis scored a major direct mail breakthrough using an outer envelope with the prospect's name written in by hand. "This is the package Mr. XXX is expecting" evidently got past the most protective secretary. (The claim was justified because of a previous letter.) One unique format for business mail uses a facsimile rubber-stamped routing form, and the prospect's initials penciled in along with others. The very successful mailing for the previous edition of this book included a hand-written yellow Post-note® with the recipients initials "AB Some great ideas here.—Bob."

And don't forget simple versioning: different letters or inserts for different lists or list segments. Elsewhere I describe the Polaroid success with different photos for different SIC codes, showing through a windowed outer envelope. Or "smart inserting," in which inserts can be varied at the inserting machine, depending on optically-read codes on the envelopes.

Involvement Techniques

Why do direct marketers make their mailings so complicated? Because they work!

With the exception of high-level business-to-business mailings, the devices of direct mail are repeated because they are successful. In some cases, though, they are so successful that they are soon over-used. When that happens, a direct mail user can outflank the marketplace by going back to once-successful ideas as easily as by coming up with new ones.

Transfer Effect.   The purpose of involvement techniques is more than to keep the reader interested. They are also used most effectively to transfer reader attention from one component of a mailing to another. If the prospect will first see the response card, it is a good idea to point out that there is a label or stamp that must be found on the letter in order to get a premium or activate the offer. This will prompt more prospects to read the letter. Or the other way around, having a seal on a letter that is to be transferred to the order form is a way of directing the prospect to the order device.

One application is the inclusion of "bonus stamps" in some Publishers' Clearing House contest mailings. The stamps, which are found on the same sheets as the magazine selections, are a way of encouraging entrants to handle and look at the offered magazines before responding.

Creative Devices.   Virtually anything can be included in an envelope or made visible through it. Virtually anything can be affixed to a mailing element for prospects to peel off, punch out, or otherwise get involved with. And most of these devices can be personalized. Here are some ideas:

- *Business cards:* For personal services, questions, warranties. Try them with a pseudo-handwritten note printed on the front or back.

- *Carbon copies:* Of a previous letter: "Did you overlook this opportunity?"

- *Checks:* A legitimately redeemable check or money order is a sure attention-getter, but see your lawyer first.

- *Coins:* A penny for your thoughts, or "Ten records for a dime, and we'll even give you the dime . . ."

- *Collectibles:* An Indian penny; facsimile Confederate money; a foreign postage stamp.

- *Facsimile photographs:* A child to help; a baby seal to be saved; a beach hammock waiting for you. Very effective if the photo is emotional.

- *Gifts:* A packet of seeds or spices; a pencil; a bookmark; a key chain; preprinted address labels.

- *Information:* Local police and fire numbers; a veteran's benefits guide; a map; a calorie counter; an after-tax investment-yield slide rule.

- *Numbers:* Serially numbered application forms, perhaps to indicate exclusivity. Often used in contests.

- *Peel-offs:* Reusable "piggy back" labels to transfer the address of any token-like symbol from one location to another.

- *Perforated stamps:* Easter seals for fund-raising; record covers for a club selection.

- *Postage stamps:* To pay for the reply postage.

- *Punched holes:* To look through, giving the impression of a computer card, bingo card, or what have you.

- *Samples:* Recipe file cards; fabric swatches; the product itself.

- *Seals:* Notary seals, certificates, etc., to indicate reliability.

- *Tokens:* To be punched out and placed in or on the order card, to accept an offer.

- *Yes, No or Maybe Symbols:* A way of asking for an immediate decision.

This list is limited only by your imagination. Some examples I've used are a string "to tie around your finger as a reminder" to call Merrill Lynch, an aspirin for executives suffering from "long-distance headaches," a pencil to note your winning contest number, a calendar to count the days left for Christmas shopping.

One direct marketer painstakingly created what looked like an antique letter from Frank Lloyd Wright to architectural firms, touting the qualities of a particular elevator company founder's ideas. (The elevator company founder was actually a friendly acquaintance of Wright's.) The direct marketer distressed the envelope so it appeared to have gotten lost in the mail for decades. Curious recipients got their questions answered ten days later when the second part of the mailer arrived.

This ingenious mailer gained a very high response. But be wary with these techniques, especially with business-to-business correspondence. The direct-mail piece looked incredibly authentic and impressed the typically stoic architects because of its adherence to authentic appearance.

ECONOMIC CONSIDERATIONS

Check with production specialists before proceeding to finished layouts. Production advice at this critical point can save the embarrassment of producing a mailing that has to be inserted by hand because there isn't clearance for automatic inserting equipment, or that wastes money by using an inefficient paper size.

Everyone in this business has made the mistake at least once of not providing enough clearance for machine labeling or inserting. An even more painful experience is watching a high-speed press print a brochure on an over-sized sheet, with literally tons of unused paper being trimmed off to be sold as scrap.

Paper comes in standard sizes, depending on the type of paper and the press it will be printed on. Some standard sizes in the United States are book paper, 25 × 38 inches; bond paper, 17 × 22 inches; cover stock, 20 × 26 inches; newsprint, 24 × 36 inches; coated paper, 25 × 38 inches; and offset paper, 25 × 38 inches. Note that standard sizes in many countries are different. For instance, while a standard letter size in the US is 8.5 × 11 inches, in Europe it is 29.7 × 21.0 centimeters.

Flyers, brochures, and letters are usually cut out of standard sizes, and can be figured by folding or cutting such a sheet accordingly. Sometimes an extra insert can be printed without added cost by using paper that might otherwise be trimmed off and thrown away. One project I saw would have permitted four additional pages in a brochure without extra cost, just by using the full size of the standard paper sheet.

On large-quantity press runs, paper companies often can prepare a special "mill run" of exactly the size and weight of paper you need, provided the quantity is large enough and you have the time to wait for it.

Art directors should familiarize themselves with paper for another reason as well. Interesting effects can often be added just by changing paper. Kraft paper portrays one feeling, bond paper another. Newsprint is good for sale brochures. Coated stock is essential where color is important. Specialty papers such as check safety papers can be very useful when conveying value concepts.

Envelopes also come in standard sizes. With rush jobs, weeks can be saved by using a stock envelope and printing a message on the face of it in simple type. Designing windows in unusual places or odd sizes requires special press runs. Usually the printing of the copy and art you provide is one job, and the subsequent conversion of the paper into envelopes through die cutting and fabricating is another. This is like two printing jobs in a row, and is usually the longest critical-path item in a direct mail job. Some standard envelope styles and sizes are shown in Fig. 12-1. Any envelope house will be happy to provide you with a complete directory of their standard envelope styles and sizes.

Mailing Weight

Postage is always one of the highest costs in a mailing. The total weight of a package is critical, particularly in first-class mail, where tipping the scale over the 1-ounce mark practically doubles the cost of the postage.

It is imperative that actual paper samples be cut to size and carefully weighed to determine mailing weight before the job goes too far. Often a slight change in paper weight or trimming will make an enormous difference in total cost.

In Standard Mail (formerly called bulk third-class) or not-for-profit mail, the weight is not as serious because costs go up in intervals for each fraction of an ounce. Check with your postmaster or letter shop for the latest postage rates.

Working with Suppliers

Many pieces have to work together: the mechanical artwork; the computer specifications; the mailing lists; paper and printing; computer processing; binding and collating; envelope fabrication; sorting; mailing and getting the mailing to the post office. If there's any field where Murphy's Law applies, it is in the execution of direct mail: "Anything that can go wrong, will go wrong."

Probably the best economy is to work with reliable suppliers. Unless you have printing specialists on staff or as consultants, let one firm—an agency or printer—coordinate the entire job from providing you with mechanical specifications to getting it in the mail. That way it's their responsibility, not yours, if the pieces don't fit or everything doesn't arrive on time. As many agencies now buy printing at so-called trade prices, their total prices, even with a mark-up, are usually no more than you would directly from printers and mailing houses.

In short, to save money on direct mail,

1. Make sure it works mechanically.

2. Design it economically.

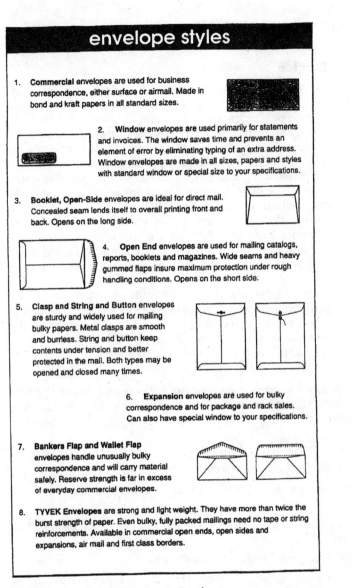

envelope styles

1. **Commercial** envelopes are used for business correspondence, either surface or airmail. Made in bond and kraft papers in all standard sizes.

2. **Window** envelopes are used primarily for statements and invoices. The window saves time and prevents an element of error by eliminating typing of an extra address. Window envelopes are made in all sizes, papers and styles with standard window or special size to your specifications.

3. **Booklet, Open-Side** envelopes are ideal for direct mail. Concealed seam lends itself to overall printing front and back. Opens on the long side.

4. **Open End** envelopes are used for mailing catalogs, reports, booklets and magazines. Wide seams and heavy gummed flaps insure maximum protection under rough handling conditions. Opens on the short side.

5. **Clasp and String and Button** envelopes are sturdy and widely used for mailing bulky papers. Metal clasps are smooth and burrless. String and button keep contents under tension and better protected in the mail. Both types may be opened and closed many times.

6. **Expansion** envelopes are used for bulky correspondence and for package and rack sales. Can also have special window to your specifications.

7. **Bankers Flap and Wallet Flap** envelopes handle unusually bulky correspondence and will carry material safely. Reserve strength is far in excess of everyday commercial envelopes.

8. **TYVEK Envelopes** are strong and light weight. They have more than twice the burst strength of paper. Even bulky, fully packed mailings need no tape or string reinforcements. Available in commercial open ends, open sides and expansions, air mail and first class borders.

Courtesy of Paul Psok at Corporate Envelopes

Figure 12-1

3. Let professionals coordinate the printing, computer, and lettershop processes.

4. Get postal approvals and permits before printing.

ELEMENTS OF THE MAILING PACKAGE

The Response Device

Everything in your direct mail package—every thought, word, and picture—is there for one purpose: to get the reply card returned to you with an affirmative acceptance of your proposition.

The format can be anything from a complex order form to a simple inquiry card. Usually a response card is about the size of the envelope, in order to permit it to be pre-addressed with the address showing through a window in the envelope. It should be large enough so that it doesn't shift around and obscure the address. It should be small enough so that it easily fits the reply envelope without having to be folded.

Often a tear-off stub or flap at the side or bottom of the form will help to solve the size problem. A flap can be useful to cover information that you don't want to be seen right away, such as complicated ordering information or a credit application, or it can contain essential sales points or immediacy incentives.

Involvement devices can be placed on the stub—a gummed stamp, sticker, punched-out token, or any of the various devices listed above. The reader usually is invited to attach the device in a specific location on the response card. The purpose is to call attention to the reply card, or to transfer interest from one piece in the mailing to another.

Implied Value. When the offer is the primary sales device, it is helpful to give the order form (or the token or stamp to be affixed to it) implied value. This can be achieved in several ways:

- Gift certificates or check-paper formats
- Borders such as those found on money orders or stock certificates
- Official-looking layouts, with punched holes, authorizations, or rubber stamps
- Engraved money-like images, indicated by choice of typefaces and decoration elements
- Notary seals, ribbons, gold embossing, signatures
- Money orders, traveler's checks, bank checks, and passbooks, all of which by convention have implied value

Other Images. Try to make the response card look like something other than what it is. If a sweepstakes is involved, dramatize the entry concept. If the product is in limited quantity, make the response card look like a reservation certificate.

Business-to-business correspondence should be on a restrained level. A simple white response card and a stamped envelope are very classy, or you can include a carbon of your letter and ask the recipient to initial it and return it.

Label Transfer. A simple, dignified device that adds to ease of response and offers a measure of involvement is the address label transfer. If you order lists supplied on "piggyback" labels—pressure-sensitive labels with a wax-finish backing so they can be easily peeled off—the prospect can take the peel-off label off the letter or catalog cover and place it on the response card. For years, *Consumer Reports* used a unique double-response card with a one-year offer on one side, a three-year offer on the other. The prospect was involved by being asked to place the label on one side or the other.

Location in the envelope also has a bearing on results. The response card can be the first thing seen or the last. Some very successful mailings have had reply devices attached to the top or bottom of a computer-printed letter, to help generate readership for both. In other cases, where the letter really is trying to "pass" as a personal letter, the reply device should not, of course, be attached to it.

The Outer Envelope

The outer envelope is the headline of direct mail. Half the battle is to get the envelope opened—and much direct mail is never opened.

Imagine an envelope that would be difficult to open, offered the prospect no reason to open it, and aroused no curiosity or interest of any kind. Such envelopes do exist—the products of dull design, poor thinking, and sloppy execution. They offer every turn-off short of saying, "Junk mail—don't bother to open this."

Fortunately, most people do open most of their mail. The problem is not just to get it opened, but to arouse enough interest or curiosity to read the contents. You want your mailing to be the one that's "saved for last," the one that a prospect wants to read because of the promise it holds forth to satisfy a basic need or interest.

Setting the Mood. My latest approach to this subject is to use the outer envelope solely to set the mood, to indicate the general field the offer deals with. My theory here is that our customer is multi-dimensional. One moment he or she is a responsible executive, later that evening a parent, or an investor watching the market. On the weekends, he or she can be a skier, a sailor, and a gardener. The envelope should have some subtle clue to let the recipient know which of his or her personae we are talking to.

For the same reason that a landscaping offer would not do well in travel magazines, we want to trigger the appropriate self-image before the envelope is opened. Sometimes I want to read about advertising, other times about investments or sailing or travel. A simple graphic or pictorial clue can set the mood so that I open the letter when I am in the mood for it and thus am more likely to respond. Tricking someone may get more envelopes opened, but in the long run it is not the most profitable way to build a business.

Pre-selling.   The obvious approach is pre-selling. It consists of putting the offer—or what would be the headline in an ad—right on the front of the envelope.

"Save 50% on *Time*" is a sure-fire headline, if the prospect already wants *Time*. If a simple offer statement is so effective, a simple turnaround document or double-postcard format will do the trick. In some cases, with pre-sold products to core lists, it's all you need, and you can dispense with practically everything else.

"Stop Smoking Fast" is another example of pre-selling that either reaches prospects or turns them off instantly. With a really good appeal, getting to the point right from the beginning can work. More often, subtler appeals are necessary in addition to or instead of a direct sales message on the envelope.

Curiosity.   The most curiosity-arousing envelope of all is the one that looks like a real business letter or a personal note. If you use a first-class stamp and a seemingly typewritten address, there is an excellent chance you'll get the letter opened.

You can also use headlines to build curiosity. Any provocative headline, ranging from "Do you make these mistakes in English?" to "Fifty stocks to avoid this year" will get people to read further to get the answer.

An incomplete statement will also get readership. Start telling a provocative story right on the outer envelope, and then just when it gets most interesting, you can . . . (Continued inside).

See what I mean? Curiosity compels you to want to know the balance of the sentence.

A quiz also will do it, such as "Which should you buy?"—a *Consumer Reports* package that was mailed to over 20 million homes.

Audience Selection.   This approach can lend itself to interesting formats as well. One package for *Self* included a plastic mirror showing through the envelope, dramatizing the kind of person being looked for as a prospective subscriber.

The type of mailing list the prospect is found on can lead to interesting concepts. For instance, a mailing to engineers for a pocket calculator presented unique diagrams and formulas that would be of interest to that audience. Another to architects dealt with blueprints and diagrams.

For Polaroid, we designed a series of mailings geared to specific types of industries. Only the opening of the letter and a buck slip, which showed through a window at the back of the envelope, changed from mailing to mailing, but to each reader the message appeared to be designed for the one particular industry. Previous mailings relating to all recipients as "Dear

Small Businessman" had failed miserably. I have used this technique a dozen times and it always does better than generic equivalents.

Personalization and Versioning.   Personalization is any message that is or appears to be relevant to the individual mail recipient. Versioning, which can be accomplished with laser or with alternative letters or brochures, is directed at an interest group, a geographic group, or some other characteristic available to the mailer.

An envelope window can disclose a large, bold name, or a message that the reader can identify with. A "Weekend Wizard" mailing I did for Avis offered weekend rentals, but dramatized the benefit of such rentals by describing specific attractions within driving distance of each city mailed to.

Anything that implies that this letter is "just for you" and not for everyone will do better. We did a self-mailer for Pilgrimage Small Group Leadership Training which high-lighted the one seminar nearest the recipient's home or church. It doubled enrollments over the previous mailings, which listed all their seminars.

In a recent mailing for a soap sample, I arranged to have the address label repeat the prospect's name three times, as in "Diana, Diana, and Diana Nash." This created a curiosity factor in itself. The three names were repeated in the letter salutation and went on to talk about "For all the women you are—sometimes traditional, sometimes romantic, sometimes adventurous." This set the stages for the introduction of a well-known bar soap in three different scented varieties.

Any aspect of personalization mentioned anywhere in this book can be adapted for use on an envelope or to show through it.

Involvement Devices.   You can use any type of token, stamp, number, or device, as listed earlier, to show through a window in an envelope, and any type of gift or enclosure can be referred to on the envelope. The simple addition of "Valuable Savings Stamps Enclosed" can increase the rate of opening, and therefore the rate of response, very substantially. Another interesting device is a zip strip on the envelope, with instructions to pull a tab and reveal a copy message or illustration.

Implied Value.   There are many ways to indicate that the contents of an envelope are of value. One obvious way is to say so. Another is to use very fine paper, an interesting colored stock, or a very professional (perhaps engraved or embossed) envelope.

Kraft paper can imply that the contents are of value. So can a seal. European direct marketers have reported fantastic results with facsimile wax-sealed envelopes. On the other end of the scale, I've often used newsprint to suggest that the brochure is a preprint of an advertisement or a special sale event.

Value can be added in other ways—rubber stamps referring to valuable contents, or stickers with added messages. One trick is to die-cut a portion of the flap to look like a seal. If part of it is left ungummed, it flaps up and looks like a real label sealing the envelope.

A show-through of something that looks like it might have value—a certificate, coin, or stamp—is of course another way of suggesting value. Or just say it, as in "Free Recipe Cards Enclosed."

The Important Look.   You can use the power of convention to make your mailing look like an official communication, providing the overall effect isn't misleading. If your client is a bank, you can be sure that the kind of envelopes in which statements usually are mailed will get attention. Another effective technique is to use official language: "Notice of Price Increase," or "Nontransferable."

However I urge readers not to suggest that your envelope is some kind of official communication from the government or the postal service. One reason is that people smart enough to make enough money to buy your product will not be fooled by such nonsense and will resent being tricked. The other is that federal and local governments are rightly protesting this type of deception and it can lead to restrictions on legitimate direct mail practices. I suggest that if you can't make money without resorting to trickery perhaps you have the wrong product or are in the wrong business.

Adding Urgency.   An expiration date is the ultimate urgency appeal. It can even be computer-printed on one side of an oversized address label. Let it show through to boost results. Another way to add urgency is to make the format look like a Teletype or wire. Or you can use headline typefaces and copy styles, as in "NEW PRODUCT SLASHES COPIER COSTS!" But if the expiration date refers to a price reduction, be prepared to justify that it really is one. It's all right to have a limited-time sale, just as retailers do, providing that the "regular price" really is higher, or that the premium is not available after the expiration date.

Bulky Contents.   Fold the inserts down, and use a smaller envelope than is customary. The added thickness will imply that something of value is included. And don't presume that all the pieces must lie flat. An uneven fold can raise curiosity as to the contents as well as provide interesting visual effects once the mailing has been opened. However, keep in mind that to meet postal requirements, the package should not exceed 1/4 inch in thickness.

John Stimolo, the expert on marketing to schools, has tested what he calls "bumpy" letters and finds that they offer a significant lift.

Transparent Envelopes.   The polyethylene envelope is the closest thing to the disappearing envelope. They hide nothing, except those areas you may want concealed under a printed area of the polyethylene covering.

Materials are not inserted into these envelopes in the usual sense. Instead, the printed polyethylene is wrapped around the collated materials and fabricated into envelopes at very high speeds.

For a four-color circular, use a clear polyethylene envelope to let it show through. It will cost less than printing similar color art on the outer envelope.

Use of transparent envelopes for certificates or other enclosures of obvious value makes them visible immediately, adding to the pulling power more effectively than merely describing the enclosure.

One caution: be sure the reader can open the polyethylene envelope easily. For some of them particularly those sealing videotapes or CDs, they seem impenetrable without a knife. This adds a preliminary obstacle: "Is this interesting enough for me to go the trouble of getting a knife." Often the answer is "No."

Envelope Sizes.   Envelopes come in many sizes. Twelve standard sizes of envelopes are usually available from most suppliers. They include monarch (3-7/8 × 7-1/2 inches), check (3-5/8 × 8-5/8 inches), the popular No. 10 (4-1/8 × 9-1/2 inches), and the more interesting No. 14 (5 × 11-1/2 inches), which accommodates a letter folded in half down the center.

Booklet envelopes come in an even wider variety of 32 standard sizes, including the popular 6 × 9 inch size. Many suppliers have stock dies with various window configurations that can be used quickly and inexpensively.

These standard sizes are very handy for test runs or small printing jobs. In larger quantities and with proper schedules, it is possible to design anything you want without any real cost disadvantage.

Convention is a vital consideration in envelope size selection. People are accustomed to certain sizes of envelopes being associated with bills, checks, invitations, personal correspondence, and business correspondence. They also expect matters of importance to arrive in No. 10, or 9 × 12 inch envelopes.

Oddly enough, the most-used direct mail size is one that has no associations except with direct mail promotions, the 6 × 9 inch envelope. It is an efficient size, and the largest that most Phillipsburg inserters can accommodate, but I prefer to use almost anything else. In fact, I have never come up against a 6 × 9 inch package that I wasn't able to beat, given the opportunity. I think it is a size that says, "We want to sell you something" and puts the reader on guard. A squarer size has more interest. A 5 × 7-1/2 inch envelope is unusual. A 3-3/4 × 6-3/4 inch envelope can contain items folded to form a very thick and apparently valuable package. Almost anything is better than a 6 × 9 inch envelope, in my opinion, and yet, because it is the easiest to work with, design for, and produce, it probably will always be the most commonly used size.

Refer to Fig. 12-1 for a sample of the variety of stock envelopes which are available in a wide variety of sizes.

Postal Regulations.   Before getting carried away with odd-shaped envelopes, be sure to check the latest postal regulations. Non-standard sizes will not only cost you more at the printer but may also bar you from using the more economical classes of postage.

For instance, a Standard Mail (A) letter can not be more than 6-1/8 inches high by 11-1/2 inches long, and 1/4 inch thick, and has a maximum weight of 3.3087 ounces. The minimum is 3-1/2 × 5 inches with a thickness of 0.007 inch thick. Larger sizes must be at least slightly thicker. It is important that designers observe the "aspect ratio" which is rectangular from 1.3 to 2.5. This means that the horizontal dimension must be not less than 130 percent of the length of the vertical dimension and not more than 250 percent.

If you want to use automated rates, which are about half the rates of first class mail, there are many other regulations as well. Some affect the address area, requiring a clear zone for barcodes of 4-3/4 × 5/8 inches at the lower right edge of any envelope. Others affect the form and style of indicias and vary for non-profit and other classes of mail. Fig. 12-2 illustrates this requirement.

There are many helpful publications available with the latest, detailed information. Contact your nearest USPS Postal Business Center or their National Customer Support Center (1-800-238-3150 or http://www.usps.com /ncsc/products)

I particularly recommend their "Quick Service Guide" (136 pages) and their plastic format templates. There is also a CD-Rom called "Postal Explorer" that contains two complete manuals, eight publications, forms, postal zone charts and rate calculators. The cost is $20, and it can be ordered by phone at 1-800-654-1905.

The Letter

How Long Should a Letter Be?   Long enough to do the job. How many pages should it have? As many as are needed to tell the story.

There have been successful letters on one side of a monarch-size page, and other successes—like Tom Collins' classic fund-raising appeal for George McGovern, which ran for a dozen pages.

True, the usual sizes are two and four pages, but this may be the result of a failure to try alternatives rather than of careful testing. As the letter is one of the least costly segments of a direct mail package, you should not skimp on it.

What Size Should a Letter Be?   Convention determines size in most cases. Business letters should be standard business sizes and should be printed on one side only with each page separate, as if it came out of a typewriter or laser printer. Consumer mail can be odd-sized just to be more interesting. It can be monarch-size to resemble a personal letter, or it can be 5-1/2 × 8-1/2 inches with an apparently handwritten message to make it resemble an informal note. It can be two pages back to back, or a four-page folder, or it can have a coupon at the top or bottom. It can be in the form and size of memo paper, a telegram, or anything that fits the tactics chosen for the promotion.

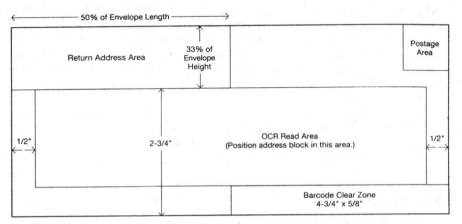

(Not Actual Size)

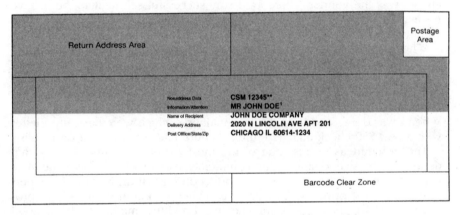

Figure 12-2. Dark shaded area indicates "free space" for nonaddress printing. Light shaded area indicates preferred clear zone to enhance readability.

What Should a Letter Look Like?   First of all, it should be readable. Readability requires either that it looks personal, with the prospect's name appearing on it, or that it looks interesting. To get readership, use a headline in handwriting or over-sized type, or add drawings or photographs.

For consumer mailings, readability means that it cannot look like a dull letter with flush paragraphs. Some sentences should be indented, some should be underlined, and others should be annotated with handwritten marginal notes. Business and professional mail requires the opposite approach to fit convention.

Formal paragraph rules can be thrown out the window. Instead, present your story in neat eyefuls of smaller readable paragraphs.

Why Imitate Typing?   A question that comes up frequently is whether imitation typing really fools anybody, and if it doesn't, why bother?

The real issue is not whether typewriter faces or book faces such as Times New Roman deceive the reader, but whether they suggest a letter by convention. The spirit of the letter format is that it is a one-on-one communication between two business executives or between a merchant and a consumer.

At one time letters set in book typefaces did not look like letters. With the widespread use of computers in the home, the convention has changed and they are now as "personal" as an old-fashioned typewriter. Convention is the standard, not deception.

The Brochure

The first question to ask is whether you need a brochure at all. I know of many successful mailings that omitted a brochure, and there have been some split-run tests of "brochure" versus "no brochure," where "no brochure" was the winner. There are many successful self-mailers, but I have never seen a split-test where a mailing with a letter lost out to a version without a letter.

Whether or not a brochure is helpful really depends on the nature of the proposition and how well the brochure is done. If the proposition is an intangible, like a newsletter on financial privacy or an appeal for a contribution, the brochure may have little to add. For philanthropy, a brochure might actually appear "slick" or "wasteful" and be a clear negative factor. When I was doing MCI long-distance mailings, which were basically a letter with a real $50 check attached, the brochure had no influence on results.

The brochure is usually one of the most expensive parts of a mailing, depending on size, quantity, and complexity. The brochure also is the most expensive part of the mechanical production cost. If a brochure is 15 percent of the cost of the mailing and that mailing without the brochure produces only 10 percent less income, the brochure might not be a good investment at all from a return-on-investment viewpoint.

When Is a Brochure Needed?   A brochure is needed most often when the sales message requires illustration, amplification, or accreditation. A brochure is the television of direct mail. Like television it offers immense credibility because words can lie but the eye cannot be fooled. It offers the prospect a chance to "see for yourself" the beauty of the product offered and how it will look at home, in the garden, or at the office. It provides space to diagram the most complex of working parts or the most elaborate of details. Unlimited except by the imagination of the artist and the skill of the photographer, it can make its presentations in full size, in color, and with dimension—from broad perspective to the finest close-up detail. In short, it provides an opportunity to use all the methods of visual, nonverbal communication discussed in earlier chapters.

What Goes in a Brochure?   Once you've decided you need a brochure, you should include, in one way or the other, every selling point that you listed in your general copy platform. Don't worry about duplicating points in the letter. In fact, use the letter as a checklist to be sure that every major point has been mentioned again. In direct mail, each piece must stand alone. Let it do the whole selling job as if the prospect will read no other piece, which may be the case.

Use the largest broadside area or brochure spread for the most impressive illustration—usually the finished product, whether it is a set of encyclopedias, a nature garden, or a completed project that your house plans or craft kit will build. The illustration can show a choice: the wide range of books, records, toys, or doll clothes you can choose from with this initial offer. Or it can show the "exploded" contents: pages from a magazine or book, materials in a correspondence course, the pieces in a set of mechanic's tools or a build-your-own-computer kit.

The opening pages or folds should be used to make the basic appeal. If the tactic chosen is to stress the offer, then this is the place to dramatize the savings, the discount, or the premium. Even the simplest free trial offer can be dramatized, with an impressive certificate warranting the return privilege.

If the mailing is benefit-oriented, then show the benefit. In a book club, dramatize the relaxation of reading through pictures of people sitting with books on the beach or before a fireplace. Or capture the spirit of the book or other product by including scenes suggesting romance, adventure, relaxation or whatever you want to associate with the product. For as intangible a product as insurance, you can dramatize the comforts of worry-free retirement, the security of knowing that the family home is secure, or the reassurance that junior will, indeed, graduate from college "no matter what."

The Information Strategy.   Whenever possible, structure the message in an educational tone, and select a format that suggests valuable information. For instance, a "Retirement Planning Guide," a booklet on "The Clear Skin Look" for an acne product, a "Fashion Fun Magazine" rather than just a catalog of Barbie premiums.

What About Format?   *Brochure* is a term that usually describes a four- or six-page printed and folded sales message. A *booklet* is eight or more pages, glued or stapled together. A *broadside* is larger than a brochure in that it is designed to unfold into a flat sheet, usually both vertically and horizontally. *Flyers, pamphlets, circulars, inserts,* and *stuffers* are all smaller items that usually unfold to a piece no larger than the unfolded letter.

Each has its own advantages. The smaller pieces are economical. The booklets and brochures are reserved, businesslike, and highly credible. The broadside is the heavy artillery of direct mail. It achieves a sense of dramatic impact that is not possible with any other format.

The principle involved in broadsides is the same as that involved in wide-screen motion pictures. If the visual image is wider or higher than the viewers' focal range they have to move their heads in order to see the whole picture. It is then perceived as more realistic than if they are aware of the edges, margins, or other reminders that it is only a picture.

Consider the possibility of making the booklet or brochure an element of apparent value in itself—something that would merit your saying something like "Helpful Booklet Enclosed" on the outer envelope.

A cookbook's brochure can include some sample recipes. A fashion catalog can include a color coordination guide. A vitamin brochure can include an article on nutrition. A grouping of several items can be presented as if it were a catalog.

For Erno Lazslo, we presented a simple dealer list as a "Directory" for travelers. Avis prepared a "confidential proposal," and Marriott Hotels did a "meeting planner's kit." Both were basically sales booklets with their own apparent value. In the case of Marriott, we eventually were able to offer the "kit" as the premium in a two-step promotion.

Other Inserts

Other than the letter, a brochure, the reply card, and the outer envelope, what else do you need to make a mailing effective? Nothing, actually. These pieces give three or four repetitions of the main selling points, and should be capable of making the sale all by themselves.

However, for many mailers, the more inserts the better. The only requirement is that each insert have a *raison d'être*, a reason for being. An insert should not be just another piece of paper, but should have an obvious message or function.

The Lowly Buck Slip.   I don't know how the buck slip got its name—maybe because it is often the size of a "buck"—but I do know it can make a big difference in results. Figure 12-3 is an example of a typical buck slip.

Figure 12-3. A "Buck Slip."

Sometimes it's used to stress a point that may have been buried in the copy, like "Remember, you'll get a free tote bag . . ." Or it can offer a special premium that may have been an afterthought. For instance "Reply by X date and we'll also send you a mystery gift worth at least $10 in catalog value."

A buck slip may also contain news. "This widget has just been granted the seal of approval of the . . ." or ". . . selected for use in the space shuttle." It can make a correction "We are out of the beige model however, we can send it to you in your choice of . . ." It might be a trade-up or referral offer: "Buy three and you'll also get . . .", "Give us the names of three friends and we'll send you a. . . ."

No doubt buck slips began as a way of adding information or sales appeal at the last minute, after a mailing had already been printed. But the occasional addition of such slips proved so effective that they are now deliberately planned in many mailings, as a way of stressing major points. Like the postscript of a letter, they are often read first. If you use buck slips, be sure that they are self-explanatory and do not presume that the letter or other parts of the mailing have been read.

The Second Letter.   The "second" letter has also been called the *lift letter* or *publisher's letter*. It has become an effective though now overused supplement to many mailings, particularly in the magazine subscription field.

As originally used, the second letter was a simple note from the publisher with a headline such as "Please read this only if you have decided to say 'No' to our offer." It went on to dramatize the no-risk aspect with copy like, "For the life of me, I can't understand why anyone would not send for . . ."

With sweepstakes mailings, second letters often reiterate the message "No purchase necessary." With insurance mailings, they stress an inexpensive introductory offer.

Today scores of variations have sprung up. Some publishers put the second letter in a sealed envelope. Others have it sticking out of the reply envelope. National Liberty Insurance used an interesting variation: a single folder printed as if it were an envelope, and held together with a spot of glue.

A new variation is the *double lift letter,* or basically two separate lift letters that may or may not be joined together. One is for people who have decided to say yes, the other for people who have decided to say no. Naturally, curiosity will lead both groups to read both letters.

Versioned Inserts.   Often it is too costly to prepare different versions of a brochure for different mailing lists. One way to take advantage of customized appeals without losing the benefits of large-quantity printing is to add customized inserts, with variations depending on list segmentation. These can be geographic in nature, referring to local conditions, local service availability, or local dealers. They can also be demographic, with special notes relating the product or service to people with different demographics.

These inserts can be related to the mailing lists and the known interests of prospects, indicated by what they have bought or subscribed to in the past. For a magazine, the insert can relate to a specific article coming up in a future issue. For a craft tool or book, it can zero in on the person's field of interest: making planes, trains, dolls, etchings, or what have you.

Selection Aids. The purpose of a selection aid is to make it easy to express a choice of one or more items offered in the mailing. It also has the effect of becoming an involvement device, and it gives you a second chance to list the products available.

In its simplest form, the selection aid can be an itemized order blank. The customer has only to check off the items desired, or indicate quantity.

Marboro Books used to list the number of each book offered, so that a customer only had to circle a number to order a book. I remember this device well, because one of my first jobs included assembling and proof-reading those lists of numbers.

Book clubs, record clubs, and magazine subscription firms routinely use sheets of gummed stamps, illustrating the selections and including the order numbers and a value comparison. Merchandisers could develop such a device for catalog sales. A department store mailer could present each item on its own sheet with a gummed, perforated order stamp that only needs to be affixed to a preaddressed order form.

Testimonial Flyers. Customer testimonials, a celebrity endorsement or other proof that your offer is sincere and valuable is often worth a separate insert.

Testimonials can be selected geographically, as in "What other Texans say about this offer." Endorsements can be in the form of a second letter.

The Reply Envelope

It does pay to have a reply envelope, even when the offer can be mailed back on a card, but this is the only simple aspect of dealing with reply envelopes.

First of all, even with restrictive postal design requirements on business reply mail, there is room to make the envelope interesting. Typefaces, reverses, patterned paper, colors, and borders all are tools that can provide a sense of design and value even with strict adherence to postal requirements. The company name and the way the envelope is addressed can help the sale as well. The USPS has no objection to adding a message or illustration at the top left of envelope face or at the back of the envelope. All they ask is that the area they have to scan be clear of distractions and the color of the paper is light enough to facilitate optical scanning of the bar code.

For envelopes other than Business Reply Mail, the only requirements are those of common sense. You must be able to fit the reply envelope into the outer envelope, and make it large enough so your customer can get your order form into it without difficulty. It can be "red-hot" to stimulate action with color, or yellow to imply telegraphic urgency. It can have a stamp affixed, or no stamp at all. For inquiry or two-step mailings, I usually prefer "Place Stamp Here" to business reply mail. The cost of a stamp is a very effective qualifier.

An interesting and effective development is the *double reply envelope,* used particularly with sweepstakes offers. One envelope is boldly marked NO, and is addressed to the contest judging company. The other is similarly marked YES, and is addressed to the mailer's fulfillment center. Sweepstakes mailings may be very different by the time you read this because of government over-reaction to people who claimed they didn't see "if you have the lucky number" or couldn't understand "No purchase required." So check with the Direct Marketing Association for the latest regulations.

Another way to accomplish the same end is to provide a window in the reply envelope so that the selection of yes or no shows through, allowing for easy sorting in the mailroom.

Some reply envelopes build in an action-now buck slip, designing it as a perforated tear-off slip at the flap or inner edge of the envelope. Even a business reply envelope can be designed in this way, as the stub will have been removed before the envelope gets to the post office.

Of course, a reply envelope doesn't have to be only an envelope. This general term might be used to refer to a Mailgram or a telegram blank—the ultimate in immediacy.

Another possibility is to help generate telephone response. Use a separate slip of paper to prominently display the phone number and the hours to call.

One trick is to provide the number on a gummed label, to be placed near the phone or in an address book or, for business mail, on a Rolodex card.

Postage

One of the largest expenses of most mailings is postage, and the choice of standard (bulk), first class, or not-for-profit mail is worth consideration. The difference in rates is substantial, and more important, so is the difference in weight requirements.

First Class Mail. This class offers the ultimate in the appearance of importance, and often is often worth the added expense for business mailings or where fast results are needed. The basic rate is applicable only to 1 ounce, and the slightest additional fraction requires almost as much. It is not difficult to take an elaborate mailing with a booklet over the 2-ounce line, and even up to the 3-ounce rate. For example, 2-1/16 ounces will require the same postage as 3 ounces.

First class mail does move faster. It has priority in the post office, and usually it travels faster. If the piece is not deliverable, it will be forwarded or returned without added cost and often with the new address that will allow you to clean your list.

First class mail varies in cost, offering substantial discounts to companies that can presort to various specifications. But even with the added delivery of the forwarding service and the added importance conveyed by first class mail, most large-scale consumer mailings would not justify the cost differential. The added cost often is worthwhile, though, in business and professional mailings.

One caution: If you are going to use first class mail, make it look like first class mail. Use stamps (for consumer mail) or postage-meter indicia rather than printed indicia (for business mail). Keep the envelope simple, except perhaps for a pseudo-stamped "First Class Mail." There are some indications that postal employees may not always notice first-class indicia, especially if the envelope looks like advertising mail.

Green diamond first class borders, or red-and-blue airmail borders, can be added to the envelope, even though they no longer have any postal significance.

Standard (Formerly Third Class or Bulk) Mail. This class is the key delivery system in the direct mail industry. Despite rates that are disproportionately high in order to enable the Postal Service to subsidize newspapers, franked mail, and individually hand-addressed mail, it is still the most effective system for delivering a printed message to American business. Some Internet enthusiasts predict that some-day all mail will be electronic, but the only applications so far are those where the consumer must find a site or where it is intrusive, called "spam." Direct mail will always be the core medium of the direct marketing business

There are many reasons that third-class rates are lower than first class ones. First, third class mail is standardized, and must be the same size and weight for convenient machine sorting. Second, it is a basic presort by zip code, and can be handled in bulk, with entire trays already tagged by the mailer for delivery to sectional centers. Third, it is paid for in bulk by the pound, and needs less handling and bookkeeping. Fourth, and most important, it is deferred, low-priority mail, delivered after first class mail and newspapers have been delivered.

Postal rates and regulations change so frequently that it would be useless to include them in a book that takes a year to produce. Today there are discounts for five-digit and nine-digit sorting, for bar codes, for carrier delivery sequence, and with different rates depending on the envelope size. Some rates vary depending on how much of your mailing sorts into carrier-route quantities. Therefore, a mailing concentrated in certain markets may be less costly than one spread throughout the country. Always check with your mailing house or the postmaster when you estimate postage rates.

The most common (read *unimaginative*) way to use bulk mail is to put a little square in the upper right-hand corner and include the required wording ("Bulk Mail/U.S. Postage Paid Permit #——") and the name of the company or the city or zip code of origin. However, there are many alternatives.

The same information can be designed into a facsimile postage-meter imprint, complete with circles simulating a postmark and a red eagle simulating the meter imprint. Also, the much-less-negative term "Standard Mail" is now permitted. There are other alternatives than printed indicia. Postal meters and pre-canceled bulk-rate postage stamps can be used instead. Most mailers can accommodate these requests, or they can affix stamps by machine for a nominal added charge.

Not-for-Profit Rates. Legitimate not-for-profit organizations such as charities, religious groups, and foundations used to enjoy significantly lower postage rates. Even these have been under attack, and the gap between for-profit and not-for-profit rates is closing fast.

The catch is that the organization has to be authorized, and the penalties are stiff for any misuse or misrepresentation of this privilege. However, many organizations—Consumers Union, the Smithsonian, and others—support major magazines with the help of this not-for-profit rate. They can successfully mail millions of pieces at response levels that would bankrupt a company paying the regular Standard Mail rate.

The effect of this lower rate is so important that organizations have been known to restructure their activities in order to qualify. For example, *Ms.* magazine, which started out as a profit-making institution, completely revised its ownership and now operates as the Ms. Foundation for Education and Communication.

Not-for-profit mail also can be mailed with meter imprints, or with pre-canceled not-for-profit-rate postage stamps.

Videotapes and CDs

In the last several years, there has been a substantial increase in the use of videotapes and CD-ROMs as direct mail vehicles. These are used for both front-end acquisition mailings and back-end acknowledgements to inquiries from other media. By the time this book is published someone will have mailed the first DVD discs for digital video presentations.

Theoretically, a video message can be accessed right on a website, particularly by consumers with adequate equipment, access, and patience. If, as I predict, cable and the home television monitor becomes the prevailing Internet access, this will become a major factor. In fact there is no technological reason why, right now, advertisers can't offer a catalog or other information in a TV spot, accessed by clicking the same remote button used for pay-per-view.

CD-ROMs. What is available right now, however, is the ability to send a CD complete with sound and search capabilities. This can contain a whole catalog, detailed specifications, competitive comparisons, Internet connections, software samples, or a sample lesson (as Video Professor does).

Format is usually not a problem, because the same CD usually has enough capacity to accommodate both the prevailing PC format and the growing Macintosh audience.

If you are sending a CD, it should take the place of the brochure in direct mail. That is, it should be self-contained and cover every copy point, perhaps in an introductory segment, and it should be accompanied by the equivalent of an envelope to get it opened and a letter to persuade the recipient to watch it.

Videotapes.   Like CDs, videotapes have a high perceived value, suggest retention, and can present a very dramatic presentation of a message. They are particularly effective where there is no substitute for "being there," as in travel destinations, cruise ships, or a demonstration of complex technology. The uses are endless. For instance, there is no better way to show views and model homes for a real estate development, or to present the convention facilities of a hotel or of a city.

The USPS and a company called Duplication Factory promoted the use of videotapes through mailings and seminars, calling it "Television by Mail." They are subject to the same low rates as printed matter and go through the mail without damage or delay. Once the shooting and editing are complete, the cost is no more than many printed brochures—often as little as $1 or $2 in large quantities.

Merrill Lynch mailed thousands of tapes to its customers to dramatize the importance of global investing, and then offered specific tapes on subjects such as retirement planning. The very nature of the medium suggests that the content is educational, and thus more likely to be watched with a positive attitude.

Using Videotapes and CDs.   There are some lessons that apply equally to both of these vehicles. The most important is the recognition that they are a means to communicate—not an end in itself which is an error common among today's Internet advocates as well.

First, they have to be easy to access. Shrink-packing may be inexpensive, but it is no bargain if a substantial percentage of your prospects give up trying to get it opened. Retail packaging should not be the model, because it was designed to discourage shop-lifting the disc out of the so-called "jewel box" or the Videotape sleeve.

Secondly, you have to re-sell people on why they sent for it and why they should put it in their computer or VCR. Even when it was requested, all the lessons of direct mail still apply. The outer wrapping and various inserts must once again generate Attention, Interest, Desire and Action— the action being watching it now not later. To do this, benefits and motivations must be dramatized once-again.

Even at the low-prices of the new "paper videocassettes," few marketers can afford to use this medium for "front end" prospecting. However, it is a dynamite addition to any two-step offer. It is the logical next step in effectiveness that began with "Send for Information" and progressed to

"Send for Free Color Brochure" or "Free Information Kit." "Send for Free Videotape or CD" has proven to be a winner over and over again, whether generating coupons, phone calls, or Internet click-throughs.

Self-Mailer Formats

The bulk of this chapter has been devoted to typical direct mail formats with letter, envelope, and various inserts. However, enormous advances have been made in the science of self-mailers.

There have been many notable successes using self-mailers in recent years, and while they must still include the basic components outlined previously, often they can do so in formats that are both clever and economical. A dozen or so major "web" printers have made these formats so economical for larger-quantity mailings that the end cost per response rivals anything a more traditional format can achieve.

For one thing, the letter, envelope, brochure, and reply card can be combined and printed in one press run, at rates far less expensive than those for printing each piece separately. And these pieces can separate when opened into several highly involving components. "On-line fabrication" can even produce a standard envelope.

For another, these suppliers have perfected the art of in-line addressing and personalization. Catalogs come off the press in a presorted ready-to-mail sequence, addressed not only on the cover but also on an inserted order form. Mailing pieces, complete with simulated closed-face or open-face envelopes, include letters, reply devices, booklets, buck slips, or what have you—in a wide variety of sizes and configurations.

One of the major innovators in these formats is Webcraft Technologies of Princeton, New Jersey. This company has provided sketches of several of the hundreds of such forms they have produced for clients. These appear in Figs. 12-4 and 12-5 for a half dozen of the hundreds of formats available.

* * *

This chapter has dealt with the physical aspects of taking a marketer's themes and a writer's words and getting them to the prospect. This physical process of format selection, design, printing, and lettershop work is often lumped together as *execution*. Creatively, it is a direct marketer's version of origami. We cut a sheet of paper, fold it, and print it to create a fascinating variety of envelopes, letters, flyers, inserts, tokens, stamps, *ad infinitum*. Perhaps we'll add a sample, a scent strip or a CD disk. Mix well with consumer psychology and effective communication. The result: not just a sale, but the prospering, growing medium that direct mail is today.

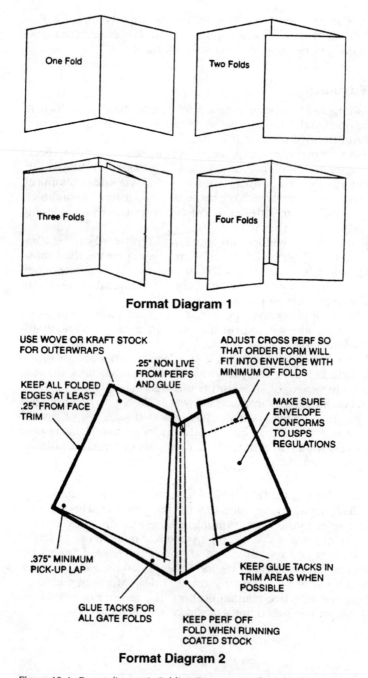

Format Diagram 1

Format Diagram 2

Figure 12-4. *Format diagram* 1: Folding Formats may be folded in many configurations to accommodate and fulfill a specific purpose or function. An enhanced in-line press offers the creative user a multitude of sizes, shapes, and format options. *Format diagram* 2: Bind-in order form/ envelopes and outwraps for use in perfect-bound and saddle-stitched publications [Webcraft Technologies, Inc.]

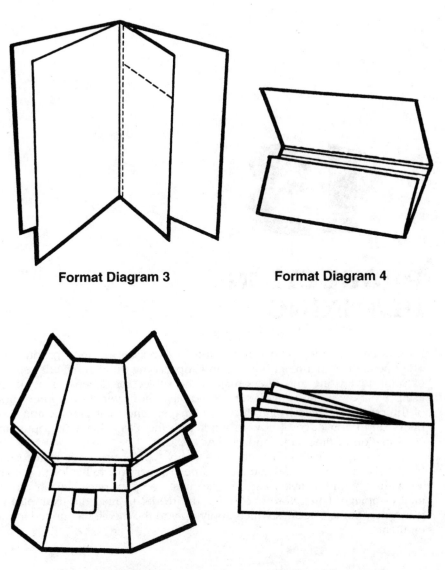

Format Diagram 3

Format Diagram 4

Format Diagram 5

Format Diagram 6

Figure 12-5. *Format diagram* 3: Mini-catalogs—versatile, multipage formats with or without a built-in reply envelope. Available with 6.8, 10, 12, or more pages in either digest or maxi size. Suitable for distribution by mail, as a take-one, a package-stuffer, or a magazine/newspaper insert. *Format diagram* 4: Round-trip mailer, the dual-purpose envelope. *Format diagrams* 5 *(open-end mailer) and* 6 *(closed-end mailer)*: Both are economical, perrsonalized web formats with closed-face or open-window envelopes. Match mailings are easily accomplished using the in-line process. Process colors, various grades of stock within a package, product samples, pop-ups, and fragrance applications are some of the capabilities Format configurations are designed for the specific user. [Webcraft Technologies, Inc.]

PRODUCTION
PLANNING

It is not necessary for every direct marketer to master the art of production. The fine craft of planning, buying, and supervising the graphic-arts aspects of print advertising and direct mail is the subject of dozens of books in itself. What every direct marketer should have, however, is an appreciation of the problems faced by production managers and their graphic-arts suppliers, and knowledge of how to work with them to achieve the optimum combination of time, cost, and quality.

The principles in this chapter apply to any type of production process—from a simple black-and-white ad for a newspaper, to a full-color magazine ad with a bound-in insert card to the most complex personalized direct-mail campaign. I therefore encourage the reader to read the examples as principles, not as specifics which apply only to the media mentioned at the moment.

NEW OPTIONS, NEW CHALLENGES

There used to be two major stages in the development of graphic arts and, consequently, in their applications. The first was the physical stage. Wood or metal type, or line etchings were coated with ink which was then transferred to paper. In time, photographs and decorative elements were etched with acid into dot patterns and added to the physical impressions. As primitive as this sounds, art directors and production managers created printed pieces that were as beautiful and persuasive as anything produced today.

The letterpress gave way to offset, which, by utilizing a simple chemical property, that oil (inks) and water don't mix, eliminated the need for metal plates, increased production speed, reduced costs, and enabled the second stage, or what I call the optical stage of development. Type could be produced and pasted on a board to be photographed. With varying degrees of precision, type proofs and photostats (for position only) were affixed to cardboard sheets called "mechanical paste-ups." Sheets of acetate defined drop-outs and surprints. Sheets of vellum indicated color breakdowns and other instructions. Skilled photoengravers put it all together, submitted proofs, made corrections, and prepared the film that the printer would turn into offset plates.

Today we are in stage three—the digital stage. Typography, design and illustration have been freed from their physical or even optical constraints. As in some ethereal science fiction scenario, all that exists are electronic impulses—ones and zeroes, whose quantity is measured in bytes and whose speed is expressed in megahertz.

The limitations are gone. Type fonts can be adjusted to precise sizes and spacing. (I was shocked the first time I asked an art director what size font she was using and got an answer that included two decimal places, something like 11.23 point.) Colors are infinite. Photos can be manipulated, stretched or combined. A hundred page full-color catalog fits comfortably on one Zip, Syquest or Jazz disk. And color proofs can be transmitted by e-mail or viewed on a website.

In some ways the printer's job is easier. Most pre-press work is now done by the advertiser or agency. But in another way it is much more difficult. Every printer is now competing with others all over the country and all over the world. Large printers with the resources to invest in the latest presses and processes are out-bidding the others, and local convenience has been upstaged by equipment, technology, competitive pricing and—most important—innovation. It is innovation that has made printers more than processors of paper and ink. They are now valuable partners in the process of creating effective direct mail and publication advertising.

THE PERSONALIZATION OPTION

Personalization has been the breakthrough tool of the 20th century. We all thrilled to be able to address letters with a name and address on a letter or response card that could show through an envelope window. The ink-jet and laser technology that did this was created to save time and money, yet still provide different versions of letters and different information for customers in different cities . . . all to create messages relevant to each prospect's known interests or each customer's previous purchasing history.

The barrier that blocked the illusion of being a true personal letter was the envelope window. We had difficult choices. We could easily address the envelope but not the contents. But to have personal elements inside the envelope and on the outside surface as well was costly and couldn't be automated. In small quantities, you could match them by hand. One company, Kurt Volk, patented the first process that could do both in quantity. Their method was to print the envelope area and the contents on one sheet, personalize them both, and then fold and trim the pieces so that the envelope was created on press, already wrapped around the letter.

Today, many printers have found a way to get the same effect. Some printers put a number on the outside of the envelope and match it with the same number on the inside by using optical scanners in the inserting process. One of the most ingenious methods I've seen is the OmniMatch, another patented process, that combines the envelope and its contents in a less costly technique that has less restrictions on formats. The key is a small window on the envelope which, after matching and inserting, is hidden by the postage stamp.

SMART PRINTING AND INSERTING

Smart inserting is the ability to vary which pre-printed insert or page of a catalog or brochure is inserted in each individual mailing piece, based on a code generated in the addressing process. This is even used in magazine advertising, where a national liquor advertiser or auto advertiser will insert a different permit based on the probable interests of the individual subscriber.

A form of "smart printing" is digital printing, which enables an infinite amount of on-press personalization. Digital printing provides economies such as "printing on demand"—for instance, books produced as the orders come in, or consumer catalogs customized according to a customer's areas of interest or the company's database information.

While some quality issues are still being worked on, this process takes personalization to a new extreme. As many as 256 fields can be specified in the database, each one generating an associated Quark XPress or similar document.

Figure 13-1 shows an example of this technique for a theoretical custom itinerary brochure for travelers. The box in the upper left corner contains four items of information supplied by the customer—name, number and ages of children, travel interests, and cuisine choices. Beneath that is the "Arrival" section with flight information and, if available, the customer's own photograph. The next panel on "Accommodations" describes and illustrates the recommended hotel. The right-hand page describes and illustrates five local restaurants that meet the traveler's specifications along with a map locating the hotel and the restaurants.

A brochure like this can be produced as needed, one-at-a-time if necessary. It is an ideal application for post-telemarketing follow-up where

Personalized information includes the Bayers' names and family data, as well as a quick summary of the itinerary and food preferences.

Welcome to Paris! Here's the Bayers' flight information, highly personalized. This includes the airline, departure and arrival airports and times, and how to get to the hotel.

A personalized activity summary reflects the needs of the Bayer children too.

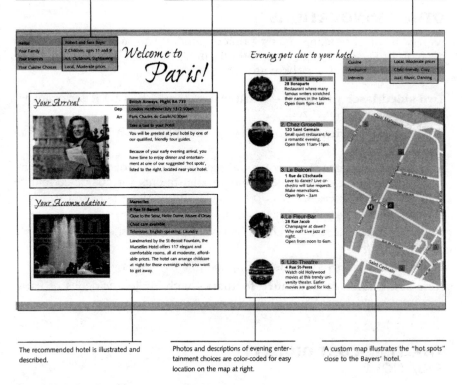

The recommended hotel is illustrated and described.

Photos and descriptions of evening entertainment choices are color-coded for easy location on the map at right.

A custom map illustrates the "hot spots" close to the Bayers' hotel.

Figure 13-1. Reprinted by courtesy of AGFA Corporation.

customized mailers can be individualized based on the results of each conversation.

The costs are not unreasonable, but this type of program obviously takes a great amount of planning and creative time. It is already available through printers who specialize in direct mail applications.

While digital is getting the press, conventional lithography has quietly stolen its thunder. Combinations of lithography and laser printing have provided personalization capability for almost any application. All that is holding it back is the imagination of the marketers who use it. For example, one application I have been exploring allows me to create a way of making it more cost effective to mail catalogs or direct mail to the 12 percent of U.S. households with a primary language other than English. By using laser-printing for all text, the same catalog can be printed in a dozen languages and still come off the press ready to mail in pre-sorted carrier route sequence. This is vastly more economical than doing separate mailings for each language group, and it has immense potential in the growing trend to global direct marketing.

OTHER INNOVATIONS

As a way of competing, many printers continue to add equipment and develop processes that give our industry more flexibility. In addition to the methods outlined above, here are some others.

Two-sided laser printing—so that two or four sides of a letter or invitation can be personalized.

Colored laser printing—so that even color photos can be changed from letter to letter.

Automated lithography—color and registration controls for quality. Plate mounting, plate washing and remote adjustments for 10- or 20-minute make-readies. Press speeds up to 15,000 impressions per hour to lower costs.

New papers—pseudo-coated, lighter weight, larger sheet sizes provide new economies.

Filmless pre-press systems—from computer to press without film.

New self-mailer or brochure formats—with endless varieties of flaps, coupons, etc.

THE TIME-COST-QUALITY TRIANGLE

Imagine a triangle with the words *time, cost,* and *quality* each written on an edge. If you press one side, another bulges. If you press two sides, the third may stretch to the bursting point.

The same principle applies to the graphic arts, and probably to most other production endeavors as well. If all three dimensions are reasonable, then there is an equilibrium. If unreasonable demands are placed on one or the other, something has to give.

Want your ad super-cheap? No problem, if you give the production supervisor the time to send it off to a printer in Taiwan, or to get bids from new, untried suppliers. There's always someone who will lose money on an initial job in hopes of getting your business in the future.

Want top quality? Then be prepared to use the best suppliers and the slower processes, and allow enough time to check proofs carefully at every stage.

Want it yesterday? Anything is possible, if you are willing to pay for it in one of the other "currencies." If time is the only criterion, a local duplicating shop can do it while you wait.

If you need both speed and quality, financial printing houses have the staff and equipment standing by on three shifts to handle rush jobs. They'll produce your color brochure in 48 hours or less, but be prepared to pay far more than what the same job would cost at a commercial printing house.

Your production manager, printers, and lettershops can do anything you want, but understand that the time-cost-quality interrelationship is a law of nature. All the haggling, screaming, bargaining, or cajoling in the world isn't going to change reality.

CONTROLLING COSTS

Each side of the cost-time-quality triangle has its own problems and opportunities. There is no trick to getting "the lowest costs." There *are* tricks to getting reasonable costs without sacrificing the other two considerations. These are the basic elements:

1. Planning the job
2. Defining the job
3. Getting estimates
4. Avoiding errors
5. Avoiding rush work

See Fig. 13-7 at the end of the chapter for a typical working budget for a direct mail project with a four-page letter and a 16-page two-color brochure.

Planning the Job

Whether you are working on a simple black-and-white ad for a newspaper, a multi-page magazine ad with bind-in card, or a multimillion-piece printing run, the problems are the same, and so is the first step: planning.

It is too late to begin production planning after the layout is complete. The time to begin is after the writer and artist have worked out rough layouts, and before either the finished copy has been written or final layouts completed. *That* is the time to bring in the production specialist or supplier who can suggest format ideas or ways to economize.

In the simplest advertisement, the production specialist should have the responsibility for determining exact sizes and the kind of halftone that is acceptable for the publication. (Halftones vary from 60 to 120 lpi (lines per inch); the lower the number, the coarser the illustration.) For a complex mailing piece, the production specialist is responsible for knowing paper sizes, envelope formats, inserting requirements, and what you can and cannot do with computer personalization.

In general planning, you should do the following:

Plan for Changes. If you have different versions for testing or are printing for different markets, plan them in advance. Usually, it is not necessary to start from scratch with each version. If you confine changing areas to the black plate, different versions can be prepared on press at a lower cost than making and setting up a whole new set of plates. If only an address or another single element changes, then an overlay on the mechanical will be less costly than new mechanicals and will save on plate-making. Production considerations should be taken into account in the creative stage as well. For example, costly changes can be avoided if different mail packages share a common window envelope, with copy changes positioned in the window rather than separate envelope styles for each.

Check Paper Specifications. Review paper specifications with publications and printers to be sure halftones are prepared correctly, ink won't show through, and your job will be cut out of the available paper with minimal waste. Even the paper's grain direction is important.

Plan for the Future. If you expect that the art will be reused for other versions, do what publishers do when preparing books that will be printed in different languages. Order a "floating fifth" film or plate. This is a second black plate containing all text matter, while the original black plate contains the black part of halftone illustrations. When printing, the two sets of film are combined into a single black plate, but the text can be changed without re-shooting the expensive halftone areas.

Avoid Inflexible Dating. More than one disaster has been averted by keeping dates off the printed area of an insert card or mailing piece. If an expiration date is mentioned in print in several places, you're up a tree if the lists come in wrong, the season turns bad, or one of the other elements is delayed. It's much better to imprint the date as part of the laser printing.

Make Dummies. Take the time to cut out blank paper representing each piece of a mailing. Fold and insert it the way you want. Errors, such as folders that open up and jam the inserter, or reply coupons that don't fit in the reply envelope, will be readily obvious and can be corrected before the final disc is prepared.

Check with the U.S. Postal Service. Always check for postal acceptability and new regulations. Don't presume tolerance, understanding, or common sense. An extra fraction of an inch on a reply card can increase your business-reply postage costs. An error in postal indicia can lead to the refusal of an entire mailing. Go by the book, or they'll throw it at you.

Defining the Job

Once you've worked out everything, write down detailed specifications. Don't count on a layout as being enough.

Bob Jurick, chairman of Fala Direct Marketing, prepared the lists of questions in Figs. 13-2a–c that should be asked by sales representatives when writing up orders for printing, computer, or mailing services.

(a) GENERAL PRINTING SPECIFICATIONS

1. *Name or subject matter of the job.*

2. *What is the quantity?*

3. *What is the size?* If a book or booklet, number of pages and the trim size of the page? Does it bleed?

4. *What is the paper stock? a.* Brand name if required. *b.* If brand name, can an equivalent sheet be used? *c.* What weight sheet? *d.* What finish is required: gloss, vellum, smooth, etc.? *e.* If a book or booklet, is there a separate cover? If a separate cover, what stock, weight and finish? *f.* Color of stock?

5. *How many colors – how many sides?* a. If two colors, are they two colors, not black or black and one color? b. If two colors on two sides, are they the same two colors? *c.* If four colors, is it four flat colors or four-color process?

6. *What type of art? a.* Printer-ready computer graphics? b. Camera-ready mechanical paste-up? c. What line screen? d. What process was it prepared in? Mac or PC? Quark or Adobe? e. Art in place or to be stripped in?

7. *If process color. a.* Size of process area or areas? *b.* If printer to strip in art, what will be supplied: chromes, wash drawings, continuous negatives? c. If *chromes*, what size, and are they all in the same focus? Are they separate units or assemblies?

8. *What is the approximate ink coverage, in percent*: 50%, 80%, 100%*?*

9. *What kind of proofs are required?* a. Blueprints? b. Color keys (or chromalins)? c. Press proofs?

10. *What type of binding? a.* Saddle stitch? How many wires? *b.* Type and number of folds? *c.* Perfect bind? *d.* Stitched or pasted? *e.* Die cut? *f.* Embossing?

11. *What type of packing?* Skid, cartons, pallet, banded? Moisture-resistant? How should cartons be labeled?

12. *Delivery.* Where? Is delivery additional? Date of delivery? Receiving department hours?

13. *Are over-runs acceptable?* If so, is there a percentage or quantity limit?

Figure 13-2a

Getting Estimates

Once the specification sheet has been prepared, getting estimates is simple. Specification sheets are simply attached to a "request-for-bid" memo and given to various suppliers.

Ideally, three suppliers should be asked to bid on each part of each job. One should be a tried-and-true supplier who helped you plan the job. Another should be an alternate supplier who is sometimes used by your firm. The third should be a new supplier who has been soliciting your work. Unless the savings are substantial with the new company, one of the suppliers who has been working with you should get the job.

It isn't cricket to play one supplier against the other, telling what another's bid is. You'll drive the prices down in the short run, as a hungry printer

(b) GENERAL COMPUTER SPECIFICATIONS

1.   *What type of job?* What is the quantity? Computer letter, list maintenance, labels?

2.   *How is it to be run?* Impact, ink jet, laser? On continuous form or cut sheets?

3.   *If computer letter. a.* Match fill-in – how many lines? *b.* Full computer letter – how many lines? *c.* Should everything be spelled out, abbreviated or exactly as on tape if tape is supplied (i.e., Ave., St., State, etc)? *d.* If prefix is not on tape, what are the rules for Mr., Miss, Mrs., Ms.? Should we look up female names on table? *e.* Type style: standard courier, wide courier? *f.* Proof and artwork information?

4.   *Computer forms information. a.* One-up or two-up? *b.* Trim size of letter, excluding pin holes? *c.* Weight of stock, color? *d.* One- or two-sided printing? *e.* Bindery: perforations, die-cuts, or tip-ons?

5.   *If labels. a.* One-up, three-up, four-up, or five-up? *b.* Type of stock: regular Cheshire, gummed, pressure-sensitive? *c.* Should match code, source code, or other information be printed on label?

6.   *Laser or ink-jet imaging.* Coated or uncoated stock. Tapes properly formatted?

7.   *If list maintenance. a.* How will client submit changes? *b.* How often is list to be updated? *c.* Will list be used for rental? If so, should test tapes of various quantities be kept "hanging"?

8.   *Tape information. a.* How many bits per inch (1600, 800, 556, etc)? *b.* What track, nine or seven? *c.* What is the blocking factor? *d.* What is the record size? Is the field fixed or variable? *e.* Are tape layout sheet, explanation of codes, sample printout, or "dump" available?

9.   *Tape information – if conversion required. a.* How much information will go onto tape: codes, dollar amounts, references, dates, etc.? *b.* What purpose will the tape be used for: letters, labels, etc.? *c.* Will the client be doing "dupe" elimination? *d.* Will the list be used for rental?

Figure 13-2b

will meet your bid. But you'll pay for it in quality shortcuts or last-minute additional charges, or by putting the supplier out of business. Most likely, you'll also suffer by not getting the job out on time.

Other Bidding Methods.   There are other ways to go, if you have a trained production person on your staff or acting as a consultant.

Some advertisers place their printing on a cost-plus basis—a fixed-percentage profit margin over the actual costs of the job. To do this, however, requires that you know how to estimate and be able to calculate press time, setup time, ink coverage, bindery, and letter-shop functions in the same way that the supplier's own estimator does.

It usually requires no more to work with a printing broker or to let your ad agency handle everything. Not only do they supervise and take responsibility for the entire job, but often they get trade prices that enable them to charge the same as if you had bid on the job directly.

(c) GENERAL MAILING SPECIFICATIONS

1. *What is the quantity?*

2. *When will material be received, and what is mail date?*

3. *Envelopes. a.* Size? Booklet or open-end? Preprinted indicia? *b.* Window or closed? (If window, open or cellophane?) *c.* Paper or polybag?

4. *Number of inserts. a.* Sizes of each? *b.* Prefolded for machine inserting (i.e., no accordion gate or open end folds)? *c.* Order of inserts – from flap to front?

5. *Addressing. a.* If labels, what kind: Cheshire, pressure-sensitive, gummed? *b.* If labels, what is labeled: envelope, BRC, etc.? *c.* If computer forms, to be burst and trimmed? Size of forms: number up, trim size? *d.* If typed address, what font? On what piece? What is the source: directory, cards, galleys, handwritten?

6. *Mailing. a.* Is list provided in strict zip-code sequence? *b.* How many lists? Sizes from smallest to largest? *c.* Class of mail: first, third, bulk? *d.* Is indicia preprinted? *e.* To be metered? *f.* If stamps, what kind: regular, commemorative, bulk-rate, not-for-profit?

7. *Bursting and folding. a.* Size of full finished sheet? *b.* Number up: one or two? *c.* Number of folds and type of fold?

8. *Shipping. a.* Where? *b.* How – what carrier? *c.* Packed in cartons? Who supplies? *d.* Is shipping included in price?

9. *Incidentals. a.* Tipping, stapling, clipping? *b.* Keying? Separately or while labeling? How many different keys? Size and position of each key?

Figure 13-2c

Purchase Orders

Award the job in writing, with the specification sheet appended and all details of price, overruns, delivery, etc., worked out in detail. The suppliers should be asked to sign an acceptance of the detailed order. (See Fig. 13-3.)

Photography

Production managers should be particularly careful about dealing with photographic suppliers. In recent years these crafts have attempted to demand royalties, even on photographs where they are simply executing a layout designed by your art director. This can result in unpleasant disputes and unexpected costs when a test ad or mailing is ready to be rolled out.

Contrary to photographers' ambitions, this practice is not universal, and there is no reason to agree to it unless you want to. Even world-famous photographers and well-known models will often agree to a "buyout" price with no restrictions, or to specifically defined terms for reuse. These are your suppliers. Insist that they agree to your terms, or get another supplier.

Watch out for bills with royalty terms on the back that you haven't agreed to, or for models who hand art directors forms that appear to be simple confirmation of hours worked, but in small type limits the use of the pho-

Production Authorization

Client: Beneficial National Bank	Job Description: Control Direct Mail
	1st Quarter - per attached
Product: Visa/Mastercard Credit	Code: specs
Date: November 9, 1984	Job No: C 91814

WORK CODE	WORK CATEGORY	ORIGINAL	REVISION	FINAL
PRINTING		1,130M + 3%		
DA	Outer Envelope	15,739.15		
DB	Business Reply Card Envelope	10,217.05		
DC	Letter S			
DD	Brochure 1	19,117.65		
DE	Brochure 2			
DG	Continuous Form	13,875.15		
DH	Response Device			
	SUB-TOTAL	58,949.00		
COMPUTER				
DL	List Rental			
DM	List Processing	16,525.00		
DN	Computer Printing	5,883.25		
DO	Reports and Analysis			
		1,180.00		
	SUB-TOTAL	23,588.25		
LETTERSHOP				
DP	Addressing			
DQ	Inserting			
DR	Meter Stamp			
DS	Sort Tie Bag Mail	16,018.75		
	SUB-TOTAL	16,018.75		
AGENCY COMMISSION		17,395.10		
T6	Shipping Air Freight			
T9	Miscellaneous (Inc. Travel, Telephone & Messenger)	500.00		
V4	Sales Tax			
DV	Postage	124,300.00		
	NON--COMMISSIONABLE SUB-TOTAL	124,800.00		
CONTINGENCY		24,075.10		
GROSS TOTAL		264,826.20		

Prepared By:	Approvals		Agency Use Only	
The above estimate is based on normal working schedules and routine corrections. Over-time author's alternatives or changes of specifications will result in increased costs This will be reflected in the final billing. Where major changes are requested a revised estimate will be submitted. According to standard printing trade practices the total quantity delivered may be subject to a shortage or overage of up to 10%. Such changes in quantity are not reflected in this estimate	Project Manager	Date	Date Received	Date
				Date Input
	Production Manager	Date	Job Number	
				To Input Group
	Client's Signature	Date	Authorization Code	Input by

Figure 13-3. Typical production estimate form for preparation of printing and mailing costs.

tographs. Whatever you do, issue your purchase order and have it countersigned before the photo shoot. It is too late to negotiate when the talent is at the studio.

Avoiding Errors

There are two ways to avoid errors. One is to check everything yourself. The other is to be sure that the client, or the senior executive in your own organization, sees and approves every detail at every stage. Do both. And use a sign-off sheet that specifies potential trouble areas such as key number, names, address, phone, copyright notices and prices. Having correct spelling and grammar for the general text won't compensate for spelling the client's name incorrectly or printing the wrong price or expiration date. Jobs and accounts have been lost over such errors.

Proofreading. Proofreaders check the text during the various stages against the original copy. If the copy is wrong, the finished job will be wrong too. But don't count on proofreaders.

My proofreader once "corrected" Barbra Streisand's name to "Barbara" at the last minute, causing understandable consternation at her record company. To avoid problems like this, a proofreader must be given a detailed list of "dos and don'ts," including spelling of all proper names included in the text, styles for numbers and punctuation, and preferred grammatical usage.

Whenever anything is corrected, don't just check the one area that contains the correction. I once saw a piece of copy prepared on a word processor that had a retyped, revised paragraph plugged into an entirely different piece of body copy. On the revised copy the changed paragraph was perfect, but everything else in the text described an entirely different product.

Getting Approvals. The most critical obstacle to cost control is revisions, whether made by the agency, designer, or client. The way to avoid excessive revisions is to be sure to obtain all approvals at each and every step of the creative and production process.

A copy change on a press proof can cost thousands of dollars; on a blueprint, hundreds; on a graphic compilation, about $50; on typed copy, nothing. Obviously, the earlier changes are made, the less they will cost.

Be sure that everything is checked. Don't count on a client or a senior executive to know what to look for. If a layout isn't clear, or the directions are confusing, be sure to point out exactly what illustration goes where, what color the backgrounds will be, and any concerns you may have about the quality of the finished product.

Avoiding mistakes involves more than simply initialing the copy or proofs. The object is not to fix blame but to avoid error. The best sign-off sheets list exactly what each person must check and require a signature next to each item on the list. For example, see Fig. 13-4.

PRODUCTION	MANAGER	DESIGNER
☐ Mock-up OK	☐ Offer clear	☐ Trim size correct
☐ Color breaks OK	☐ Prices correct	☐ Bleed size correct
☐ Traps OK	☐ Shipping info	☐ Live area OK
☐ Address window	☐ Prominent phone	☐ Folds indicated
☐ Coupon fits BRE	☐ Correct URL	☐ Correct photos
☐ Personalization	☐ Expiration date	☐ High res scans
☐ Indicia checked	☐ Return address	☐ Disclaimer
☐ Image quality OK	☐ Legal OK	☐ Postal regs
☐ No moires	☐ Copyright notice	☐ Easy to read
☐ Paper quality OK	☐ Key Codes OK	☐ Easy coupon
	☐ TMs in place	
	☐ On schedule	

Figure 13-4. Sample checklist of elements during production.

I once saw a $30,000 printing job rerun because a client company president didn't realize that computer lettering didn't look a secretary's hand-typed letters. I saw another job rejected because an executive didn't like the very subtle perforations on a letter produced in a pre-fabricated format. The fact that no one else was bothered by these characteristics is irrelevant. The clients were not made aware of these details and had not been asked to sign off on samples as well as on artwork. If they had, the projects would not have become victims of what has been called "the expectation-realization gap."

Avoiding Rush Work

Overtime costs money, and overtime for digital processors, film-makers and printers costs more than overtime for writers and artists. If you must rush a job, put the pressure on the early stages and the approval process, not on the very costly graphic arts stages.

Schedule your job carefully, as described next, and then stick to the schedule. "Walk through" approvals and corrections, and be sure that everyone concerned knows the effect on timetables. It's amazing how often the people who insist that a job be finished on a certain date are precisely the same people who keep making changes or delaying approvals.

Each approval process should have a deadline, just as any other step does. The approver should be notified that delays past a due date will result in extension of the final deadline or perhaps even missing a deadline.

If the basic schedule is adhered to, most rush work can be avoided.

CONTROLLING TIME

When submitting a project for approval, I always make it a practice to submit a timetable as well as an estimate of costs. In some ways, the timetable is more difficult to control than the costs.

Time Requirements

Table 13-1 shows some timing allocations—a composite of schedules used by various graphic arts suppliers and ad agencies. It is important to note that no two are the same.

Though any of these steps can take less time under rush conditions, these are reasonable guidelines for careful cost and quality control. They add up to six to eight weeks for preparing a color ad for a magazine, half that for

TABLE 13-1
OPTIMUM PRODUCTION TIMING

	Black-and-white ads	Color ads	Ads with cards	Labeled mailings	Computer mailings
Orientation and planning	2–4 weeks	2–4 weeks	2–4 weeks	2–4 weeks	2–4 weeks
Copy and rough layout	2–4 weeks	3–5 weeks	3–6 weeks	3–6 weeks	4–6 weeks
Comprehensive layouts	3 days	5 days	5 days	7 days	10 days
Approval and revisions	5 days	7 days	7 days	7 days	7 days
Typesetting and mechanicals	7 days	10 days	14 days	14 days	16 days
Mechanical approval and revisions	3 days	4 days	4 days	4 days	7 days
Color preparation, engraving, and proofing	5 days	10 days	10 days	15 days	15 days
List order and delivery				4–5 weeks	4–5 weeks
List preparation, including merge				3 weeks	4 weeks
Printing, including computer forms			3 weeks	4 weeks	5 weeks
Envelope conversion				1–4 weeks	1–4 weeks
Labeling or computer printing				5 days	10 days
Inserting and mailing				10 days	10 days

Note: These optimum schedules include scheduling and waiting time. On tightly scheduled projects, most of these steps can be cut in half if suppliers with available time are prescheduled. Very complex projects or mail quantities over 1 million pieces may take more time during the last two or three stages. Of course, very simple projects can take much less time. It is possible to get a simple ad or letter produced in a day or two if that is the objective.

a black-and-white ad, and between two and four months for direct mail, depending on whether or not it is computerized.

These are optimum schedules, within which costs and quality can be carefully budgeted and controlled. Unfortunately, such schedules seem to be the exception rather than the rule. The need to get a new product on the market before competition does, or before waiting for results of a previous mailing before sending out the next, often requires that time allocations be reduced substantially. My experience is that the schedules can be cut in half without serious effect on costs. Much tighter schedules can require severe quality risks or "crash" costs necessitated by night and weekend work.

Critical Path Scheduling

Critical path method is a business planning technique originally developed as part of a process called Program Evaluation and Review Technique (PERT). It has been used to plan complex research and development projects such as the space program and major construction projects. In its most advanced usage, every step is programmed into a computer, progress is reviewed, and "critical dates" are called to the attention of appropriate managers.

Basically, the critical path method involves placing a time factor on each phase in a process, figuring what the necessary preliminary steps are for each, and laying the phases out in the indicated sequence.

This is sort of a "backward timetable," beginning with the finished project and working back step by step, perhaps plotting the time factors with lines on a sheet of graph paper.

Figure 13-5 is an example of this process applied to a complex direct mailing on a 16-week schedule. Note that this project was completed in four months only because several steps were conducted at the same time, so that lists and mechanicals would both be ready on the same date.

Different companies will have entirely different schedules. For instance, large corporations may require a week for legal approval. A mutual fund may need four weeks to get the NASD or other officials to pass on a simple letter. Companies with in-house computer facilities may be able to cut time on list processing. If only house lists are being used, the two or three weeks of waiting time for delivery of rented lists can be cut to a week or so.

WAYS TO SAVE TIME

There are many ways to shorten a schedule or, at the very least, to prevent a job from getting behind schedule. Here are some that may be helpful.

Use Good Suppliers.   A rush job is no place to use untested or out-of-town suppliers. Use people you can count on.

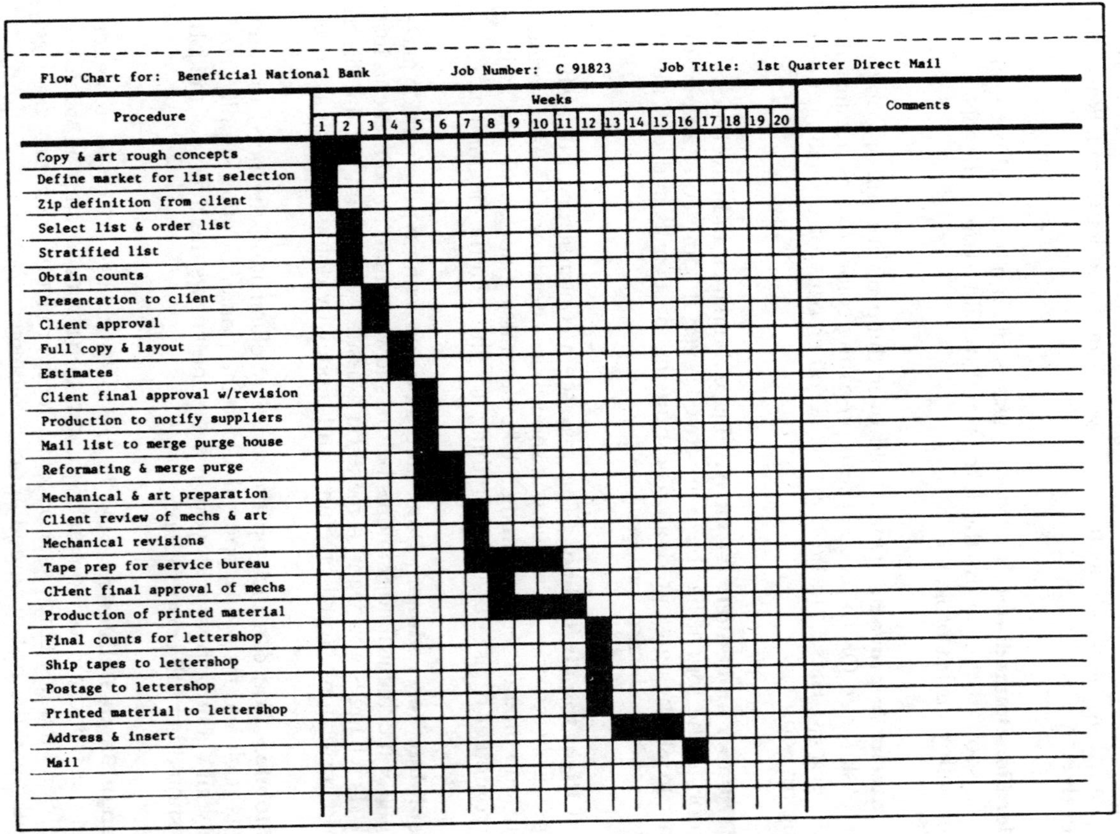

Figure 13-5. This flowchart provides a convenient way to plan any promotional project.

Count Everyone In.   Let everyone—client, staff, and supplier—know what the deadline is and why it's important. If possible, bring all these people together in a "starter" meeting so that all of them will know what is expected of them and how their part of the job affects everyone else. You'll be amazed by the shortcuts they can work out if you let them talk to each other directly.

Order Lists Immediately.   Ordering lists is often the critical path on any job. As soon as you know the format and the lists you want, place your order with your list broker.

Get Interim Approvals.   Don't hold everything up for minor copy revisions. Ask for an OK to proceed with preparing color artwork, for instance, or envelopes. These can be done while other parts of a mailing are still being revised.

Order Paper and Envelopes Early.   Place the paper and envelope orders as soon as the format has been approved, even if some copy and art elements are still being worked out. These are the most costly and least flexible parts of the production process.

Get It Right the First Time.   This may seem contradictory, but rush jobs are precisely the ones on which you should slow down and be extra careful. There's no time to redo anything. Make dummies. Check with the mailing and computer firms. Be sure everything is right from the beginning.

Consolidate Corrections.   Don't take time correcting type errors or making minor mechanical adjustments before showing them to your client. Just mark the changes you want to make on a tissue overlay and ask the client to add corrections. You'll save time and money by doing them all at once.

Be Mobile.   You can pick up days just by eliminating the need to send proofs back and forth for approval. Go to the printer or other supplier, and take your client or boss with you. If everyone knows the timing of the job, you should get full cooperation.

Arrange Batch Deliveries.   On large jobs that have to go to a binder, envelope fabricator, or computer printer, don't wait to ship all copies at once. Send the first batch as soon as it's ready, to let the next processor get started. Send the rest in agreed-upon increments.

Pin Down All Interim Dates.   Be sure that delivery dates—and sometimes even the time of day—are indicated in writing and pointed out to each supplier. "As soon as possible" and even "rush" are meaningless. If suppliers have a specific time to aim for, they are more likely to make it, and will be less likely to bump your job for some larger customer's rush job.

CONTROLLING QUALITY

Presuming that the layout of the ad or mailing represents what you really are looking for, the problem of quality control in the production process is one of fidelity—being faithful to the original design.

Text Additions.   Good design includes a good type-specification process. A frequent problem is that lawyers or others add long phrases that were not in the original copy.

The wrong solution to this problem is to "make it fit," with illustrations reduced, spacing omitted, and type set small and crowded. This can impair the overall style of the ad or mailing. A better solution is to sit down with all parties concerned, including the copywriter, and make deliberate choices as to what can be cut or omitted.

Catalog Corrections.   In all catalog companies, the most critical element is the choice of merchandise. Somehow this is never "final." Despite planning and deadlines, there is always a hot item someone wants to add, or one included that is no longer available.

Rather than risk missing a printer's scheduled press time or a critical seasonal mailing date, I suggest planning for the inevitable changes. If you must drop a product and no replacement is available, repeat an item from another page. Oddly, offering it in two places will result in added sales.

Taking advantage of last minute additions is another story. You can plan for this by leaving a space which can be used to feature a "special" item or to announce a new one.

Illustrations

If you're using photography, go to the photography session and look at all the details that the photographer might miss. Chances are, the photographer will be concentrating on lighting and composition. You should look at how the model is dressed and posed, whether your product is displayed at the best possible angle, whether the background is distracting, and whether the props create the right image. The photo will be no better than the scene at the moment the picture is taken.

Cropping and retouching usually can't add quality that's not in the photo. You can remove some defects or mask out an error, but the best bet is to get the picture right at the beginning.

Consider using digital cameras for new illustrations. While the most popular digital cameras won't reproduce in fine screens as well as scanned prints, newer, more expensive professional cameras are available which will meet the most exacting standards.

If you're using original artwork, then have it drawn oversized and insist that it be right. Revise it as many times as you have to, until you know it's what you want. This is not the time to keep quiet to spare the artist's feelings.

Be sure to scan any artwork and look at it in the size that it will actually appear. Embarrassing details can suddenly show up when a 35-mm chrome is blown up to a larger size. On the other hand, a computer composition that looks exciting on a large screen can lose all its detail in a smaller size.

Photographic Processes

Color separators and digital processors have the common objective of converting the computer output or mechanical paste-up into a form that can be turned into press plates and printed at a newspaper, magazine, or printing plant. The processes vary according to the end use and the artwork provided, but the objective is the same: fidelity.

The way to get what you want is to be sure that everyone knows what that is before starting. You have to supply good examples and clear instructions. For instance, if you are shooting gold coins and want a specific tone of gold, then be sure to show the photo processors a sample. They are not mind readers. If two photos of the same product start with different colors, the finished printing job will not be consistent either. Computer imaging can perform virtual miracles with illustrations, combine scenes from different photographs, change colors, and create any illustration fantasy one can envision.

When seeing proofs, insist that press proofs be pulled on the stock specified. Usually the only adjustments that are possible without substantial expense are color specifications, but the overall quality of the printing job can be no better than the artwork you provide. Whenever possible make adjustments in the computer, not at the printer.

Printing Adjustments

It would take years for an advertiser to learn everything a printer knows about achieving quality. All you have to understand is that by the time the job gets on the press, the printer's options are very limited.

Quality begins with the computer output. By the time the piece gets on press, all that can be adjusted is the impression, the speed, and the color. Yet it is always the printer who gets blamed if the job doesn't look right.

Impression is a function of the make-ready process, in which the pressure between the printing cylinder (whether letterpress or offset) and the base cylinder behind the paper being printed is adjusted slightly.

Speed can affect the ink application and how fast the printed sheet passes through a drying station.

Color can be lightened or darkened on press, but it will turn out better if it starts out right in the proof stage

Other Processes. If quality is the supreme requirement, then consider— when first planning the job—using letterpress or gravure printing rather than the more common offset lithography. These processes sometimes are used when printing illustrated books, photography magazines, and fine-art reproductions. The differences are dramatic, and the costs are not excessive. The problem is that most printers have converted to the higher-speed offset process and will discourage letterpress and gravure printing which cannot be produced in their own shop.

Mailing Lists.   The simplest process should be placing orders for the previously selected mailing lists. Unfortunately, because there are so many sources and sub-suppliers involved, such orders frequently are mishandled. I once ordered ten lists for a test of a new product that included both sex-select and sectional center zip-select. Over 40 percent of the names did not meet specifications and had to be reordered.

The only way to catch many errors is to examine a "dump" or printed output of the lists. To wait until they are ready to be merged for labeling or computer printing is a mistake, as it can then be too late to rerun incorrect lists.

Shipment.   Here's another apparently simple process—but what disasters can take place! Be sure to specify whether a job is to be banded, in cartons, or stacked on skids, and choose how you want it shipped. I've shared many anxious moments with production managers, waiting for news that a magazine insert, last seen on a loading dock in St. Louis, had finally arrived at the publication only hours before final closing. In an early night job at a lettershop, I experienced first hand the extra work and time required because inserts arrived from a printer in cartons without separators. It was impossible to stack them into an insert feed tray. Each piece had to be sorted and re-stacked by hand.

Shipping and freight are not to be taken for granted and should be considered, planned, and executed correctly. Any shipping instructions to suppliers should be sure to include not only when something should be shipped, but how.

Lettershop.   What can go wrong in a lettershop? Plenty. For one thing, there have been plenty of horror stories about mailing the wrong insert to the wrong list. For another, it's easy to completely omit one of the pieces of a mailing.

Careful written instructions and clear insert coding must be provided. Each and every piece should include an item number that is clearly visible without unfolding. Your inserting instructions should clearly list the sequence, the facing, and the nesting of the various pieces. A sample package, stapled together so that the sequence will not become confused, should be provided as soon as printed samples are ready.

A Phillipsburg inserter stacks one piece on top of another using suction. A Pitney-Bowes inserter uses rollers to nest one inside another. Inserting equipment can have 6, 8, 10, or even 14 "stations," each inserting a single component. The more stations you need, the more costly the inserting will be and the more difficult it will be to find a supplier with the right equipment. The same for the envelope size. Most inserting machines can't handle 9 × 12 envelopes.

Also, if you don't want your mailing-date delayed, be sure to send the lettershop a certified check to cover postage. They can't send bulk mail or buy postage stamps until the Postal Service is paid. As a rule, mailing services will never mail until they have the postage in their hands.

Proof of Mailing.   How do you know the mailing went out on time, the way you wanted it? The final test is to see how and when it arrives in the mail.

Always "seed" a list with names of some of your key executives, and be sure they are merged into the list at the computer house, not at the lettershop.

It's also a good idea to include in your seeding of the list some people in other parts of the country, so that you can get an idea of the Postal Service's delivery at the time of the mailing. It will make a difference when you're trying to read results if you discover, for example, that your mail still has not been delivered on the other coast.

U.S. Monitor is a company that was created to handle seeding and monitoring for both domestic and international mailings. Their costs are very reasonable considering the value of their service. Other firms have announced that they will also be providing this service.

SUPPLIERS ARE PEOPLE TOO

Choosing graphic arts suppliers is more than a matter of getting three bids and picking the lowest one. You might save 5 or 10 percent with strict purchasing procedures, just as you might save a small part of the commission by not using an ad agency, but these economics can cost you 50, 100, or 200 percent or more where it really counts: in response rates.

Of course, get competitive bids; but put service, cooperation, and creative contribution into the mix when you make your final decision.

Your suppliers are not servants, and they are not the enemy. They can and should be part of your team, involved in the creative process at as early a stage as possible. The contributions they can make are enormous.

For instance, a printer can suggest a slight change in size that will make better use of paper sizes, or can help you develop a format that will do a better job of presenting your particular message at a better price.

A lettershop may offer ideas that can save you both time and money, such as widening an address window or changing a fold so as to facilitate inserting.

Too many marketers simply prepare their specifications and send them out for bids, without making suppliers part of the process. Different printers, for example, may vary only slightly in price. But one of them may show you how to combine two elements in the package and save 25 percent of the total cost. Isn't *that* the real economy?

Great North American Widget Corporation, Consumer Solo-Mailing Campaign Two-for-One Widget Offer (Approx. Net Quantity, 100,000 [100M]; Scheduled Drop Date, 7/28/97)

A. CREATIVE

1. Preliminary roughs and dummies	$ 420
2. Copy, including revises	3,925
3. B&W Computer Mockup (headlines & text in place; illustrations & photos—position only)	940
4. Contingency	575

Total $ 5,860   (6.27%)

B. ART & PREPARATION

1. Photography	$ 940
2. Model fees	420
3. Photo direction	520
4. Line illustrations (7)	365
5. Color Computer Mockup (final copy & art elements in position, incld. low res scans of photography)	630
6. Color separations (2 randoms)	420
7. Colorkeys	260
8. Image Assembly of Film	625
9. Contingency	1,150

Total $ 5,330   (5.70%)

C. PRINTING PRODUCTION

1. 4-pg. litho let., 8-1/2" x 11" 2 colors (105M @ $31.26/M)	$ 3,285
2. 16-pg. booklet, 5-1/2" x 8-1/2" 2 colors (105M @ $112.16/M)	11,775
3. Reply card, 3-1/2" x 5-1/2" 2 colors (105M @ $18.90/M)	1,985
4. BRE, #7-3/4" one color (105M @ $18.30/M)	1,920
5. Outer env., 6" x 9" 2 color, cello window (105M @ $66.24/M)	6,950
6. Contingency	1,500

Total $27,415   (29.34%)

D. MAILING LISTS

1. Mail order respondents (tape) 70M @ $100/M	$ 7,000
2. Active magazine subs (tape) 45M @ $65/M	2,925
3. Contingency	1,210

Total $11,135   (11.92%)

E. COMPUTER PROCESSING

1. Reformatting, data conversion, etc.	$ 470
2. Merge/Purge (115M @ $11.25/M)	1,295
3. Code and run 4-up labels (100M @ $4.35/M)	435
4. Reports & directory printout	220
5. Contingency	550

Total $ 2,970   (3.18%)

F. LETTERSHOP PRODUCTION

1. Insert, label, sort, mail, etc. (100M @ $35.38)	$ 3,540
2. Affix bulk-rate stamps (100M @ $6/M)	600
3. Audit & pull samples (100M @ $2.15/M)	215
4. Contingency	375

Total $ 4,730   (5.06%)

G. ALLOCATED FEES

1. Ad Agency	$ 6,200
2. Consultant	1,800
3. Contingency	1,000

Total $ 9,000   (9.63%)

H. POSTAGE

1. Automation (Presorted & Barcoded)/Basic @ 270/M	$27,000 (28.90%)

Budgeted Grand Total $93,440   (100.00%)

[Courtesy of DMA *Statistical Fact Book* 1998]

Figure 13-6. Direct mail—Sample working budget.

The way to build a relationship with your suppliers is to make them part of the team and to let them know that they have work from you as long as they keep their prices in line. You want your account to be important to them, and it won't be important to them if they have to low-ball their bids to get each and every job. My suggestion is to take bids on every job from new suppliers, but to change suppliers only when you can save at least 10 percent. In that case, *change suppliers*; don't rotate them or play one against the other. When you find good suppliers, be good to them as long as they're good to you.

14

MAILING LISTS

Direct mail is the world's largest advertising medium, and mailing lists are the key to its success. It is an industry axiom that a poor mailing to a good list can be profitable, but that no mailing—no matter how well conceived—will work if sent to the wrong list.

In all direct marketing, the medium is the market. In direct mail this applies doubly. The mailing list is not a way to reach a market—it *is* the market.

Direct mail is a communications medium in its own right, and can justify its place in the world of advertising media even when not used to generate responses. It is unfortunate that advertising agency media departments don't analyze this medium as they do all others. If they did, millions of dollars would switch from publications and broadcast to direct mail, just as they are switching funds to Internet applications.

TWO KEY FACTORS

The economic facts of life are that on a cost per circulation basis direct mail costs about ten times the cost of print advertising, and 50 to 100 times the cost of broadcast. Why should an advertiser pay $500/M for direct mail rather than $50/M for a magazine advertisement? There are two reasons: selectivity and space. To compensate for the higher cost, direct mail has to be ten times more selective or offer ten times the space, or some combination of the two factors.

Selectivity

Mass advertisers are perfectly willing to pay more for a specialty magazine, like Golf World, than for a general publication. If we look at CPTM (cost per thousand target prospects) it is obvious that the CPM figures are useless. If you want to reach female readers, a women's magazine at $50/M costs you just that, while a mass magazine with equal gender distribution and the same CPM rate actually costs you $100/M for the audience you want. Add a specific age group, or a specific interest of lifestyle, and the usable circulation narrows even further and the CPTM begins to approach the cost of mail.

Space

The same general agency media departments will admit that a full-page ad is worth twice the cost of a half-page ad, and twice again for a spread instead of a page. But what would you pay for a magazine or newspaper ad with no limits on size, and almost total flexibility in format. What if the ad was eight-pages in full color? With a bound in order form? With a letter inserted? And personalized? And what if you could tip-on a sample or a scent strip? Or perhaps enclose a CD? Or a videotape? How many "pages" would that be the equivalent of?

The Combination

When you combine the two elements the cost advantages become very clear. Say you have five times the selectivity, and five times the space, for a combined factor of 25. Multiple your $50/CPM by 25 and you have $1250/M. Suddenly the $500/M, or $750/M, or even $1000/M direct mail package looks like a very sound investment.

But the advantage is good only if you use elements which justify the cost. Send mail to everyone in the phone book and you are no longer selective. Limit the scope of your mailpiece and you no longer have the space advantage.

Tactically, the need to make good use of the added "space" dictates the objectives. With all that space, why stop at getting recall? Or creating an impression? You have the ability to take the prospect further—to demonstrate features, dramatize benefits, overcome objections, provide argument and assurances—all leading to asking for the order or, at least, a decision to buy. Using Starch terminology, why stop at "recalled" or "read most" when you can go all the way to "intent to buy" or, better yet, "check enclosed."

Sometimes print and broadcast are called "the big guns" of marketing. Direct mail, then, is the sharpshooter. With the high cost of direct mail, you can't send your messages wildly into the night as in broadcast. You have to decide who is your best target, where to find that target, and then take careful aim.

Those who know how to use this medium—how to select from over a billion names on 50,000 different mailing lists—have in their hands the most powerful and profitable tool in the world of marketing.

WELCOME TO LISTWORLD!

How is it possible to choose from and deal with the vast and flexible array of media possibilities? An equally vast and flexible industry of compilers, managers, brokers and processors has emerged to help.

List Owners are the companies whose offers generate responses that are compiled into lists. The lists may be "actives," or "expires." They can consist of magazine subscribers, charity donors, book club members or mail order buyers. If generated within the last three or six months, they may be called "hot line" names. They may be segmented by the item they bought, the size of their donation, their gender, marital status, age, and any of a number of other factors. They may also be "enhanced" with information from various databases or the demographics of their household location. But they are still basically the names of people who responded to a direct-marketing offer.

List Compilers are, in a sense, also list owners. The difference is that their lists are not usually respondents to offers, but compilations taken from other sources. On a mass scale, they can be based on car registrations, marriage licenses, birth records, property transfers or voting registration lists. Or they can be special compilations for special needs—donors to charities, members of corporation boards, owners of large barbecues who filled out warranty cards. One kind of compilation has grown so important that I list it as a separate category—survey names, or the information on category usage, brand preference, buying intentions and even physical ailments that makes modern database-marketing possible.

List Managers market the lists for the owners, in return for part of the list rental fees. They maintain advertising campaigns and sales organizations to bring the lists to the attention of large mailers, agencies and list brokers. They are also responsible for screening and approving rental requests, processing orders, collecting payments, preparing tapes to customer specifications, and getting the information shipped in time. They prosper by building the list-rental revenues of the owners they represent.

List Brokers work for the mailer, not for the list owner, though they retain part of the rental fee as their commission just as the manager does. It is their job to help the mailer select appropriate lists, to obtain information and rates, and to obtain rental approvals. The list brokers draw on their experience with other clients to provide informed advice to their customer, the mailer. Unlike the manager, they should be unbiased in their recommendations even when a list is managed by an affiliate of the broker, as is often the case. Often advertising agencies have fully staffed list departments that supplement or replace the list broker. Both brokers and agencies compete by helping list renters locate lists that are profitable to the mailer and are thus likely to be used again and again in larger quantities, called "roll-outs."

List Processors may be independent or may be affiliated with the list owner, mailer, list broker, manager, printer, agency, fulfillment house or lettershop. These are basically data processing facilities, sometimes called Service Bureaus. They receive lists from various sources, conform formats and address styles, merge the lists, enhance them, add key numbers, and prepare final "output tapes" for the printer or lettershop.

The process includes eliminating people who have notified the DMA or the list owner that they do not wish to receive such mail, people who have moved and have left no forwarding address that can be corrected (the Postal Service's National Change Of Address service), or those with bad credit. From a direct marketing perspective, no matter what a person's assets or income, if they have not honored previous obligations to a direct marketer they are "bad credit." The Credit Index and Experian companies compile these lists and make them available through list processors.

Anyone starting out in this business should make consulting a good broker a priority. Most brokers are staffed with experienced professionals using custom computer systems. Not only is their information up-to-date, but they are in a position to make recommendations based on their knowledge of which lists have been selected for other clients and which have been tried but not repeated. The advertiser gets irreplaceable advice and service, yet pays no more than if ordering directly.

LISTS OF LISTS

There are many ways to learn about what lists are available. Brokers will send you "List Cards," like magazine Rate Cards. Some publish their own mini-catalogs. The trade papers devote whole sections to announcements of new lists.

The reference source I find most convenient is SRDS *Direct Marketing List Source,* published by Standard Rate and Data Service, Wilmette, IL. This is the same organization that produces the standard reference works on newspapers, consumer magazines, business publications, broadcast and a dozen other media categories.

This huge two-volume directory contains over 1700 pages of detailed information about more than 24,000 lists organized in 212 market classifications. A subscription costing about $500 a year includes six bimonthly issues, interim updates and access to an on-line version which contains real-time updates and hot links to brokers, managers and compilers. SRDS also offers an Internet service with advanced functionality called DirectNet, designed for list brokers and agencies.

SRDS Contents

The lists in the main sections of the directory are divided into three broad categories: *business, consumer,* and *farm.* Both compiled lists and response lists are included. Other sections cover Canadian lists, international lists, co-op mail programs and package insert programs.

Consumer lists include more than 60 broad interest categories with every type of demographic, geographic, and psychographic breakdown, including responders to every type of solicitation imaginable. Anyone who has ever joined, subscribed, inquired, donated or answered a questionnaire is on one or more of these lists.

Business lists include over 150 categories with both compiled lists of different kinds of businesses and response lists of buyers of business products, subscribers to business publications, and professionals in various business specialties. There are also seven categories of farm lists.

These categories appear in full in Fig. 14-1.

RESPONSE LISTS

Other than a company's own house lists, response lists are the workhorse of consumer direct mail. Sometimes called *buyers' lists,* or *mail-order lists,* they include every classification related to a consumer's previous response to a direct marketing offer.

The names can be those of buyers, subscribers, inquirers, donors, members, or depositors. They can be new customers, active ones, or former ones. They can and do represent every conceivable area of human interest.

All have two things in common: 1) they have identified themselves, by an action, as people with a specific interest, and 2) they have demonstrated that they are willing, when properly motivated, to respond to an offer in a direct-response communications medium. This medium may or may not necessarily have been direct mail, however.

It is the knowledge that the people on the list are responsive which sets these lists apart from other types of lists. This becomes an even more accurate indicator if they have responded recently, if the value of the order resembled the one sought, if they have responded frequently or to many similar offers (such names are called *multi-buyers*), and if the source is similar to the one being used. By source I mean direct mail, telemarketing, television, e-mail, or other forms. This similarity is a big positive when added to the common-sense "affinity" of similarities to the product or service.

For example, for a new ad for a mattress, try a list of buyers of a book on back pain. For a catalog of religious books, rent the names of members of a religious music club or subscribers to an appropriate magazine. For fundraising for a multi-purpose research institute, go after donors who have given to causes relating to specific goals, and version your letters to stress the work in that field being done by the institute.

Thousands of mailing lists are available, and each one usually can be further selected and segmented.

Figure 14-2 is an example of a consumer listing—the Columbia House Music Club. Note that this is just one of the lists offered by this major direct marketer, which also has lists of video buyers and record and tape buyers.

BUSINESS LISTS

3	Advertising & Marketing
5	Air Conditioning, Heating, Plumbing, Sheet Metal & Ventilation
7	Amusements
9	Appliances
11	Architecture
13	Arts
15	Automatic Data Processing - Computers
17	Automotive, Automobiles, Tires, Batteries, Accessories, Service Stations, Garages
19	Aviation & Aerospace
21	Baking
23	Banking & Financial
25	Barbers
27	Beauty & Hairdressing
29	Boating
31	Books & Book Trade
33	Bottling
35	Brewing, Distilling & Beverages
37	Brick, Tile, Building Materials
39	Brushes
41	Building
43	Building Management & Real Estate
45	Business Executives
46	Business Firms
47	Camps & Camping
49	Cemetery, Monuments & Funeral Suppliers
51	Ceramics
52	Certified Public Accountants & Accountants
53	Chain Stores
55	Chemical & Chemical Process Industries
57	China & Glassware
61	Clothing & Furnishing Goods (Men's)
63	Clothing & Furnishing Goods (Women's)
65	Coal Merchandising
67	Coin-Operated and Vending Machines
69	Confectionery
71	Control & Instrumentation Systems
73	Corsets, Brassieres & Undergarments
75	Cosmetics
77	Dairy Products
79	Dental
169	Insurance
171	Interior Design/Space Planning
173	International Trade
175	Jewelry & Watchmaking
177	Journalism
179	Landscape, Garden Supplies, Seed & Nursery Trade
181	Laundry & Dry Cleaning
183	Leather, Boots & Shoes
185	Legal
187	Lighting & Lighting Fixtures
191	Luggage & Leather Goods
193	Lumber & Forest Industries
195	Maintenance
197	Maritime, Marine, Shipbuilding, Repair & Operating
201	Materials Handling & Distribution
203	Meats & Provisions
205	Medical & Surgical
207	Metal, Metalworking & Machinery
213	Mining (Coal, Metal & Non-Metallic)
215	Motion, Talk, Sound, Commercial Pictures, Etc.
217	Motor Trucks & Accessories
219	Motorcycle & Bicycle
221	Moving & Storage
223	Music & Music Trades
225	Notions & Fancy Goods
229	Nursing & Health
233	Ocean Science and Engineering
235	Office Equipment & Stationery
236	Office Equipment Mail Order Buyers
237	Office Methods & Management
241	Optical & Optometric
245	Packaging (Mfrs.) Paperboard
247	Packaging (Users)
249	Paint, Painting & Decorating
251	Paper
253	Parks, Public
255	Petroleum & Oil
257	Pets & Pet Supplies
259	Photographic
261	Plant & Manufacturing Executives

CONSUMER LISTS

502	Almanacs & Directories
506	Art & Antiques
508	Automotive
510	Aviation
512	Babies
514	Boating & Yachting
515	Book Buyers - Consumer
516	Brides
518	Business Leaders
520	Children
520A	Collectibles
521	College & Alumni
521A	Consumer Electronics, Video & Video Games
522	Contributors (Philanthropic)
524	Crafts, Hobbies & Models
525	Credit Card Holders
527	Disabilities
528	Dogs & Pets
530	Dressmaking & Needlework
532	Education & Self-Improvement
534	Entertainment
536	Epicurean & Specialty Foods
538	Ethnic
544	Fashions - Clothing
546	Fishing & Hunting
548	Fraternal, Professional Groups, Service Clubs & Associations
549	Game Buyers, Contest & Puzzle Participants
550	Gardening (Home)
551	Gay & Lesbian
552	General
553	General Merchandise Mail Order Buyers
554	Gifts - Gift Buyers
556	Health
558	Home & Family Service
558A	Home Computers & Software
559	Horses, Riding & Breeding
560	Insurance Buyers
561	Investors
562	Labor - Trade Unions
563	Land & Real Estate Investors
564	Magazines

Figure 14-1. Table of Contents of SRDS *Direct Marketing* List Source.

81 Department, General Merchandise & Specialty Stores
83 Discount Marketing
85 Display
87 Draperies & Curtains
89 Drugs, Pharmaceutics
91 Educational
93 Electrical
95 Electronic Engineering
97 Engineering & Construction
99 Engineers
101 Farm Implements & Suppliers
107 Feed, Grain & Milling
109 Fertilizer and Agricultural Chemicals
113 Fire Protection
115 Fishing Commercial
117 Floor Coverings
119 Florists & Floriculture
121 Food Processing & Distribution
123 Funeral Directors
125 Fur Trade, Fur Farming, Trapping, Etc.
127 Furniture & Upholstery
129 Gas
133 Giftware, Antiques, Art Goods, Decorative Accessories, Greeting Cards, Etc.
135 Glass
137 Golf
139 Government Administrative Services & Public Works – Municipal, Township, County, State, Federal
141 Grocery
143 Hardware & Housewares
145 Home Economics
147 Home Furnishings
149 Hospital & Hospital Administration
151 Hotels, Motels, Clubs & Resorts
156 Human Resources
161 Industrial Distribution
163 Industrial Purchasing
165 Infants', Childrens' & Teen Age Goods
167 Institutions

263 Plastics & Composition Products
265 Plumbing
267 Police, Detective & Security
269 Pollution Control, Environment, Ecology, Energy
271 Poultry & Poultry Products
273 Power & Power Plants
275 Printing & Printing Processes
277 Produce (Fruits & Vegetables)
279 Product Design Engineering
281 Public Transportation
283 Radio & Television
285 Railroad
289 Religious
291 Rental & Leasing Equipment
295 Restaurants & Food Service
297 Roads, Streets, Etc.
299 Roofing
301 Rubber
303 Safety, Accident Prevention
305 Sales Management
309 Schools & School Administration
311 Science, Research & Development
315 Selling and Salesmanship
316 Small Office/Home Office
317 Sporting Goods
319 Stone Products, Etc.
323 Swimming Pools
327 Telephone & Communications
329 Textiles & Knit Goods
331 Tobacco
333 Toys, Hobbies and Novelties
335 Trailers & Accessories
337 Transportation, Traffic, Shipping & Shipping Room Supplies
339 Travel
341 Venetian Blinds/Storm Windows
343 Veterinary
345 Water Supply & Sewage Disposal
347 Welding
349 Wire & Wire Products
351 Woodworking

566 Mechanics & Science
568 Men's
572 Military, Naval & Veterans
578 Music & Record Buyers
584 Occult, Astrological & Metaphysical
586 Occupant & Resident
588 Opportunity Seekers
590 Photography
592 Political & Social Topics
593 Premium & Catalog Buyers
594 Professional
596 Religious & Denominational
598 Senior Citizens
600 Society
602 Sports
604 Teenagers
606 Travel
612 Women's

FARM LISTS

700 Dairy & Dairy Breeds
702 Diversified Farming & Farm Home
704 Farm Education & Vocations
710 Field Crops & Soil Management
714 Land Use & Conservation
716 Livestock & Breed
718 Poultry

Figure 14-1. (*Continued*)

COLUMBIA HOUSE MUSIC CLUB
Data Verified: Feb 24, 1999.

Location ID: 10 DCLS 578   Mid 611386-000
Columbia House
  1221 Ave. of the Americas, New York, NY 10020. Phone
  212-596-2428. Fax 212-596-2475.

1. PERSONNEL
  Dir. Sales—JoAnna De Gennaro, Phone 212-596-2428.
  Asst Acct Exec—Patty Diaz, Phone 212-596-2431.
  Client Service Asst.—Eddie Ahmad, Phone 212-596-2427.

2. SUMMARY DESCRIPTION
  Members in good standing from music clubs.

3. LIST SOURCE
  Direct mail, space ads.

4. SELECTIONS WITH COUNTS
  Updated: Feb 24, 1999.

	Total Number	Price per/M
CD active members	6,800,000	*95.00
Cassette Club active members	400,000	*85.00
Monthly paid hotlinenew members	225,000	+10.00
Monthly hotline payers	1,000,000	+15.00
PC owner	1,200,000	+5.00
Merchandise buyers	600,000	+15.00
Change of address (monthly)	250,000	*95.00
Lifestyle interest selections:		
Collectors	295,000	+10.00
Contributors	130,000	"
Cooking/gourmet foods	480,000	"
Crafts	395,000	"
Gardening	705,000	"
Investors	345,000	"
Sports/fitness	715,000	"
Pet owners	510,000	"

(*) Fundraiser Rates: 10.00/M off base rate for cultural/
membership fundraisers; 20.00 off base rate for all others.
Minimum order 10,000.

4A. OTHER SELECTIONS
  Listening preference:, Christian, country, easy listening, jazz,
latin, popular, rock, classical; key coding, 1.00/M extra; geo,
gender, title only, PC owners, multi buyers 1+, 5.00/M extra;
multi buyers 2+, multi buyers 3+, 6.00/M extra; multi buyers
4+, 7.00/M extra; multi buyers 5+, credit card buyers, exact
age, 10.00/M extra; incidence of children, 12.00/M extra.

6. METHOD OF ADDRESSING
  Cheshire labels, 4-up; pressure sensitive labels, 6.00/M
extra; mag tape, 25.00 fee.

8. RESTRICTIONS
  No political fundraisers.

Figure 14-2

Those lists, like the one shown from the music club, have names in the millions.

Note that the list is useful in several ways. People on this list are not only likely to be interested in music, but also to be "new triers" or "early adopters" because they own the latest tool for music reproduction. Accordingly they are more likely to try other new products. In addition, the music preferences tell you something about the personality of the member, to the extent that music preferences are consistent. For example, classical music members are more likely to respond to an art offer, and country music members are more likely to honor their obligations than members in some other categories.

As you can see, this listing includes the owner of the list and the names of their staff list sales personnel. Most list owners use a list manager—a company retained to manage and promote the list on a commission basis. (See Fig. 14-5 and 14-6.) The list manager is the source of specialized information and the clearinghouse for rental availabilities. However, the customer need not contact the owner or manager. Instead, you should work with your agency or a list broker—a company specializing in recommending and coordinating list rentals for customers. Such companies usually have all the data you need in their own files, plus experience on how the list has worked for their other clients. They will contact the manager for clearances and orders.

These listings include the rental price per thousand names for each of several subcategories, plus surcharges for additional segmentation. Usually there are notations on minimum test quantities and on requirements for advance approval.

Many advertisers find it convenient to assemble their own file of list data, usually pages or cards with this same basic information. List brokers usually provide such cards as backup for their recommendations.

COMPILED LISTS

People not familiar with direct marketing often think of compiled lists first. These might be names and addresses drawn from the telephone book, automobile registrations, association memberships, directories, warranty-card registrations, or any similar source. The defining characteristic—what dramatically differentiates compiled lists from response lists—is that there is no indication of previous willingness to subscribe, buy, donate, or otherwise respond by mail.

Such lists provide expanded coverage of market areas, including certain psychographic and demographic characteristics as well as large quantities of names in precise definitions not available in response lists.

There is a theory in direct marketing that people who have recently made one key decision in their lives, or a basic change of any type, are more likely than most to make other changes. Consequently, very successful lists have been established identifying new parents (births—families with children: 275,000 new names per month), newlyweds (couples—newly married: 50,000 names per month), and recently moved families (new movers: 800,000 names per month). This type of psychographic characteristic can be successful for a wide range of products and services. Obviously, children's products do well with new-parents lists; but so do cameras, correspondence schools, and self-help publications. Evidently, the new addition to the family adds a new sense of ambition and responsibility as well.

Automobile-owner lists, in those states where compiling them is still permitted, are an extremely valuable means of selecting prospects, not just for automobiles, but for any product whose audience may vary by the personality factors indicated by the model (minivan or sports car, for instance), and age of car.

Some compiled lists are actually pooled lists, where list-owners have combined data or enhanced their lists to make them more interesting to renters. One factor which may be available, and which can narrow the gap between response lists and compiled lists, is "recent mail-order purchase."

Figure 14-3 is an example of a typical compiled list of families who have changed addresses during the year or, for a higher price, of those who have moved within the previous two weeks.

EXPERIAN NEW MOVER DATABASE

experian

Location ID: 10 DCLS 586   **Mid 043064-000**
Experian Information Solutions, Inc.
   701 Experian Parkway, Allen, TX 75013-3718. Phone 972-
   390-5000. Phone 800-527-3933. Fax 972-390-5100.
1. PERSONNEL
   Nat'l List Sales—Raelyn Wade
   Mktg Mgr—Gary Laben
2. DESCRIPTION
   People who have recently moved.
2A. SELECTIONS AVAILABLE
   Dwelling type, head of household; age, exact, 13.00/M extra;
   ethnic markets, 10.00/M extra; age, combined, 7.75/M extra;
   presence of children, 6.50/M extra; distance of move, distance coordinate select, dwelling moved from-to (mfdu-sfdu),
   mail responder, 5.00/M extra; household income, geographic
   income percentile, 3.50/M extra; married, length of residence, gender, 2.50/M extra; census data, carrier route code,
   prioritizing, state, Zip, SCF, county, census tract/bg, msa,
   dma, 2.00/M extra; resequence/breaks, keying month/year of
   birth, key coding, 1.00/M extra; splits, bar codes, radius
   select available.
3. LIST SOURCE
   Derived from trw consumer information, customer notification
   of change of address and recorded deed information.
4. QUANTITY AND RENTAL RATES
                       Updated: May 14, 1998.

	Total Number	Price per/M
Total list (1-12 months)	14,399,053	55.00
14-day file	683,578	75.00
Hotline (30 days) (monthly)	1,119,612	65.00

   Minimum order 5,000.
5. COMMISSION, CREDIT POLICY
   Cancel charges: Orders cancelled within ten days of mailing
   date charged full price; already processed and cancelled
   before ten days of mailing date subject to 5.00/M running
   charge and stock. 20% commision to all qualified brokers on
   base price only.
6. METHOD OF ADDRESSING
   Cheshire labels, 4-up; pressure sensitive labels, (under
   50,000), 6.00/M extra; pressure sensitive labels, over 50,000,
   5.00/M extra; 1-up, 10.00/M extra; 3 x 5 cards, 15.00/M extra;
   mag tape, or cartridge, nonrefundable, 15.00 fee; diskettes,
   20.00 fee; running, 5.00/M extra; electronic delivery, 50.00
   fee; cd rom, 35.00 fee.
7. DELIVERY SCHEDULE
   Next day. Hotline names available, approximately 10th of
   each month. Electronic delivery available.
8. RESTRICTIONS
   Sample mailing piece required. One time use only. Mailing
   dates required in some states.
11. MAINTENANCE
   Updated monthly.

Figure 14-3

Selecting Compiled Lists

The two major considerations in selecting direct-response lists are mail responsiveness and affinity. Neither of these is presumed when working with most mass-compiled lists. Why, then, is this such a large industry, and how do these lists fit into the world of direct marketing?

Compiled lists offer two attributes ordinarily not available in the direct-response list field: *saturation* and *precision segmentation*. These attributes are interdependent. It is only the large quantity of compiled lists that makes precision segmentation economical, and it is only segmentation that makes it profitable for advertisers to use compiled lists.

There are two major types of segmentation: *area selectivity* and *individual household selectivity*. The former is based primarily on information about individual postal areas, sometimes organized into clusters with similar attributes. The theory here is that people in similar neighborhoods tend to have similar tastes and attitudes, independent of their income.

The latter is based on individual or household information, a source that has become increasingly more sophisticated since the previous edition of this book was published. Where we once had only demographic data or lifestyle changes such as "new parents," we now have all the results of the database marketing phenomena—individual interests, hobbies, health problems, product usage and brand preferences—and all in significant quantities.

For more information about using or building marketing databases, I refer the reader to my book devoted to this subspecialty of direct marketing, *Database Marketing* (McGraw-Hill, 1993).

SURVEY LISTS

Over half of the households in America have filled out questionnaires that ask about interests, lifestyles, brand preferences, product buying intentions, occupations, hobbies, and even what ailments they have and what medicines they take.

This data, often enhanced or pooled, is the foundation of the entire database marketing industry. These lists and how to use them are discussed in greater detail in Chapter 20 on Database Marketing. It is listed here not only in the interest of completeness, but also because they represent enormous potential for traditional direct-response promotions that can get a satisfactory response rate. Nowhere else can you get lists, in quantity, of people who suffer from a specific ailment, or who intend to move, marry or have a child in the near future. Yet many direct marketers who have tried these lists for non-database use have been disappointed.

The key is to remember that these lists behave like compiled lists, even though filling out the questionnaire was a response of sorts. The difference is that it wasn't a purchase or even an inquiry leading to one. It was an accommodation in the hope of getting some free samples and discount coupons. Like a sweepstakes "No" response, it is not an indication of willingness to buy by mail, phone or Internet. One factor which may make a difference is the same as for other compiled lists—a survey answer saying that the person has bought something through direct response, or a match against other lists indicating the same.

Figure 14-4 is a typical survey list, also from SRDS. It offers names of people who have indicated an interest in one of eleven sports. Further segmentation with demographics and psychographics is available.

BUSINESS LISTS

The area of business-to-business selling is very different from consumer selling. As with consumer marketing, prospects from a list of individuals

BEHAVIORBANK SPORTS

 **BehaviorBank**^{SM}

Location ID: 10 DCLS 602   **Mid 035548-009**
     Member: D.M.A.
Metromail Corporation.
     360 E. 22nd St., Lombard, IL 60148-4989. Phone 888-446-
     3611 Ext. 6170. Fax 630-889-5010.
     URL: http://www.metromail.com
     **NOTE: For basic information on the following num-
     bered listing segments 1, 3, 5, 6, 7, 8, see Behavior-
     bank listing under classification No. 552.**
2. DESCRIPTION
     Consumers who completed a product coupon questionnaire
     indicating their interest in outdoor activities and their psycho-
     graphic lifestyles and demographics about themselves and
     members of their households.
2A. SELECTIONS AVAILABLE
     Each additional life style/psychographic category, 7.50/M
     extra; demographic, 6.50/M extra; hotline, 10.00/M extra; Zip,
     state, SCF, 5.00/M extra; title only, title coding, 2.50/M extra;
     key coding, 2.00/M extra; phone numbers, 15.00/M extra.
4. QUANTITY AND RENTAL RATES
                    Updated: May 12, 1998.

	Total Number	Price per/M
Total list	28,000,000	60.00
Camping/hiking	4,249,080	"
Cycling	1,526,440	"
Fishing	4,815,070	"
Fitness/exercise	13,567,290	"
Golf	2,200,650	"
Hunting/shooting	3,165,940	"
Motorcycles	792,420	"
Rugged outdoor enthusiasts	7,713,260	"
Snowskiing	1,281,080	"
Tennis	860,630	"
Watching sports on TV	2,576,520	"

Minimum order 10,000.

Figure 14-4

who have already responded to another related offer are much more likely
to accept your offer than prospects on any compiled list. Unfortunately for
most business propositions, there simply are not enough such lists.

The great bulk of business mailing activity involves compiled lists, usually
sorted by NAICS or SIC codes (discussed on p. 350). The need for this
selectivity is obvious for products that are usable by only one or two industries. However, if you are selling a general business product, such as
imprinted business forms, small computers, typewriters, copiers, office furniture, or consulting services, then you have a different problem.

Often an advertiser will mail to a typical cross-section of SIC codes, company characteristics, and geographic areas. They will then analyze responses by every relevant factor. In this way, subsequent mailings can
exclude names with unresponsive SIC codes or other factors. Several segmentation factors can have a bearing on your results:

- *Age of business.* When it was founded
- *Size of indicators.* Sales volume or number of employees
- *Type of business.* The primary or secondary SIC codes
- *Ownership.* Private or public

- *Headquarters or branch office.* Or the fact that this might be a single-location business
- *Credit.* The Dun & Bradstreet credit rating, and the general trend of the particular business.

One particular advantage is the large number of individual officer names and titles available through this supplier, especially when personalized letters are appropriate for the mailing. They have already offered the names of presidents and chief financial officers, and have over 15 million names of individuals with various titles including vice president, secretary, manufacturing director, and purchasing agent. They are listed by name, title, job function and company size.

Unfortunately, no one supplier can give you the name of every vice president of manufacturing in every type of company. It will probably be necessary to deal with several list suppliers. Publishers of trade publications in specific fields often have very complete lists of the industries reached by their publications. IDG, for instance, produces a very good list of subscribers to various technology magazines that a technical manager might subscribe to. This type of list is frequently used by computer software and hardware companies.

Figure 14-5 is an example of a pooled list—IDG Communications Database—comprising suppliers to all of their computer-oriented magazines.

Financial propositions can sell to the substantial subscriber lists of *Money, The Wall Street Journal,* and *Boardroom Reports* readers, as well as to smaller but very responsive lists of subscribers to newsletters and advisory services. There are lists of buyers of business equipment, inquirers about business services, subscribers to trade publications, and attendees at trade conferences. SRDS provides information on lists of this type in exactly the same way as consumer response lists. See Fig. 14-6—Active Medical Marketing & Media—personnel in segments of the health care industry. Note that this list is segmentable by business classification or by job function within the medical industry. This list rents for $141 per thousand names, with a minimum purchase of $247. Selecting by job function, location (state and zip) and other selections cost an additional $30.

Whereas such response lists are the keystones of consumer direct-mail efforts, usually they are a secondary consideration in business selling. The primary list sources for business selling are so-called compiled lists—those prepared by Dun & Bradstreet, Database America, and others. The basic selectors of such lists are size and type of business.

Also called *vertical lists,* these lists reach all types of executives in all sizes of businesses within a specific industry. The narrower the category, the more precise you can make the message, the offer, and the product offering.

Such lists were originally compiled from the Yellow Pages from the telephone companies, with all the obvious limitations and inaccuracies such a list would include. A look at Yellow Pages directories will show you that many categories are inconsistent, repetitive, and hard to define.

IDG COMMUNICATIONS DATABASE
Data Verified: Mar 16, 1999.
Location ID: 13 ICLS 15   Mid 037202-000
1. PERSONNEL
   List Manager
   American List Counsel, Inc.
      88 Orchard Rd., CN-5219, Princeton, NJ 08543. Toll Free
      800-252-5478. Fax 908-904-6219.
   Key Contact: Greg Jarrow, Phone 908-904-6218.
   E-mail: gcj@amlist.com
2. SUMMARY DESCRIPTION
   Unduplicated subscribers to CIO, ComputerWorld, Game
   Pro, Infoworld, Infoworld Electric, JavaWorld, Netscape
   Enterprise Developer, Network World, Network World
   Fusion, NC World, PC World, PC World Online, Publish,
   Civic.com, Computercurrents, Computerworld IT Users, Fed-
   eral Computer Week, MacWorld, PC Games, Sunworld, Web
   master and the exposition lists of Electronic Entertainment
   Expo, Comnet, Macworld Expo, Telcommuting and Home
   Office Expo and internet Commerce Expo.
   76% male, 16% female.
3. LIST SOURCE
   Direct response.
4. SELECTIONS WITH COUNTS
                Updated: Mar 9, 1999.
                                          Total   Price
                                          Number   per/M
   Computer/technical rate 3,157,223 *120.00
   Hotline (last 3 month) 755,167   +10.00
   Computer type:
   CD ROMS 625,238   +35.00
   PC 2,356,864   "
   Mainframes 280,763   "
   VARS/VADS 197,150   "
   Workstations 568,030   "
   Windows 979,368   "
   Minis 446,916   "
   Laser printers 556,781   "
   UNIX 531,504   "
   (*) Business rate 105.00/M; Consumer rate 85.00/M; Fundraiser
   rate 75.00/M.
   Minimum order 5,000.
4A. OTHER SELECTIONS
   State, SCF, Zip, 5.00/M extra; home/business, gender,
   hotline, canadian, 10.00/M extra; title only, # employees,
   industry, 15.00/M extra; mainframe, mini's, micro's, 35.00/M
   extra; laser printers, 40.00/M extra; vars/vads, unix, workstations, 35.00/M extra; multi-subs, 25.00/M extra; key coding,
   1.00/M extra; zip set up, 25.00 fee.
5. COMMISSION, CREDIT POLICY
   20% commission to brokers. Payment due 30 days after mail
   date. Cancel charges: Cancellations after mail date require
   payment in full.
6. METHOD OF ADDRESSING
   Cheshire labels, 4-up; pressure sensitive labels, 7.50/M
   extra; mag tape, 20.00 fee.
7. DELIVERY SCHEDULE
   Delivery from 3 to 5 working days.
8. RESTRICTIONS
   Sample mailing piece required.

Figure 14-5. From SRDS *Direct Marketing List Source.*

SIC and NAICS Codes

For decades Standard Industrial Classification (SIC) codes were the basic segmentation tool of business to business marketing. These four digit SIC codes identified business categories and were the basis for compilations of names and addresses offered by virtually every list compiler.

As of 2000, Census Data for businesses will be organized by the North American Industry Classification (NAICS) system, and undoubtedly most list compilers will adopt the same system as fast as the files can be revised. The new system is a major improvement in several ways. It has been adopted in Mexico and Canada as well.

For one thing, it includes about 350 new industries recognized for the first time. These range from high-tech industries such as fiber optic cable

ACTIVE MEDICAL MARKETING & MEDIA SUBSCRIBERS

Data Verified: Mar 4, 1999.

Location ID: 13 ICLS 3   Mid 107143-000
CPS Communications

1. PERSONNEL
List Manager
Medical Marketing Service, Inc.
  185 Hansen Ct., Suite 110, Wood Dale, IL 60191-1150
    Phone 800-633-5478. Fax 630-350-1896.
    URL: http://www.mmslists.com
    E-mail: c-morrison@mmslists.com

2. SUMMARY DESCRIPTION
Marketing personnel employed by health care manufacturers, as well as the suppliers who serve them: advertising agencies, publishers, services suppliers and others allied to the field.

3. LIST SOURCE
Circulation of medical marketing & media magazine

4. SELECTIONS WITH COUNTS
              Updated: Jul 8, 1998.

	Total Number	Price per/M
Total list	11,676	141.00
Business/Industry Class:		
Health care manufacturer	7,329	141.00
Health care agency	2,803	"
Publisher/publisher's rep	294	"
Service/support company	244	"
Others allied to the field	44	"
Healthcare market:		
RX/ethical pharmaceutical	3,259	141.00
OTC consumer/proprietary pharmaceuticals	1,637	"
Medical products/equipment	2,810	"
Diagnostic products/equipment	1,603	"
Hospital products/equipment	2,454	"
Dental products/equipment	515	"
Other (including Biotechnology)	1,054	"

Minimum order 247.00.

4A. OTHER SELECTIONS
Job functions, state, SCF, Zip, key coding, 30.00 fee.

5. COMMISSION, CREDIT POLICY
20% commission to brokers. 15% commission to agencies. Cash with order unless credit established. Payment for 3rd-party contracts must be guaranteed.

6. METHOD OF ADDRESSING
Cheshire labels, 4-up, east-west; pressure sensitive labels, 8.00/M extra.

7. DELIVERY SCHEDULE
24 hour turnaround available.

8. RESTRICTIONS
Sample mailing piece required. List owner's approval required. Lists not returnable for credit or refund.

10. LETTER SHOP SERVICES
Available.

11. MAINTENANCE
Updated monthly.

Figure 14-6. From SRDS *Direct Marketing List Source.*

manufacturing and satellite communications to warehouse clubs, pet supply stores, and diet centers. For another, the economy is now grouped into 20 sectors instead of 10, enabling more precise sub-definitions. Over 18,000 separate industries and independent occupations are sorted down to six digits replacing the old 4-digit SIC system.

The first two digits represent major economic sectors, such as Agriculture or Construction. The remaining digits, in descending order, represent economic sectors, economic Subsectors, Industry Groups, and specific industries. For a detailed list and more details go to the web at www.gov/naics.

It is important to note that not all compilers use exactly the same coding, or have the same standards for data storage, pricing, and segmentation. A particular dilemma is the depth of coverage. Some compilers offer mostly presidents and financial officers, while others can provide information on

Two-Digit NAICS Codes and Titles

11. Agriculture, Forestry, Fishing and Hunting
21. Mining
22. Utilities
23. Construction
31-33. Manufacturing
42. Wholesale Trade
44-45. Retail Trade
48-49. Transportation and Warehousing
51. Information
52. Finance and Insurance
53. Real Estate and Leasing
54. Professional, Scientific and Technical
55. Management
56. Administrative and Support
61. Educational Services
62. Health Care and Social Assistance
71. Arts, Entertainment and Education
72. Accommodation and Food Services
81. Other Services (Except Public Administration)
92. Public Administration

Two-Digit Standard Industrial Classification Index

Division A. Agriculture, Forestry and Fisheries
01. Agricultural production crops
02. Agricultural production livestock
07. Agricultural services
08. Forestry
09. Fishing, hunting and trapping

Division B. Mining
10. Metal mining
12. Coal mining
13. Oil and gas extraction
14. Nonmetallic minerals, except fuels

Division C. Construction
15. General contractors and operative builders
16. Heavy construction, except building
17. Special trade contractors

Division D. Manufacturing
20. Food and kindred products
21. Tobacco products
22. Textile mill products
23. Apparel and other textile products
24. Lumber and wood products
25. Furniture and fixtures
26. Paper and allied products
27. Printing and publishing
28. Chemicals and allied products
29. Petroleum and coal products
30. Rubber and miscellaneous plastics products
31. Leather and leather products
32. Stone, clay, and glass products
33. Primary metal industries
34. Fabricated metal products
35. Industrial machinery and equipment
36. Electronic and other electronic equipment
37. Transportation equipment
38. Instruments and related products
39. Miscellaneous manufacturing industries

Division E. Transportation and Public Utilities
41. Local and interurban passenger transit
42. Trucking and warehousing
44. Water transportation
45. Transportation by air
46. Pipelines, except natural gas
47. Transportation services
48. Communication
49. Electric, gas, and sanitary services

Division F. Wholesale Trade
50. Wholesale trade - durable goods
51. Wholesale trade - nondurable goods

Division G. Retail Trade
52. Building materials and garden supplies
53. General merchandise stores
54. Food stores
55. Automotive dealers and service stations
56. Apparel and accessory stores
57. Furniture and homefurnishings stores
58. Eating and drinking places
59. Miscellaneous retail

Division H. Finance, Insurance and Real Estate
60. Depository institutions
61. Nondepository institutions
62. Security and commodity brokers
63. Insurance carriers
64. Insurance agents, brokers and service
65. Real estate
67. Holding and other investment offices

Division I. Services
70. Hotels and other lodging places
72. Personal services
73. Business services
75. Auto repair, services and parking
76. Miscellaneous repair services
78. Motion pictures
79. Amusement and recreation services
80. Health services
81. Legal services
82. Educational services
83. Social services
84. Museums, botanical, zoological gardens
86. Membership organizations
87. Engineering and management services
88. Private households
89. Services, NEC

Division J. Public Administration
91. Executive, legislative, and general
92. Justice, public order, and safety
93. Finance, taxation, & monetary policy
94. Administration of human resources
95. Environmental quality and housing
96. Administration of economic programs
97. National security and int'l. affairs

Division K. Nonclassifiable Establishments
99. Nonclassifiable establishments

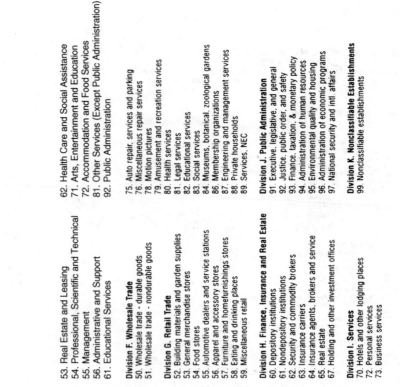

Figure 14-7. NAICS codes and "SIC" broad categories, from SRDS *Direct Marketing List Source.*

a wide range of executives. Compilers, particularly publishers of business publications, are constantly striving for greater penetration of an industry or occupation. One publishing group announced the availability of over 5 million business names "at hundreds of managerial levels." Of these, less than half were individual names, the others required title addressing (e.g., "Production Manager," et al.). McGraw-Hill, the publisher of this book, offers a business-leaders masters list.

Primary and Secondary Codes.   As many firms are in more than one business, another variable exists in the designation of companies. Usually credit services will have a classification for the companies of the business the company considers the primary one and others that are considered secondary. Usually a business firm is looking to sell to everyone engaged in a particular business, regardless of whether it is their primary or secondary field.

An advertising agency, for instance, might be classified as SIC code 7311. If they consider themselves to be in the public relations and direct mail business as well, they may carry secondary codes of 7392 and 7331.

Ordering a list of companies with a particular SIC code would give you both the companies with the primary business and secondary ones. However, there are times when you may want only those firms that consider a business their primary one, or vice versa.

There are many refinements in working with classification lists. Of importance are the varying techniques for seeking out individuals you need within each corporate address. These are discussed later in this chapter.

HOUSE LISTS

No discussion of direct marketing would be complete without including the most obvious but most neglected list of all: a company's own house list.

As *Direct Marketing* magazine points out, "Every transaction in the direct marketing field, whether it begins with direct mail, print, broadcast or telephone selling, always ends up on a [house] list—of inquiries, of orders, of sales leads, of contest entrants, or whatever."

While building a list may not be the primary purpose of entrepreneurs running their first mail-order ad, it is the beginning of the process that makes the difference between a one-shot mail-order sale and a long-term direct-marketing business. Even the smallest, newest company should begin at the outset to make the most of its mailing list. The same applies to *any* business asking for direct responses.

First of all, a house list is the most profitable source of future sales. Second, list-rental income or the ability to exchange names can be very important. For these and other reasons, a house list can be a company's single greatest asset. Ways of protecting and utilizing this asset are discussed later in this chapter.

Recency, Frequency, Unit Sale and Source. These four factors should always be identifiable in a company's house list, for its own internal promotions as well as to enable renting the list. In addition, a company should always have its own data on types of purchases or other transactions, payment and credit history, and other important factors. Also, a list can always be enhanced with external data, based on location or survey information. Or it can be pooled with other lists to refine it further. (See *List Pooling* later in this chapter.)

This type of data enables a company to decide what kind of promotions to send to what parts of the list. For instance, a banking customer who uses several bank services is more likely to buy another than someone with only a checking account. A business which sells by catalog may send six catalogs a year to one segment but only one or two to others. Another marketer may use telemarketing exclusively for TV respondents, and only e-mail for web customers.

Some companies have even more data—from application forms, bank records, club transactions, or other records. A grocer knows every purchase that was paid for with a check-card or credit-card. A stockbroker knows what stocks you bought and sold. A cable company knows what you watch on TV. A music club knows what kind of music you like. A phone company knows where you call. A web marketer can tell what you clicked on before you visited their site.

But, just because you have access to data doesn't mean that it is proper to use it or that it will be profitable. Blockbuster was severely criticized for proposing to make video-rental data available. Whether or not legal restrictions are placed on the use of customer data, ethics and good taste are always in order.

The Neiman-Marcus data, in Fig. 14-8, is typical of the way a company might segment their own list. In this case it is broken down by type of merchandise, price of purchase and frequency.

CHOOSING AND USING LISTS

After consultation with a list broker and independent examination of list cards, a perusal of SRDS resources, or examining the data in a house list, every list or segment worth considering should be listed and sorted by category. These categories can correspond to SRDS categories, or they can be arbitrary. See the discussion of "Media Constellations" in the next chapter, which can also apply to list planning.

Lists should be grouped by the common denominator that makes them of interest to you, whether or not it is their basic identity. For instance, some groups could be purely affinity-based. Groups can include readers of magazines in related fields, buyers of similar products, buyers of books on the subject, buyers of items in a related price category, or any other segment.

Some owners sort their lists by size of purchase and whether or not the buyer has made more than one purchase. Almost all of them have a time

NEIMAN-MARCUS MAIL ORDER BUYERS

Neiman-Marcus

Data Verified: Mar 2, 1999.
Location ID: 10 DCLS 553   Mid 031597-000
NM Direct
  5950 Colwel Blvd., Irving, TX 75039. Phone 972-969-3205.
  Fax 972-969-3192.
1. PERSONNEL
  List Mgr—Tina Carter
  Ass't—Clarkie Choice, Phone 972-969-3197.
2. SUMMARY DESCRIPTION
  Mail order catalog buyers of clothes and accessories, jewelry, gourmet food, home furnishings, gifts, etc.
  70% female; ages 40-45.
  Average unit of sale 160.00.
3. LIST SOURCE
  Direct mail.
4. SELECTIONS WITH COUNTS
        Updated: Mar 2, 1999.

	Total Number	Price per/M
Buyers:		
Last 24 months	427,280	*100.00
Last 12 months	255,606	+10.00
Last 6 months	112,708	+15.00
Last 3 months	54,728	+25.00
50.00+		
24 months	383,586	+22.00
12 months	234,105	"
6 months	105,909	"
3 months	50,196	"
75.00+		
24 months	358,858	+27.00
12 months	220,378	"
6 months	100,522	"
3 months	47,612	"
100.00+		
24 months	332,085	+35.00
12 months	205,805	"
6 months	95,051	"
3 months	44,800	"
Multis		
24 months	261,636	+10.00
12 months	164,038	"
6 months	76,951	"
3 months	36,316	"
Single purchase		
24 months	165,644	+10.00
12 months	91,568	"
6 months	35,757	"
3 months	17,962	"
Cat subs:		
24 months	25,211	+65.00
12 months	9,675	"
6 months	4,289	"
3 months	3,935	"

Men's product:		
3 month	2,900	+25.00
6 month	5,106	+15.00
12 month	12,318	+10.00
50.00+:		
3 month	2,891	+22.00
6 month	5,096	+2.00
12 month	12,303	+22.00
75.00+		
3 month	2,879	+27.00
6 month	5,078	"
12 month	12,260	"
100.00+:		
3 month	2,832	+35.00
6 month	5,023	"
12 month	12,139	"
Women's All:		
3 month	36,960	+25.00
6 month	82,832	+15.00
12 month	176,103	+10.00
50.00+:		
3 month	68,535	+22.00
6 month	112,478	"
12 month	170,427	"
75.00+:		
3 month	66,846	+27.00
6 month	110,036	"
12 month	166,348	"
100.00+:		
3 month	64,007	+35.00
6 month	105,538	"
12 month	159,649	"
Hardgoods:		
3 month	64,654	+25.00
6 month	107,028	+15.00
12 month	144,302	+10.00
50.00+:		
3 month	58,101	+20.00
6 month	95,262	"
12 month	128,803	"
75.00+:		
3 month	54,503	+25.00
6 month	89,355	"
12 month	121,283	"
100.00+:		
3 month	51,494	+35.00
6 month	84,217	"
12 month	114,610	"

(*) Fundraising/publishing rate, 65.00/M.
Net name arrangement (minimum 100,000). 85% plus 8.00/M running charge.
Minimum order 5,000.
4A. OTHER SELECTIONS
  State, SCF, Zip, 7.50/M extra; gender, 5.00/M extra; product categories: (women's, wapp, women's acess, men's hardgoods, home furnishing, tableware, linen-bath, child, collectibles and food), multi-buyers, single purchase, 10.00/M extra; 100.00+ buyers, 35.00/M extra; 75.00+ buyers, 27.00/M extra; 50.00+ buyers, 22.00/M extra; volume discounts.
5. COMMISSION, CREDIT POLICY
  Cancel charges: Cancellation before mail date 8.00/M plus shipping charges, Minimum charge, 50.00. After mail date full charges. Prepayment required for new customers.
6. METHOD OF ADDRESSING
  Pressure sensitive labels, 6.00/M extra; mag tape, 25.00 fee.
7. DELIVERY SCHEDULE
  Delivery from 3 to 5 days.
8. RESTRICTIONS
  Sample mailing piece required.
11. MAINTENANCE
  Updated monthly.

Figure 14-8. From SRDS *Direct Marketing List Source.*

frame built in, so you can start with the most recent names and work back to the older ones if results justify.

Lists can be selected by sex, by state, and by zip codes chosen for geographic or demographic criteria. Large mailers can identify clusters of zip codes where response rates and quality are exceptionally rewarding, and concentrate on those when sending out their mailings. Conversely, clubs or other credit propositions can screen out zip codes with historical bad-debt problems. Some magazine publishers select zip codes that will deliver the demographic mix that will best appeal to their advertisers.

Virtually every selection factor costs a bit more—maybe 10 to 15 percent—than the basic list, and many list owners charge a premium for gender or geographic selection. Considering that these charges are an even smaller percentage of the total mailing cost, and that selectivity is the essential ingredient of making the campaign work, such extra charges are a small price to pay.

There are different approaches to selecting segments for list testing. One school says that hotline names and particularly favorable geographic areas or buyer classifications should be avoided, in order to make the test as "fair" as possible. This is true if research is the objective. My approach is to put the best foot forward and give the list every chance of working by selecting the most favorable segments. If those are not successful, the list will be dropped anyway.

The exception would be a campaign where, for competitive or other reasons, a major rollout must be conducted in the next season with no time for extensive testing. In that case I would go with a list segment that is representative of the quantity that would be needed in the rollout.

The factor here is the total anticipated rollout quantity. If it's moderate, then the list program can be built gradually, beginning with the best segments, which should supply enough names without reaching into the bulk of the list. If the plan requires an ambitious rollout, then by all means test only large lists in typical segments.

Pilot Lists

Once the lists have been sorted into categories, the next step in preparing a test mailing is to select one or more lists that are most likely to succeed in each category, lists called "pilot lists." These pilot lists should be representative not only of the potential of the whole list, but also of the entire group.

Quantities should be considered, of course. Test factors with the potential to roll out into much greater numbers, or else the test isn't really worth it. For example, if you have a list of only 20,000 names, using 10,000-name test cells leaves you only another 10,000 to roll out to—essentially nowhere to go if the list does succeed. The pilot lists should be larger lists or, at least, representative lists from a group of smaller lists with a substantial total.

Recency, Frequency, Unit Sale and Source

Recency is the time element between the date the list is rented and the date the people on the list sent in their order, inquiry, donation, or subscription. The more recent, the better.

Frequency is the number of times a prospect has purchased from the list owner, or the length of the subscription, membership, or other association. The greater the frequency, the better.

Unit Sale or Purchase Amount, is the amount of the highest transaction the customer has made through the mail. If your offer involves a substantial commitment, it is more likely to be accepted by people who have made other substantial purchases than by people who have not.

Source is the origin of the name in the first place—recently recognized as a factor deserving of equal consideration with the original R-F-P standard—Recency-Frequency-Purchase Amount.

Lists of people who bought by direct mail will be most likely to work for other direct-mail offers. People who responded to telephone or television solicitations may not necessarily be accustomed to responding to mail offers. If the list has been built with sweepstakes offers, they are likely not to be responsive except to other sweepstakes offers.

The Principle of Affinity

In selecting mailing lists, the most important principle is the need for *affinity,* a logical connection between your offer and the prospects on a mailing list.

Some are easy. If you are selling gourmet cookware, you might try buyers of sophisticated cookbooks. If you are soliciting money for a charity, lists of donors to similar causes like health and religious organizations or the arts are the first place to look.

If you are soliciting leads for an expensive, high-performance automobile such as a Porsche, you have several options based on personality indications. For example, you can assume that owners of yachts and airplanes are affluent and love fine possessions. You can mail to engineers because you think they would appreciate the performance of the car. You can speculate that readers of *Road & Track* and *Playboy* and top executives in advertising and entertainment might identify with the imagery associated with this kind of car.

Fortunately, direct-mail methods permit the testing of a wide variety of lists with some possibility for success. A list does not have to be a "sure thing" to be worth testing. It only has to have some logical affinity.

It's helpful to remind yourself, when picking lists to test, that not every person on a list has to be right for the offer. If you're looking for a 5 percent response, you can probably get it if 25 or 30 percent of the list consists of reasonable prospects. You can afford to build in a "waste factor" of people who definitely are not prospects, as long as there are enough people who are. The total quantity of prospects in the list counts for less than the quality of the prospects. It's better to have twenty very good prospects out of a hundred than forty so-so prospects.

LIST SEGMENTATION

Once a mailing list has been chosen, there are still other alternatives available to the media manager. Mailing lists can be segmented in any way the list owner chooses and the computer can execute.

Some of the largest companies make their lists available according to the type and dollar value of merchandise purchased by their customers. Note the Neiman-Marcus data in Fig. 14-8.

In addition, many of these lists can be further segmented not only into the fairly common sex, age, state, or zip code, but also to their unique characteristics such as these:

- Credit-card buyers
- Cash or credit buyers
- Single or multi-buyers
- Nielsen market
- Sweepstakes "yes" responses
- Type of product

The last item means you can select buyers of apparel, home furnishings, appliances, automobile accessories, stereos, cameras, power and hand tools, etc.

Doubleday Book Clubs, for instance, offer a wide variety of similar sub-sections, but also another exceptional aspect: the type of book that members of their various book clubs have selected. (See Fig. 14-9.) So if you're interested in a list of people who relate to any of the subjects, they can give you names of people who have purchased a book in exactly that subject area.

Doubleday Direct Inc. Masterfile Categories

- Art, Coffee Table
- Classic, Poetry and Drama
- Entertainment, Biography, History
- Gardening
- Household, Cooking and Crafts
- Juvenile
- Military
- Mystery and Suspense
- Nature, Exploration, Outdoor Sports
- Personal Finance, Current Affairs
- Romance
- Science Fiction, Psychic

Figure 14-9. A list of book-buyers available by category of purchase.

Hotline Names

So-called Hotline Names are eagerly sought after. These are people who have recently bought, subscribed to, ordered, or inquired about the product from the company that is renting the list, and have done so usually within the last 90 days. The hottest of the hotline names are those that are less than 30 days old. Such lists have been shown to do very well, and some advertisers contract for such names on a year-round basis.

Here's one caution to watch for in hotline names: some lists include "trial orders" or "inquiries." In this case the hotline names will be of poorer quality than the names in the regular file.

Telemarketing Lists

This phrase, when used correctly, refers not to the availability of phone numbers, but to the past buying mode of the names on the list. These should be people who have responded to a telephone solicitation—perhaps to a magazine renewal or a charitable campaign.

These are more than simply lists with phone numbers. Many lists are available with phone numbers for a slight surcharge. And telemarketing firms can use various methods to get phone numbers when they are not already on the list.

Of course, many telemarketing efforts use the same lists and list criteria that anyone would use for a direct mail-campaign. While some list owners will not allow their lists to be used for telemarketing, these are exceptions.

THE MAILING PLAN

An initial test probably might include 50,000 names testing various pieces of copy. These names might be taken from one or two lists that appear to be very logical choices. Another 50,000 names might be divided among 5 or 10 pilot tests representing substantial list categories.

An ongoing campaign would have three major groupings. The most important would be the rollout of lists that have been successful in previous testing. Then there would be list extensions: re-tests in larger quantities of lists that have proven successful in previous testing, but during a time when it is not yet considered safe to roll out the full quantity. Then there is additional list testing, which is divided into two areas. One area of list testing for an ongoing campaign would be the exploration of additional lists in categories where the pilot list was successful. The other is in searching for new list categories.

Let's say that 10 lists were tested in an initial campaign, and 5 were successful. Those 5 would be rolled out or re-tested as extensions, depending on the quantities involved. Then additional lists in the successful categories would be tested, plus some new categories. The original unsuccessful test lists would be dropped, as would any other lists in the same categories.

Such a hypothetical schedule might look like the chart in Fig. 14-10.

In this schedule, the original 100,000 mailing is now built up to 442,000, of which over 80 percent are rollout or extension. The percentage of testing is kept to less than 20 percent, so that even if all the tests did only half as well as the rollouts and extensions, total results would be depressed only 10 percent. Even this is unlikely, as most of those tests are in categories that have already been proved successful.

This type of evolution—from a highly subjective initial test to a logical combination of tests, extensions, and rollouts—quickly converts the direct marketing manager from a chance-taking gambler into a statistician and scientist. However, no growth is possible without some risk.

Taking Chances.   While some lists have a history of being very responsive to certain categories of offers, there is almost always a need to make some choices based on common sense and old-fashioned hunches. If a mailing costs $700/M the "risk" of using an unproven list of 5M names would be $3500, but in fact it is even less. It is unlikely that the new list will produce no responses at all. If it produces only half the responses of a proven list,

Hypothetical Schedule of a Mailing Plan

List A	Rollout	125,000; full list, less previous tests
List C	Rollout	87,000; full list, less previous tests
List E	Extension	50,000 of possible 1,250,000
List G	Extension	50,000 of possible 650,000
List I	Extension	50,000 of possible 325,000
List K	List test	10,000; same category as A
List L	List test	10,000; same category as A
List M	List test	10,000; same category as A
List N	List test	10,000; same category as C
List O	List test	10,000; same category as E
List P	List test	10,000; same category as G
List Q	Category test	10,000; new category pilot list
List S	Category test	10,000; new category pilot list

Figure 14-10. Hypothetical schedule of a mailing plan

the experiment in fact costs only $1750. It is more likely a "bad" response would be only 20 percent less, costing only $700.

On the other hand, the upside potential far exceeds the risks of testing. For instance, take the worst case example just offered of the $1750 "cost." If three such lists are tested and one with 100,000 potential names is successful, you have spent $3500 on testing and found a new audience where you can mail to all 100,000—a profitably invested $70,000!

E-MAIL LISTS

Ideally, these lists—like telemarketing lists—should be of people who have bought something from an e-mail solicitation. However, as of this writing, such lists are few and far between. Instead so-called e-mail lists are the Internet's equivalent of phone-book names. They are usually a list of e-mail addresses gathered from directory listings or from sellers of computer modems or Internet access services.

Most lists so far are e-mail addresses of people who have bought something through direct response, but not necessarily as the result of an unsolicited e-mail communication. Or they are past-purchasers who have the capacity to receive e-mail or who say they use the Internet. Some lists are people who have downloaded free software, another dubious qualifier. One of the largest lists offered is called "Internet User Consumer Buyers" which sounds like a gold-mine until you discover that they did not necessarily do their buying on the Internet. One should question the origins of lists in this new category very carefully. Another problem is e-mail list rental rates are two or three times the rental cost of comparable direct mail lists.

One exception is On-line Superstore Customers, a list of over 100,000 names of people who have purchased and downloaded software on-line. But even these are buyers through a website, not through e-mail. Considering that e-mail is intrusive, limited in format for most computer owners, and limited in selectivity, it is no more suitable for mass communication than an "Occupant" mailing. Like telemarketing, it is best used when there is a previous relationship, and when the customer has provided the e-mail address.

So-called "Opt-in" or "permission" lists may be of people who gave permission to *one* e-commerce site to send bulletins or newsletters. It doesn't mean they knowingly permitted their names to be offered to others. Such lists are necessarily only e-mail addresses. Usually, there is no way to enhance the lists with demographic or even geographic data.

LIST LOGISTICS

List Cleaning

Every "nixie" should be removed from the file immediately. Nixies are mailings returned by the Postal Service with notations such as "No longer at this address." When new addresses are known, the listing can be updated and put back in the active file.

Address changes also should be entered promptly. This is vital, as bulk mail is never forwarded, and even first-class mail seems to have a mixed record for forwarding reliability.

A "match code" can help you spot new inquiries or orders from people who are already on the list, possibly under the name of another family member. The new order should supersede the previous file, but must be matched in order to avoid the expense of sending two mailings to the same household. The customer name should supersede the similar prospect name.

List Rental

The list-rental business can be very profitable. There is no reason to worry about "protecting" your customers from other mail offers. They will be getting them anyway. The only question is who will be getting the list-rental income. You won't have to worry about directly competitive offers because you can refuse to rent to any offer you feel is competitive with you or offensive to your customers.

The first step is to set up your segmentation and pricing structure so as to make it appealing to other list-rental customers. The second step is to get a list-management company to handle the promotion and administration of your list-rental business. A good list manager will have a decent administrative operation and—more important—a strong sales organization to promote your list to likely users.

Figure 14-11 is an estimate of rental income for a list of 250,000 names rented ten times a year. Expenses and commissions leave a 50 percent profit margin, in this case $50,000 a year.

Using Your List

In addition to using your list for your own products or renting it out to others, you may find that your list will be so important that you will be looking for new ways to "mine" it.

One way is to use syndicated mailings—offers of products prepared and packaged by others for mailing to your list. It could be an insurance plan, a language course, or any other product. The letter goes out under your name to your customers, but the expenses are the responsibility of the syndicator. All you do is handle the list and the orders. The syndicator will pay for the mailing, handle the product, and ship it out to your customers. You get your commission on each sale, and it can amount to a substantial sum if the product is the right one for your list.

The ultimate use of your list is to develop products that fit the reputation your company has built and the interests of the people on your list. As you are working toward a known customer base, it is relatively simple to work with researchers to arrange focus panels, questionnaires, or other forms of pre-testing to help you develop an offer that will sell. The chances are that,

List Rental Income

	250,000	names
×	10	turnover
	2,500,000	annual quantity rented
×	$40.00	per thousand rental price
	$100,000	gross rental
−	$20,000	minus broker commission (20%)
	$80,000	

	$80,000	
−	10,000	minus managers fee (10%)
	$70,000	
−	10,000	minus service bureau and overhead
	$60,000	
−	10,000	minus net name guarantee (10%)
	$50,000	net income

Figure 14-11. List rental income
[Source: Allan Bilofsky in "Direct Marketing Handbook—First Edition"].

if the offer appeals to your current list, it will also appeal to the readers or viewers of the media that you used to build your list.

PROTECTING YOUR LIST

Anyone in the field will tell you at least one horror story about attempted list fraud. The value is just too great for some people to avoid temptation. When I was at one company I personally received a phone call from the president of a competitor who had been offered my list for sale. It took a detective less than two days to track down the dishonest employee and, with the help of the competitor, turn him over to the police. But don't let it come to this. Your competitor may not be as ethical.

The first protections are obvious ones. The data storage area must be protected from theft as well as from fire or vandalism. Tapes or discs should be stored in a locked room with tightly enforced access restrictions and a sign-in–sign-out system. Alarms should be built into the room, as well as fire extinguishers. Most important, a "grandfather system" should be instituted, in which original tapes and the latest update tape are sent to a remote location for storage. Once a working database has been updated, it replaces the previous database in storage. The idea is that there should always be, in another location, the basic data for reconstructing the current working tape.

"Seeding" names is another important step. Place some names and addresses on the list—your own, and those of several key employees and friends—with deliberate misspellings as codes. Whenever the list is used, you'll be able to spot the source of the list by the coded name. If an unauthorized mailing comes in with the coded misspelling, then you'll know something is wrong.

ORDERING MAILING LISTS

Selecting the right mailing lists may be a fine art, but ordering and processing them correctly is an exact science. As in every direct marketing activity, excellence requires the best of both worlds.

Ordinarily, lists are rented through a list broker. A good list broker should be a willing and enthusiastic part of your marketing team. Select the best, regardless of whether they are a local company or across the country. Sometimes the best company for your needs is not in your back yard, but easily accessible by phone or e-mail.

Then you will need a list processor. This is sometimes subcontracted by your direct mail letter shop or advertising agency. Many suppliers are tempted to increase their own profit margins by trying to do this type of work themselves, but often they don't have the computer capabilities or the depth of experience of the companies that specialize in list processing: companies such as Hibbert, MBS/Multimode, Printronic, and Creative Automation. An ideal place to search for these companies are the back pages of the industry magazines.

Placing the List Order

List orders should be worked out with the list broker. There are many details to be worked out, and often they vary from list to list. Treat your list broker like a partner, not just a supplier.

List Description. For each list, you have to define exactly what you want. Include the name of the list and an exact specification of the segment you are ordering, such as "2001 Buyers" or "1999 Expires" or "Latest HotLine."

Quantity. Usually, you want to test a fixed quantity or utilize a previously ordered quantity of direct mail packages. Often, though, you may want all available names in a geographic area, or hotline names as available, or as many names as are available within recency parameters. In such cases, specify that instruction and be sure the list owner is told to provide an actual list count.

If you must estimate the amount of a mailing designated for a geographic area before the list is run, one handy way is to use state or Standard Metropolitan Statistical Area counts published by the Census Bureau. Your list broker can supply this information, or go to www.census.gov.

This data includes the percentages of population, manufacturing, and retail sales for each state. Use the population figure for consumer lists, the manufacturing figure for business lists, and the retail-sales figure for retail or professional lists. Just take the appropriate percentage and apply it to the total national list size.

Manufacturing and retail sales figures may not be available by individual SMSA market. To get these, take the state figure you need and then apply the "percentage-of-state" population figure to the manufacturing or retail figure. It's far from perfect but usually it's close, with an error margin of 5 or 10 percent.

Sampling. If you want a typical cross-section for test purposes, the usual practice is to ask for an "Nth-name sample, to be taken from all reels." This means you want the total list size divided by your test quantity: a 300,000-name list used for a 10,000-name test would require that N = 30, or every thirtieth name.

I would avoid testing with what is called a *fifth-digit zip select*. Arbitrarily mailing to a last number of zip codes does not give you 10 percent of the entire list. I have had this checked, and there is a dramatic difference in response by fifth-digit zip number. The reason is that lower numbers, such as 0, 1, and 2, often are the downtown areas of major cities, while the higher numbers are more likely to be suburbs away from the city center. Also, many areas do not have the higher zips at all, and so a smaller postal area may have only the first few last digits.

On a test extension or rollout, you may want to specify certain geographic areas that you believe to be the most responsive to your offer, or you may designate a list of zip codes to be selected from or suppressed, as the case may be. You can also select by city size, seeking either urban or non-urban buyers.

You can designate sex by asking for "males only" or "females only." If your letter refers to the recipient by gender, you may want to avoid offending the opposite sex by adding this phrase: "Omit unidentified gender names." This will drop out those with only initials for first names and those names that could be male or female.

Compiled and business lists can, of course, be selected by all the criteria indicated in the previous parts of this chapter. Such specifications should be clearly stated. If names are not available individually, you may instruct the supplier to add a specific title such as "purchasing agent" or "stationery buyer."

Key Coding. Your key numbers should be assigned at the very beginning, so that your lists can be supplied with key numbers already included.

Dates. You must indicate the planned drop date and advise the list house if there are any substantial delays. Usually you will receive protection against competing use of a particular list one week before and one week after your scheduled mailing date. During this time another company will not be able to mail to this list. This parameter should be indicated on the order. If a longer protection period is necessary, it will have to be negotiated in advance.

Your list processor should have your order indicate both the scheduled drop date and the date you want the lists.

Telephone Numbers. Some compiled lists can be supplied with telephone numbers. This is a great convenience if you are using a list for telephoning instead of, or in addition to, direct mail.

Multiple Use. If you are planning a second or third use of the same list, order them all at the same time. Most list owners will agree to a reduced rental rate (usually 50 percent) for repeat uses of the same tape as part of a series mailing.

If you are preparing a master prospect list, some list compilers will lease their list, at a higher price, for unlimited use during the contract period.

Seed Names. A list of seed names—names and addresses that you have access to that are to be intermixed for checking mail delivery—should be included from the beginning and attached to each list order. These will be valuable in checking on the accuracy of the mailing house and the delivery time of the post office.

Deliverability Guarantee. Your printed list order form should include a standard line requesting a guarantee of deliverability by the list owner. A figure such as 95 percent should be acceptable, and the list owner should be willing to pay the minimum third class or nonprofit postage rate on all returned mail over the 5 percent figure.

Such a guarantee should provide an incentive for the list owner to have the list cleaned regularly, and to drop the names on returned mail from the list for future mailings.

Mailing Identification. The mailing order should clearly identify the product being offered and should be accompanied by a sample mailing piece. All orders are subject to the list owner's acceptance. Scrupulous honesty in regard to identifying mailings and barring reuse is expected not only by the list owner, but also by the entire direct-marketing establishment.

Figure 14-12 is a typical agency list order form. Note the specifications.

Protecting Your House-List Investment

The single most valuable list used by the majority of advertisers is their own house list. Sadly, it often is the most neglected. For most direct-marketing companies, it is their single most precious asset—the one whose loss could put them out of business. Usually it is the list most responsive to a company's additional offers.

There are several important ways in which this investment can be protected and maximized. The first is to set the list up correctly in the first place. Too many companies, when first starting out, simply copy a cus-

TeamNash, Inc.   **LIST ORDER**
275 Madison Avenue • New York 10016   Phone: 212-376-6274 • Fax: 212-376-6277

ORDERED FROM   SHIP TO MAILER

List Name And Specs: _____$ Per M:_____

Extras: _____

Gross Quantity (M): _____Est Net (M): _____

Date Ordered: _____Date Needed: _____Mail Date: _____

Format: ☐Labels   ☐Mag Tape   Other: _____

Imprint Key:	YES___NO___	☐**Nth name sample across entire file.**
Omit Canada:	YES___NO___	☐**Tab names for possible continuation.**
Omit Foreign:	YES___NO___	☐**Omit names used on previous order.**
Omit APO/FPO:	YES___NO___	☐**Tape Layout & dump: Now___With Order___.**
Phone Numbers:	YES___NO___	☐**Special instructions below:**

_____
_____
_____
_____

GUARANTEE: Mailer hereby guarantees the list will be used only one time for the offer and date stated and will not retype or copy names. List will not be telephoned unless so indicated on this form.

WARRANT: List owner warrants that the list is as described, that it has full rights to rent this list, that it has been cleaned using NCOA or nixies within the last six months, and that opt-out requests have been removed.

BILLING: Send statement including our order number and exact quantity. We will bill client and remit, less commission, after receipt of payment from mailer.

FOR CLIENT:_____OFFER:_____KEY#:_____
TEAM NASH JOB #:_____SAMPLE ENCLOSED: YES___   NO___

Figure 14-12. Typical agency list order form.

tomer's name and address off a coupon the way it comes in and preserve this name on labels, address systems, or at a computer service.

Even the best computer service can be a mistake if they do not have specific experience in direct marketing list management. Companies such as Polk, Metromail, MBS/Multimode, and other specialists in list-management should be considered. If you are publishing a periodical, by all means talk to Neodata in Boulder, Colorado, and similar magazine fulfillment specialists. Reinventing the wheel is not a good idea. There is just too much that can go wrong.

Your lists should be carefully edited to conform to the DMA bulletin "Standards for Computerized Mailing Lists." This details exactly how many characters to allow for prefix, first names, titles, addresses, cities, and other information according to accepted industry standards.

Abbreviations, codes, and tape formats should be worked out so that they are compatible with other tapes used in this field, in order to enable you to use matching, updating, and suppressing techniques as discussed later in this chapter. Also, if you're going to rent the list, you don't want a reputation for having a "dirty" list (one that is not updated or not in a consistent format). Such a reputation would lower your rental income substantially.

LIST FORMATS

Cheshire Labels.   The original addressing vehicle was the Cheshire label, a continuous form containing four labels to a line, side by side (or "east to west"). These labels are 1 inch by slightly less than 3½ inches wide. Ungummed and unperforated, they can be affixed only by machine.

Peel-off Labels.   At slightly higher cost, list owners can supply adhesive labels on a waxed-paper backing, each label being slightly smaller than a Cheshire label. These can be machine-affixed in the same manner, in situations where you want the customer to peel off the label and place it on an order form. They also can be hand-affixed very easily when labels are supplied to retailers or salespeople for local mailings.

Sheet Listings.   Printouts of data in listing form, sheet listings usually consist of 50 lines to a page. It is usable only for reference or checking, or for telephone selling operations.

Card Files.   Each individual record can be printed on a 3 × 5-inch card, or on a form having one or more parts, for distribution to salespeople or for similar uses. Such formats often include additional information. Dun's sales prospecting cards include sales volume, number of employees, lines of business, telephone numbers, and the chief executive's name in a format intended for convenient use by field sales personnel.

Magnetic Tape.   Larger mailers often prefer to order lists on magnetic tape, in a format specified by their list processor. These tapes can then be sent to a list processor for any of the services outlined in the following paragraphs, or they can be sent to mailing houses for the preparation of personalized computer letters using high-speed chain printers, laser printers, or ink-jet printing.

Delivery Instructions. The list broker should be told exactly where the lists are to be shipped and how they are to be marked. Usually you will have the lists or tapes shipped directly to the mailing house or computer service. The tapes should be clearly marked with key numbers, purchase-order numbers, drop dates, and your company name.

Other Items. Your list broker also will want to clarify such questions as how the lists are shipped, what the cost is with tax and all surcharges, and what payment terms are mutually acceptable. You may also be required to sign an agreement not to reuse the names except as specifically agreed upon.

LIST PROCESSING

Most large mailers eventually will need the services of a list processor. These firms offer even the smallest advertisers the type of sophisticated computer equipment and advanced programming that otherwise only a handful of direct marketers would be able to afford.

The advantages of these processes are directly related to volume. Duplication may not be an important factor if you are mailing only 100,000 names nationally. But it can add up to a lot if you are sending out 10 or 20 million names a year.

Duplicate Elimination

Duplicate elimination, or "de-duplicating," is the most common list-processing service. Sometimes called *merge-purge,* it basically consists of matching names and addresses from several lists against each other, searching for similarities (including family members at the same address), and consolidating duplications.

List processors usually have their own systems to maximize overall de-duplication accuracy. Some systems use phonetic logic, which spots similar names although spellings are slightly different; transposition logic (which detects transposed characters); data entry error logic (for address keying errors); and zip-code logic (to correct incorrect zip codes). The best ones have different patterns for matching urban, suburban, and rural addresses.

With most systems, duplicate names can be combined and merged into a separate multi-buyer tape. Such names, because they appear on more than one logical list, usually have a higher response rate.

A duplication allocation system produces a report showing the duplication by list. This can be done on a priority basis, matching new names against a house list or other master list, or by *stratification allocation,* which distributes duplication evenly.

Other by-products of the system are suppressions, if desired, of names outside the continental United States, APO/FPO military bases, prisons, and other unique zip-code categories. Postal bag tags are computer-generated and printed to meet Postal Service requirements for various zip sorts. A report of "net counts by key" is also prepared.

Net Name Arrangements

When ordering names from many lists to be "merged" into one file and "purged" of duplicates, how do you pay the list owner? And what about when you are eliminating names that are already your customers?

In such cases you must ask your list broker to secure an "85 percent agreement" beforehand. This means that you agree to pay the list owner for no fewer than 85 percent of the names on the list mailed. Some also charge $3 per thousand deleted names, to cover computer costs. If the actual percentage after the merge-purge has been completed is higher, then you will have to pay the higher rate.

Such agreements customarily are granted only on orders of 50,000 or more names of a large list, or the full run of smaller lists. Without such an advance agreement, you will be expected to pay the full rate regardless of the number of unused names.

The computer house must submit proof of the number of names purged from the list. If 93 percent of the list is mailable, the renter has to pay for 93 percent of the names. But if only 65 percent of the names are mailable, the renter is still obliged to pay 85 percent, as per the agreement. This system protects the list owner and broker and also provides some discount for the list user.

Large-scale mailers sometimes can negotiate a 75 percent agreement. On the other hand, some list owners permit no discount at all.

List Cleaning

Any mailer or list owner must keep its list "clean" to eliminate wasted duplication of "nixies" in its own use of it, and to give renters fair value. While there are other, privately maintained techniques, the most popular one today is the postal system's NCOA (National Change of Address) Service. Large computer-processing firms are licensed by the post office to match lists against post office files of active recipient addresses and move notices. While even this process isn't perfect, it is almost always worth the small cost. According to MBS/Multimode, this list-cleaning process can eliminate 10 to 20 percent of otherwise wasted mail that would be better sent to "live" prospects.

Two valuable types of information can be added to a mailing list as a by-product of the matching process. One add-on is carrier route codes, which can result in faster mail handling in the short term and probably postage savings later on. Another is demographic data by census tract or individual family characteristics, to be used in list-suppression or data-overlay processes.

The savings resulting from a "clean" list will pay for the address-correction process from the first large mailing, and it is certainly cheaper than current postal service charges for individual address correction.

The significance of this type of service lies in the fact that one out of five Americans moves each year, so that if your list is not updated, 20 percent of it becomes obsolete. Statistically, a one-year list is 80 percent accurate, a two-year list 64 percent, a three-year list 51 percent, and so on.

Name Suppression

Another process that has become standard for many large mailers is the suppression of selected names, performed by computer matching techniques. The names that might be suppressed from a mailing include:

- DMA Mail Preference Service "opt-outs"—people who have asked that they not be sent mail of any kind.
- Customer lists, to avoid sending introductory offers to names already on your house list.
- Any other characteristic, individually or by zip code, selected because of credit history, poor response records, or simple inappropriateness for the particular offer.
- People who have indicated that, while they wish to receive mail from a company they do business with, they prefer not to have their names rented to or exchanged with other companies. The Direct Marketing Association now requires member companies to offer this option to their customers.

Note that the elimination of unmailable or duplicate names reduces the number of names. Also these extra charges add up. Figure 14-13 shows a typical example where a $90 CPM list actually costs $139/M.

Customer History Files

When list processors are used for maintenance of a company's own list of active customers, they can perform many valuable services in addition to list maintenance and the preparation of labels for mailing.

Business mailers can add to their customer lists any Dun & Bradstreet information, as discussed earlier, plus information on specific sales, sales commissions, purchases, and relative rankings.

Consumer catalog mailers can add a product-preference code, average and latest purchase amount, credit history, gender, birth date, ages of children, census tract data, and a profitability index taking into account the number of catalogs mailed.

List Name Selection		BMG Direct Classical Music Service Active Members, $25+	
Quantity Ordered-Recieved	100,000	100,000	
Edit Fails	2.50%	(2,500)	
Good Names	97,500	97,500	
% Duplication	40.00%	(39,000)	
Net Names	58,500	58,500	
Net Name %	80%		
List CPM	$90.00	(78,000*.001) * $90	$7,020.00
Regular Selection Charges	$0.00	Not applicable	$0.00
Across the Board Selection Charges	$10.00	(97,500*.001) * $10	$975.00
Running Charge	$7.50	((97,500-78000)*.001) * 7.50	$146.25
Total Base List Cost	$7,020.00		
Total Selection Charges	$975.00		
Total Running Charges	$146.25		
Total Invoice	$8,141.25		$8,141.25
Invoice CPM	$104.38		
Actual CPM	$139.17		

Figure 14-13. Calculating actual list rental cost

Fundraisers can compile similar information for contributors, including interest groups, initial and subsequent contributions, date of last gift, and individual and census information.

Circulation promotion mailers can add subscription term, renewal information, income, advertising cost, additional purchases, and anything else that might be of value.

Reports can be compiled by source, customer type, product category, month, state, or Standard Metropolitan Statistical Area. Virtually any type of data can be produced, provided it is in the system in some form in the first place.

Special Systems

Some list processors and compilers have prepared total systems for list management, lead procurement, or direct marketing.

There are too many suppliers to try to mention all their services. At least one company supplies a business-lead system integrated with mailings, reports, sales follow-up, and lead distribution. Another has a special program for the insurance industry, where local agents may select demographic specifications within their own areas and order mailings sent to their immediate neighborhood, with related lead follow-up systems.

Some companies have stock systems for continuity programs or card-file mailings. Others have software ready to go for catalog operations, with or without credit sales. Your best bet is to talk to many potential suppliers and to find those who have learned how to handle your problem. They became experts the hard way—by making their mistakes at some other client's expense in the past. It is much easier to adapt an existing computer program to meet your needs than to teach a company the basics of list processing.

OUTBOUND RENTALS

Don't overlook renting out your own mailing list, as an added source of income. It's easier than it seems, because a list manager will handle all the details and give you a "turnkey" new profit source. They advertise your list and promote it to list brokers and end users, then handle all the requests for rental. They will even handle the approval process, screening out uses you would not want and submitting questionable requests to you.

In some countries, companies hesitate to rent their lists for fear it will be copied. Fake names, called "dummy names," added to the list will reveal if this happens. To avoid it happening, list rental agreements between owners, brokers, and renters should stipulate what in the United States is an unwritten understanding—that anyone copying a list or mailing it without permission will be cut off from ever renting a list again, or from renting out their lists. National direct marketing associations should agree on this type of penalty and enforce it.

OTHER MAILING-LIST TECHNIQUES

Here are some of the list-buying and list-processing techniques used by some large advertisers. Most of these will be necessary only for companies that have exhausted conventional sources and who require very substantial mailing lists. In some cases, however, they may help a marginal company get bigger, if employees have the time and patience to work out some of these methods.

Category Pooling

Earlier in this chapter we discussed how catalog companies and other direct response firms use recency-frequency-purchase size, source and type of product purchased to refine their mailing lists. Certainly reducing a predictably less-responsive number of names is a practical way to improve profits. However, there is only a limited amount of data that will indicate this for the names in each company's file.

Firms like Abacus came up with an innovative solution, one now offered by other list brokers as well. They offered to analyze a mailer's list based not on just their own data but on the customers' patterns dealing with—in the case of Abacus—100 different catalogers. The mailer could determine that a customer who might not be buying a lot from them might actually be an active buyer from other catalog companies, and therefore worth mailing to. The "catch" is that each mailer company must contribute its own mailing lists and data to the combined database at Abacus.

While this is theoretically an advance in predictive capability, there have been some concerns. For instance, is everyone now mailing to the same people, thus producing a decline in responses for each participant? Are there just too many catalogs? Are we mailing too frequently? Or is everyone now buying on the web?

Multibuyer Match

One way to pretest a mailing list is to match it against either your customer list or other known profitable lists. The higher the match factor, the more likely it is that the total list will be successful. This is used to predict the likelihood that a list will work.

Data Overlay

It is possible to match response lists against either the census tract or the individual characteristics of compiled lists and producing a list that combines both known response history and demographic factors. For instance, for a home-repair book, you might overlay the factor of "individual residence" against known mail-order buyers to produce a list of mail-order buyers who live in single-family homes. Or you might match a list of people who have responded to any book offer against other lists of families with children, to send out a mailing offering a set of children's books.

Title Conformance

If you are looking for female mail-order buyers and have exhausted all known female names on your best lists, you can try arbitrarily adding a "Mrs." before the male names on the lists. The chances are that "Mrs. John Jones" will reach the woman of the household, even though a certain amount of such mail will be wasted on bachelors.

In neighborhoods with children, you can correct a title to read "To the children of Mrs. Smith" with a reasonable chance of successfully reaching your prospect. When you have the names of children, there's no problem in having the computer print out "To Amy Nash's Mom" or something similar.

You can direct the list manager to print out names in any format and type size, providing an opportunity for creativity. For a three-scent sample pack of a new soap, I once addressed the envelope to the first name three times—"Diana, Diana and Diana Jones." The letter then referred "to all the women you are"—practical, romantic, etc.

Cluster Analysis

Companies such as Claritas and Database America have perfected systems that enable you to analyze your customer data and determine which zip codes have the greatest chance of success for your mailings. Gross response, credit performance, buying patterns, and other factors are used to pick out which areas are worth mailing to and which are not.

Waste Factor Calculation

Some advertisers back off from using lists because their message is too narrow. An example might be a special credit offer to college graduates. Such lists are difficult to obtain in quantity, yet in some neighborhoods more than half the household heads are college graduates.

The waste calculation strategy deliberately ignores the off-target addresses and concentrates on the doughnut instead of the hole. Sure, some people will get mail with an offer that they will not be qualified for. But if the mailing produces an overall 2 percent response, and if that 2 percent is acceptable, then it is no longer important that a pure college-graduate list might have produced twice the response if there isn't one around, or the ones that exist aren't of sufficient size. A half-efficient list is better than none at all.

Skimming versus
High-Penetration Strategies

"High penetration" is needed when you have few prospects and a high-unit sale. Companies such as Avis Rent-A-Car and International Gold Corporation did well with a series of letters at a CPM over $1000. On the other hand, some mailers—especially philanthropies—do better with inexpensive mailings.

Other Techniques

The more advanced techniques in this field are often carefully guarded secrets. Even some of the examples used here have been changed to respect confidences. We urge you to look at the techniques discussed here more as a way of thinking—of stretching your mind to the potential of what can be done with mailing lists—than as specific ideas for your company. I strongly recommend that you read some of the articles by list specialists in *The Direct Marketing Handbook* (Second edition, McGraw Hill).

PACKAGE INSERTS AND
CO-OP MAILINGS

Two mediums that are often lumped with mailing lists are *cooperative mailings* and *package inserts*. Like mailing lists, both are listed in SRDS Direct Mail, and like mailing lists, they are ordered through list brokers.

Package Inserts

Several companies sell the right to insert an offer in their package mailings, or their statement stuffers. Because they get a free ride with postage that would have had to be paid anyway, such stuffing opportunities can be made available very inexpensively.

Figure 14-15 shows an SRDS listing for the Eddie Bauer package insert program as listed in SRDS along with quantities and prices. Note that the rate of distribution varies according to the each company's own business cycles.

These inserts have stringent weight and size limitations and so are most useful where a skimming strategy has proven effective. A disadvantage is that it is difficult to coordinate them with other media or seasonal plans. They may be inserted in packages over several months. I have used them very successfully for two-step offers and catalog requests where timing was not critical.

Cooperative Mailings

Probably the best-known cooperative mailings are Donnelly's Carol Wright, which sends out some six mailings a year to over 20 million people, and Supermarket of Savings by Larry Tucker Associates, and those by Madison. An illustration of a typical co-op mailing appears as Fig. 14-14. There are also many specialized cooperative mailings to teenagers, seniors, ethnic groups, and specific occupations or business types. NIA, for instance, has a very successful mailing to affluent Afro-Americans. The Tucker organization has been particularly helpful in providing flexibility to help test solutions for special marketing situations. Their rate card appears as Fig. 14-16.

Costs can range from $25 to $50 per thousand inserts, depending on the degree of selectivity, the amount of clutter, and the number of inserts. Rates vary with the size and weight of the pieces inserted. Printing is extra. Some advertisers, especially those offering mass general magazines, recipe cards, or film processing, consider this medium very important and reserve choice dates and geographic areas years in advance.

Clutter is the result of too many other pieces inserted with yours in a cooperative mailing. The number of pieces, as well as the perception of the quality of the products and services offered, will dilute attention and therefore response. The execution of the other inserts and the perceived quality of the products offered will "rub off" on your insert.

The advantage is, of course, the low cost. For products employing a "skimming strategy" or where the offer can be expressed in limited space, they are often very effective. They are also inexpensive to test. They are a media category that should not be overlooked.

* * *

This is easily the longest chapter in the book besides Chapter 22 on the Internet. It should be. No other medium is as important, varied, or complex.

Figure 14-14. A typical co-op mailing package. This one features ads of interest to people over 50.

Working with mailing lists will never be as dramatic as designing a new mailing package, but it is more challenging. Suppressing or segmenting out the unproductive half of a mailing list is as important as doubling a response rate. It is just as profitable (actually more so), just as feasible, and just as worthy of our time, attention, and talent.

EDDIE BAUER PACKAGE INSERT PROGRAM

Data Verified: Feb 8, 1999.

Location ID: 10 DCMI 544   Mid 038495-000
Member: D.M.A.
Participant D.M.A. Mail Preference Service.

1. PERSONNEL
List Manager
Direct Media Insert Management Div.
200 Pemberwick Rd., Box 4565, Greenwich, CT 06830.
Phone 203-532-1000. Fax 203-531-1452.

2. SUMMARY DESCRIPTION
Inserts in packages to mail order buyers of men's and women's outdoor apparel and equipment.
29% male, 71% female; average age 47.
Average unit of sale 95.00.

4. SELECTIONS WITH COUNTS
Updated: Feb 8, 1999.

	Total Number	Price per/M
Total list	4,599,000	65.00
1998:		
January	386,000	65.00
February	326,000	"
March	363,000	"
April	297,000	"
May	385,000	"
June	477,000	"
July	189,000	"
August	208,000	"
September	335,000	"
October	354,000	"
November	504,000	"
December	775,000	"

Minimum order 10,000.

5. COMMISSION, CREDIT POLICY
20% commission to brokers. Cancel charges: A 50.00 cancellation fee with 60 days notice from want date applies.

6. METHOD OF ADDRESSING
Maximum size 5.5" x 8.5". Maximum weight .25 oz.

8. RESTRICTIONS
Sample mailing piece required. Non-competitive offers have to be consistent with Eddie Bauer image. Inserts must be delivered by the first of the month previous to mailing. Ship to instructions will be given upon approval of mailer's piece. Maximum inserts 6.

Figure 14-15. From SRDS *Direct Marketing List Source.*

SEARS PORTRAIT STUDIO

(SPONSOR)

SUPERMARKET OF SAVINGS
"YOUNG FAMILY"

RIDE-A-LONGS

(To Heavy Coupon Users)

DESCRIPTION:

A "Ride-A-Long" is a mailing targeted to a special list, generally to customers or members where other advertisers "ride-a-long" in the envelope. The benefits to advertisers who participate (versus a Co-op) are generally a <u>much higher response / redemption, a strong "implied third party endorsement,"</u> projecting instant credibility for all advertisers, and an <u>exclusive distribution channel</u> not available elsewhere.

This "ride-a-long" is personally addressed in a 6 x 9 envelope mailed nationally to heavy coupon users. Your offer will "ride-a-long" with very special and valuable offers from Sears Portrait Studio. The strongly implied third party endorsement insures that your offer will be received with excitement, read with special interest and responded to—because the valuable package of offers is coming from **Sears**.

Up to 28 advertisements, cents-off coupons and samples are mailed in the attractively designed, four-color, personally addressed envelope from Sears Portrait Studio indicating that there are 25 "great offers inside."

A combination of proprietary and high response lists are used to reach the most responsive young family households in America. These families have **consistently** demonstrated their desire to receive, read and respond to the valuable offers inside.

3 OPTIONS: **ANNUALLY:**

1.	2.5 Million New Parents with a newborn up to 12 months old	10 Million
2.	10.0 Million Parents of Preschoolers 1-6 years of age	40 Million
3.	12.5 Million Young Parents (unduplicated)	50 Million

SPECS:

Maximum Size:	5 ½ x 8 ¼
Maximum Weight:	.1 oz (Overweight-Inquire)
Maximum Inserts:	28
Stock:	45# Coated

DEMOGRAPHICS:

Parents with children in the 0-6 age range
Average household has 2.2 children
Age of adults in the household 18-39
Average HHI $36,140
Mail responsive households nationwide

Working Mothers:		64%
Coupon Usage:		
Redeem Coupons:		92%
Heavy Users (5 or more per week):		83%
Education: 58% graduated college		

In-Home Dates	Inserts Due	Film Due	Closing Date
07/12-07/17/99	05/10/99	04/15/99	04/08/99
10/04-10/09/99	08/09/99	07/15/99	07/08/99
01/03-01/08/00	10/22/99	09/27/99	09/20/99
03/06-03/11/00	01/07/00	12/13/99	12/06/99
07/10-07/15/00	05/03/00	04/08/00	04/01/00
10/02-10/07/00	08/09/00	07/15/00	07/08/00

DATE

February 17, 1999

CPM

$35/M

SELECTING

$5.00/M SCF

MINIMUM ORDER

100,000 - $5,000

LISTS USED

Proprietary sources

COMMISSION

15% commission to accredited agencies

ADDITIONAL SERVICES

Print & creative available

CONTACT

Jill Cook
Sales Coordinator

Phone: (201) 307-8888 x 125
Fax: (201) 307-0888
E-mail: <u>SuperSav1@aol.com</u>

Figure 14-16

15

PRINT MEDIA

In the fast-changing world of direct marketing, newspapers and magazines are the Cinderellas of media. While these communication tools have lacked the instant stardom of broadcast, or the high-tech mathematical and personalization tools of direct mail, or the instant interactivity of telemarketing or the Internet, they are still productive and—when used correctly—can be profitable for every kind of direct marketer.

True, little has changed when it comes to the classic uses of print media. Small-space ads are still in shopping sections. Inquiry-pullers in financial, travel, real estate and other newspaper sections still exist. Special-interest business and consumer magazines are commonplace. Multi-page music club sections, and other freestanding inserts in the Sunday papers, still fall out of the paper each Sunday morning.

The change here is that direct-marketing methods have become the key to the survival of these media. Advertising lineage has declined in many once-prosperous publications, as marketing funds have been diverted to direct mail and other accountable media. Yet direct marketers know that well-done print advertisements have the power to reach and identify prospects who can't be identified on existing mailing lists.

Business advertisers need print media to reach the elusive "initiators" and "approvers" who play a key role in purchasing and supplier decisions. Consumer advertisers need it to reach the fresh, highly responsive prospects who have not already been worked over by their competitors: the newly prosperous, the recently married, or the enthusiastic new adopters of an interest or activity.

Don't despair if tacking on a phone number to your clever "image ads" hasn't generated the response you expected. Instead, have direct marketers design an advertisement where response-generation is a prime objective rather than an afterthought, and see the difference. It is no more accurate to say, "Print media doesn't work" than to apply that to any other media category. All that means is that you haven't figured out how to make it work. Newspapers and magazines will always be with us, and will always be an effective if not glamorous communication tool. They cannot be ignored.

WHEN TO USE PUBLICATION MEDIA

The principles of planning newspaper and magazine schedules are not unlike those that apply to selecting direct-mail lists. The medium is the market, not just a way of reaching a market. There must be a logical affinity between product and audience. The quality of audience is more critical than the quantity. Divisibility permits segmentation and, therefore, fine-tuning of profitability and limitation of downside risk. The principles are the same, but the practice is significantly different.

Many businesses are launched in direct mail or on the Internet, and some giant firms use direct mail as their single most important way of reaching potential audiences. However, in every marketing situation some important role is played by other media. Some examples follow.

Extending Direct Mail

A frequent problem with successful direct mail users is that they reach a point where the list universe is exhausted. Despite tailored appeals, segmentation refinement, and the testing of alternative direct-mail strategies, there simply are no more names to be tested.

At this point many advertisers, particularly magazine subscription managers, try to increase the frequency of mailing, but they find that lists that did well on an annual or biannual frequency roll over and die when mailed too often. The highest-affinity core list simply has only so many fresh names or old names ready to accept a product offer—and no more.

In such situations, print media extends direct mail. If subscribers to a magazine are an effective list, for instance, then an advertisement in that magazine enables you to reach not only the subscribers, but also the newsstand buyers of the magazine. You'll also reach the publication's pass-along readership. According to some studies, this can be two or three times the circulation and up to six times the number of subscribers.

If a list such as Lillian Vernon is highly effective, then it is often possible to do well by going into the same magazines that Lillian Vernon did to build their list in the first place. This is another approach to extending mail.

Advertisers usually discover that, except for house lists and a limited group of core lists, print or broadcast media are the most effective media sources. Non-core lists take up the next position in effectiveness.

An Alternative to Direct Mail

There are some propositions and situations that are simply solved much better with print media than in direct mail. The four situations where this usually occurs are (1) economics, (2) credibility, (3) a need for coverage and (4) a need to create new markets.

Economics.   Print media reaches a much larger number of people, at much lower cost, than direct mail. The trade-off is that they possess a much lower percentage of the desired audience for most propositions. Previously I've discussed skimming as a strategic alternative to high penetration in direct mail. The skimming approach is often best executed in print media, where a message can be presented to a larger number at less expense.

Skimming is particularly appropriate for offers involving a low unit-cost or for two-step propositions with initial free offers. There is simply not enough margin to support a 50-cents-per-unit ($500-per-thousand) mail contact on an offer that has no more likelihood of getting a response from any one prospect than a 5-cents per-contact ($50 per thousand) print-media message. In other words, unless there is 10 times the likelihood that a list addressee will respond, either because of list affinity or the added impact of a longer, more involving direct mail message, an alternative media like print might be more economical. It will be more profitable to reach that prospect and others in a less involving, less expensive print-media message.

Need for Credibility.   Some direct-marketing offers, from unknown companies, are helped by the implied endorsement of a publication, just as some direct mail programs need the *imprimatur* of a well-known company. Readers presume, and rightly so, that a magazine or newspaper will stand behind the products advertised in its pages. Some publications, such as *Good Housekeeping* and *The New York Times,* are very strict about this, and so have greater credibility than publications that may not be as stringent in their requirements.

If your company is unknown, and especially if your product raises health or safety concerns on the part of the consumer, it may do much better in established magazines than in any direct mail other than that endorsed by a well-respected third party.

Coverage Need.   Some companies have a product or service that can afford a highly targeted, high-penetration direct mail effort, but simply do not have enough good lists. This is frequently the case in the business-equipment and financial fields. The print medium's wide coverage is an effective way to reach out and attract new customers.

Mailing lists that identify key executives by name will do well for a maker of computer software, or a solicitor of investments in gold, gems, or money-market funds. But there are just not enough of those names. Dun's Decision Makers, for instance, can provide the names of half-a-dozen top executives in a corporation, but hundreds more may have the authority to buy a new fax machine, choose an air-freight service, or plan a plane trip. While direct mail may be much more effective on a cost-per-order basis, such products still require extensive print-media campaigns to reach all of their potential prospects.

Finding New Markets. Starting something new often requires going into the widest possible marketplace and letting the product seek its own level or find its own market.

In some cases—such as prepaid health services, a magazine for tennis buffs or a club for indoor gardeners—there are not enough mailing lists to build a business, no matter what the strategy is. That's where print media can be extremely useful. In fact, I sometimes recommend using general publications for an initial round of ads, followed by a regression analysis of respondents to find unexpected list-affinity areas.

A valuable by-product of this approach is the building of a unique mailing list of buyers of your own product. This should have high value in the list-rental marketplace or as a foundation for additional product introductions.

Remember that direct mail is a sharpshooter's medium, while print media and broadcast are like shotguns that spray over a wide area. If your targets are few, worthwhile, and identified, nothing beats a sharpshooter like direct mail. But if they are hard to find, small in number, or hard to identify, then there's nothing like a shotgun. That way you will be sure to hit something.

I had occasion to survey mattress advertising for one client who used only television and telemarketing. It turned out the competitors were spending the bulk of their budgets in print media. The client refused to even test print because of bad results from one test many years ago. The correct approach would be to test new offers and creative until something worked, rather than writing off the bulk of his potential marketing media.

SOURCES OF INFORMATION

Before we go into selecting newspapers and magazines, the first step is to know where and how to get the information you need. This includes not just rates and circulation but type of circulation (paid or free) page sizes and mechanical specifications.

Both newspapers and magazines will have different rates for different classifications, such as Retail and Mail Order. Both will have regional and other types of editions. Either will or will not have capabilities to do split-runs and inserts, or may charge different rates for different sections of positions.

Rate Cards

The basic information source is the publication itself. For a small, simple schedule, pick the publications you are interested in from the displays at a major newsstand. Then call the publication and ask for a rate card or "media kit." Usually you'll get everything you need, along with sample copies, circulation breakdowns, and lists of special editions. The publications can also give you valuable research studies about how often your competitors use various publications.

The advertising sales representative, like all sales executives today, is expected to be knowledgeable and helpful. Treat representative as allies. The more they know about your product and your plans, the better advice they can give you.

Media Brokers

Many magazines, and some newspapers, offer discounted rates in return for flexible insertion dates or for advertising during their slower seasons. Sometimes the special rates are available for last-minute "stand-by" insertions when the publication has a cancellation. As these discounts can run as high as 30 percent or 40 percent off the rate card, the savings can be significant.

The media directors of specialist direct-response agencies know of many of these "deals." Others are available only through media brokers, such as Steven Geller in Greenwich, CT or Novus in Portchester, NY. They often are the exclusive sales agents for the direct-response category of a magazine, and offer low rates that the publication's sales representatives may be unaware of. Even ad agencies buy through these brokers when the rates are advantageous, passing the savings along to their clients.

Standard Rate and Data Service

As with direct mail, the directories published by Standard Rate and Data Service are essential tools of the trade. They publish separate editions for consumer publications, business publications and weekly newspapers as well as reference books which provide detailed printing specifications and market-by-market circulation breakdowns.

The consumer magazine directory alone contains data on thousands of magazines sorted into 63 classifications. The main classifications are worth noting. (See Fig. 15-1.)

Most people are surprised at the wide range of little known and highly specialized magazines. When we deal with publications that are not as well known, such as the 8,000 or so magazines in the classifications in *SRDS Business Publications*, the challenge is even greater. Media buying cannot be done "off the top of your head." It is a rigorous and demanding science that demands the best tools of the trade.

Each listing of a single magazine incorporates, in a standardized format, all the objective data needed to analyze potential media. Unlike rate cards supplied by the magazines themselves, SRDS listings are always comparable, point by point. Each listing includes all of the information shown in Fig. 15-2. See Fig. 15-3 for an actual sample listing in an SRDS Consumer Magazine Advertising Source.

SRDS has several other specialized features that are also very helpful.

0.	Affluence	23B.	Home Office/Small Business
1.	Airline Inflight/Train Enroute	24.	Home Service & Home
1A.	Almanacs & Directories	25.	Horses, Riding & Breeding
2.	Art & Antiques	25A.	Hotel Inroom
3.	Automotive	27.	Labor, Trade Union
4.	Aviation	28.	Literary, Book Reviews & Writing
5.	Babies	28A.	Mature Market
5A.	Black/African-American	29.	Mechanics & Science
6.	Boating & Yachting	29A.	Media/Personalities
7.	Bridal	30.	Men's
8.	Business & Finance	30A.	Metropolitan/Regional/State
8A.	Campers, Recreational Vehicles	30B.	Metropolitan/Entertainment
8B.	Camping & Outdoor Recreation	31.	Military & Naval
9.	Children's	31A.	Motorcycle
9A.	Civic	33.	Music
9B.	College & Alumni	34.	Mystery, Adventure & Science Fiction
10.	Comics & Comic Technique	35.	Nature & Ecology
10A.	Computers	36A.	Newsweeklies
11.	Crafts, Games, Hobbies & Models	36B.	News – Biweeklies, Dailies, Semimonthlies
12.	Dancing	36C.	Newsweeklies (Alternatives)
12A.	Disability	37.	Newsletters
13.	Dogs & Pets	38.	Newspaper Distributed Magazines
14.	Dressmaking & Needlework	38A.	Parenthood
15.	Editorialized & Classified Advertising	39.	Photography
16.	Education & Teacher	41.	Political & Social Topics
17.	Entertainment Guides & Programs	41A.	Popular Culture
17A.	Entertainment & Performing Arts	42.	Religious & Denominational
18.	Epicurean	43.	Science/Technology
19.	Fishing & Hunting	44A.	Special Interest Publications
19A.	Fitness	45.	Sports
20.	Fraternal, Professional, Veterans	45A.	Teen
20A.	Gaming	46.	Travel
21.	Gardening (Home)	47.	TV & Radio/Communications
21A.	Gay Publications	49.	Women's
22.	General Editorial	51.	Youth
22A.	Group Buying Opportunities		
23.	Health		
23A.	History		

Figure 15-1. SRDS Categories of Consumer Magazines

Magazine and Farm Publication Representatives. Shows name, address, and telephone number of home and branch offices of firms representing consumer magazines and farm publications.

Three-year Media Buying Calendar. Shows purchasing dates in bold.

Geographic Index. Shows the cities where the magazines are published.

Magazine Group-buying Opportunities–Domestic and International. An alphabetical index of all group titles appearing in Consumer magazine and Farm Publication Rates and Data, with reference to editorial classifications in which listings have been assigned.

Magazines with Geographic and/or Demographic Editions of Split-run Advertising. A two-section index, listed in alphabetical order. Shows international listings as well.

General Information

Title of publication
Printed in Spanish or English; Bilingual
Frequency of issue
Name of publisher
Address of publisher

Specific Information

Personnel
Executives responsibile for national accounts

Representatives and/or branch offices
  Company name (representatives only)
  Name/Title
  Address

Commission and cash discount
  Amount of agency commission
  Cash discount or no discount

General rate policy
  Contract cancellation clause
  Policy on rate protection and revision
  Conditions and/or regulations
  Effective date and of rate card in force

Black/white rates
  National advertising rates
  B/w discount structures

5a.*Combination rates*
  Rates when sold in combination

5b.Discounts *(gross expenditures)*
  Discounts applicable to total dollars

Color rates *(if available)*
  Rates for standard colors
  Rates for selected colors
  Color discount structures

Covers
  Availability
  Rates

Inserts
  Base rates
  Special charges
  Tip-ons

Bleed
  Availability and rates

Special position
  Availability
  Rates

Classified/mail order
  Classified rates

Display classifications
Mail-order rates

Split-run
  Rates
  Requirements
  Circulation data and source

Special issue rates and data
  Special or thirteenth issue.
  Issuance dates for special issues
  Circulation data and source

13a.*Geographic or demographic editions*
  Rates
  Requirements
  Issue and closing dates
  Circulation data and source

General requirements
  Trim size, number of columns to page
  Binding method
  Color available
  Dimensions – ad page (width and depth)
  Minimum depth R.O.P. (run of paper)

Issue and closing dates
  Frequency of publication
  Closing dates for: black-and-white, color,
  inserts, set copy, and special feature issues

Special service
  ABC Supplemental Data Report
  Ad readership studies
  Advertising preparation services
  Direct mail services
  Direct-response services
  Merchandising services
  Reprints
  Reader service card
  Special stock printing

Circulation
  Single-copy and annual prices
  Circulation data and source
  Territorial distribution
  Publisher guarantee or "rates based on"

Distribution
  Year established
  Distribution data and source

Print order
  Copies printed and offered for sale

Figure 15-2. Information available in SRDS *Consumer Magazines*

MAINE ANTIQUE DIGEST

Location ID: 8 MLST 2   **Mid 360582-000**
by Maine Antique Digest, PO Box 1429, 911 Main St., Waldoboro, ME 04572. Phone 207-832-7534. Fax 207-832-7341.
E-Mail mad@maine.com
URL http://www.maineantiquedigest.com

PUBLISHER'S EDITORIAL PROFILE

MAINE ANTIQUE DIGEST focuses on the marketplace for Americana, encompassing antiques, accessories, and art form the seventeenth century to the twentieth century. Heavy auction and show coverage with pictures and prices, what sold, how much, who bought, condition, etc. Frauds, seminars, help-needed, stolen, legislation, and other topics directly relating to the antiques trade are also included. Rec'd 2/8/99.

1. PERSONNEL
Adv Mgr—Alice Greene.
Pub—Samuel Pennington.

3. COMMISSION AND CASH DISCOUNT
15% to recognized agencies. 10% prepaid or 10 days. Late payment charge or 1-1/2% a month for bills unpaid 30 days after billing.

ADVERTISING RATES
Effective January 1, 1999. (Card)
Rates received February 8, 1999.

5. BLACK/WHITE RATES

1 page	750.	1/3 page	265.
3/4 page	595.	1/4 page	215.
2/3 page	530.	1/6 page	150.
3/5 page	450.	1/8 page	110.
1/2 page	380.	1/16 page	80.
2/5 page	310.	Per col inch	16.

9. BLEED
No bleed.

11. CLASSIFIED/MAIL ORDER/SPECIALTY RATES
CLASSIFIED:
1.00 per word, 25 word minimum. Photos extra 10.00.

15. GENERAL REQUIREMENTS
Also see SRDS Print Media Production Source.
Printing Process: Web Offset Full Run.
Binding Method: Fold.
Colors Available: Black and white.

NON-BLEED
AD PAGE DIMENSIONS

1 pg	9-3/4	x	14-1/2	1/4 v	3-3/4	x	9
3/4 v	9-3/4	x	10-7/8	1/4 h	9-3/4	x	3-1/2
2/3 v	9-3/4	x	9-11/16	1/4 sq	5-3/4	x	6
3/5 v	5-3/4	x	14-1/2	1/6 v	3-3/4	x	6
1/2 v	4-3/4	x	14-1/2	1/6 h	4-3/4	x	4-3/4
1/2 h	9-3/4	x	7-3/16	1/8	3-3/4	x	4-1/2
1/3 v	4-3/4	x	9-11/16	1/8	4-3/4	x	3-1/2
1/3 h	9-3/4	x	4-3/4	1/16	3-3/4	x	2-3/8
1/3 sq	5-3/4	x	8	1/16	1-3/4	x	4-3/4
1/4 v	4-3/4	x	7-3/16	2/5	3-3/4	x	14-1/2

16. ISSUE AND CLOSING DATES
Published monthly.

Issue:	Closing	(**)	Issue:	Closing	(**)
May/99	4/7	4/6	Sep/99	8/4	8/3
Jun/99	5/5	5/4	Oct/99	9/1	8/31
Jul/99	6/2	6/1	Nov/99	10/6	10/5
Aug/99	7/7	7/6	Dec/99	12/1	11/30

(**) Electronic

18. CIRCULATION
Single copy 3.75; per year 43.00.

SWORN 12-31-98 (6 mos. aver.)

Total	Non-Pd	Paid	(Subs)	(Single)	(Assoc)
31,234	...	31,234	28,598	2,636	...

Unpaid Distribution (not incl. above):
Total 1,039

Figure 15-3. Typical magazine listing from SRDS

Market Data by Census Regions.   Listings by regions, then by state.

Demographic and Geographic Editions.   Guide that lists magazines that can be segmented by type of reader or by area of the country—a valuable way to target expenditures to a specific market or to minimize downside risk on a test.

Split-Run Availability. Section that shows magazines that will accept split-run advertising, facilitating copy testing with or without combination with geographic or demographic editions.

Some Other Tools of the Trade

While SRDS is the indispensable tool of the media planner, other tools can sometimes be very useful.

Audit Statements. Audit statements began as a way of verifying circulation claims and providing an independent verification of publishers' sworn statements. The best-known individual magazine statements are those published by the Audit Bureau of Circulation. Today their most valuable function is their breakdown of circulation by source. An ABC statement will disclose whether a magazine is subscription-sold or newsstand-sold; whether it has been sold at cut rate, with premiums, or with a sweepstakes; and whether it has been sold by direct mail or through agents such as Publishers' Clearing House. All this data can be analyzed to indicate the quality of a publication's circulation.

Direct mail-sold readers who have come in through full-price subscriptions can be the most meaningful circulation if your own product is sold the same way. However, if you have a reduced-price introductory offer or are selling with a sweepstakes, it may be important to know that similar offers were successful in attracting the magazine's readers in the first place.

Usually, the data is helpful the other way around—in tailoring the offer. If a magazine ad has been marginal in response despite a logical affinity of editorial matter, it may be helpful to look at how the magazine was sold in the first place. For instance, if the publication was sold by sweepstakes, it might be successful if you have a sweepstakes offer.

Another factor revealed by audit statements is the status of the circulation, as opposed to the source. If most readers are new, they may not be reading the magazine intensely if it is not what they expected. However, a large percentage of renewed renewals (RRs) indicates that the publication is being read thoroughly, giving your advertisement a better chance of being read as well. From a direct marketer's point of view, the quality of a magazine might be represented by the formula MS% × RR% = QF, or percentage of direct mail-sold times percentage of renewed renewals equals quality factor. MS stands for Mail-Sold, RR for Renewed Renewals and QF is Quality Factor.

The quality factor can be applied to total percentages or to cost per thousand readers to produce a quality-adjusted circulation or cost per thousand. There should be a correlation between quality-adjusted cost figures and resulting cost-per-order data from actual insertions.

PIB Reports. Another tool is *PIB Reports,* issued by Publishers' Information Bureau. As discussed in Chapter 3, The Marketing Plan, the primary reason for reading *PIB Reports* is to check on the competition by seeing what publications they are using repeatedly.

Simmons Reports. Simmons reports, available in voluminous binders at great expense, are the most sophisticated application of research to publication-media buying. Simmons conducts extensive surveys, asking readers what magazines they read and what their hobbies and interests are, and draws valuable conclusions about magazine readership and reader interests.

Many agencies have this data on computer, and can quickly run through categories to produce media efficiency studies. For instance, if you wanted to run an ad selling golf clubs by mail, they would correlate readers who play golf and readers who buy by mail. They could then combine the results with income, education, age, family size, or any other factors to produce a media list based on *cost per thousand targeted* readers. This "CPMT" factor is discussed in more detail later in this chapter.

Figure 15-4 is an excerpt from a Simmons report. The category is "Cruise Ship Vacation Within the Last 3 Years," and is also available by male and female readers of magazines. The A column is a projection of their samples to the actual number of readers of each magazine who fit the description. The B "Down" column represents the estimated percent of all cruise ship travelers that can be reached by advertising in each magazine. Not surprisingly, larger magazines like Parade reach more of this market. The C

	TOTAL U.S. '000	A '000	ADULTS B % DOWN	C % ACROSS	D INDX
TOTAL	182456	10340	100.0	5.7	100
THE N.Y. TIMES MAGAZINE	3859	292	2.8	7.6	134
OMNI	2338	*110	1.1	4.7	83
1,001 HOME IDEAS	3771	308	3.0	8.2	144
ORGANIC GARDENING	2544	*186	1.8	7.3	129
OUTDOOR LIFE	7310	*366	3.5	5.0	88
PARADE MAGAZINE	67853	4386	42.4	6.5	114
PARENTING	1947	**58	0.6	3.0	53
PARENTS	6643	247	2.4	3.7	66
PEOPLE	28488	1855	17.9	6.5	115
PLAYBOY	8337	386	3.7	4.6	82
POPULAR MECHANICS	5655	206	2.0	3.6	64
POPULAR SCIENCE	4555	276	2.7	6.1	107
PRACTICAL HOMEOWNER	1281	**97	0.9	7.6	134
PREVENTION	6154	308	3.0	5.0	88
READER'S DIGEST	36930	2267	21.9	6.1	108
REDBOOK	10533	683	6.6	6.5	114
ROAD & TRACK	3838	275	2.7	7.2	126
ROLLING STONE	6154	318	3.1	5.2	91
SCIENTIFIC AMERICAN	1835	*98	0.9	5.3	94
SELF	2957	*190	1.8	6.4	113
SESAME STREET MAGAZINE	3606	*161	1.6	4.5	79
SEVENTEEN	3532	*131	1.3	3.7	65
SHAPE	1664	*108	1.0	6.5	115
SKI	1764	*95	0.9	5.4	95
SKIING	1535	*80	0.8	5.2	92
SMITHSONIAN	6299	466	4.5	7.4	131
SOAP OPERA DIGEST	6437	205	2.0	3.2	56
SOUTHERN LIVING	7213	553	5.3	7.7	135
SPORT	3012	*195	1.9	6.5	114
THE SPORTING NEWS	3348	218	2.1	6.5	115

Figure 15-4. Sample of Simmons Listing. Source: © 1991 by Simmons Market Research Bureau, Inc.

"Across" column is the percentage of the magazine's readers who are in this market. The D "Index column" is a convenience for comparison. The 5.7 average of the total population is set at 100 and is the base for the Index. Note the lower index for magazines read by parents, and the higher figures for publications that appeal to older and/or more affluent readers. Conde Nast Traveler, Golf and the New Yorker (not in shown in this excerpt) had the highest scores at the time this particular report was released.

For each category not only magazine readership is studied but also newspapers, outdoor, radio (by type of music) and television by program or event. Demographics are also provided for every category, and every category you can think of is covered. I have found it particularly useful to combine two categories—mail order purchase within the last year and the product I am advertising. This and similar types of research are part of the tools of mass advertising that are extremely useful to direct marketers as well.

THE MATHEMATICS OF MEDIA

Someone said a rose is a rose is a rose, and Aristotle is famous for A is A. But rates aren't always rates. Rate haggling at an ad agency media department is a necessary skill akin to buying a carpet from a Middle Eastern rug dealer.

For companies new to this field, a review of some of the basics will be helpful before going on to selection of magazine and newspaper media.

CPM versus CPR

The basic tool of media buying is cost per thousand (CPM, using the Roman numeral 'M' for thousand), meaning that advertising cost divided by one-thousandth of the circulation gives you the cost per thousand in circulation. This is a traditional index, and at one time SRDS used to quote CPM for a typical black-and-white page at the end of each listing. However, it is not the only index and certainly not the most important one.

CPR (Cost per Response)

The figure that counts, in the long run, is one that correlates results—or at least expected results—as *cost per response* (CPR) (or per order, or per lead, or per subscription). The CPR, the ultimate index for direct marketers, is simply advertising cost divided by number of responses.

Some advertisers and agencies also use a figure called *orders per thousand* (OPM) to provide a constant figure for responsiveness of a given media space unit against all propositions and all advertisers whose data they can compare. OPM eliminates distortions due to volume discounts, remnant rates, or exchange space deals, and indexes the potential "life" of the magazine's audience without cost distortion. The value of the OPM factor becomes very clear if you presume that each publisher is reasonable and negotiable, as most are, and that—given the facts—they will bring their costs into line with other publications to make their magazine attractive to advertisers.

The OPM factor is also important when conducting tests in split-run or regional editions. Such smaller segments are always more expensive on a CPM basis. The use of the OPM factor evens out the premium cost and provides a consistent standard for comparing results.

A more precise standard is CPMT (Cost per Thousand Targeted Audience), discussed later in this chapter.

Volume and Frequency Discounts

Many publications offer lower rates, called *frequency discounts,* for multiple insertions, either in a single issue of a publication or over a period of time. Publications also offer volume discounts, based on the total lines or dollar amount of space used during a fiscal or calendar year. Such discounts often allow large advertisers to support marginal propositions where other advertisers would not be able to make them work. In some cases, however, such discounts are not available if a mail-order discount is also being taken. Check with the publications.

At the end of a contract period, it sometimes pays to run some additional advertising that will help the entire schedule to reach a lower rate breakpoint. Columbia House, for instance, is able to run advertising for its magazines and for specialty mail-order clubs in the same *TV Guide* issues it runs its music club ads, making a much lower rate available to the smaller proposition than it would enjoy if it were independent.

One unfortunate by-product of such volume and frequency discounts is their tendency to accelerate the decline of small individual direct marketers. Such rates make it possible for a giant advertiser to buy a smaller competitor or overwhelm their advertising.

Mail-Order and Other Special Rates

Many magazines and newspapers offer special reduced rates for classifications of advertising that they consider particularly desirable, or where competition with other publications is particularly severe. Philanthropic rates, cultural rates, publishers' rates, and retail rates are all common, and can make a big difference in projected CPR.

I know of one mail-order book advertiser whose most important medium was *The New York Times.* The advertiser opened a retail store just to get that paper's retail rate. The retail store prospered unexpectedly and became the forerunner of half-a-dozen such stores.

One caution: lower rates are sometimes not a good deal if they require a "back of the book" position or other inferior placement. I know of two philanthropies that did better at full rates in the front of major magazines than in the back. And it is often better to pay the full rate in the Friday/

Weekend edition of *USA Today* than to get discounts for placement in other weekdays.

Printed Inserts

In direct marketing media, advertisers often buy units with bound-in or tipped-on insert cards, multi-page sections, or newspaper inserts. In such cases the printing cost should be considered part of the overall cost in all schedules, even though it is usually not billed by the magazine. A media schedule and subsequent analyses of results should always include printing costs as if they were part of the media cost.

In general, the old rule of thumb that motivates advertisers to use this format still stands. The rule: a bound-in insert costs 2½ times as much and results in four times the responses. This also applies to free standing inserts (FSIs) in newspapers. Whether it's a simple bound-in response card or an elaborate multi-page section, the problem is usually not the cost, but the availability. Publications usually can accommodate only a limited number of such units in any issue, so they must be planned well in advance.

Premium Rates.   Almost all publications charge a higher CPM for regional or demographic editions than for full-run advertising. This is only fair, as a publication is segmented at great cost and difficulty, and only for the convenience of advertisers. However, the resulting CPR will be higher than if a full-run insertion had been used. This should be kept in mind and appropriate budget adjustments made when determining whether regional or split-run advertisements can be rolled out to the full circulation and do well.

Remnant Rates.   Many publications offer various kinds of remnant deals, particularly in the Sunday supplement field. The offer applies to units that remain unsold after premium regional edition buyers have made their pick. In some cases, publications will offer unsold space on a remnant deal, subject to preemption if a full-price advertiser comes along. Even the prestigious *New York Times* has had a half-price offer contingent on permitting the *Times* to select the date within a certain time frame, and *Time* magazine has offered flexible-date advertising at less than the full rate.

Surcharges.   Another rate consideration is the cost of surcharges. Most publications will charge extra for a premium position such as a back cover, although few will charge for (or guarantee) positions such as the front of the magazine. Some newspapers charge different rates or surcharges for ads in a specific Sunday section, such as a magazine section.

One of the most common surcharges is for "bleed" pages: the right to run your advertisement to the edge of the page, rather than just to the margin. Many progressive publishers, recognizing that four-color bleed ads make their magazine more interesting and colorful for readers, are discontinuing this charge.

Agency Commissions and Cash Discounts

Most magazines and newspapers in the United States grant recognized advertising agencies a 15 percent agency commission. In other countries this is often 20 percent. This practice dates back to the days when agencies literally bought space in blocks and resold it to advertisers. Today agencies earn this commission by providing planning and creative services that used to be supplied by individual publications.

There was a time when any recognized member of the American Association of Advertising Agencies would be expected to work strictly on the commission system. Today that expectation applies mostly to very large advertising accounts that require a full range of agency services. Some large clients who demand less than full service—perhaps excluding the agency from marketing planning or media buying—negotiate arrangements where the agency is paid only a partial commission. Or agencies may be paid on a fee or hourly basis, rebating all or part of the commission to the advertiser.

With smaller accounts, this agency commission may be only part of the compensation paid by the advertiser to the agency for marketing, creative, media buying, and executional services. A minimum income-guarantee or supplementary fee often is required in addition to earned commissions. Sometimes the commissions are credited against a guaranteed monthly income.

It is possible for an advertiser to set up a "house agency" to keep the commission, thus lowering advertising expenses by 15 percent. Generally this is a false economy, due to the cost of the staff required and the loss of the professionalism and objectivity provided by an outside agency. Any client who thinks a house agency is a good investment has probably never worked with a first-class advertising agency. In the direct marketing field particularly, any agency that can't lift its clients' results by much more than the 15 percent commission isn't doing its job. The best solution in such cases is not a house agency, but a different outside agency.

Production Costs

The costs of preparing artwork—photography, computer graphics, etc.—can be substantial. Should these costs be figured into the media budget and the result analysis? My recommendation—and the general industry practice—is no.

If an ad runs only once, production costs will be substantial in relation to the overall budget. If it runs many times in many publications, production costs may be insignificant. I have never seen a formula that anticipates this problem. The general practice is to treat production costs as a separate "below-the-line" budget against the total advertising appropriation—not against individual advertisements. The costs should be controlled, and economies should be related to the extent of intended use as a control on the production budget, not as a burden to individual media expenditures.

Whatever rates your company can earn, and whatever fees, surcharges, commissions, or discounts are involved, the bottom line remains the same: cost per response.

SELECTING THE RIGHT PUBLICATIONS

How do you pick the best magazines or newspapers in which to place your first advertisements? If you have already proved that print media works for you, where do you run your next ads?

No matter what stage you're in, the selection process is the same, and the principles are very similar to those we explained for selecting direct mail lists. If the media is the market, you want to know which media will pay off for you. The "affinity" approach is a logical place to start—with some exceptions.

CPMT (Cost per Thousand Target Audience)

I try to rank publication costs by CPMT, which means cost per thousand targeted circulation. This counts only that portion of the circulation that has the desired demographic characteristics, to the extent that these factors are known and the data is comparable.

For example, let's say we have a product for women between the ages of 25 and 44. Let's say one magazine is a mass publication that costs $50/M. Half the readers are women, and half of the total circulation is in the desired age group. Combining these figures indicates that only 25 percent of the circulation is "targeted." The cost per thousand of that portion alone is therefore $200/M.

It is likely that another magazine expressly published for women in this age group costs $100/M and that 90 percent is usable. Therefore this CPMT is $111 and is a better choice, using this standard, then the mass magazine.

This way of looking at media is particularly valuable when you look at so-called "Vertical" magazines—magazines that reach everyone involved in a specific industry, sport, interest, political view, etc. (Horizontal magazines refer to business publications which reach an occupation or management level across many industries, such as Sales Management, Meeting Planner, or Office Manager.) If you are looking for women who sail, a magazine called *Sailing for Women* will always produce a better CPMT than any non-specific publication. The same goes for any sports or other special interest publication such as travel, gourmet cooking, or designer fashions.

Magazines included in Simmons will have circulation breakdowns that are based on their research data and indicate estimated circulation in terms of various breakdowns, such as "Has More Than $100M of Life Insurance." Two percentage figures are shown: *vertical,* or percent of such households reached by the publication, and *horizontal,* or percent of the publication's circulation with the sought characteristic; i.e., the "target" audience. In addition, an index is provided that gives the user a quick indicator of the circulation efficiency for that characteristic as compared with other listed publications.

In addition to the percentage figures, there are also estimates of the readers of each characteristic in actual numbers. The planning process used by the account executives I train is to compare these actual numbers with the applicable rates, usually discounted ones or rates that can be purchased through a direct marketing media service such as Stephen Geller Company. The rates are divided by the target circulation figures on a spreadsheet to produce "Cost Per Thousand Target Audience." See Figure 15-4.

This CPMT ranking is a valuable directory of media efficiency in terms of cost. But it doesn't become a media schedule in itself. We must still take into consideration such experience-based questions as editorial affinity, audience responsiveness, and the availability of economical and reliable testing options. These are all discussed later in this chapter.

Responsiveness

You might think that any art publication would be the right place to advertise art supplies or prints. It seems logical because of the affinity between audience and product. Most likely, however, you'd be wrong.

When you're selecting from lists of mail-order buyers, the factor of responsiveness is already built in. That's where the list came from. But that's not necessarily the case with magazines.

Certainly look first at those publications where there is a clear relationship between their editorial subject and your product or service, but within that group of magazines, look for the factor of mail responsiveness. That's where you'll need either the ABC statement or a space salesperson who's willing to do more than take you to lunch.

Is the magazine sold by subscription or on the newsstand? Subscription buyers have at least responded to the subscription offer. Is the magazine sold by mail? That's a good sign for any direct marketer. Is it sold through association memberships or sweepstakes-based agents? That's bad. Whether you observe them empirically or go to the trouble of calculating the Quality Factor discussed earlier, these factors have to be taken into account.

A simpler approach is to play follow-the-leader. Look at several issues of the magazine and see if it carries a great deal of other direct-marketing advertising. Then look up some of the advertisers in PIB and see if the ads are first-time insertions or repeats. If the latter, you can presume the earlier ad was successful. You might even talk to some advertisers who are not direct competitors and ask how the magazine pulled.

Ask whether the advertising is paid space. Don't be misled into going into a publication at full rate when the bulk of its previous direct-response space has been on an exchange or remnant basis.

And if plenty of other advertisers have been repeating coupon advertising or if the publication has a high quality factor by observation or calculation, then it's worth a try—provided the audience is the right one.

Editorial Environment

How do you determine whether a magazine's audience is right for you? The key is *editorial affinity*, or an observation of the editorial environment—an observation that relies entirely on the subjective judgment of the person responsible for making the media recommendation or decision.

A vertical publication that deals directly with the field your product aims for may not be right if the readership is too advanced or too amateurish for your particular product. A general magazine with a strong mail-order advertising representation may be too downscale or upscale, or may exclude the audience or market segment you need. This is where judgment comes in, and is one of the ways direct marketing is still an art as well as a science.

It is just as much of a mistake to go by audience demographics alone and ignore the editorial environment. Just as business direct mail does better when sent to business addresses, and personal offers are sent to consumers, so too it is dangerous to ignore the context of the advertisement.

When I read *Cruising World* or *Popular Photography* or *Condé Nast Traveler,* I am thinking about an interest that gives me pleasure, not profit. While I might be interested in investments or insurance or a new long-distance service, it is an intrusion at that particular time. To a large extent, I would probably not even be interested in a travel ad when I was reading a sailing magazine. On the other hand, you would be unlikely to sell me a new dinghy while I was reading *Advertising Age*.

If all you want to do is associate a brand with the special interest, then a BMW or Mount Gay Rum ad in *Sail* makes sense. But if you want an immediate response, don't fight your advertising environment.

There is no substitute for examining the actual magazines and getting a feel for the editorial content and the level of other direct marketing advertisements. The environment has to be right for your particular advertisement. Maybe you will have to prepare a special offer and advertising approach that will make this particular medium work for you.

The Elusive Audience

The people you are trying to reach read many magazines and newspapers. They get direct mail. They listen to radio and watch television. There is no single way to reach them, but usually there is a best way.

It is essential to remember that usually we are trying to get a response from less than one-half of 1 percent of a publication's readership. That means we are concerned with only 10 or 20 percent of the publication's circulation at best. Our target market segment does not have to be the majority of a magazine's readers. They just have to be there somewhere.

That "somewhere" doesn't have to be in the mainstream of the publication's circulation. They could be at the lower edge of an upscale publication or the upper edge of a downscale one. A mass-market mutual fund, for instance, can do equally well in *Barron's,* which is primarily directed at sophisticated investors, or in *Money,* which deals largely with budget planning and shopping guidance rather than investments per se. Both may have attracted enough prospects to be successful for you. The only way to find out is to examine the magazine, use your own judgment, and—if you're not sure—take a chance and see what happens.

Media Constellations

If the total potential media for a proposition is called a *media universe,* then the logical subcategories of that whole might be termed *constellations.* Just as astronomers arbitrarily group stars into constellations, so advertisers arbitrarily group publications into categories.

Once you've examined SRDS, considered the wide scope of possible magazines, examined the data and reviewed the magazines themselves, you can sort the publications by any common attributes you desire. Your categories are as good as anyone else's.

Perhaps you'll have vertical publications, downscale ones, prestige magazines, city or regional publications, newspaper Sunday supplements, foreign language papers, women's magazines. If your market is narrower, you might break down a category such as women's magazines into even finer sub-constellations such as women's homemaking magazines, women's career magazines, women's cooking publications, and women's escapism magazines. With newspapers you might use categories such as size of market, area of country, level of editorial, and political slant. Any category can be refined down to the ultimate subcategory: an individual publication.

The categories in SRDS are a handy place to start, but they are as subjective as the categories you would invent. That's why many magazines list themselves in more than one SRDS category, and that's why categories must be broken down into those that are relevant for you and your business.

Pilot Publications

Once you've established the categories, you're ready for the next step: picking one representative magazine within each constellation to be your pilot publication. This is the magazine or newspaper that you will advertise in, the one that will enable you to make a decision about the entire grouping that it represents. As such, it must be typical of the constellation.

A pilot publication should not be the place to experiment with a magazine that might be new or untried by others. You want to give this pilot every chance of succeeding and representing its group, so it should be the publication that appears to be most used by other direct marketers and most representative, editorially, of the group as a whole.

To minimize downside risk, a pilot publication does not have to be a full run of a given magazine or newspaper. It can be a region or a split run, provided that the publication will not double-handicap you—not only charge you a premium rate but also place your ad in a marginal back-of-the-book position.

Don't be concerned about picking a publication that is likely to do a bit better than most other publications in the constellation. For instance, if you

are considering news magazines and you are looking for older, more serious readers, then by all means start with *U.S. News & World Report*. A *Time*
regional buy might be more representative, but if your offer doesn't work
in *U.S. News* it won't work in *Time* or *Newsweek*. So give yourself the edge
by going with the most relevant magazine and then rolling out cautiously
after you see the results.

TV Guide.   This single magazine is a media constellation in itself, and no
discussion of media would be complete unless its unique attributes were
reviewed. It is the key medium for some of the nation's largest direct marketers, and it has been an important test medium for many others.

Because *TV Guide* reaches an audience whose common denominator is
simply ownership of television sets, it covers an almost universal audience.
In 1999 its total circulation exceeded 12 million households.

The magazine has 109 local editions, distributed according to TV markets,
and offers a perfect A-B split in each of those markets. It is a weekly, which
means you can get fast turnaround for testing. You can test a wide variety
of copy appeals very quickly, sometimes in advance of a general national
campaign.

This publication's readers have many interests: the outdoors, decorating,
shopping, entertainment. It is a unique place to use the skimming strategy
and let a proposition seek its own audience.

Inserts and fold-out units are eagerly sought after, but they are very sensitive to position, timing, and competitive factors, With printing costs, a
typical book club or encyclopedia insertion can cost over $300,000 an in-
sertion—yet there's usually a waiting list for the most responsive issues.

Letting the Consumer Make the Decisions

In general advertising, expert opinion and statistical data lead to a high
budget to schedule each magazine for several insertions and to build frequency. In direct marketing, each ad has to stand alone and a small budget
is appropriated for pilot publication testing, with one insertion per publication. Then the direct marketer waits to read the results. The balance of
the appropriation is held in reserve for a campaign to run during a good
season after getting the results of the pilot test. In an ongoing campaign
these tests might alternate with rollouts. Summer tests, for instance, sometimes are intended to influence the following summer schedules, not the
winter campaign. Turnaround time becomes very important in integrating
tests and rollouts.

Fast closing dates might influence the selection of a pilot publication.
Weekly rather than monthly publications offer a plus in testing. Weekly
magazines are readable just after the sale date, a full month sooner than
monthlies, and usually have faster closing dates as well.

General advertisers often have difficulty in accepting the constant change
and step-by-step decision making of direct-marketing media plans. They

are accustomed to taking $1 million and scheduling it all at once. A direct marketing schedule might commit a fourth of that to testing and put the other three-fourths in reserve.

MAGAZINE CONSIDERATIONS

Circulation numbers and characteristics are only one consideration in planning a magazine schedule. You also have to know what kind of space unit to use, what position to ask for, and whether or not to use some type of segmentation.

Space Units

Let's look at the space unit first. Should it be large or small? One page or two? What about those spectacular units like multiple-page inserts or heavy-stock preprinted bind-ins, perhaps with a reply-card flap?

The traditional rule is to use as little space as possible to get your message across, and to avoid wasting money on white space and irrelevant illustrations. That's a good starting place, but it's not a rule without exceptions.

On one end of the spectrum, a small 3- or 4-inch one-column advertisement in a shopping section can be the safest and most profitable insertion you can make, on a return-on-investment basis. After this unit is placed in every applicable publication, as often as results are positive, what's the next step?

Running larger ads seems to be the obvious solution, but often the larger ad produces little more response than the original ad. That's because space alone is not an attention-getter. As I explained in Chapter 11 on Art Design, the perceived size of an ad is not the size of the space unit, but the size of the largest single element in the advertisement. Just blowing up an ad to a larger size gives you a larger element, but not necessarily more selling power or more impact.

A larger ad should be redesigned and conceptually thought through from the beginning. If the ad is to have proportionately greater result-getting appeal than the original ad, it must use the space better. Perhaps the larger version can add testimonials, or dramatize a guarantee or product features that there wasn't room for before. Or perhaps the main attention-getting element—a headline or illustration—can be made even more dramatic so as to multiply the stopping power of the ad even more than the increase in the size of the space.

For some types of products or services, standard fractional units like a half-page or page can be important because of the credibility size adds to the advertisement. This is the only case where sheer size can improve results. An "exciting announcement" is much more exciting in a full-page ad, as a message from a company that purports to be large and important. This theory is more important with companies that are not well known. A major institution that already has a widely established name can get away with smaller space units than a newcomer to the field.

Once a space unit reaches its optimum level of responsiveness, increasing the space unit to a larger size can still be worthwhile. For example, a philanthropic advertiser soliciting contributions used double-page spreads in the best-pulling magazines, rather than single pages. The cost per donor was slightly higher, but the incremental return for the second page was still greater than if the same money had been spent on a marginal medium or greater frequency.

Spectacular Units

So-called *spectacular units* are very substantial investments that produce equally substantial improvements in results. As I've said before, the old rule of thumb is that a page with an insert card costs two and a half times the cost of a page alone, but produces four times the results.

There are several kinds of spectacular units. The simplest is the bound-in reply card. The greatest importance of this unit is the ease of reply that it offers the reader interested in your proposition. But it also "indexes" the magazine, causing it to open at that page while being thumbed through.

Full-page inserts, with your ad printed on both sides, also offer the same advantages, plus even more impact due to the sheer weight of the inserted page.

When it is necessary to offer a large choice or a long presentation of copy points, four-, six-, or eight-page inserts, or even longer ones can also be bound in. Such units are often on coated stock, card stock, or standard magazine coated paper. They may or may not include a reply card, but some advertisers deliberately omit the business reply card as a way of trading response rate for quality improvement.

Such units often are hard to schedule, as publications have relatively few such positions available in each issue. Advertisers who have used them before generally have an option to continue to use the same unit on the same date in subsequent years.

Color or Black-and-White?

There's no hard-and-fast rule to this question either. Color is particularly valuable if used well—especially to illustrate a colorful product. The only test I have seen that tested color versus black-and-white showed that color paid for itself, although it did not lower the cost per order. The rule is to use color only if it adds to the visual appeal of the product or the impact of the advertisement—both highly subjective evaluations.

One alternative that is always wrong is limiting the ad to two or three colors. If your message isn't appealing in black-and-white, a color headline or background isn't going to make a difference. And certainly it's not worth the money just to put your company trademark in a second color. Either go with black-and-white, or go all the way to four-color with lifelike illustrations.

Magazine Positions

Virtually all advertisers agree on the relative ranks of various positions in most magazines, although they disagree on the exact percentage difference between them. However, everyone agrees that position is an important influence on results.

In magazines, insert-card positions are the most effective, with the first better than the second and so on. Pulling power declines until just before the back of the magazine, where the last insert card does only 10 percent less than the first. This is a general rule, and results vary depending on the type of magazine. Fashion publications, handicraft magazines, and financial publications seem to hold up better throughout the magazine than other types of publications.

In general space, right-hand pages pull better than left-hand, with the first right-hand page the very best and others declining in response for each subsequent right-hand page.

Back covers are particularly desirable, and will do as well as a first right-hand page if the publication does not impose a punitive surcharge for the position. The inside back cover or the page facing it on the right will do almost as well. These unique back-of-book positions are more likely to be available than first right-hand pages, and should always be considered when negotiating with a space representative.

One of the errors direct-marketing beginners make is presuming that the magazine will give them the best possible position, or that nothing can be done to influence the choice of position. It may be easy to mail out an insertion order reading, "Far forward right-hand position requested," but this is not doing everything you can. Talk to the ad sales representative from the publication and stress the importance of position, particularly in terms of potential repeat insertions. You should negotiate for specific pages and reach an understanding with the magazine, even if the positions cannot be guaranteed. One insertion order clause that is sometimes accepted by magazines is "Page xx or better right-hand position urgently requested, or notify agency prior to cancellation date."

Segmented Editions

As previously discussed, it is not necessary to buy a full national circulation of a magazine. There are many times when it will be desirable to pay a higher rate per thousand circulation in order to target a specific area or demographic group, or to limit downside risk.

Magazines offer a wide variety of options. Here are some examples of the alternatives available.

Better Homes and Gardens is a good example. With a 7.5 million circulation, it offers the following choices:

■ 84 regional marketing editions, generally states, with circulations ranging from as little as 15,000 to almost half a million, with any combination available.

- 58 top markets, generally metropolitan areas, with circulations as little as 29,000 (Providence, Rhode Island) or as much as 386,000 (New York).
- Better By Design. An edition with 1.2 million circulation that represents a market for upscale products and services.
- Focus V. An edition of 5 million covering the 35 top markets (typically the 35 top city/regions.)
- Travel sections. State circulations grouped for the convenience of the travel industry, each comprising more than one million people in travel origination areas such as East, Great Lakes, West, South, Central.

Time has been particularly innovative in segmentation, and offers 50 state editions, 50 spot-market (city) editions, and 11 general geographic regions. The magazine can reach different markets in editions of as little as 9,000 copies (for readers in the state of South Dakota) to large regions up to 1.3 million (for the Eastern edition that includes the New England states, the tri-states around New York City, the tri-states around Washington D.C., Puerto Rico and the U.S. Virgin Islands). *Time* also offers some unique demographic editions:

Time Business	1.6 million	Business executives
Time Top Management	725,000	Top management heads
Time Top Zips	1.3 million	Subscribers in high-income zip codes
Time Women Select	975,000	Affluent, professional women who may be hard to reach through other magazines. Names taken from *Time* Top Management and Time Business
Time Digital	989,293	An editorial feature that goes to professional/managerial.

This example represents only one of the thousand segmentation opportunities available from hundreds of magazines.

Personalized of Segmented Issues

Some advertisers have been able to arrange applications of personalization to the field of magazines, particularly magazines that are mostly sold by subscription and addressed on press.

In such an arrangement, the subscriber data not only creates the address on the cover, but also generates a message inside the magazine or arranges for a different ad to be printed depending on computer data.

Minolta copiers printed the address of a local Minolta dealer on insert cards in a national news magazine. A liquor company varied the product advertised depending on individual or zip code data about drinking preferences. An upscale community would see an ad for Chivas Regal while a mid-scale area would see a promotion for another brand of Scotch. Automobile marketers have a similar opportunity. Daimler-Chrysler, for example, could advertise Mercedes in doctor's editions and upscale areas, offer Jeep Cherokees in second-home areas, and Dodge Trucks in farm areas.

NEWSPAPERS-ROP, SUPPLEMENTS, AND PREPRINTS

In general advertising, the most important attributes of the newspaper medium are its ability to achieve a very high penetration of each market, its high credibility, and its immediacy.

These same attributes are of interest to direct marketers, but overall they are offset by the medium's lack of "mail responsiveness." Very few newspapers are sold by mail, and few carry significant amounts of direct-marketing advertising in relation to other advertising. This trend is changing, as newspapers use direct mail and telephone calls to solicit home-delivered subscriptions.

ROP Newspaper Advertising

There are very few national direct marketers who advertise ROP ("run of paper") in daily or Sunday newspapers in preference to national magazines or other forms of newspaper advertising. When such ads are not specified for a specific section (such as the financial section) they are ROP.

Gerber's life insurance division has been running full and double-page ads offering term policies for many years, and other insurance companies seem to be following suit. It is more common for continuity and collectible advertisers to use Sunday rotogravure sections or photo-finishing and magazine circulation offers to appear as free-standing inserts.

In addition, newspapers are used when the product or service is local, or when a specific newspaper editorial section targets a needed audience. Newspapers also provide a believable environment for an advertisement that appears to be "news," perhaps announcing a new product feature or new test results.

As a whole, newspapers lack the "editorial environment" edge of magazines. But this can be offset by placing direct response ads in specific sections of a newspaper related to the subject matter. For instance, many newspaper financial sections are profitable sources for investment products. Sports sections do well for sports books. Home decorating products sometimes are profitable when placed with related editorial matter.

For example, schools and seminars advertise in newspapers to build enrollments for their classes. In such advertising, location and starting date should be prominently featured, as in "Fayetteville Classes Start October 1." This makes the ad a news item in itself, with its own elements of local interest, immediacy, and newsworthiness. In effect, this adapts the ad style to the media environment.

Many advertisers use newspapers to tie in with local dealers, particularly where the product must be sold through a dealer. This is not strictly a direct marketing application but more of a sales promotion scheme, although direct marketing agencies work with such projects frequently.

The most effective use of local newspapers by national direct marketers appears to involve "reader notice" advertising, where 50- or 100-line ads are designed to resemble newspaper items. (There are 14 agate lines to an inch; this is a standard way of expressing newspaper sizes. A 100-line ad can be 100 × 1 or 50 × 2, the second figure indicating the number of columns.)

Successful newspaper "reader notice" ads include many self-improvement subjects in areas such as memory, vocabulary, and conversation. An interesting application was Bradford Exchange's schedule of advertisements, with testimonial headlines like "Claremont woman buys dish in garage sale for $1—worth $1100."

Newspaper advertising rates are covered in a *Newspaper SRDS* that is very similar to the one previously described for magazines. Newspapers are listed by market area, with rates generally expressed in agate lines. Most newspaper advertising is sold ROP. Your ad can be placed anywhere. Specific classifications or sections of the paper, such as "Food Editorial," "Main News Section," "Sports Section," "Financial Pages," and "Business News" usually have a separate higher rate or require a position surcharge. There are also surcharges for specific positions such as "top of column."

Newspaper positions can and should be negotiated in the same manner as magazine positions. A prominent, far-forward or top-of-page position is often worth any extra surcharge. In buying newspaper ads, caution should be taken before automatically placing advertisements in "appropriate" classifications. The education section often is not the best place for a school ad, just as the stamp and coin page would not be the best place for an ad selling coins to investors—especially if you were seeking to bring new people into the market.

Both placement (location in the newspaper) and position (location on the page) should always be tested.

Sunday Supplements

The two principal newspaper supplements, *Parade* and *USA Weekend,* together deliver over 50 million households in hundreds of newspapers. This is a big medium, and one that is often used by direct marketers.

Sunday supplements are published on a large scale, usually in a magazine format, sometimes as comics. They are distributed in newspapers around the country. The larger ones can be broken down into regions or "target groups." Because Sunday supplements usually are printed on calendar stock, their four-color reproduction rivals that offered by magazines.

The larger national Sunday Supplements are distributed in hundreds of newspapers, and consequently offer circulation in the millions. However there are many regional and split-run opportunities. The largest are USA Weekend, Parade and Sunday. The Metro-Puck comic sections have a huge circulation. There are also regional and special interest supplements, including one for older families.

Some excellent Sunday supplements are published by newspapers in many large cities. The magazine sections of the *New York Times, New York Daily News, Chicago Tribune,* and *Los Angeles Times* are excellent editorial vehicles and have been successful for a wide variety of direct-marketing advertising. Some specialized publications, such as the *Los Angeles Times Home Section* and the *New York Times Book Review* are recognized as important media in their own right, for all types of direct-marketing products, not just those that are "home-" or "book-"related.

A new supplement, *American Profile*, should do well for direct marketers. It will reach 10.5 million readers of Sunday newspapers in C and D counties—smaller communities that historically do well for direct response.

Sunday supplements have a very different readership pattern from newspapers in general. The supplement is likely to be treated as a magazine and kept around the house for several days until it can be read leisurely.

Consequently, many ads work in supplements that do not work in newspapers. Many advertisers place half- and full-page ads on a standby or remnant basis at a substantially reduced rate.

Newspaper Preprints

Sometimes called *free-falls* or *freestanding inserts,* newspaper preprints are the big guns of modern direct marketing. They offer all the impact of the most spectacular magazine or direct-mail unit, complete with envelopes, reply cards, pop-ups or membership cards.

Preprints are exactly what the name implies. The advertising unit is printed by the advertiser, generally in large quantities, and shipped to individual newspapers for insertion with the Sunday paper. It is like a separate "section" of the Sunday paper and most likely tumbles out when the paper is opened; just as a blow-in card falls out of a magazine. The reader has to handle the preprint, even if only to throw it away—and if it is handled, it is likely to be looked at.

The range of propositions that work in preprints is truly amazing, from the most general of book club, insurance, or magazine propositions to highly selective invitations for ballet subscriptions or mutual funds.

The cost of preprints is high. If you include space costs, printing, and freight, a preprint campaign can cost $100 to $200 per thousand circulation, depending on the format. However, the results are higher still.

Preprints offer the opportunity to use a reply device and to have enough space to tell the entire story and ask for the order. There are booklet formats, gatefold formats, and envelope formats. The choice is so versatile that the medium is sometimes considered closer to direct mail than to print advertising. The main difference is that the newspaper, rather than the post office, delivers the message to the customer.

There is another advantage as well. Many newspapers can permit preprints to be distributed to specific geographic areas within the newspaper market. You can often specify the kind of neighborhoods you need. An investment product might go into higher-income areas only. A home repair or gardening product might be advertised only in suburbs rather than in apartment building areas. Banks or real estate developers might select only their own trading area.

The Starrett City apartment complex in New York utilized newspaper preprints by concentrating on the most likely target areas. The same budget that had been spread over the whole metropolitan area in routine ads was reallocated to preprints to be disseminated in select neighborhoods. There was no increase in budget, only a redistribution of it. The improvement in cost per response was over 500 percent.

BUSINESS MEDIA

The same principles apply to business magazines and business newspapers as to general publications. Some general business magazines such as *Business Week* and *The Wall Street Journal* can be very responsive. Some general publications, such as airline magazines or *USA Today,* can also produce impressive results for business propositions. This section deals with magazines and newspaper primarily addressed to business readers.

There are two basic kinds of business publications. "Horizontal" ones cut across industry lines and address themselves to job titles or management levels, financial officers, engineers, purchasing agents, and marketing specialists. "Vertical" publications such as *Hardware Age* and *Modern Plastics* talk to everyone within a specific industry.

Most specialized magazines do not do well for direct-marketing offers, at least not as compared to renting the lists of the same publications and addressing the readers by mail.

However, specialized business publications often are keys to reaching influential executives not found on mailing lists. They can also be valuable aids in building a custom prospect list. Consequently, an overall communications campaign should cover this media category even if the campaign cannot be totally justified on the basis of cost per response.

The Wall Street Journal and *Business Week* straddle the fence between being general business publications and business-oriented consumer magazines. They are listed in both editions of *SRDS.*

If you do use specialized business publications, I suggest that you ask the publication not to list your product in their "bingo" card—the reply card that the magazine provides to readers so they can easily request information about products. The ease of reply is so great, and the temptation to circle a few more numbers while filling it out so inviting, that such bingo leads have a reputation for very poor quality. This doesn't mean that all the responses are bad—only that the good ones are lost among the curiosity-seekers. This applies to any type of publication, but the cards are much more common in business publications. Figure 15-5 is a sample.

Increasingly, business decisions can be made at any level of a corporate structure, and it is important to reach every potential buyer. This requires covering a wide range of media. In the last few years, air-express and telephone-service marketers have been using television to reach the wide number of people who make day-to-day business purchases in those areas. Such campaigns are fully rounded out, with advertising in both horizontal and vertical business media and with extensive use of direct mail. Today, virtually any medium can be used for business campaigns.

WHAT'S THE BEST SEASON?

After you pick the right magazines for your direct-marketing program, you still have to decide what time of the year would be the best for your advertising campaign. Seasonal influences can cause substantial differences in results.

Many advertisers have tested direct-mail seasons and have been able to precisely plot the best times of the year for mailings. However, testing is not as easily done in print advertising. If the same ad runs month after month, a fatigue factor sets in, automatically making the first months look better than the later ones.

Receive the information you need to market smarter instantly!
Go to: **www.targetonline.com** and click on the icon. Advertiser Information

Or... Fill out this card and either FAX your request today: **215-238-5388 or mail.**   February 1999 • Expires August 1999

Free Subscription	Free Information

Do you wish to receive (continue to receive) a FREE subscription to TARGET MARKETING? ❏ **YES** ❏ NO

Signature _____ Date _____

Name (please print) _____ Title _____

Company Name _____

Address _____

City/State/Zip _____

Telephone _____ FAX _____

Internet/Email Address: _____

1. TYPE OF BUSINESS AT THIS LOCATION: (Check One)
10 ❏ Catalogers, Mail Order Companies, Retailers, Wholesalers
03 ❏ Financial Services: Banks, Insurance, Credit Cards, Investment
21 ❏ Fund Raisers: Non-Profit Groups, Charities
33 ❏ High Technology (non-catalog): Computers, Software, Telecommunications, Office Equipment
12 ❏ Manufacturers, Package Goods and Other Business-to-Business Marketers
31 ❏ Non Financial Services Marketers: Associations, Clubs, Educational, Government Agencies, Health Care, Membership Organizations, Personnel Services, Real Estate, Utilities, Communications, Tourism and Travel
13 ❏ Publishers: Magazines, Books, Newsletters, Newspapers, Book & Record Clubs
01 ❏ Advertising/DM Agencies, Freelance Creative and Consultants
09 ❏ Mailing List Professionals: Brokers, Compilers, Owners
20 ❏ Other: (Please Specify) _____

2. JOB FUNCTION: (Check One)
10 ❏ Corporate and General Management (Excluding Sales, Marketing and Advertising Management)
02 ❏ Marketing, List and Sales Management
01 ❏ Advertising Promotion and Public Relations Management
08 ❏ Operational, Technical and Telemarketing Management
06 ❏ Circulation Management
11 ❏ Other: (Please Specify) _____

Circle the free info number for the products and services that interest you

001	002	003	004	005	006	007	008	009	010	011	012
013	014	015	016	017	018	019	020	021	022	023	024
025	026	027	028	029	030	031	032	033	034	035	036
037	038	039	040	041	042	043	044	045	046	047	048
049	050	051	052	053	054	055	056	057	058	059	060
061	062	063	064	065	066	067	068	069	070	071	072
073	074	075	076	077	078	079	080	081	082	083	084
085	086	087	088	089	090	091	092	093	094	095	096
097	098	099	100	101	102	103	104	105	106	107	108
109	110	111	112	113	114	115	116	117	118	119	120
121	122	123	124	125	126	127	128	129	130	131	132
133	134	135	136	137	138	139	140	141	142	143	144
145	146	147	148	149	150	151	152	153	154	155	156
157	158	159	160	161	162	163	164	165	166	167	168
169	170	171	172	173	174	175	176	177	178	179	180

3. MY FIRM'S MARKETING ACTIVITY: (Check All That Apply)
1 ❏ Catalog   5 ❏ Consumer
2 ❏ Direct Mail   6 ❏ Business-to-Business
3 ❏ Telemarketing   7 ❏ International
4 ❏ Alternate and Electronic Media/Internet   8 ❏ None of the Above

4. IN THE PERFORMANCE OF YOUR JOB, CHECK THE ONE THAT BEST DESCRIBES YOUR PURCHASING AUTHORITY: (Check One)
1 ❏ Authorize/Approve Purchase
2 ❏ Recommend/ Specify Purchase
3 ❏ No Purchasing Authority

Figure 15-5. Bingo card

However, here's the "state of the art" agreed to by most major advertisers:

1. The best month is January, meaning January magazines with on-sale dates just after Christmas, or January weeklies or newspapers.

2. February and October tie for the number 2 position, about 10 percent behind January.

3. July and September also are acceptable, with only another 10 percent decline behind February and October.

4. March and November are possibilities, especially if you can't find an open date anywhere else. Another 10 percent drop.

5. The second quarter—April, May, and June—is the worst part of the year, along with December and August. Another 10 percent drop, so avoid these months if you can.

To translate these comments into a scale would produce an index like Fig. 15-6.

100 equals January, typically the most successful month. The other num

represent the percentage success of January.

January	100
February	90
March	70
April	60
May	60
June	60
July	80
August	60
September	80
October	90
November	70
December	60

Figure 15-6. Preferable months to advertise in magazines

Theories about why certain months do better than others are plentiful. Prevalent is the "change-of-season" theory, which says the second quarter is when people are looking forward to summer, and October is when they are finally "back to work" in the new fall season. Everyone agrees on the reason for January—another "back-to-work" feeling after the hectic Christmas season, plus a sense of affluence from Christmas bonuses and the feeling that the New Year is the time to start new projects or fulfill newly adopted self-improvement resolutions.

There are many other factors as well. Weather can play a big role in results, particularly in newspaper schedules. Bad weather is good for periodical advertising, as people will stay in and read the paper—provided the weather is not so bad that they can't get the paper at all. Good weather is bad, for people may go out on a Sunday drive instead of staying home to read your advertisement. Broadcast is even more sensitive to weather factors. Newspapers are sometimes saved to be read another day. Magazines almost always are. But usually a missed radio or television announcement is missed forever.

Elections can have an influence. Just after a hotly contested presidential election, about half the country will feel a letdown because their candidate lost, and this can show up in ad results. Before an election, there may be too many interesting items to read in a newspaper. In fact, anything worth reading can depress ad results. A major news event of any kind that's worth reading leaves your prospect less time to look at ads. The Gulf War, California brush fires, the conflict in Kosovo and Monica Lewinsky all produced marked reductions in response rates in all media, but particularly in newspapers, television, and news magazines. Fortunately, these are not frequent occurrences.

* * *

Now that we've covered the *science* of media planning, let's conclude with a word about the *art*. There's no way to plug in a computer and produce an ideal media schedule. There's still a great need for subjective judgment in evaluating editorial environment, selecting audience targets, and picking the best publication and the best season—particularly when the ones you really want have already been reserved by some other advertiser.

There will always be a place for instinct in media buying. An executive's hunch may be too complex to explain, but more often than not turns out to be right. That's why there is no substitute for professional direct-marketing media specialists. Just as a good list broker should be part of any company's team, so should an agency with a top-notch media staff.

16

BROADCAST MEDIA

When the first edition of this book was released, it made news as the first book on direct marketing to recognize that there are other ways to generate responses than direct mail.

Not only are radio and television advertising logical expansions for successful mail-order or database-building programs, but there are many propositions that work in broadcast that do not work at all in direct mail.

BROADCAST IS UNIQUE

Every medium is unique, with it own strengths and weaknesses, and broadcast is no exception. Nothing else reaches mass audiences so cost-effectively to identify new prospects. Nothing else permits the advertiser to demonstrate, prove, dramatize. And nothing else provides the ability to portray emotion and self-image—the powerful selling tools direct marketing has borrowed from the toolbox of national general advertising.

No one can describe broadcast as a new or experimental media in this field. Indeed, today it is fully recognized, widely used, and the subject of entire books devoted to this specialty.

It is no longer even possible to describe direct response media as an exclusive tool of direct marketers. An increasing number of retail and general advertisers are adding phone numbers and website locations to their commercials to take advantage of lower costs and the ability to measure responsiveness.

General advertisers seeking lower rates often discover that the responses generated are potentially so useful that making direct response offers would be worthwhile even without the rate advantage.

On the other hand, direct marketers often discover that the awareness by-product of a good direct response commercial strengthens their response rates in all media and eventually facilitates successful retail distribution.

WHAT'S DIFFERENT?

Radio and television require a very different approach from direct mail or print. On the one hand, they lack a "hard-order" device; there's no card to fill out, and not even a coupon. On the other, they offer incredible impact, coverage, and credibility.

The opportunities are fantastic. Broadcast goes into the home and talks to your prospect. It finds a viewer. It doesn't wait for a page to be turned, an envelope to be opened, or a website to be accessed.

Broadcast is Perishable

It can't be torn out and read carefully at a more convenient time. It's now or never.

Broadcast is Impatient

You have seconds to tell your whole story—to attract attention, offer a benefit, demonstrate your product, and motivate a desired action. Then you still must communicate an address, website location or telephone number in a way that will make it memorable. In direct response broadcast, you have to say it quickly, say it simply, say it effectively—or save your money.

Broadcast Offers Sight, Sound, and Motion

It communicates 100 percent, not 10 percent. The body language and tone of voice that must be simulated by copy style and graphics in other media are available to support your message with appropriate degrees of sincerity, enthusiasm, conviction, or urgency.

Broadcast has Credibility

In focus panel research, the most often repeated objection to buying by mail order is the wish to see the product. On television it can be seen from every angle. Consumers can see it working. They can see what it does, what makes it tick, and how to operate it. Television is the ultimate illustration, and it does its work at the lowest cost per thousand of any medium.

FOUR KINDS OF BROADCAST

There are four basic different kinds of broadcast direct marketing, each of them applicable to both radio and television. They are

1. *Direct Response Short Form.* Direct response applies to advertising designed to produce an immediate inquiry, order, or donation. By definition, it must offer an address, website and/or a telephone number. By necessity, it must be lengthy enough to accomplish several creative objectives—usually 60 or 120 seconds in length, compared to the 30-second ads most used by conventional advertisers.

2. *Direct Support.* This is exactly the opposite of direct response. It needs no address or telephone number. It can be effective in very short units, even 10 or 30 seconds. It is bought in the same way, and usually at the same rates, as conventional advertising commercials.

3. *Direct Response Long Form.* Often referred to as Infomercials, these are currently 30-minute formats, purchased in marginal time periods for a fixed price, usually paid in advance. They usually cost about 12–15 times the cost of a one or two minute spot—e.g. $3000 instead of $250, for a smaller station.

4. *Shopping Channels.* Like Infomercials, where you must supply the entertainment or other content to attract an audience to your 30-minute segment, here you buy a channel and arrange for cable stations to carry it by offering them stock, fees or a percentage of the sales. While Home Shopping Network and QVC (Quality-Value-Convenience) are the best known and established operators, in reality there is no reason why a multi-product advertiser like Damark or Sharper Image couldn't do the same and promote their own products.

These four types of broadcast are as different as night and day. They require different formats, different copy treatments, and different media strategies.

DIRECT RESPONSE TELEVISION (DRTV) SHORT-FORM

Direct-response television is not for every product. It requires products or services that either appeal to very general audiences or to audiences segmentable by program adjacencies. A kitchen knife or a set of pots may work because everyone who cooks is a prospect for it.

More specialized products often work only if the spot is adjacent to relevant programming. For example, a set of books on World War II will typically work only on the History Channel or when it is adjacent to a war movie, a violent sports program, or another form of violence—in some cities, the local news. Such specific program adjacencies are usually not available in quantity. However, many special-interest propositions can now be successful during general programming if the allowable margin is adequate and sophisticated audience analysis techniques borrowed from general advertising are used.

The "old" rules of direct-response television dictated formats and placements that made this medium successful only for mass-market products. In recent years, new media buyers have been able to use sophisticated general agency analysis methods to make direct-response broadcast effective for investments, fine-arts publications, intellectual magazines, business products and services, insurance, and the entire range of upscale direct marketing propositions.

In the last few years a major direct response category has opened up with the liberalization of FDA regulations on pharmaceutical advertising. An estimated half a billion dollars is being spent on pharmaceutical direct response, offering educational material and incentives to "Ask your doctor about . . . ."

Television stations offer "day-parts" the way newspapers offer different editorial sections. Daytime shows—often soap operas and game shows— appeal to homemakers. News and sports shows deliver predominantly male viewers. Tennis and golf deliver smaller but more upscale audiences than baseball or boxing. Children's shows and family-appeal movies attract their own unique audiences. Late night re-runs and old movies are effective at reaching older people. Usually selectivity in direct response is limited mostly by the day-part that is available.

Most radio stations have adopted single-format programming. Each station generally has a reputation for a type of news or music, rather than the original concept of balanced programming with a little of everything. Rock stations reach teenagers, easy-listening stations find older adults, country and western stations select blue-collar workers, and news programs reach more general audiences. In radio you reach specific audiences by selecting the station that aims at your audience.

It is sometimes possible to reach specific audiences on radio by sponsoring a specific show, such as farm or stock news, if the programming is relevant to your product.

As in all other direct-response media, the medium is the market, and your offer will be successful in broadcast only if the market is the right one for your product.

Direct-Response Offers

Just as different propositions do well on broadcast rather than in print or direct mail, so do different offers. If your conventional offer requires a great deal of explanation or legal copy, it won't fit on a radio or television spot. If it requires a signed agreement, you won't have a form to give out. If you usually give people a choice of 50 records or 15 sizes and colors, it will be too complicated.

Credit quality is another problem. If your offer involves a free magazine or other premium, the percentage of people taking the gift and electing not to buy or pay for the rest of the offer will usually be greater with broadcast than with any other medium. Broadcast, as the name itself indicates, casts a broad net over a wide variety of people and personalities. It will pull in the deadbeats along with the good customers, unless your offer is designed to be selective. Fortunately, there are many ways to do so.

More often than not, successful offers in print or direct mail have to be changed in order to be successful in radio or television. Choices have to be eliminated or reduced. Credit has to be simplified. Offers have to be attractive and easy to understand. Here are some examples:

- A magazine that generally sells a full-year subscription in print media offers a short-term introductory offer on television.

- A book club that usually offers a wide choice of gift books for new members offers a pre-selected library.

- An appliance usually sold "off the page" is featured in a two-step offer, offering a free information kit.

- A special-interest club offers a single book at a nominal price—a straight deal that does not require explanation or legal copy. The buyers then are converted with a letter that suggests they "tear up the bill" and take the book free as part of a standard club offer, which is explained in full in the letter.

- A major catalog merchandiser, who usually sells only on a prepaid basis, makes an exception and accepts credit card orders on television in order to get qualified prospects.

- An insurance company offers low-cost term life policies, qualified during the phone call, and achieves greater profitability and volume than direct mail. For another type of policy, this same insurer offers information and price quotes to be given to their agents as highly qualified leads.

- A collectible manufacturer sells coins related to a current event, and generates hundreds of thousands of new customers.

Integrated Advertising Offers

Today's growing trend to integrating all forms of advertising to achieve marketing goals has fostered some dramatically effective uses of direct-response broadcast.

While most advertising budgets have traditionally allocated funds between different marketing disciplines—advertising, public relations, sales promotion, direct marketing—the modern approach is to define objectives and allocate funds to achieve them according to which tools appear to be the most effective. That's one of the reasons why some advertising agencies include all disciplines in their planning and services without favoring one over another.

The result has been the evolution of techniques that use media to achieve short- and long-range goals simultaneously. Applied to broadcast, this often results in advertising that gets leads for immediate sales and builds brand equity at the same time, or that offers further information or free samples as a by-product of budgets originally devoted exclusively to image building.

One sees offers like this now for a wide variety of products—phone services, computers, travel destinations, automobiles, and packaged goods. And it works. In effect, they use broadcast to build awareness and at the same time identify prospects meriting further communication or sales contact. As this aspect of database marketing increases as part of direct marketing, the use of broadcast also becomes more important.

Pre-emptible Time-Buying

In its early days, direct-response media buying required a kind of guerrilla media operation. While general agencies massaged audience figures and paid card rates, direct-response agencies wheeled and dealed for good buys. "Who you know" was a more important credential than "what you know."

The best buys went to advertisers and agencies that could pay cash, had good credit, and had "clout." It helped if the buyer had a personal relationship with a station time-buyer. In those good old days, station representatives seldom got involved in direct response, and most buying was conducted by phone directly with executives at the station.

Today, all that has changed. While some entrepreneurs still do business the old way, more sophisticated practitioners have made direct-response buying much more of a science. For one thing, getting the lowest rate is often not as important as achieving clearance goals. Run-of-station frequency has been replaced by pressure to reach those day-parts that deliver the specific audience type most likely to be profitable.

Even cable stations, once dominated by direct response advertisers, have been fully discovered by all types of general advertisers. The result has been both an increase in rates and a decrease in availability. While the number of cable stations keeps increasing, those that have been proven to be the most profitable are in great demand.

In addition, numbers influence decisions today more than "connections" or personal experience. Many agencies have developed systems which correlate past results from a wide variety of advertisers to forecast probable results for new advertisers. One that I've used inputs rates and demographics for 2400 day-parts on 300 stations to generate a ranking by cost per thousand for any demographic characteristic

While the approaches have changed, the basic theories and goals have not. For one thing, most direct-response propositions cannot afford the same rate cards paid by general advertisers, even with the discounts often negotiated for them. Typically, our clients can afford only 25 to 33 percent of the general rates. Most stations are willing to accommodate this need by offering pre-emptible availabilities.

The trade-off in pre-emptible availabilities is that the station will give you a very low rate providing they can use your ad as a standby for unsold time. Time is a perishable commodity for stations. Magazines can cut back on the number of pages, but broadcast stations can't reduce the number of seconds they have for sale.

Advertising agencies often cultivate personal relationships with station managers. Media buyers are assigned to groups of stations and keep in touch with them every week, putting together mutually advantageous deals. Buyers visit the stations and attend conventions of station managers to reinforce these contacts.

Officially, the deals often are for run-of-the-station spots, with day-parts requested but seldom guaranteed. Unofficially, not only day-parts but also even particular adjacencies are often verbally agreed upon.

The catch is that they are always pre-emptible. If a general advertiser comes along and offers full rate, the direct response spot is moved to another time slot or bumped altogether. During busy seasons it is necessary to order 20 or 50 percent more time than is really needed in order to get the desired coverage.

The personal contact between media buyer and station manager continues after the spots are run. Each week, and sometimes on a daily basis, the buyer checks the results and calculates the cost per order. The commercials are continued as long as the order cost is satisfactory. If the response is inadequate, the buyer "pulls" the schedule. Sometimes an effective buyer can get a marginal station to throw in "bonus spots," in order to bring the station to a profitable level so the campaign can continue. When arranged in advance, this becomes a *de facto* result guarantee.

The bottom line is the only consideration. The media buyer must have the responsibility and authority to spend a given budget as effectively as possible, in any stations in that buyer's area of responsibility. Neither the client nor the account group can be consulted on every decision. The buyers must make decisions on the spot, while talking on the phone, to revise schedules or pull them.

Contemporary Media-Buying Techniques

The object of the time-buying activity described in the previous section used to be getting the most Gross Rating Points (GRPs) for your money. Gross Rating Points are the sum of the percentage of homes viewing the group, or "flight," of commercials in a given market. Ten spots with a 7 percent AA (average audience) have 70 GRPs. This is sometimes expressed as

$$\text{GRP} = R \times F$$

where R is reach (the average audience coverage, expressed as a percentage) and F is frequency (the number of times the commercial is aired).

GRPs are the currency, so to speak, of the broadcast industry. Just as circulation is what magazines have to sell, GRPs are what stations have to sell. (The equivalent magazine formula to the one for GRPs is circulation times frequency is equal to impressions.)

Until recently, getting the most GRPs was the simple goal of some of the best-known agencies and media-buying organizations, and the results of using this method led to the conclusion that only downscale, low-priced mass-market products could be sold by direct-response television. But the science of direct response analysis has advanced significantly. Particularly with non-mail products such as telephone services, Internet access, credit cards and insurance, the "quality" of the respondents is frequently more important than the cost-per-response.

Today's audience-selection media-buying beats the bargain-hunting "haggle method" which once characterized this business. At that time, most television and radio time was bought on an "ROS" (Run of Station) basis, meaning any spot, day or night, that the station has available.

It is important to work with good DRTV media specialists, and to check references. For instance, Si Sanders of Corinthian Media showed me the results of a home mortgage commercial for which they produced leads at a very acceptable $21 CPR each. The same spot, previously tested at another agency, came in at $48—more than double the cost!

Airtime is now valued in terms of the characteristics of the audiences delivered, not just the number of sets turned in. Just as general agencies do, direct marketers now request specific day-parts and adjacencies, sometimes paying premium rates. "Day-parts" refers to time segments such as Early Morning (6 A.M.–9 A.M.), Daytime (9 A.M.–4 P.M.), Early Fringe (4 P.M.–7 P.M.), Access (7 P.M.–8 P.M.), Prime Time (8 P.M.–11 P.M.), and Late Night (11 P.M.—conclusion). "Adjacencies" refers to specific programs that the commercial appears before, during or after.

In all fairness, I should point out that state-of-the-art time buying is not the only key to making a direct-response campaign work. Another has to do with the station owner—an often forgotten factor in the media equation. The owner or manager is sensitive to the opinions of viewers and, understandably, to the opinions of other advertisers. It has been my experience that direct-response commercials with music, entertainment value, believable announcers and credible situations—all presumed in general advertising but often omitted from direct response—get placed in better time spots and program adjacencies.

I do not mean to say that there was, or is, anything wrong with the old approach. It still works for sets of records and offers of pots and pans, as it always has. But those who have defended it as the *only* way to go have been proved wrong. It is right for some kinds of products, but not for others. Modern time-buying methods, combined with creative techniques that result in commercials that don't insult the viewer's intelligence, are a proven alternative—one that has opened up television to a wider range of advertisers than ever before.

Commercial Length

How long should a direct-response commercial be? The industry started with sponsored 15-minute programs, which were whittled down to 5 minutes, then 2 minutes. When I wrote the first edition of this book, the unchallenged consensus of the field was that a direct-response commercial should be 120 seconds.

Today, the answer to the question of length, like everything else in the business world, is more complex. It depends on a number of factors.

It has been demonstrated that 60-second commercials out-pull :120s on a cost-per-response basis and on a quality basis for some products, but not for all products. There are now indications that :30s may be workable for some propositions. In the case of infomercials, many advertisers have achieved enormous success by going full circle to 30-minute and even one-hour sponsored advertising programs. There are several considerations:

- *What do you need to get the story across?* Some propositions can be expressed only in a :120 spot. On the other hand, successful continuity offers have been done, complete with all required legal copy, in a :60 spot. And they worked.

- *How narrow are the placement opportunities?* If the proposition is a general one that can work on almost any kind of station, in any day-part, length may not matter. But if the audience is a narrow, highly specialized one, the 60-second format will give you access to better program adjacencies.

- *Can you hold the viewer's interest?* Some messages actually come out better in a shorter format, and there is less risk of boring or antagonizing the viewer. This is especially true if the commercial is part of a high-frequency market saturation effort. For clients such as Mutual of Omaha, I have placed as many as 20 spots a week in some markets to meet lead-acquisition goals. This high a level of activity could never be sustained with long, drawn-out :120 formats. Musical themes, or a variety of interesting situations in rotation, lend themselves better to a 60-second format.

- *What works best?* The ultimate question is always, "Which length produces the lowest cost per response?" This applies to broadcast media, as it does to any medium. Where possible, my preference is to produce both a :60 and a :120, try both, and see which works best. In many cases the two can be produced during the same "shoot" at little additional cost. Often the :60 is just edited out of the :120, but both versions should be planned in advance in case some different scripts must be shot for the shorter version.

Setting Up a Broadcast Test

I've found that $100,000 can get a good initial reading on the potential of short form DRTV for a proposition. This includes about half for the time purchased and half for the production of the commercial, professional marketing and creative counsel. However, that is a bare-bones budget requiring a lot of shortcuts.

Infomercials can cost even more—usually $200,000 to $300,000 for the production alone, which makes sense only if the advertiser has at least the same amount available for the initial placements, which must be paid in advance.

Fortunately the cash flow from there on is very positive. With credit-card propositions the media investment is usually recovered within days and can be reinvested in a quickly expanding schedule.

The choice of cities and stations should be made on the same basis. A new-offer viability test is not the place to experiment or succumb to "deals" offered by untried stations. It should be placed with proven stations that have worked well for other direct-marketing propositions. Day-parts and adjacencies are a different matter. There can be very dramatic differences in response by day-part, including weekday versus weekend. Testing several day-parts within the selected stations will be necessary.

Awareness of television builds, and a two- or three-week flight is necessary in order to assess the ultimate potential of the station. Unlike direct mail and print, there is no statistical curve by which you can forecast early results. The building of response rates is erratic, but once it reaches the full response level it usually holds at that level as the flight is extended for several more weeks. After a while a noticeable downward curve develops. The schedule is continued only as long as it is profitable.

Three-week flights generally are scheduled, with the third week pulled from stations where initial results are disappointing. The buyers then transfer that money to other stations to reach fresh audiences. Usually the client agrees to keep providing additional advertising funds as long as the CPR is holding up.

A typical campaign in a medium-size market might build like this:

Week	1	2	3	4	5	6	7	8	9
Responses	110	190	270	390	410	380	400	270	130

In this example, if 250 orders per week were needed to make the station pay, it would have been a mistake to pull the campaign after only two weeks. This is the most common error made by companies using broadcast media for the first time. They pull out too soon and draw the sweeping conclusion, "Broadcast doesn't work."

In this case, the campaign should have been pulled at the end of week eight, demonstrating the need for prompt result reporting and continuous decision making. Once pulled, the proposition can be taken to other markets or "rested" for a year or so.

As test results come in, day-part selection should be adjusted and adjacencies revised. Weak cities are dropped. Trends are identified for the successful stations, day-parts, and adjacencies. A pattern soon emerges for the best size of city, type of programming, and the relationships to other direct marketing results. An index is established, based on cost-per-thousand target audience, to guide future negotiations. When the first results come in, the schedule can build rapidly as fast as cash flow permits, and a modest test schedule can become a million dollar campaign in a matter of weeks.

In direct-response broadcast, one typical error seems to come up frequently: imposing personal taste on scheduling. It happens that the top-rated or most intellectual shows often are not the best place for direct-response broadcast. We cannot sneer at schedules that include reruns and old movies because such schedules often are the best buys.

Response Options

Every direct marketing message ends with a request for some type of action. But what kind of action do we ask for on radio and television? There are currently only two choices: mail and telephone.

Eventually, there will also be a significant number of viewers who will be able to order or get more information on screen by simply pressing a button on their remote control. For more information on this, see Chapter 21 on the Internet.

Telephone Responses

Telephone response has become the prevalent reply device of mass direct marketers. Despite some problems, telephone numbers now are used with the great majority of direct marketing commercials.

The greatest problem is the busy signal customers get when hundreds of people call the same number immediately after a commercial has run. The impulse factor vanishes quickly, especially if the television program gets exciting and lures your customers back to the television set. Jammed telephone lines are a major consideration in setting up a means to handle telephone orders or inquiries.

A more detailed discussion of inbound telemarketing appears at the end of Chapter 18 on Telemarketing.

Mail Responses

Addresses are desirable when you're trying to screen out unqualified respondents or when you are asking for a token payment to ensure quality. Also, older people are more likely to respond by mail. If you use mail, you may have to prepare a "super" for each station, including the product name, the address, the price, and a key number. ("Super" is a shorthand for a super-imposed phone number or other text—usually appearing at the bottom of the television screen). The station will add this at the end of your commercial. If the address or U.S. Postal Service box number is complicated, the chance of errors increases. Usually you'll also have to reveal the actual name of the sponsoring company and state some type of guarantee, in order to satisfy station requirements.

Many such companies use Postal Service box numbers, but I feel that they should be avoided unless the sponsoring company is well known. Boxes have a suggestion of impermanence and don't inspire consumer confidence. I'd rather include a real address, where people can walk in if they have a mind to, even if that address is a bit more complicated.

Reporting and Analysis

One of the great advantages of direct-response television, in both short form and long form, is the speed at which calls and cash flow come in. Consequently the advertiser can expand or contract a schedule very rapidly. While some orders may drag in over the next few days, most will be recorded at the end of the day the spot ran.

A successful radio or television effort can easily produce thousands of orders within an hour of the broadcast. Many of the later orders are from people who tried to get through but found the lines busy—one of the reasons why most companies should not handle their own phone responses, but should instead place the task with one of the huge telemarketing firms who are equipped to handle this kind of peak volume. These companies train their people to handle calls quickly and efficiently and, at the same time, to effectively present any trade-up offer. (Telephone trade-ups are an important contributor to the success of such propositions.)

Because you want media buyers to be able to quickly respond to result data, daily "flash reports" by the station are a necessity. These reports present raw numbers per station—number of calls, number of orders, number of trade-ups. Note that a significant percentage of callers end up not buying at all. The media buyers who already have unit sale and other data translate the numbers into go-no go decisions. To do this they also must know what actually ran and when it ran. Agencies usually subscribe to services that obtain this data or have arranged for e-mail or fax reports from the stations themselves.

Weekly reports are generally prepared by the advertising agency or media service. These sum up the results by stations in terms of number of spots, each day-part, and each station. They report on how many spots cleared and how many were pre-empted. They apply the cost of the spots that cleared and the trade-ups and express the results in cost-per-order and profitability.

Usually the report incorporates recommendations, based on experience as well as observation. Some station's spots may be continued despite apparently poor results because pre-emptions prevented achieving the frequency goal. Profitable ones may be dropped because the response is weakening, or because the availability has changed.

Per Inquiry Arrangements

A surprisingly large number of radio and television stations will place spots on a per inquiry basis—extending the availability of broadcast to both companies on a tight budget as well as larger companies looking to extend their reach. In such an arrangement, a fee-per-order or per-call is negotiated. The advertiser collects on the basis of the phone center's credit-card bookings, and pays the agency or media broker each week who in turn pays the stations. My own agency, TeamNash, has been running such a program on a year-round basis for Video Professor and other clients, producing thousands of orders from stations that would ordinarily be too small for an advertiser to bother with.

While most of such stations are in smaller markets or during less desirable time periods, there are hundreds of them and the sales can be substantial.

DIRECT SUPPORT

The purpose of direct support is not to get inquiries or orders, but to increase the effectiveness of other media. I've called direct support a *media extender,* the "Hamburger Helper" of direct marketing. It is always used in conjunction with direct mail or print campaigns that would still be effective without broadcast. It makes a good medium larger, not necessarily better.

Support commercials are closer to general advertising than any other area of direct marketing. As in general advertising, shorter commercial spots (30 second or even 10 second spots) are bought to achieve the most economical combinations of reach and frequency. As in general advertising, the creative theme must be single-purpose, chosen to be easily dramatized and remembered. There is only one action request: Look for this offer in your newspaper or mailbox.

Broadcast support is not a medium in itself, only an adjunct to other media. As such, it always must be planned in terms of its effect on the media it supports.

Probably the best example of this type of advertising is its use by Publishers' Clearing House and its competitors, running support commercials during the week their heavy mailings are due to arrive in homes around the country.

In recent years this device has not been used as often as it once was, largely because direct mail has become more effective. Also, it has been found that there is an improvement in response rate simply by coordinating the timing of broadcast commercials, whether image-building or direct response, with the arrival of direct mail. Nevertheless it is a valuable tool, and can be used whether the support is of mail, newspaper inserts, or even door-to-door distribution of samples.

No matter what the use, such campaigns always must be planned in terms of their effect on the medium being supported.

When to Use Broadcast Support

With few exceptions, support does not lower cost-per-order. What it does is increase the number of orders that can be obtained from other media.

If a $100,000 preprint insertion ordinarily would produce 20,000 responses at $5 each, the addition of support cannot be counted on to lower the cost to $4. What it can do is increase the number of $5 orders from that insertion, in proportion to its own added cost. If the preprint in this example is supported by a $50,000 television support campaign, the objective should be to garner 30,000 responses from the combined insertion.

In order for such an investment to be effective, the coverage of the supported media within the television market must be substantial. Unless you are deliberately spending out of proportion for testing purposes, a proposed support program must be measured in terms of broadcast support cost per thousand prospects (BSC/M). But what is a prospect in this case? Not every television viewer reached by the station is a prospect, for the commercial is relevant only to people who receive your ad, preprint, or direct-mail piece.

If your newspaper preprint reached 250,000 households in a city of 500,000, you would have 50 percent market coverage in that medium. If you supported this with broadcast that produced an average rating of 25 percent, you would be reaching 25 percent of homes using television (HUT).

If the HUT is 80 percent, for example, then 80 percent, or 400,000 homes, are watching TV, and 25 percent of them see your commercial. That's 100,000 homes. Expressed another way, this means a "reach" of 20 percent. This 20 percent reach applied to the 50 percent preprint coverage gives you a "support penetration" of 10 percent. Fifty thousand homes in this market will see both the preprint and the TV commercials supporting it.

Let's say the preprint costs $12,500, and the purchase of 300 GRPs in this market (to give you 20 percent reach) costs $5000. The $5000 is effectively reaching only the 50,000 homes that are getting both. The BSC/M is $100. If the supported preprints cost $50 per thousand, the combined cost is $150 per thousand—200 percent more than the preprints alone. Therefore a 200 percent lift is required—usually an impractical objective for support advertising.

Putting it another way, if the support cost is applied to the total preprint cost, the investment is 250,000 × $50/M or $12,500 for the preprints, plus $5000 for the support. Divide 5000 by 12,500, move the decimal point two places to the right, and you get 40 percent—the overall lift required to make the support investment pay.

This is the way the total campaign will be measured, but the BSC/M method is the best way to test the reasonableness of expecting a particular support investment to achieve a desired lift. A 200 percent lift on the BSC/M method is unreasonable, a conclusion you would not get from the 40 percent overall lift requirement.

We have an entirely different picture if we use direct mail instead of preprints in the same hypothetical market. If direct mail costs $400 per thousand, reaching the same 250,000 households would require $100,000. The same 300 GRPs still cost $5000, and the broadcast reach is still 20 percent, producing a support penetration of 10 percent.

The BSC/M is still $100 for the 50,000 households, but this is now only 25 percent more than the cost of the mailing alone to the supported households, and only a 25 percent lift factor is required. Compare the 200 percent lift required in the previous example. On an overall basis, the $5000 support investment is just 5 percent of the $100,000 mail cost, so only a 5 percent overall lift is required to justify the expenditure. The likelihood of success is much greater here.

One major advertiser buys as many as 3000 GRPs in prime seasons—ten times this example. This advertiser aims for a 50 percent overall lift and usually gets it. Increasing the GRPs, the reach, and subsequently the penetration level is effective, provided there is a sensible relationship to the media being supported.

One rule of thumb is that the mailing or other supported medium must reach one of three homes in a television area for support TV to be cost-effective. Often a combination of media is used to accomplish this. I'm told *Reader's Digest* mails to as much as 50 percent of some markets, combining several product offerings under the same support umbrella.

Theoretically that means that, if we can invest 25 or 50 percent in support dollars instead of 10 percent, we should be able to get 25 or 50 percent more orders. This presumes that the additional support dollars are spent effectively to get increased reach and penetration. But how do we know if we are spending it effectively?

Support Media Buying

As indicated in the previous section, all support schedules must be in relation to the media being supported. The more media that can be concentrated under one support umbrella, the more effective the support program will be.

One advertiser uses common sweepstakes to send out various product offerings to different people in the same market and thus widen the coverage. This enables the support program to cover all the products by referring to the sweepstakes instead of the product. I have proposed similar tactics for multiple-product book club groups, using a copy theme or response device as a common supportable theme.

The examples given here had a penetration factor (supported media coverage times support media reach) of no more than 10 percent. A good media buyer should be able to achieve between a 30 percent and a 50 percent penetration factor by making a comparable investment in the support media. Some advertisers believe this is a minimum range for support to be worthwhile.

The budget for support is developed by working backward from the media coverage and expenditure, and calculating how much penetration is available in various TV markets for a given level of expenditure.

Let's say a market has $75,000 in all supported media, and a decision has been made to aim for a 33 percent lift for a comparable expenditure. The media buyer then determines what can be bought for 33 percent of the $75,000, or $25,000.

The budgeted sum then is spread over a variety of targeted day-parts in a very precise pattern over a period of three days adjoining the expected on-sale date of the publication or the date a mailing is expected to be delivered. The objective is to see how many GRPs (gross rating points, obtained by multiplying reach times frequency) can be purchased in the particular market.

Advertisers with access to audience composition forecasts can go a step further, and work with GRPs or TGRPs (target audience gross rating points) to reach a target audience. Estimates are prepared indicating the type and number of individual households reached by the number of GRPs obtained, and calculations quickly indicate whether the penetration of target households receiving the supported media is sufficient to justify the expenditure.

In some markets this may not be feasible. In others, it may be relatively simple. No matter which comes first—GRP level, penetration level, or support budget as a percentage cost of media supported—all the factors must interact before final recommendations can be assembled.

In direct response, a campaign can be run a few weeks later or in a different market. But support schedules must be precisely timed. To be effective, the campaign must run as scheduled. This means that at least the foundation of the schedule usually has to be placed at negotiated, but non-pre-emptible, rates. This is closer to 80 percent of the rate card rather than the 20 percent paid for direct-response campaigns.

Direct-response campaigns flourish on marginal programming and midnight movies, but support must produce raw audience counts in the same manner as general advertisers. Thus prime-time day-parts and top-rated shows must be part of the schedule.

One method used increasingly is to set up a minimum schedule, say at the 30 percent budget level, with orders placed at negotiated card rates, and then arrange a campaign in direct-response programming, at 120-second or 60-second length, to supplement the minimum schedule. The full-rate minimum schedule guarantees the required penetration, while the preemptible direct-response schedule adds additional exposure at bargain rates if time is available.

Major advertisers have found that direct-response commercials, while not referring at all to "look in your mailbox" or other support references, do as well as pure support commercials on a dollar-for-dollar basis. Planning this requires concentrating a heavy schedule of direct-response commercials just before the mail is expected to arrive.

Another problem involves direct-mail support. When a campaign is being supported, it is critical that the mailing arrive on time. This requires close coordination and special arrangements with Postal Service customer representatives. If the mailing is delayed, the support campaign will be delayed too. One of the very largest users of TV support had a major snafu in timing, with their multimillion-dollar support campaign appearing just when a competitor's mailing was arriving instead of theirs. A major management shakeup took place soon afterward.

Does this all sound complicated? It is. It's very time-consuming as well, which is why agencies and time-buying services seldom will handle broadcast campaigns of any kind—support or direct-response—without getting a full commission and sometimes even supplementary fees or incentive arrangements.

INFOMERCIALS

In recent years the infomercial, or "long-form" commercial, has become one of the most exciting developments in broadcast media, not only for direct-response advertisers, but for many general advertisers who have become fascinated with its unique ability to explain and convince.

Over the years well-done infomercials have built multimillion-dollar businesses for products ranging from cosmetics to car polish and Dean Martin monologs. Organizations such as Synchronal and TMI created omnibus formats such as *Amazing Discoveries*, which enabled them to sell enormous volumes of juicers, broilers, mops, irons, paint rollers, and countless other items. For example, try to imagine this success story—11 million Smart-Mops!

The success or failure of a given infomercial usually is most dependent on three factors.

1. The proposition, meaning what is being sold or given away and at what price

2. The media, meaning whether it is appearing on a station and at a time of day that will affordably reach the right market

3. Sufficient interest values to attract or hold attention while still effectively presenting the sales message

The key is finding or having the right product. Many infomercial companies have built their reputation not on the quality of their communication or media buying, but on their ability (or luck) in finding a product that has "the right stuff." Often they take over the idea, arrange for manufacturing, pay for the advertising, and pay the originator a royalty. Here are some of the attributes such promoters look for:

- Five-to-one mark-up
- Blue-collar, mass-market appeal
- Easily demonstrated
- Unavailable in retail stores
- Available testimonials
- Price of $49.95 or less
- Promises a better life in some way
- An impulse, not a considered, purchase
- Possibility of "back-end" repeat sales

Whereas it took 20 years for general advertisers to recognize and respect the applications of direct marketing in general, it took no time at all for all kinds of general advertisers to rush into infomercials. Automobile manufacturers, investment counselors, record producers, and many others have rushed into the category. Companies like Braun, Singer, and Nordic Track have sold tens of thousands of appliances directly to the public, while at the same time increasing demand at retail. The result has accelerated both the opportunities and the problems in this field.

Unfortunately the power of this format has appealed to the unscrupulous marketer as well. For some consumers, infomercials are indelibly associated with the get-rich-quick schemes. One such marketer is now serving a 24 year prison term.

Opportunities

The chief opportunity is the upgrading of the quality of infomercials. Just as with short-form spots, advertisers have found that quality counts. Infomercials with talented actors, unique story concepts, and genuinely interesting formats have proliferated, building the public's confidence in the format itself. This has also opened up previously unavailable dayparts on important cable stations and major-market local stations.

This quality improvement in turn has attracted more Fortune 500 or 1000 clients. One infomercial agency, Tyee, which serves Hewlett Packard, Hanes and Phillips Electronics, reported that 80 percent of their business now comes from such clients.

Media Buying

One source estimates that there are 500,000 hours per year available for long-form direct response on broadcast stations alone, not counting cable. A highly successful product could be placed on 200 broadcast stations and 10 major cable networks, with as many as 600 airings in one week. The media cost of such a schedule could run to $500,000 a week, but it would be bringing in between two and four times that amount in immediate income. And most amazing of all, a successful infomercial can run for *years*. No wonder some infomercial producers have made $10, $20, even $50 million dollars in profits from a single production!

As with direct-response television, rate cards are meaningless. The buyer must negotiate the cost and placement of each individual insertion. While a rate may be for an entire day-part, such as "overnight," there are dramatic differences in audience levels as each half-hour passes. I have seen 100 percent differences in response rates for the same spot scheduled only an hour earlier. Often a station will require a rotation package, i.e., 3 A.M. placements along with desirable midnight ones.

Compounding the scheduling problem is the fact that the most proven stations and times often are the most expensive. In order to run a schedule on the better stations, a substantial investment often must be made. Therefore infomercial planners generally have developed, through experience, smaller stations where results are predictable.

One advantage of infomercials is that they are sold on a firm basis, rather than a pre-emptible basis as with direct-response spots. This enables them to be planned and promoted. One disadvantage, at least for smaller entrepreneurial firms, is that stations generally demand payment in advance.

Media rates vary from season to season, and probably will escalate each year as more and more advertisers use this format. Different rates are charged for different day-parts—late night, Friday through Sunday, and daytime Saturday and Sunday. Table 16-1 shows some typical rates, as of this writing, for a variety of markets, stations, and day-parts. All are for a half-hour.

MANAGING A BROADCAST SCHEDULE

Broadcast has to be planned, projected and analyzed very much like all other direct response media. However there are some differences.

In planning, you have to allow for pre-emption. Depending on the season, between a quarter and a half of your scheduled spots will not run. The reason is simple: the station got a better offer, perhaps from a local retailer. (National advertisers seldomly place their spots at the last minute.) You won't know until after the air date, so you have to allow for spots

TABLE 16-1
TYPICAL ONE MINUTE DRTV RATES

Type of station	Low	High
SPOT (Local stations)		
Large Markets (Rank 1-20)	$300	$2,000
Mid-size (Rank 20-50)	100	600
Smaller (Rank 51-100)	50	350
CABLE (National)		
Large Network (50-75MM)	500	3000
Mid-size (30-50MM)	300	1000
Smaller/Newer	20	100

Rates shown are for daytime or overnight. Prime time and fringe would be higher. Size of station or audience level are not necessarily significant. Available inventory is often more important. For example smaller stations are often a better value because national advertisers bypass them and so better time-slots are available for direct marketers. For the same reason, mid-December through January and the summertime are best for direct marketers.

Source: Pam O'Dell, PJO Direct, Gardiner, NY

"Booked" and "Cleared." However you are responsible for the amount booked. If 100 percent of your spots run, you have to pay for them even though you may have only budgeted for 66 percent.

Table 16-2 shows a DRTV Media Plan, allowing for spots booked and spots cleared for each station, based on the media buyer's experience and best guess.

Projections are not a problem. The "half life" is measured in hours, not weeks. The bulk of your orders will be in the same day, mostly within the same hour. The few orders that come in the next day or later in the week are referred to as "drag."

Result analysis is a bit more complicated. If only one or two spots cleared, and the results were disappointing, you can't conclude the station is not right for you. Usually you need five or six spots in one week to get your maximum result level. You have to look at what day parts the spots ran in and ask if the audience ratings were off for any reason. If a war breaks out or the big game is on, the ratings for old movies will be much worse than usual. That's why media buyers call the stations and discuss the results before canceling. Sometimes the station will offer some free "bonus spots" to encourage another test or to keep running on a marginal station.

The schedule can also be compared with audience demographics. Often the stations and/or day-parts that did well have a higher concentration of a particular audience segment (e.g., parents or college graduates) that will help determine which other stations are most likely to succeed in a roll-out.

Profit and Loss is still the final judge of whether a campaign worked. Table 16-3 is the final report of one-week of a campaign for an item with four multiple trade-up options, suggested by the operators during the incoming call. In this example about half of the callers did not place an order, but a third of those who did accepted an upgrade.

Problems

In the rush to use this media tool, it is too often overlooked that most infomercials haven't worked, and that most individual long-form media options haven't worked.

Infomercial monitoring company Jordan Whitney Inc. reported that of 600 commercials produced in 1998, only 12 percent were successful.

The problem is that the increase in infomercial use has limited the inventory of effective day-parts. Sure, it's possible to buy half-hour segments on prime time if you're Ross Perot and price is no object. But experience shows that, as in all direct marketing, the final determination of success depends on cost-per-response.

The best buys often have been sewn up by advertisers and agencies who place a variety of infomercials for different products, and who can book blocks of time on a seasonal or year-round basis. Williams Worldwide credits much of its success not just to planning and creative work but to what they describe as "clout"—placing so much broadcast time that they get the first crack at the better availabilities.

TABLE 16-2
SAMPLE CO. DRTV MEDIA PLAN

Network	Daypart	# Spots ordered	# Spots cleared	Cost/spot	Tot. G $ booked/wk	Tot. G $ cleared/wk	% $ cleared	Weeks on air	Total G booked	Total G cleared	Total % cleared
Core Network A :60's 12/28-3/28	:60's M-SU 6:30A-6P	14 14	10 10	$825	$11,550 $11,550	$8,250 $8,250	71% 71%	13	$150,150	$107,250	71%
Core Network A :30's 12/28-3/28	:30's M-SU 6:30A-6P	14 14	8 8	$400	$5,600 $5,600	$3,200 $3,200	57% 57%	13	$72,800	$41,600	57%
Core Network A Fixed 1/4-1/10	:30's M-F 6:30A-9A	2	2	$225	$450	$450	100%				
	:30's Sa/Su 6:30A-9A	2	2	$900	$1,800	$1,800	100%				
	:30's M-F 9A-4P	2	2	$650	$1,300	$1,300	100%				
	:30's Sa/Su 9A-4P	1	1	$2,175	$2,175	$2,175	100%				
		7	7		$5,725	$5,725	100%	1	$5,725	$5,725	100%
SUBTOTAL Core Network A									**$228,675**	**$154,575**	**68%**
Core Network B 12/28-3/28	:60's M-SU 6A-12M	21	11	$650	$13,650	$7,150	52%				
	:60's M-SU 3-6A	7	4	$250	$1,750	$1,000	57%				
		28	15		$15,400	$8,150	53%	13	$200,200	$105,950	53%
Core Net C 12/28-3/28	:60's M-F 10A-8P	10	6	$1,200	$12,000	$7,200	60%				
	:60's Sa/Su 6A-12N	2	1	$550	$1,100	$550	50%				
	:60's Sa/Su 12N-8P	2	1	$1,100	$2,200	$1,100	50%				
		14	8		$15,300	$8,850	58%	13	$198,900	$115,050	58%
Core Net C Test 1/4-1/17	:60's M-F 6-10A	5	5	$200	$1,000	$1,000	100%				
	:60's M-Su Prime	1	1	$1,500	$1,500	$1,500	100%				
		6	6		$2,500	$2,500	100%	2	$5,000	$5,000	100%
SUBTOTAL Core Network C									**$203,900**	**$120,050**	**59%**
TOTAL ALL CORE NETWORKS									**$632,775**	**$380,575**	**60%**

Source: Pam O'Dell, PJO Direct, Gardiner, NY

TABLE 16-3
RESULT RECAPITULATION

Date range:	8/10–8/16/98	Conv.
Estimated Media Dollars Spent:	$21,605.00	
Regular Orders—Total Orders:	1,160	100%
Option 1—Basic Plus:	756	65%
Option 2—Classic:	127	11%
Option 3—Silver:	34	3%
Option 4—Gold:	140	12%
Estimated CPO	$18.63	
Total Calls:	2,218	
Estimated CPL	$9.74	
Conv. of Total Calls to Total Orders	52%	

Source: Williams Worldwide

I predict that Victoria Jackson's infomercials, in which Cher and other celebrities calmly discuss makeup and beauty, will be around much longer than the screaming antics of Richard Simmons' exercise tapes. The television format mirrors life itself. Weirdness will get attention, and there's a sucker born every minute for aptly-named "incredible buys," but in the long run it is civility and common sense that will endure.

They say that most strengths also are weaknesses. The great strength of the infomercial format is its length. Like direct mail, when it is used properly, it uses the time to tell the whole message: to explain, to demonstrate, to dramatize, to provide endorsements from users and authorities. But length is also the problem. As of now, no one looks up infomercials in their program guide because they want information on a product or service, although eventually I believe they will. In the meantime we have to appeal to what I call "accidental audiences," viewers who fell asleep during one program and woke up to find our spokesperson on the screen, or channel-surfers skipping around during commercials and looking for something interesting to watch.

"Interesting" is the key to the creative process for infomercials. There is some tendency to rely on gimmicks or formats, as in badly done direct mail. With the infomercials I have worked on, I have found it to be no problem to simulate an interview show, or a game format, or other audience participation show. It also is not a big problem to find an appropriate celebrity to endorse a product and act as a spokesperson. However, these are no guarantees that a sufficient audience can be stopped and held long enough to make the sale.

As with all advertising, we must respect the AIDA rule: attention, interest, desire, action. To turn interest into a buying decision, the product or service itself has to provide the fascination for the viewer. In my experience, a skilled direct marketing copywriter—accustomed to the long-copy requirements of direct mail—has a better chance of accomplishing this than a slick television scriptwriter.

In the end, direct-response infomercials are not a different kind of commercial message, simply a longer one. The terms *short-form* and *long-form* ultimately refer only to the amount of time being bought.

SHOPPING CHANNELS

The President of "Home Shopping Network" summed it up nicely. "We don't sell advertising." he said. "We're all about dollars per minute."

While QVC and HSN may not technically be advertising media, they are definitely 100 percent direct marketing, and represent a different type of opportunity for direct marketers. No longer outlets only for cheap jewelry and discontinued electronics, these channels now can move $5000 Michael Jordan jerseys or tens of thousands of well-priced fashion items or gift merchandise.

Basically, they are both like big (very big) catalogs, constantly searching for merchandise that will pay off their investment in space (or time). Like catalogers, they need items that are "hot"—in style, in price, in story value, in uniqueness. But unlike a catalog company with 40 or 50 pages to fill every other month, they have to fill 30,000 five-minute time segments a year!

To do this they have developed their own approaches to pre-testing. They have grouped merchandise into showcase-like segments. They have created brands with celebrities, sports figures, and organizations (such as NASCAR), to keep their content fresh and inviting.

The result? QVC reported over $1 billion in sales in 1998, and HSN probably did as well or better.

It is obvious that these are outlets worth considering for anyone selling merchandise directly to the consumer. Unfortunately, whether they accept an item of merchandise is strictly up to them. And their needs are often not the same as your company's desires.

It seems that the format could lend itself to any enterprising multi-product company, first to sell their own merchandise and, secondly, to either accept advertisers or sell others' merchandise complementing your own. It is a logical extension for any marketer who has developed a successful multi-product website or done well on a co-op Internet "shopping mall."

Why haven't more such channels opened? Because it was hard to get the cable operators to add another channel. But that has changed, now that satellite transmission and fiber-optic cables have made possible dozens of new channels that need some kind of income-producing content. There are some windows of opportunity—for a teen shopping channel, a fashion channel, a travel marketer, a business equipment outlet, a home maintenance company. (For example, a Home Depot family handyman channel is a natural!) This is a big idea for someone. Remember who suggested it!

RADIO ADVERTISING

In most of the previous sections, television has been the representative example of the various broadcast tools. I do not want to overlook radio, which has similar tools, methods, and objectives.

The differences in radio lie in the nature of the medium itself. Radio is not visual, but this is not a handicap for business services or products that the consumer is already familiar with. Radio is often heard outside the home, when it is not convenient to write down a phone number. But this is no problem when the radio message is being used for support purposes. A recent exception is "drive time" in areas where mobile phones are widely used.

One great advantage of radio is the nature of its programming. Whole stations are often devoted to a specific kind of music or to news, bringing the advertiser a very predictable type of listener. And special-interest programs—business news, farm news, ski reports, even advertising news—give us access to specific interests and occupations.

Radio can be particularly effective for business products or services, lending audio impact and immediacy to offers appearing only in business publications and business sections of newspapers. With radio, as with any other medium, creative copy must be tailor-made for radio, taking into account its strengths and limitations. Because radio often is a "background" sound, you must attract listeners' attention and sustain their interest. And because many people don't focus on radio as they do on television, it is often necessary to repeat messages more frequently.

Creative Approaches

Often, radio is an afterthought of a successful television effort—added to a broadcast schedule in an effort to find more outlets for an effective spot. In such a case, it is tempting to take the successful television spot and adapt it for radio. However, without visual impact, such messages sometimes are effective, and sometimes not. There is no problem with the reasoning to try such a creative approach. The only problem is concluding, if it is not successful, that "radio doesn't work."

As is true of all media, radio has its particular strengths and weaknesses. Its strength is based on its programming consistency. On some stations the listener expects entertainment, and in those a musical spot or comedy script is more likely to maintain attention. On others, the listener expects news and commentary. To the extent that the product or offer has news value, such a style is more likely to succeed on such stations.

Though the programming itself is a selection factor, day-parts still have to be considered. Often, audiences are very different at different times of day. Also, many stations have radio personalities. These commentators or "disc jockeys"—to their audiences—are trusted authorities. Try a commercial that is simply read and even ad-libbed by the radio announcer. This will often out-pull your regular "canned" radio advertisement.

One minor but important piece of advice: Don't write your spot so tightly that the message must begin at the first fraction of a second. Give listeners a break so that they can differentiate your spot from the previous one. Then get their attention with a "stopper statement" or sound effect. And another suggestion: A whisper is often louder than a shout as a way of getting attention. As with direct-response broadcast, don't feel you have to shout your message. The sound of sincerity is always more winning than that of forced enthusiasm.

When you are ready to consider radio, go back and read the previous paragraphs on television, but substitute the word radio. Radio is different in many ways, but the same as TV in others.

* * *

In the first edition of this book, 15 years ago, I wrote: "Direct-response television is a multimillion-dollar medium, but it is still in its infancy technologically. It is somewhat like a baby elephant: big, strong, but not yet housebroken."

Part of the problem was that the initial users of this medium were often those with the least regard for the public. In some cases, product quality left something to be desired. In others, there was simply contempt for the taste level of the viewing audience.

I went on to say that "'in New Jersey call . . .' should not be the public's only impression of direct marketing on television. There is room for creativity and imagination, for adding entertainment values that not only attract and hold an audience but also make selling points subtly, memorably, and effectively."

Today, I am delighted to report that creativity, imagination, and entertainment values are the rule rather than the exception. Direct-response advertisers are producing both radio and television spots that are as good as anything coming out of the finest general agencies.

Today's direct-response broadcast doesn't just bring in the orders. It adds measurably to the image and reputation of the advertiser and to all its products, building credibility and desire that will make all its future advertising more effective, no matter what medium is being used.

17

BROADCAST CREATIVE

Many propositions that are unsuccessful in direct mail and other media work well on television (and vice versa). Television can demonstrate, convince, and rouse enthusiasm as no other medium can.

This chapter assumes that strategy, tactics, and copy platforms have been prepared just as they might be for print media or direct mail, but of course recognizes the opportunities and limitations of broadcast. It concentrates on the differences, and details the creative and production steps needed to convert a script into an on-the-air communication.

The Primary Goal: Action *Now!*

Direct marketers do not measure success by awareness or changes in image or attitude, though these are valuable secondary benefits. We should also not be concerned with cuteness and cleverness, with winning awards, or with whether or not the public "likes" our commercial. Direct response is epistemologically a branch of sales, not of advertising. Therefore our primary objective is, and must always require, *Action!*

A direct-response commercial is intended to generate an immediate order or inquiry. Unlike general broadcast advertising, which only aims to impart awareness or change attitudes, it must convey enough sales argument and ordering information to generate a letter or phone call. Because direct marketers have discovered that "later means never," that action we seek must be immediate—as soon as the spot is viewed, if not sooner.

But Don't Ignore Image

In the early days of direct-response broadcast, little consideration was given to the attitudes being created toward the product, the company, and direct marketing in general. Consequently, broadcast direct marketing developed an image of loud, tacky, amateurish, and sometimes dishonest commercials for poor-quality records and gimmicky kitchen appliances.

Today the immediate objective of getting an answer must be tempered with the long-range goal of building credibility for the industry and the sponsor. This will pay off in the short term too, as each airing of a commercial builds awareness and attitudes that may lead to improved response at the next airing.

The Power of Emotion

One of the great strengths of television is its ability to convey and arouse emotion and present characters that the viewer can identify with and take seriously.

Figure 17-1 is from a Mutual of Omaha spot I worked on at Bozell, which has run for years with a variety of situations. The format is classic P&G style—two people anyone can identify with at home, talking about a problem anyone can identify with and the solution "I'm so glad I got that insurance policy that protects you."

Figure 17-2 dramatizes the threat of robbery by introducing the criminals who stay away from houses with an ADT security system. The dialogue is almost too realistic. "Dey didn't even know we wuz in the house." "If I had a nice home I'd want to protect it from, well, from people like me."

Figure 17-3 relies on a celebrity, astronaut Buzz Aldrin, to promote a space exploration commemorative coin, legal currency in the Marshall Islands, for our client Unicover. This spot sold over a million dollars in coins.

Figure 17-1. "Gardening" spot for Mutual of Omaha begins with a "life-and-death" discussion, but in a calm, nonthreatening setting, before turning to the price/benefits message. |COPYRIGHT BOZELL WORLDWIDE|

Figure 17-2. This "Faces of Crime" commercial for ADT Security Systems was designed to dramatize the consequences of not having alarm systems |COPYRIGHT POPPE TYSON|

Short Form or Long Form

First, should you use short-form or long-form formats, as defined in the previous chapter? One authority draws the line at price. If it's less than $50, use short form. If it's more, use long form. Others say it's a matter of capital. It costs more to get an infomercial produced and tested, and often it must be paid with cash. Short form is a less expensive option.

Still another expert says it depends on whom you're trying to reach. Infomercials and 120-second short form spots are both hard to place in day-parts and stations that reach more affluent and educated audiences. For most investment or upscale products and services, they prefer 60-second spots.

I consider all the elements rather than just the media type. For instance, say you have a complex product or a highly entertaining celebrity who needs more than seconds to build viewer rapport, but the product price is only $19.95. Perhaps you should turn the offer into a continuity program, or add other elements to justify a higher unit sale. For example, if you have a face cream, sell a regimen and a complete care kit rather than a single item.

Figure 17-3. "Celebrate the rebirth of the space program" says astronaut Buzz Aldrin in this Unicover spot for Marshall Island commemorative coins "marking this historic event." |COPYRIGHT TEAM NASH|

SHORT-FORM CREATIVE FACTORS

:60s or :120s—or Both!

There used to be two distinct philosophies about television direct-response strategies. The traditionalists, sometimes called "the Chicago school," believed that only 120-second spots work, that television produced poor-quality buyers for low-price products, and that production quality is less important than the availability of cheap time.

The so-called New York school, heavily influenced by the experience of the general advertising agencies with which they or their agencies were affiliated, took a completely different tactic. Their premise is that 60-second spots will often work better than :120s (particularly in terms of quality of respondent). They reasoned that shorter spots could be placed in better day-parts reaching younger, more-affluent buyers than the classic late-night spots.

Some argued that long, involved propositions or difficult-to-explain products or services always needed :120s. Others said that the greater ability to secure good placement for :60s was more important. My current conclusion is that both lengths are usually needed. With some exceptions, I usually recommend creating both versions and testing them in time slots with reasonable rates, which usually confines the :120s to early mornings and late nights. The exceptions are propositions based on price or on taking action now. (See discussion of Horizontal Positioning in Chapter 9.) Examples are a subscription to a magazine that viewers are already familiar with, or a telephone or Internet service being sold on the basis of price.

Production Values

The old direct-response cliché is an announcer sitting at a desk in front of a fake bookcase, next to an American flag or a potted palm, holding up a booklet about life insurance, desert land, or an effort to save whales, dolphins, or trees. A later cliché was "Judy," the smiling phone operator waiting for your phone call and the opportunity to send you a free calculator, telephone or portable radio—depending on the type of magazine or book club requesting subscriptions.

Today's professionally prepared direct-response commercial uses story value, entertaining or interesting characters, and emotional intensity or excitement. They use mood lighting, music and songs. Today's direct-response spots are often comparable to the best national spots on their television sets at any time of day or night.

Viewers are more likely to believe the messages, more prone to trust the advertisers, and—not to be overlooked—more likely to make positive long-range associations with the products and the companies. The awareness by-product effect, discussed in Chapter 2, is a free bonus.

Yet you still see direct response spots in short from and long form that lack both production values and good taste. Some of them are very successful. They are products of what I call the old school and they succeed by buying time slots during late, late movies and afternoon game shows. They spend less on production and buy only the cheapest time slots. Their rule: "The program must be less interesting than the commercial."

The new school seeks more affluent, more educated evening audiences and invests in first-quality production values. Their rule: "The commercial must be more interesting than the program." The statements may sound similar, but the difference in emphasis underlines two fundamentally different approaches.

Which approach should you use for your company? The old school was established to sell records, knives, and pots and pans—and it does a fine job for such mass-market, low-priced products. In fact, these direct-response methods were applied successfully to opening up retail distribution in discount stores, drug chains, and auto supply stores. If your product would ordinarily be found in such a mass-market environment, my opinion is that this approach will work fine—unless you are concerned about the long-range image of your brand name.

My own experience indicates that commercials that were interesting, credible and included user imagery (see Imagery Triangle in Chapter 9) outperformed the old approaches hands-down. In test after test, 60s beat 120s.

Poor-quality television spots are fine if you can settle for poor-quality viewers. It seems obvious that intelligent television advertising will attract intelligent television viewers, and that such viewers are more likely to be interested in upscale magazines, investment products, books, real estate, or luxury items for their homes.

Once the length and production value issues have been established, the creative process begins. In television, as in any other medium, the basic creative strategy must be established, preferably in the form of a creative work plan. But the creative skills required are more demanding than those needed for one-dimensional, silent media. These skills must include an understanding of the unique requirements and capabilities of the medium itself.

A Modular Approach to Creativity

The first objective is to stop the prospect from getting up and going for a snack or visiting the washroom. In the AIDA formula, *attention* is the first requirement, then *interest,* followed by *desire* and *action.*

The message can begin with an attention-getter: a diver jumping off a cliff, a display of fireworks, a tiger's roar, an airplane taking off, or any high-energy situation involving interesting characters. Or it can be a headline-like statement from an interesting announcer, or a situation people can identify with. Classic Procter & Gamble commercials often had two women in a kitchen. Mutual of Omaha used the same approach for life insurance spots that still ran five years later.

Once the viewers are pulled in, they must be involved. Visual images and scripts must be interesting and relevant, and portray real and emotional benefits. I prefer to bring in this element before revealing the dirty truth that we are trying to sell something. Save the sales pitch until after the benefit is established, and then do it dramatically and execute it well. State the benefits, and later summarize them. Repetition helps get the message across, and getting the phone number on the screen early gives the viewers a better opportunity to *act now!* And where possible, use testimonials. People trust what "others" say more than what your company says.

Towards the end, add the "zinger"—the inevitable, irresistible reason to call right then rather than later. Maybe it's a special price, a great premium, or a limitation on availability. Remember, in direct marketing, "later means never."

Credibility Requires Sincerity

Because we are usually asking people to order products they have never seen from an advertiser they have never done business with before, credibility is an absolute requirement. Even if the company is well known, we direct marketers must be sure we are adding to their reputation, not detracting from it.

There are many ways to build credibility. The obvious ones are to state why a product is a good value, that it is well built and backed by a reputable company. But television, unlike almost any other form of communication is mostly nonverbal. No matter what you say, the tone or mood of the message will do more to establish or destroy credibility than any of the words in the script.

If an announcer is used, he or she must look reliable and sound sincere. This is no place for a flashy sports jacket or the bravado of most used-car commercials. (I don't believe used-car commercials are the right place for such devices either, but that's another story.) The setting, the music, the rates at which scenes change and the camera moves—all this must contribute to credibility.

Action Requires Immediacy

Credibility might ordinarily lead you to a relaxed, soothing pacing of the commercial. The challenge is that we also are trying to elicit an immediate action, and that requires a sense of urgency. The announcer must deliver the message in a manner that sounds sincere and that suggests that he or she really believes the offer is a once-in-a-lifetime opportunity. The skill required to accomplish this is the reason why some announcers demand premium rates while others find it hard to get work at all.

Casting

The choice of actresses and actors is crucial to the finished product, just as it is to a finished movie or television show. Characters in a dramatization or demonstration must be believable, likable, and convincing to the audience. In addition, they must reflect the aspirational goals of the audience, so that the audience can identify with them.

For example, if the commercial shows a magazine being handled by a reader, the actor chosen to play the part should not represent precisely where the prospective viewers are, but where they hope to be. The character portrayed should match the aspirational goals of the audience. Age, sex, and occupation need not be taken literally, but disposition, personality, confidence, and pride must be. Audiences identify with feelings more than with physiques.

The aspirational image must be achievable. Most people can imagine retiring in Florida or the Caribbean and enjoying a comfortable lifestyle, but not in formal wear at a society ball. They can envision being a bit thinner, younger, richer—but they don't expect to become supermodels.

Basic acting talent is essential. A model with a pretty face, for example, is not appropriate on television today unless she is also an actress and can play a convincing role. And you can't judge acting ability from headshots or composites. That's why it's worth the investment to use an agency casting department or an independent casting service that will audition actresses and actors, have them read lines, and record them on tape. You can then, at your leisure, review the tapes and see how each person comes across, not in the flesh, but where it counts for you: on the video screen.

Cost Relationships

How much should a TV commercial cost? It is possible to spend anywhere from $15,000 to $150,000 on a television spot. Usually, $50,000 will do the job nicely. It is also more economical to produce several spots at the same time.

The cost should be related to the size of the schedule and the type of programming. To compete for attention with an old movie requires much less talent and gimmickry than running in the midst of prime-time programming.

If the commercial is a new one for a product line that has already been proved effective in direct-response broadcast, no expense should be spared to make it as effective as possible. As in direct mail, measure increased production costs against the probability of generating increased revenue.

But spending more on production doesn't guarantee better results. When I handled ITT Longer Distance the client asked us to use their regular TV producer. They did a $100-thousand spot which produced only 20 percent of the response rate of our previous $25,000 spot. It was cancelled after the first week.

Table 17-1 shows typical production budgets for a low end and high end DRTV short-form spot, not counting agency or other creative fees. It also excludes talent. If a celebrity is involved the celebrity minimum alone can be as much as the costs shown here, plus a fee for each order generated.

To keep costs under control, the scriptwriter should be aware of basic economics. It's expensive to have large casts with speaking parts or hordes

TABLE 17-1
SHORT-FORM DRTV PRODUCTION COSTS
The following cost breakdown is for two hypothetical short-form DRTV
productions. Low end refers to a budget production shot using video where
costs are kept at an absolute minimum. High end is a more extravagant
production using film and graphics. Dollar figures are averages from numbers
provided by producers interviewed for a *Response* TV article, as well as other
sources. Mark up refers to the percentage a producer charges to cover
overhead and to make a profit. Note: The industry average is around 30
percent.)

Expense*	Low end	High end
Script	$3,000	$5,000
Music/Audio	1,000	3,500
Crew/Equipment	5,000	26,000
Location/Studio	1,000	4,000
Art Direction/Stylist	500	3,300
Props	300	700
Film	0	5,300
Editing	5,000	18,000
Make-Up	350	600
Catering	150	400
Director	500	1,500
Voice Over	500	1,500
Animation/Graphics	1,000	2,800
Mark Up (25%/30%)	4,575	21,780
Total*	**$22,875**	**$94,380**

*Because the cost of talent varies widely, it has not been included here.
Source: Rebecca Thompson, *Response TV* magazine, 1997.

of extras. Distant locations and complicated sets add to the cost. Night
shooting can more than double a commercial's budget. Most important, stay
away from the big-name production houses that look down their noses at
direct-response television and its cost realities. They often act as if spending
less than a quarter million dollars on a 30-second spot is an insult. There
are plenty of fine production houses all over the country that specialize in
direct response, and will give you what you want at reasonable cost. If you
are working with an agency, let them select someone they are used to
working with.

Asking for the Order

If you are going to ask someone to remember an address or a telephone
number, make it easy to remember and give them time to write it down.
Fifteen or twenty seconds should be devoted to the actual presentation of

the address or phone number, broken up by a premium sell or a basic offer resell.

Advance warnings help, particularly on radio where there is no visual reinforcement of the number. "Get your pencil ready" may be a cliché, but it's a cliché that works.

It's a good idea to plan a commercial so that these ask-for-the-order segments are self-contained. Eventually you may want to test a new price, change the phone service, or work out per-inquiry deals with stations that want to insert their own local telephone service rather than your 800 number.

It's possible to edit the commercial so that the closing and any supers (superimposed text) of price or phone number can be changed later without having to re-shoot the entire commercial. But you have to plan for it in advance. For example, if you have a spokesperson, do not have them vocalize the number or price while their image is visible, but rather while the product or other image is being shown and their voice is a voice-over, either by the actor or an announcer. That way the commercial can be modified easily for price, telephone and other differences.

Offer Modification

Often you cannot use the same offer in broadcast that was developed for print or direct mail. But many offers can go the other way. A proven television offer can often be adapted for other media.

As discussed in earlier chapters, an entirely different strategy typically must be developed to make the broadcast medium successful—perhaps even pulling for inquiries rather than orders, or changing the basic proposition completely.

Multiple add-ons are effective. "If you act now, we'll also send you this . . . and this. . . . And if you call right now, even *this!*" Sets of knives, dishes, towels, and tools all look impressive when the camera pans the merchandise or as additional elements are added to the offer.

Simplified responses are necessary. If you ordinarily give prospects a choice, you may want to offer only one version on television. You can always tell them about an alternate when they call in the order.

SUPPORT BROADCAST

Today, support broadcast is used only by advertisers to support saturation mailings or for large-scale print-media campaigns. The economics simply do not work out for others.

Two current examples of large-scale uses of support broadcast are Publishers' Clearing House and Readers' Digest. For most other advertisers, however, simply coordinating direct-response television efforts with direct-mail drops or other advertising can achieve a response lift. While the broadcast spots are justified by the responses they produce, there is a measurable increase in response from other media appearing at the same time.

Length

Support commercials are not expected to make the sale at all, and need little time to ask for the desired action, which is to look for an ad or letter. Consequently they need much less time than direct-response commercials, and can be handled well in 30-second and even 10-second formats. For some complex propositions, :60s may be used as well. The 10s, however, usually are used only in combination with the :30s, as an added reminder of a message that is being presented in the longer format. They don't provide enough time to do very much on their own.

Variety

When there is a high frequency of support commercials, it is usually advisable to present a few different versions in order to avoid fatigue. Generally these commercials present the same theme, but use different examples or settings. Publishers' Clearing House, for instance, used a series of interviews with prize winners for their direct-mail support campaign. The subject matter in each interview was different because of the interviewee, but the theme—demonstrating that people really do win contests—was the same.

Television in support of a catalog mailing, for example, could present a different item in each commercial, but the main theme would be the value of the forthcoming catalog.

Cost Standards

It would seem that a support commercial should be much less expensive to produce. After all, if :120s costs $60,000, shouldn't :30s cost one-fourth as much? Logically, yes, but in reality, no.

It's possible for support commercials to cost even more than longer response commercials. The main reason is the difference in quality required. Support commercials are placed against the best programming in the dayparts. The adjoining commercials for packaged-goods products will be first-class, highly creative, well-executed commercials. If you have a short support commercial, you aren't up against the local furniture dealer or other direct marketers. The commercials surrounding yours are of a different production quality, so you've got to be good. And being good costs money.

Credibility versus Immediacy

Because you are not asking for an order or response in support commercials, credibility is less of an issue than with direct-response commercials, but immediacy is more of an issue.

In most cases, the medium that is being supported is a direct-mail piece that is timed to arrive within one or two days of the commercial. It can also be a newspaper preprint or a TV Guide advertisement that appears during the same weekend that the commercials run. Prospects have to get that publication or look for that mailing piece, and act on it right then. The message to get across is that there is no way for them to write down a phone number and call when they get around to it.

As a result, direct-response commercials can go all the way to put stress on immediacy. This is the place for the breathless enthusiasm, the proclamation of "big news," the thrill of presenting a wonderful offer.

Support "Offers"

In the simplest sense, the immediate "offer" is simply "Look in your mailbox" or "Look in this Sunday's paper." However, the need to make a sufficient impression to get the message across is as important here as is giving the phone number during a response commercial.

If you are supporting a mailing, marketers agree that it is essential that you actually show the mailing piece. If it is a preprint or other ad, you must show the ad and name the newspaper. "Look in your Sunday newspaper" isn't enough, particularly as there may be several newspapers in any one station's viewing area.

The newspaper should be identified by name in a super or closing panel. (See Video Techniques in this chapter for descriptions.) One economic method is to have your announcer say "in your Sunday paper," but have the super show the specific newspaper's name. You can change visuals at will, but changing the words the announcer says will require all kinds of extra costs.

The basic principle here is that there must be a visual association between the media. An excellent example is Ed McMahon appearing on both the envelope and on the television commercial for Publisher's Clearing House.

The Transfer Device

One important innovation in support advertising is the *transfer device*. Attributed to Lester Wunderman, this device offers a premium "just because you are watching this message," as a reward for placing a secret mark on the card in the ad or mailing.

In one move, this ingenious device provides play appeal, immediacy, involvement, and a way of directing attention not only to the advertisement but right to the order form.

Transfer devices have become a mainstay of support commercials. Doubleday offers maps. Time-Life offers a number of items, including posters. Their Home Repair Library commercials offer a handyman's apron, and their magazines offer an extra issue or a free book. Music clubs offer an extra CD. The premium possibilities are endless.

To increase involvement, extra play-appeal is added by directing people to turn an S on the card into a dollar sign, or to circle the correct plane or animal, or to write a number in a box. As a plus, the transfer device can be used to measure the relative effectiveness of different commercials. One ad asks people to circle the panda, and the other asks them to circle the polar bear.

Transfer results cannot be "read" in the classic sense. The commercial has to be evaluated on the combined effect of the media being supported and the support costs, independent of the number of people who use the transfer device.

INFOMERCIALS-LONG-FORM

Just as some early direct-response commercials looked as if they were shot on a home camera in someone's garage, some early infomercials looked equally primitive. It only makes sense, when there is no certainty that a format will be successful, to limit the production investment.

But even within these budget limitations, the early infomercial producers developed formats that looked as good as—if not better than—some of the talk shows and other formats produced for conventional programming. Most had one or more of the following components:

- Inventor or author as guest
- Interviewer, lecturer or emcee
- Studio audience
- Celebrity or other authority
- High energy and fast pacing
- Enthusiasm, excitement, sincerity
- Interesting demonstration
- People who have succeeded with the product or service
- Details and demonstration of the product or service
- News announcer
- Traveling demonstrator
- Documentary
- Multi-product home shopping mart
- Anticipation of all possible objections
- Promise of significant benefit: success, good looks, popularity, material comforts
- An immediacy incentive: for example, a gift sent only if the call is received before the program goes off the air

While many of the formats were similar, they varied greatly in production values. Some had large audiences. Some were shot in exotic locations, such as a Hawaii beachfront home. Others had celebrity participants who added real value to the show.

Probably some of the best-done infomercials, and the most successful, were for the Victoria Jackson cosmetic line, which included Cher as an enthusiastic endorser. A very creative execution was Richard Simmons for his Deal-a-Meal diet program, traveling around the country "surprising" customers who had used his program successfully. And who can forget Susan Powter, the former fat lady with the close-cropped haircut, screaming "Stop the insanity!"

Note that all these direct-response infomercials not only sold direct to the consumer, but built brands and personalities that can add value to magazine covers and retail products alike.

Susan Powter, for example, became so well known as a result of her infomercial appearances that she has been featured on the covers of national magazines and had a book on the best-seller charts. In general, infomercials are one of the best examples of the idea that new products can best be introduced through direct marketing, where the advertising-to-sales ratio is ten times that of a retail-distributed product.

The Length Factor

One common denominator of all infomercials, past and present, is that they have to make good use of the longer programming time. Just as direct mail can work so much harder than a print ad, so an infomercial must work harder than a one- or two-minute spot. The infomercial is best used, therefore, precisely when it is essential to cover much more ground in order to make the sale.

To a large extent, the unique role of the infomercial lies in its ability to tell the whole story the way direct mail does, but in situations where there are not enough specifically targeted mailing lists. It therefore combines two concepts discussed in earlier chapters: *high-penetration selling,* and a *skimming media opportunity.*

The Channel-Surfer Factor

A very important creative consideration for most mass-market infomercials is the recognition that most viewers have not tuned in to watch your show, but have stumbled across it while zapping a remote controller looking for something to watch.

This means that, as far as many viewers are concerned, there is neither beginning nor end to the presentation. And there is no assurance that even those who develop an interest in the proposition offered would stay to the end.

Therefore all the AIDA elements must be present in each five- or six-minute segment. There has to be something unusual—the setting, the personalities, the tone of the dialogue—to get *attention.* You need enough of a product story value to develop an *interest,* then enough of a benefit message to create *desire.* And last but not least, the *action* element: call this number now, and here's what we'll do for you.

Production Values

In theory, the offer and the product story are more important than the form in which the message is delivered. This is true, to the extent that even the most elaborate presentation can't sell something that people don't want. But for a successful product, a quality commercial can sell much more than a cheap one.

There are two reasons for this. One is that production values that resemble those of general advertising are reassuring to the viewer. They suggest that the sponsor is a big, established, reputable company, and that therefore he or she can believe the promises made and implied.

The other is that, as with direct response, station managers often are more willing to give better placements to programming that reflects well on their station, meaning infomercials that look more like "real" programming rather than obvious sales harangues.

Testing and Revision

Although infomercial production can represent an investment averaging $250,000 for a half-hour (about the same as some 30- or 60-second general commercials), it is never considered finished. If the test is marginal, and even if it is successful, it usually requires some form of re-edit or revision.

Some of this is generated by reports from the telephone operators, possibly indicating that there is some confusion about the offer. Focus panels often reveal a problem or opportunity—especially when the participants are callers who did not order.

Such research is much more meaningful after the first results are in, as the respondents can be profiled and analyzed so that focus groups represent typical customers.

The usual process is to:

1. Expose consumer groups to the product and general message prior to final scripting and production.

2. Produce a commercial for on-air testing.

3. Research the responses and revise as required.

4. Roll the infomercial out as fast as results justify and good media buys become available.

A word of advice, from my own experience: Be sure to test the reaction to the spokesperson or host as well as to the product. A skin-care product created by a woman with a Hispanic accent and a fitness product endorsed by a champion African-American athlete failed to realize adequate responses from general audiences. While there were more respondents than expected of similar ethnic backgrounds to the spokespersons, overall response was disappointing. Somehow these spokesperson choices seemed to trigger a "not-for-me" reaction in other prospects.

Production Considerations

What's involved in producing an infomercial? And how much should it cost? The answer to both questions is, "It depends."

At one extreme, you can start with a copy platform and travel around interviewing people trying your product at interesting locations, the way Joe Sugarman did for his BluBlocker sunglasses. It would have been impossible to script such interesting characters and enthusiastic endorsements. One participant even wrote a rap song about his glasses. It was all assembled with great creative skill in the edit room, to become one of the most creative infomercials I've seen.

I don't know what this particular commercial cost, but my agency produced infomercials with top-grade talent for less than $50,000, and I suspect this one was in that price range.

On the other hand, you can hire a production company to plan the entire production—concept, script, sets, and casting—and easily spend between $250,000 and $500,000. Often it's worth the expense, especially if it's a continuation of a successful campaign or there are secondary uses, as described later in this chapter.

Table 17-2 presents figures compiled by Response TV magazine for a low-end and high-end infomercial, thirty minutes in length. Talent is not included, and usually requires a substantial fee. Many celebrities have taken part in DRTV spots in return for a fee per item sold, which can be substantial.

The trick is to get real value for whatever amount of money is spent. The infomercial specialists responsible for past successes are not the only choice, though they may be the safest ones. New users of this format will have to break the mold and come up with fresh, creative approaches as this format becomes not just popular but over-used.

I have seen very fine work produced by companies whose past credentials were in documentaries, news productions, industrial films, and of course, advertising commercials. All that is needed is a general knowledge of direct-marketing basics if a response is needed, and a creative plan that assures that correct imagery objectives are established and delivered. Companies with integrated full-service advertising agencies on retainer should certainly leave the direction and supervision of this medium to the experts, just as they would any other medium.

RADIO PRODUCTION

Everything I've said about television applies to radio, except the obviously visual aspects. Sound studios and radio producers work the same way and should be interviewed and asked for estimates in the same way. They will always use tape, of course.

The key difference is in the creative aspects, where sound effects become more important and the creative challenge is more difficult.

TABLE 17-2
LONG-FORM DRTV PRODUCTION COSTS
The following cost breakdown is for two hypothetical 30-minute infomercials.
Low end refers to a budget production shot using video where costs are kept at
a bare minimum. High end refers to a much more extravagant infomercial. This
figure does not represent the most expensive infomercials ever made; some
corporate high-end productions have cost more than $1 million to produce.
Mark up refers to the percentage a producer charges to cover overhead and to
make a profit. (Note: The industry average is around 30 percent.) Dollar figures
are averages from numbers provided by producers interviewed for a *Response* TV
article, as well as other sources.

Expense*	Low end	High end
Feasibility Study	NA	$7,500
Script Consultation/Concept	NA	5,000
Script	$4,000	22,000
Music/Audio	2,000	15,800
Crew/Equipment	23,000	57,000
Location/Studio	6,000	192,400
Art Direction/Stylist	2,000	68,400
Props	1,000	6,000
Editing	30,000	66,700
Catering	2,000	5,000
Director	4,500	21,700
Voice Over	3,000	5,000
Animation/Graphics	2,000	10,000
Audience	3,000	10,000
Mark Up (25%/30%)	20,500	147,750
Total*	**$102,500**	**$640,250**

*Because the cost of talent varies widely, it has not been included here.
Source: Rebecca Thompson, *Response TV* magazine, 1997.

Some radio commercials are done live, but this is very risky. If you listen
to monitored tapes from live announcers in several cities, you'll be amazed
at the differences in the style and the quality of the delivery. The only time
when it's to your advantage to have live announcements is on a personality
show, where a well-known announcer will deliver your script in a style that
implies a personal endorsement of the product. For such shows, provide
fact sheets and product samples to encourage improvisation.

OTHER USES OF VIDEO SPOTS

In creating and shooting television spots, keep in mind that you may want
to use the footage you are shooting for other purposes as well. As long as
you are paying to bring together sets, talent, equipment and production
team, perhaps some extra takes and expenses will be worthwhile.

A successful TV spot can often be used in other media besides television,
either by itself or supplemented with out-takes and supplementary footage

shot at the same time. But you won't be able to utilize this extra material if your actor release is limited to television. You should anticipate other uses, provide for them in your contract, and plan for them when you write your scripts. Some of these uses include:

Print and Direct Mail.   It is often effective to use stills from the shoot in other media selling the same product. For instance, I used a still from the TV spot on the envelopes containing a Mutual of Omaha offer advertised on television. The idea is that the stills will remind the recipient of the commercial and that this is the information they requested.

Also, if you are running in other media or sending mail for the same product, stills or characters will be memorable and help build the cumulative effect of the multi-media impressions. For example, consider the memorability of Ed McMahon in recent direct response advertising for American Family Publishers. Be sure to get signed releases from the talent. This is always easier and less expensive to get when the TV spot is being cast than if you go back later on a shoot day or right before the spot is supposed to run.

Videotape Mail.   Mailing videotapes have become an important and effective direct mail method. Some companies have mailed millions, reaching many more customers that the original TV spots or infomercials.

Mailed videotapes can reach exactly the right audience—either of selected outside prospects or of names on a database. Depending on length and quantity, videotapes can be produced and mailed for as little as $2 including packaging, postage, and reply forms. The decision to use videotapes in the mail depends on the extent to which mailing lists offer greater selectivity and penetration of a target audience than television

The narrower the desired audience, the more likely mail will be a better investment than television. In some cases, such as for travel destinations, television is used in the markets most likely to produce visitors. For example, videotapes are often offered in travel magazines.

For one client we mailed over 300,000 videotapes presenting a sophisticated investment alternative, with very impressive results in new and enlarged accounts. In such a case where affluent investors were the objective, a mass medium like television would not have provided either the coverage or the cost efficiency.

Internet.   As carrier capacity and modem speeds increase, more and more Internet users will be able to link to a site to see and hear your commercials—at least in a miniature size.

Movie Theaters.   More and more movie chains are showing commercials prior to their feature films. While I doubt that this will be a direct response medium, I see no reason to give up the right to use a spot or infomercial this way if you want to.

Kiosks.   Trade shows, airports, doctor's waiting rooms and other places are high traffic locations, and kiosks are often effective at reaching transient or captive audiences. Here again, you should have the rights to use this medium if an appropriate opportunity presents itself.

WRITING A TELEVISION COMMERCIAL

All of the steps and disciplines outlined in Chapter 10, The Art of Copywriting, go into the writing of a television script, but the dimension changes radically. If we liken an advertisement to a drawing, then a direct-mail piece is like a sculpture and a commercial is like a motion picture.

You have infinitely more than words to create with. The 90 percent of communication that words on a printed page fail to utilize all come into play on television. A narrator's personality and sincerity can come across, or not. Character, through actors' personalities, can relate to the viewer's self-image. You have realism, motion, and emotion with television—the ability to bring words to life. In addition, you have sound effects, music, lights, and special effects to add allure, excitement, and entertainment value.

However, all this is no substitute for the sound thinking that has to go into any kind of direct-marketing selling in any medium.

Figure 17-4 shows and describes a classic direct response television spot for what was then called the Weekly Reader Book Club. It was one of the first DRTV spots to incorporate general advertising production values and the results of psychological research.

Timing the Script

First, take the time you are allotted—:60 or :120 for a response commercial or 28 minutes for a long-form infomercial—and set up a matrix on a blackboard or a sheet of paper.

Draw a line representing the length of the commercial and divide it into segments as if it were a ruler, using seconds, not inches, as your unit of measurement. Then break out the main components of your commercial—the "must" ingredients—and see how long each of them will run. Here are two examples of a :120, expressed in seconds,

Opening	10	Opening	10
Subject sell	20	Problem	20
Product sell	20	Solution	20
Offer sell	20	Testimonial 1	10
Guarantee	10	Testimonial 2	10
Restatement	10	Testimonial 3	10
Phone	5	Offer	20
Premium sell	10	Phone	5
Phone	5	Premium	10
Immediacy copy	5	Phone	5
Final phone	5		

These are not formulas, just examples of how to approach this problem. The contents might consist of examples, demonstrations, case histories, applications, exhibits—any of the most graphic materials available to make the point. Scene ideas should be listed first, before trying to write the script.

Here are some time breakouts for :60s that lend themselves to more contemporary formats, also expressed in seconds.

Situation	10	Introduction	10
Dramatized Solution	30	Testimonials	30
Offer	10	Offer	10
Phone	5	Phone	5
Immediacy	5	Immediacy	5

Arrange the blackboard or paper in time segments, such as a frame for every 3 seconds. If you use this measure, draw 60 or 120 lines across the page—one for each second. For infomercials, do the same for each minute.

Then draw a line down the page, dividing it into two horizontal sections. Label the left-hand column "Video" and the right-hand column "Audio," and start writing your storyboard.

Under "Video," describe what pictures will be on the screen. Examples are an announcer, a product shot, a close-up of a product detail, some footage of the product in use, a picture of the factory where it's being tested, or a home or office where it's being used. Include any words you want to show on the screen.

Under "Audio," write your text: the words the announcer will be saying on camera or off, the statements of others, sound effects, and musical effects that you know you want. The video and audio should work together and reinforce each other.

Once the first draft is done, read it out loud. Time it with a stopwatch. You'll probably discover that it's way too long. This is where the 10 percent inspiration gives way to the 90 percent perspiration: the careful, calculated selection of what must fit and what can't.

Every visual image requires a few seconds to be comprehended, unless it's part of a flurry of images designed to create an impression rather than a rational point. Every phrase can be measured in seconds, every word in fractions of seconds. Rigorous selection of what goes and what stays is critical. The writer must play Solomon and decide which copy point can stay, which must go, and which favorite slogan or play-on-words has to be sacrificed to nuts-and-bolts copy.

The temptation will be to cut down on those terribly uncreative phone numbers at the end, or to plan for an announcer who can talk faster—which is fine if you don't care if anyone understands anything. In broadcast, the essence of creativity is in the choices you make.

(MUSIC) ANNCR:(VO) Weekly Reader Books hopes this happens in your home some time soon.

WOMAN: Shall I read to you? CHILD: I'll try myself.

"Hooray for fish," said the seal.

Mom, I can read! KIDS SING: I CAN DO IT, YES, I CAN READ. AND THE LETTERS

MAKE SUCH PRETTY THOUGHTS INSIDE OF ME.

ANNCR:(VO) Weekly Readers "I Can Read" Books have already helped millions of children

get excited about reading. The sooner you call us, the sooner your child can say-- CHILD: Dad, I can read!

ANNCR.(VO) We'll start your 4 to 8-year-old off with a free "I Can Read" Book

Just call now. We'll also send your first "I Can Read" Book

on approval for only $3.49 plus delivery. If you like it, you'll get two new books about every six weeks at the same low price

You can cancel after just three shipments

Call now and we'll add a free tote bag and sticker set too.

What you'll really value is the solid foundation

your child will get for school for life CHILD (READING)

KIDS SING: I CAN DO IT, YES, I CAN READ. MAN: We did it.

Figure 17-4. "I Can Read" spot for Weekly Reader, by BBDO Direct. Note the emotional messages—a. mother freed from reading to children. b. Pride in child's accomplishment. c. Father/son bonding. Half the message makes the classic direct response offer of a free book, free tote bag, free sticker set, but the real reward in dialogue and song is the satisfaction of "We did it!" This ran for four years.

VIDEO TECHNIQUES

Once the basic script has been worked out, you can indicate some of the wide choice of effects that are available. The skills and facilities of the production company can give you any effect you have ever seen in a television show or motion picture, including all the effects listed below.

Close-ups.   You can indicate exactly how close you want to get to a person or product. You can show a room full of people, close in on one of them, and then focus on something the person is holding.

In the jargon of the production industry, the group in the room would be shown with a long shot or a medium shot. The single person would be a medium close-up (MCU). A shot of the person's face would be a close-up. And focus on something in a hand would be an extreme close-up (ECU).

Panning.   Panning is moving the camera sideways, to follow action or simulate it.

Zooms.   If you know what a zoom lens is, the term *zoom* speaks for itself. You can bring the scene closer (zoom in) or move back from it (zoom out). This technique lets you set a scene and focus on one person or object. In reverse, you can start with a close-up that arouses curiosity and pull back to show what it is.

Freezes.   Stop the motion with a *freeze* when you want to call attention to something. A freeze is a good way to relate an exciting scene to its photograph in a book.

Dissolves.   One scene fades out, the other in—a much smoother way of changing scenes than the abrupt "cut."

Superimposition.   More commonly called a *super,* a superimposition is the placing of one image on top of another—usually a written message appearing at the same time as photography. Often it's a phrase under or across an image.

Split Screens.   You can show two images at once on a split screen, or four on a quartered screen. The images are combined in the editing stage and can be used to add a feeling of motion to an otherwise static still shot.

Other Special Effects.   A technician in a good production house can simulate anything you can think of. You can make images larger or smaller, add type, change backgrounds; you can speed scenes up or slow them down. You can paste scenes together to make new ones, change night into day, and mountains into oceans. If you've seen it on your home television set, there's someone who can do it.

Now that we've covered what you can do, let me add a word of caution, particularly to those producing their first commercial. Just because you *can* do something doesn't mean you *should*. Too many good scripts are ruined because they get "gimmicked up" with flashy technique that distracts from the main theme.

Pacing. The pacing of a commercial requires a pulsing of high and low involvement points, particularly in 120s and long-form commercials. You can't keep the viewers in a continuous state of excitement. You have to bring up their interest, pay it off, bring it back again, and pay it off again— usually five or six times in one announcement.

AUDIO TECHNIQUES

There are three audio techniques that should be used together, in the proper balance: *voice, music,* and *sound effects.*

Voice

The announcer's voice, or on-screen dialogue, will be the primary delivery vehicle for your message. How a message is delivered is as important as what is said. The tone can convey enthusiasm or boredom, sincerity or duplicity. The manner of delivery cannot be specified in the script, except by means of occasional instructions such as "with enthusiasm." Voice is an essential consideration in casting, direction, and editing.

Music

Music offers almost as wide a range of communication as voice, except that it reaches emotions rather than logic. No one will ever remember your musical backgrounds, behind the voice or as fill-in between spoken passages. They will remember that the commercial was soothing, thrilling, gentle, or powerful. All of these ideas—setting the tone for your message and conveying aural images to your product—depend on the music selected.

Most direct marketing budgets will not be able to afford original scored music, but there is an enormous range of stock music available, particularly in New York and Hollywood, to meet virtually any need. A skilled director can select from available music tapes to give your commercial any feeling you want.

Sound Effects

Since the earliest days of radio, sound effects have been used to convey images: the creaky door for suspense shows, horses galloping and livestock sounds for westerns, bullets ricocheting and sirens in the distance for detective shows—plus bells, explosions, traffic sounds, and anything you can think of that makes a sound.

Sound effects can be used to inexpensively suggest an action that the viewer never actually sees. For example, do you want an announcer to bring a kitchen gadget to a home by helicopter? Do it this way: "*Whirring noise.* Boy: Look, ma, it's a helicopter! *Pilot makes entrance.*"

Want Santa Claus to make an entrance? You can get bells, reindeer hoofs, and the sound of Santa sliding down the chimney.

All of these sounds are available on tape, and it's very simple to arrange to hear the ones you want and to get permission to use them for reasonable fees.

For one commercial we used scenes from old newsreels, but the sound tape had a news commentary and was therefore unusable. We were able to use stock sound effects to simulate the original sounds.

PRODUCING A COMMERCIAL

In print advertising or direct mail, it is customary to treat production as if it were simply an execution process: setting the type that has been indicated, ordering the illustrations specified, and assembling the pieces into mechanical paste-ups for later printing.

In television, the creative process is only half done with the completion of the storyboard. Television production is a highly subjective process requiring artistic talent, skill, and experience to translate the storyboard into the message that will appear on the air. A professional producer is essential, regardless of the budget, the length, the medium, or any other variables.

Choosing a Director

A full-service advertising agency will have worked with production companies or freelance directors, and can help recommend one based on past experiences. Because of the volume of production work they handle, they will usually have some "clout" to assure the best prices and other arrangements.

If you are trying to produce television on your own, there are several ways to go.

The local television station usually will know some independent producers and directors, and the station itself may even do television production. A TV station's prices usually are unbeatable, but the productions are often very poor. The problem is that stations are geared to simple news shows or local interview-type programs and don't have the exacting standards of commercial production houses.

Production firms are in business to provide professional production of documentaries, training films, commercials, and other expressions of the cinematic arts. There are very large production firms and very small ones.

The larger firms may have commission representatives who do a wonderful selling job, and they may have one or two chief executives who have a fine reputation, but the only people who count are the producer and director they plan to assign to your project. Many of the larger, better-known companies may consider a direct-marketing commercial a crass, inartistic venture, or they may resent having to work with budgets that don't permit taking the entire crew to Rome for a 3-second segment. The result is that your particular project may be delegated to a very junior manager who is learning the craft on your job.

A smaller firm usually is run by the principals who serve as both director and sales representative. You'll be working with the top people, but their crew may be assembled for each job. They may have technicians who have never worked together before, somewhat like the "pickup musicians" who make up the bands that play at weddings.

However; there is no reason why even a freelancer can't rent the same facilities and assemble the same quality crew as a larger production firm.

My choice is usually a small, independent production company that specializes in direct marketing, and that can assign a producer and a director with an appreciation of direct response broadcast production

Screening the Reel.   Usually a production company seeking your business has one presentation and one only: a reel of work they've done for others. When you call a director you find in a telephone book or through referral, they will send you a tape or you'll be invited to a "screening."

Knowing how to watch such a screening is a skill in itself. It is a classic *caveat emptor* situation. First of all, take notes as you watch the work. You may be particularly impressed by some of the projects because of "big-name" clients or big-dollar budgets. Such projects are included to impress you. After the screening, refer to your notes and ask the production company representative:

- Did you make this film at this company, or when you worked for someone else?
- Who was the producer? The director? Are they still with you? Are they available for my projects?
- What was the budget? Is it comparable to the one I have in mind?

Then ask yourself these questions:

- What did I like about the reel? The acting? The special effects? The music? The humor or story line?
- Are the things I liked relevant to my project?
- Did the commercial come across as a well-integrated, continuous, consistent message, or were there good parts and bad?
- Do the producer and director seem enthusiastic about my project, or are they acting like they're doing me a big favor?

Once you've seen enough reels, you'll develop clear-cut standards of your own for comparing reels. Choose two or three companies you like best, discuss the specifications generally, and then ask for an estimate on your job.

Getting an Estimate

Always, without fail, get more than one company to give an estimate for your project, and always put your specifications in writing and make them identical for all bidders.

Begin by reviewing the storyboard, which should be self-explanatory, but usually isn't. If you're showing a kitchen set, who will provide it for the filming or videotaping? Can the studio find a kitchen that generally fits your story? Or do you have such specific requirements that a set will have to be built to accommodate your needs? Obviously, the costs will be entirely different in these two cases.

Will the shoot be on film or videotape? With union or nonunion talent? These factors also will make a big difference. The bid should ask the production company to specify exactly what crew will be used and whether the actresses and actors are figured on the basis of scale or above-scale fees. Also, are there usage limits or residuals?

Many of the questions about specifications for your particular commercial will arise in discussions with directors who are estimating for you. Directors can be very helpful in suggesting ways to cut costs or add creative strength to the finished product. Willingness and ability to make such suggestions should definitely be a factor in your final decision, even if the most helpful director's bid is a bit higher. Low cost certainly should not be the only criterion. In television production especially, you get what you pay for.

The proposal also should indicate, and make a commitment to, the shooting schedule and the completion date. Problems should be anticipated, such as what happens if bad weather spoils an outdoor shot, or who's responsible if an actor turns up drunk and can't work, yet the rest of the crew still has to be paid. That's what "contingency allowances" are for.

There are two ways to get such bids: *cost plus* and *completion bid*. Cost plus means that the director gets a flat fee or a percentage of costs of what the actual charges come to. This gives you a great deal of flexibility if you want to "play Hollywood" and get several takes on each scene, but it also means that you are signing a blank check because you have no way of knowing what the finished cost will be.

The most responsible bid is the completion bid, in which the producer quotes a price on the finished product regardless of problems. Re-shoots, editing problems, and uncooperative talent are paid for by the production company at no extra expense to you. Under this arrangement, producers may skimp when it comes to re-shooting a scene, but they probably won't because they too want to produce something they can be proud of.

Film versus Videotape

Almost every producer and director will have a strong feeling about the choice between film and videotape, and there are pros and cons to each. You should be familiar with both media even if you decide to leave the choice to the producer or director.

Advertisers with large budgets generally use film to do this shooting. Most directors are comfortable with this mode, and so are their camera operators and other technicians.

The equipment is more readily available, less bulky, and more portable. You don't need to rent expensive mobile control units if you're shooting indoors. Direct marketers generally use videotape. The advantage is that it is instantaneous. "Takes" can be played back while everyone is still on the set, and problems can be spotted and scenes re-shot without having to call back the talent and crews. Special effects—"chroma-key" combinations of scenes, superimposition of text over photography—are much simpler to arrange.

Shooting on video is far less expensive than film, especially if digital video (DVD) is used. For example, a 10-minute roll of 16mm film costs approximately $110, while a two-hour tape on DVD costs $55. Minute by minute, l6mm film is 24 times as expensive as film. Traditional video is even cheaper, but has become outdated because of the ease and relative low-costs given production value of digital video. And even if the commercial is shot on film, the editors will transfer the image to tape and edit that way, since making film dubs is rather expensive.

If very fine quality is required, as in food or cosmetic commercials, you may not only want to use film but 35mm film instead of 16mm. The extra cost will be justified in details and depth that are hard to achieve in less professional formats.

Regardless of what format you choose to go with, remember: the traditional rules of editing and post-production costs still apply, whether you're talking about film, DVD or regular video. Creative people, clients and others put in long hours until the editing has been completed—costs that quickly add up.

The Shooting or Editing Session

Once the director has taken over, the advertiser's main concern is to respond to the queries, copy-revision requests, and schedules set by the director. This is no time for second-guessing. The director is in charge—at preproduction meetings and casting sessions, on the set, and in the editing room.

That doesn't mean you have to abdicate responsibility. It does mean that you should respect the authority-responsibility structure and work exclusively through the director.

It is sheer disaster to have agency or client personnel on a set making suggestions directly to lighting people or camera operators, and it is worse yet to allow them to offer friendly advice to an actor who may be fighting off stage fright.

Be there, at every session. Watch, listen, and scan the takes if they're on tape. Listen to the sound playbacks in either medium, but keep quiet. Pass your comments along at appropriate times, preferably in note form, to the director.

If there's a serious problem, ask to speak to the director privately. Never embarrass producers or directors in front of their staff and associates, or they will have to resist your suggestion in order to save face. This is the time for protocol, courtesy, and strict observance of the channels of communication.

Try to confine your comments to your areas of interest and experience, and to staying true to the agreed marketing strategy. Try to resist the temptation to play movie mogul. Sure, shooting a commercial is a new experience for many advertising executives. It should be a fun experience as well. But let's remember that, in direct marketing, the fun that counts is counting orders.

18

TELEMARKETING

While the Internet and global expansion dominates the trade headlines, and clever mailings and DRTV spots win the awards, "the invisible medium" of telemarketing has quietly grown into the largest and perhaps most profitable direct marketing medium.

According to statistics complied by Simmons Market Research Bureau, over half the population in the U.S. ordered some kind of product by telephone—over 100 million people. Some may have been responding to an ad, mailing or TV offer, called "inbound" telemarketing; others may have been solicited by a phone operator, called "outbound" telemarketing.

The "boiler rooms" of yesterday are today sophisticated, computerized "call centers." While most began taking phone orders or reservations for car rentals or airlines, they have logically extended their experience and facilities into customer service programs and "technical support." Today telemarketing call centers are big business. The top two hundred call centers accounted for approximately $100-billion in gross-sales volume, as estimated from a *Telemarketing Magazine* survey from 1997. One recently merged telemarketing company was reported to have 11,000 employees manning 6,000 phones at 18 different call centers. And they're only the seventh largest!

There is nothing new about using the telephone as an advertising medium. The "boiler room" filled with telephones has been a sales institution as far back as anyone can remember. Insurance agents have called newlyweds, compiling their lists from the wedding announcements in the local newspaper. Stockbrokers have called newly promoted executives, scanning trade papers for names of prospects. The most aggressive users of all have been politicians, whose paid and volunteer workers canvass voters, raise funds, and get supporters to the polls on election day.

The first major telemarketing user was Ford Motor Company, who made 20 million phone calls to produce automobile leads—in the 1960s! Today even the U.S. Census Bureau is a telemarketing customer. For the year 2000 census they contracted for 11 million outbound and 4.5 million inbound calls, over a five-month period. Banks, credit-card companies and Internet access companies allow "affinity marketers" of insurance, travel and other propositions to call every one of their customers.

Its techniques have become more efficient. In many cases telemarketing is a substitute for other direct-marketing efforts. Some campaigns use it as a supplement to other direct-marketing media. There are companies, large and small, that build their own telemarketing capabilities. Others use one or more of the telemarketing firms that, like co-op mail, serve the needs of many companies more cost-effectively than on an individual basis.

ATTRIBUTES OF TELEPHONE SELLING

Like direct mail, telephone selling is highly selective. Like direct mail, it is expensive, even with low-cost WATS lines (Wide Area Telephone Service) and independent long-distance networks. Its high cost is justified by two factors: 1) maximum selectivity, and 2) maximum inter-activity. Like direct mail, it can be precisely targeted. Like broadcast, it can't be ignored. Like the Internet, it enables the ultimate in ease of response.

To get the entire message, all the customer has to do is not hang up. A muttered "Okay" will replace filling out a coupon, finding a stamp, and going out to the mailbox. A recited charge-card number will prepay the order. In terms of simplicity of response, it is rivaled only by the click of a key or a mouse in an Internet transaction.

However, unlike all other media, the telephone call is involuntary for the prospective customer, who cannot simply turn the page, look away from the TV set, or toss a letter into a wastepaper basket. Prospects are contacted—one-on-one, usually by another human being. For consumer products and services, the contact is in prospects' homes, at a time when they might have been enjoying a nap or eating dinner. For a business call, it is in offices, at a time when the prospects are presumably working, in a meeting, or making their sales calls. There is no doubt that it is intrusive—just as television commercials are intrusive in the middle of a sports event or an exciting televised movie. Yet, most people feel some obligation to be courteous. One study reports that only 4% of people called just hang up.

The power to capture and hold the attention of the prospect is the strength of telephoning—and its weakness as well. Nothing will irritate a consumer quite as much as a poorly timed, poorly conceived, or poorly executed telephone call. Nothing will terminate a long-term customer or donor relationship as quickly.

When to Call

For this reason, the telephone must be used with caution and with good taste. Late calls should be avoided, as well as Sunday calls, with particular attention to local custom. Farmers should not be called after nine o'clock in the evening, as they retire early so they can attend to farm chores in the morning. Seventh Day Adventists, if their religious affiliations are known, should not be called on Saturday. Observant Jewish families should not be called on Friday evening or on Saturday. Most people should not be called early in the morning when they are scrambling to leave for work, nor should they be bothered at the office about personal matters. Maintaining the good will of the consumer is the responsibility of everyone in direct marketing who uses the telephone.

PROPER USES OF THE TELEPHONE

The best uses of this medium are for pre-existing relationships. A phone call from a company to its customers may be positioned and perceived as a service. The same call to a stranger may be an intrusion. Though there have been very successful mass telephone campaigns, I recommend utilizing this medium with caution except where there is some prior relationship. Also, because of its cost, it generally should be used only after less expensive media such as direct mail has been utilized. In fact, the combination of direct mail followed by telephone may be the most profitable way to use this medium

Service Calls

The most effective appropriate uses of the telephone are calls that offer information or a reminder that can be perceived as a service. Some examples: "Your order has been delayed." "The color you wanted isn't available, may we substitute another?" (Note that delayed orders must still be confirmed in writing as well, according to FTC procedures which, for some reason unknown to anyone in business, do not recognize this effective form of customer communication.)

Trading Up and Cross Selling

For outgoing phone selling, as well as inbound, scripts should be written and operators should be trained to make the most of each positive response. Magazine offers routinely push for longer-term subscriptions. A cosmetics offer might recommend a companion product. A book publisher can offer the deluxe binding. A credit-card offer can be upgraded to the gold or platinum version.

Direct Mail Follow-Up

"We haven't received your reservation yet for our hummingbird collector's plate, and before we close out the edition . . ." "We have been saving a place in the next excursion bus to our resort development for you, and before we release it . . ." "There is still time to take advantage of the introductory offer we wrote you about . . ." These are all examples of direct-mail follow-up appeals that can be effective. Not only does the phone call bring a sense of immediacy, but the calls bring the offer to the prospects' attention if they haven't picked through that particular pile of mail yet, or if they started to fill out the card but forgot to mail it in.

Business Contacts

Personal sales visits can cost a great deal of money in employee time and transportation costs, depending on the time involved and the distance traveled. Costs can actually be in the hundreds of dollars per visit. Telephone contacts may cost about $5, and produce fast and substantial results. Purposes can range from sales calls positioned as restocking reminders to old-fashioned collection calls. Help is available in the form of "phone power" training courses and brochures from most telephone companies. And most direct-marketing agencies and consulting firms will write scripts and train staff if you need outside help.

"Summer is coming, and you might want to check your stock on our . . ." "We've had reports that our . . . is selling out, and we wanted to see if you need more." "Our ad campaign is about to break, and we thought you might need some of our . . ." "We know you like to be among the first to stock new items, and so I wanted to tell you about . . ." Calls to dealers, sales agents, and franchises are the most effective way of exchanging information—getting it out fast and getting a fast reply. Sometimes a simple, "I'm not calling to sell you anything, just to thank you for last year's business" can be one of the best long-range investments a company can make.

Renewals and Reactivation

Telephone selling is uniformly recommended as part of a magazine's renewal series. After a series of letters has gone out, another label is generated and sent to a telephone center rather than a mailing house. "Your subscription is expiring, and we wanted to give you a last chance to renew." Reactivation of inactive customers is another use: "We've enjoyed having you as a customer, and wonder why you haven't bought from our catalog lately."

"Immediacy" Situations

The telephone offers a very believable sense of immediacy, and fits well with efforts such as these: "Have you read about the plight of the refugees from Kosovo? We're raising a special fund to help, and we thought you, as one of our past donors . . ." "The election looks very close, and if we can just raise another $100 from each contributor for a last-minute TV campaign . . ." "We only have a limited supply of this product, and wanted to give you a chance to place your order." "The price is about to go up, but if you get your order in now you will only pay . . ."

Prospecting

In both consumer and business selling, telephone lead-solicitation is a widespread application that has proved very effective. In some cases the telephone is used to ask for the order, usually for a low-unit sale—newspaper or grocery delivery, a magazine subscription, or a trial examination of the first volume in a set of books.

Another common telephone use is *bird-dogging*. The term refers to hound dogs trained to "point" at birds or game. Cold-canvass field salespeople used to have trainees set up their appointments for visits later in the evening, and the trainees were called "bird dogs." Today the term applies to telephone lead-prospecting.

The end product of a bird-dogging call is not a sale, but an appointment. The mailing list uses every appropriate type of list selection, as described in Chapter 14, Mailing Lists. The offer can be any of the lead-generating approaches described in Chapter 6, Propositions. The caller can offer information, a free booklet, a valuable gift, a discount—anything that proves to be effective—but they don't attempt to close the sale on the phone.

Insurance salesmen now offer financial planning. Health club salesmen offer free visits. Real estate agents call owners of desirable homes and offer free appraisals or tell of a buyer who has expressed interest in their home. Coincidentally, the same offers that work on broadcast are likely to work over the telephone.

ECONOMICS OF THE TELEPHONE

As a direct marketing medium, the cost of a telemarketing effort can be measured in relation to its results. The concepts of CPR (cost per response), conversion rates, and allowable margin, as well as every aspect of mail-order math, apply in exactly the same way.

If you deal with one of the established suppliers of telephone-contact services, you will know your costs exactly. They can give you an all-inclusive estimate based on your own particular needs and taking advantage of their established systems, telephone automation, and trained personnel.

If you plan your own telephone campaign, you will have to anticipate a variety of costs, including:

- Renting and processing of mailing lists
- Phone number acquisition, from a list supplier or a phone directory in CD or website form
- Telephone operator costs, including time, overhead, supervision, and any incentive bonuses
- Phone company equipment and toll charges
- Management, creative preparation, forms, scripts, operator training, meetings, and results analysis

In determining costs, a great deal will depend on the selectivity of the list, the percentage of valid telephone numbers that can be obtained, and the efficiency of the telephone operators. The operators must be trained to convey friendliness, enthusiasm, professionalism, sincerity, care, authority or whatever style is appropriate. They must also learn to handle rejections, terminate unproductive conversations, and stick to a proven script.

Telephone number look-up costs are an important consideration. Few mailing lists are available with the numbers already provided, and those that are charge extra. For most mailing lists you'll have to rent your list from one source and then add the numbers provided by another. Metromail computer-matches phone numbers to lists with an average 60 percent match-up rate. Additional names then can be obtained from other look-up services at a cost between 7 and 10 cents a name.

Wide Area Telephone Service (WATS) is most efficient when calls are made in rapid sequence with little downtime. Some large telephone services maintain computer switchboards that automatically select the most economical calling route, depending on time of day, utilization of phone lines, and other factors. "Automatic dialers" dial prospect lists automatically, connecting operators only to numbers where the party is at home and answers. Skilled operators need not waste time dialing or waiting for an answer.

As a general rule of thumb, telephone responsiveness can average ten times that of direct mail—as high as 25 or 35 percent of all calls made. This, of course, is for a successful campaign. At the same time, the cost of making calls (depending on the length of the call, the distance, and the cost of lists, among other things) can average between $2 and $5 a call.

The advantages become obvious. Your costs are four to ten times that of direct mail, but your response rate is ten or fifteen times better. However, such figures usually apply only where there is a pre-existing relationship. As always, there is no such thing as an "average" proposition. Yours will do better or worse depending on its applicability to telephone selling. This medium, like any medium, requires its own evaluation.

Of course, cost-per-response will be the ultimate criteria. But there are also ways of measuring the efficiency of a phone service or the quality of a phone prospect list. Peter Theis of Conversational Voice Technologies recommends that companies calculate "yield." This is defined as the percentage of total calls that result in completed calls.

OUTBOUND CONSUMER SALES OPERATION ANNUAL COSTS
(EXAMPLE)

BASIS
Call Schedule:

M - Th:	3 four-hour shifts (9 to 9)
Fri:	2 four-hour shifts (9 to 5)
Sat:	2 four-hour shifts (9 to 5)
TOTAL:	**64 Hours of Operations**

STAFF
For adequate use of a dialer the need is estimated for at least 14 reps per shift. The staffing basis includes a 20% non-phone factor: absences (10%), breaks (6%), and coaching (4%).

Rep staffing calculation costs:
- 16 shifts x 4 hours = 64 shift-hours
- 64 shift-hours x 14 workstation-hours/shift = 896 workstation-hours/week
- 896 hours ÷ 20 workstation-hours/rep/week = 45 reps
- 45 reps x 1.20 non-phone factor = 54 PT reps needed

Reps Base @ $9.00/hour

Management and clerical staffing and schedules:

(1) FT Manager:	M-F	10:30 - 7:30	@ $40K
(1) FT Supervisor:	M-F	8:00 - 5:00	@ $25K
(1) FT Supervisor:	M - Th & Sat	12:30 - 9:30	@ $25K
(2) FT Clarks:	M - F & Tu - Sat		@ $16K

Commissions:

Manager	$6,000 Annual
Supervisor	$8,000 Each, annual
Reps	Average $3.00/hour, each

Tax and Fringes:
FT @ 30%
PT @ 10%

TELEPHONE
(17 reps [for peaks] and 5 other stations)

Network @ .08/minute of connect time for average day, evening/weekend (dialer) connect per rep hour of 43 min.

Blended system of 17 stations (small installation) @ $16,000 per station depreciated over 5 years plus maintenance of 15% of total cost per year: $54,400 plus $40,800 annual.

AUTOMATION
H/W - 22 stations @ $2,500 each over 3 years plus annual maintenance of 10%: $18,333 plus $5,500.

S/W - 22 stations @ $2,000 each over 3 years plus annual maintenance of 15%: $14,666 plus $6,600.

RENT
17 reps stations @ 120 sq. ft. each = 2,040 sq. ft.

2,040 x $15.00/sq. ft. (includes LHI): $30,600

WORKSTATIONS, FURNISHINGS & OFFICE EQUIPMENT
22 workstations @ $2,200 average each over 8 years plus annual maintenance of 5% of total: $6,050 plus $2,420.

Furnishings: $12,500 over 8 years plus annual maintenance of 5% of total: $1,500 + $600.

Office Equipment: $12,500 plus annual maintenance of 10% of total over 4 years: $3,125 plus $1,250.

Mail sent as follow-up to calls estimated at $1.50 per rep phone hour.

Figure 18-1. Source: Oetting & Company, Inc., 1997. DMA *Statistical Fact Book* 1998.

OUTBOUND CONSUMER SALES OPERATION ANNUAL COSTS

	Annual	Rep Hour
Annual Rep Workstation Hours @ 896 per Week		46,592
STAFF		
(1) Manager	$40,000	
(2) Supervisors	50,000	
(2) Clerks	32,000	
Commissions	22,000	
Tax and Fringe (30%)	43,200	
SUB-TOTAL	187,200	4.02
54 PT reps @ 1,000 hours/year each		
less 105 absences @ $9.00/hour	437,400	9.39
Commissions: $3.00/workstation hour	139,776	3.00
Tax (10%)	57,718	1.24
SUB-TOTAL	634,894	13.63
STAFF TOTALS:	822,094	17.65
TELEPHONE		
Network	160,276	3.44
Equipment	95,200	2.04
	255,476	5.48
AUTOMATION		
H/W & Maintenance	23,833	.51
S/W & Maintenance	21,266	.46
	45,099	.97
Furniture & Equipment	14,945	.32
Mail/Follow-up to calls	69,888	1.50
TOTAL DIRECT EXPENSE	$1,207,502	$25.92
Plus		
CORPORATE G & A (10%)	120,750	2.59
TOTAL	**$1,328,252**	**28.51**

Figure 18-1. (*Continued*)

Costs

Time is the commodity—long-distance service time, operator time, service and supervision time. Most phone services, both inbound and outbound, either charge by the minute or by the call. Even when they charge by the call their rate is based on time. Take this into account when you do your scripting. The more the operator or the customer talks, the more expensive the call. Figure 18.1 demonstrates a breakdown of costs for a telemarketing operation.

Predictive Dialing

Before predictive dialers became available, the typical call center was only able to reach about 30 people for every 100 attempts. The time it took to look up a number, dial, and wait to see if the phone is answered resulted in between 25 and 30 minutes of billable talk time per hour.

High-volume automated-dialing systems changed these figures dramatically. A true predictive dialer chooses the next party to be called, looks up the number, dials, and listens for a voice. Then it transfers the call to the next available operator who is ready to begin a conversation immediately.

More sophisticated dialers calculate the average call length and work to keep ahead of the operators—often dialing 100 numbers an hour to yield 30 calls. As a result, the operators are able to talk 45 or 50 minutes an hour—a 50 percent increase in productivity. Multiply this by the salaries of 500 or 1000 operators in a large center and the savings are obvious. Even smaller call centers often find the investment in a predictive dialing system will more than pay for itself.

Qualifiers

"Qualifier" is a term borrowed from field selling. It refers to a short introduction and a few key questions to determine if the person being called is really a prospect. With one reaction, they go into the full pitch. With another, they move on to another and hopefully better prospect. I am always amazed at the callers who start reading a long script without first determining if I'm interested. It wastes their time and mine.

Inbound calls are qualified easily, by asking, "How can I help you?" If the caller refers to a previous purchase, they are referred to customer service. Outbound calls require that the operator ask a few questions before proceeding.

Affinity Marketers

Some of the largest and best-known marketers get their best results by sharing the revenue with another company in return for using their list (which already has phone numbers) and their credit-card accounts (which facilitates payment). Many of the country's largest banks, oil companies, department stores and internet-access providers have made their lists available on this basis.

The usual offer involves three or six free months of insurance, a service, or a subscription which is then charged to the customer's credit card. Some companies fail to make clear the amount of the fee that will be charged and the fact that it will be renewed annually. While customers can cancel the charge, some fail to notice it. There have been many complaints, particularly from senior citizens, about this type of marketing technique. What I personally find so amazing is the way substantial organizations such as Citibank allow their lists of customer names to be used for such irritating and often deceptive promotions.

Telephone Preference Service (TPS)

Every telemarketer should have phone lists matched against the DMA's Telephone Preference Service, to remove names of people who have requested that they not be solicited by telephone. Some phone companies will also be introducing DNC, or "Do Not Call" lists of customers who have expressed this preference.

At this writing, there are a dozen states where legislation is pending requiring telemarketers to honor such requests, and it is being considered at Federal agencies as well. While industry leaders are arguing that self-regulation is a better alternative, the outcome is uncertain. In any case, it just makes good business sense to respect these requests and to compile your own list of people who have expressed negative reactions to telemarketing calls.

THE TELEPHONE SCRIPT

The presentation of a telephone message has become a unique and highly creative art form. The script must never be clever, tricky, or gimmicky. It must sound sincere and courteous. This is no place for dramatics.

A phone message generally begins with a simple introduction, including the name of the caller and the company being represented, followed by a request for or confirmation of the identity of the person called. The next statement is a qualifier or screener—a statement or question that gives enough information to get a reaction as to whether this call is worth continuing.

There has to be room for the person to respond if the call is not going to sound like a one-sided lecture. Once the qualification response has been obtained, the basic message is delivered.

The script is not simple. Depending on answers at various points in the conversation, the script must provide for various alternate messages. In some cases, it moves to "Thanks anyway. Good-bye." In other situations, it asks other questions or provides more information. Questions have to be answered and objections overcome. The operator cannot improvise. Everything has to be provided for in the script.

The late Murray Roman, recognized as the pioneer of large-scale outbound telemarketing, had great success with one technique that still has merit. Operators would tell the party being called that they had a brief message from a celebrity—perhaps a TV star or political office-holder. Once they obtained the permission of the party called, they would play a recorded message, perhaps an appeal to vote or to contribute to a cause. The operator would then return to make the appeal or present an offer.

The following is an example of a classic type of telephone script—a style that was in use years ago and that is still very effective. The purpose of the script was to ask Consumers Union subscribers for contributions. The call format included the fund-raising appeal in a concise, logical, warm, person-

to-person interaction, with detailed, truthful responses to questions and objections. Several fund-raising strategies were tested, and the one finally
chosen included a $35 donation request, with an appropriate drop to $25
and then a further step-down to $10.

CONSUMERS UNION FOUNDATION FUNDRAISING COMMUNICATOR SCRIPT ©CCI

1. INTRODUCTION TO HOUSEHOLD
    Hello. May I speak with (NAME ON CARD)?
    IF ASKS WHO'S CALLING: This is (YOUR NAME) calling for Con-
    sumer Reports Magazine. Is Mr(s)_____in?
    IF ASKS WHAT ABOUT: We're calling our subscribers about some
    help we need. Is he/she there?
    IF NOT AVAILABLE: Fine. We'll call again. Can you tell me when is
    a good time to reach him/her? (NOTE) Thank you.

2. INTRODUCTION TO SUBSCRIBER/MEMBER
    Hello, Mr(s)_____. This is (YOUR NAME) calling for Consumer Re-
    ports. How are you (today/this evening?) (LISTEN AND RESPOND).
    I'm calling because you're one of our subscribers. I'd like to thank
    you for your subscription and take a minute to talk to you about a
    difficult situation we're in right now. May I do that?
    IF NO/TOO BUSY: May I call you back at a more convenient time?
    (LISTEN AND RECORD)
    IF NO/IS VERY IRRITATED: I'm very sorry to have disturbed you
    Mr(s)_____. I hope you have a pleasant (day/evening).
    IF YES: We're asking our subscribers for help Mr(s)_____, because
    regrettably Consumer Reports is in a financial crisis. As you know,
    we're a nonprofit organization, and unlike any other consumer mag-
    azine we refuse to accept any advertising. This guarantees that we
    remain impartial in our testing and stay independent from any com-
    panies or retailers we evaluate in the magazine.

3. FIRST REQUEST
    As you may have read in the January issue, all nonprofit organiza-
    tions were hit with a huge and unexpected postal rate increase. Be-
    cause of this increase, we're now faced with a $2 million deficit.
    That's why we must appeal to our friends, Mr(s)_____, and ask them
    for their help. We need your contribution to help us surmount this
    present crisis. A tax-deductible contribution of $35 will go a long way
    in helping us through these difficult financial times. If you're able to
    help us with a pledge, don't send us any money yet. We'll send you
    a pledge acknowledgment in the mail and we'll enclose a reply en-
    velope for you to send your pledge back to us. So, can you help us

with your support by making a tax-deductible contribution of $35 or more, Mr(s)_____?

> IF YES: Thank you. GO TO CARD 8
> IF NO: I see. GO TO CARD 4
> IF RETIRED OR MENTIONS LACK OF FUNDS: GO TO CARD 5A

4. SECOND REQUEST

Of course, a contribution of *any* amount would be greatly appreciated. Our ability to maintain the high cost of quality testing requires that we turn to you and ask you for help. Even $25 will go a long way in helping us continue to provide the best in product testing and reporting. As we mentioned in our January issue, we've been calling our subscribers all around the country and so many of them have been responding to this appeal. Can we also count on you for a $25 tax-deductible contribution, Mr(s)_____?

> IF NO: GO TO CARD 5
> IF NO (VERY ADAMANT/IRRITATED): GO TO CARD 10
> IF YES: Thank you. GO TO CARD 8

5. THIRD REQUEST

I can certainly understand the way you feel, Mr(s)__. If we could count on you for just $10 at this time we'd be that much closer to overcoming our present deficit. Can you support us with a $10 pledge?

> IF YES: Thank you. GO TO CARD 8
> IF NO: GO TO CARD 10

5A. REQUEST/RETIRED

Mr(s)_____, many of or subscribers are retired and I certainly understand your position. We hope that Consumer Reports has helped you to be able to get the best buys for your money. Our ability to continue to provide all consumers with the very best in product testing requires that we do ask for your help.

If we could count on you for just $10 at this time we'd be that much closer to overcoming our present deficit. Can you support us with a $10 pledge Mr(s)_____?

> IF YES: Thank you. GO TO CARD 8
> IF NO: GO TO CARD 10

6. WILL CONTRIBUTE—AMOUNT NOT SPECIFIED

Mr(s)_____, I understand. I'll send you a donation form and a pledge reply envelope so that you may make your decision at a more convenient time.

Let me make sure I have your correct name and address. Is it (NAME & ADDRESS ON CARD)? (RECORD ANY CHANGES)

Thank you, and have a good evening.

6A. HESITANT ABOUT SPECIFIC DOLLAR AMOUNT

The only reason we're asking for a specific dollar amount, Mr(s)_____, is because it is so critical for us to know how close we are to meeting our $2 million dollar deficit. (PAUSE SLIGHTLY FOR RESPONSE)

     IF GIVES AMOUNT: GO TO CARD 8
     IF STILL REFUSES TO GIVE $ AMOUNT: GO TO CARD 6

7. MAY CONTRIBUTE

Mr(s)_____, I realize you may want to know more about this fund-raising effort, so I'll send you some information. Let me make sure I have your correct name and address. Is it (NAME & ADDRESS ON CARD)? (RECORD ANY CHANGES) Thank you. I hope that after you've had a chance to give it some thought, you'll decide to make a contribution. Thank you for your time.

8. CLOSE/PLEDGE

(RECORD AMOUNT OF PLEDGE) That's very generous of you, Mr(s)_____.

We'll send you a pledge acknowledgment in the mail—along with a reply envelope for your contribution of $_____. Okay? Let me make sure I have your correct name and address. Is it (NAME & ADDRESS ON CARD)? (RECORD ANY CHANGES)

Thank you again for your pledge, Mr(s)_____. Before you hang up, I'd like to make sure you have my name in case there are any questions when you receive your pledge acknowledgment in the mail. (GIVE YOUR NAME, AND WAIT IF NEEDED FOR SUPPORTER TO RECORD) Thanks, and have a good (day/evening).

(IF ASKS WHEN THEY WILL GET THE PLEDGE ACKNOWLEDGMENT, SAY:) Mr(s)_____, we'll be sending that out in the next day or two.

9. NOT NOW—UNEMPLOYED/SICK

I understand, Mr(s)___. We want to thank you for supporting us by subscribing to Consumer Reports—and we hope we've been able to help you with important buying decisions. (LISTEN AND RESPOND) Thank you for your time. Have a good (day/evening).

10. CLOSE/WILL NOT CONTRIBUTE

I understand. There is, however, something you can do for us, Mr(s)_____. (PAUSE) When you get your renewal notice, would you let us know right away that you'll be renewing your subscription to Consumers Union? That will save us the expense of mailing more notices. Thank you. I hope we can continue to count on your support.

The script went on to include 25 or more "cards" with additional dialogue, responding to specific questions or situations. However, this type of scripting is now used only by company-owned telemarketing departments, where operators can be intensely trained in a single company's policies and products.

Commercial telemarketing organizations, particularly inbound ones, today serve dozens of clients. The general practice today is to simplify the script and let a supervisor handle objections or problems. It is also possible to use "on-line transfer," in which a specific prospect can be connected to the client's own customer service staff, or to a local agent or dealer, to make an appointment, close the order, or resolve problems.

One classic use of outbound telemarketing was planned by National Marketshare, which made over one million calls on behalf of Pizza Hut, mostly to reactivate customers who had not ordered recently. The script asked about prior service and quality, and then made an offer to deliver pizza that evening at a special price. Other mail and telephone offers followed up these calls, varied according to the information received and the policies of the local Pizza Hut outlet. A custom computer program planned the calling so as to correspond to slow days and hours at each outlet, when the special-price offer could easily be implemented.

INBOUND TELEMARKETING

Inbound telemarketing is a marketing discipline in itself, with its own suppliers, its own standards, and its own techniques.

While some suppliers offer both inbound and outbound telemarketing, most have particular strength in one or the other.

Though outbound telemarketing is a medium to be evaluated as part of the overall media mix, inbound telemarketing is a service, the costs of which are added to cost per lead as another fulfillment expense.

However, inbound phone services do much more than act as order-takers. With proper planning and careful testing, they can be used to "qualify" a lead, prescreen credit, and—most commonly—trade up the customer to a deluxe option, a longer term, or a larger quantity.

Selecting Inbound Telephone Services

If you are selling with catalogs, direct mail, print media or from a website, phone calls from each effort will come in over several weeks. You may be able to handle these with your own operators or with smaller phone services. However, if using short form or long form television or large-scale radio campaigns, all but the largest companies will need to use an outside service. Broadcast calls are concentrated within moments of the airing of each commercial. Some prospects will call back if the line is busy. Others won't. The phone service or your phone company can give you a report detailing how many calls didn't get through.

The key considerations when deciding on telephone services are the number of phones available, how many of them are staffed, and what their load factors are. Before selecting a telephone service, get a list of the company's clients and check references. Also, call in on a broadcast offer for one of their clients to see how long it takes to get through and how courteously and efficiently the telephone is answered. If you have a bad experience, go elsewhere. Don't let anyone argue that you reached the one exception. There shouldn't be any exceptions if the staff has been properly selected and trained before being placed at the phones.

Because jammed telephone lines can cost you an estimated one-half to two-thirds of your potential response, selection of a telephone service is serious business. Take the time to pick the right telephone supplier for your needs and to check out every detail in person. The available numbers should be easy to remember and unique to the particular advertiser if at all possible.

Phone answering companies should have efficient systems—manual or computerized—for indicating all necessary information about the offer and the order. The best systems are those in which every operator has a computer terminal that can display the script and input an order. The operator says exactly what is on the screen, giving information or asking for it as necessary. Questions to be asked to the caller appear on the screen. If there is information to be checked, such as available inventory for a particular item being ordered or the validity of a credit-card number, the checking is done automatically and simultaneously while the customer is still on the phone. The customer's answers are punched right into the computer, displayed on the screen, and stored in memory.

Professional telephone suppliers can do more than just answer the telephone and capture name, address, and item ordered. They can train their telephone operators to be salespeople as well. They are also your company's goodwill ambassadors. For this reason, care in the selection of a telephone supplier and training of operators is essential. The operators must be able to deal with all their customers and prospects, regardless of age, language or level of product knowledge.

For example, one insurance firm who dealt with AARP members had their operators get special sensitivity training in dealing with senior citizens. Another insurer out-sources such callers to a telemarketing firm which specializes in this market segment.

Here are some tips when looking for a phone-services company:

- Ask prospective phone services what their staffing is at different times of the day and night.

- Ask how they handle source coding. Do they have multiple numbers available? Can they reliably capture a verbal or dialed "extension number."

- Look at some of their reports. Are they complete? Are they useful?

- Can you "listen in" on phone calls by dialing a special number from your own home or office, anytime you wish? Many services offer this now.

- Can you use the supplier just for overflow calls from your own facility? Do they have a back-up for their own over-flow?

- Can they accomplish on-line transfer for calls they can't handle to a dealer or customer service center?

- Can they handle calls from languages other than English? Can they handle call from international customers?

- Do they have *automatic call routers* (see below) and how are they used?

Automatic Call Routers

Just as predictive dialers have revolutionized outbound calling, automatic call routers have done the same for inbound.

This system evaluates the caller's keyed response to inquiries about the nature of the call. In a multi-client environment, it determines which phone number generated the call, and hence for which client the call is for.

Sophisticated routing systems go far beyond sending the call to the correct department. They take into account the waiting time for each operator and the experience and specialties of each operator. If one department is backed up, subsequent calls are automatically routed to anyone in any department who has the knowledge to be able to handle the call.

This system also works with multiple-office situations. Calls can be transferred to an office in another time zone if it will help reduce waiting time.

One company, Carnival Cruises, takes this application a step further. When their calls peak, their system will not only route calls to other sales operators but will assign calls to reservations agents, group booking agents, customer service agents—whomever is qualified to handle a particular call. The agents are evaluated in ten areas of skills and knowledge to define the qualifications. The company credited this system with a 16 percent reduction in their call abandon rate.

Trade-ups

Telephone trade-ups are a growing trend, but they require trained salespeople. Some magazines offer short-term subscriptions on the air and then offer "added savings" on the telephone to try to convert the respondent to a longer subscription. Some companies invite COD or to-be-billed orders on television and then have the telephone operator offer a premium if the customer pays by giving a credit-card number on the telephone. Some advertisers invite viewers to mail cash or checks to a certain address but suggest that only credit-card holders may call and order by phone.

Many telephone services now offer total fulfillment services, or everything except the actual shipment of merchandise. Some of those we use for our clients handle mailed orders, fax orders and Internet orders as well as telephone orders. Some even handle customer service calls. Some full service shops not only input data, but also maintain the mailing lists, issue reports, and handle returns as well.

Inbound Telephone Scripts

Here is an example of an inbound telephone script for a one-shot mail-order proposition being sold by COD or credit card. Note that in this script no questions are asked to determine the source of the call, as the called number activates the computer program automatically to tell the answering service operator the nature of the product and the proposition.

PRODUCT: $19.95 widget
PAYMENT: Credit Card—MasterCard, Visa, Amex, Discover, COD—$5
SCRIPT:

1. HI, THIS IS _____. MAY I HELP YOU?

2. MAY I HAVE YOUR POSTAL ZIP, PLEASE?

3. YOUR LAST NAME? FIRST? MISS OR MRS.? (if female)

4. YOU LIVE IN _____, _____ (city, state)

5. MAY I HAVE YOUR STREET ADDRESS?

6. WHICH CREDIT CARD WILL YOU BE USING? (MC, VISA, AMEX)

7. (If Customer says "none") DID YOU KNOW THAT YOU CAN SAVE
    $5 COD POSTAGE AND HANDLING BY USING YOUR CREDIT CARD?

8. MAY I HAVE YOUR CREDIT CARD NUMBER, PLEASE?

9. YOUR AREA CODE IS _____. MAY I HAVE THE REST OF YOUR HOME
    PHONE, PLEASE?

10. YOU CAN HAVE TWO WIDGETS FOR $35.00—AN ADDITIONAL
    SAVINGS OF ALMOST $5.

11. THANK YOU FOR CALLING. YOUR WIDGET WILL BE DELIVERED
    IN 4 TO 6 WEEKS.

The zip code is punched into the computer, and the city and state are revealed so that the operator can confirm the zip code. The same information also gives the telephone area code to facilitate getting the home phone number, which is mandatory for this company before either credit card or COD shipment will be accepted. The credit card question is presented as a presumption: "Which credit card will you be using?" rather than "Will you be using a credit card?"

Note the trade-up suggestion in line 10—additional savings for multiple purchases. I have had exceptional results trading up $5 coin collectibles to multiple orders or a $25 silver version.

Similar suggestions can be made to turn company credit orders into cash, one-year subscriptions into two-year ones, and information leads into qualified appointments for salespersons. The creative opportunities for telephone scripts are much greater than most people realize.

OTHER OPTIONS

Internet Integration

In Chapter 21 on the Internet, I will be discussing the various ways leads and inquiries can be generated directly over the web. However, it is important to note that the communications channel that reaches the customer is not necessarily the one the customer prefers to use in return.

For example, Honeywell generated tens of thousands of inbound contacts for their home heating equipment by featuring both their 877-

4COMFORT phone number and the identical web URL in their advertising. Those making contact through the web page were able to click through to a voice connection directly to local dealers.

800 Numbers

As we write this, the toll-free 800 number has expanded to include 800, 888 and 877 numbers. The expansion was necessary because long distance services offered 800 numbers free for the asking, even to residential customers. As might be expected, they soon ran out of numbers.

There are indications that the public is not fully aware of the newer numbers. Therefore the words "toll free" should be used to reassure skittish callers.

Another consideration is the protection of vanity numbers. If you are using a number like 800-FLOWERS be sure to get the same number in 888 and 877 to head off imitators. If your website URL is using a similar screen name, then try to protect that as well. For example, 800-FLOWERS also has a website at www.800flowers.com. Some quick-thinking and technology-minded employee was smart enough to register that web address before the competition did. Other companies with catchy phone numbers have not been so lucky. The need to protect your number is becoming as critical as the need to protect your name.

When you do use a letter-based phone "number," I suggest you also list the numeric version nearby. While the vanity numbers are easy to remember, some people seem to get confused finding the right keys to press.

900 Numbers

Billing charged automatically to a phone bill was, when introduced, supposed to be the ultimate convenience to the direct-marketing customer. It is a convenience, but the phone companies and the media poisoned its usefulness by letting its first users include sex phone services and similar embarrassments.

Another problem is that phone companies do not have the conflict-resolution systems offered by credit card companies. If buyers dispute a charge on an American Express Card, they are given automatic credit until the question is resolved. With a phone charge, they must pay the bill or have their phone service cut off, and there is no help at all from the phone company.

As a result, the mere use of a 900 number raises a credibility question about an offer. While this method has proved useful for applications in which the sponsor is well known such as memberships in public service television, I generally do not recommend it.

Electronic Answering

Several in-bound phone services now offer automated data-entry services, which are generally less expensive than systems that use live operators.

These systems generally prompt replies by asking the caller to press a touch-tone button on the phone. This facilitates multiple questions, as for database surveys, and has even made possible complex games such as sports contests and stock market selection games.

Checks-by-Mail

Many consumers, particularly older ones, prefer not to give anyone their credit-card numbers over the telephones, severely restricting the total sales resulting from television offers. Others simply do not have credit cards. One answer to this has been the development of services that can accept the customer's check number and arrange to debit the account.

While it is too early to determine the impact this will have on the direct-marketing industry, I find it difficult to imagine that consumers who do not want to give their credit card number will be willing to give their check number. There should be some incremental convenience for those consumers who simply do not have credit cards, but I'm skeptical about how large or valuable that segment would be.

TELEMARKETING'S FUTURE

The problem with telemarketing is that, while it is an industry in itself, it largely uses the same type of mailing lists used by direct mailers. The few bad apples have exacerbated negative attitudes toward both mail and telemarketing, leading to serious legislative threats to the collection and use of both business and consumer prospect lists.

Eventually, telemarketers will have to band together to clean their own house, or mailers and advertisers will have to distance themselves from telemarketing. We are not in the same business. Our messages arrive in a mailbox, a magazine, on the air or on a computer channel. A prospect has the right to toss the envelope, turn the page, or change the channel. We do not incur a prospect's anger at having to leave the dinner table to answer the telephone, nor do we interrupt the prospect during a busy business day by the need to deal with a supposedly "personal" call.

Like it or not, telemarketing is here, and it has its legitimate uses, particularly where a prior relationship exists or where there has been a request for information. It can be used and used well in these circumstances. As direct marketers, we have to do our best to create legitimate offers and sincere messages for telemarketing purposes. We don't have to use it. But we do have to understand it.

19

FULFILLMENT

The term *fulfillment* derives, as with most modern direct marketing, from this field's roots in mail order. Originally it referred to "fulfilling the order." The original scope was confined to opening the mail, typing a label, keeping track of the orders and deposits, and mailing the merchandise.

Direct marketing has, of course, evolved into much more than simple mail order. The "mail" response might be a phone call, an Internet response or a coupon delivered at a retail store. The "label" is more likely to be the input onto a computer record of not just a name, address, and key number, but answers to a complex database questionnaire. The "merchandise" is likely to be a membership, a donation, a subscription, further information about a product or service, or the activation of a sophisticated interactive service.

The common denominator is not what is being sold, but the advertiser's response to the consumer's response: the process of fulfilling the promise or offer made in the advertising. Today this process is better viewed as a function of customer service or "relationship marketing."

MEETING EXPECTATIONS

The mailing piece is attractive and inviting. You open the envelope and find yourself involved in an offer of a product that will make your job easier or your life more satisfying. Eagerly, you mail in the coupon. Like most customers, you then impatiently wait . . . and wait . . . and wait.

Finally, weeks later, a battered-looking carton arrives. Your name is misspelled. You break your fingernail opening the carton. You rustle through a mass of yellowed pages from an old newspaper, and there it is—broken!

Maybe it's not even what you ordered. The instructions may be in Pidgin English. Sometimes the item doesn't come at all, but a polite postcard arrives six weeks later to tell you that it has been out of stock, or not available in your size.

Whether you keep this item or not, or whether your return or refund is handled efficiently or not, you've already lost your enthusiasm for the product, for the company, and probably for buying by mail at all.

Avoiding this all too common scenario is what mail-order fulfillment is all about. Fulfillment should be concerned, but too frequently isn't, with fulfilling not only the order but also the customer's expectations. This subject is, technically, a matter of operations rather than marketing, but it can dramatically influence return rates, collections, reorder rates, and the entire future of direct marketing.

Good fulfillment practices, including prompt shipment, can significantly affect conversion and acceptance rates. Fulfillment costs, including order processing, shipping, and service functions, are always a significant expense that, unmonitored, can eat up your profit margin. Fulfillment problems, whether handled in house or by an outside supplier, can get your company in trouble with the Better Business Bureau, the DMA Ethical Standards Committee, the Postal Service, the press, and the law. More important, it is unfair both to your customers who trusted you and your fellow direct marketers whose reputation you tarnished along with your own.

DATABASE AND LEAD GENERATION

Most of the advice in this chapter deals with mail order, the most complex form of fulfillment. But the principles—particularly those involving speed and service—apply to any type of direct-marketing effort. A direct marketer has to perform similar functions, whether it involves developing leads, a sales force, a consumer or business proposition, or just building a database.

Leads must be coded and transmitted promptly and accurately. They must be assigned to the correct geographic or specialty salesperson and transmitted by mail or by wire transmission in a usable form. In addition, there must be provision for information feedback: Did the party purchase the product or service? Is a follow-up necessary? Should the party be sent information about a different product? If no sale was made, why not?

An information-tracking system should be set up that analyzes the leads from every perspective: conversion by source, type of prospect, geographic region, type of industry (if a business lead), advertising source, and the outlet or salesperson.

Usually there is a direct mail or telephone follow-up, in addition to simple transmission of the lead. List maintenance comes into play here. So do economic decisions concerning how many letters to send, how long to continue sending letters, and whether letters should supplement or replace the field-sales effort.

SUBSCRIPTION AND CONTINUITY PLANS

Other forms of fulfillment involve subscriptions—the method used by most magazine publishers—and continuity or club plans—used by book clubs, record clubs, and other businesses selling on a continuing basis.

These methods are even more complex, as they involve the continuing shipment of merchandise or the provision of services to a direct marketing customer.

Besides promptly handling each shipment, the fulfillment organization has the added responsibility of administering a two-way contract, to be sure that both the company and the customer honor their obligations to one another.

Subscription expiration dates, club commitments, and continuity cancellation privileges must be honored to the spirit and letter of the agreement entered into during the original transaction. Sometimes an entire correspondence series must be created to persuade customers to honor their commitments—to pay for the last shipment, to buy the required additional item, or to renew the agreement.

Lead generation, clubs, subscription plans, and continuity plans could each occupy an entire chapter, and they do in *The Direct Marketing Handbook* (McGraw-Hill, First ed. 1984; Second ed. 1992). I recommend that those readers concerned about these specific approaches read the appropriate chapters. The general principles described here—particularly those involving the need for accuracy, speed, and service—apply to any form of fulfillment.

FULFILLMENT PROCESSES

Each fulfillment process involves a complicated decision-making process. There are usually many compromises, depending on the standard of customer service you set as your goal.

Direct marketers aim for a high level of personalization, promptness, and performance—the three Ps of fulfillment. At each phase these must be weighed against the realities of time and cost, as expressed in added personnel, inventory risk, computer capability, and the expense of communicating with your customer by mail and telephone. Let's look at each step individually (see Fig. 19-1).

Opening Mail

Most firms count or number the mail first, to establish a control against loss. If there is cash involved, a "caging" process takes place, in which remittances are removed and the amount noted. The money is handled under supervision within a security area and deposited each day. Fulfillment suppliers deposit payments in their customers' banks each day.

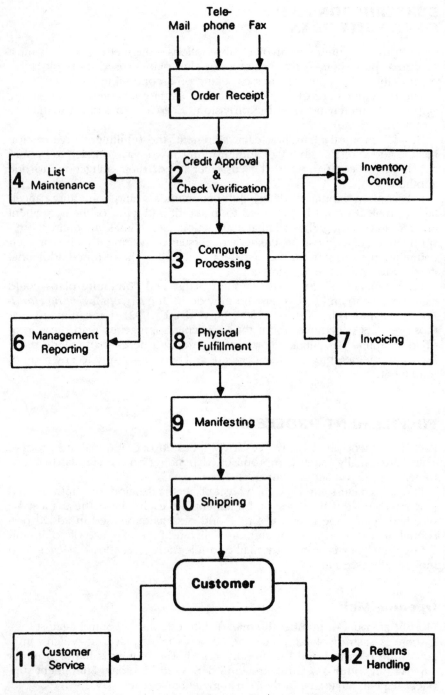

Figure 19-1. Twelve basic steps in the fulfillment cycle. |Courtesy of Fenvessey & Associates, New York.|

Large fulfillment operations also use very ingenious machinery that slits open envelopes and exposes the contents for easy removal. Other machinery can imprint checks with source and amount. This enables (1) generating deposits that can be quickly processed by the bank and (2) efficiently recording and controlling cash intake.

Often the mail is sorted into types: payments, credit-card orders, general correspondence, returns, catalog requests. Advertising responses are sorted or counted, so that daily counts by key numbers can be supplied to marketing personnel. If the volume is large, the sorting and counting process can be helped by using different sizes or colors of reply envelopes, bold tag marks on envelope edges, windows with code number show-through, or optically scannable imprints on the envelope faces. Many companies use different locations or post-office boxes for each type of mail, in effect letting the postal service do their sorting.

Each type of mail is batched into work groups of 25 or 50 items and logged in.

Handling Telephone Responses

For most types of propositions, the ring of the telephone is becoming as important as picking up the mail. The growth of telephone usage brings with it both problems and opportunities.

Toll-free WATS (Wide Area Telephone Service) lines are the usual technique for providing such service. Marketers must provide not only for enough lines to handle the normal flow of inbound phone calls, but also for skilled and trained operators on all shifts.

To take full advantage of this medium, the phones should be answered day and night, seven days a week, whenever people are likely to be reading your message in their mail, in publications, or on your website. This is also necessary because, as direct marketing becomes increasingly global, your caller may be in a time zone anywhere on the planet.

If your message is offered on television, however, usually it is uneconomical to have your own company handle the inbound calls. The intensive peak demand for inbound lines would result in expensive idle capacity most other times. Outside phone services are geared to handle peak usage at advantageous rates.

An exception would be companies that are maintaining large telephone operations for out-bound calling, reservations, or tech support services. When a DRTV spot produces a flood of inbound calls, they simply switch from outbound to inbound. Of course, the personnel must be trained to handle both functions. A simple system used for the long distance service I handled was to have green, yellow and red lights. Green had almost everyone on out-bound. Yellow ceased outbound calling and switched all operators to in-bound. Red indicated that the system was over-loaded, and directed operators to take names and phone numbers and call back later.

Most companies, especially those using direct-response television with its intense calling patterns, find it preferable to use a company that specializes in handling telephone responses. Neither their rates nor the quality of their service is necessarily equal, so competitive bidding and reference checks are strongly recommended. At the very least, find out what propositions the companies are currently handling and investigate by responding as if you were a potential product or service customer. This is the best way to really see how the company handles different phone calls.

The ideal situation is to be able to maintain your own 24-hour telephone service customized to your own needs. With today's technology, a catalog company can identify callers automatically and have their name and history on a screen before they've even answered the phone. "Hello, Mr. Jones, how can we at XYZ help you today?" is now entirely possible, as well as instant confirmation that an item is in stock and ready to ship. Some Internet direct marketers are already doing this electronically.

One recent innovation is "on-line transfer," used in both outgoing and inbound telemarketing. This enables a caller to be connected, instantly, from the initial contact person to a customer service representative who can handle more complex questions, or to a local dealer, insurance agent, stockbroker, or repair service who can make an appointment.

Whether your company handles its own phones or uses a service, the telephone contact is an opportunity to make a positive impression for your company by the way the call is handled. A courteous, efficient operator can do a lot to inspire trust. While on the phone, the operator can offer special trade-up offers or sell related items. Alternate colors or sizes or replacement items can be recommended. With credit-card orders, the entire transaction can be confirmed and entered on the spot.

Order Acceptance

Telephone operators can also be helpful in reducing fraud. They should be trained to question orders billed to one address and shipped to another, to spot callers who are under 18, or who appear to be under the influence of alcohol or drugs. Simply asking for a day and night phone number or the zip code a second time will often discourage a prank caller or a crook. Operators should remember that whenever the call sounds suspicious they should find an excuse to call one of the phone numbers at a later time.

Credit-card orders for large amounts should be verified by calling the issuing bank, checking both the shipping address and the status of the card.

Checks should be examined carefully. Does the Federal Reserve number correspond to the location of the bank? Is the optical-scanning code dull, meaning printed with non-metallic ink? Do the numbers smear? Are the check numbers low, meaning it is a relatively new account? Does the check lack a preprinted name or address? These are all warning signs.

The "exceptions" department should verify all suspicious transactions before shipping. If a check bounces, or a credit card charge is contested, the appropriate steps should be taken to re-deposit the check or send verification to the bank.

Data Entry

Fulfillment is a lot more complicated than newcomers imagine. The order or inquiry must be edited—examined for completeness and clarity.

- Are the item numbers correct? The prices? The shipping charges?
- Is the source code right? Does the zip code match the city name?
- Is the credit card number complete? Is the expiration date present?

Any discrepancies with phone and Internet orders are caught instantly, while the customer is still on-line or on the phone. For mail and fax orders, a phone call or some additional correspondence may be needed to enable the order to be processed. These "exceptions" are usually handled by a customer service representative.

Then the order information is put into a form where it can be compared with lists of former customers, credit-risk clients, zip-code verification, and other data. Key numbers are counted and reports are compiled and perhaps even analyzed, depending on the sophistication of the system. The data from the customer file then is used to send out acknowledgments and generate shipping documents, invoices, statements, and offers of other items. Payments are recorded, and so are returns. All along the way, reports are generated that tell management whether the customer, the promotion, the product, and the business itself are sound.

Order-processing systems also guard against mail-order fraud, particularly with larger checks and credit-card purchases of valuable merchandise. Many companies have manual or data-transmission systems enabling them to call banks to verify balances and to obtain credit-card authorization on purchases over $100.

However, not every company faces the same problems, nor does every company start out on a scale requiring large-scale computer applications or sophisticated outside services. As recently as the first edition of this book (1982), many companies still were using label and ledger card systems. Today, however, minicomputers and software packages are available for various types of direct marketing applications. Consulting firms and computer services can help a company set up all the procedures it needs, on relatively simple data processing equipment with customized software. There is no need for any company today, of any size, to use manual procedures.

Many companies prefer to use an outside computer firm to handle order processing and list maintenance during the startup period, and then bring the functions in-house when their systems have been debugged and their needs fully identified.

Maintaining the Database

The heart of any direct-marketing program is the database, or mailing list. Everything that comes in or goes out is part of some sort of list and, as I have already pointed out, a mailing list is likely to be a company's greatest single asset.

A customer list or prospect list must include data to guide future marketing efforts. This includes source codes, shipments, payments, returns, items ordered, and dates of transactions. Even the simplest system should be capable of quickly determining whether you want to make new offers to the customer (depending on credit), what the customer has bought, and when it was bought. Recency, frequency, and unit-sale data will be vital segmentation data for future promotions. A prospect list should include the source, any data provided by the customer, and a record of the mail, phone, e-mail or salesperson follow-ups. If a business, the SIC code (showing type of business), the size or number of employees, and the names of decision influencers or approvers will be valuable as well.

If you plan to rent the list out, you will need to be able to "tag" rentals, so that the same names are not used for every test mailing. This enables you to omit the tested names when a customer rents the list again. You should also be able to tell a renter how old the name is (when it was put on your list), whether it is active or not, and how recently it has been active. They can also make use of source information, as names from different sources have been proven to respond differently, have different "quality" characteristics, and merit different types or lengths of promotional efforts. For example, previous direct-mail customer names are generally more responsive to direct mail offers than the general public. Mailers will also want to know if names came in from a sweepstakes offer.

In any event, the customer list should be maintained using standard formats and abbreviations, from the very beginning. Consult "Postal Addressing Standards" (Publication #28) available free from any Postal Business Center.

List rentals can be a very profitable source of income. Direct marketers should plan their systems to handle rentals in a manner that will render the type of fast, reliable, accurate service they want when they rent lists from others.

Shipping Orders

Assuming that you have hand-addressed, duplicated, or computer-generated the shipping labels, the most important action yet remains—shipping the customers what they ordered.

Shipping is a separate function from order entry and processing. The label may be created in one building and the merchandise shipped from another—maybe a warehouse close to the customer, or "drop-shipped" directly by a supplier. If outside suppliers are used, separate firms may be used for fulfillment and shipping.

In a warehouse, there are several major functions. One is receiving– keeping track of shipments that are coming in, spot-checking merchandise quality, verifying quantities, and getting the incoming merchandise to the right section of the warehouse.

Inventory control keeps track not only of everything that comes in, but also of everything that is *supposed* to come in. Late orders have to be followed up, and the appropriate party notified when quantities appear to be low. To be effective, inventory systems cannot confine themselves to tracking the inventory as it is shipped, but must include a sophisticated forecasting function based on the expectation of new promotions. Reorders must be placed while there is still time to get additional merchandise. Customers must be promptly notified that the item ordered is not available, so that they can order something else.

Inventory and forecasting control is one of the most critical functions in the fulfillment process, and often makes the difference between profitability and loss for a mail-order company. This function concerns not only the quantity of merchandise received and shipped, but also its quality. Incoming merchandise and drop-shipped merchandise must be inspected, tested, or measured (as in apparel and other sized products) and reviewed for conformance to the original order. What goes out of your shipping department is *your* reputation, not your vendor's.

Once in the warehouse, the merchandise must be clearly marked and assigned locations so that it can be found again. I have seen desperate warehouse managers frantically tearing open cartons because a shipment couldn't be found. Marking cartons clearly and storing them so that the markings are visible can save your sanity.

Often the main bulk of merchandise—books, printed material, or whatever—is in cartons or on skids in one area of the shipping facility. A lesser quantity is on shelves in a compact area closer to the shipping area. It would take too much time for order pickers to go through the entire warehouse to find a single item. Instead, a "pick rack" keeps some of each handy so as to minimize walking, searching, and time wasting. Some larger firms have more complex systems with pick areas for different lines of merchandise, multiple documents, and high-speed belts or conveyor systems. The objective is the same—minimize walking so as to increase orders picked per hour.

Once the order has been assembled, it goes to a packer. The packer checks the item picked against the shipping document and, if correct, places it in a bag or carton. For most companies, pickers and packers are the heart of the shipping process.

Address labels are affixed. Cartons are sealed. Then the packages are weighed, and postage or an air express sticker is affixed. Some systems have the weight and dimensions in their data bank, so they can print the shipping charges and even specify the ideal carton size. Some larger warehouses have postal or UPS facilities right in the warehouse to expedite shipping.

The choice of shippers can result in substantial savings, cost reductions, or both. The USPS now has Account Representatives who will help mailers choose the most economical choice, or the fastest, or the most efficient. For some applications, they can even arrange to supply the shipping cartons and arrange for scheduled pick-ups. For international operations, they have many innovative ways to save time and money and avoid customs delays.

A meeting with a USPS account representative is an essential step for any company that sends out mail or ships merchandise.

UPS also competes for shipping business, but has systems and rate structures geared to large shipments to and from retailers. Direct marketers, usually as an extra charge to customers, also use FedEx and other air-express services. All things being equal, mailers should give precedence to the USPS because their shipping revenue helps them provide economical mail delivery. Where would direct mailers be without the postal service? Despite the fantasies of some Internet enthusiasts, direct marketers will always need a healthy and efficient postal system. Does any direct marketer really want to rely on a communications system that "crashes" or "unexpectedly loses contact" as frequently as most Internet carriers? Not me.

The invisible part of a warehouse operation is administration—the managers, personnel, and security guards who keep the whole thing together behind the scenes. Unless you've been involved in warehouse management, you can't imagine the variety and complexity of problems that are handled by administrators.

One important administrative area is security—guarding against unauthorized use of mailing lists, protecting goods from damage or vandalism, preventing loss through inventory pilferage or larger-scale fraud, detecting computer scams that would divert payments from customers or to suppliers, and protecting vital records. I know of one club that went out of business largely because of the accidental erasure of its commitment data during a tape-to-tape transfer. Good security procedures could have saved 500 jobs.

Another important area for administration concern is quality assurance: making sure that the fulfillment task is being done according to the procedures that have been laid out. This usually involves testing one's own service as well as the competitor's, sampling customer opinion (at least through questionnaires inserted in packages), monitoring return and cancellation rates, and conducting in-house audits and quality checks.

Much of this discussion does not apply to items such as single books, card sets, or magazines. These can be mass-packaged on automated equipment with automatically affixed labels.

Back-Orders and the 30-Day Rule

No one likes back-orders, but they are inevitable. The customer is disappointed. The marketer has extra paperwork and some degree of cancellations and lost sales. But that's just the beginning.

The Federal Trade Commission has something called the 30-day rule which is not to be taken lightly. In essence, it requires a written notice within 30 days if an item can't be stocked, offering an option for the customer to cancel. If at 60 days it hasn't been shipped, a different notice is required that advises the customer the order will be cancelled unless they send back written authorization to keep the order open.

Notice, the rule says written. Not e-mail, not telephone. One company was fined a small fortune because they called customers instead of writing to them. Yes, calling is a better form of customer service, but common sense has no role in law-making or law-enforcement. Check with your lawyer for the latest interpretation of this and other legislation.

INQUIRIES AND LEADS

While most fulfillment processes were developed to handle mail orders, it is just as important to assure speed and service for inquiries, leads, and questionnaires.

Certainly, sales leads require the fastest possible processing. Most companies fax or modem such contacts the same day they are received directly to the sales office or dealer most qualified to handle them. In some cases, outgoing phone calls are made within hours to try to set an appointment or to qualify the prospect. Several companies with field sales forces have been very successful in having their phone department make appointments for the sales representatives, using computers to keep track of individual schedules and the layout of sales territories.

It is just as important to respond promptly to booklet requests or other database-building requests. The interest or excitement generated by the direct-response effort in mail or other media fades quickly.

Recently I filled out a "bingo card" in a travel magazine for information about a dozen vacation destinations that interest me. Three or four responded within a week, and we selected one of those for a vacation trip. But more than half of the booklets arrived at our home while we were away on our vacation or after we had returned—a waste of the entire promotion. If you are going to offer information, send it promptly or don't bother making the offer in the first place.

CUSTOMER SERVICE

Theoretically, customer service should be an unnecessary function. If everything went right all the time, there would be no need to handle complaints, inquiries, replacements, and special problems. The cost of maintaining a customer service department is one of the incentives to get it right in the first place. Hire people who will prevent fires rather than wait until they occur and then try to put them out.

Correspondents are, basically, the human beings who read customer mail. They make note of problems for management attention, and direct those who operate the computers or other systems to make an adjustment, accept a return, correct an address, or reship a damaged item. And, yes, they also do correspondence.

Once upon a time that meant they wrote personal letters to customers. This still happens, but very rarely, in the case of complex adjustments or explanations, or in companies where a highly personal approach is part of the image to be maintained. More often the correspondence is a form letter, a preprinted postcard or, at best, standard paragraphs from a word-processing system.

In a well-run business, customer mail—all of it—is answered within two days of its receipt. Any slower schedule will result in aggravated correspondence, cancellations, returns, and a bad reputation. To monitor speed of response, each letter should be marked with the date received.

Today most customer inquiries come in by telephone. Customers expect the person answering the phone to have instant access to their account record, and instant authority to make a required adjustment. They want to know when their order will be shipped, when their return will be credited—and they want it immediately. While maintaining on-line accounting records is expensive, it may eventually be less costly than the cost of lost customers.

Aggravated complaints are another problem and particularly troublesome when customers sign up for programs involving commitments, automatic shipments, or automatic credit-card charges. At Capitol Record Club, I made it a point to accept one or two calls a day from callers who demanded to talk to the President. After they got over the shock of learning that they really had gotten through, I was able to learn a great deal about what was important to our customers and about the enormous anger and distrust that an incorrect shipment or unanswered letter can cause. I recommend that any executive concerned with customer service spend some time dealing directly with customers in this way, in order to find out what kind of feelings lie behind the cold statistics in customer-complaint reports.

INTERNET FULFILLMENT

Whether or not the initial order came in through some sort of Internet marketing, websites and e-mail offer enormous opportunities to build a customer relationship and render fast, accurate, user-friendly fulfillment services.

At the very least, customers who provide an e-mail address can receive a quick, automatic acknowledgement that their order has been shipped. Businesses who maintain on-going accounts can make the latest, up-to-the-minute statement available for inspection by website. Business customers can access records of their past business, what they bought, who they shipped to, and any other pertinent information.

For example, an air shipping service can record the address of a company that was recently shipped to, so a subsequent shipment requires just a click in the custom address book. Detailed rates and prices can be instantly available. So can lists of parts or dealers. And, with more and more technology-based products, instruction manuals and help services can be available around the clock.

There is a great deal of discussion at Internet conferences of how to develop what they call "customer-centric" applications. These include Dell and Gateway building computers to order, or on-line book retailers services recommending new titles based on those you previously bought. I particularly like Amazon's opportunity to comment on a book you read, almost as you might to your friendly local bookseller, except that your comment is available worldwide to anyone interested in the book. (Try it. If this book is helpful, place a customer review at www.Amazon.com.)

FULFILLMENT REPORTS

In other chapters I have discussed the role of reports, results, and statistics in evaluating promotions. Many reports can be generated within the fulfillment process. They can evaluate customer quality, the value of the customer base as a whole, the acceptance of the company's product, the reactions to company service, expense forecasts and the intrinsic health of the entire business

Any business, large or small, simple or complex, should record all needed data in some type of regular reporting or review system. The data should be examined by the highest levels of management and by all relevant operating departments. They should be available to consultants, ad agencies, or other suppliers in a position to influence the operations. Not all these kinds of data will be applicable to all businesses of course, but the list below may serve as a checklist for your own operation.

Types of Reports Needed in Fulfillment Process

- Response and Access Records
- Customer "Quality" Reports
- Shipments and Postage
- Inventory Data
- Returned or Refused Merchandise
- Work in Progress
- Customer Service Reports
- Credit and Billing Information
- Quality Control
- Productivity and Employee Reports
- Continuity Reports

Response and Access Records

The simplest and most obvious record is the number of responses received. While this appears to be simple and superficial, it is more complex and critical than newcomers realize.

It is necessary to know exactly how many mail and phone-order responses came in each day, so that trends can be graphed and accurate forecasts prepared.

One critical but frequently overlooked report is a record of the phone calls or website access attempts that didn't get through. Phone companies can give you the exact number, day by day, hour by hour. We must presume that a large percentage of such attempts are not repeated and, therefore, represent lost opportunities. Since remedies are available—more phone operators or better outside services, larger servers or more access lines—identifying and remedying access problems can be the most important marketing step you take all year.

Customer Quality Reports

It is highly desirable to find out not only how many orders or other responses are produced, but also what kind of responses they are. In mail-order catalogs, this is obvious. What items sold, and what didn't, is the heart of the merchandising process. And it is just as important to learn what orders had to be unfilled as the quantity of items that did not sell. Older types of sales reporting systems sometimes omitted unfillable orders.

For leads and inquiries, the mix is also critical. Often I have helped a company not by increasing the number of responses but—by using more intelligent communications—attracting customers who bought more stock, bigger insurance policies, did more traveling, etc.

For business responses, ask what size and kind of companies are replying? Are you reaching the people who really make the decisions? For consumer promotions, ask where the orders are coming from. Analysis will tell us that your better consumers come from certain size cities, particular regions, or specific psychographic clusters.

For example, one might expect that the success of television commercials for Mutual of Omaha would simply have been measurable by the number of calls received. But some calls came from states where a particular policy was not available. And even those who bought policies were not all the same, according to the client's actuaries. Depending on age and area, some were more or less likely to have a life expectancy that will turn out to be profitable for the company. And all of this varied by the kind of television spots aired, the stations they ran on, and the dayparts where they were finally seen. Decisions to pull unprofitable stations and add new tests were made every day, as soon as data was available. An extra few days on a weak station or the wrong daypart can be very costly, so this data was compiled and analyzed on an urgent basis, with custom software to expedite the compilations and analytical work.

Other Reports

Inventory Data.   What's on order, what's needed, what's overstocked, and how much it all represents as cost of goods. Some companies obtain this data monthly, some weekly, some on a real-time basis with instant updating on a computer terminal.

Returned or Refused Merchandise.   A cost factor, an inventory factor, and most important, an indication of promotional overselling or product deficiency. Alternatively, if the returns are because of incorrect shipments or poor arrival condition, you know you have to review your packaging and shipping.

Work in Process.   Orders awaiting entry. Correspondence awaiting answers. Shipments stacked up in the warehouse. Promotional mailings held up. Reports on these matters will measure the efficiency of operating departments, and the likelihood of customer dissatisfaction.

Customer Service Reports.   Tabulations of complaints, inquiries, unfilled orders, and damage claims—to help point out problem areas for future correction.

Credit and Billing Information.   If you're selling on credit, you have to track the percentage of customers turned down. You have to know how many are paying and how many are not, what credit cards are being used, and how many customers are being turned over to collection departments.

Quality Control.   Spot checks should be made of all operations and departments to determine how well work is being done, in addition to other reports that indicate how fast it's completed. Computer programs should be checked. Work in process should be sampled and reviewed. Dummy orders should be put through the system and compared with the service being offered by the competition, which should be similarly monitored.

Reports should be compiled on everything for the information of department heads and management. Error rates should be recorded, since a report can spot a trend while a single error is usually not significant. An increase in error rate is a cause for concern in any function.

Productivity and Employee Reports.   Since fulfillment operations often are personnel-intensive, cost controls depend on the proper utilization of employees. Workloads must be forecast by department, and employees must be reassigned or staff levels revised to meet changing demand requirements.

In addition, the output of employee work groups or individual employees has to be monitored in order to identify exceptional producers or those who may need additional training.

Large mail-order companies such as Sears, Montgomery Ward, and Hanover House were pioneers in establishing productivity standards for office and warehouse tasks. In some such companies, most of the employees are on some sort of incentive plan—one of the major reasons for their fast service and the low costs the company incurs in handling orders.

Continuity Reports.   Organizations selling on continuity, club, or sub-scription basis need many additional reports, including acceptance rates by cycle, renewal rates, commitment status, attrition rates, and sales projections.

This list does not include the financial and budget reports that would ordinarily be produced by the accounting department or by the analysts in the marketing group. However, all reporting will depend on these fulfillment reports as input data for reliable financial projections.

Report Design Considerations

In setting up a direct-marketing company's reporting system, there is one standard that is paramount: *usability*. Reports must be in a form that genuinely helps those who must use them, and must quickly indicate significant trends, events, and exceptions that require management action.

The definition of *usability* depends on the level of management. Operating foremen and department heads may need every detail that pertains to their department. Interfacing departments and senior management may need only the highlights.

Most sophisticated reporting systems include comparisons with previous months, previous years, annual budgets, and variances for each—for every single expense line. Other reports turn everything into trend lines, or relate each action to a plan or profitability standard.

Every department circulating a report should have the responsibility for preparing a one-page summary in simple language of changes, exceptions, and variances—the information that should be called to the attention of management. Whether the summary is distributed on paper or on an Intranet or secure Internet site, it must still be in a usable and understandable format. Technology may provide speed and access, but reports must still be comprehended and acted upon by human beings—at least for now.

FULFILLMENT PHILOSOPHY

Fulfillment is an operations process with a profound effect on marketing results, and an impact on profitability. The standards of fulfillment practice within a given organization are subject to a series of strategic decisions that, in total, derive from a company's philosophy.

This philosophy must be consciously and deliberately chosen by top management, not left to the sometimes myopic preferences of line managers. Let's look at some possible extremes as a framework within which commonsense midpoints can be defined.

"Stop the Deadbeat"

Not a year goes by when I don't find that a zealous credit manager has guided ever-obliging programmers and customer service personnel on a course of "throwing out the baby with the bath water."

If credit is the priority, the philosophy begins with the offer. No credit at all is permitted. Merchandise is shipped only after checks have been received, deposited, and cleared. The weeks this adds to shipping time materially increase returned merchandise. More important, orders and reorders are materially decreased from a credit proposition.

Under this policy, a customer's claim that an item arrived broken may become the subject of lengthy correspondence, or a false claim that a billed item never arrived will be looked up and invalidated, and a collection process begun.

"The Customer Is Always Right"

This is preferable in terms of short-term expense reduction and long-term corporate reputation. With this philosophy, account reviews are minimized, returns are accepted without checking shipping dates, and credits are issued on the customer's word.

The problem is that there are always some bad apples in the customer barrel that will take advantage of this policy. However, depending on the relative costs of products and fulfillment practices, it may actually be less costly to overlook the abuses and concentrate on pleasing the 99 percent of honest folk who are the bread-and-butter customers.

"Cost Efficiency Über Alles"

Let the engineers and cost accountants reign supreme and you'll have a different emphasis: cutting costs ahead of all else.

Maximum efficiency in managing operating costs is important, of course. But it should not be attained at the expense of customer service. Daily batches are more efficient than continuous processing, and weekly batches more efficient than daily ones. This reasoning can lead to filling orders once a month.

Personal letters and phone calls are costly, both outgoing and incoming. One company, after finding that customers objected to having collect complaint-calls refused, solved the problem by having their phone number unlisted. Very efficient! But is it smart?

Manpower planning finds peaks and valleys a nuisance. It's a lot easier to let a backlog of orders, payments, returns, and entries stack up so that personnel are fully utilized. One company built a wall to hide unprocessed returned merchandise from visiting management, rather than hire the people to process the returns. No, this is not a joke. I've seen the wall!

"A Rolling Stone Gathers No Loss"

"Keep it moving. Get it out. The customers are waiting." This should be the cry of every supervisor and department head.

Fast order turnaround and shipping materially increases customer satisfaction and sales levels. Slow handling leads to customer correspondence, refusals, and returns. Slow handling of correspondence leads to more correspondence, with higher and higher levels of anger and annoyance.

The industry standard is to deliver merchandise to the customer within two weeks of mailing the order and in even less time if the order is phoned, faxed or e-mailed in. "Allow six to eight weeks for delivery" is a phrase that may legally permit inefficiency and poor planning, but that doesn't justify it from the customer's point of view. One industry joke tells of the customer who goes down to the corner to mail an order and then, upon returning home, looks in the mailbox to see if the package has arrived yet. The joke may not be funny, but the expectation is a real one in the mind of the consumer. The closer we can all come to realizing this fantasy, the stronger our entire industry will be.

Every marketer should read through aggravated complaint reports and letters to government regulators. Such letters almost always begin with a phrase like "I've written three times and no one answered." Often there has been some kind of form response—but one so vague, so impersonal, so noncommittal that the customer did not even realize it was a reply.

"If I'm Your 'Dear Friend,' Why Don't You Know My Name?"

Nothing can so quickly destroy the illusion of a personal communication or a relationship-building program with customers as spelling the recipient's name incorrectly. The same applies to company names.

We know that the first thing people look at when they look at an envelope is their own name. And we also know that there is genuine annoyance if it isn't right, or if a Mr. becomes a Ms. or if an executive's incorrect title is listed. People's names are icons representing themselves. They deserve to be treated with respect. Yet errors are rampant in direct mail.

One problem is the tendency to have large-scale data-input projects assigned to offshore countries where labor rates are lower. Though the operators may be efficient, they cannot be expected to spot names that seem uncommon, or to interpret the notoriously bad handwriting of most Americans. Where possible, they should be matched to other lists, such as compiled phone lists, before adding them to the file. Where there are contradictions, a decision should be made as to which source is most likely to be accurate. They also should be scanned by people with reasonable familiarity with common names, and the odd ones compared with the source document. In situations where each prospect has a high value, these names should be confirmed by telephone.

The simplest solution is to get the name right in the first place. Coupons should be large enough so that a name can be printed clearly. Some companies even insist on providing separate blocks for each individual letter, to encourage careful printing from the potential customer. If the name isn't legible, the easiest way to check it is with a phone call or postcard inquiry when the inquiry first comes in.

Telephone responses should be keyboarded directly, which eliminates visual errors but adds phonetic ones. It is thus up to the operator to listen carefully and confirm spellings, particularly unusual ones. Yet most phone staffs are pressured to finish each call quickly, with no bonus for accuracy. Perhaps this emphasis should be reversed.

THE BIG PICTURE

If our service is not what we'd like, it may be because we have not set standards, defined policies, and established correct criteria. Systems designers and programmers, like copywriters, can be infinitely creative in meeting objectives and solving problems, but someone has to tell them what is wanted.

Computers originally were introduced in direct marketing as a way to improve customer service. Today, they are more often the excuse given for slow, inaccurate service. Don't blame computers. They do only what we tell them to do.

The place to begin good customer service is in the original selling message. Don't make promises you can't keep, or guarantees you can't fulfill. Make the coupon clear and easy to fill out, with plenty of space so your customer can print clearly. If you are on the Internet, keep it simple! This is not the time to build a customer profile with research questions. Do that after you fill the order, as part of a customer satisfaction inquiry.

Screen out the deadbeats before they get on your books. Maintaining a small number of deadbeat lists or using outside services is cheaper than collection efforts. Offers that require some payment will knock out the professional coupon-clipper, and quality media and lists usually will produce quality business.

Figure 19-2 is a detailed chart of the fulfillment process from one of the best fulfillment agencies, MCRB. The elements in this chart are essentially the same as the ones in Figure 19-1 at the beginning of this chapter, only in more detail. Following these guidelines and treating your customers— potential, current and previous—is an essential element for any direct marketer.

Go after the right customers in the first place, and treat them right in return. Good service is good business.

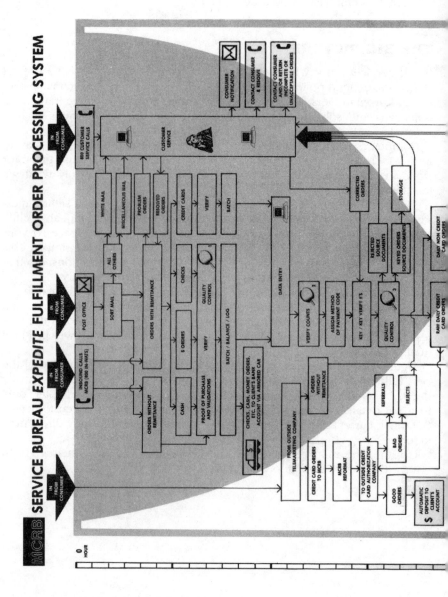

MCRB SERVICE BUREAU EXPEDITE FULFILLMENT ORDER PROCESSING SYSTEM

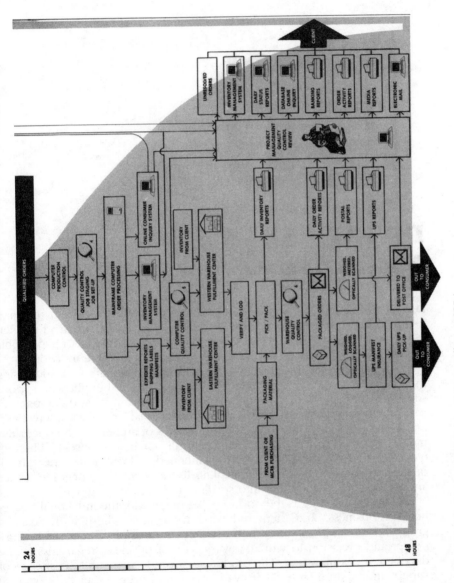

Figure 19-2. (*Continued*) [Courtesy of Craig Collins, MCRB.]

20

DATABASE
MARKETING

Database marketing is the most sophisticated selling process in the marketing world today. Its foundation is the highest level of the direct marketing craft, with one big difference. Instead of relating to media or geographic groups, it relates to the smallest media segment of all—the individual.

The goal of selecting common interests of individuals and addressing their needs is not new. Every major mailing list can be bought with various selects or characteristics, based on gender, age, education, and demographics. Most newspapers and magazines offer regional or special interest editions. Broadcast day-parts reach different types of audiences. Internet sales messages can now be placed geographically or in response to different types of interest areas through sites maintained by local newspapers. In all of these media, we start with a mailing list, a circulation, or an audience and we seek to divide them into smaller, more precise segments.

Database marketing is the opposite. We begin with the individual household or business, and then find ways to organize these individuals in groups. This simple change has enabled us to apply direct marketing's power and precision to virtually every type of business, regardless of the distribution channel used. The producers of products that fill the shelves of supermarkets, drug stores, hardware stores and every other type of retail store now have as much to gain from our field as the catalogers, charities, banks, utilities and others who sell directly to their customers.

Database marketing hasn't made headlines the way the Internet has. No political office-seeker has taken credit for its invention. No one has become an instant millionaire because of wild stock market optimism. But it's here.

It's growing. And it works—so well and so often that many of its most frequent practitioners go to great lengths to keep their successes secret.

WHAT IS DATABASE MARKETING

The word *database* has come to mean any collection of information, including collections of marketing results or sales data. Direct marketers use the term differently. Let's look at the two parts of the word separately.

Data

As we refer to it, *data* is information about individual prospects or households, along with enough information to select those most likely to respond to a given promotional idea.

Developing data is the key to database marketing. There are many ways to get names and addresses, and other ways to add useful information. But none of them are perfect and none of them provide 100 percent coverage of the potential customer base. That's why our database marketing plans can only be based on "identified" customers or prospects—those whom we can contact through their home or computer address.

Notice that I am saying *individual*. For direct marketers, there is nothing new in finding *groups* with a high probability of responding. Let's say a mailing produces a 5 percent response—five out of a hundred names. If the 20–80 rule is true, four of these responses came from twenty of the names—a 20 percent response from our "real" customers! Only one came from the other 80—a 1.2% response. Imagine if we could just mail to the first five! Theoretically this is possible. To bring reality as close as possible to this goal—and to not waste our time, money and efforts on people who will *never* buy—is the objective of professional database marketing. Figure 20-1 illustrates this dramatically.

In database marketing we are dealing with the ultimate micro-market—one household or even one individual at a time.

Does this seem unlikely? Too optimistic? An exaggeration? Not to those who are actually involved with database marketing rather than just talking about it. That's why my book, *Database Marketing* (McGraw-Hill), includes statistical variation tables to 30 percent.

With this kind of arithmetic, the whole game changes. Database-driven mailings can often be more cost-effective than mass advertising, any way you measure it. Impressions. Intent-to-buy. Improvement in market share. And, the ultimate edge for all direct marketing programs—actual sales!

What kind of data? The unique edge of database marketing is that you know, with a 90 or 95 percent certainty, whether a customer really is a customer. You know whether a prospect really is a prospect—that he or she is someone who already uses the category of product, or who has asked for information, or who has an immediate need for what we are selling.

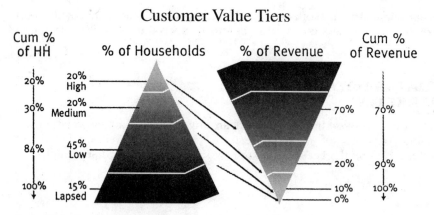

Figure 20-1. Typical Customer Value Tiers. *Courtesy of Epsilon.*

Of course you must also have the basics of any mailing list. The name must be in proper format. Addresses, cities, zip codes must be in formats than can be merged and which are deliverable. You must also check names against "Do not mail" or "Do not call" lists. Fax and e-mail addresses must not only be in the right format, but you must be able to demonstrate that you have the consent of the addressee. Direct marketing associations in each country can advise you of the accepted standards in their country.

Base

The other part of the word is *base*. More than anything else, this suggests a starting point, a place to begin. It does not mean a collection of academic information to go into research reports. Nor does it suggest a repository of names and addresses as part of some corporate archive.

A database is a *tool*. It should be designed actively to achieve goals—distribution goals, share goals, sales goals, profit goals. Names should be collected and transcribed into electronic formats only if they will produce a profit. Information should be added to these lists only if the added effectiveness can be cost-justified. In database marketing, information should be *actionable*!

In an article I wrote for *Sales and Marketing Management*, I described "Common Database Disasters." The number one disaster: building a database without deciding on marketing goals. Time after time I find that companies have made major investments collecting data that is not useful, or they have omitted data that can make a difference in sales numbers. Often it is because the database project was managed by the company's market-research department instead of by direct marketers.

BUILDING YOUR DATABASE

Whether you choose to communicate by mail, phone, e-mail or with door-to-door salespersons, the most critical part of your program will be the size and quality of the database you work with.

There are many ways to buy or build a list. Some are easier to work with and less expensive than others. As with any direct marketing program, it pays to test on a limited basis—perhaps in geographic test markets—before investing in a more complex list-building program. Following are the basic four categories of lists.

Company Lists

Most companies start with their own customer lists. Companies dealing directly, with the public such as utilities or banks, will have large and accurate lists to work with, often with data that will prove useful in planning a marketing strategy. Retail stores with charge accounts or supermarkets using scannable cards presented at the register keep a record of actual purchases. For manufacturers, customer warranty cards often have enough information to build a solid database-marketing program.

Other companies might work with responses to past promotions, such as premium or rebate offers. Obviously the type of offer that generated the names in the database will make a difference in how the information can be used. An offer requiring the accumulation of proofs of purchase will produce names of customers, while an offer of a free sample or a deep discount to try the product can only be counted on to produce prospects.

At least once a year, I still find companies with names that are not stored electronically, but are just coupons or sales slips stacked in shoeboxes. One U.S. jewelry client delivered a hundred thousand hand-written sales slips when we asked for their list. Though the information had to be inputted and formatted, the sales slips included types of purchases and sales amounts. Even with all the work involved this was still more valuable than a list from another client that had names on computer tape, but had discarded information on sales and purchases.

Promotions

Even if you have access to a large in-house database, or if there is one commercially available that fits your needs, there will always be times when you will want to expand your database's size, or at least improve it with new names.

If you are in a battle for market share, or otherwise in a situation where incremental customers are virtually all profit (such as a phone company or Internet access provider), the more names the better. There is another reason to add to your list. New, fresh names mean new eyes to view your marketing materials. Chances are these new individuals will respond better than the ones on previous lists that may already have received materials for similar promotions. They are the database equivalent of "hotline names" which marketers are willing to pay 10 percent to 20 percent more than for ordinary names.

Whether you compare the cost of buying a name from an outside compiler or an estimate of the long-term profit potential, establish an "allowable cost" for each name added to your database. You can then test alternative ways of building your list. Often it will pay for you to develop promotions in which the primary or secondary objective is to obtain names for future promotions.

One assignment my agency handled for a Procter & Gamble product was to test every possible way of adding to their already substantial database. We used small space ads and inserts, magazines and Sunday supplements, co-op mail and solo mail. The offers ranged from simple questionnaires to sample offers. In the meantime, their regular television advertising added a phone number and a free sample offer. All the methods were tested and then ranked in order of "Cost Per Incremental Name." Note the use of the word *incremental.* Because their list already contained a large percentage of category users, the program to be rolled out was not the one with the largest total response, but the one that most cost-effectively added new names to their lists.

List Building

Here are some ways of building a list:

Direct Mail. These are offers of premiums, discounts, rebates or contests that require a mail, telephone or e-mail response. These are sent to individuals on lists with a high probability of producing names of customers, heavy category users, or imminent prospective buyers. This last category is particularly important for customers of moving services, automobile sales, vacations and similar purchases that take place no more frequently than once a year.

One advantage of direct mail is that a store coupon can be coded with electromagnetic numbers or a scannable bar code that reveals the name and address of the customer redeeming it. The identification is laser printed when the mailer is prepared, and the data is then retrieved after the stores redeem the coupons.

Alternative Media. Low-cost, high-circulation media are excellent for reaching mass markets with list-building promotions. These include co-op mail from Direct Marketing's "Madison," Direct Media's "Carol Wright" or Larry Tucker's "Supermarket of Savings" programs. These are often segmented into categories such as "over 50," "over 65," "new parents," "affluent families" and various ethnic markets. There are also many specialized co-op opportunities, such as Nia Direct's African-American and NCRA's Hispanic programs. Package-insert programs, such as those marketed by Leon Henry, take several months to bring in a quantity of names, but the respondents are current mail-order shoppers. There are also bulletin-board programs that will put your offer into supermarkets, colleges and doctor's offices. These alternative media are particularly effective for magazine subscription offers and catalog requests.

Newspapers and Magazines. Any offer you can make in direct mail or alternative media may be effective in print media as well. But direct marketing experience must be brought into the media planning. For instance, most mass advertisers immediately think in terms of pages. Database builders are often successful only in small space units (⅓ or ⅙ of a page in magazines) or in "hard space" (page or reply card inserts in magazines, or free-standing solo inserts in Sunday newspapers). Newspaper supplements are often successful as well—both the magazine formats such as *Parade* and *USA Weekly* and the co-op coupon inserts from companies such as Media Marketplace and Valassis.

In-Pack and On-Pack Offers. An often overlooked "medium" is a company's own packages—a recipe offer on a soup can, jam on an English muffin package. These can generate names of buyers for retention and resell programs, but also of prospects for other products or services produced by the same company. For instance, you can offer a free newsletter, an update service or accessories.

If your company only has one product, consider making a deal with a manufacturer of another product used by the same businesses or households. For instance, make a deal where you offer a "Paint selection guide" with your brushes if a paint company offers your "Brush selection guide" with their paint. This is where sales promotion and direct marketing work well together. Making a deal like the paint and brush companies may not even be necessary. For example, "$2 savings coupon on cheese" will help sell your package of ham whether or not a cheese company reciprocates with an offer on your ham.

If name generation is the primary objective, then the redemption process should be as simple as possible. For instance, demanding a cash register receipt in addition to proofs-of-purchase may eliminate some fraud, but the savings may not offset the value of the reduced number of new customer names.

Advertising Add-Ons

For companies that maintain advertising programs designed to build awareness, change customer attitudes or develop brand equity, there is no reason why database offers cannot enjoy a free ride as part of that advertising. On the simplest level, it costs nothing to add a phone number or website address to an advertisement or television spot. Doing so can develop valuable database names and, at the same time, provide a relative index of the effectiveness of the various ads and media.

I suspect that one reason many general agencies resist this suggestion is nervousness over what such comparisons would reveal. Another is that art directors with their eye on awards instead of sales often resist any added element.

Despite the objections, this kind of integration is gaining in popularity. Other than the cost of a booklet or a premium, adding a database-marketing ride-along costs next to nothing. For some clients I've added such mail-in offers to sales promotion ads which had the primary objective of distributing store coupons. In others we paid for a reply card insert to accompany an image ad that the brand was running anyway.

If the purpose of the ad is to seek customers, the offer can request a proof-of-purchase in return for something of value. For some clients I've suggested free "subscriptions" to a promotional publication and how-to guides as gifts in return for proofs-of-purchase. I've also suggested contests, especially when the contest prize can emphasize a feature of the product or dramatize its imagery. For example, a Ford Explorer's outdoor image to Eddie Bauer, or a trip to Rio de Janeiro for a romantic perfume.

Such offers, when supplementing an image ad, are necessarily not the dominant elements in the ad. However, the responses can be multiplied by making the offer as attractive as possible. Consider these alternatives: *Free information. Free booklet. Free 16-page color booklet. Free guide to . . . Free poster. Free jumbo 20″ × 40″ poster. Free video or CD . . . Free half-hour video starring . . . Free membership in . . . Free subscription to . . .* All of these promotions represent advertising material with nominal costs, yet, as with any other form of direct marketing, the offer expression will make a major difference in response rates.

Custom Compilations

There were only two kinds of lists in the earliest days of direct marketing— a) response lists and b) compiled lists. Both are still available, yet database marketers often overlook them in favor of the larger, easier to manage "survey lists," discussed in the next section.

Response lists are of people who bought something from another company, subscribed to a different magazine, or inquired for information about another company's product. Such response lists are very effective because the people on the list have a characteristic that is not available on compiled lists. They are responders! If they responded to someone else's offer they are more likely to respond to yours than the general public that includes many non-responders. A problem with these lists—both then and now—is that often there are not enough names.

Compiled lists are also usable in database marketing. These include:

Directories. There are hundreds of industry and professional directories and membership rosters that can be used to put together a list of people with specific interests.

Credit reports. Some companies develop credit information. The best-known ones are Experian for consumers and Dun & Bradstreet for businesses. Both can provide data based on income, credit reports, and other factors. These lists aren't only of the individuals or companies with good records; some businesses such as lenders prefer or gear their business towards people or companies with bad credit.

Subscribers. Business magazines can often provide lists of subscribers to one or more trade magazines. Many free publications require the subscribers to supply specific information on their responsibilities and the size and scope of their businesses.

Phone books. Other compilers have taken every phone book in the country and entered the data in their computer systems. For their business lists they have entered every yellow-page category. For their consumer lists they have tracked how long the person has lived at the most recent residence, as well as other useful data.

Public records. Some of the largest database-building companies began by compiling data from public records. They produced lists of new home-owners, newlyweds, and new parents as well as public data from voting records, drivers' licenses, car registrations, boat and plane ownership and other data. All of this information is available and is often very successful for marketers. Some of this information can be used in unique ways. For example, car registrations can be used as a personality indicator and compared with brand personalities.

Telephone surveys. In business to business marketing it is often difficult to identify the job title or individual in charge of recommending or purchasing a specific product or service. This information is so valuable and so specific in nature that many companies have hired telemarketing firms or set up their own in-house phone rooms to call and ask, "Who in your company is in charge of buying . . ."

All of these kinds of lists are best purchased through direct marketing agencies or list brokers—companies who have built their businesses and reputations on their ability to recommend and supply lists that will give direct-marketing companies the results they need.

"Survey Names"

Some of the most useful tools that a database marketer can use are the growing number of what I call "survey names." In more than half of the households in the United States—and in a growing number in other countries in the world—someone has filled out a questionnaire that he or she has received in the mail or in a newspaper that asks about purchase intent, category usage, or brand preference.

These lists were originally sponsored by cigarette companies that arranged for questionnaires to be sent to millions of people asking about cigarette smoking and brand preferences. The cigarette questions were presented in the context of questions about other purchase categories. The information concerning the other categories was then made available in lists and sold to other companies—companies that at the time saw these lists mostly as research tools.

National Demographic Lists pioneered this list category. Now available through Polk, they offer manufacturers a series of research studies about their customers in return for allowing National Demographic Lists to add a series of questions to the company's warranty cards. Some of these questions ask about the customer's interests, others about demographics. These interest questions are then offered as direct mail lists to other companies.

These two sources were the first lists that gave direct marketers information about what people bought, how often they bought the products, and what brands they preferred. For the first time direct marketers could identify prospects who were using their brand, or who used a type of product, but a different brand. The value was obvious, but it took several years before the major packaged-goods advertisers (other than cigarette companies) saw the potential of the lists—the ability to concentrate advertising effort and couponing against the 20 percent of the market that accounts for 80 percent of sales.

Eventually the packaged goods advertisers themselves conducted surveys, and later made the information available though list compilations to companies that did not compete with their products. Then more and more list compilers distributed questionnaires with an ever-expanding range of questions. After some time the questionnaires were distributed more inexpensively—in co-op mailings, as inserts in newspapers and magazines, and on the Internet. At least one company used the telephone to get answers to key questions for their clients.

While the original emphasis was on developing specific data for survey sponsors, eventually the speculative questions became increasingly useful. Category and brand questions were included on any subject the compilers thought might be "rentable" to direct marketers. They added soaps, food and fashion. They asked about intended purchases, likes and dislikes, and favorite hobbies.

Currently most surveys include the question "Does anyone in your household suffer from any of the following ailments?" and a companion question about prescription drug use. I have been amazed at the willingness of those filling out these forms to reveal their hemorrhoids, incontinence and other private matters. I know of cases where the list compilers knew of a consumer's problems that were carefully hidden from the respondent's own family!

Figure 20-2 is an example of a typical survey. Some of the questions, such as the one's regarding smoking and hair coloring, are undoubtedly sponsored—customized to a company's needs in return for a guaranteed payment. The others, such as the questions about hobbies, are included in the expectation that database advertisers will find ways to use such information if it is available. To paraphrase the key line in the movie *Field of Dreams,* this is the database industry's equivalent: "If you build it (the database), they (the marketers) will come."

Carol Wright® Wants To Know.

"Help me tell major manufacturers what's right for you. They'll be able to send free samples, money saving coupons and special offers that meet your particular needs. Please complete and mail this survey today."

A1

I am 18 years of age or older and agree to accept a free, non-prescription medicine sample.

First Name [_____]
Last Name [_____] M ☐ F ☐ Age [___]
Address [_____] Apt # [____]
City [_____] State [__] Zip [_____]
Spouse's First Name [_____] M ☐ F ☐ Age [___]
Married 1.☐   Single 2.☐   Rent Home or Apartment 3.☐   Own Home 4.☐
Please send me your completed survey no later than March 31, 1993

1. How many glasses of carbonated soft drinks are consumed in your home each week?

0-5	5-10	10+
1.☐	2.☐	3.☐

1a. Which brand(s) are consumed? (check all that apply)

	Regular	Diet	Caffeine Free
Coca-Cola	01.☐	11.☐	21.☐
Pepsi	02.☐	12.☐	22.☐
Dr. Pepper	03.☐	13.☐	23.☐
Cherry Coke	04.☐	14.☐	24.☐
Cherry 7-Up	05.☐	15.☐	25.☐
7-Up	06.☐	16.☐	26.☐
Slice	07.☐	17.☐	27.☐
Sprite	08.☐	18.☐	28.☐
Gatorade	09.☐	19.☐	29.☐
Other	10.☐	20.☐	30.☐

2. Which brand(s) of beer have you purchased in the last month?

	Number of Six Packs		
	1-3	4-7	8 or more
Bud Light	01.☐	11.☐	21.☐
Coors Light	02.☐	12.☐	22.☐
Miller Light	03.☐	13.☐	23.☐
Budweiser	04.☐	14.☐	24.☐
Coors	05.☐	15.☐	25.☐
Miller High Life	06.☐	16.☐	26.☐
Miller Genuine Draft	07.☐	17.☐	27.☐
Busch	08.☐	18.☐	28.☐
Imported	09.☐	19.☐	29.☐
Other	10.☐	20.☐	30.☐

3. Which brand(s) of pain/fever relievers have been used in your household by adults in the past three months?

	Have Used (Check all that apply)	Use Most Often (Check only one)
Advil	01.☐	11.☐
Anacin	02.☐	12.☐
Bayer	03.☐	13.☐
Bufferin	04.☐	14.☐
Excedrin	05.☐	15.☐
Motrin IB	06.☐	16.☐
Nuprin	07.☐	17.☐
Tylenol	08.☐	18.☐
Store Brand	09.☐	19.☐
Other	10.☐	20.☐

3a. How often are pain/fever relievers used?

Daily	1.☐	Monthly	4.☐
3-5 Times a Week	2.☐	Occasionally	5.☐
1-2 Times a Week	3.☐		

4. Which brand(s) of cold and allergy/sinus remedies are used most often in your household?

Actifed	01.☐	Nyquil	12.☐
Alka Seltzer Plus	02.☐	Sine Aid	13.☐
Benadryl	03.☐	Sine-Off	14.☐
Comtrex	04.☐	Sinus Excedrin	15.☐
Contac	05.☐	Sinutab	16.☐
Co-Tylenol	06.☐	Sudafed	17.☐
Dimetapp	07.☐	Sudafed Plus	18.☐
Dimetapp Plus	08.☐	Triaminic	19.☐
Dristan	09.☐	Tylenol Sinus	20.☐
Drixoral	10.☐	Store Brand	21.☐
Drixoral Plus	11.☐	Other	22.☐

4a. How often are cold and allergy/sinus remedies used?

Daily	1.☐	Monthly	4.☐
3-5 Times a Week	2.☐	Occasionally	5.☐
1-2 Times a Week	3.☐		

5. Please write the ages of all persons in your household. Please circle your age.
Female Ages _____
Male Ages _____

6. Check all interests or hobbies pursued in your household.

Fishing	01.☐	Gourmet Cooking	13.☐
Camping	02.☐	Physical Fitness/Exer.	14.☐
Hunting	03.☐	Diet Conscious	15.☐
Tennis	04.☐	Photography	16.☐
Golf	05.☐	Stamps/Coins	17.☐
Snow Skiing	06.☐	Gardening	18.☐
Cycling	07.☐	Foreign Travel	19.☐
Casino Gambling	08.☐	Woodworking	20.☐
Sewing	09.☐	Needlecraft	21.☐
Books	10.☐	Quilting	22.☐
Do-it-Yourself	11.☐	Scuba Diving	23.☐
Sweepstakes/Lottery	12.☐	Symphony/Ballet/Opera	24.☐

7. Please check all that apply to your household:

Have a Cellular Phone	01.☐
Support Health Charities	02.☐
Have a Compact Disc Player	03.☐
Have a VCR	04.☐
Have a Personal Computer	05.☐
Have American Express	06.☐
Have MasterCard/Visa	07.☐
Have a Dog	08.☐
Have a Cat	09.☐
Military Veteran in the Household	10.☐
Recently Donated by Mail	11.☐

8. What types of magazines/books do you or your family members read?

Best Seller	01.☐	Fashion	09.☐
Business/News	02.☐	Mystery	10.☐
Classics	03.☐	Romance	11.☐
Cooking/Wine	04.☐	Science Fiction	12.☐
Crafts/Needlework	05.☐	Sports	13.☐
Devotional/Bible	06.☐	Travel/Entertain.	14.☐
Home/Gardening	07.☐	Young Children	15.☐
Health/Beauty	08.☐		

9. Does anyone in your household suffer from: (check all those that apply)

Allergies	01.☐	Gastritis	14.☐
Alzheimer's Disease	02.☐	Heart Disease	15.☐
Angina	03.☐	Hearing Difficulty	16.☐
Arthritis/Rheumatism	04.☐	High Blood Pressure	17.☐
Asthma	05.☐	High Cholesterol	18.☐
Bladder Control/ Incontinence	06.☐	Migraines	19.☐
		Osteoporosis	20.☐
Bleeding Gums/ Gingivitis	07.☐	Parkinson's Disease	21.☐
		Physical Handicap	22.☐
Blindness/Visual Impairment	08.☐	Sensitive Skin	23.☐
		Sinusitis	24.☐
Diabetes	09.☐	Thinning Hair/ Balding	25.☐
Emphysema	10.☐		
Epilepsy	11.☐	Ulcer	26.☐
Frequent Headaches	12.☐	Yeast Infection	27.☐
Frequent Heartburn	13.☐		

10. If you or anyone in your household colors their hair, which brand(s) is used most often?

Nice & Easy	1.☐	Ultress	4.☐
Loving Care	2.☐	Color at a Salon	5.☐
Miss Clairol	3.☐	Other	6.☐

10a. If you or anyone in your household perms their hair, do you?

Perm at a Salon 1.☐   Perm at Home 2.☐

11. How many times have you shopped by mail in the last six months?

Once or Twice 1.☐   Three or More Times 2.☐

11a. In total, how much did you spend?

Under $50 1.☐   Over $50 2.☐

FOR SMOKERS ONLY
"By completing the following questions you are certifying that all smokers listed are 21 years of age or older, and want to receive free samples of cigarettes and incentive items in the mail, subject to applicable state and federal law."

12. You
First Name [_____]
Last Name [_____]
Birth Date (required) [__] [__] [__] Month Day Year
Gender Male 1.☐ Female 2.☐
What is your regular brand of cigarettes?
[_____]
What other brand, if any, do you smoke?
[_____]
Is your regular brand? (check one in each column)

Filter	3.☐	Menthol	5.☐	Reg./King	7.☐
Non-Filter	4.☐	Non-Menthol	6.☐	Long/100s	8.☐
				Extra Long/120s	9.☐

How many packs of cigarettes have you smoked in the last month?
Regular _____ Other _____
X_____ Signature (required)

13. Other Smoker
First Name [_____]
Last Name [_____]
Birth Date (required) [__] [__] [__] Month Day Year
Gender Male 1.☐ Female 2.☐
What is your regular brand of cigarettes?
[_____]
What other brand, if any, do you smoke?
[_____]
Is your regular brand? (check one in each column)

Filter	3.☐	Menthol	5.☐	Reg./King	7.☐
Non-Filter	4.☐	Non-Menthol	6.☐	Long/100s	8.☐
				Extra Long/120s	9.☐

How many packs of cigarettes have you smoked in the last month?
Regular _____ Other _____
X_____ Signature (required)

Thank you for completing this questionnaire. Your responses benefit manufacturers and marketers of goods and services who are interested in satisfying your wants and needs. The information collected (unless you choose otherwise by checking this box ☐) may later be shared with other reputable businesses.

Mailing is as easy as 1-2-3!

Figure 20-2. An example of a survey mailing.

There are several sources of such lists with many more categories than shown here. These are available to any marketers who recognize the value of focusing on their customers and their best prospects. The availability of this type of category and brand list has been a major stimulus to the growth of database marketing.

LIST ENHANCEMENT

Many companies find that they have names to start with, perhaps from an old promotion or simply a list of present and former customers. Sometimes these names are properly collected in electronic form. Other times they are original documents stored in a warehouse somewhere.

Editing. Whether you're dealing with electronic information or data from original documents, the first step is to edit the list and get it in proper order. Every direct marketing computer service firm can handle this type of project. If the list has to be entered into the computer, the firm's employees may be able to use optical scanning with new character-recognition software. Or they may subcontract to one of the very capable data-entry firms in Ireland, Jamaica, India, and elsewhere, to keyboard-enter the information in the traditional way.

For many reasons, lists should be maintained in standardized formats, with separate fields for first name and last name, proper zip codes, and standardized abbreviations. A nonstandard list cannot effectively be matched with other lists, even if the name and address are accurate. Standard formats are needed in order to eliminate duplicates through what is called a *merge-purge process*, as well as to efficiently add enhancement data from outside lists. And the standardization is essential if the list is going to be exchanged with others or placed on the list-rental market. In the U.S., refer to USPS publication #28.

Internal Data. To the extent that other usable information is available, it should also be preserved in the basic list. At the least this would include the date when the name was acquired, and the source of the name. It would be valuable to have any information about what kind of purchase or service was provided, or the price and type of any transaction. Ultimately the use of the lists will be influenced by the mail-order standard of recency-frequency-price (of transaction), regardless of the intended use. With promotions to outside lists, companies will want to separate present customers (who should be given incentives for multiple purchase or trade-up) from prospective customers.

External Data. Any list can be enriched by adding information from commercially available sources. There is an incredible wealth of such information, but I suggest that you resist the temptation to load the list with data that may be interesting, but will not make money for your business. Remember that you are building a marketing tool, not a research report.

If your list is older, your computer service can match it with NCOA (National Change of Address) lists provided by the post office, or the various telephone and resident lists compiled from telephone directories. These will give forwarding addresses for a substantial portion of the consumers who have moved, and let you remove the names of those individuals whose current addresses cannot be confirmed.

Demographic data can be added as well. Some will come from available individual information, and the remainder from the characteristics of the consumer's neighborhood. Some people opt to skip the individualistic information and use just the neighborhood lists, which for most uses is more than adequate. These suppliers can add any information that has ever been asked on a warranty card, survey program, or census questionnaire. This includes age, occupation category, estimated income, home value, education, and many other factors. Finer geographic delineations often are available, down to individual postal carrier routes.

Present product use and intent-to-buy information can be added from many sources. Survey sponsors have so much data on file that it is preferable to presume something is available and try to find it, rather than having the opposite, pessimistic opinion and not search for the information you need, regardless of how unrealistic the request might seem. I have found prescription usage, personal health ailments, oil-change preferences, cereal preferences, and car-buying intentions. When you see such a survey, study it carefully; you'll be amazed at the diversity. Of course, some categories of information are blocked from various suppliers because the data was sponsored by another advertiser on an exclusive basis. But then chances are you can find it from a different supplier, or you can sponsor questions yourself for a fee and control your own, new information source.

While most response lists are too small to be used for enhancement, there are some notable exceptions in some special categories. Huge multimillion-name lists such as Spiegel, Fingerhut, Warshawsky auto accessories, or Boardroom publications are large enough to make it pay to combine their data with yours. Such overlays can provide specifics that can make the difference between success and failure in a database application.

Other suppliers have combined data from many lists, so that the names on your list of individuals who have responded to any direct-response offer within the last year or other time period can be coded as such. These will respond to your own company's offer at a much higher rate than those who have not. Recent car buyers, type of car owned, recent appliance purchased, recent residential moves, music and book preferences—any of these may be valuable if the information is significant to the purchasing profile.

Regression Analysis. Which data is worth adding? That is what regression analysis is all about. It is a mathematical process to determine the degree of matches between known buyers and available enhancement data. This is an important process—one that should be conducted by all major mailers in the early stages of marketing development.

Basically it compares the characteristics of the people you want to reach (presumably your best customers) with the characteristics from a survey list, a compiled list, or a group of response lists. Those lists or survey answers that most frequently match the characteristics of your target group are isolated and tabulated mathematically.

A penetration report ranks which characteristics of likely customers are found most often. This enables the marketer to specify the lists or the survey questions so that the resulting list produces the same kind of customer. Often the key factors turn out to be unexpected characteristics of psychological and personality coincidence rather than specific category or brand usage, but they are just as valuable for list selection as more obvious differences.

My book *Database Marketing: The Ultimate Selling Tool* (McGraw-Hill) has an entire chapter devoted to this single subject. I also recommend Arthur Hughes' *The Complete Database Marketer* (Probus).

TYPES OF DATABASE MARKETING

Database marketing is the "missing link" between advertising and sales. Today, when all kinds of advertisers (not just direct marketers) are demanding accountability in advertising, database marketing is one of the few tools that can make a direct connection between money expended and sales realized.

Sometimes called *integrated marketing* or *relationship marketing* or even *maxi-marketing*, the principle seems simple. Make every marketing communication work twice as hard—building brand identity at the same time as asking for an order or at least an expression of interest. In other words, build brand equity and a marketing database at the same time.

When customers or prospects are identified, marketing funds should be allocated to influence to them, usually by mail promotions. Mass advertising should be directed at everyone else, with a secondary objective of getting new names or information for the database.

Mass advertising—whether it's broadcast, print, or even badly designed mail and door-to-door media—usually only has the ability to get across a single message or image. That message therefore must be addressed to the lowest common denominator of prospect. Also, mass advertisers must rely on package design, store display, or retail clerks to close the sale. With the growth of megamarkets and the decline of both service and salesmanship, the relationship between "intent to buy" and "share of market" has become increasingly distant. Database marketing is the answer.

Conquest Marketing

The most exciting application of database marketing is the ability to concentrate promotional efforts in exactly the right target markets. During a time when mass advertising agencies are under pressure to justify themselves, direct or database advertisers have no problem in doing so. But mass advertising and direct marketing are linked. The need to develop names for database marketing is the missing link between general advertising and direct marketing. Combining the efforts makes both more cost-effective. This process is called *conquest marketing*.

In general, conquest marketing involves sending highly persuasive communications and incentives for trial to select businesses or consumers who are more likely to be interested than readers or viewers of mass media.

As with all direct-marketing efforts, conquest marketing is not a panacea. The cleverest ideas must still take a backseat to the simplest spreadsheet forecast. To be effective, a database-marketing offer should include most the following elements:

- Clearly defined prospects or self-defined inquirers
- Product or service stories that require space for demonstration or the ability to provide samples
- Product or service advantages that would be obvious to someone who tries the product or service, and therefore lead to additional sales
- A substantial "lifetime value" to a product user—in either long-term value of smaller purchases (e.g., shampoo) or high-profit individual sales (e.g., an automobile)
- A creative approach that is genuinely interesting and that uses the mail format effectively—something that's not just "an ad in an envelope"

Conquest advertising can be addressed to users of the same product category but different brands, or simply to people who are likely to respond to the offer. Sometimes the offer is selected to fit a specific market segment. Often a conquest offer can be combined with the name-generating advertising described earlier, or it can be used to promote more than one type of product. I am amazed at the number of major corporations—including one of the big-three cereal makers—that use databases to send out single or multiple coupons, as if the prospect can simply be bribed into trying the brand. They overlook the demonstrated research that shows that the consumers who respond to such offers will just as easily switch back when someone else's coupon comes into their possession. As Procter & Gamble has stated publicly when they announced their value-pricing policy, sending coupons indiscriminately simply trains customers to buy products with anyone's coupons, including the competition's.

It is also accepted practice to assume that most coupons are redeemed by people who have already tried the product, and that perhaps only 1 of 10 represents a new trial. That's why conquest marketing is most effective by mail when you can identify new prospects and eliminate present customers from your coupon list. Don't trust research results that conclude that the extra creative effort of identifying new prospects isn't worthwhile. Most likely these results are faulty—a product of the core-market fallacy discussed in Chapter 4 on Research. The present users polled don't need the extra selling, and are not the payoff of the promotion. It is new customers whom we want to try the product or service, and we want them to try it because of its merits, not just because of a bribe. We can find these new customers who do appreciate and respond positively to a well-done creative execution.

One factor that successful conquest advertisers currently emphasize is that brand users selected must be "conquestable"—that is, susceptible to switching. Unless the product or service you are promoting is superior in some way, save your money. For instance, for a Seagram's Gin promotion, we didn't bother mailing to households who drank Tanqueray or Bombay gin because we knew they would not be attracted to our client's milder product.

Many "conquest" database programs today are coordinated with the company's dealers or sales agents. Mailings that appear to come from a local dealer have been very successful. The added benefit is that the dealer relationship is strengthened at the same time. Sometimes the dealer is offered such a mailing program as an incentive to stock the full line. Responses from consumers are sent to the dealers for follow-up. This has been very successful in the sale of new cars.

Some examples of conquest marketing:

- Dove sending litmus paper and a product sample to Ivory users, with a suggestion that they test the soap residue on their own face

- Pepsi-Cola sending whole cases of their product to heavy users of Coca-Cola

- Kellogg's sending discount coupons to families with more than one child who live in the vicinity of stores where a lower priced competitor was being introduced. The discount offsets the price advantage of the lesser-known competitor.

Up-Sell and Cross-Sell

While conquest marketing is the exciting end of the database business, often the most profitable programs are those that address present customers. One maxim of database marketing is that it is easier to get ten customers to make one more purchase between them then it is to find one new customer.

The logic of this is obvious. To reach the ten present customers you only have to mail ten pieces. All that is needed is a usage suggestion or a promotional motivation to make one more purchase. It is reasonable to expect a 10 percent response from your present customers. To reach one outside new customer, you may have to mail to 50 or 100 people to get a 1 percent or 2 percent response. Not only are you mailing more pieces, but you also have to pay for the list, while your own list has no added rental expense.

Multi-product companies can get the positive associations the customer has with one product to "rub off" on another. One major packaged goods client used cross-brand newsletters for this purpose with great success.

Some of the most successful promotions from my agency are cross-brand promotions, sending multiple communications to people with certain age or lifestyle similarities.

Frequency and Loyalty

Here again the relationship between mail-order and database marketing is indisputable. In mail order, it is common practice to design programs that may do no more than break even on the initial customer acquisition. The profit is in the "back end"—magazine renewals, repeat donations, sales from subsequent catalogs, the fulfillment of a continuity obligation, etc. Business-building comes from the "front end" investment. Profits come from the "back end." Striking a balance between these two programs is the key decision that management must make each and every year.

I have seen several financial studies in which companies not only received the proverbial 80 percent of their sales from the top 20 percent of all customers, mostly repeat buyers, but this group produced 100 percent of the company's profits. One consultant reports that actual figures from his clients are not 20–80 but 30–75—that is, 30 percent of the customers produce 75 percent of the sales. But the principle is the same.

One book I recommend is a work by Kevin Clancy and Robert Shulman entitled *The Marketing Revolution*. In it the authors explain a new way of thinking about advertising—retain current customers as a first priority and gain new ones as a second. I share these authors' amazement that general advertisers have given so little attention in the past to retaining customers as opposed to winning new ones.

The approach I advocate, which many companies are beginning to adopt, begins with budgeting marketing funds. It is as simple as making the "first cut" of the money an allocation for "identified customers" based on the percentage they represent of customers, sales volume, or profit margins. The second category is identified category users or imminent buyers. The third step then is to take what's left and invest it in advertising that builds brand equity and/or at the same time identifies new customers and prospects. Some companies separate these last two functions as well, with different budgets assigned to each priority.

Database programs (and in my opinion all marketing) should be looked at in the same way. Mass advertising should appropriately be bringing in new triers and first-time customers, with a secondary objective of identifying high-potential prospects and current customers. There are countless ways to motivate new trials from consumers, especially if you're willing to invest a large part of the income from the initial sale in doing so.

There is a different standard, however, for present customers. The object here is not volume but profits, and therefore the investment to induce incremental sales must be limited. Remember, these are the people who are likely to buy your product anyway, and the promotion investment must be appropriate to the profit goals. The object here is to either

1. Increase frequency of usage or purchase
2. Upgrade to a more profitable variation of the product or service
3. Extend product loyalty to related products
4. Defend market share against competitive conquest efforts

Obviously, sampling and extensive argument should not be needed for present customers. However, it is often beneficial to give customers information to support their original decision, and to reassure them that they did the right thing. Mostly, however, present customers are successfully motivated in one of two ways: *relationship* and *reward*.

Relationship. The object here is to build a bond between the company and the customer. Publications are often used. Sometimes these share information and give advice, with the objective to show the customers that they are important to the company. Sometimes they are entertaining, with stories, games, and other editorial material. Or they can provide news about a related interest and reinforce the product's association with its imagery. An example of this would be news of off-road adventures sent to Jeep customers, a guide to new hairstyles for Vidal Sassoon shampoo users, and a magazine with advice for parents to households that use Pampers.

Publications may be in any format. A database archive service has reported such efforts in the form of newsletters, newspapers, magazines, booklets, and even bound books. Similar promotions have increasingly been offered in videotape or computer software form.

Some companies send gifts. Small businesses have been sending gift calendars, pencils, and notebooks for years. An oil company uses baseball caps with their logo. A laundry product sends its best customers a convenient dispenser unit. These often have a secondary objective of keeping the advertiser's brand or phone number visible. In most of these cases it's not the value of the gift that's important, but the idea of it.

And don't overlook common courtesies. A thank-you letter. Winter holiday card. A letter celebrating the anniversary of a business relationship. Advance news of a product, service or sale before it is offered to the general public. While some of these may come with reminders to buy the product or contain plugs for related products, the main objective is to build the relationship and make customers feel they are "family."

Reward. "This free gift if you send three proofs-of-purchase!" "Save ten proofs-of-purchase, and get this accessory at half price!" "A discount coupon if you buy a carton of our cigarettes instead of a pack!" "Try all three flavors or scents and get a rebate!" All of these are approaches to combining incentives to buy more with a reward for being a present customer.

Often this takes the form of a whole catalog of products—free, or at a discount price for proof of various levels of purchase. Such gifts can be self-liquidating; that is, priced at a level that represents a significant saving to the customer, but is really at or near the advertiser's actual cost. Or they can be free to the customer.

My preference is a two-level pricing program. The lowest price requires substantial quantity of usage, and represents the actual cost or even a subsidized cost. In this case the customer might get interesting items at half-price. But each item also has what I call a "Speed Plan." Fewer proofs-of-purchase are required but the discount is only a third or so. Promotions of this type, for Betty Crocker and Kool-Aid and many others, often involve millions of customers and enormous volumes of merchandise.

Some sales promotion specialists put together programs such as this for manufacturers—on either a single-product or a catalog basis—and will even supply the promotional materials, as long as they can handle the sales and take a small profit margin. While it is more costly than setting up your own program, some companies prefer to have a turnkey arrangement where they don't have to concern themselves with the details of merchandise selection, inventory levels, fulfillment practices, and customer service.

Certainly the frequent-flyer or buyer programs have to be considered in this category. I have reservations about giving away the same product you are trying to sell, but in most of these cases the plane seats or hotel rooms would be empty anyway, and so have little incremental cost. Also, the flights taken often are vacation trips that do not displace business trips anyway.

Most plans offer merchandise that is related but not the same as that being sold. The Barbie pink-stamp plan earned points with purchases of doll clothes, toy cars, and other accessories, but could be redeemed only for items such as Barbie-branded clothes, book bags, and portable radios intended for use by the girl herself. AT&T's Opportunity Calling and Citibank's Citidollars offered neither phone nor banking services, but merchandise at discounted prices from a catalog.

There are other variations as well. A program I did for Beneficial Finance offered a contest entry every time the card was used. Banks offer personal banking conveniences (no standing in lines) and reduced rates if you consolidate all your accounts in one place so as to keep a minimum balance. Even supermarkets offer price specials to those who join their club plans and use them consistently.

Advocacy

The most neglected lesson from the world of direct marketing is the use of *advocacy programs,* sometimes called *member-get-member* (MGM) or *get-a-friend* (GAF) *programs.*

Offers that are to be passed along to friends and requests for friends' names have been very successful in database offers, mostly as a way of building the database. Some major programs have generated an additional 20 to 40 percent in added responses.

Usually your new customers are your most enthusiastic word-of-mouth generators, especially during the "honeymoon" period soon after the initial purchase. A program I once recommended for Nissan included a coupon book that new customers would keep in their glove compartment. If friends admired their new car, the owner could give them coupons that introduced the friends to a local dealer. The coupon entitled both the friend and the car owner to extra accessories if a sale resulted.

My usual approach is to offer a gift to both the referrer and the referee if a sale results. Other approaches might be that the customer can send a free sample of a product or a promotional booklet or a publication to the friend. For instance, every issue of *The Jolly Times*, a family-fun newspaper Bozell did for Jolly Time popcorn, invited the reader to send in the name of a friend who would like a copy. The copies sent to the friends then suggested that they continue the subscription and send in proof-of-purchases.

HOW THE PIECES FIT TOGETHER

While working on this chapter, one of my Asian associates called to discuss a database program for an airline based in a European country. We had to work out a strategy right there, over the phone. While it is not as thorough as it could have been if we had had more time, it's a concise example of how the pieces fit together. Here's what we recommended:

■ *List-building*. Identify several thousand nationals who had flown with the airline before from the customer lists. Include members of a business group dealing with the European country and senior executives of major international corporations. Also identify those planning business trips through a small-space advertising program in business publications offering a booklet on "How to Do Business in Europe."

■ *List enhancement*. We recommended two projects. One, a questionnaire with an offer of several thousand mileage points just for filling it out. The other, a win-a-trip-to-Europe contest asking contestants which country they would like to visit and at what time of the year, if they win.

■ *Loyalty/frequency*. We suggested a typical frequent-flyer campaign, but one recognizing that most visitors from this country flew only on business trips and those free trips revert to their companies in this country. The plan we worked out emphasized other personal rewards—especially trips for companions and pleasure-trip extensions to other cities in Europe.

■ *Conquest/trial*. This recommendation was mostly aimed at the more flexible vacation travelers, and included a program of special offers during seasons of high vacancies—upgrades, or hotel and recreation perks. These would apply only for trips taken during specific seasons or leaving on specific days. The offers were sent to prospects based on the information provided in the list-enhancement questionnaires.

This proposal is an example of how database marketing can pinpoint the potential customers and customize the separate campaigns. Each element of a database program must work together with the others in a continuing cycle, as illustrated in Figure 20-3. In many ways, database marketing—selling to individuals rather than groups—is the most sophisticated form of direct marketing. Its uses are just beginning. But its roots are as wide as the many applications of direct marketing in use today and as deep as the

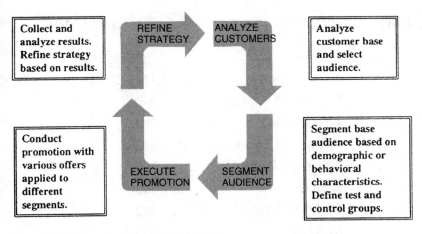

Figure 20-3. Campaign Management Process

earliest ads, catalogs, and mailings that unashamedly offered goods by mail order.

Project or Program?

Figure 20-4 shows some of the major corporations who have been using database marketing as an on-going tool for their various brands. At companies like these, database marketing is treated an on-going program— building lists, enhancing them, sending conquest mailings, maximizing their relationship with present customers. This leads to the kind of on-going trackable profits shown in Table 20-1. (Further explanation and additional calculations for lower priced and higher priced goods can be found in my book *Database Marketing*.) The return on database marketing is a long-term investment, just like investments in building share.

"DATA MINING"

While direct marketers were building database marketing on the foundation of mail order and mailing lists, a parallel universe was developing called *data mining*. The term *knowledge discovery* also describes this. A decade ago, a less glamorous phrase was used for the same process—*data dredging*. Epsilon, Oracle and IBM have been very aggressive in promoting this methodology to the direct marketing industry.

By whatever name you call it, the objective of database marketing and data mining is the same. But they are not competitive processes; each simply emphasizes a different starting point in the process. Data mining does, however, facilitate some types of program that could not be possible with traditional analysis methods.

Leading Companies (Syndicated File to 3/31/99)

Rank	Company	# Efforts
1	Kraft Foods	1,154
2	Procter & Gamble	942
3	Perrier Group	655
4	Campbell Soup	575
5	Johnson & Johnson	564
6	Nestle	496
7	Philip Morris	462
8	Kellogg	455
9	Ralston Purina	446
10	R.J. Reynolds	420
10	General Mills	420

Source: John Cummings & Partners DBM/SCAN®   9   5/3/99

Figure 20-4. Leading Users of Database Marketing in the U.S. as of March 1999.

Definitions

Knowledge Discovery. This is defined as an interactive process turning data into information and information into business solutions. *Data mining* is defined as the application of statistical and artificial intelligence techniques for discovering patterns and actionable information in large volumes of data. *Data warehousing* is a related term, which refers to the accumulation of data.

Process

This process starts with any available data, without preconceptions. It could be the mass of information in banking transactions, stock brokerage transactions, and insurance-company applications. It could be the rental patterns and selections of Blockbuster video rental customers, or the record of where you went on the Internet or the programs you watched on cable television. It could be purchases in a catalog or in department store. Or it could begin with the mountain of purchase data generated at a supermarket checkout counter where customer ID cards are scanned.

The analytical service probes for patterns and trends through a variety of computer algorithms and mathematical transactions that are preceded by a careful deletion of anomalies or non-variable data. To do this with such a large mass of data and so many variable elements, "artificial intelligence"

TABLE 20-1
FIVE YEAR ECONOMIC VALUE OF TYPICAL DATABASE PROGRAM

Assumptions

Name acquisition cost:			
Data base assembly	500,000 names	$0.21 per name	$105,000
Incentive/promotion	500,000 names	$1.50 per name	$750,000
Total Acquisition Cost (Yr. 1)	500,000 names	$1.74 per name	$855,000
Ongoing database costs:			
Database maintenance		$0.08 per record	
On-going relationship management		$2.25 per record	
Total On-going Costs (Yrs. 2–5)		$2.33 per record	

Economic Value Analysis

	Year 1	Year 2	Year 3	Year 4	Year 5
Revenues:					
1. Total customers	500,000	800,000	1,000,000	1,100,000	1,200,000
2. Percentage of customers cross-sold		5.00%	5.00%	5.00%	5.00%
3. Sales price		$100	$100	$100	$100
4. Annual unit sales per customer		2	2.25	2.5	2.5
5. Total Revenue = (1) × (2) × (3) × (4)		$8,000,000	$11,250,000	$13,750,000	$15,000,000
Direct Costs:					
6. Name acquisition costs (assumptions)	$855,000	$513,000	$342,000	$171,000	$171,000
7. On-going database costs (assumptions)		$1,165,000	$1,864,000	$2,330,000	$2,563,000
8. Total Database Costs = (6) + (7)	$855,000	$1,678,000	$2,206,000	$2,501,000	$2,734,000
9. Cost of goods sold 60% × (5)		$4,800,000	$6,750,000	$8,250,000	$9,000,000
10. Total Direct Costs = (8) + (9)	$855,000	$6,478,00	$8,956,000	$10,751,000	$11,734,000
Gross Profits:					
11. Gross profits = (5) – (10)	($855,000)	$1,522,000	$2,294,000	$2,999,000	$3,266,000

TABLE 20-1
FIVE YEAR ECONOMIC VALUE OF TYPICAL DATABASE PROGRAM (Continued)

Operating Expenses:					
12. Selling G&A = 15% × (5)		$1,200,000	$1,687,500	$2,062,500	$2,250,000
13. Taxes at 34%		$109.480	$206,210	$318,410	$345,440
Net Profits:					
14. Profit After Tax = (11)-(12)-(13)	($855,000)	$212,520	$400,290	$618,090	$670,560
15. Cumulative PAT	($855,000)	($642,480)	($242,190)	$375,900	$1,046,460

Discount factor:	12%
Economic Value (NPV):	$464,246
Return on Investment (IRR):	33%

is brought into play. Instead of seeking particular elements from the beginning, the computer sorts and resorts the information, compares it and reacts to the patterns that evolve. Millions of combinations and trial-and-error tests take place, sometimes using methods similar to those that forecast the result of the next thirty moves in a chess tournament.

Applications

Though it seems as if the computer is replacing instinct and practical experience, that's not the case. Once data mining is fully perfected, it gives marketers a more precise, more powerful, and more accurate forecasting and prospect selection tool. But the decision on how to use the data still demands the brain-power of executives who understand the roots and principles of direct and database marketing.

What can we use it for? Whatever you can imagine! We can identify potential customers we can win over, or present customers who are likely to use our products or services again. We can use it to enhance our understanding of usage patterns and predict reorders and renewals. We will be able to suggest to customers a variety of books, tools or business services they need or might like—and be right every time! We will be able to analyze purchasing behavior to predict where a catalog company should open its next retail store, or what specialty catalog is most likely to succeed in a particular market, or which foreign market is the best bet for expansion. We will have better tools to judge which credit card applicant to accept, and what credit limit is most likely to be both safe and profitable.

This still emerging analytical tool, when harnessed to the still developing world of interactive marketing, may finally fulfill direct marketing's potential. We can look forward to more personal, more customized and more convenient customer relationships than the combination of retailing and traditional marketing ever was or ever could be.

21

INTERNET MARKETING

When the first edition of this book came out, the word "Internet" was unknown. "Interactive" was a term that applied to any direct-response effort. Five years ago when the third edition was written I devoted one slim chapter to this emerging curiosity; other books on direct marketing didn't mention it at all.

At that time, a respected and very successful president of a major ad agency made what may have been the one wrong call of his career. He referred to "the money that is going in the toilet in the name of building the Information Superhighway. It's going to make the financial fiascoes of the eighties," he said then, "look like small change." He must have reconsidered because today his agency owns some of the leading resources in the Internet field.

IT'S EXPLOSIVE GROWTH

In that five years, the Internet expanded from a "techy" novelty to an accepted tool of communications and commerce. The number of users in the U.S. went from 6.5 million in 1994 to 62 million in 1999. Worldwide it went from 19 million to 129 million during the same time period. By the year 2002, analysts estimate that between 85 million to 175 million people in the U.S. will have access to the Internet, and at least twice that number worldwide.

Looking at it another way, it took 13 years for television to be in 50 million homes; ten for cable TV to do the same. The Internet achieved this same growth in only five years! The excitement reported in the previous edition has turned into reality:

> "Nothing has captured the imagination of marketers, media, and the communications world as much as the Internet. Not millions but billions of dollars have been put at risk by investors who see this development as the communications and media herald of the twenty-first century. Telephone companies, cable companies, and movie studios engage in mergers and legal battles, fighting for the high ground in the inevitable shakeout. Press releases, each heralding the newest "ultimate" system, flood the desks of editors and executives."

How Is It Different?

But what *is* it, really? It depends on whom you talk to. Yet what the Internet is today pales in comparison to what it is becoming. Within the next five years it will take on new dimensions, provide new consumer and business services, and create new fortunes. It will change cultures and lifestyles around the world.

However, as a marketing channel and an advertising medium, it will still be subject to the lessons of 100 years of direct-marketing experience. It will be those marketers and Internet service providers who recognize and respect its inter-relationship with direct marketing that will dominate this field in the years to come.

I recently sat in on an informal debate that asked this question: "Who will be the most successful Internet marketers? Internet technologists who learn direct marketing? Or marketers who learn the Internet technology?" I offered my own opinion: "It doesn't make any difference, as long as they acquire *both* skills—the art of manipulating this new medium and the science of motivating action through communications."

Like all other new media, the Internet initially attracted the "New Triers." It has already grown beyond that stage. Within a few years the Internet will reach and maintain a share of the media world and co-exist side-by-side with publications, outdoor advertising, broadcast and, yes, even what some in the Internet world insist on calling "snail mail." (I prefer to use the term "tortoise mail," and to remind audiences about the tale of the "Tortoise and the Hare.") As an advertising medium, the Internet can and will reach the same people who read newspapers, watch television and respond to direct mail. And as a direct marketing medium, the lessons on how to reach and motivate consumers are as applicable as ever.

It is too often forgotten that ease of response is only one aspect of generating a lead or an order. We must still attract attention, generate interest, involve prospects, motivate them, overcome objections, and give them a reason for acting *now*. That is exactly what direct marketers understand better than anyone in the world of marketing, and why any Internet marketer that disregards this body of experience will be among the first to vanish from the scene.

Background

The Internet originated in the 1980s when the U.S. Defense Department's Advanced Research Projects Agency sought a disaster-proof communications system. The result, called ARPAnet, was designed to distribute military data over packet-switched networks connected by telephone lines. If one of its six centers was destroyed or a connection became congested, data could still flow to the others. In 1985, control of this network was turned over to the National Science Foundation, which in turn expanded it to 16 super-computer sites linking universities and research centers doing military research. A few commercial services emerged, generally fee-based business services on Prodigy. It was not until the early nineties that control passed to the private sector. Since then, under free enterprise, the Internet exploded with chaotic but spectacular growth.

A number of very important changes took place in the late 1980s and early 1990s that would change the Internet forever. 1989 witnessed the creation of the World Wide Web, the part of the Internet that is represented by the "www" in web addresses.

At the same time, a new program called Mosaic took the basic computer language of the Internet—hypertext markup language, or HTML—and put it into a graphical format. Mosaic enabled Netscape, which became the most popular Internet browser until Microsoft started giving its Web Explorer browser away free, bundling it with software.

America Online (AOL) specialized in providing e-mail services and enabling access to consumer-oriented websites. In the mid-1990s, to build their subscriber list, they made major direct-marketing investments using direct mail and DRTV. Millions of computer owners received their first Internet software in floppy disks—and later CDs—from AOL. The former leaders, Prodigy and CompuServe, followed suit, but too little and too late. AOL enjoyed explosive growth and today serves over half of all the computers in the United States and a growing share of those in other countries.

A Year 2000 Snapshot

Today's fundamental Internet structure is as invisible to its users as are the studios and satellite dishes and transmission towers of television. First a computer user—called a "client" in the computer world—dials the local access number of an Internet service provider (ISP) or other services that provide Internet access. (Services such as America OnLine or CompuServe are different than ISPs because they are their own mini-networks with *access* to the Internet, while ISPs link the users *directly* to the Internet.)

One of the company servers takes the call, checks the password from the user's computer, and converts the e-mail or website address to a computerized digital format. For example, the text uniform resource locator

(URL) "www.info@myexample.com" is typed into a URL box of a browser like Netscape or Microsoft Explorer. It is then converted to a number, called an IP address that all the networked computers recognize. The URL is essentially the web page's digital "address" that tells all the computers where to look to find that page.

Routers from the Internet-service host transmit this digital signal to another series of servers until it finally reaches the computer that hosts the information for www.info@myexample.com. This host responds with the digital information requested, whether it's a series of e-mails or a web page, and sends it back to the user sitting at his or her computer. In our example, the host computer would return the HTML coding that produces the web page www.info@myexample.com. Each new click by a client-user starts this process over again.

Any computer can be a host, whether it's a powerful Sun, IBM or Oracle server capable of handling thousands of Internet connections at one time, or someone's Mac or PC sitting on a kitchen table. Estimates are that there will be two million small-computer "kitchen-table" Web hosts by 2000.

WHO HAS WEB PAGES?

It will soon be easier to ask "Who doesn't?" Host servers can be set up for any application the mind can imagine. On one hand it could be a family's newsletter or a teacher's homework assignments, or a local coffee shop's menu and delivery service. Most of these sites can be hosted by an Internet company's server along with hundreds of other pages, so the site owner doesn't have to keep his or her computer hooked up to a phone line all day. Most ISPs also will host web pages for a modest cost, averaging around $25 a month—a price that include the ISP services like e-mail and dial-up Internet connection.

On the other extreme, a host server can be a big corporation's customer service department or a mail order company's catalog—tasks that require one or more large servers. These enable such services as ordering an airline ticket, requesting an air express pick-up or even downloading tax forms. It can answer a buyer's inquiry with videotaped information about a product, a service or a travel destination—and it can accept the order or book a reservation. It can already download a college professor's lecture, complete with the ability to ask and answer questions live or in writing. Users with fast connections can even download a music CD or a full-length movie.

Scores of businesses and organizations are using websites to facilitate access to an information, training or education source or to provide news, services or entertainment designed to generate viewership. Their motivation? Perhaps to add value to an association membership or magazine subscription. Perhaps to generate viewers of advertising that others will pay for, just as any advertising-supported magazine or television station creates "content" to attract readers or viewers.

Other servers are used to support businesses providing enhancements to Internet connections that, as a by-product, can support advertising or marketing ventures. The access companies themselves provide such services, charging advertisers for exposure or selling retailers preferred-position links from their site.

One such service is called a "search engine"—a way of finding a website that meets a viewer's information or product needs. These are operated by companies such as Netscape (also the provider of the browser software), Alta Vista, Excite and Yahoo, which compete for viewers by making their searches easier, faster and more responsive.

Every day companies find new applications. Dow Jones offers corporate information and security filings for a modest fee. Daily newspapers offer restaurant listings (and ads), theater reviews (and ticket ordering), sports news (and tickets.) Conducent offers advertising services on software and game downloads. Flycast enables national advertisers to direct messages only to areas or homes that meet their demographic requirements. Orb helps advertisers sell products and services—advertisers that pay only for actual orders, "per inquiry" advertising applied to the Internet. Today, without leaving the Internet, you can play a game, go to an auction, get a mortgage, buy a car or even a house, and then look for a better job to pay for it all. To more easily understand the Internet and its potential, think of it as three different Internet businesses—each one a light-year advance over the traditional formats, but each subject to the realities of the basic business. They are Publishing, Retailing and Advertising.

Figures 21-1 through 21-6, scattered through this chapter, illustrate some of the basic types of web pages.

Publishing

Today's biggest profit-makers are not the websites of advertisers and new businesses, but the companies who provide editorial content, conveniences or services to attract the equivalent of circulation.

I am using the term publishers, as in newspapers and magazines, but it could just as well be the stations, channels and producers of the broadcast industry. As with all of these, the Internet "publishers" make money in two ways: they sell subscriptions (as with magazines or premium TV channels), one-time access (as in newsstand sales or pay-per-view TV) or they sell advertising space.

The equivalents of subscription sales are the fees paid to access providers such as AOL and MindSpring. Some information providers and research services charge a fee per use or an annual fee for access to their database. And some make money by selling software or hardware that speeds up or otherwise enhances Internet access. For example, one of the most interesting features justifying the purchase of the Mac OS 8.5 operating system is Sherlock, a tool that permits using several search engines simultaneously as well as searching the individual computer drives and network memories.

Some free attractions are portals that attract audiences by conveniently linking them to web sites with the information they need or a product they are interested in buying. When searching for information, portals may cor-

Figure 21-1. E-COMMERCE
E-Commerce sites are often linked to financial services which process credit-card orders securely and enter the order. The web operators never see the credit-card information. Other firms handle it themselves, using various encryption techniques.

respond to a library or a set of reference books. For shopping, as a direct marketer I think of portals as catalogs. Others relate the category to real estate, and talk of portals as stores and shopping malls.

The most visited websites at this time are access providers, browsers and search engines. These include AOL, Netscape, Microsoft, Excite and Yahoo.

Retailing

The Internet can be looked at as simply another channel for any type of commerce on the face of the Earth—with some powerful plusses. It can be a bank, an insurance company, a mortgage lender, or a stockbroker. It can be a clothing store, a florist, a supermarket, a lumber yard, a restaurant's delivery or catering service, or just about anything you have ever heard of or can imagine.

As in mail order, some product categories lend themselves to Internet marketing more than others. One survey indicates that at the present rate of growth Internet marketers will cut deeply into certain categories of retail selling. This study predicts that by the year 2002 over 35% of software, 13% of computer hardware, 11% of books and 8 percent of air travel will be sold directly over the web. There are many reasons for this growth:

- Your store can be as large as your server's memory bank, and you have no rent to pay except for your computer services.
- Your market is not local or regional but national and international. The tiniest website can be reached from any place on earth.
- You can stay "open for business" 24 hours a day, seven days a week; you don't even close for holidays.
- You can change your "store window" instantly to meet competition or to feature new inventory.
- As with all direct marketing, you know the name of your customers and can easily solicit repeat business.
- You can display your wares or present your case in text, photos, voice, music and—increasingly—in video formats.

But the Internet is not a free lunch.

- You must have inventory and a fulfillment system that meets the Internet users unrealistic expectations of almost instant delivery. (You can do this with downloadable products such as music or software.)
- Your "store" and your prices are open to constant monitoring by your competition. It's difficult to get an edge.
- Fraud and security are problems, as are the fear of loss of privacy and being flooded with spam (unsolicited e-mail).
- You are competing with huge companies that have raised so much investment capital that they don't have to show a profit for years. It's hard to match their prices.

- Most important, you can have the most unique store and the best values in the world, but it will do you no good if no one can find you.

And don't overlook the huge advantages in business-to-business marketing. *Business Week* magazine reported that Internet commerce between businesses are five times the dollar volume of consumer applications—$43 billion in 1998; predicted to $1.3 trillion by the year 2003. That will be 9 percent of all U.S. business trade, ten times the estimate for consumer e-commerce and more than the entire gross domestic product of Britain or Italy. Some reasons:

- Instant inventory and ordering of supplies or replacement parts.

- Intranet private systems for clients and customers, vendors and service companies.

- On-line support and supervision of dealers, distributors, sales agents or franchises.

- Repair manuals and common technical-support answers always available to customers and technicians at much less cost than telephone support.

- Vendor searches. Many companies look at websites when they are looking for consultants, ad agencies, package designers or other specialties.

Advertising

The Internet can be looked at as simply an advertising medium. The advertising can be for brand image or for direct response—to generate orders on the web or by phone or by visits to a retail store. But it is still advertising, and advertising agencies will continue to look for rate structures and measurement tools comparable to those available for other media.

As of 1998, advertising revenues on the Internet were expected to exceed $2 billion—more than one percent of all U.S. advertising spending and about 25 percent of cable-television advertising revenue.

As most readers of this book will know, print media is sold on the basis of cost per thousand circulation or some variation of cost per thousand target circulation (discussed in Chapter 15 on print media.)

The Internet has its own equivalents of circulation:

Impressions or "page views." The number of times any page that happens to contain the advertisement is requested. The ad can be on the bottom of a page that requires scrolling and is never viewed, or it can require downloading . Nevertheless it is a standard for determining reach and frequency.

In early 1999, the cost per thousand (CPM) impressions had slipped from almost $50 per thousand two years earlier to about $35. However, rates are subject to extremes of supply and demand. At one point Procter & Gamble refused to pay more than $5 per M impressions for advertising banners. Banner costs are running between these extremes. As with direct marketing

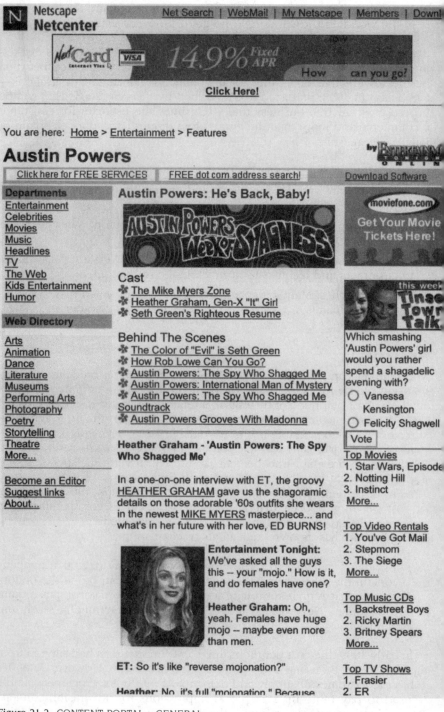

This Netscape page is a portal to different entertainment pages. Paid banners and buttons appe
the top of the page.

media buying, many orders are on a preemptible basis at reduced rates for unsold space.

CPM rates vary widely. Search engines will often charge a premium for a keyword. Content sites will charge more to make the listing look as if it was editorial. Highly targeted sites understandably cost more on a CPM basis than general portals, category rotation placement, or ROS (scattered, based on the TV term Run of Station). For instance, *The Economist* was charging as much as $85/M. One advertiser's mortgage rate page had a CPM rate of $150.

Hits. The total number of Internet files selected, counting each page and each source file (illustrations, graphic headlines, sounds, illustrations) as a hit. Each single customer who goes to a homepage, clicks to a portal, and then selects one page is generating a "hit" not just for the page but for each file that is opened. Each image counts. A file with a major graphic headline, two illustrations, six icons, two product shots and two ads is measured as a dozen "hits." This is why few advertisers want to pay "per hit."

Clicks. Any interaction with an advertisement, listing, button or banner that links a website visitor to the advertiser's URL.

Before the current proliferation of websites on almost every subject, some sites reported click-through rates of as much as 2.5 percent or 3 percent of impressions. In 1999, the same sites had click-through rates only 0.5 percent and rates of less than 0.1 percent are widely reported.

"Responses." This refers to inquiries, enrollments, orders, downloads of a store coupon or any other action relating to a sale.

For classic mail-order sales, "responses" are the only ultimate measurement. With over 50 percent of web space unsold, some websites are accepting what would ordinarily be called per-inquiry deals based on actual results. However, a 1998 Price Waterhouse Cooper study showed that only 5 percent of revenue was generated on this basis; 40–45 percent of ad revenue was generated on a straight cost-per-thousand impression basis. Half of all deals were on a "hybrid" basis—a mix of impressions and some type of revenue sharing.

TOMORROW'S INTERNET

It is already obvious that the Internet of tomorrow will have a totally different dimension than the one in use today. The world's largest corporations are paying billions of dollars to stake their claim on this future. Investors are supporting these decisions. Billions of dollars are riding on advertisers' expectations of attractive costs per thousand impressions and on direct marketers' hopes for low cost-per-response figures.

The New York Times
ON THE WEB

NYC W
61°

FRIDAY, JUNE 11, 1999 | Site Updated 1:50 AM

QUICK NEWS
PAGE ONE PLUS
International
National/N.Y.
Politics
Business
Technology
Science/Health
Sports
Weather
Opinion
Arts/Living
Automobiles
Books
CareerPath
Diversions
Magazine
Real Estate
Travel
ARCHIVES
SITE INDEX
FOR LISTINGS, VISIT
NEWYORKtoday
● Movies
● Restaurants
● Theater
● Music
● Shopping
● Yellow Pages

The New York Times
ON THE WEB
Learning
Network
FOR STUDENTS,
TEACHERS & PARENTS

Text Version

Archives
Classifieds
Forums
Marketplace
Services

Help
Site Tour

Home Delivery
-Order Online
-Service

NATO SUSPENDS BOMBING OF YUGOSLA
AS SERB FORCES BEGIN LEAVING KOSOV

NATO suspended the bombing of
Yugoslavia on Thursday after confirming
that Yugoslav troops had begun
withdrawing from Kosovo hours earlier.
Go to Article
•ISSUE IN DEPTH: The Conflict in Kosovo

NATO Officials Expect a Distinct
Kosovo With No Serbian Control

U.S. and NATO officials envision for
Kosovo an international protectorate that
will be part of Yugoslavia in name only and
that may eventually become independent.
Go to Article

Loitering Law Aimed at Gangs
Is Struck Down by High Court

The Supreme Court, voting 6 to 3, struck
down Chicago's anti-loitering law, saying it
gave the police too much discretion.
Go to Article

President Clinton in the Ov
Office on Thursday night a
13-minute address on Koso
Go to Article

TECHNOLOGY
New Infection Is Killi
Files Through E-Mai

SPORTS
Show Time for Fema
Soccer Star

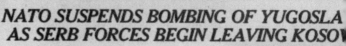

computers
electronics
music
and more!...
choose a store at jandr.com!
Computers ▼

HOME DELIVERY
1-800.NYTIMES.COM

MARKETS		
Dow	10621.27	-6
Nasdaq	2484.62	-3
S&P 500	1302.82	-1
Russell 2000	442.27	-
NYSE	622.85	-

SEARCH THE SITE
[   ] Search
Tips

GET STOCK QUOTES
[ ][ ][ ] Go
Look Up Symbol

BREAKI
NEWS F
A.P.

Questio
Kosovo
Answer
a.m. EDT

FILM REVIEWS
Current Film
Janet Maslin reviews "Austin Powers: The Spy Who
Shagged Me" which opens Friday. Other new movies
include "Return With Honor" and "The Red Violin."

Figure 21-3. CONTENT PORTAL—NEWS
This web operator offers free content that will attract viewers to their page. This editorial co
supported by advertisers, just as the print newspaper or magazine.

536

Connections

For one thing, your home or office telephone line will probably not be the medium that connects your screen to the servers that eventually connect to websites all over the world. Most telephone lines have a maximum transmission speed of 28,600 (bits per second)—one of the reasons why the "World Wide Web" has been nicknamed the "World Wide Wait."

The relative slowness of today's Internet affects connection speed, search speed and downloading speed. As a result, most sites irritate users who must wait for illustrations and large graphics and can't handle motion at all. Bell Atlantic compiled the following comparison in Table 21-1.

As you can see, the speed of the Internet transmission depends upon the telecommunications technology. T-1 fiber-optic phone lines that are directly connected to Internet hubs are about 30 times the speed of an ordinary phone line. DSL (Digital Subscriber Lines), which are ordinary phone lines using a modified digital transmission format, can receive data between 1 and 6 megabits per seconds and—at their highest transmission speed—are a little faster than T-1. Dual-channel ISDN is a little over twice as fast as a 56.6 modem. (ISDN services are typically installed as dual channel.) The fastest modem capability with normal phone lines is 56.6 kilobits because of analog phone-line limitations

Many of these services are already available through local phone companies or other telecommunication companies in various parts of the United States, especially in urban areas. While the United States is typically the leader in telecommunications technology, some other areas are much farther along in their introduction of these services into the general public infrastructure. T-1 service is much more common for the general public in Hong Kong, for example. In the U.S., the installation and maintenance expense of anything beyond a 56.6 modem limits the most advance technol-

TABLE 21-1
COMPARISON OF TRANSMISSION SPEED

These tables, compiled by Bell Atlantic, compare the speed of downloading ten full-sized newspapers (a 10-megabyte file) using different Internet technologies.

Process	Time
Dial-up modem (56K)	25 minutes
ISDN*	10.5 minutes
Home satellite dish	3.3 minutes
DSL (Digital Subscriber)	2.5 minutes
Cable TV modem	1.3 minutes
T-1 Line	51 seconds

*Integrated services digital network, dual channel.
Source: Bell Atlantic

ogies to businesses that can afford them or consumers who want faster download speed and install DSL or ISDN in their homes. T-1 lines can cost over $1000 to install and over $1000/month in service fees, and are typically used only by businesses. DSL monthly fees can run between $100/month for service similar to the speeds from ISDN, to over $500/month for something closer to T-1 transmission capability, not including installation and equipment expenses.

One alternative to telephone lines is the same cable companies that bring television signals into homes. More than 70 million Americans are already connected to such cables. These bring in data at the same speed as the fastest phone lines, but at half the cost. Table 21-2 shows a comparison of transmission speeds with different technologies.

The most likely solution—for the next decade at least—is fiber-optic cable versus the older coaxial. In cable television, this technology permits buying a pay-per-view movie or sports event with a click of a remote. It will soon go one step further and enable the TV remote control to be used for both phone and Internet services in addition to television. Users will be able to respond to polls, order products, or access the Internet as easily as changing television channels—with the click of a remote. The Internet will suddenly become accessible to couch potatoes as well as computer techies.

Digital electronics is already state of the art. You can hear the difference on a telephone or CD player. Whereas analog records and transmits degrees of sound or picture, digital breaks the signal into tiny bits with fixed values, assuring the same quality on the receiving end. Digitally-based HDTV (High Definition Television) is already available and may become the standard within the decade. A European transmission system called multiplexing is also well established and may rival HDTV in the U.S. market as well.

Telephone companies and cable companies are competing to become the primary source of data transmission, buying related companies, investing in technology, laying fiber-optic cables. The outcome of this race will determine if the next generation is watching TV on their computer or making phone calls from their television sets. Either one will incorporate the Internet.

TABLE 21-2
DATA TRANSMISSION SPEEDS
USING COMPETING CAPABILITIES

Technology	Speed	Speed (bits per second)
56.6 Modem	56.6 kilobits/sec	56,600 BPS
ISDN (single channel)	64 kilobits/sec	64,000 BPS
ISDN (dual channel)	128 kilobits/sec	128,000 BPS
DSL	Varies—160 kilobits/sec to 6 megabits/sec	160,000–6,000,000 BPS
T1 Fiber-optic	1.544 megabits/sec max	1,544,000 BPS max
Cable Modem	10 megabits/sec max	10,000,000 BPS max

Source: *Internet Resources* magazine.

It would seem that a simpler solution would be satellite or microwave transmission, as with Direct TV or cellular telephones. This technology mostly has only a one-way signal at the moment, and the tech wizards in the industry say that the limited resources today that do have dual-signal capability have the transmission-speed capacity of a relatively slow modem (28.8 kilobits/sec). But who knows? Cable companies had the same problem only a few years ago, but are rapidly changing the scene by replacing their outdated cables. Somewhere, in a big corporation's multi-million dollar R&D building, a team of technicians is working on the satellite issue. And somewhere else, in a garage or basement, two guys or gals are working on the same thing. Tomorrow, anything is possible.

Convergence

Two days before I wrote this chapter, I attended a presentation by WorldGate Communications, introducing their Channel HyperLinking© technology and its applications. Their unique cable box and signal-processing system is already enabling TV viewers in test markets to connect to the Internet directly from their television.

But using the TV instead of a computer is not the big news. Working with major cable content providers such as CNN, A&E and Showtime, WorldGate has also made it possible for television viewers to instantly access a website—without using an Internet access provider such as AOL, without a computer, and without even selecting a website URL. The service will be available for a monthly fee, probably marketed in the same way premium channels are made available to cable subscribers.

The applications are awesome. See an infomercial, click once and order the item. See a short form commercial (perhaps a :30 which in this medium will be feasible) and the detailed sales story is on your screen. See a good movie, click and order a videotape. Get excited about a news item, click and record your views in a poll (which can be reported on in seconds), or send a note to your Senator. Hear about a new product, click and download the address of the nearest outlet and a personalized store coupon.

Now imagine all these applications at the same speed as the TV show itself—apparently instantaneous. This new technology enables the same range of sound and motion communications options, along with the flexibility of the Internet. Forget scrolling, buttons and website pages. Whether they are accessed as part of a TV program or directly from a website, the messages available at this speed can be presentations, demonstrations, testimonials, or anything else you might send in a videotape or on a CD. The viewer can select the specific information they want, just as on any good website. They can calculate a new car's lease cost or their home-mortgage payments. And they can do this instantly—either during a television program, or later by downloading after the program is over.

Another form of convergence may take place between the telephone and the computer, and perhaps the TV set as well. Simple software additions already enable anyone to call anywhere in the world at local phone rates by using the Internet. I know several people from other continents who keep in touch with family and friends via their computers. Video conferencing between parties, using compatible software and the same communications protocol, can be enabled simply by a small camera at each location. How this will affect the use of the Internet as an advertising and marketing tool is anyone's guess. But it certainly enables the addition of the personal contact that half of current Internet buyers say they miss.

Convenience

One problem keeping Internet e-commerce companies from growing even faster is the reluctance to accept that technology must take second place to customer service. The missing link in all the grand schemes is the distance between the buyer and the computer screen.

Direct marketing on the Internet is no different from any other media we work with. Just as an ad must be readable, a website or e-mail must be easy to find, easy to navigate, and easy to read. Just as coupons must be easy to fill out, the order-taking process must fit consumer preferences, not the other way around. Cold electronics is not enough. If Internet marketers are to succeed, they must have a human face as well.

Customer service may be the key to the survival of the small businessman who doesn't have millions to buy preferred positions on the major portals. Lynn Bowlin, in Cedar Rapids, Iowa went into the mail-order book business as www.positively-you.com. "You'll never be able to compete with Amazon," his friends told him.

Operating the business from a spare bedroom, he contacted the same wholesalers Amazon.com uses and offered to sell to consumers any book at even lower prices—up to 35 percent off. When he started, his monthly expenses were $150 a month, mostly for service from an ISP (Internet Service Provider), fees from a credit-card processing service, and various miscellaneous bank charges. His business has grown to $2000 a day, with orders coming from all over the world.

His "secret?" He handles every order personally, writes to the customer, thanks them for the order, and discusses books with his customers. It's the mom-and-pop bookshop combined with modern technology—and it works.

GETTING TO THE STORE

Access is another barrier that must be overcome, using both direct-marketing experience and Internet technology. Websites must be easy to access and easy to order from.

Often websites are designed by professionals in studios equipped with T-1 lines and large high-definition monitors and sound systems. The sites they design look great—on their screens. There's voice, music, and motion. And lots of great original artwork. They'll win the awards, but they won't get the customers.

Those beautiful photos often cause useless delays. The design that looked great on a big screen now requires endless scrolling. Try to print the page and an inch of text on the side of the web-frame doesn't print. The company President—whose welcome speech was so eloquent on those expensive speakers—may sound like Donald Duck on a PC's built in speakers.

Not every customer has the most powerful computer, the largest screen, or the latest software. Try downloading your brightly colored website on a black and white printer and see what comes through. One of the largest direct marketing agencies in the world has a website where nothing is readable when printed in black-and-white.

Until the majority of users have high-speed access, over-designed sites simply add to the frustration and disillusionment of customers. Let's impress our peers with sales figures, not graphics.

Ordering

Ordering is another part of the same problem. The mail order rule is to recognize that different people prefer different ways to order, just as they prefer different ways to shop.

Recently I searched for a book on Barnes & Noble's much heralded website. I found it and tried to order a book, but got a message that said that they couldn't process an order through my Internet software (AOL 3.0 at the time) and that I should order by phone. OK, no problem! But I searched in vain for the phone number on the website. I finally gave up and ordered the book from Amazon.com, with no difficulty or delay.

Other "shopping carts" have an identity crisis. They don't know if their function is sales or research. Just as the K.I.S.S. rule (Keep It Simple, Stupid!) applies to ordering from a mailing, ad or broadcast, it applies to the Web as well. Research questions about the customer's occupation and other interests can come after the first sale, as part of a later relationship-building contact by mail or e-mail. The first goal is to make the cash register ring.

Web marketers report that as many as two-thirds of Internet customers who indicate an item for their "shopping cart" don't follow through and actually order. Just as direct marketers in traditional media found that the design and wording of the order device can make a difference, their experiences apply to Web marketing as well. One concept, proven again and again, is that different people prefer different ways of ordering, which is why we list phone numbers and fax numbers on mail-in order forms.

On website programs I have been involved in, I always give the buyer an option to order by phone as well as through the Web. In some cases, phone orders out-pulled Internet orders!

Land's End goes even further. You can order from a salesperson aurally and visually, right through your computer.

Confidence

Another of today's limitations is that many potential customers fear sending credit card information over the net. Despite this, the amount of web commerce is expected to grow—from $2.6 billion in 1996 to more than $220 billion in 2010, according to International Data Corporation, an Internet research company. There was a time when consumers had similar fears about giving credit-card numbers over the telephone, or even simply ordering by mail. There are still people who must be assured that they will really get the merchandise ordered. The bad apples in the mail-order business keep this fear alive.

The fact is that there is little to worry about. Most transactions, especially for small- to medium-size companies, are encrypted over the network and are not readable until they reach the site's own server. Other credit-card transactions are transmitted directly to financial institutions from the "Shopping Cart" order page. Companies like MacAuthorize, CyberSource, and SoftCart handle such transactions directly for the advertiser or website owner. Even the advertiser doesn't have the actual credit-card number that is transmitted through the Web, only the financial institution.

As there is more understanding of the "secure" ordering systems the Internet offers, consumer resistance will fade. It would help if the U.S. government would permit 128-bit encryption system for even greater security, as other countries do.

More "firewall" research is needed to block distant hackers who can access transaction data or place counterfeit e-commerce orders. With all this, Internet ordering is already as safe as a phone order and needs only the customer's acceptance of this fact.

DIRECT MARKETING APPLICATIONS

Many of the news and articles in *iMarketing News* and *Internet World* might give you the impression that the Internet is a world unto itself. Some practitioners write and give talks expressing wonder at the Internet's ability to get responses, measure the figures, and enable decisions based on actual results and statistical projections.

In the previous part of this chapter I have tried to cover what the Internet is, how it is changing, and how it is being used as a tool of communications and marketing. In this section we will review some elements of Direct Marketing and show how they relate to the Internet.

E-MAIL: THE INTERNET'S "DIRECT MAIL"

What's the difference between direct mail and what we'll call "direct e-mail?" In principle, nothing at all.

Both rely on mailing lists—the more targeted the better. Both do better with people who have responded to a previous communication. Both get better results when they can make the message personal or relevant. Both lend themselves to a wide variety of formats and creative approaches.

Economics

The biggest attraction has been the low cost. At one point mass faxes—including the list rental—could be sent out for as little as $150/M, or 15¢ each. In less than a year later the list cost *alone* was $250/M for opt-in lists with any type of selectivity, plus another $100/M to $150/M for the transmission of a simple letter. By the time you read this book, the cost for mass faxing may be even higher.

This could be worth the expense, depending on your product margins, the effectiveness of your offer and your creative execution. Some e-mail brokers are claiming response rates "as high as 5 to 15 percent." One article claimed 20 percent. I suspect that these are free, no-obligation offers such as a downloaded store coupon or a contest entry.

On the other hand, one on-line electronics store e-mailed 75,000 people offering discounted TVs, stereos and camcorders. The owner reported "good" click-throughs in the 5 to 10 percent range which brought people to his website. Sales were between .2 to .8 percent of those who clicked through. Even if you take the high end of these figures, you have 10 percent of 75,000 or 7,500 click throughs, Eight-tenths of one percent made a purchase, which brings it to 60 orders. If the e-mailing cost as little as $200/M, the 75,000 e-mails cost $15,000—for a CPO (cost per order) of $250.

However, many advertisers are turning to e-mail because the curse of proliferation has caught up with Internet banner results. Advertisers are complaining that banner-click rates had fallen to less than 1 percent, compared to claims of "double-digit" response-rates for e-mail. As a result, even the largest banner-placement networks such as DoubleClick and WebConnect were negotiating to buy companies that specialized in e-mail.

E-mailing Lists

Lists with e-mail addresses are generally marketed the same way as mail phone lists. There are list managers and list brokers. List compilers and list processors can do a merge-purge just as with any other kind of list. There are lists of people who actually bought something and lists of people who asked for information or otherwise indicated an interest in the subject. The problem is that there are still not that many lists to choose from, and that the quantities available on most e-mail lists are quite small.

For most lists, the only selection factor you have is the list source—subscribers to a free on-line magazine or newsletter, people who asked to be updated on travel bargains, consumers who asked that information be sent to them about a certain category of product, or members of an association. In very rare cases, such as an on-line magazine subscription, you may have the age or gender of the customer. If the customer didn't provide a zip code, you may not know where they live—meaning you can't refer a local dealer and you can't append census characteristics. In most cases you don't even have the potential customer's name—only an e-mail address.

Format

Anyone whose introduction to e-mail was a casual note from a friend or a business memo will be amazed at the creative potential of an e-mail message today.

Type fonts, colored type or backgrounds can be transmitted on some ISPs as easily as a black and white sentence, and at no additional cost. Drawings and simple illustrations can be part of the basic message as well. Because all ISP's don't use the same coding, this usually works best when both the sender and receiver use the same ISP—an AOL subscriber to another AOL subscriber, for example.

E-mail has always had the capacity to enclose a document that can be downloaded, in a theoretical "envelope" that travels with the basic message. Some attachments can be opened—with a simple text editor—directly from the e-mail host. But most are more complex documents that require downloading to your computer's memory and opened later when your basic software is up. However, this is not always as simple as it sounds. Different ISP's and e-mail servers have different mail protocols. Often color, images, and type fonts sent by MindSpring, for instance, to another MindSpring subscriber come out perfectly, but can barely be downloaded using AOL's current version of MIME—and vice versa. Currently, if I send a client a colored or formatted e-mail message using Outlook 97, and the client reads it with Eudora 1.0, it will not look the same at all. As a result we have had to use multiple ISPs with different protocols. Hopefully, by the time this book is out, there will be some type of standardization or at least better translation capability.

However, enough subscribers can download to support some attempts to enclose photos, software, documents or whole catalogs. Today, an e-mail message can include one or more URLs, usually in a contrasting color, which only have to be clicked on to bring up a website or to activate a download process. This therefore combines the advantages of e-mail with all the resources of the Web, assuming that a reader is connected to the Internet when reading the e-mail.

Depending on the software and capacity of the receiving computer, the e-mail and its enclosures can contain a full-color catalog, a video clip, or an entire infomercial. It can talk to listeners or even play music. It can print out a coupon to take to the store, a ticket to a movie or a concert, or an application form for a beauty contest or a research grant. (Sorry, it can't deliver your lunch or do your research project—yet!)

The Insight Company's e-Catalog service arranges to e-mail whole catalogs to customers of major merchandisers. The catalogs include color illustrations, real-time pricing and links to detailed product information and shopping pages. Recognizing that Internet companies should consider other direct-marketing media as well, they use direct mail and telephone calls to solicit e-mail addresses, product interests, and permission to send e-mails.

The applications to the music industry are enormous. Club customers can actually play a sample of a new recording and decide on the spot if they want to accept it, take an alternate or buy nothing. If they are in a hurry, they can download a single CD instantly. However the industry has serious concerns about the potential for fraud and piracy which have, as if this writing, not been resolved.

Creative

It seems most of the early users of e-mail have relied on curiosity, free services, contests or exuberant hard-sell messages to get responses. Early direct mail and DRTV did also.

This is changing for the better, as more experienced direct marketers and image-building agencies get involved in e-mail and the Internet. Just as most websites are "designed" with little evidence of creative writing, most e-mail communications have been written with little evidence of creativity in copy or design.

An e-mail message, to the extent it is intended to generate a response, should consider all the dos and don'ts and tricks of the trade of direct-mail copy and design. I will not repeat them here, except to suggest, to those who skipped ahead to this chapter, that they should go back now and read about positioning, copywriting and design.

What most e-mail writers seem to need are the discussions of personalization—not just using the recipient's name (which is not always available with e-mail) but making the message as specific and relevant as possible to the reader's interests.

Opt-in e-mail Lists

Elsewhere in this book I will write about the dark cloud of government restrictions and regulation which threatens not only the Internet but also all direct marketing. One aspect of this specifically relates to e-mail lists.

Despite the advanced educational level of Internet and e-mail users and the ease of deleting an unwanted message, legislators are threatening damaging new laws if direct marketers don't "self-regulate." The consequences of some impending legislation would close thousands of direct-marketing companies, cost the jobs of hundreds of thousands who work in our industry, and severely slash the revenue and the survivability of every postal service in the world. It is imperative that we follow the lead of the Direct Marketing Associations in our respective countries, follow reasonable privacy and "Do Not Mail or Call" suggestions, and support industry lobbying and political fund-raising requests.

The immediate application for e-mail is the need to use "opt-in" lists, meaning lists of people who have "stated and not rescinded their desire to receive the type of mail being sent." Most e-mailers are confining their sales efforts to so-called "opt-in" lists, but there are many interpretations as to what "opt-in" means exactly.

Some marketers use a very tight definition, and use their lists for only their own and affiliate's promotions. Some presume that permission to send their particular e-mail means they can make the list available to outside companies as well, sometimes by claiming that they are "partners" or "affiliates."

Other companies are specifically in the business of acquiring such permission, as well as specific information on the interests of each business or household. This is the e-mail equivalent of "survey names" discussed in the direct-mail chapter. Every renter and list user should establish the standard they believe is correct and verify the definition of opt-in used by list providers.

What is not an option is that every list-owner is obligated to disclose their policies at the time the name or e-mail address is acquired. For example, compare the privacy statements of Amazon (which really is one) and Yahoo (which tries to obfuscate the fact that their customer information is not private at all). It is just good business for consumers to know what information is being collected and how the information will be used, just as consumers have the right to "opt-out" of telemarketing and direct-mail lists.

WEBSITES AS PRINT MEDIA

The Internet was an advertising medium before it was a virtual retailer. But, as an advertising medium, it has been burdened with unrealistic expectations and unprofessional creative efforts.

Internet operators began with "impressions," as if an inch-high button or banner was somehow worth as much as a 7 × 10 inch page in a magazine or 10 seconds on television. It's not. At best, it's worth as much as similar small space advertising.

Then Procter & Gamble and other companies insisted on a different measurement. They would pay only if someone "clicked" on a banner and reached a P&G website. This quickly became a standard. Access companies, browser companies and popular websites such as those operated by local newspapers started to charge by the "click-through."

But this is somewhat like paying a radio station for generating calls, with no consideration given for how many of the calls are legitimate prospects and how many will result in sales.

With clicks as the standard of success, curiosity became the creative tactic of choice. "Win" or "Free" buttons and banners can generate clicks. But what are they really worth?

To stimulate these scores, designers use clever cartoons, waving flags, and morphing characters. One company is now adding sound to their banners—like a store "barker" calling to passers-by who are heading for another store down the block. This will be a new high (or is it low) point in advertising intrusiveness. Internet advertising was meant to be informational—selling by convenience. I predict that the introduction of loud unsolicited "commercials" will exceed the outrage created by e-mail "Spam" (unsolicited e-mails.)

Alliances

In many cases, it is not about "buying" space, but a matter of creating affiliations in which the website that is accessed pays a fee to the website that generated the link. These fees can be a percentage of sales. But, just as a magazine will charge extra for a cover position or a newspaper will charge for top of column or adjacency to specific editorial content, the proprietors of high-traffic portals, online services and Internet browsers charge premiums for the best locations.

For example, America Online, which controls access to 16 million members, collected $75 million dollars from e-Bay to be the lead auction-site for four years, $150 million from Tel-Save for a five-year preferential position as a long-distance provider, and $300 million from First USA for the credit-card category for five years.

These preferences show up on its home pages and browser searches.

Even Amazon.com collects a fee from publishers in return for preferential position when its books, authors or book subjects are searched for. Compaq's Alta Vista search engine leads off each search-results category not with the most popular or most relevant site as people might expect, but with the two highest bidders. The *Los Angeles Times* lists restaurants in the order of who bought the biggest ad on their CitySearch website. If you are looking for travel resources on the Yahoo! search engine, the first thing you'll see is "Travel Agent," which leads you to their paid "official" travel service. You have to scroll below their page to get to airlines or other non-affiliated travel agents.

Increasing Response Rates

It is interesting to note that some advertisers are complaining that click-through rates on banners have fallen to "only 1 percent or 2 percent" and so they are turning to mass e-mailings. For many propositions this is a respectable return-rate, provided that people are responding to an offer, not because of curiosity.

What too many Internet users are forgetting is that the key strength of the Internet, other than its convenience, is interactivity. In this regard the Internet is a pure direct-marketing medium, and therefore subject to all the experience of what makes people respond.

If we compare buttons and banners to envelopes, the parallels fall into place. Yes, you can get an envelope opened with curiosity or by promising rewards. But the best bet is to get it opened by appealing to the same interest or self-image that the product appeals to, and then following through with benefits, information and reasons to act now.

I note that web creative-directors seem to always be referred to as "web designers." Perhaps that's where the problem lies. Good direct-marketing communications, in any medium, must be *written* as well as *designed*.

The same kind of thinking that goes into a direct mailing or a coupon advertisement must go into every web ad. And the goal of that Internet ad must be a direct-marketing goal. Customers who have "noted," or "read some" of an ad—the Starch equivalent of a click-through—aren't the goal. It's customers who "responded." Consequently, the standard of measurement for web advertising should be nothing less than "Cost Per Response." (Starch is a research service used by magazine advertisers which measures how many readers of a magazine actually saw each advertisement.)

Conversion

Two-step direct marketing has always been limited by the time required to get the videotape or information kit to the prospect who has asked for it. The "joke" was that the typical direct responder mailed a request at the post office and then went home and looked in the mailbox to see if the answer was there. Customers barely tolerated that fulfillment embarrassment: "Allow 4-6 weeks for reply."

When most inquiries came in by mail, the expectation was that it would take at least several days for it to arrive. Now that most responses, at least in the U.S., come in by telephone, patience is an even rarer commodity. A frequent dilemma is whether to spend what it takes to send a big colorful 4-ounce booklet by first-class or standard mail. We usually advised our clients to compromise by immediately sending a brief response with basic information first class, followed by the bigger package sent a week or so later by bulk mail.

Phone follow-ups often indicated that when the package reached the customers, the people didn't remember it was something they had asked for, so we had to tell them, right on the envelope, "This is the information about XXX you asked for." This is obviously not a problem with referrals to a website.

One of my consulting projects for MCI involved studying "post-telemarketing follow-up." We noted what information was sent and when the customer received it—not only for competitive long-distance suppliers, but for other major direct marketers as well. There was an enormous difference in the formats, presentation, degree of personalization and ease of response in all of the packages. Most striking was the difference in timing, ranging from same-day responses by fax to three week responses by mail. When consumers' reactions were added in to our research study, it was clear that for most products the same-day response by fax or e-mail was far superior to a four-color brochure sent weeks later.

The only more desirable alternative seems to be an informed operator who can be reached without long waits. The phone is still the preferred way for customers to get dealer locations, product specifications or to place orders.

The best solution is to give the customer a choice of how to respond. Call this number (or send this card) for a catalog or free brochure has always been a staple of direct marketing. Now the website URL can be added as well. But it may not always help response rates.

Should You Always Give Your URL?

A referral to the website if fine *if* your customers write down the URL, have nothing better to do when they get on their computers, have no problem getting to the website, and if they maintain the impulse that got them interested in the first place! You wouldn't tell a broadcast viewer to wait and see your magazine ad. Direct-marketing common sense indicates that you shouldn't tell an imminent buyer to do anything except "Order Now!"

For now, only inbound phone and direct mail will give you the name and address you need to send a personalized follow-up or phone call to every respondent. You can't do that if all you have is their e-mail address. Half to two-thirds of the people who go to websites do not fill in the enrollment forms.

One important point! Referring someone to your website is appropriate *only* when soliciting an inquiry—when you are offering information and the website has all the selling power of your catalog or information kit. Do not use your website address in an ad or mailing asking for a mail order, subscription or continuity offer. It will very likely lower the number of net prospects, which will reduce your sales volume.

If I haven't gotten across the importance of immediacy—the idea that in direct marketing "later" means "never"—then you the reader and I the writer have both wasted our time. A phone number in or near a coupon is fine. You are giving the customer a faster response method than filling out a form and remembering to mail it. But adding a URL is going the opposite direction. You are saying, in effect, "Hold it! Don't order now. Instead go see how cleverly we designed our website and read some more."

A study by Response Marketing Group concluded that only 15 percent of magazine ads displayed their website URL prominently, compared to 34 percent who featured a toll-free telephone number.

CATALOGS

Website designers often compare the offering of merchandise or service over the Internet with opening a "virtual store." Groups of such stores are called "shopping malls" in the e-commerce industry, and there are many parallels to the real ones. However, it is safer and more profitable to look at these businesses from the perspective of mail-order catalogs.

A *directory-type catalog* is often an annual or quarterly. It is common in business and industrial use, and might include a manufacturer's total inventory or a complete list of spare parts. Examples include Warshawsky's auto parts and West Marine's lists of lines, pulleys and other boating supplies.

To use the store analogy, this type of catalog is like a 7 day/24-hour specialty store with everything one could possibly need. The only difference is that the store is not around the corner.

Home > Men's > Sport > Swim   << >>

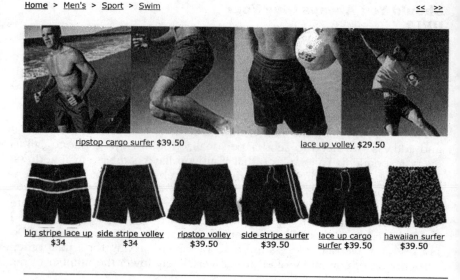

ripstop cargo surfer $39.50   lace up volley $29.50

big stripe lace up | side stripe volley | ripstop volley | side stripe surfer | lace up cargo | hawaiian surfer
$34 | $34 | $39.50 | $39.50 | surfer $39.50 | $39.50

Home > Men's > Sport > Swim > Lace up cargo surfer   << >>

Lace up cargo surfer

Quick-drying cotton/nylon. Unlined. Sits on hip. Velcro® fly and back pocket. 8 1/2" inseam. Imported. Machine washable.
24083CG $39.50.

Color ▼

Size ▼

1 Qty

OK

click for larger view

Figure 21-4. CATALOGS
Catalog companies can display categories of items (top), with links to a more detailed description and ordering information (bottom).

This type of catalog is a perfect fit for the Internet. It is available to new buyers of a product category—buyers who might not have known of the company before seeing them online. The web-page catalog can be updated daily, if not hourly. It can be accessed wherever the customer happens to be, given that he or she has Internet access. And, unlike paper catalogs, it doesn't represent a costly investment to make it available.

A *savings catalog* offers a limited selection at lower prices, sometime of off-brands or closeouts. Damark is a good example of this, as is Mac-Warehouse and other computer suppliers. If you're looking for the best price, it's handy to have this kind of catalog available.

A *boutique catalog* does not try to be the most complete or the cheapest. Instead it offers merchandise selected to appeal to a special interest. Examples would be a catalog of cigar or golf accessories, a catalog of left-handed tools, or a catalog of large size or petite clothing.

These catalogs depend on reaching the narrow audience that will appreciate their product. Often entrepreneurs open such a website counting on their customers to find them with search engines—an extension of the "better mousetrap" theory.

Catalog Access

Any type of website catalog has to be concerned with the Internet equivalent of street traffic. Just as regular stores need to be in a neighborhood where people come to find such a store, a website has to get a steady flow of traffic of viewers cruising by their site. It has to be visible and capable of being entered (linked) from the right "neighborhoods."

They say the three keys to success in real estate are location, location and location. This applies to the Internet as well. That's why access providers, browsers and popular sites are justified in charging (and advertisers in paying) for preferred positions.

After all, don't we pay print media to be on pages relevant to our product, or for top-of-page positions? Don't broadcast stations charge more for prime-time and desirable adjacencies? And, to use the retail store analogy, wouldn't you pay more for a "downstairs near the entrance" location in a shopping mall? Whether the commodity is audience, circulation or traffic, it's worth paying for.

On the other hand, yes, you can succeed in a lower-priced out-of-the-way location where you have to develop your own traffic. But your product or price must be so attractive that publicity and word-of-mouth will spread the word. Otherwise you must advertise heavily to bring in those customers.

Targeting

You may not save any money by restricting your message to a target audience, as a Website costs the same to build and maintain whether you make it available to a narrow audience or to the whole world. However, it must be targeted in a creative sense.

To use the store analogy again, if you were a brand new store opening on a main traffic street, would your sign just say "Smith & Co," or would it indicate what you sell—for example, "Antiques." As in every other form of direct marketing, your reader is impatient and will not bother to read the small type to figure out what you are selling. Too many banners seem more interested in getting clicks from curiosity than from real orders.

Immediacy

If everything is always at a discount, what's the incentive to buy now rather than later? The lack of "specials" or "sales" costs website marketers a substantial share of business. As long as they are making money, or living off the IPO (Initial Public Stock Offering), they aren't concerned. But attention should be given to why so many people access their site but don't buy. One survey indicates that two-thirds of customers who reach the Shopping Cart order-page don't complete their purchase.

Cross-Sell

Despite the use of the phrase "browser," the opportunity for impulse sales just doesn't compare with the retail shopping experience. Websites are great at making available an item you are looking for, but fail to attract people to "walk through the store." More attention should be given to creating incentives to browse on the Internet.

In fact, in some categories, total sales of products have gone down as the Internet share of the remaining sales increases. For example, one survey indicates overall book sales in the United States have gone down as Amazon.com's share has gone up. This is precisely due to the loss of the browsing factor. Any web marketer should attempt to replicate browsing, perhaps by adding links to pages with "our best-sellers" or "just in!" or "special values" sections of the site.

RELATIONSHIP-MARKETING

One of the most impressive functions of the Internet is its ability to provide a higher level of relationship-building, not only for customers obtained from websites but for any type of customer relationship.

For services or on-going accounts, it is a great convenience for the customer to be able to access status reports, billing information, lists of accessories, services or other information—whenever they want or wherever they are. The extreme example of this would be banking or investing, where the entire transaction and up-to-the-second statements can be accessed at will.

FedEx maintains a website that will look up zip codes, keep track of our customers' addresses, print out shipping labels, and call for a pick-up, as well as keeping track of shipments and bills.

Several Internet marketers build relationships by simply adding a simple "thank you." Others enroll customers into a "preferred" status that may entitle them to previews of new items, discounts, or other courtesies. Some effective benefits to steady customers may be Internet access to some type of game or entertainment, a private on-line newsletter, or a personal convenience such as a downloadable calendar program.

For most routine inquiries, it is much more economical to steer customers to website manuals or trouble-shooting sites. Fax-on-demand services are also used extensively, and are a desirable service for that segment of the market that doesn't use the Internet.

Customer Service

However, no system can anticipate every inquiry or every customer problem, so some type of phone or e-mail service is still needed to provide customer satisfaction.

Companies like General Electric and Procter & Gamble long ago chose to put customers first by building extensive customer service telephone systems. Any kind of question is handled by well-trained operators any time of day or night. Later they applied these lessons to their customer-service websites.

It is ironic that, so far, most Internet providers have been slow to supplement their interactive programs with easy access for the customer to initiate a dialog. It's almost like the customer is being told to "speak only when spoken to."

Zona Research reported that a survey of recent online shoppers indicated that 28 percent of them said that completing their purchase was "somewhat difficult" or "extremely difficult." A survey by NFO Interactive surveyed 2300 consumers, and more than one-third said they had made an on-line purchase, but would have bought more if they could communicate with a company representative while they were shopping. And 14 percent said they had never made an online purchase, but would if they could contact a representative by e-mail or phone.

Need for Research

Relationship-building programs must begin with understanding the Internet user.

All the tools of modern face-to-face research are called for. One-on-one interviews. Focus panels. Telephone interviews. The needs and attitudes of active customers must be identified and compared with marginal prospects or non-buyers.

But don't make the mistake of relying on Internet questionnaires, even about Internet use. You need trained interviewers to let people free-associate and answer the questions you didn't think to ask. You need to read emotions and degrees of enthusiasm (or complaint) to draw reliable conclusions.

For example, one trade association sends out inquiries on how many companies use the Internet for various purposes, asking for details in more than a dozen questions. Not surprisingly, they report positive trends in the 90% range. But most recipients don't respond at all! The non-respondents include those people who simply don't care or who are embarrassed to admit they haven't done anything yet!

On more than one occasion I have arranged for phone follow-ups to question non-respondents and have always, without exception, found their attitudes to differ from the respondents.

Once you have decided what will work, use all media to promote it, not just electronic media. For example, if you have a catalog of premiums, print and mail it to your customers as well as posting it as part of your website.

GETTING STARTED

There are many sources for help if you are a large company committed to building and promoting a professional website. Equipment and software manufacturers such as Microsoft, Sun and Oracle will not only sell you what you need but will also provide advice and service so it all works together. IBM has a department called E-commerce Services that can handle a program that includes everything from website-design strategy to hosting to management, anywhere in the world.

Virtually every advertising agency—large and small— worldwide has either a subsidiary or an associate that serves their clients' Internet needs. *Business Marketing* magazine reported that the costs of developing a full site were averaging between $78,000 for a smaller site to $440,000 for a larger one. A different survey indicated that most customized e-commerce sites cost more than a million dollars.

For a simpler start-up, you can hire a smaller consulting or design firm for much less than the figures in the previous paragraph. My own firm, TeamNash, charges development fees closer to $15,000–25,000 for strategic and marketing planning and the same for executing copy, design and graphics. But if you have some design and writing talent, go ahead and do it yourself to get started. You can always bring in the professionals after you know your business idea is viable.

There are also some very substantial independent website developers who will work with agencies or directly to create solutions beyond the ordinary. Three I have worked with are Rare Medium's Joshua Glantz, Andy Pakula of Orb Communication and Fergus O'Daly of Fergus O'Daly Associates.

Starting Small

Most newcomers out-source the essentials, so they can concentrate on the basics of product and promotion without getting tangled up in computer technology.

However, the do-it-yourselfer can get started with a modest investment in equipment, software and training. A dedicated PC or Macintosh will do just fine. Even the $1200 iMac can handle thousands of hits and hundreds of orders per day. Web-server software will cost under $500. There are plenty of computer books available that can instruct those technically inclined, or consultants can be hired on a temporary basis.

The Internet-dedicated phone line or other Internet connection will be an additional expense—the largest one. A regular analog phone line can cost no more than an additional line for a fax machine and is very inexpensive in the United States because most phone companies charge a flat rate for service. But the analog connection is only adequate for an *informational* home page, not an Internet service that will be providing e-commerce transactions. A more expensive digital connection like ISDN, T-1 or DSL is necessary—and even ISDN may be considered too slow. Prices for a T-1 line can run in the thousands for the initial set-up fees and routers, and anywhere between $700 to $1300 for monthly service.

Symetric DSL with a high bandwidth is a new substitute for the T-1 lines and can be less expensive, but an adequate set-up will still require some heavy costs. As of this book's writing, DSL service in midtown Manhattan costs include an installation fee of between $300–$500, a router between $700–$1000 for purchase or $30/month or more for a rented one, and monthly services that run between $300–$600/month, depending upon the amount of bandwidth needed. (Bandwidth is another way to describe the number of bits/second that can be transferred via the various telecommunication technologies. A good e-commerce site needs a "high" bandwidth of at least "one meg," or the capability of transmitting 1 megabit—1 million bits—per second.) Some DSL services may cost less, but make sure the bandwidth is adequate for your needs. And remember, both T-1 and DSL can take weeks or even months to install, and are not available in all areas.

On the other extreme, you can simply hook up with a shopping "mall" and let them handle it all for you. Yahoo's store, for instance, requires less than $300 in start-up fees and the same amount in monthly fees for up to 25 items. You can design it yourself from home with the help of step-by-step prompts. Your site will also be listed in their shopping area, which will produce some visitors at no extra cost.

The most popular solution is to use a hosting service and a shopping cart service and let them handle it all. MindSpring will set up a 100-product site for $50 and a $100 a month fee. Sitematic in San Diego charges $40 a month to host up to 20 products. IBM's "Home Page Creator" starts at just $39.95 a month for a 50-item site, with free setup.

For most services, you will have to purchase shopping cart software or hook up with a shopping cart service like CheckItOut for about $40 a month.

Other expenses will be the cost of registering a domain name, various software costs and account fees from your bank. Don't forget that credit-card charges will take between 2–4 percent of your gross income. Credit-card companies charge more for e-commerce transactions, claiming a higher risk for Internet sales.

One option for a small business that expects significant sales and intends to build ongoing customer relationships is IBM's Start Now program. The program leases hardware and software, and provides set-up and consulting services for $1,100–$2,000 a month.

BUILDING AN AUDIENCE

Whether you are starting big or starting small, you still have to get people to visit your website. The size of your budget will be different, but the options are similar—here are several: publicity, search engines, affiliations, Web advertising, print and broadcast advertising, and direct mail.

Publicity

A newspaper or magazine article, or a mention on a news program, is worth a small fortune in free advertising. You should send a press release to the dozens of computer magazines and special sections of newspapers that can help you reach Internet enthusiasts.

But your emphasis should be on the publications that appeal to the same interest as your site does. Want to reach parents? Investors? Fashion-conscious women? Create a list of relevant media and go after them with news-releases, personal visits, and press parties. Or, better yet, hire a professional public relations agent to do it for you.

Don't forget websites of relevant subjects! They are the competition. But there's room for all of you to succeed. Offer reciprocal promotions. You plug them, they plug you. You carry their ad, they carry yours. Competing magazines do this all the time.

Search Engines–Finding Your Page

Approximately 75 percent of Internet users navigate the Web with search engines or Yahoo! (Yahoo! is actually an *index* created by people, versus a search engine that complies lists by computer.) If you're not one of a category's top-ten search results, you're finished anyway. Few people have the patience to keep scrolling and clicking for the next group of ten, and the next one, and the next one. . . .

In the early days of the Internet, anybody who actually had a web page was easy to locate with a search engine. A candy shop in Sacramento didn't have to do too much work in 1995 to get Internet exposure, since searching with the key word "candy" brought up a list of less than a hundred sites. Type the word "candy" into AOL's "Netfind" search engine today and the number of sites listed is 113,271. (Yahoo, which is edited by humans, shows the most relevant—or the highest paying—18 sites.) So how does someone on the Internet get to be at the beginning of AOL's list, or get on Yahoo's list at all?

The key is a general understanding of how search engines work to create their lists. A search engine will go onto the web and stops at each page. These parts of the search engine process that investigate the pages are often called "spiders," since they "crawl" along "strands" of the web to each page. Once on the page, the spider collects the page title, content summary and key words from coding called "meta-tags." The spider also collects the first 25 words or so of the text from the page. All of this information is then

Figure 21-5. TYPICAL SEARCH ENGINE PAGE
Note that the page can do word or sentence searches, in a variety of languages, and give the options for specialty and category searches.

stored with the search engine. If a particular word is found a number of times within this information, the search engine will rank it "high" when the search results are displayed.

For example, if the page titled Bob's *Candy* Store says that the store stocks thousands of different types of *candy* in its page description, includes the word *candy* as a meta-tag, then mentions the word *candy* in the first 25 words on the site, chances are that a search engine will rank Bob's Candy Store high—given that two thousand other candy stores haven't done exactly the same thing.

You can do some of the search-engine spiders' work for them. Table 21-3 is a list of the submission pages for some of the top search engines. You can go to these URLs and provide the company with information about

TABLE 21-3
WEB ADDRESS FOR SUBMISSION PAGES OF POPULAR SEARCH
ENGINES

Alta Vista	http://www.altavista.com/av/content/addurl.html
AOL Netfind	http://www.aol.com/netfind/info/addyoursite.html
Excite	http://www.excite.com/info/add_url
HotBot	http://www.hotbot.com/addurl.asp
Infoseek	http://www.infoseek.go.com/AddUrl?pg=submitUrl.html
LookSmart	http://www.looksmart.com/aboutus/devcenter/subsite.html
Lycos	http://www.lycos.com/addasite.html
Northern Light	http://www.northernlight.com/docgurl_help.html
Snap	http://www.snap.com/main/help/item/0,11,-8450,00.html
WebCrawler	http://www.webcrawler.com/info/add_url/
Yahoo!	http://www.yahoo.com/info/suggest/

your site. Yahoo! actually has people looking at and reviewing sites (versus the computerized search engines), and an invitation to view a site might get a faster response than just waiting for them to find it.

When writing the text for a web page, *get to the point quickly.* Brainstorm what search words a potential customer might put into a search engine to find your site, and use those words in the title, description, meta tags and the first 25 words on the site. Don't "back in" to your subject. This isn't a brochure, it's a web page. There's plenty of other places to describe your product or service in detail on the page. I prefer a short and sweetly written homepage with links to different detailed aspects of the product or service.

Don't think that writing a description of "Candy, candy and more candy" will put your candy-store page at the top of a search-engine list, either. More likely you'll be dumped from it altogether. Search-engine companies have gotten smart and programmed their software to avoid just this type of stacking. A clearly written description and tight list of keywords will serve you much better.

And another hint: search-engine spiders cannot read the text in a graphic. They can only read the HTML text. Don't put your key points only into a logo, graphic, or even an HTML table or frame on the page, because a search engine will not find them. Check with your web-page designer and ask whether these important elements are in plain HTML. And put all links to other pages on the bottom of your page. It's nice to provide information for your viewers, but you don't want someone else's page to be considered part of your content.

Domain and URL Names

A small business can get started by arranging with one of the larger portals to host their site, using a name such as Newcompany@Yahoo.com. However, this will not enable them to build a brand identity. They have no protection from a competitor using a name like Newcompany@Earthlink.com. Most Internet enterprises begin with registering their own domain name, which is actually very easy and inexpensive.

Originally Networksolutions.com had a franchise from the U.S. Federal government to register .com, .net and .org names. Other designations, such as .edu, .gov, .mil and .us, were registered through other sources. Competition is now permitted and new companies, such as register.com, now offer the same service. You simply go to their website and enter the name you want. Within seconds you learn if it is available and you can register it for as little as $70—if you already have an Internet service provider. Or you can pay about $250 for your name plus enough services to get a simple site "on the air." If you deal with a total site hosting service, they will arrange to register the name, but it is not always included in their fees. Ask.

If the name is taken, you can click to learn who owns it, their address and e-mail contact, when it was registered, and when it was last active. You may be able to buy this name from the original owner if they are not using it actively.

If you are planning to go global, you may want to register your name in other countries, which may be the same name (if still available) but with a uk (England), or similar designation, replacing the .com. Different countries have different systems. Brazil has a very sensible one—in addition to names for commercial, organization, educational and other categories; they have them for personal, dentists, lawyers, retailers, and many other categories, expanding the supply of names while helping to identify the type of business.

It will help if the domain name you choose is easy to remember and indicates what you're selling. Mnemonic names, such as used for toll-free 800 numbers, are the right choice. If possible, use the same one. For instance, 1-800-Flowers is the same company as www.800flowers.com. If possible, imply a benefit too. Examples: Any CD, OmniTalent, 1800Healthy or ValueAmerica. You will want to register your own domain name so that you are not tied to one Internet service provider. You will also want to register similar URLs and link them to your site—for example, any-cd or anycd@aol—for the potential customers who get your URL *almost* right.

Affiliations

Make deals with other websites. Help refer customers to them, and vice versa. Sometimes you can each position the other's services as a benefit. Or you can pay a fee for each contact that comes to your site from theirs. Computers that are linked through the Internet are all "talking" to each other, and the links and click-throughs can be recorded and tracked. An Internet host knows which computer was the last one contacted.

Usually you display your banners on a website and let affiliates choose what they want to display. They will use their own unsold space when it is available, and select banners that they think fits their own image. You may want to stay in control, and be able to restrict what websites your banner appears on, especially if you are concerned with image or creditworthiness.

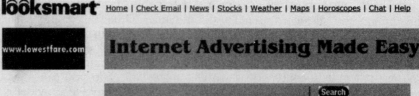

**1-1 category matches for ""Direct Marketing in Japan""
from LookSmart**

World - Work & Money - Business - Int'l Business - Countries &
Regions - Asia - Countries H-L - **Japan**

**1-1 site matches for ""Direct Marketing in Japan"" from
LookSmart**

US **Marketing in Japan**
Article covering the use of distribution channels, agents,
franchising, **direct marketing**, licensing, and joint ventures.
From LookSmart category - ... - Countries H-L - **Japan**

**1-8 matches for ""Direct Marketing in Japan"" from the
entire Web**

"Direct Marketing in Japan" - the direct web address for company or
product names from RealNames.

Direct Marketing in Japan
The Challenge With a population of 125 million people and the
highest per capita income, **Japan** is the most sought-after market
in the world. Companies...
Size 3K - 08-May-98

Direct Marketing in Japan
Now's the time to enter the Japanese market! **Direct marketing in
Japan** is currently undergoing rapid growth. Read this book and
find out how to succeed **in**.
Size 3K - 08-May-98

WELCOME TO DM **IN JAPAN**!
.. WELCOME TO OUR SITE! The **Japan Direct Marketing**
Association. Japanese page is here. .. *ABOUT US (THE **JAPAN
DIRECT MARKETING** ASSOCIATION) New President.
Size 8K - 05-Apr-99

Japanlist.html
Recommended Reading List: **Japan**. I. General Background.
Learning to Bow, Bruce S. Feiler. Ticknor & Fields, 1991. **In** this

Figure 21-6. SEARCH ENGINE RESULTS
Even with the bulk of the page showing search results, there is still a banner ad available. The
search engine first returned category matches from its databanks, then sites from the search
engine databanks. Finally the results from the entire web are displayed.

One suggestion: make long term deals with other companies while they're starting up. Later on, some other company may be willing to pay millions of dollars for a priority position that can shut you out. Or some access or search-engine company may decide to go into the same business you're in.

Internet deals are being made with all the finesse of a 19th century robber baron so don't count on a handshake or a simple confirming letter. Business is business, so let your lawyer draw up the deal.

Web Advertising

Certainly look at websites that are likely to give you the audience you need, but avoid paying card rates. List price and card rates are obsolete terms. You will probably save money by dealing with an agency that specializes in Internet-media placement.

Print and Broadcast Advertising

You'll want to use any appropriate media to let people know what you have to offer and why they should access your website. Certainly many companies are doing this. *Marketfacts* reported that 62 percent of web users say they have visited a site because they saw it mentioned in a print ad, while 53 percent say a TV spot referred them.

One of the best users of print advertising is ValueAmerica, which gives specific examples of products and prices they offer. They started with full pages and some spectacular offers on computers, then gradually introduced the rest of their product line in smaller space. Their ads always list the impressive array of brands they carry.

On the other hand, early Amazon and Barnes & Noble ads seemed more interested in their comparative claims on how many titles they carry. Both were lacking any motivation for the consumer to visit their site, and no reason at all for potential customers to do it immediately.

Still other advertisers run space ads, but treat them as if they were the kind of curiosity web-banner ads I mentioned and criticized earlier. Readers have no idea what the site contains, are offered no benefits and no motivation to spend time finding it.

Direct Mail

Just as direct mail remains the precision tool of direct marketing, so it has the greatest potential for building traffic on a website or attracting buyers to an online retailer.

Skeptics should keep in mind the virtual flood of free CDs from AOL and other Internet access companies that built those franchises in the first place.

Let's look at some of the opportunities:

- *For specialty sites,* there is no better way to reach people with specific interests. The entire world of response lists and compiled lists is available, usually by the millions. Though some can be reached through e-mail, most households are likely to be identifiable only by mailing address and phone number. While there are a growing number of e-mail user lists, including opt-in names, they usually lack the quantities or the detailed segmentation available to traditional direct mail lists.

- *For lifestyle sites,* the whole world of new parents, newlyweds and new home-owners is available and is constantly being replenished.

- *For narrow interests,* not only do you have a wealth of response lists for most subjects, but you can "sponsor" a question on a survey mailing (discussed in Chapter 14 on mailing lists) for any subject you want. Most survey compilers will (or should be) adding a request for phone numbers and e-mail addresses, giving you access that way if you prefer not to use the mail.

- *For business and professional sites,* here too the mailing list availability far outweighs the access possibilities within the web itself. If you only reach people who are already using the web, you are only fighting for share of market. If you go to "outside" direct mail lists, you will not only be getting your share, but also helping to expand the market at the same time. If you are the first source of news about a benefit available on the Internet, you will automatically get that new user at a more cost-effective price than getting someone to switch from a competitive site.

- *For mass markets,* such as anyone who buys books, or clothing, you will still get better responses by reaching people who are accustomed to ordering such items by mail or phone. The willingness to order "by mail" will produce an Internet customer faster than someone who prefers to shop and browse in a retail store.

- *For imminent buyers,* such as for autos or moving services, survey names will reveal buying intentions of millions of prospects. Even a non-Internet user will find a way to reach your autos for sale site if you explain the benefits.

- *For local traffic.* If you are selling in one neighborhood or one city, all the same tools are available, except on a geographic basis. Internet services such as CitySearch and Flycast will let you buy advertising on websites or services that provide information for the local area. Local news and weather sources are also local. Consider city magazines for upscale audiences. Remember that many magazines have city or regional editions, and many newspapers have area or neighborhood editions. Direct mail is available for any local area, as is telemarketing. Local radio and television can also be effective.

CREATIVE TACTICS

No matter what medium you use to attract readers to your website, you should read and re-read the sections on Propositions and Creative Tactics in Chapters 6 and 9. The "web designers" artistic needs aside, you are "selling" and not "entertaining." And you are asking for an action, not building awareness to influence the next time you are at the store. Even the super-modern technology-rich Internet is not immune from the A-B-Cs of Direct Marketing 101. Let's review a few basics:

Attention. Stop the people you want to reach with words or a picture targeted to their interests.

Interest. Involve them with some fascinating news-worthy advantage or site feature.

Desire. Elaborate on the benefits. What will it do for you? How will it enhance your self-image?

Action. Give the reader a reason to act now rather than later. Make it easy to recall the URL or give them an incentive to access your site immediately. Some examples:

- The first 100 people to access our site and enter this code name will get a box of floppy disks or a free tote bag. (Yes, tote bags work even on Internet offers.)
- The special price shown in the ad/mailing is only good until the sale ends on (date).
- Click on this symbol on our site before (date) and you can win . . .

Impressions

If your objective is not immediate action, but getting people to use your site next time they have a need for some type of information or service, then you need the tricks of the trade for image-building direct mail. Some of the most obvious ones are a refrigerator magnet with your URL, a sticker to put on a rolodex card, a mouse pad, a pencil or notepad.

You can offer more elaborate items as free gifts or with a slight fee for mailing. A small calculator, a set of novelty stickers, and a CD-ROM with royalty-free clip art are some examples. Other items like a clever screensaver or fun freeware can be down-loaded and delivered instantly, perhaps in return for an enrollment.

Tracking Responses

Of course you want to know which creative treatments and which advertising buys worked best for you. With internet advertising, the "cookie" can tell you which website the respondent was using before he or she went to yours.

(Cookies are small programs that are downloaded from the Internet when users go to certain sites. The downloads are quick—they take a couple of seconds.)

Most cookies are information packets that just let the website have access to the web browser's history list—the listing of which URLs the browser has viewed. Others can actually be dangerous—like viruses—or can give other websites access to tons of information in your computer. Most Internet software gives you the ability to refuse or erase "cookies," but some e-commerce sites will then refuse to take your order—another example of putting "research" ahead of salesmanship.

In most direct marketing, we can use "department numbers" or "extensions" as key codes. It's more complicated on the Internet. A cookie can tell you which site was in use prior to yours, but not which version of your ad or offer was on that site. For on-line advertising, you can simply use a unique link to a page or to a "pointer site" which counts the response and automatically forwards it.

For off-line media, you are in the same situation as a phone number in a national TV spot. The customer must be prompted to give you the equivalent of a "department" or "extension" number. For our Internet clients, for off-line traffic building in print or broadcast, we use an "offer code" which must be entered to "get this special offer" (or premium). In e-mail and direct mail, we usually include a card or sticker with a unique number which not only identifies the media and message but the individual to whom it was addressed. It is positioned as a special access code, and must be entered to gain the benefit of the site.

A LONGER-RANGE VIEW

I mentioned earlier that the Internet is not an island, or an isolated space station. It is a media and a communication tool available to men and women all over the world—some technologically proficient and some not, some affluent and some not, some patient and some not.

As the Internet becomes easier and faster to use it will reach larger numbers and an even wider range of needs and interests. It may be as easy to use as making a phone call or turning on a TV set. As the Internet evolves from a fad for technology addicts into a mass communications tool, things will change. Not all the changes will be good for today's Internet entrepreneurs.

For one thing, there will be more competition—not just for viewers but for access to the best portals and search engines. Already many preferred locations are being tied up in multi-million dollar deals. For another, reality will set in with the investment community. All it will take is one major downturn to scare off the speculators in Internet stocks and drive the remaining investors back to bonds and blue chips.

Companies are trying to justify investor confidence by going after "share" or sales volume. A study by e-retail trade group shop.org, reported in *Internet World,* reveals that e-commerce retailers spend an average of 76% of their revenue on acquiring more customers, compared to 3.5% by traditional retailers in brick-and-mortar locations. Average customer acquisition costs are 1.5 to 2.5 times the *gross* amount of the total order! A study by Jupiter Communications notes that the average health and beauty products order is $30 to $60, but the online merchant spent $60 to $90 to attract the sale. The average clothing order is less than $80, but the cost to acquire the customer is $100 to $120! How many repeat orders will be needed to make these transactions profitable?

Direct marketers have always "bought" customers this way, and it is certainly possible that additional sales and profits will follow the initial one. But when? For their sake, and for the sake of the wonderfully optimistic investors who made the Internet's rapid expansion possible, I hope it is before the following aspects of reality set in:

Novelty. How popular will they be when they're not the newest "killer app" (application)?

Exclusivity. How will they do when more and more sites "rip off" their unique idea?

Ad Rates. As more companies compete for preferred positions and advertising locations, rates will go up. Who will benefit? Who will be hurt?

Proliferation. As more and more companies compete for the buyer's attention, will response rates hold up? Will cutomers remain loyal? It will be more and more difficult to provide "the world's largest selection" and "the world's largest discounts" at the same time.

Competition. A handful of giants will dominate each Internet subcategory, and it will more difficult for newcomers to break in. It will be more difficult to build a business relying on the Internet alone.

INTEGRATING THE INTERNET

One direct marketing maxim says "To reach all your customers, you must use all distribution channels." That's why department stores went into the catalog business and catalogers opened retail outlets. It is also why those Internet companies—having stumbled into the direct-marketing world to make use of a technological marvel—will find that their inventory, their fulfillment systems, and their customer service staff can be used more efficiently if they add additional media that will reach additional markets.

Your competitors, who have been using traditional media for years, are adding the Internet as another option for their customers. Shouldn't the E-commerce folks add traditional media?

Another business maxim revolves around the question "What business are you really in? The railroad business or the transportation business? The newspaper business or the advertising sales business? Today's Internet purists will face the question sooner or later, and many of them will discover that, after all, they are in the direct-marketing business.

WELCOME TO REALITY

Having just returned from the 1999 Internet World Conference, I can understand why the technology innovators and entrepreneurs in this exciting world see themselves as pioneers on the leading edge of communications and commerce. Many of the people I spoke to, though, seemed to think that they were operating on a different planet. To them, there *was* no prior marketing experience, no need for other communications options, no appreciation of the idea that there will always be customers who prefer to drive to the mall or place their order by mail or phone. In the midst of today's Internet "high," it is understandable that one executive would even question if the post office will always be needed.

I've seen such euphoria before—on behalf of database marketing, infomercials, and telemarketing. At one point a colleague predicted that "one day all advertising will be direct marketing." But direct marketing (and all its sub-specialties), while growing, eventually encountered reality and took its place as just one of the many tools of marketing—so will the Internet. Its specialists are very welcome to join us. When the chaos calms, they will find we are still here, still working to perfect our crafts, and that mutual respect and cooperation will turn out to be the ultimate "killer app."

GOING GLOBAL

It wasn't too many years ago that the "adventure" for many businesses was "going direct." Despite fears of reprisals from retailers and mistakes due to not respecting the differences between direct response and other forms of advertising, more and more companies got their feet wet. Now, where it was once rare to find a major corporation selling by mail order or a major agency offering direct-response services, today it is rare to find one that isn't.

Global marketing is in that first stage today. Yes, there are some direct-marketing programs that have successfully expanded internationally, but the great majority of direct marketers act as if their market ends at their borders. As international consulting represents more than half of Team-Nash's current activity I frequently meet executives who have been innovators within their home country, but who express absolute fear at crossing borders. Perhaps this is some kind of genetic impression left over from the days when our ancestors expected to fall off the edge of the Earth if they went too far.

ONE WORLD, ONE MARKET

It is no longer news that the Earth is round, and that our friends in Australia are not hanging from it upside down. The headline today is that most borders are only lines on a map for marketers—simply marketing inconveniences that can usually be dealt with one way or another.

Today most people in the world have similar needs and aspirations. They have access to impressions about the food, clothing, lifestyles, and cultures of the rest of the world. They read newspapers, watch television, read their mail and surf the web. In some countries they use technology to a much larger extent than in the United States.

Some regions are better off economically than others, some countries have citizens who are more or less educated, and some nations' citizens speak different languages than the others—just like within the United States! Go to Argentina, India or Thailand and you'll see denim jeans with both the Levi's and Calvin Klein logos. Go to Japan, Brazil and Russia and you'll hear the same songs that are on the Billboard charts here. Make a list of the products and services sold by direct marketing, and you'll find very few differences from those sold in the United States.

And in the United States, you'll see the store windows filled with Godiva chocolates and Sony electronics, with fashions from France, designs from Italy, cutlery from Germany, and electronics from Japan. Go to a toy store or a mass-market clothing store and try to find a product that isn't made in China, often at near-zero labor costs in that country's prisons and army bases.

Yes, of course there are creative differences. And of course you must know which media work best and what lists are available. But just as you solved these mysteries in your home country, the resources exist to do it in other countries as well.

The rule of thumb today is that international markets can represent twice the sales and profits that a direct-marketing company can realize in the United States! As of 1998, it is estimated that U.S. direct marketers are doing over 4.7 billion dollars in sales in foreign markets—three fourths with business products such as computers.

A general rule of thumb is that the worldwide potential for most businesses is twice that of a company's U.S. sales. This is especially relevant for mature businesses that have rolled-out to their logical markets and are struggling to find more responsive media or creative approaches. It's somewhat like scraping the bottom of an over-explored gold mine when there are two unworked mines nearby.

It may not be easy to go global, but it's certainly worth the trouble.

The Statistics Trap

The first step is to read between the lines of statistics. Yes, only a tenth of the middle-class households in India can afford a television set. But that adds up to 33 million households! In China, the number of households is even more astounding—a whopping 75 million. If VCR ownership is only 10 percent of these television owners, that's still seven and a half million video machines!

Yes, only one out of ten homes in Brazil has a telephone. But there are millions carrying cellular phones, and millions more waiting six to twelve months to have a normal analog phone installed. In Brazil, it is not a problem of demand but of supply, which is why the world's telephone companies bid hundreds of millions for a chance to help fill these needs when the national telecommunications industry was privatized in 1998. An impressive 30 percent of the telecommunications services in the country are provided by foreign companies. "Problems are opportunities in disguise!"

In Singapore, more than half the homes have a personal computer—a larger percentage than in the United States! What's important is not how much people make, but how much they spend and what they spend it on. The term "average consumer" is meaningless.

The Internet Factor

Another stimulus to the growth of international direct marketing is the worldwide reach of the Internet. We helped one company set up a modest commercial site. Their first offering was a Leatherman multi-purpose tool. With no special effort, 30 percent of the first week's orders came from other countries. We later increased the percentage even more by providing an international phone number for inquiries and customer service. (A US toll-free 800, 888 or 877 number can't be dialed by foreign customers.)

Any offer you make on the web can be reached by any Internet user in the world, and vice versa. All the software and service providers have set up marketing units in other countries. Often, the "better mousetrap" which is not particularly new or well priced in one country is particularly attractive in another.

As great as the "spillover" potential is, there is even more business awaiting those who use the Internet in another country with the local language and local media. For example, Brazil's Universe Online or UOL (www.uol.com.br) has a larger share (80 percent) of Internet users in the Brazilian market than America's America Online has in the U.S. (54 percent). As of December 1998, they were racking up 300 million page-views per month.

Expansion by Acquisition

One way to take advantage of global markets is, if you can afford it, to simply buy companies in other countries. Although the investors have not blessed international expansion with the same zeal as the Internet, it remains a great opportunity for those companies who have the resources or can raise the money.

Germany's Otto Versand bought Spiegel and Eddie Bauer. France's Redout owns the Lerner catalog. Bertelsmann bought some of America's largest and most famous direct marketers, including Doubleday and RCA Victor (now BMG Music).

At one time it was easier for foreign companies to buy U.S. companies than the reverse because of U.S. tax law, most notably the treatment of "good will"—the difference between the book value of a company and the price paid for it because of other assets. The real-market value of a company may be augmented by the value of a brand name or the loyalty of a customer list, but U.S. companies were not permitted to treat it as an asset until 1993. When Congress changed the tax law in 1993, American companies breathed a sigh of relief and started treating good-will characteristics as real assets, putting them on equal footing with their foreign counterparts.

Advertising agencies, while sharing the same accounting limitation, have been more willing to purchase direct marketing and other agencies in other countries. Certainly Young & Rubicam's Wunderman, Omnicom's Rapp & Collins and Interpublic's Relationship Marketing have been very aggressive in doing so. But the agency business has considerations that its clients don't necessarily share. For one, an agency often must have a capability in a particular country in order to provide full service to a multi-national account. Despite the possible lack of immediate profitability of the new subsidiary, it may need the new office to hold on to its very profitable business in the U.S. or elsewhere. Also, with direct-marketing talent still scarce, they have to buy the agency to get the skills and reputation of the local expert.

Buy or Build?

While American ad agencies and foreign marketing companies have been achieving their global potential through acquisition, other types of companies have been building their foreign resources rather than buying them.

Publishers.   Time-Life Books and Reader's Digest are all operating in a score of countries. They not only sell translations of U.S. books and programs, but also develop products that are unique to some of the countries.

Catalogers.   Neiman-Marcus, Saks Fifth Avenue and Victoria's Secret have all successfully expanded their markets overseas.

Continuity Businesses.   A model of efficient international expansion for a continuity marketer is International Masters Publishing, a Swedish marketer of card programs such as My Great Recipes or MasterChef. They took their Swedish card programs and adapted them to one country after another. They not only changed marketing material to fit each country, but also revised the product to fit national tastes. When I helped this company enter the U.S. market, International Masters Publishing was in only four or five European countries. Today they are all over the world.

To enter the U.S. market, they brought over one editor and one marketing manager. Then they hired an ad agency, a fulfillment house, and a food photographer. Their unique laminated cards were produced and packaged in Sweden, shipped here in bulk, and then fulfilled by a local U.S. company. I doubt that their start-up costs were in excess of $200,000, yet their profits today must be in the millions.

Universality

Interwood, a Canadian infomercial company, has tapped world markets through licensing. They test new products in Canada and roll out the successful ones into the United States. Once the effectiveness of the product and the commercials are established, they arrange for companies in other countries to translate the scripts, dub in the local language and place the spots on local television. It is rare for a commercial that is successful in the U.S. to fail in other markets, as long as local traditions and customs are adhered to in the ad.

Two of my international clients, Oak Lawn in Japan and Sprayette in Argentina, built their business on imported products. Today they handle products from many countries and also develop their own products.

In television, print, mail or on the Internet, products that have been successful in one country have a high probability of being successful all over the world. There are exceptions, of course, and they usually occur when not enough thought has been given to adapting the advertising to local needs. For example, one international infomercial company bought time on one of Brazil's largest station for a product that did particularly well in Europe. Someone decided to economize and use the same commercial that they ran in Portugal, not knowing that there is a world of difference (particularly in pronunciation) between European Portuguese and the softer, more melodic Brazilian Portuguese. The commercial failed miserably. Later interviews indicated that there was no problem understanding the offer, but that people were offended by what appeared to be a lack of respect for their language. Most Brazilians can understand Spanish as well, but I recommend not using Spanish in Brazil for the same reason.

The products in these cases are the same in every country, and range from steam irons and paint rollers to miracle mops and exercise equipment. These are products that were designed for the mail-order market and have some universal benefits. But worldwide marketing has a unique advantage for any product or service, even those which are sold in retail stores in their home country.

"Leap-Frog Marketing"

Global direct-marketing is not only a logical step for products sold direct in the home country, but is often the simplest way for any company to open new international markets. The term *leapfrog marketing* is from a speech I have given in a half-dozen countries and which has generated enormous interest. It refers to a "leapfrog," a type of amphibian noted for its jumping ability, and is used here to suggest leaping over borders by using direct marketing to open a new market, whether the final goal is a direct-marketing or retail business. In Argentina it became a lead story in the major business newspaper.

For a manufacturer to enter another market there are several obstacles that must be overcome. One is the prejudice of the purchasing agent at the retail outlets, who are generally not as open to new designs, new products or new vendors as consumers. Often our focus panels indicate an enthusiastic reception from potential customers, but a long list of negatives from retailers. They are concerned with the ability to get reorders, with a need for credit (often called "dating" of invoices), and with their relationships with their tried-and-true present suppliers. For the manufacturer or distributor, overcoming these objections requires free merchandise, co-op allowances, return privileges, couponing, shelf-stocking allowances, and other inducements. What it really means is buying your way onto the retailers' shelves.

Even if this obstacle is overcome, there is the "pipeline" problem. Let's say a Canadian company wants to enter the U.S. market, which is ten times the size of Canada. To advertise in national media, the company needs national distribution. To get national distribution it has to produce typically ten times the amount as in their home country. This can be a daunting task. But to distribute the same product in the United States by any direct-marketing technique, the company simply has to produce enough of the product to support whatever size mail or print or television campaign the company's marketing team chooses to use. The company is in control of the investment it chooses to make and the speed at which it chooses to roll out distribution. And since direct marketing has split-testing capability, the best positioning, pricing and creative offers can be determined with negligible extra expense.

Not only is downside risk reduced, but there is also a huge bonus in free advertising when a product is distributed by mail order. (See Table 22-1.) Note that when the product is distributed in a traditional manner, the manufacturer might allocate perhaps 10 percent of their wholesale income to advertising. In this example, the 10 percent equals only $50,000, which is not enough to make any real impact or build any brand awareness through general advertising.

But in direct marketing, the *entire* retail mark-up is used for advertising and creating brand awareness while building the initial acceptance of the product—three tasks all accomplished in one swoop. The advertising

TABLE 22-1
RETAIL VS MAIL ORDER
(100,000 units. Retail price $10)

	Retail	Mail order
Sales to end user	$1,000,000	$1,000,000
Retailer's share	500,000	0
Net income	$ 500,000	$1,000,000
Advertising budget	50,000	500,000
Product cost	250,000	250,000
Distribution costs	50,000	100,000
NET	$ 150,000	$ 150,000

In this theoretical example, both distribution channels produce the same contribution to overhead and profit, but Mail Order has a bonus of $450,000 in advertising which will build awareness and demand among both consumers and retailers.

budget not only sells merchandise but also creates demand. Eventually the retailers will ask the company to please let them stock the product because their customers are asking for it. Obviously the company is in quite a different negotiating position.

Response Rate

Recently I attended a meeting of some of the top catalog companies in the United States. They had a common complaint: that catalog results were off about 15 percent from the previous year. And they agreed on the cause—too many different catalogs mailed to the same over-selected "prime prospects" too many times each year. Yet less than half of them had expanded into international markets, where the market is anything but over-saturated.

Those companies that have gone global, and done it right, are enjoying response rates four or five times as high as in the United States! Even adjusting for higher start-up costs, they are doing better than if they put out still another catalog in the U.S.

Why are response rates higher? Figure 22-1 shows the number of mailing pieces per household per year (for the last year measured) in eight major

Mailboxes Are Less Crowded in International Markets

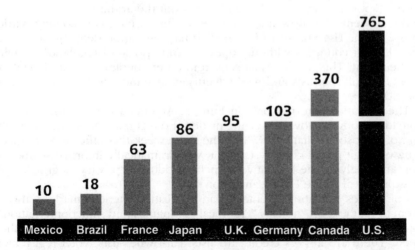

Figure 22-1. Direct mail saturation comparison. Number of direct mail pieces per household per year. [Households or businesses which receive one or two catalogs a week obviously will spend more time looking at them and are more likely to order from them. Compare this with the U.S. where the average is 10 catalogs a week but prime prospect households can often get that many in a single day, especially when they all choose the same mailing seasons.] Source: USPS.

international markets. An American household gets twice as much mail as a home in Canada, 40 times as much as a home in Brazil, 75 times as much as in Mexico!

There are other advantages reported by mailers who have gone to countries outside the United States. Renewals are higher, and customers are willing to pay higher prices. For instance, it is not necessary to offer 50 percent off introductory offers. More modest incentives will turn out to be more profitable, achieving very good response rates at a higher price.

WHAT'S DIFFERENT

So far I hope I've made two points. One, going global is worthwhile. And two, it's possible. But I haven't said it's easy. While you usually don't have to change your product, and while consumer motivations are usually the same, it's important to know what's different. Later in this chapter I'll tell you how to get the answers you'll need. For now, let's focus on the questions of what you need to know to be successful.

Lists

Some countries, including Australia and the largest nations in Europe, have list-management and list-brokerage services as good as any in the United States. While mail and phone lists tend to be more expensive, they are also more responsive, which in the end evens out the arithmetic.

But it seems that now that it's easier to find lists, it is becoming harder to use them. The European Union (EU) has legislation denying the use of their lists to countries without "opt-out" and "privacy" regulations similar to their own. This restricts mail sent from other countries, but a direct marketer can still rent lists and mail advertisements and packages from within the EU.

The limitations are not only in Europe. Argentina is an example of the spread of both the advances being made for direct marketers, and the problem of imposed limitations. Within the same week that officials announced a new 8-digit postal code system that will dramatically improve segmentation and analysis, the legislative branch introduced "privacy" legislation almost identical to the European Union's.

Companies hesitating to enter Asian and Latin American markets always seem to blame it on "no lists." Yet local companies and skilled international marketers such as Reader's Digest always seem to find all the lists they need. There are always credit-card lists, car-owner lists, voter-registration lists, and newspaper and magazines subscription lists. Business lists are available almost everywhere, usually from a directory publisher.

A global direct marketer has to be creative and has to work with local people who are trusted. For example, one direct-marketing company offered to help a county's regional and national governments collect taxes by phone in return for access to tax rolls. The lists are there, but they often require negotiating with each individual list owner and, when found, they will typically be 50–100 percent higher than comparable lists in the U.S.

But the lack of list brokers should be looked at as an opportunity, not as a problem. For one of my agency's international consulting clients, one of our first recommendations was to open a list-brokerage division. It becomes a way of marketing the company's own lists and finding outside lists they need as well as creating a new profit center.

Direct marketers operating in the country you're trying to start business in usually have assembled mailing lists which can be exchanged or joint-ventured, if not rented. And the situation is improving every day in every country.

For example, in Japan there are over 100 different lists that are readily available, but many of the best lists are only available on a reciprocal basis. In Brazil, the Abril publishing house's database program is under the direction of a respected direct marketing expert, Peter Rosenwald. His organization has compiled and enhanced lists from their many magazines, made them available, and then created new direct-marketing programs. In Argentina, the Clienting agency has invested in identifying neighborhoods by affluence. In Costa Rica, my client La Nacion, can reach the entire country with precision targeting by using information tabulated by carrier route rather than postal district.

When talking with an automobile manufacturer, I heard that the Mexican government did not permit compiling automobile-registration lists. I wanted this information clarified, and with a few inquiries we found that to be true. But I also found out that similar data is available through automobile insurance companies. The lesson learned is that there's always a solution, but one needs a positive attitude and investigative mind to find it.

Companies are recognizing the profit potential of list building. It will not take long for more of them to make the investments to be the first to fill this need. I have met with some newspapers in Latin America who are already considering building database "survey" lists. In every country, creative solutions are being invented, services are being made available, and new fortunes are being made by those who are among the first to use them.

Other Media

People who tell you "there are no lists available" are just saying they don't know where to look for them. Anyway, to the extent that lists are not large enough or segmented sufficiently, this is an opportunity. You can build your own lists with newspaper offers, on-package offers, or through door-to-door delivery systems. Newspaper and magazine inserts in some countries produce surprisingly high response rates. Television advertising—both short form and long form—also builds lists as a bonus by-product.

Regardless of the status of mailing lists, print and broadcast media are used very extensively in some countries. For instance, in England it is often more profitable to run "send for catalog" ads in Sunday newspapers followed by the catalog mailings, then to simply send out "cold" catalogs as is done in the U.S.

Mail and phone costs are relatively high in Japan, and so some companies do very well by making television offers and then selling other products and services on the incoming call.

Address and Mail Formats

Special attention must be given to address formats. You cannot expect to force-fit foreign addresses into the format you use in your own country. Is the building number before or after the street name? Is a postal code before or after the city name? Is the floor or suite number a mandatory requirement or an option?

If you are dealing with one country at a time, or mailing from within the country, you must adapt your format to local requirements. The problem usually surfaces if you are compiling your own worldwide customer or prospect list. Most list programs will not print out all foreign addresses in a mailable format.

You'll need to modify your mailing program to reformat the address so it is deliverable in the country being mailed to, or use a mailing service that provides this facility. One company that specializes in this, Data Services Inc. in Virginia, has services and software to help companies with this problem.

Note that some countries don't even use addresses in the classic sense. For my first project in Costa Rica I learned that "Direcciones" literally meant directions, not addresses. Try to do a merge-purge with "300 meters north of the house with green shutters" or "house to east of where library used to be." Yet this mail was deliverable and, using other indicators, capable of being compiled for database marketing programs.

Not only the list, but envelope and other specifications may vary. Some countries prohibit self-mailers, and require that even a catalog or magazine must have an envelope or at least a wrapper.

Some countries require that the source of a list-name be disclosed on the label or in the mailing package. Others prohibit sweepstakes or contests of any kind. Each country's postal service branch has its own rules and regulations which must be observed if you want your mailing to be delivered or your phone calls to go through to the customers. In many countries, the telephone system is run by the same branch of government as the post office.

Orders

Even though credit-card ownership may be high in some countries, it doesn't mean that this is the preferred way of placing an order there, and it is certainly not the only way to do so. Some countries work only with pre-paid orders. In others, COD shipments are very common.

In some countries, mail orders far out-pull phone orders. In Japan, half of a direct-marketing company's orders will come in by fax. In Germany, most shipments are invoiced in advance or on a C.O.D. (Cash on Delivery) basis.

Credit experience also varies, which particularly affects club and continuity programs. In some parts of the world "Send no money now" is read as "Don't pay ever." In other countries it is simply not honorable to have unpaid debts, nor is it good manners to pressure someone who cannot pay.

If you are mailing directly from the U.S, it is not a problem to request payment in U.S. dollars for most of the world. The exception is Europe, where the local currency should be requested, and even the EU currency is still not always welcomed.

Telemarketing

As in the United States, telephone orders have become the preferred way of placing an order or getting customer service. But there are differences from country to country.

Not every country has the equivalent of toll-free 800 numbers, but it has not been a major deterrent. Mail order grew and prospered in the United States long before toll-free was available here.

In most countries, commercial call-centers are available to handle order-taking and fulfillment functions within the country. Multi-lingual call centers can handle order-taking for multi-national companies. And some, as those in Ireland for instance, are so cost-efficient that publishers in the U.S. use them to handle all data entry as well as inbound phone calls. Even IBM's huge call center routes over-load calls to international call centers.

Smaller multi-lingual marketers have other options. One of our clients was soliciting catalog inquiries from Brazilians who live in the U.S. We had difficulty finding an affordable service with Brazilian Portuguese-speaking operators in the United States. The problem was solved with electronic messaging, a system where if a customer was interested in a free catalog, he or she called a U.S. toll-free number, with a Portuguese recorded message. The caller gave the name and address they wished the catalog sent to, and punched their phone number in on the keypad so we could call back for any untranscribable information. If the client wanted to place an order, the call was routed directly through the toll-free number to our client in Rio.

Delivery

Some postal systems are so reliable that you need not hesitate to mail or ship anything, at least by insured mail. The U.S. post office, for instance, will insure a package up to $25,000 for a very reasonable rate. For example, the $25,000 insurance total is only $20.50, plus postage costs for delivery within the U.S. For a South American jewelry client, we delivered packages by private courier to Miami and then reshipped them across the U.S., using this type of insured mail.

But it is the other extreme that is more common. In many countries, neither businesses nor consumers feel that the national mail systems are secure. However, in those countries, alternate systems have been created to accept payments or to deliver merchandise.

In Mexico, for example, book clubs simply advise members that their next shipment is ready. The customer goes to a contracted retail location (often a check-cashing service) to pick up the merchandise and pay for it at the same time. My client in Costa Rica uses its own local newspaper offices to collect payments and deliver merchandise for customers of its database services.

Alternate delivery systems are the rule rather than the exception in many countries. This applies not only to packages delivered by the local equivalent of UPS, but also to the mail. In Mexico, even telephone companies distribute mail by private courier services rather than through the postal system. In Australia, such services place advertising right in the mailbox—a practice not permitted in the U.S.

Customs

Today most countries encourage international trade and work to make tariffs mutually inexpensive and customs clearance a quick and simple process. However, many good intentions in these areas have not yet been realized.

The U.S. Postal Service and the postal system of another country recently worked out a simplified process to encourage international mail for one of our clients. It looked great on paper, and provided 48-hour delivery from overseas to a U.S. residential customer. Great! But the first test mailing took over a week. The two postal systems and the customs office finally got it all together, but it wasn't easy.

Contrary to some first impressions, postal systems and customs departments want to make things work better. It's good for them as well as you. Bring them into the picture early, ask for help and advice, and cooperate with their systems. But don't make unrealistic delivery promises to your customers until you and the delivery systems have worked out all the bugs.

Creative

Yes, people everywhere have the same emotional needs. They want to be thinner, richer, healthier, younger, smarter, etc. Some companies can simply take a TV spot that was successful in one country, dub in the message in a different language, and have it be a success. Some can run their catalogs with the same pictures but a different black plate for copy and prices, and make a profit.

This will work if the country of origin is one of the selling points. An offer of French cosmetics can look as if it was written and designed in France, the country where the goods are made. The same principle applies to Chilean wine or American golf equipment. At times I've even sent such mail from the country, with a foreign stamp, just to reinforce the image of an exclusive foreign-made product made by the best in the world.

The simple approach can also be effective if you're trying to inexpensively determine the relative success of your product line in different countries. You can always refine your ads or mailings later.

In the long run, regardless of whether you want your product to look local or like an import, you will want to use the techniques that work best in each country. This may include local models, local product applications, local testimonials, or local figures of speech in the headlines and copy.

And you'll want to be aware of local images and associations. For instance, red is a lucky color in Japan. The Chevrolet Nova ran into difficulties in South America, since "no va" means "Doesn't Go" in Spanish. Brazilians prefer a gentler approach than Americans. Most mail asks politely for a response, and "Hurry, Act Now!" is considered rude and generally avoided.

Not only are language subtleties different, but so are formats. Hand assemblies, which are prohibitively costly in the U.S., are common in some Asian countries. Paper sizes are different; the generic size of 8 × 10 inches doesn't apply to countries on the metric system. It may take more space or less space to say something in another language. This may be especially true if the other language has a completely different alphabet.

It is essential than the creative process be shared by the company in the originating country and someone in the destination country. Although we in the United States often have foreign nationals on our staff, and while Berlitz and other translation companies maintain excellent services, my company prefers to have local associates from the country we want to market in review copy from a *selling* perspective, and not just for language accuracy.

We generally write an ad or mailing piece in English and send it, along with a rough layout, to associates in each country we do business in. The associates edit it and translate it into the local language and than finalize the layout using available illustrations. We then do a back-translation to English to see if anything was lost in the process.

In this way we (representing our client) are in control of product description and the use of direct marketing fundamentals. Our local partners have final responsibility for adapting it to their market. We work the same way in reverse when we are helping a foreign company introduce a product line into the U.S.

GETTING STARTED

Know Thyself

Entering a new world market is not unlike starting a business in the first place. It begins with a plan, and the plan begins with an understanding of where you are and what you are trying to accomplish.

First, what is it about your product, service or company that you believe will most appeal to a new, foreign audience? It will probably be the same as for the home country, but do you really know what that is? What technology, management or other strengths do you think will give your company an advantage over others?

Second, what is your goal? Will more sales enable you to lower your manufacturing cost-per-unit? Are you trying to widen your profit margin? Are you hedging against possible deflation in your home country? One suggestion: don't go to another country because you are having problems with your home market. Solve those problems first.

Know Thy Market

Next, select the markets you are most interested in. Do you have key staff members who know one country or another? Is there a country where you have friends and enjoy visiting? If you have retail stores, see what items foreign tourists buy and which country they call home. If you are on the Internet, make an effort to track links and see the nationality of many of your viewers.

Talk to your own country's postal service. They most likely have a department that specializes in building international trade. Ask where other exporters are having the greatest success, and see where they are getting the best cooperation from other postal services.

Above all, go to the country you want to market to. Talk to the people who might be your potential suppliers and partners. Go to retail stores and see what prices similar products sell for. If you have something new, show it to people you meet and get reactions. Better yet, arrange for some focus panels conducted by professional researchers.

Brand Names and National Imagery

Do your potential customers know your product? Your brand name? That will help. If they don't, what is your home country's national image as it affects the product? Is it romantic, like Italy? High fashion, like France? High tech, like Japan? Is it noted for the product category—cookies from Belgium, beer from Germany, wine from Chile? Is it direct from the gold mines of Africa? Is it the clothing that feels cool even in Sumatra? Is it the engine that doesn't quit even in northern Finland? Is it the coffee hand-picked in the mountains of Colombia? Or, one of my own favorite copy lines, a romance-positioned Vodka from Alaska, "where the nights never end."

National imagery has been particularly useful for my clients from Brazil who wish to bring their products to the United States. The American preconceptions of Brazil helped to market gemstones from the heart of the Amazon, lingerie with the spirit of the girl from Ipanema, and a swimsuit line suggestively called *Carioca!* with ads of gorgeous Brazilians wearing the suits against a background of Rio de Janiero's beaches. With imagery like this, who needs a brand name?

If you have a well-known national brand, by all means use it. Certainly a new publication from *Time* or fashion from Ralph Lauren can be marketed anywhere in the world. If your name is not known, consider using the national imagery of the country to give you a head start, as in the preceding examples.

The size of the market is also a consideration. It costs the same amount of time, energy and capital to market to little New Zealand as to Australia, to tiny Paraguay as to Argentina. Brazil is my first choice in South America because it represents almost as much buying power as the eleven countries in the rest of South America. I like Costa Rica in Central America because what works there can be easily expanded to the rest of the isthmus. As Macmillan's Raymond Hagel used to tell me, "Put your priority where the money is."

In Europe you can theoretically start anywhere, but the restrictions and regulations can be discouraging. Also, the local marketers in major European countries are tough competitors.

Many American companies will want to start with English-speaking countries. Canada, England, Australia and South Africa have all been good export markets for American companies, and vice versa.

There are large numbers of mail-order buyers who speak English all over the world. If you want to get your feet wet in international commerce, particularly in the financial or technology fields, consider the many lists of Americans and Britons living and working in other lands, or the publications that cater to them. They can be reached by advertising in the international editions of *Time, Newsweek,* the *Miami Herald* and the *Wall Street Journal* —many of which are printed locally in foreign countries and read avariciously by English-speaking residents.

There are also local papers in foreign languages. For example, in the United States, we found five Portuguese publications, plus websites and a videotape service of Brazilian soap operas. New York newsstands have locally-published newspapers in forty different languages and dialects! If you're exporting your product, you can presume that almost every country has some English-language publication—*Athens News, Bangkok Post, China Daily, Cairo Gazette, Caracas Journal, Jerusalem Post, Japan Times,* and many others.

Other than reaching expatriate English-speakers, you can always mail to foreign nationals who happen to be proficient in English. For instance 53 percent of Belgians, 55 percent of Netherlanders, 51 percent of Danes and 19 percent of Greeks all speak English, using it mostly for business to business correspondence. For business use, English is also acceptable in India, Hong Kong, Taiwan, Japan, Israel and most of South America, depending upon the business. But even if your target market in the business world speaks English, my experience has taught me that you will get twice the response if you communicate in their own language. In some countries— France, Italy, Spain, Germany, and others—English is never an acceptable option.

Know Thy Suppliers

You will want to out-source as much as possible during your initial test. Your first step is to determine sales potential. Maximizing profits can come later. I strongly recommend against hiring a large local staff or building your own telemarketing or fulfillment center until after you are sure that you want to stay in that country. It is much safer to go into three countries with minimal investments than one with an all-out expenditure. Then, after the test, you can drop one of the countries and invest more in the one that looks best.

You will need a direct-response advertising agency, preferably one that is independent and small enough so your test is an important opportunity for them. Then you will need to make decisions on how to handle orders. Theoretically, the advertising and fulfillment supplier can handle it all and deposit the proceeds in a bank of your choice. However, it's a good idea to have a company officer assigned to make routine decisions and report on progress, and a local accountant or lawyer assigned to review operating reports and financial statements.

POSTAL SUPPORT

I cannot underestimate the enormous help that postal systems can provide to companies planning to enter international marketing. I have had occasion to deal with the postal service in Singapore, Brazil and France as well as the International Business Unit of the U.S. Postal Service. All of them have made enormous contributions to the success of the marketing programs we worked on together.

In every case they have demonstrated creativity and positive thinking, and found ways to minimize expenses and cut through red tape. One recent innovation developed with the U.S. Customs Department ended with the creation of a system called Global Package Link, a program that eliminated the need for individual customs forms by pre-clearing shipments.

As far as I can tell, the world's postal services are all working to educate businesses for international commerce through direct marketing. The U.S. Postal Service (USPS) has been sponsoring seminars on "Going Global," both in the U.S. and in other countries. Correos Brasil, the Brazilian postal service, is co-sponsoring my leap-frog marketing talk on a national video-conference to a thousand small businesses in their country. The Australian Post and Israel Post have printed some of the best guidebooks I've seen on the basics of direct marketing. And the USPS has publications like "The World Business Advisory and Calendar" and their "Global Shipping Solutions Kit." Call 1-800-THE-USPS, Ext. 2055 for a copy, or go to www.uspsglobal.com on the Internet.

INFORMATION SOURCES

It is impossible, in one chapter of one book, to even attempt to outline the specifics of markets, media, customers, tariffs and postal regulations which should influence your decision on which country or countries are right for your company.

If I've succeeded in whetting your appetite for the wide world of international marketing, there is one book I recommend enthusiastically. It is *Multinational Direct Marketing* by Richard N. Miller (McGraw-Hill 1995).

TABLE 22-2
USEFUL INTERNATIONAL DIRECT MAIL RESOURCES

USPS Int'l Mailer Assistance	202-268-5731	www.USPSglobal.com
U.S. Dept. of Commerce, Int' Trade	202-482-0453	www.ita.doc.gov
U.S. Chamber of Commerce	202-463-5460	www.uschamber.org
U.S. Small Business Administration	202-205-6720	www.sbaonline.sba.gov
Direct Marketing Association (US)	212-768-7277	www.the-dma.org
Team Nash, Inc.	212-376-6274	www.teamnash.com

I also recommend participating in the various seminars created by the United States Postal Service and postal systems in other countries. Bill Mc-Nutt of International Direct Marketing Consultants (224 443-9494) sponsors a series of Trade Missions—highly regarded tours for direct marketers and telemarketers to Asia, Europe, Mexico, Canada and South America. I will also be happy to answer inquiries by phone at 212 376-6274, by fax at 212 376-6277 or by e-mail at nashnet@aol.com.

In Table 22-2, there are a few phone numbers and Internet addresses or fax numbers of organizations that are good places to start for both mail-order imports and exports for the United States. Each country will have equivalent services, which can be located either by contacting their U.S. partners listed below or the International unit of the local post office.

Virtually every country now has it own direct-marketing association, which is usually a valuable resource and a good way of meeting local agencies and other suppliers as well as local managers of other multinational companies. If you cannot locate the association or the appropriate postal office in the country you are interested in, consult the DMA or USPS at the numbers above and they will refer you to a local resource.

* * *

I will summarize the point of this chapter with a headline I wrote for the *Direct Marketing News International* DM Conference, an event I chaired and helped organize:

"If you're not competing globally, you're not competing at all."

INDEX

ABOUT THE AUTHOR

Edward L. Nash heads up Team Nash Inc., direct marketing consulting and creative firm based in New York City handling Internet, direct marketing and database clients in the U.S. and five other countries. He also teaches direct marketing at New York University and Virginia Commonwealth University. Prior to forming Team Nash, he was Executive Vice President of Bozell Worldwide, Inc., where he oversaw the strategic development of U.S. global direct marketing programs.

Ed began his career as a copywriter and has been marketing Vice President for LaSalle Extension University, President of Capitol Record Club, Executive Vice President of Rapp Collins, and President/CEO of BBDO Direct, which he founded and ran for five years. He is the author of *Database Marketing: The Ultimate Selling Tool* and editor-in-chief of *The Direct Marketing Handbook*, both published by McGraw-Hill.